CHRISTIANITY IN THE MIDDLE EAST

Studies in Modern History, Theology and Politics

edited by

Anthony O'Mahony

MELISENDE
LONDON

Christianity in the Middle East:
Studies in Modern History, Theology and Politics
First published 2008 by Melisende
London
England

ISBN 978 1 901764 49 9

Melisende Publishing Ltd, London
and
Rimal Publications, Nicosia

For information on our publications, visit our website
www. melisende.com
and for
Rimal Publications, Cyprus, www.rimalbooks.com

Editor: Leonard Harrow
Printed and bound in England at the St Edmundsbury Press

CONTENTS

CONTRIBUTORS

Sebastian Brock, Oriental Institute, University of Oxford, a leading expert on Syriac Christianity, he has written a series of important publications on the subject including *The Luminous Eye: The Spiritual World Vision of Saint Ephrem* (1992), *The Wisdom of Saint Issac the Syrian* (1997) and the following volumes in the Variorum Collected Studies Series: *Syriac Perspectives on Late Antiquity* (1984); *Studies in Syriac Christianity: History, Literature, Theology* (1992); *From Ephrem to Romanos: Interactions between Syriac and Greek in Late Antiquity* (1999); *Fire from Heaven: Studies in Syriac Theology and Liturgy* (2006).

Giuseppe Buffon, a member of the Franciscan Order and lectures at the Pontifical University of the Antonianum. His doctorate from the École des Hautes Études, Paris, was published as *Les Franciscains en Terre Sainte(1869-1889): Religion et politique. Une recherché institutionelle*, Éd. du Cerf, Paris, 2005; 'Les franciscains en terre sainte: de l'espace au territoire, entre opposition et adaptation', *New Faith in Ancient Lands. Western Mission in The Middle East in the Nineteenth and Early Twentieth Centuries, (Studies in Christian Mission 32)*, H Murre-van den Berg (ed.), E J Brill, Leiden, 2006; 'Les Franciscains en Terre Sainte au 19e siècle: de l'espace au territoire, entre opposition et adaptation', *Revue d'histoire ecclésiastique*, 2005.

Helen Bryer, studied history at the University of Cambridge and has a research interest in the modern history of Eastern Christianity.

John Flannery, undertook postgraduate studies in Christian Theology and other religious traditions which formed part of a research project on the Jesuit encounter with Islam and Buddhism in Asia at the Centre for Christianity and Interreligious Dialogue Heythrop College, University of London. At present he is working on the history of the relations between the Holy See, the Augustinian Order and Persia in the 17th century. His publications include, 'Through a Glass Darkly: the Jesuit Encounter with Buddhism in Tibet, in *Catholics in Interreligious Dialogue: Monasticism, Theology and Spirituality*, Leominister, Gracewing, 2005; 'The martyrdom of Queen Ketevan in 17th century Iran: an episode in relations between the Georgian Church and Rome', *Sobornost: Eastern Churches Quarterly*, Vol. 27, 2005; 'Christ in Islam',

One in Christ: a catholic ecumenical review, Vol. 41, 2006; 'Christian-Muslim relations in the Sudan', *Christian Responses to Islam: Muslim-Christian relations in the modern world*, Anthony O'Mahony and Emma Loosley (eds), Manchester University Press, 2008.

Guita G Hourani, University of Notre Dame, Lebanon and The Maronite Research Institute. She is Editor of *The Journal of Maronite Studies* and has a special interest in the emigration and the global Maronite diaspora community. Her publications include, 'The Maronite Eremitical Tradition', *The Heythrop Journal*, Vol. 45, no. 4, 2004.

Antoine B Habchi, The Maronite Research Institute, has a special research interest the Maronite Church and spirituality. He co-authored with Guita Hourani 'The Maronite Eremitical Tradition', *The Heythrop Journal*, Vol. 45, no. 4, 2004.

Fiona McCallum, Department of International Relations, St Andrew's University; 'The Coptic Church, Islam and Muslim-Christian Relations in Egypt', *Christian Responses to Islam: Muslim-Christian relations in the modern world*, Anthony O'Mahony and Emma Loosley (eds), Manchester University Press, 2008; 'Desert Roots and Global Branches : The Journey of the Coptic Orthodox Church', *Bulletin of the Royal Institute of Interfaith Studies*, Vol. 7, no. 2, 2005; 'The Role of the Maronite Patriarch in Lebanese History: the Patriarch of Lebanon?', *Chronos*, no. 15, 2007.

Leonard Marsh, is an Anglican priest to a London Parish. He has a specialist interest in the contemporary theological, especially Liberation theology, and political movements within the Palestinian Christian community in Jerusalem and the Holy Land. He did postgraduate research and study at the School of Oriental and African Studies, University of London. He has published many articles on contemporary Palestinian Christianity and theology including 'Palestinian Christians', *One in Christ: a catholic ecumenical review*, Vol. 41, 2006; 'Palestinian Christianity: A Study in Religion and Politics', *International Journal for the Study of the Christian Church*, Vol. 5, no. 2, 2005; 'Palestinian Christians and Liberation Theology', *Christianity and Jerusalem: Studies in Modern Theology and Politics*, 2007.

Leon Menzies Racionzer; after a long career in business, he completed postgraduate study and research into contemporary Christian-Jewish relations in modern the State of Israel at the Centre for Christianity and Interreligious Dialogue at Heythrop College, University of London. His publications include:

'Christian communities in Contemporary Israel: A Study in Religion, Politics and Church-State Relations', *One in Christ: a catholic ecumenical review*, Vol. 41, 2006; 'Hebrew Catholic Thought and Theology in Israel', *The Heythrop Journal*, Vol. 45, no. 4, 2004; 'Christianity in Modern Israel', *International Journal for the Study of the Christian Church*, Vol. 5, no. 2, 2005. He is writing a monograph on Christian theological reflection in the modern State of Israel based upon the life and work of the Dominican scholar Marcel Dubois OP.

Anthony O'Mahony, Heythrop College, University of London, has a specialist interest in contemporary Christian theology and politics and Christian-Muslim relations. His publications include *Palestinian Christians: Religion, Politics and Society in the Holy Land*, 1999; *The Christians communities in Jerusalem and the Holy Land: Studies in History, Religion and Politics*, 2003; *Eastern Christianity: Studies in Modern History, Religion and Politics*, 2004; *World Christianity: Theology, Politics, Dialogues*, 2003.

Sotiris Roussos, is Lecturer of Near East Politics and International Relations, at Panteion University and Co-ordinator of the Centre for Mediterranean and Middle Eastern Studies at the Institute of International Relations in Athens. He did postgraduate research and study at the School of Oriental and African Studies, University of London, entitled *Greece and the Arab Middle East: The Greek Orthodox Communities in Egypt, Palestine and Syria, 1919-1940.* His recent publications include, 'The Greek Orthodox community in Jerusalem in international politics: international solutions for Jerusalem and the Greek Orthodox community in the 19th and 20th c.' in *Jerusalem: Its Sanctity and Centrality to Judaism, Christianity and Islam*, 1997; 'The Greek Orthodox Patriarchate and Community in Jerusalem: Church, State and Identity' in *The Christians communities in Jerusalem and the Holy Land: Studies in History, Religion and Politics*, 2003; 'Patriarchs, Notables and Diplomats: The Greek Orthodox Patriarchate of Jerusalem in the modern period', *Eastern Christianity: Studies in Modern History, Religion and Politics*, 2004.

Nicolas Servas works for the World Council of Churches and is a BA candidate in Arabic at the University of Geneva. He has a double Master in Ancient History from the Universities of Heidelberg and Lyon, and a Master in Middle East Politics from the University of Exeter. He taught French in Cairo between 2000 and 2002.

William Taylor is Vicar of St John's, Notting Hill, in the Diocese of London, and a graduate of Heythrop College, having studied Syriac Patristics under Robert Murray. He is Chairman of the Anglican and Eastern Churches

Association, Secretary of the Anglican-Oriental Orthodox Regional Forum, and a member of the Anglican-Oriental Orthodox International Commission, and the Middle East Forum of CTBI. His publications include: 'Christianity in Modern Iraq', *One in Christ: a catholic ecumenical review*, Vol. 40, 2005 and *Antioch and Canterbury: The Syrian Orthodox Church and the Church of England (1874-1928)*, Gorgias Press, 2005.

Dominique Trimbur, Centre de Recherche Français de Jérusalem. He is the author numerous studies including *De la Shoah à la reconciliation? A question des relations RFA-Israel (1949-1956)*, CNRS Editions, Paris, 2000; and edited *De Bonaparte à Balfour. La France, l'Europe occidentale et la Palestine, 1799-1917*, CNRS Editions, Paris, 2001; 'Une lecture politique de la mission pour l'Union: la France et la mise en place de la Sacrée Congrégation Orientale, 1917-1922', *La mission en textes et en images XVIe-XXe siècles*, Karthala, Paris, 2004; 'L'Église catholique et le sionisme au temps de Theodor Herzl, 1897-1904', *Mélanges de Science Religieuse*, Vol. 61, no. 4, 2004; 'Exil et retour: l'impact de la législation française sur la présence tricolore en Palestine, 1901-1925', *Le grand exil des congrégations françaises 1901-1914*, Éd. du Cerf, Paris, 2005;

John Whooley, a Catholic priest in a London parish. His specialist research interests are in the modern and contemporary history of Armenian Christianity and in particular the Armenian Catholic Church. His publications include: 'The Armenian Catholic Church: A Study in History and Ecclesiology', *The Heythrop Journal*, Vol. 45, no. 4, 2004; 'Armenian Christianity: An Historical and Theological Overview', *One in Christ: a catholic ecumenical review*, Vol. 41, 2006; 'The Mekhitarists: Religion, Culture and Ecumenism in Armenian-Catholic Relations', *Eastern Christianity: Studies in Modern History, Religion and Politics*, 2004.

INTRODUCTION

Anthony O'Mahony

It is all too easy to be the bearer of bad news about Christianity in the modern Middle East. A profound series of crises has overtaken Middle Eastern Christianity in contemporary times. Displacement by war, genocide, interreligious conflict, leading to loss, emigration and exile would seem to be the main experience of Christianity in the Middle East. The Churches have had to respond to the crisis not just in political position, but in theological and ecclesial terms; for example, partially witnessing to this displacement experience, 'The Guidelines for Admission to the Eucharist between the Chaldean Church and the Assyrian Church of the East' (the two principal Iraqi Christian communities) issued by the Holy See in 2001 would allow for a Chaldean Catholic or a member of the Church of the East to take communion at each other's liturgy if 'pastoral necessity' required, 'as there cannot be a priest for every local community in such a widespread diaspora.'

Against this background of displacement, when allowed, Christians have sought to resettle and build anew. They have been able to make a significant cultural, political and economic contribution to Middle Eastern society. Some observers have suggested that there is a 'Christian barometer' which provides the world with an accurate measurement of the political atmosphere in the Middle East. Progress toward freedom in the Middle East can be gained by focusing on the status of the large Christian minorities. Most are highly educated and multilingual and have studied and worked in Europe and North America where they also have a large diaspora. The Christians in the Middle East also tend to be more open to the world and less inclined to join religion and politics together as ideologically contemporary currents of Islamist thought among the surrounding Muslim majority.

The theory goes that as the Middle East becomes more free and prosperous, linked to the West and hospitable to minorities, the higher the probability that the Christians will continue to live and even return from abroad to countries like Lebanon, Egypt and Syria. And vice versa, if Christians sense that things are getting worse, if the Middle Eastern countries they live in are losing their commitment to political, economic and religious freedom, they would tend to emigrate from the Middle East.

After the fall of the Ba'athist regime in 2003 the Christians in Iraq became 'the canaries in the coal mine' for the greater Middle East. The extent to which they are tolerated in the new Iraq was being watched closely by the Maronites of Lebanon, the Copts of Egypt and other non-Muslim populations of the region. The Christians in Iraq are deeply troubled by the rise of radical Islamic tendencies in both the majority Shi'ite and the former ruling class, the Sunni minority. For Iraqi Christians the continuing spectre of growing insecurity, which has lead to church bombings, kidnapping and assassinations has created a situation in which they have left in large numbers.

Maybe as many as 200,000 have left Iraq never to return, others are refugees in the region, some 60,000 in Syria and maybe up to 40,000 in Jordan. Some states have welcomed these newcomers and hope that they will stay, bringing their skills, and that their presence will add to a diversity in society which in turn will help support 'moderate' politics. In fact previous generations of displaced Christians, particularly Armenians and other oriental Christians, arrived in Lebanon and made that country (before the Civil War 1975-1990) a leading cultural and economic space for the region.

Christian identity in the Middle East is a contested one caught between an Arab Christian identity and an 'Eastern Christian' identity—Assyrian, Chaldean, Coptic, Maronite. The late Jean Corbon in his well-known work, *The Church of the Arabs*, called for the Christians of the Middle East to actualize this vocation. Voices from within the Christian communities in the Arab world have been raised that their co-religionists stand against a minority complex that would lead them to withdraw into a ghetto and that they live and act as conscious Christians and as fully committed citizens, so together with their Muslim fellow-citizens they are active builders of their respective countries. In order to fulfil this double mission, the Christians of the Arab world can build on the richness and diversity of their religious and cultural traditions. It is often forgotten that it was initially the Syriac Christians who handed on the classical heritage of science from the ancients through their translations into Arabic to the West.

The Churches of the Middle East can be grouped into five families: Oriental Orthodox, Eastern Orthodox, Oriental and Eastern Catholic, Anglican and Protestant, and the 'Assyrian' Church of the East, together representing about 25 million Christians of whom approximately 10 million are residing in the Middle East.

If we take the framework of the Middle East Council of Churches (MECC), namely the four families of Churches, we have the following representations:[1]

1 The Oriental Orthodox family

- The Armenian Orthodox Church
- The Syrian Orthodox Church
- The Coptic Orthodox Church
- The Ethiopian Orthodox Church

2 The Eastern Orthodox family

- The Greek Orthodox Patriarchate of Jerusalem.
- The Greek Orthodox Patriarchate of Antioch.
- The Greek Orthodox Patriarchate of Alexandria

3 The Catholic family: six Oriental, one Latin, one Hebrew

- The Latin Patriarchate of Jerusalem (restored in 1847)
- The Greek Catholic Church
- The Maronite Church
- The Syrian Catholic Church
- The Armenian Catholic Church
- The Chaldean Church
- The Coptic Catholic Church
- Hebrew Catholic

4 The Evangelical and Anglican-Episcopal family

- The Anglican and Episcopal Church (in Jerusalem and the Middle East)
- There are various Protestant, Presbyterian and Lutheran

[1] Frans Bouwen, 'The Churches in the Middle East', in ed. L S Cunningham, *Ecumenism*, University of Notre Dame Press, Notre Dame, Indiana, 1998, 25-36.

Churches throughout the Middle East, who have emerged from Eastern Christian communities or from converts from Islam to Christianity.

5 The fifth family is, in terms of independent history, one of the oldest and most self-contained of the Middle Eastern Churches: the Assyrian Church of the East. Sometimes identified by its historical tradition as the Church of the 'East Syrians' or the Church of Persia. Its Catholic counterpart is the Chaldean Catholic Church. It is mainly found in Iran, Iraq, Syria and Lebanon.

The long centuries of Ottoman domination fossilized the Churches in their division. Initially these Muslim rulers centralized all Christian authority within the patriarchate of Constantinople (followed a few years later by an Armenian patriarchate). It was not until the 19th century that reformist measures allowed these ancient Churches to be formally recognized. Modern crisis, which has made Christian unity a priority, and contemporary ecumenism are beginning to bring down the barriers. In the course of the last decades, remarkable developments have taken place in the ecumenical relations between Churches in the Middle East, both on the bilateral and multilateral levels—agreements that allow partial mutual participation in sacraments, formation of future priests and catechesis. Christian theologians have been calling for a new discernment to evaluate the theological and ecclesiological meaning of this new form of communion that is growing among Churches of the Middle East. The Christian Churches have become part and parcel of each other in some mysterious way.

Too often Christianity in the Middle East is obscured from view, especially in the West. The Christological controversies of the 5th and 6th centuries produced a three-way split among the Christian Churches which still continues to this day (as Sebastian Brock has reminded us),[2] although it is only among the Churches of Syriac liturgical tradition that all three doctrinal positions are represented. The divisions were originally caused by controversy over how best to describe the relationship between the divinity and the humanity in the incarnate Christ. For the Orthodox

---

[2] S Brock, 'The Syriac Churches in Ecumenical Dialogue on Christology', in A O'Mahony (ed.), *Eastern Christianity,* Melisende, London, 2004, 44-65.

and Catholic (and derived Reformed) traditions the matter had been settled by the carefully balanced doctrinal formulation produced by the Council of Chalcedon in 451. This situation was effectively fossilized by the Arab invasions of the 7th century, at the time of the birth of Islam, when the Churches of the Middle East were politically cut off from those of the (much diminished) Byzantine empire and the West.

The situation was further exacerbated in the 19th century with the splitting off of small Protestant bodies from the various non-Chalcedonian Churches. Given such a history, it is not surprising that historically there has been a good deal of rivalry between the various Churches traditions, and it is only in the last four decades or so that there has been any sustained rapprochement and dialogue. Three main factors can be identified as being responsible for these developments: the ecumenical movement of the 20th century and the establishment of the World Council of Churches (in 1948), the Second Vatican Council, and the large-scale emigration from the Middle East to Europe, the Americas and Australia.

Although this large-scale emigration has in general been disastrous from the point of view of the life of the indigenous Christian Churches in the Middle East, there have at least been two good consequences: emigration to Western countries has provided the possibility of publication without censorship, and it has brought the existence of these non-Chalcedonian Churches more into the awareness of the Western Churches, thus providing an opportunity and incentive for theological dialogue.

The rich pluralism of traditions in the ancient patriarchate of Antioch (covering the territories of Lebanon and Syria) has suffered many divisions in the course of history. As a result, today, five patriarchates bear the title of the see of Antioch. The Latin Patriarchate of Antioch founded during the Crusader state of the Principality of Antioch was abolished in 1964. During the last decades a growing awareness of the absurdity of this situation has induced new efforts to re-establish communion among the different traditions. The Greek Orthodox patriarch, Ignatius IV Hazim, has sought to revive a synodical process involving all the Churches of the region. Without waiting until visible unity can be reached, Churches can start meeting and working together on a regular basis, in the social and pastoral fields. Such a dynamic would bring the Churches closer to each other and at the same time would be an empowering factor in difficult tasks.

The most remarkable initiative in this sense is the pastoral agreement between the Greek Orthodox and the Syrian Orthodox patriarchates of Antioch in 1991. This agreement provides for collaboration in practically all pastoral and liturgical fields, except eucharistic concelebration and ordination. Again in the territory of Antioch, as far back as 1974, meetings took place between the synods of the Greek Orthodox and the Greek Catholic patriarchates with a view to re-establishing unity on the local level, without waiting for an agreement on the universal level. The Holy See and representatives of Eastern Orthodox authorities expressed concern about certain aspects of these relations and reminded the Antiochene Churches that theological exchange must not limit itself to the two direct interlocutors but must involve the wider Catholic and Orthodox confessions to which they belong.

However, both Churches have continued to develop their mutual relations. The Syrian government allocated in a new urban development two areas for the construction of a mosque and a church. For Christians this presented an awkward problem: which Christian community would build the church, who would be the owner? The former Greek Catholic patriarch, Maximos V Hakim, and Ignace IV Hazim signed an agreement that they would construct the church together. On the 4 February 2005 the Church of St Peter and St Paul in the Doummar quarter in Damascus was jointly consecrated by Ignace IV Hazim and the Greek Catholic patriarch, Gregory III Laham.

Modern times have brought about a profound change in the configuration in Christian presence in the Middle East. In the last days of the Ottoman empire Christians made up 20-30 percent of the population. The Armenian genocide, the massacre of the Syriac Christians and the exchange of populations between Greece and Turkey (there is still debate about numbers but approximately a million and half Orthodox Christians and half a million Muslims) means today there are barely 200,000 Christians in a population of seventy million of the modern Turkish republic—although there might be up to two million people of Armenian descent who issue from the large numbers of Christian women and children taken as slaves or forced into Islam at the fall of the Ottoman empire. A number of these re-trace each year steps to their original grandmothers' Christian faith. Christians in Syria are down from 20 percent before the Second World War to fewer than 10 percent (800,000). During the Lebanese Civil War some 670,000 Christians had been displaced as opposed to 160,000

Muslims. Lebanon always had a Christian majority, but not now. This has allowed the Shi'a community to emerge as the majority community and its political organizations, such as Hizbullah, to try and capture the state and challenge traditional Maronite dominance. Since the beginnings of the 1960s and the internal Kurdish-Iraqi war some one million Christians have left their northern Iraqi mountains and homelands to emigrate. During this period Baghdad gained large numbers of Christians and the Chaldean patriarchate relocated there in 1950. In Egypt several hundred thousand Christians—mainly Greek, Armenian and Syrian—left in the 1950s, the large Coptic Christian population in Egypt, has traditionally not undertaken emigration until very recent times; one estimate is that maybe 12 percent of Copts now live abroad. Since 1948 some 230,000 Christians have left the Holy Land. The Christian population may be down from 30,000 in 1948 to 5,000 today in Jerusalem. There maybe fewer then 150,000 Christians in left in Iran as many departed after the 1979 Islamic revolution.

The Christian communities have obviously lost many of their most educated and young members. The Churches not only lose part of their future but also the potential leadership that should be charting the community's fortunes. In some communities this has seen more men leave than women and this has changed the gender balance. Christian women marry Muslim men and this fractures the Christian population and diminishes it, with implications for property rights and the education of children.[3]

All are aware that Churches have lost many millions of their people to emigration, and that their diaspora communities have grown correspondingly, but the question of presence is a dynamic one. Today large numbers of non-indigenous Christians, brought by the global economy have come to live and work in the region. 250,000 Christian workers are estimated to be in Israel and have been there for some time. These are made up of Eastern European (for example 60,000 Rumanians) and Asian workers. There are large numbers of Filipinos, and increasingly Sri Lankans, Indians and Africans in the region, for example approximately 140,000 Asian workers in Lebanon, 80 percent of whom are women. At times the traditional Churches are slow to provide for them.

---

[3] A O'Mahony, 'Christianity in Modern Iraq', *International Journal for the Study of the Christian Church*, vol. 4, no. 2, 2004, 121-42.

In this changing situation, patterns of authority have altered in modern historical times; somewhat marginalized by secular politics, the patriarchs of the different Churches have emerged as significant voices for Christianity in the contemporary political 'public square'. In the context of profound social and economic dislocation created by modernity, political upheaval and lack of 'legitimate' political structures, religious revival has brought these traditional points of authority to the fore; we think of the public role of the Coptic Patriarch Shenouda in Egypt, the Maronite Patriarch Sfeir in Lebanon, Michel Sabbah, the Latin Patriarch in the Holy Land to name but some.

To sum up Christianity has its historic roots in the Middle East. The Christian presence bears witness to the global Church, the unicity of its origins and the diversity of its expression. Christians also help maintain and sustain diversity in the Middle East. Christianity in the Middle East has a witness beyond itself; let us hope that the Churches of East and West rapidly rise to this challenge for the key to the future of this important region may lie with the few.[4]

---

[4] See the following studies on Christianity in the Modern Middle East: A O'Mahony (ed.), *Palestinian Christians: Religion, Politics and Society in the Holy Land*, Melisende, London, 1999; A O'Mahony (ed.), *The Christian Communities in Jerusalem: Studies in History, Religion and Politics,* University of Wales Press, Cardiff, 2003; A O'Mahony (ed.), *Eastern Christianity: Studies in Modern History, Religion and Politics*, (London: Melisende 2004; A O'Mahony (ed.), *Christianity and Jerusalem: Studies in Christian Theology and Politics in the Modern Holy Land*, Gracewing, Leominister, 2007; John Binns, *An Introduction to the Christian Orthodox Churches*, Cambridge University Press, Cambridge, 2002; Michael Angold (ed.), *The Cambridge History of Christianity: Volume Five—Eastern Christianity*, Cambridge University Press, Cambridge, 2006; Suha Rassam, *Christianity in Iraq,* Gracewing, Leominister, 2005.

THE SYRIAN ORTHODOX CHURCH IN MODERN HISTORY

Sebastian Brock

At the end of the 19th century the Syrian Orthodox Church of Antioch was only to be found in the Middle East and in south-west India. By contrast, at the end of the twentieth century there are dioceses and churches to be found in all five continents. The primary cause of this major change can readily be identified: during the course of the twentieth century the Syrian Orthodox Church has suffered from two traumatic experiences, the massacres that have taken place, above all in 1915, 'the year of the sword *(Sayfo)*', and the large-scale waves of emigration from the Middle East, first mainly to the Americas, and more recently to countries of western Europe and to Australia. And then, in recent decades the presence of the (non-Chalcedonian) Syrian Orthodox Church in the West has led to the renewal of theological dialogue with the (Chalcedonian) Catholic and Orthodox Churches after a break of over thirteen centuries. It is upon these three features, the massacres, the emigration (especially that to Europe), and the renewal of theological dialogue, that the present chapter will focus.[1] Among the more important matters that are not covered here is the complex 20th-century history of the Syrian Orthodox community in south India and its relationships with the Patriarchate.

The historical background in brief

The Syrian Orthodox Church, along with the other Oriental Orthodox Churches (Armenian, Coptic and Ethiopian), has always objected to certain parts of the Definition of Faith issued at the Council of Chalcedon (451),

---

[1] The section on theological dialogue is, however, very brief, since I have described this elsewhere (see note 36).

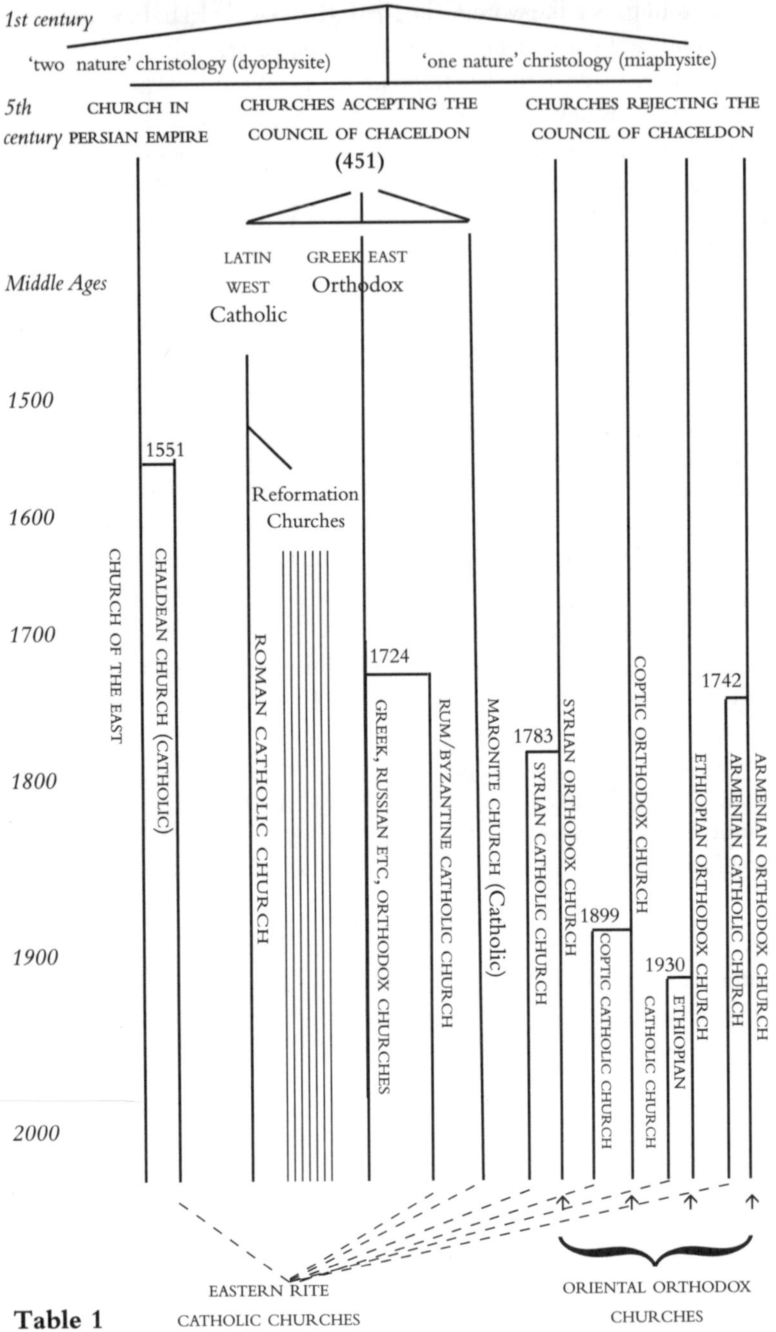
1st century
'two nature' christology (dyophysite)
'one nature' christology (miaphysite)
5th century
CHURCH IN PERSIAN EMPIRE
CHURCHES ACCEPTING THE COUNCIL OF CHACELDON (451)
CHURCHES REJECTING THE COUNCIL OF CHACELDON
Middle Ages
LATIN WEST
Catholic
GREEK EAST
Orthodox
1500
1551
Reformation Churches
1600
1700
1724
1742
1783
1800
1899
1900
1930
2000
CHURCH OF THE EAST
CHALDEAN CHURCH (CATHOLIC)
ROMAN CATHOLIC CHURCH
GREEK, RUSSIAN ETC, ORTHODOX CHURCHES
RUM/BYZANTINE CATHOLIC CHURCH
MARONITE CHURCH (Catholic)
SYRIAN CATHOLIC CHURCH
SYRIAN ORTHODOX CHURCH
COPTIC CATHOLIC CHURCH
COPTIC ORTHODOX CHURCH
ETHIOPIAN CATHOLIC CHURCH
ETHIOPIAN ORTHODOX CHURCH
ARMENIAN CATHOLIC CHURCH
ARMENIAN ORTHODOX CHURCH
EASTERN RITE CATHOLIC CHURCHES
ORIENTAL ORTHODOX CHURCHES

Table 1

on the grounds that the wording implied an excessive separation between the divinity and the humanity of the incarnate Christ. Although various attempts were made in the late fifth, the sixth and early seventh centuries to heal the divisions between those who accepted the Council (today, the Orthodox, Catholic and Churches of the Reformation) and those who rejected it (today, the Oriental Orthodox Churches), the division effectively became fossilized as a result of the Arab conquests of the 630s, since the anti-Chalcedonian Churches, located in areas which came under Muslim rule, were now cut off politically from the Byzantine Empire and the Christian West which henceforth remained solely Chalcedonian. A regrettable consequence of this separation was that the polemical terms used in the heat of the christological controversy also got fossilized in the consciousness of the Chalcedonian Churches and have regularly been used up to—and including—modern times: it is only in the context of recent ecumenical dialogue that it is beginning to be realized that the traditional terms 'Jacobite' and 'monophysite' (for the Oriental Orthodox Churches) and 'Nestorian' for the Church of the East, are not only offensive but also positively misleading.

The designation 'Syrian' for the Syrian Orthodox Church of Antioch antedates the creation of the modern state of Syria. Although it so happens that the seat of the Patriarchate is in modern Syria, the designation 'Syrian' in fact refers to the Syriac liturgical tradition of the Church. In the Diaspora, because many members of the Syrian Orthodox Church originate from other countries of the Middle East (Iraq, Turkey, Lebanon etc), and not from the Syrian Arab Republic, the term 'Syriac Orthodox' has sometimes come into usage, in particular in North America.

At the end of the 19th century the Syrian Orthodox Church was present only within the Ottoman empire and (since the late seventeenth century) in south-west India. Some idea of the demographic distribution of the Syrian Orthodox populace in the Middle East, c.1870, can be gained from the figures given in two manuscripts in the Mingana Collection

Table 1: The place of the Syrian Orthodox Church among the other Churches.
(Nb: for reasons of space, the Evangelical offshoots of the different Churches of the Middle East have not been included; likewise, the complicated history of Syriac Christianity in southern India is left out of consideration.)

(University of Birmingham).[2] The figures are given by diocese ('eparshiyah = eparchy); see Table 2. At this time, it should be remembered that that Patriarchate was located at Deir ez Za'faran (Dayro d-Kurkmo), just outside Mardin.

Table 2: The Syrian Orthodox populace in the Middle East, c. 1870

Amid/Diyarbakir and villages	13,500
Mardin and villages	30,000
Gargar, Siverek, Viranshehir and villages	10,000
Deir al-Mu'allaq, Maifarqin [= Silvan], Lice district and villages	10,150
Bsheriyeh, Deir [= Monastery of] Mor Quryaqos, district of Radvan and Garzan, and villages	30,800
Jebel Tur 'Abdin: (1) Deir Qartmin [= Mor Gabriel] (2) Deir Mor Malke (3) Deir Mor Ya'qub of Salah (4) Deir Mor Abraham, Midyat	52,080
Deir Mor Ya'qub, Nisibis, Aznawor district and villages; Deir Mor Awgen	16,500
Cizre, Azakh, Esfes, Basbirina, Midun, 'Ain Sari	10,200
Jebel Quros, district of Sawur, Qellet, and villages	8,000
Melitene and Vilayet of Kharput, district of Hisn Mansur, Adiyaman and villages	8,400
Bitlis, Siirt, Sirvan, Deir Mor Gurgis and villages	13,000
Vilayet of Adana ('TN')	1,500
Syria: Homs, Hama and villages	18,000
Jerusalem, Deir Mor Marqos, Bethlehem	150
Istanbul	600

[2] Mingana Syr. 161, f.245b-246a (dated 1872), and Mingana Syr. 310, f.1b-2a (of *circa* 1894). It seems likely that these tables go back to a 'Statement of Register of the Syrian Orthodox people', compiled in 1870 by 'Abdallah Stoph, a monk from Sadad (near Homs).

Mosul, Balad, Deir Mor Mattai and villages;	
Bahshiqa, Bahzani, Bartelli, Qaraqosh	10,000
Urfa and villages, Aleppo	5,000
Total	237,880

The massacres

As is well known, the Armenian population of Anatolia suffered from a series of massacres in the last years of the Ottoman Empire, especially in 1895/6 and 1915. The reasons for this, given by the Ottoman government of the time and still maintained in many Turkish official publications today,[3] lay in Armenian nationalist aspirations and the accompanying revolutionary actions. Although it is certainly true that some Armenians did have such aspirations and a small number did commit acts of terrorism, the massive scale of retribution, extended in 1915 to the entire Armenian population was totally unjustified. While this much is generally recognized, what is much less recognized is the fact that the Christian populace of eastern Anatolia belonging to the various Syriac Churches also suffered in the same way as the Armenians.

(a) 1895

Information, sometimes very detailed, concerning these massacres, which occurred mainly in the last three months of 1895, is to be found in several published Syriac accounts, in both prose and verse.[4] Some further details are preserved in the colophon of another manuscript in the Mingana Collection, written in Mosul in May 1896, a translation of which is given in Appendix 2. According to this account, the number of Syrian Orthodox who were killed in the course of these massacres of 1895/6 was 25,000, while that for the Armenians was 80,000.

---

[3] See, for example, K Gurun, *The Armenian File: the Myth of Innocence Exposed* (London, 1985).

[4] See the sources for the massacres of 1915, below; the most important is Abdmshiho Na'man, *Dmo Zliho* (1997), 42-50 (German tr. 39-43), based on a contemporary narrative by the priest of Qarabash, Paulos son of Abdulahad.

(b) 1915

Even more dire were the widespread massacres of 1915, during the First World War. Again, besides the Armenians, Christians belonging to the Syriac Churches were also victims, and in Syrian Orthodox oral tradition 1915 is known as 'Sayfo', '(the year of) the Sword', or 'Firmano', '(the year of) the Firman (sc. to kill the Christian population)'. Until recently there has been hardly any documentation for these massacres available in print. An account, in Arabic, had indeed been published in Beirut in 1920 by the Syrian Catholic priest Isaac Armalet, who had been living in Mardin at the time.[5] In the last few years, however, a number of new sources, mainly Syrian Orthodox, have been made available:

JY Çiçek (ed.), 'Seyfe'. *Das Christen-Massaker in der Türkei*, 1714-1914 [in Syriac] (St Ephrem Monastery, Holland, 1981). This is a collection of verse texts by different authors; several contain material of historical interest.

Suleyman Henno, *Schicksalschlage der syrischen Christen im Tur-Abdin 1915* [in Syriac] (St Ephrem Monastery, Holland, 1987); a Turkish translation has been published in Germany, *Ferman: Tur 'Abdinli Suryanilerin 1914-1915 Katliami*, 1993. This contains a very detailed account, village by village, in part based on oral information from survivors. Exact figures and names are often given.

'P.V.M', 'Documents sur les evenements de Mardine 1915-1920', *Studia Orientalia Christiana, Collectanea* 29/30 (1996/7), 5-220.

'Abdmshiho Na'man d-Qarahbash, *Dmo Zliho* ['Spattered Blood'; in Syriac] (Augsburg, 1997; St Ephrem Monastery, 1999). German translation by G. Toro and A. Gorgis, *Vergossenes Blut. Geschichten der Greuel, die an den Christen in der Türkei verubt, und der Leiden, die ihnen 1895 aund 1914-1918 zugefugt wurden* (Bar-Hebraeus Verlag, Glane, 2002). In 1915 the author was a boy of 12 studying at the Seminary School in Deir ez-Za'faran (the

---

5 Ishaq Armaleh, *Al-qusara fi nakabat an-nasara* (Beirut, 1920); cp. also Joseph Naayem, *Les Assyro-Chaldeens et les Arméniens massacrés par les Turcs* (Paris, 1920; English translation, *Shall this Nation die?* (New York, 1921). For the massacres in eastern Anatolia of the Assyrians, see G Yonan, *Ein vergessener Holocaust. Die Vernichtung der christlichen Assyrer in der Türkei* (Göttingen/Vienna, 1989); also G Davis (ed.), *Genocides against the Assyrians* (Washington DC, 1999) [a collection of documents; non vidi] and S R Sonyel, *The Assyrians of Turkey: Victims of Major Power Policy* (Turkish Historical Society Publications, VII.168; Ankara, 2001) *[non vidi]*.

seat of the Patriarchate, just outside Mardin). His book contains detailed information on the massacres of 1895 as well as on those during the First World War.

Na'man Aydin, *Gedshe w-Shabte d-Tur'Abdin* [in Syriac] (St Ephrem Monastery, 1997). Poems, with introductions containing information on monasteries and churches.

Asmar al-Khoury, *Sulfotho qashyotho d-'al Suryoye* [in Syriac] (Södertälje, 1998). Prose and verse accounts, village by village.

S de Courtois, *Le génocide oublié. Chrétiens d'Orient, les derniers araméens* (Editions Ellipses: Collection l'Orient politique, 2002); English translation: *The Forgotten Genocide*, Gorgias Press, Piscataway NJ, 2004. This is focused on Mardin, and makes use of French official documents from the time.

From the various sources it is possible to discern a general pattern underlying the massacres: initially the younger men were conscripted, originally (August 1914) into the army, but from March 1915 onwards into forced labour under harsh conditions, as a result of which many died (one source says that the survival rate was only 30 percent[6] survived). The leading men, including the clergy, in both towns and villages, were first summoned (or simply rounded up) and then imprisoned, only to be taken off in droves and killed in some secluded place. Thus, for example, on 9 April 1915 the governor of Diyarbakir ordered his deputy to seize the leading Christians. In the course of three days 1200[7] men had been rounded up; these were imprisoned and subjected to various tortures. Finally, on 25 April they were roped together and taken by 15[8] boats, allegedly to go to exile in Mosul, but in fact the governor had given secret orders for them to be taken ashore at the village of Shkafto, after two days' journey, and there to be stripped and killed by the local headman, 'Omarkay son of Farikhaneh. Once the men were all out of the way and disposed of in this sort of manner, those who remained, especially in the villages, where only women and children left, could be attacked and pillaged with impunity.

6 Abdmshiho Na'man (1997), 80 (German tr. 61).

7 See Abdmshiho Na'man, pp 81-2 (German tr. 61-2). There is some understandable variation in the figures given in the different sources: a second account on p. 192 (German tr. 124) gives '807', and Henno, 10, has 'about 700'.

8 The second account in Abdmshiho Na'man gives '17'.

In 1919, after the First World War had ended, Bishop Severios Barsaum (who was to become Patriarch, 1933-1957) presented figures for the number of Syrian Orthodox villages affected and persons killed in the massacres (see Table 3);[9] when these figures are compared with those in Table 2, it becomes evident that the Syrian Orthodox Church lost well over one third of its people in the Middle East. Eight out of the twenty dioceses in the Middle East were either totally, or very largely, wiped out, and whole areas which had formerly had a sizeable Syrian Orthodox population were now left with none, since those who had escaped being killed had fled elsewhere.

Table 3: Bishop Severios Barsaum's figures for Syrian Orthodox losses in the massacres during the First World War

Town	villages affected	families	persons	churches	priests
Amid/Diyarbakir	30	764	5,379	5	7
Bsheriyeh	30	718	4,481	10	10
Bitlis	12	130	850	1	
Cizre	26	994	7,510	13	8
Derik		50	350	1	1
Garzan	22	744	5,140	12	9
Kharput/Elazig[10]	24	508	3,500	5	2

[9] The table can be found reproduced in a number of different places (the figures differ minimally; those given here are based on the original document as reproduced by S de Courtois).

[10] Although it concerns the far more numerous Armenian population, a very important contemporary account of the massacres in this region is to be found in L A Davis (ed. S K Blair), *The Slaughterhouse Province. An American Diplomat's Report on the Armenian Genocide, 1915-1917* (New Rochelle, 1989). Davis was the American Consul in Kharput from 1915-1917. That the Syrian Orthodox were also included is clear from his passing references to them, alongside the Armenians, in his Dispatches (to the American Ambassador, Henry Morgenthau), of 30 June 1915 (p. 144) and of 30 Dec 1915 (pp. 179-80). On the massacres of the Armenians, particularly important is his comment in his Dispatch of 24 July 1915, where he says: 'I have written strongly about the situation and proceedings here because it is impossible to write about them at all and not do so. It is not that I am in any way a champion of the Armenian race. It is not a race one can admire or among whom I should chose to live. But whatever the faults of the Armenian people may be and however conclusive may be the proof that some of them have been involved in a revolutionary plot, the punishment inflicted upon these people is so severe, the tragedy is so terrible, that one cannot contemplate it and certainly cannot live in the midst of it without being stirred to the depths of one's nature. ..... [I]t is impossible to conceive of any justification that can be urged for a measure so severe.' (p. 160). A moving account by a survivor from a village in the Kharput region is given by Elizabeth Caraman, *Daughter of the Euphrates* (New York, 1939).

Lice	10	658	4,706	5	4
Mardin	8	880	5,815	12	5
Midyat	47	3,935	29,830	60	60
Nuseybin	50	1,000	7,000	12	25
Baravat	15	282	1,880	1	1
Sirvan	9	283	1,870	2	4
Savur	7	880	6,164	2	3
Siirt		100	650	1	2
Siverek	30	897	5,725	12	12
Urfa (Edessa)		50	340		
Viranshehir	16	303	1,928	1	
Total	345/6	13,350	90,313	150	154

The Kurdish uprising of 1925/6 caused much further suffering to several of the Syrian Orthodox villages in parts of Tur 'Abdin.[11] Among the bases that Kurds took over were two famous monasteries, that of the Cross, and Mor Malke. Both were eventually taken and destroyed by the Turkish army. There had also been plans to sack Mor Gabriel monastery too, since it had been alleged to be another Kurdish stronghold, but fortunately a Syrian Orthodox serving under the army commander learnt of the plans, informed the bishop who managed to get a counter order from the army general in Diyarbakir, thus saving this ancient monastery which, in 1997, celebrated the 1600th anniversary of its foundation.

Emigration

It was this first traumatic event, the massacres of 1895/6 and 1915, which led to the second traumatic event, the large-scale emigration from Eastern Turkey. Prior to 1895 there had been very little emigration of Christians of the Syriac Churches, but in the late 1890s, and again after 1915, large numbers fled from their homes and either settled in other parts of the Middle East (notably modern Lebanon and Syria), or emigrated to the West, and in particular North America. It was in this initial wave of emigration

[11] The following is based on the Syriac account by Na'man Aydin in *Qolo Suryoyo* 62 (1988), 155–53 [sic]; also his article in *Qolo Suryoyo* 117/118 (1997), 226–19 *[sic]*. (*Qolo Suryoyo/Kolo Süryoyo* is the very informative magazine of the Archdiocese of Central Europe, and has been published on a regular basis since 1978).

that many Syrian Orthodox from Diyarbakir settled in New Jersey, those from Kharput in Massachussets, those from Tur 'Abdin in Rhode Island, and those from Mardin in Canada (Montreal and Sherbrooke). Yet others went to Brasil (San Paolo, Campo Grande) and Argentina (Buenos Aires, Cordoba, Frias-S.Estiro). The first priest for North America was ordained in 1907, and the first two Syrian Orthodox churches were consecrated in 1927 (New York) and 1928 (Worcester, Mass.).[12]

Although the second massive emigration from Eastern Turkey did not get under way until the early 1970s, two political events of the intervening years resulted in Syrian Orthodox emigration from two other parts of the Middle East. The creation of the State of Israel in 1948 had led to many Palestinian Christians being driven out of their homes, and among those who emigrated to the West were a number of Syrian Orthodox, including the Bishop of Jerusalem, Mor Athanasius Samuel, who had been one of the first people to recognize the importance of the Dead Sea Scrolls, buying a number of them from the Beduin finders.[13] In 1957 Mor Athanasius was appointed Metropolitan of the newly created Archdiocese of North America, and he subsequently played a very important part in the development of the Syrian Orthodox community in America: new churches were acquired, or built, and the main liturgical books were translated into English and published in bilingual editions.[14] When Mor Athanasius died in 1995 the number of Syrian Orthodox parishes warranted the division of the Archdiocese into three separate Patriarchal Vicariates (Eastern US, Western US, and Canada). There are now some 35,000 Syrian Orthodox in North America as a whole.

Further emigration from Israel and the West Bank has taken place as a result, especially, of the June War of 1967, and the First and Second Intifada. As a result, the number of Syrian Orthodox left in

---

12 The information on North America is derived from an unpublished typescript on the history of the Syrian Orthodox in North America by the Very Revd John Meno.

13 Athanasius Y Samuel, *Treasure of Qumran. My Story of the Dead Seas Scrolls* (London, 1968). Further information, based on information from the diary of the author's father, a friend of Mor Athanasius, is to be found in G Kiraz's (Syriac) colophon to his *Comparative Edition of the Syriac Gospels*, IV (Leiden, 1996), 371-4. G Kiraz has also given an account of the Syrian Orthodox community of Bethlehem in his *'Iqd al-Juman fi Ahbar al-Suryan* (St Ephrem Monastery, Holland, 1987).

14 Bilingual volumes of the Services for Baptism, Marriage and Burial were published in 1974 (Hackensack NJ), of special services for Festivals in 1984 (Lodi NJ), and of a collection of anaphoras in 1991 (Lodi NJ); for the latter, see my review in *Sobornost/Eastern Churches Review* 15:1 (1993), 71-3.

Jerusalem (focused on the Monastery of St Mark) and Bethlehem is now very small.

Emigration of Syrian Orthodox (along with other Christians) from Iraq has been caused by a number of political events in that country: the revolution of 1960, the Iraq-Iran War, and the Gulf War along with its aftermath.[15] In Lebanon, the troubles of 1961 and especially the Civil War, likewise led to considerable numbers of Syrian Orthodox (and of course others) seeking a new and more peaceful home in the West.

Unlike these earlier smaller waves, the second massive wave of emigration again came from eastern Turkey. This time it did not have its origins in turmoil caused by the political situation, but its roots go back to the agreement between the Turkish and West German governments in 1961 whereby encouragement was given to Turkish workers to go to Germany as Gastarbeiters.[16] Among those who went were a number of young Syrian Orthodox men from the economically depressed area of Tur ʿAbdin. In the late 1960s and early 1970s the momentum increased considerably, with whole families settling in the Netherlands and Sweden as well as Germany. This was because the situation in Tur ʿAbdin deteriorated seriously as a result of Kurdish insurgence in the region. The Syrian Orthodox were caught up in the turmoil between the Turkish Army and the Kurdish insurgents (the PKK), and as a result of the Turkish Army's scorched-earth policy a large number of villages were forcibly evacuated. This situation lasted until 1999 when a ceasefire eventually came about. In the early 1990s the situation in Tur ʿAbdin had actually become even worse, due to the activities of Islamic extremists who targeted leading figures in the Syrian Orthodox villages, as a way of instilling fear in the community, the aim being to get the people to leave. Thus, for example, on 29 November 1993 the Mayor of Hah (a village famous for its ancient and beautiful church) was assassinated, and a year later, on 18th Decmber 1994, the only remaining Christian doctor in the small town of Midyat, in

---

[15] The destruction of many villages in the north, in the course of the government's campaign against the Kurds, led to a massive forced emigration of Christians from the north to Baghdad. Many Assyrians, of course, had left, or were driven out, in 1933; for this, see especially R S Stafford, *The Tragedy of the Assyrians* (London, 1935). For a well documented account of Christians in Iraq in recent years, see B Dumler, 'Zur aktuellen Situation der Christen im Irak', *Ostkirchliche Studien* 48 (1999), 107-43.

[16] For details on the diaspora in Germany, see K Merten, *Die syrisch-orthodoxen Christen in der Türkei und in Deutschland* (Hamburg, 1997); also H Acar, *Menschen zwischen Kulturen: Aramäische Jugendliche in Deutschland* (Paderborn, 1997).

the middle of Tur 'Abdin, met a similar fate. Following a regular pattern, their murderers were never brought to justice. It has only been since the time when Turkey was first notified of the possibility of its eventual entry into the European Union, that the local situation in Tur 'Abdin has markedly improved.

In 1973 the West German government terminated its agreement with Turkey over Gastarbeiters. This came precisely at the time when conditions in Tur 'Abdin were becoming intolerable for many Syrian Orthodox, and so the flow of would-be immigrants to Europe actually increased, coming by way of the ever increasing Syrian Orthodox community in Istanbul. Those who still made for Germany now had to claim refugee status (which in effect barred them from returning to Turkey). Because this was not easy to acquire, many people now turned to Sweden as a place of refuge.[17]

In Sweden the first Syrian Orthodox immigrants had arrived as refugees from Lebanon in 1966, along with some Assyrians (of the Church of the East). Owing to the government authorities' failure to distinguish between the two Church groups, the Syrian Orthodox were also described as 'Assyrians'. This subsequently gave rise to much trouble and conflict within the Swedish community: once in Europe, where ethnic identity, rather than ecclesial (as in the Middle East) predominates, many Syrian Orthodox laity wanted to find an appropriate ethnic label that would be recognized in a secular western society; some wished to keep the (historically mistaken) identity as 'Assyrians', while others strongly objected to it, and adopted instead 'Aramean' as their ethnic identity. The issue remains one on which feelings still run high.

Numbers

It is possible to gain quite a good idea of the numbers involved from a variety of different sources. In the Introduction to his book on Turoyo, the Modern Aramaic dialect of Tur Abdin, published in 1967, Helmut Ritter provides figures for the number of families and persons in all the villages

---

[17] U Bjørklund, *North to another Country: the Formation of a Suryoyo Community in Sweden* (Stockholm, 1981). For the Netherlands, see F Sumer, *De Syrisch Orthodoxe Gemeenschap* (Hengelo, 1982), and for the community in Istanbul, R Roldanus, *De Syrisch Orthodoxen in Istanbul* (Kampern, 1984).

(43 in all) which had a Syrian Orthodox population.[18] This will represent the situation before the emigration had started on any large scale. Figures, for the same villages, are next available for 1978, 1979, 1981 and 1987.[19] Then, finally, there are figures for 1995 [20] and 1997;[21] these last two more or less represent the culmination of the emigration. This is not the place to give the full details;[22] the general pattern, however, can readily be seen from the figures for some of the more prominent villages (figures denote families,[23] unless otherwise stated):

Village	1966	1978	1979	1981	1987	1995	1997
Anhel/Yemishli[24]	1306	152	140	135	82	7	
Arkah/Uckoy	120	103	92	88	70	38	
Aynwardo/Gulgoze	140	96	91	93	60	7	
Bekusyone/Alagoz	155	73	62	63	30	15	17
Bsorino/Haberli	120	78	70	63	40	22	18
Hah/Anitli	73	67	55	52	42	19	18
Kafro Tahtoyto/ Elbeğendi	37	44	37	23	15 (forcibly evacuated)		
Kerburan/Dargeçeit	150	16					

[18] H Ritter, *Turoyo, die Volkssprache der syrischen Christen der Tur 'Abdin*, I (Beirut, 1967), pp. *10*-*15*. For the Syrian Orthodox of Tur 'Abdin in general, see H Anschütz, *Die syrischen Christen vom Tur Abdin* (Würzburg, 1985). A wonderful collection of illustrations is to be found in H Hollerweger, *Turabdin. Lebendiges Kulturerbe/Living Cultural Heritage/Canli Kultur Mirasi* (Linz, 1999).

[19] The sources for 1978 and 1979: *Qolo Suryoyo* 11 (1979), 25-7; for 1981: *Qolo Suryoyo* 19 (1981), 19-17 [sic]; for 1987 (and 1915): *Qolo Suryoyo* 56 (1987), 140-41 (also Henno, 178-81). Figures for 1966 and 1995 concerning the towns can be found in the table in S P Brock (ed.), *The Hidden Pearl: the Syrian Orthodox Church and its Ancient Aramaic Heritage*, III, *At the Turn of the Third Millennium: the Syrian Orthodox Witness* (Rome, 2001), 94. The annually decreasing figures for the Syrian Orthodox in the Province of Mardin from 1972 (17,340) to 1989 (4,829) are given in Merten, *Die syrisch-orthodoxen Christen in der Türkei und in Deutschland*, 249.

[20] For 1995: *Zur Lage der Christen in der Sudosturkei, in Syrien und Irak* (Augsburg, 1995), 88.

[21] For 1997: *Qolo Suryoyo* 117/118 (1997), p. 216, where it is stated that only 300 families were left.

[22] For a Table giving the figures for all the villages (and including figures for 1915, given by Suleyman Henno, *Gunhe d-Tur Abdin*), see *The Hidden Pearl*, III, pp. 92-3.

[23] To judge by the figures given for both families and persons in Ritter, the families mentioned vary between 5 and 10 persons.

[24] In the 1960s the Turkish government systematically renamed all the villages with Turkish names. This act of cultural suppression was presumably aimed at wiping out the memory of the past history of the region.

Kfarze/Altintash	130	68	64	42	27	12	12
Marbobo/Gunyurdu	57	67	38	28 (forcibly evacuated)			
Midyat	700	403	400	400	250	108	70
Mzizah/Doğançay	100	80		56	35	8	7
Zaz/Izbirak	75	69	62	53	25		

On the receiving end, in Europe, it is said that by the early 1970s there were about 2,000 persons in Germany, the country which received the majority of the early emigration. By contrast, Sweden only had about 1,000 by 1974,[25] although this was soon to change rapidly, as can be seen for the rounded-off figures (of persons) given by Mor Julius Çiçek for the different countries for 1977:[26]

Sweden	10,000
Germany	7,000
Austria, Netherlands	700 each
France, Switzerland	600 each
Rest of Scandinavia	500
Great Britain	250
Belgium	100

By the end of the millennium these figures had increased markedly, as the very approximate figures for 2000:[27]

Germany	50,000+
Sweden	45,000+
Netherlands	12,000
Switzerland	5,000
Belgium	800 families
France	1,000
Austria	300 families
Great Britain	140 families

According to Mor Julius Çiçek the present to tal of Syrian Orthodox in Western Europe is approximately 150,000 persons.

[25] Bjorklund, 63.

[26] The figures are based on Mor Julius' paper at a conference on the Syriac tradition held at the Ambrosian Library, Milan. on March 28th 2003. I am most grateful to His Eminence for a copy of the original Syriac text of his paper, now published in *Qolo Suryoyo* 139 (2003), 86-81 *[sic]*.

[27] The figures are those I gave in *The Hidden Pearl*, III, 99-103, based on information gathered from a variety of Church sources.

The establishment of new dioceses in the diaspora in Europe

The creation, in 1957, of an Archdiocese for North America has already been mentioned. In Europe, by 1977 the growing numbers in the emigre communities warranted the creation of two new dioceses, one of Central Europe (covering Germany, the Low Countries, France and Austria), the other of Scandinavia (under which Britain was included). For the former, a Patriarchal Vicar was appointed, Rabban Isa Çiçek (the former abbot of Mor Gabriel Monastery in Tur 'Abdin), while for the latter Mor Timotheos Afrem Aboudi was appointed, taking up his residence in Sodertalje, near Stockholm, where most of the Syrian Orthodox had settled). Two years later Rabban Isa Çiçek was made Metropolitan, taking the name Mor Julius (Çiçek), with his seat, from 1983, at the newly founded Monastery of St Ephrem, near Hengelo in the east of the Netherlands.

In Sweden, partly due to the large increase in numbers, and partly to the conflicts over the designations 'Assyrian' and 'Aramean', a new Patriarchal Vicariate was established in 1994. Three years later, in April 1997, the Archdiocese of Central Europe was divided into two, with Germany as a separate diocese under a Patriarchal Vicar (Mor Dionysius Gurbuz).

Monasteries and churches

Throughout history, monasteries have always played a very important cultural as well as spiritual role in the Syrian Orthodox Church. In the mid-twentieth century monasticism was at a rather low ebb, but in the latter half of the century a considerable revival has taken place, although by no means on the same scale as has happened in the Coptic Orthodox Church. In this revival a particularly important role has been played by the Monastery of Mor Gabriel in Tur 'Abdin, the seat of the Metropolitan of Tur 'Abdin, Mor Timotheos Samuel Aktash. Besides having both monks and nuns,[28] the monastery complex also includes a school for young boys which has, for over three decades now, been under the inspiring guidance of its head teacher, Malfono Isa Gulten. This school provides an excellent training both in the liturgical services and in Classical Syriac. Many of the young men now teaching Syriac in church or state schools in Europe

---

[28] For the rebirth of women's monastic life at the monastery, see E Gulcan, 'The renewal of monastic life for women in a monastery in Tur 'Abdin', *Sobornost* 7: 4 (1977), 288-98.

have received their training at this school.[29] Although the Monastery receives many visitors from emigres returning for holidays as well as from tourists, the huge scale of the emigration has seriously dried up the pool of children from local villages in Tur 'Abdin, from which in the past the school drew.[30]

Other indications of revival of Syrian Orthodox monastic life in the Middle East are physically visible in the newly built Monastery (cum seminary) of St Ephrem, in Ma'arret Saidnaya, north of Damascus, which was consecrated in 1996, and the Monastery of Mary, Yoldat Aloho (Bearer of God); the latter, consecrated in 2000 and situated at Tel Wardiyat, to the west of Hasseke (E Syria), is also of considerable architectural interest.[31] In Iraq, the ancient Monastery of Mar Mattai, not far from Mosul, has undergone much renovation in recent years.

In contrast to the situation in America where no Syrian Orthodox monasteries have yet been founded, the emigré community in the Archdiocese of Central Europe has been been very active in this respect. This has primarily been thanks to the initiative of the Metropolitan, Mor Julius Çiçek. In 1981 the opportunity came of buying a former Catholic monastery at an advantageous price; situated just outside the village of Glane, on the Dutch/German border, and not far from Hengelo, the building was converted and consecrated as the Monastery of St Ephrem in 1984.[32] Besides serving as the seat of the Metropolitan, it also provides a religious and cultural focus for the emigre community (in 1994 a large new church was built in the grounds in order better to serve these needs). Since 1986 it has also been the location of the Bar Hebraeus Verlag, which is very active in publishing both liturgical and cultural books in Syriac; before the advent of printing Syriac by computer technology, many of these books were reproduced from Mor Julius' own beautiful handwriting.[33]

---

[29] In state schools in Sweden (since 1976), the Netherlands (since 1982), and Germany (since the 1990s) Syriac can be taught as a cultural language when there are sufficient numbers of Syrian Orthodox pupils.

[30] See Hollerweger, *Turabdin*, 59-91.

[31] Illustrated in *The Hidden Pearl*, III, 83-5.

[32] Illustrated in *The Hidden Pearl*, III, 145-6, 150 (top).

[33] *Ewangelyon Qadisho d-'ide Moranoye* (Bar Hebraeus Verlag, 1987), with 16 illustrations taken from a thirteenth-century Gospel Lectionary in Tur 'Abdin. An illustration of Mor Julius at work writing out a manuscript can be found in *The Hidden Pearl*, III, p. 147, while a sample of his calligraphy is on p. 182 (top left; an edition of Anaphoras, published in 1985, whose contents are described in my 'Two recent editions of Syrian Orthodox Anaphoras', *Ephemerides Liturgicae* 102 (1988), pp. 436-45).

Much more recently, Mor Julius Çiçek was given the possibility of buying a former Capuchin monastery in Arth (Switzerland), again at a generously low price, and this has now become the Monastery of Mor Awgen (an early monastic saint), consecrated in 1999. Meanwhile in Germany (which had become a separate diocese in 1997), a former Dominican monastery was acquired in Warburg, and this was consecrated as the Monastery of Mor Ya'qub (Jacob) of Serugh in 2000.

Prior to the founding of these monasteries, however, numerous churches had been acquired or even built in the various countries of the European diaspora. In the early years, especially, much help, both financial and practical, was afforded by both the Catholic and the Reformed Churches. Today the European diaspora has some 60 churches and is served by 125 priests.[34] Besides the various Church associations, there is now a considerable number of secular lay organisations, many of which produce their own cultural magazines.[35]

In very recent years, thanks to the much improved situation in Tur 'Abdin, a few families have started to go back to their ancestral villages. Whether or not this will continue and grow will very much depend on the political and economic situation in Turkey in coming years. But, in any case, it would seem likely that the vast majority of the European diaspora will remain where they are.

Theological dialogue[36]

On a purely practical and local level, the Syrian Orthodox emigration in Europe has received a great deal of assistance of one sort or another from the different Western Churches. This was already the case in the very early years of the emigration, and has continued to this day. It was certainly in part due to this large-scale presence, for the first time in history, of Syrian Orthodox in Europe that the need for theological dialogue between the Chalcedonian Western Churches and the non-Chalcedonian Syrian

[34] Derived from information by Mor Julius in *Qolo Suryoyo* 139 (2003), 86-81 *[sic]*; see also *Qolo Suryoyo* 126 (1999), 306-288 *[sic]*. Some of the churches are illustrated in *The Hidden Pearl*, III, 169-71, 176-7.

[35] For these, see The Hidden Pearl, III, 124-8, and illustrations on 180-1, 183.

[36] This is only covered here in very summary form since I have given a much fuller account in 'The Syriac Churches in ecumenical dialogue on christology', in A O'Mahony (ed.), *Eastern Christianity. Studies in Religion, History and Politics* (London, 2003), 44-65.

Orthodox Church became more apparent. The Syrian Orthodox Church had joined the World Council of Churches in 1960, and from 1964 onwards there had been Non-Official (and later, Official) dialogue between the Syrian Orthodox and other Oriental Orthodox Churches with the (Chalcedonian) Orthodox Church.[37] But it was not until 1971, however, that Non-Official dialogue between the Syrian Orthodox (and other Oriental Orthodox) Churches with the Catholic Church commenced, thanks to the initiative of the PRO ORIENTE Foundation in Vienna.[38] The two most prominent outcomes of dialogue with the Catholic Church were the meetings in Rome of Pope Paul VI with Patriarch Mar Ignatius Ya'qub III in 1971, and of Pope John Paul II with Patriarch Mar Ignatius Zakka I Iwas in June 1984, on both of which occasions a common declaration signed by both hierarchs was issued.[39] The latter declaration is particularly important, since allowance is made for intercommunion in cases where a priest of the individual's own Church is not available.

In all these theological dialogues it already became clear at an early stage that the differences over christology were only surface deep; once one takes the trouble to penetrate beyond these surface differences (which sometimes involve verbally conflicting formulations), the existence of an underlying orthodox faith in Christ held in common becomes apparent. In the light of this, it is clearly an urgent task on all sides, not only to convey a sense of this commonality of faith to both ordinary clergy and people, but also to ensure that the standard textbooks on doctrine and Church history are rewritten, or at least revised, in a spirit of ecumenical openness.

★ ★ ★

This rather rapid survey of certain aspects of the history of the Syrian Orthodox Church in the 20th century has of necessity been very selective, and

---

[37] The most important documents are reproduced in C Chaillot and A Belopopsky (eds), *Towards Unity. The Theological Dialogue between the Orthodox Church and the Oriental Orthodox Churches* (Geneva, 1998).

[38] The communiqués and main papers are republished in PRO ORIENTE, *Five Vienna Consultations between Theologians of the Oriental Orthodox Churches and the Roman Catholic Church* (Vienna, 1993). From 1994 onwards PRO ORIENTE has organised a series of 'Syriac Dialogues', involving all the Churches of Syriac traditions; five volumes of the proceedings have so far been published.

[39] See, for example, A Stirnemann and G Wilflinger, *Ortskirche und Weltkirche* (Innsbruck/Wien, 1999), 305-6, 311-13.

it should be recognized that many important features, such as developments in the Middle East and in Kerala, have been left aside entirely.

APPENDIX 1

SOME KEY DATES

(A useful 'calendar' of events of importance for the Syrian Orthodox diaspora in Europe, covering 1977-2003, is given by Mor Julius Çiçek in *Qolo Suryoyo* 139 (2003), pp. 75-61 [sic].)

1895/6	Massacres, above all in Diyarbakir area
1915	The 'Year of the Sword' (Sayfo): large-scale massacres in eastern Anatolia
1957	Archdiocese of North America created
1960	The Syrian Orthodox Church becomes a member of the World Council of Churches
1960s	First Gastarbeiters from Tur 'Abdin go to Germany
1970s	Emigration from Tur 'Abdin to western Europe on a large scale
1971 (27 Oct)	Common Communique of Pope Paul VI and Patriarch Ignatius Ya'qub III
1973	Germany ends agreement with Turkey over foreign labour
1977	New dioceses of Central Europe and Scandinavia
1984 (23 Jun)	Common Declaration of Pope John Paul II and Patriarch Ignatius Zakka IIwas
1984 (7 Jul)	Consecration of Monastery of St Ephrem, Holland
1986 (5/6 Jul)	Opening of Bar Hebraeus Verlag, Monastery of St Ephrem
1994	New Patriarchal Vicariate in Sweden
1995	Archdiocese of North America divided into 3 Patriarchal Vicariates
1996	New Patriarchal Seminary of St Ephrem, Ma'arret Saidnaya, Syria
1997	Archdiocese of Central Europe divided, with separate Patriarchal Vicariate of Germany
1999 (20 Jun)	Consecration of Monastery of Mor Augen, Switzerland
2000 (15 Aug)	Consecration of Monastery of Yoldat Aloho (Theotokos), Tel Wardiyat, Syria
2000 (27 Aug)	Consecration of Monastery of Mor Ya'qub, Warburg, Germany.

APPENDIX 2

Historical notice in Mingana Syr. 95 concerning the massacres of 1895.

Mingana Syr. 95, containing a variety of different texts, was completed by a well-known Syrian Orthodox scribe, the deacon Mattai son of Paulos, in Mosul on 2nd May, 1896. On ff. 122a-123b he provides a notice (probably his own) concerning the massacres that had taken place in October and December the previous year. Since this notice was only written a few months after the events, it is translated here. It should be noted that the dates given are likely to be by the Old Calendar (the New Calendar was officially adopted by the Syrian Orthodox Church in November 1954). For other sources on the massacres of Syrian Orthodox in 1895, see note 4.

Translation

In this year, in the month Teshrin I (October) there was fear and trembling in all the regions and cities and villages where there are Christians (Nasraye), while the remnant of the Christians (Mshihaye) living among the Muslims were in terror that they would kill them. They began to kill the Christians (Mshihaye), plunder their houses and burn their possessions, from the city of Trebizond to the city of Amid (i.e. Diyarbakir; above the line, the scribe adds 'and Edessa'), along with the towns and villages around them. In every town the Muslims rose up against the Christians and massacred them: wherever there were Christians, they massacred them wholesale, without mercy or pity, killing men, women and children, old and young. But anyone who became a Muslim they did not kill—and there were a few people who did turn Muslim. Let us beseech the Lord our God that he spread over us his holy hands, so that the Muslims may not harm us, and that he may deliver us from the hands of the insolent Kurds, by the prayer of Mary, Bearer of God, and of the holy prophets, amen.

This took place in the days of Sultan 'Abdulhamid, when he sent his son-in-law Sakr Pasha (i.e. Musir Shakir?) to pacify and put in order the nations (i.e. millets). He sent him deceitfully: he left Byzantia (i.e. Istanbul) secretly, and he ordered him to do what he liked. When he arrived at Trebizond by sea, he sent telegraph messages to every region and city to the judges (i.e. Qadis) and governors to kill every Christian, catching them by surprise. But an order (publicly) went out from the Sultan about the community of the Armenians: because the Armenians were wanting to set up self rule (lit: a king and a house), the Ottoman Sultan Abdulhamid, not wishing them to govern their own state *(bayta)*, commanded that they be killed. Of the Armenians, 80,000 were killed in the towns and villages, and from our own people, the Suryoye (i.e. Syrian Orthodox), they massacred about 25,000—that is, those that were known (sc. to have been killed), and from the Chaldeans, and apart from them (others) were killed.[a] The pretext (for this) being the Armenians. This took place on Friday 12th October in the year 1895, in the regions of the towns Trebizond, Erzurum, Bitlis and Severek, (margin: + and Edessa) and in the villages around them; also in Amid and the surrounding villages, the villages around Mardin, Seert, Urfa (Edessa), Kharput, Malatya, Mar'ash and Bshiriyeh, and all the regions and villages whose names are Anadwar (sic; = ?) and Gezirta d-Qardu (i.e. Cizre).[b] Some were massacred, others turned Muslim. And those who hid to escape massacre had their houses plundered. They dragged people from the churches and houses. This was the work of Kurds, a people without mercy: they sacked the houses of Christians (Nasraye), and their markets and shops. Those who had any life left in them were naked and without food, with no bread or anything else to eat.

The Patriarch and the Syriac Christians (lit. saints), and the faithful people, collected money, wheat and clothing from the towns to send to those of the faithful Christians who had survived in every region and village, because they were all in great affliction and fear.

Now in Edessa there was a second occasion when the command went out from the (local) governor to massacre the Armenian community; and they massacred them and plundered their houses and possessions, (seizing them) from the markets and shops; and they tore down their villages, and everything they had planted in the villages they uprooted—trees, crops and such like. This second occasion took place on 28th Kanun I (December) of the year AD 1895.

Christians suffered persecution and affliction in every city, region and town. And he who survived the slaughter had become Muslim, and many Christians became Muslims out of fear of slaughter and the sword in the villages and towns: they apostasized (to escape from) plunder and rapine, so as to save themselves from slaughter and plunder. Whoever was saved from slaughter and the sword had all his property and possessions in his house—down to the corn in his house—plundered, and they did not leave them anything to

[a] The official government figures of those killed in 1895 were: 1,828 Muslims, and 8,717 non-Muslims (Gurun, p. 150; for the wildly conflicting figures given for the period 1890-1896, see p. 160).

[b] There had been incidents involving Armenian revolutionaries in most of these towns. The scribe's subsequent addition of Urfa suggests that he only learnt later of the appalling massacres there (for these, in October and on December 28th-29th, 1895, see the account, based on the witness of Gerald Fitzmaurice, the chief interpreter at the British Embassy, in Sir Edwin Pears, *The Life of Abdul Hamid* [London, 1917], pp. 249-53). Many of these regions were visited by the biblical scholar J. Rendell Harris in 1896; he and his wife Helen have left an account in their *Letters from the Scenes of the Recent Armenian Massacres* (London, 1897).

eat, or any clothes to wear. They lived on the ground, without beds, in the dust, and because of the great amount of hail, cold and snow that year, they began to die; because many had fled to the mountains (to live) in caves to escape from the sword, they died of cold and hunger. The rich in the cities and villages who received the poor and needy into their houses, giving alms to those in want, were suddenly impoverished and left with no food to satisfy and fill their bellies. They had to beg for food like the poor, and to beg for help from those who had some pity to show them. Deliver us, O Lord God, from the hands of the shameless murderers who shed blood for no reason and without any cause.

Our Syrian Patriarch, Ignatius Abdulmasih, was in Amid, and after the massacre had abated, about the third day, he sent a report to the governor, and (the latter) brought soldiers to keep guard over the Christians who had survived the massacre. The governor made an agreement with our Patriarch and told him: In every case where your people have suffered from kidnapping of wives, daughters and young children, I will send for them and return them to you. And in every case where they have plundered any of your people, I will have it returned, because you are among those loyal to the Sultan.

Wherever the Patriarch heard that someone's daughter or wife was in such and such a place, the governor began to send orders concerning them, together with messengers to bring them back. He also began to collect the plunder from the Muslims, but he did not bring back one thousandth of it, and what was lost was lost (for good). And the order went out from the Sultan that whoever had apostasized out of terror of massacre should return to his former confession. And people began to return, little by little. And the sovereign, that is the Sultan, sent a 'prime missive' to our Patriarch, with the seal (sigillion), in all solemnity.

THE MARONITE PATRIARCH IN THE CONTEMPORARY ERA—TRADITION AND CHALLENGES

Fiona McCallum

In examining the political role of Christianity in the Middle East, the case of the Maronites provides an enlightening study. The Maronites have long been associated with their spiritual homeland Lebanon—the only country in the region to have a Christian Head of State. In the past, the Maronite patriarch has exercised both religious and temporal authority but the establishment of a strong presidency in the independent Lebanese state was regarded as restricting the political role of the patriarch. The consequences of the civil war have provided the Maronite hierarchy, especially the patriarch, the conditions in which to rediscover this role and act as the legitimate representative of the community. The church has attempted to satisfy these needs by using all the resources available—spiritual, practical and political. The realities of the 21st century have also ensured that the patriarch must act on an international stage—both in political developments and in response to the expanding Maronite diaspora.[1] Hence, the following article will seek to provide an analysis of contemporary patriarchal authority in the case of the Maronite church.

The origins of the patriarch

The term patriarch which is used to describe the head of many Eastern Christian churches originates from a combination of Latin and Greek—*pater* meaning father, *patria* meaning lineage, race, people, nation and lastly, *archos* meaning leader or chief.[2] Originally the title was given to Christian

---

1 Estimates of the number of Maronites outside of the Middle East range from 4-5 million. Maronite dioceses have been established in Mexico, Brazil, Argentina, Australia, Canada, Europe and two in the United States (Brooklyn and Los Angeles).

2 Aziz S Atiya, *The Coptic Encyclopaedia*, New York, 1991, 1909.

dignitaries as an honorific title but once Christianity had become the official religion of the Roman Empire, it was applied to church hierarchs only.[3] The early ecumenical councils recognised this title regarding the metropolitans of the five major sees—Rome, Constantinople, Alexandria, Antioch and Jerusalem. It was no coincidence that the chief bishops resided in the main urban centres of the Roman Empire. Corbon states that the patriarch was the church equivalent of *patrick* (governor) and thus, exercised temporal power in the territory under his jurisdiction.[4] The acceptance of the dual role of the patriarch as the head of the church and the community was accentuated after the Islamic conquest in the 7th century. The new rulers preferred to deal with one representative for each collective group. Under the *dhimmi* system, the patriarch was deemed responsible for the conduct of the entire community, collected taxes and in exchange was given substantial political autonomy especially relating to personal status matters. Consequently, through tradition and the new Islamic environment, patriarchal authority over the community became an established norm in Middle Eastern Christianity.

Origins of the Maronites

The name Maronite is derived from a 4th century hermit Maron whose ascetic life attracted disciples who founded a monastery in his memory—Beit Maroon.[5] Although there is controversy regarding the doctrinal beliefs of these monks after the Council of Chalcedon in 451, the Maronite Church firmly states that they adhered to the Chalcedonian Christological definition of one person in two natures.[6] As this doctrine was rejected by many in Syria and Egypt, the monks of Beit Maroon were subject to persecution including the massacre of 350 monks in 517 by followers of Patriarch Severus of Antioch.[7] Church historians claim that

3 'Our Patrimony of Patriarchs', *Catholic International 6(8)* 1995, 365.

4 Jean Corbon, 'The Churches of the Middle East: Their Origins and Identity, from their Roots in the Past to their Openness to the Present' in Andrea Pacini (ed.), *Christian Communities in the Arab Middle East: The Challenge of the Future*, Oxford, 1998, 94.

5 Elias el-Hayek, 'Struggle for Survival: The Maronites of the Middle Ages' in Michael Gervers and Ramzi Jibran Bikhazi (eds), *Conversion and Continuity: Indigenous Christian Communities in Islamic Lands Eighth to Eighteenth Centuries*, Toronto, 1990, 408.

6 Ronald Roberson, *The Eastern Christian Churches: A Brief Survey*, Rome, 1999, 23.

7 George T Labaki, *The Maronites in the United States*, Beirut, 1993, 6.

because the last Orthodox patriarch in Antioch died in 609 and due to the Arab conquest, later patriarchs resided in Constantinople; the Maronite community was in grave need of a leader and thus filled this vacant see in the late 7th century.[8] Thus, the Maronite monastic community evolved into a 'church' with its own hierarchy and ecclesiastical autonomy.[9] Given the title of Maronite Patriarch of Antioch and All The East, the first patriarch John Maron is regarded as the founder of the Maronite Church. Having lost Byzantine protection either due to electing their patriarch without the consent of the emperor, or as some historians claim, due to their following of the compromise Monothelitist doctrine,[10] John Maron was credited with winning a decisive battle against the Byzantine army. Continual conflict resulted in waves of emigration to the safety of Mount Lebanon. Here, the Maronites developed their own ecclesiastical and community identity, resembling what Salibi terms *sha'b* (people) wherein the patriarch was seen as the tribal chief rather than just the head of the church.[11] The arrival of the Crusaders in the late 11th century halted the isolation of the community and allowed links with the Catholic Church to be re-established. In 1215, Patriarch Jeremias al-Aanshitti was the first Maronite patriarch to visit Rome, attending the Council of Lateran IV and relations were reaffirmed in 1439.[12] A gradual 'Latinization' policy was encouraged with the founding of the Maronite College in Rome in 1584 and culminated in the 1736 Synod of Mount Lebanon which undertook vast restructuring of the Maronite Church in accordance with Roman practices from the 1562 Council of Trent.[13]

---

8 John D Faris, *Eastern Catholic Churches: Constitution and Governance*, New York, 1992, 50.

9 Shafiq Abouzayd, 'The Maronite Church' in *The Blackwell Dictionary of Eastern Christianity*, Oxford, 1999, 305.

10 Jean-Pierre Valognes, *Vie et Mort des Chretiens d'Orient*, Paris, 1994, 371; Seely Beggiani, 'The Patriarchs in Maronite History' *Journal of Maronite Studies 5(1)* 2001, www.mari.org/JMS/january01/The_Patriarchs_in_Maronite_History.

11 Kamal Salibi, 'The Maronite Experiment' in Michael D Gervers, and Ramzi Jibran Bikhazi (eds), *Conversion and Continuity: Indigenous Christian Communities in Islamic Lands Eighth to Eighteenth Centuries*, Toronto, 1990, 425

12 Robert Brenton Betts, *Christians in the Arab East*, London, 1979, 48.

13 Labaki, *The Maronites in the United States*, 30.

TEMPORAL AUTHORITY OF THE MARONITE PATRIARCHATE UP TO 1990

Due to the relative autonomy of Mount Lebanon under Islamic rule, the Maronite patriarchate has always had a political dimension as the leader of the community. According to Picard, historically, 'Ultimately the task of placing the claims of the people before the civil powers lay with its leader, the patriarch'.[14] In fact, Labaki asserts that the capture of the patriarch was more prized by enemies that the capture of a town.[15] However, the temporal authority of the patriarchate was repeatedly challenged by the Maronite lay elite. Under the feudal system of the Maan and Shihabi emirs, notables such as the Khazen family acted as liaisons between the civil leaders and the church. The Khazens claimed to be patrons of the patriarch and clergy by ensuring no external interference. Yet through this position, they countered the traditional predominant role of the patriarch by intervening in patriarchal elections and church administration, especially the supervision of monasteries.[16] By the mid-19th century, class conflict between the feudal lords and peasants allowed the patriarchate to reclaim temporal authority. Led by Patriarch Boulus Masaad (1854-1890), the first of a new generation of patriarchs from peasant backgrounds, the church leadership secretly supported peasant revolts against the feudal regime and then acted as mediators between the two groups, thus illustrating Maronite unity was achievable only through the patriarchate.[17] The subsequent decline of the Maronite feudal aristocrats, the defeat of Yusuf Karam—a charismatic leader of the peasant movement, the 1860 massacres and the consequent new political order of the *mutasarrifiyya*, guaranteed by foreign powers, allowed Patriarch Massad and his successors to consolidate temporal power.[18]

---

[14] Elizabeth Picard, 'The Dynamics of the Lebanese Christians: From the Paradigm of the Ammiyyat to the Paradigm of Hwayyek' in Andrea Pacini (ed.), *Christian Communities in the Arab Middle East: The Challenge of the Future*, Oxford, 1998, 210.

[15] Labaki, *The Maronites in the United States*, 19.

[16] Richard van Leeuwen, 'The Political Emancipation of the Maronite Church in Mount Lebanon (1736-1842)', *Middle East Research Associates Occasional Paper No. 8*, Amsterdam, 1990, 7.

[17] Engin Deniz Akarli, *The Long Peace: Ottoman Lebanon 1861-1920*, London, 1993, 164.

[18] David A Kerr, 'The Temporal Authority of the Maronite Patriarchate 1920-1958: A Study in the Relationship of Religious and Secular Power', Ph.D Thesis (Oxford, St Anthony's College, University of Oxford, 1973), 80.

The patriarchy of Elias Hoyek (1899-1931) illustrates the political dimension of the office. After safeguarding his community during the wartime Ottoman occupation, his activities as head of the Lebanese delegation to the 1919 Versailles Peace Conference, were instrumental in securing the establishment of Greater Lebanon under French protection.[19] Kerr states 'With the inauguration of the new state, the patriarchate witnessed the realization of a dream for which it had struggled for more than a century'.[20] While the patriarchs tended to be firm supporters of France, this affection did not prevent them speaking out when Lebanese interests were not served. Patriarch Hoyek deplored the anticlerical attitude of High Commissioner General Sarrail. His successor Patriarch Antoine Arida also criticised French policy, for example regarding the tobacco monopoly and the suspension of constitutional government, as being in French not Lebanese national interests.[21] The desire of the patriarchate for full independence resulted in an unlikely alliance with Syrian nationalist leaders. Speeches by the patriarch calling for each community to receive its rights in an independent Lebanon were instrumental in persuading Muslim leaders to accept Lebanon as a separate entity from Syria. This resulted in the patriarch becoming the focal point of opposition to French policies.[22] The National Pact which allocated executive powers to the president—who was Maronite—reintroduced the rivalry between the patriarchate and civil leaders. According to Moosa, 'this is not to say that the National Pact destroyed the status of the patriarch as the spokesman of his own people; it rendered it secondary to that of the president in civil matters'.[23] However, under Patriarch Boulos Meouchi (1955-1975), the Maronite Church continued to voice its opinion on all aspects of life. In particular, Meouchi played a major role in the 1958 crisis over both the pro-Western foreign policies of President Chamoun and the attempts of the president to gain a second unconstitutional term of office.[24] By opposing Chamoun, Patriarch Meouchi demonstrated his awareness of the tense

---

19 Valognes, *Vie et Mort des Chrétiens d'Orient*, 379.

20 Kerr, *The Temporal Authority of the Maronite Patriarchate*, 133.

21 Farid el Khazen, *Papers in Lebanon 12: The Communal Pact of National Identities*, Centre for Lebanese Studies, Oxford, 1991, 9.

22 Philip Khoury, *Syria and the French Mandate*, London, 1987, 452.

23 Matti Moosa, *The Maronites in History*, Syracruse, 1986.

24 Paul A Jureidini and James M Price, 'Minorities in Partition: The Christians of Lebanon' in R D McLaurin (ed.), *The Political Role of Minority Groups in the Middle East*, New York, 1979, 170.

regional environment which was dominated by Nasser's Arab nationalism and therefore, ensured that the conflict did not divide along sectarian lines. Frankel states that during this period, it appeared as if the patriarch was the 'leader of the predominantly Muslim opposition'.[25] Consequently, this example illustrates that the relationship between the president and the patriarch depended on the personalities of the men concerned.

The Lebanese Civil War (1975-1990) witnessed the collapse of patriarchal temporal authority. Unlike his predecessors, Patriarch Antonios Khreich (1975-1986) attempted to stay out of politics, stating 'In the past the Maronites were alone and the patriarch was everything. When we gained our republic, the function and role of the patriarch changed ... I am the Head of a Church not of a community'.[26] However, as the state had disintegrated, many Maronites still looked to their church to provide leadership, especially in times of crisis. Consequently, power within the church shifted from the patriarchate to the Maronite monk orders. Monks such as Sharbel Kassis and Abbot Boulos Naaman were key contributors to Christian 'ethnic' nationalist ideology that stressed the Islamic threat to Maronite identity.[27] After the retirement of Patriarch Khreich, the Secretary of the Maronite patriarchate Nasrallah Sfeir, a man known for his moderate political views, was elected Maronite patriarch in 1986.

Born in Rayfoun, Kesrouan in 1920, Nasrallah Sfeir was educated at the St Maron Seminary in Ghazir and studied Philosophy and Theology at the University of St Joseph in Beirut. In 1950, he was ordained into the priesthood and served in his home parish of Rayfoun. From 1956 until 1961, he was professor of translation in literature and philosophy at the Maronite Brothers School in Jounieh. After being ordained bishop in 1961, he served as a Patriarchal Vicar and continued to be the Secretary of the Maronite patriarchate until his election as patriarch. His position as head of the Catholic communities in Lebanon was reinforced when he was made a Cardinal by Pope John Paul II in 1994 and appointed President of the Special Assembly of the Synod of Bishops for Lebanon one year later. [28]

---

[25] Ephraim A Frankel, 'The Maronite Patriarch: An Historical Review of a Religious Za'im in the 1958 Lebanese Crisis', *The Muslim World 66(3)*, 1976, 213.

[26] Picard, 'The Dynamics of the Lebanese Christians', 212

[27] Walid Khalidi, *Conflict and Violence in Lebanon: Confrontation in the Middle East*, Cambridge, 1979, 70. Raymond G Helmick, 'Internal Lebanese Politics: The Lebanese Front and Forces' in Halim Barakat (ed.), *Toward a Viable Lebanon*, London, 1988, 312.

[28] *CV of His Beatitude Cardinal Mar Nasrallah Boutros Sfeir*, www.bkerke.org.lb/Sfeir1e.html.

Elected at a difficult time for the Maronites when both the community and the church hierarchy were divided over what factions to support, Patriarch Sfeir continued the previous efforts to achieve reconciliation. Acknowledging the grave situation of the Christians, he supported the 1989 Document of National Understanding (known as the Taif Accord) which was a revision of the National Pact but sanctioned the presence of the Syrian army. In doing so, he gave the agreement enough legitimacy in Christian circles to allow it a chance to succeed.[29] However, his position contrasted with many ordinary Maronites, especially the followers of General Aoun (the caretaker Prime Minister), whom Patriarch Sfeir criticised for launching his War of Liberation in 1989. Incensed at the acquiescence of their patriarch to what they perceived as Syrian hegemony, the patriarch was jostled by demonstrators and consequently sought refuge in the Syrian occupied sector.[30] Furthermore, the patriarch publicly condemned the subsequent intra-Christian fighting between the Geagea (leader of the Lebanese Forces) and Aoun factions, deeming it 'collective suicide'.[31] By the end of the civil war, the patriarchate resembled the wider Maronite community—weakened, disunited and defeated. Therefore, the main aim of the patriarch in the post-war era was to oversee the rejuvenation of the Maronite church and as a consequence, the entire community.

Post-war situation in Lebanon

In post-war Lebanon, all communities are concerned at the political and economic situation of the country. However, Christian, especially Maronite worries are becoming increasingly existential. Lebanese population figures since independence have been based on the 1932 census which registered 793,426 citizens, of which 28.7 percent were Maronite, 22.4 percent Sunni and 19.6 percent Shiite. Christians enjoyed a slight majority—51.3 percent compared to 48.8 percent.[32] However, decreasing Christian birth rates and steady emigration have resulted in demographic changes. Although

---

[29] Farid el Khazen, *Prospects for Lebanon: Lebanon's First Postwar Parliamentary Election 1992: An Imposed Choice*, Oxford, 1998, 13.

[30] Valognes, *Vie et Mort des Chretiens d'Orient*, 399.

[31] Charles Winslow, *Lebanon: War and Politics in a Fragmented Society*, London, 1996, 278.

[32] Elizabeth Picard, *Lebanon—A Shattered Country: Myths and Realities of the Wars in Lebanon*, London, 1996, 66.

now emigration affects all the communities, it is estimated that around half of those who left during the war years were Christian. Furthermore, few Christians have returned since peace occurred and the still steady flow of emigrants affects the already smaller community. All Lebanese are aware of these developments but due to the political sensitivity regarding population statistics, no official census has been undertaken in the post civil war years. However, it is widely regarded that the Shiites are the largest community—estimated at around 30 percent, with the Sunnis around 27 percent and the Maronites at 22 percent.[33] If current trends continue, there are fears that the Christian population, currently not more than 30 percent of the population, could decline to 15 percent within ten years.

This decline in numbers has been experienced in an environment where many Maronites feel they have lost power in a country they perceive as being created as their homeland. Although Maronite acceptance of the Taif Accord was limited at best, the failure to fully implement the agreement, has ensured that the Maronite masses no longer feel that they enjoy active participation in Lebanon. One key grievance is the lack of representation in the political system. While the other communities have credible leaders e.g. Sunnis—Prime Minister Hariri, Shiites—Speaker Berri, Amal and Hizb'allah, Druze—Deputy Walid Jumblatt; the leaders who genuinely represent Maronites are either in exile (General Aoun) or imprisoned (Samir Geagea).[34] Although the President remains a Maronite, his powers have been reduced and the two post war presidents, like many of the Maronite parliamentary deputies, are dismissed by the community as lightweights indebted to Syria for their positions. The pre-war political parties also lack credibility due to their violent past as militias, lack of political programmes, internal division and failure to gain power.

Although three parliamentary elections have been held in the post-war era, these have not eased Maronite concerns. Electoral laws have minimised the impact of Christian voters by changing the size of electoral districts to the extent that in 1992, 35 percent of Christian candidates were elected by Muslim voters: this is not reciprocated.[35] A predominantly Christian boycott ensured that only 5 percent of eligible Christians participated, with one seat in Mount Lebanon won with 41

---

[33] Valognes, *Vie et Mort des Chretiens d'Orient*, 637.

[34] Hussein Sirriyeh, 'Triumph or Compromise: the Decline of Political Maronitism in Lebanon', *Civil Wars 1(4)*, 1998, 63.

[35] Farid el Khazen, 'Lebanon—Independent No More', *Middle East Quarterly*, 2001, 48.

votes out of 60,000 registered voters.[36] While the boycott was successful in illustrating Christian discontent, no changes occurred and thus, by 2000, only three main opposition parties still refused to participate. Pro-government candidates continue to win the majority of seats although in 2000, due to the increase in Christian voters, a handful of opposition members were elected.[37] However, it is clear that elections have little impact on government policy. Instead, power is concentrated in the 'troika'—consisting of the President, Prime Minister and Speaker of Parliament.[38] When these three agree, government institutions are bypassed, while disagreement results in stalemate, thus paralysing the governing system.

The Syrian role and the question of Lebanese sovereignty are also a major Maronite concern. A key provision of the Taif Accord was the withdrawal of the Syrian army within two years, yet the Syrian military presence and just as importantly, political and economic influence is still present. A Maronite critic illustrates their understanding of Syrian-Lebanese relations. 'All major decisions are to be arrived at 'jointly' between the two unequal partners, which of course translates into the stronger (Syria) dictating to the weaker (Lebanon) on every level'.[39] Regarding freedom, there is also a sense that the Lebanese system is being 'Syrianized'.[40] A pattern has emerged of government crackdowns whenever the opposition gains momentum. The judiciary has become politicised. For example, investigations were re-opened into alleged abuse of public funds by former president Amin Gemayel and Michel Aoun. The Constitutional Court annulled the by-election victory of a leading opposition politician Gabriel Murr due to apparent violations of the electoral law. This decision came shortly after his television station was forcibly closed down.[41] The government also refuses to permit opposition demonstrations which is a marked contrast to the frequent legal marches by movements such as Hizb'allah. The issue of Hizb'allah causes concern as unlike other militias, Hizb'allah was not disarmed and instead has been

---

36 Augustus Richard Norton, 'Lebanon: With Friends like these', *Current History*, January 1997, 7. Augustus Richard Norton and Jullian Schwedler, 'Swiss Soldiers, Ta'if Clocks and early elections: Toward a happy ending?' in Deirdre Collings (ed.), *Peace for Lebanon: From War to Reconstruction*, London, 1994, 56.

37 'Hariri's Half-Triumph', *Middle East International*, 1 September 2000.

38 Maurus Reinkowski, 'National Identity in Lebanon since 1990', *Orient 38(3)*, 1997, 500.

39 Habib C Malik, 'The Future of Christian Arabs', *Mediterranean Quarterly 17(2)*, 1996, 92.

40 El Khazen, *Prospects for Lebanon: Lebanon's First Postwar Parliamentary Election*, 73.

41 'Opposition Nadir', *Middle East International*, 8 November 2002.

promoted by the authorities as the official resistance against Israel.[42] Not only do some Lebanese regard this as double standards but they also fear the consequences of such activity on the future stability of the country. Furthermore, the use of repression against unrest has become common. The army is regularly used to disperse opposition demonstrations, resulting in injuries and detainment of the predominantly student protestors. Members of the two main opposition groups—the Free Patriotic Movement led by Aoun and the Lebanese Forces loyal to the imprisoned Geagea—are frequently the targets of crackdowns including the questioning of over 150 in August 2001, which led to over 75 receiving prison sentences.[43]

The grave economic situation is a major concern for all Lebanese, not just Christians. Although economic growth was initially fuelled by the post-war reconstruction boom, this faltered by the mid 1990s due to overspending, the failure to collect taxes or clamp down on corruption and lack of investment due to regional instability. Consequently, the post-war economic situation has become characterised by a vast national debt of around $32 billion and rising, high unemployment—with youth unemployment estimated at 34 percent, minimal economic growth, high cost of living, inadequate welfare services and frequent strikes protesting against these conditions.[44] Government policy has appeared inept at dealing with this ongoing crisis. Instead, economic inequality has increased and corruption remains rampant. Indeed, many Lebanese believe that the power struggle between the President and Prime Minister is contributing to the economic crisis as it paralyses government institutions. The severity of the situation was highlighted in May 2004 when a protest against rising fuel prices, denigrated into a riot in a predominantly Shiite impoverished suburb of Beirut, leaving six dead and fifty injured.[45] The grievances outlined above serve to illustrate what many Maronites perceive as the contrast between the pre-civil war era, when they enjoyed political supremacy and the present post-war situation where that power has been usurped and political and economic conditions have declined. Consequently, the community has turned to the one institution which still serves its interests—the Maronite Church.

---

[42] Magnus Ranstorp, 'The Strategy and tactics of Hizballah's Current 'Lebanonization' Process', *Mediterranean Politics* 3(1), 1998, 125.

[43] *BBC News*, 'Lebanese court releases Christians', 20 August 2001.

[44] 'Does the gateway to the Middle East lie in ruins?', *The Daily Star*, 10 February 2004. 'Conference examines youth unemployment dilemma', *The Daily Star*, 30 January 2004.

[45] 'Questions flourish in the aftermath of the Beirut riot', *The Daily Star*, 1 June 2004.

Spiritual and social dimensions of the Maronite Church in the post-war era

In the post-war era, the Maronite Church, aided by the Vatican, has attempted to address the issues raised by the civil war. In particular, the identity and mission of the church has become an important concern. The Vatican perceived Lebanon as a model of coexistence between Christians and Muslims. While papal missions during the war were unsuccessful in achieving reconciliation, the personal involvement of Pope John Paul II in recent initiatives, has given impetus to the Church renewal process. The Special Synod for Lebanon (1991-1995), instigated by the Pope, stressed the need for all Catholic communities in Lebanon to join together to attain spiritual renewal. It also outlined the Papal vision of the Lebanese future—one where Christians and Muslims work together to rebuild their country. A quote from the Pope 'Lebanon is more than a country: Lebanon is a message' became the inspiration for many Lebanese—Christian and Muslim alike.[46] This was followed by the Apostolic Exhortation 'A New Hope for Lebanon' which was signed by the Pope during his visit to Lebanon in 1997. The Apostolic Exhortation acts as a guide to the situation of the church, its mission and Lebanon, calling for dialogue between the Christian churches, the Muslim communities and the need to work together for national reconciliation.[47]

These Papal initiatives have particularly concentrated on the need for interreligious dialogue in Lebanon. Although the country has long been regarded as an example of Christian-Muslim coexistence, in the pre-civil war era, few efforts were made to acquire a solid national identity.[48] Although some Lebanese mixed on a personal level, confessional identity remained strong, especially because it was reinforced through the political system.

While conferences promoting inter-religious dialogue were held, both sides were often wary of such activities, regarding them as a means for one side to acquire doctrinal or political advantages at the expense of the other. Instead, the communities preferred to co-operate

---

46 Antoine Najm, 'Envisioning a Formula for Living Together in Lebanon: In Light of the Apostolic Exhortation', *Journal of Maronite Studies* 2(2), 1998, www.mari.org/JMS/april98/Envisioning_a_Formula.htm.

47 Beggiani, 'The Patriarchs in Maronite History'.

48 Annie Laurent, 'Le Dialogue Islamo-Chretien au Liban a la Lumiere du Synode Special des Eveques' in Marie-Therese Urvoy (ed.), *En Hommage au Pere Jacques Jomier*, Paris, 2002, 308.

on the humanitarian level, making welfare services accessible to members of all confessions.

During the civil war, both religious leaders and lay representatives tried to continue Christian-Muslim dialogue. For example, the Institute d'Études Islamo-Chrétiennes (IECC) was established by Christian and Muslim scholars in 1977 to create academic space for mutual understanding between the adherents of the two religions.[49] Throughout the war years, Patriarch Khreish and his successor Patriarch Sfeir, maintained contact with other spiritual leaders, receiving Muslim delegations whenever possible.[50]

The Special Synod for Lebanon provided the impetus to institutionalise these relations in the post-civil war era. At a Spiritual Summit of the religious heads of the communities held in 1993 at Bkerke—the winter residence of the Maronite patriarch—it was decided to create a National Committee for Muslim-Christian Dialogue.[51] The seven committee members are directly appointed by their religious leaders and although well respected by the political establishment, are deemed separate from other actors e.g. the government. The group regards its mission as acting as a bridge between the communities, settling misunderstandings and participating in relevant conferences.[52] In 1995, after approval from the religious heads, the committee published a Working Paper calling for the full implementation of the Taif Accord and affirmed that Islamic-Christian dialogue is 'Lebanon's mission to the world'.[53] Furthermore, in certain issues, the religious leaders have allied together against apparent secular moves. For example, Patriarch Sfeir stated that he could not support a 1998 bill to allow civil marriage because the Muslim communities were against it and such a proposal must be accepted by either all Lebanese or none.[54]

Other post-civil war initiatives have been concentrated in universities such as academic programmes, conferences and publications. For example, the Greek Orthodox University of Balamand established the Centre for Christian-Muslim Studies in 1995, while the IEIC has continued its efforts including the creation of a website to allow on-line

---

[49] *Institute d'etudes islamo-chretiennes*, www.ieic.usj.edu.lb.

[50] Valognes, *Vie et Mort des Chretiens d'Orient*, 394.

[51] *Islamic Christian National Dialogue Committee,* www.chrislam.org.

[52] Interview with member of the Islamic Christian National Dialogue Committee, Beirut, April 2004.

[53] *Islamic Christian National Dialogue Committee,* www.chrislam.org.

[54] Simon Haddad, 'Christian-Muslim Relations and Attitudes towards the Lebanese state', *Journal of Muslim Minority Affairs 21(1)*, 2001, 474.

discussion on Islamic-Christian dialogue.[55] There has also been an increase in Muslim led initiatives which were rare before the Special Synod for Lebanon. For example in 1997, the Faculty of Imam Ouzai for Islamic Studies established regular debates for students of the different faculties and institutes of religion in Lebanon. The necessity of Christian-Muslim dialogue has also been recognised by one of the institutions previously regarded as a bastion of the Maronite isolationist current. The University of the Holy Spirit in Kaslik, associated with civil war era publications supporting the notion of a smaller Christian state, has now joined the Association of Arab Universities, co-operates with Mokassed (a Sunni Islamic Institute), has entered dialogue with Hizb'allah and welcomes Muslim students to its courses.[56]

While it is clear that the Papal initiatives mentioned above, have encouraged more inter-religious dialogue, it is less certain what impact these have had on ordinary Lebanese. At the rhetorical level, many conferences have been held and the comment by the Pope that Lebanon is a message has been oft-quoted by religious leaders, politicians and intellectuals. Yet, outside of these elite gatherings, many are concerned at the lack of integration among Lebanese, especially the youth. The segregation of the communities which occurred during the civil war is proving difficult to overcome. Thus, at a practical level, little progress has been made to further dialogue and national unity as is espoused by the above initiatives.

The post-civil war era has also seen the Maronite Church enact its own initiatives for church renewal. For many decades, elements within the church have called for a Maronite Synod to take account of the many changes since the last council in 1856. In 1921, Bishop Bechara Chemali sent a report to Pope Benedict XV petitioning for the founding of a new Maronite seminary which could provide impetus for Church renewal and undertake preparatory work for a much needed Maronite Council. Various associations were formed to lobby for reform such as the Sacerdotal League. These groups issued publications to convince the Church hierarchy and faithful that a Maronite Council was necessary to achieve this process and provided detailed information on topics to be covered.[57] The Vatican Council (1962-1965) had a further impact on Maronite calls for reform.

[55] See Hiwar, http://hiwar.net.usj.edu.lb.

[56] Laurent, 'Le Dialogue Islamo-Chretien au Liban', 318.

[57] Patriarch Nasrallah Boutros Sfeir Lent Message 2003, www.maronitesynod.org/English/intro/pat-letter.htm.

Unlike previous ecumenical councils which were normally held to combat heresies and define doctrine, Vatican II was regarded as being of a predominantly pastoral and ecumenical nature. In particular, the council addressed the issue of internal renewal of the universal church, its relations with society, other Christian churches and members of other faiths. Many Maronites believed that in order to implement these changes, it was necessary to hold a separate Maronite Council. Writing in 1983, three years before he was elected patriarch, the then Bishop Sfeir stated that in the past, councils had great influence on Church life, especially the 1736 Mount Lebanon Synod. As the Church was in need of renewal, not only because of Vatican II but also due to events in Lebanon, he argued that the best way to achieve this was through a new council.[58]

Consequently, the mid 1980s found a favourable environment for supporters of a Maronite Council. In 1985, an instrumental figure in the reform movement, Father Youakim Moubarac was appointed by the Synod of Bishops to undertake a pastoral survey regarding potential topics for the council. While Father Moubarac was an ardent believer that significant church reform could only occur under the auspices of a Maronite Council, he also stressed that spiritual renewal was vital to achieve this reform.[59] The preparatory period included involvement by bishops and clergy through the Maronite Council Commission established by Patriarch Sfeir. Lay experts were also involved in examining the proposed content of the Council. However, this work was delayed, firstly due to the intra-Christian conflict in 1989 which affected the ability of participants to meet and then, due to the Papal announcement of the Special Synod for Lebanon as mentioned earlier. Although work on the Maronite Council was temporarily shelved, the hierarchy agreed that the two synods addressed different issues. Thus, preparation for the Maronite Synod recommenced in 1997 and in 2002, the Synod of Bishops announced that the first session of the long-awaited Maronite Council would take place in June 2003.

The Maronite Synod is being regarded by the faithful as a defining moment for the modern Maronite Church. Its importance is shown by the opinion of one participant who viewed it as 'something like Vatican II for the Maronite Church'.[60] It is the first time that members of the 'Maronite

---

58 *Ibid.*

59 Mounir Khairallah, 'Le Synode Patriarcal Maronite: Periode Preparatoire (1985-2003)', *Proche Orient Chrétien* 53 (2003), 58.

60 Interview with member of 2003 Maronite Synod, Beirut, April 2004.

family' have been brought together from around the world to discuss the affairs of their church. Patriarch Sfeir has also been keen to encourage the involvement of all Maronites in the event. Thus, the faithful are invited to pray for its success, seek spiritual renewal in their personal lives and discuss the topics addressed by the council.[61] The Synod has also enjoyed media coverage and set up its own website to inform those interested in the latest developments. Following the precedent established at the Special Synod for Lebanon, representatives of other religious communities in Lebanon—Christian and Muslim—were invited to attend.

During the first session in June 2003, the participants at the Maronite Council discussed the preparatory texts, agreed amendments and will examine these revised texts in the next session in November 2004. This methodology differs significantly from that of the Special Synod for Lebanon where the Synod followed the guidelines set by Pope John Paul II. Instead, the continual consultation and revision of texts by all members of the Maronite Council, emphasises that this process is *by* all the Maronite faithful *for* the Maronite faithful.

The topics addressed in the first session were divided into five files. The first file examined the identity and mission of the Maronite Church, affirming its Eastern identity, Antiochian roots and Syrian tradition. Reflecting the tone of the Apostolic Exhortation, the Synod also stressed the ecumenical vocation of the Maronite Church and sought to continue efforts to reconcile the different Christian churches and to fully participate in Christian-Islamic dialogue.[62] The second file covered issues relating to pastoral renewal, stressing the importance of education among the clergy. This section also affirmed that the office of patriarch acts as a reference point for all believers and combined with the liturgy, ensures Maronite unity. The third file entitled 'The Maronite Church in Today's World' addresses issues relating to political, social and economic questions. The Synod clearly defined its view on the Maronite role in Lebanon, confirming that Maronites have chosen 'coexistence and intercommunity harmony'.[63] They stated that in the political sphere, the Maronite Church has no wish to be seen as 'a national church and its vocation has never been to lay hands on a land of its own to the exclusion of others'.[64] The

---

61 Patriarch Nasrallah Boutros, Sfeir Lent Message 2003.

62 *Final Communiqué of the First Session of the Patriarchal Synod*, 21 June 2003 www.maronitesynod.org/English/session1/final-communique.htm.

63 *Ibid.*

64 *Ibid.*

contents of the fourth section were more in line with previous church councils, examining canonical matters. However, the fifth file reflected the changes which have occurred in the Maronite Church by addressing the important topic of emigration and the consequent expansion of the Maronite Church outside of the traditional homeland. The Synod agreed that it was vital to preserve Maronite identity and stressed the need to retain close links between the church in Lebanon and its adherents outside the patriarchal territory.

Consequently, it is clear that this Maronite Synod in the 21st century has the potential to be as significant for the Maronite Church as the influential 1736 Mount Lebanon Synod. The continual calls for church reform through the holding of a Maronite council, voiced since the 1920s, have eventually been answered. Its participants are eager that their efforts to reform the church from inside will not only allow spiritual renewal but also bring new hope and impetus to the community, whether in Lebanon or elsewhere. However, it must be noted that it took over one hundred years to implement the changes agreed by the 1736 Synod. Therefore, it is hoped that the Maronite Church will experience the benefits of the reforms of this council significantly quicker than occurred regarding the preceding one.

The Maronite spiritual renewal is also apparent when examining the devotion to the saints. At the recent canonization of the 19th century monk Neamatallah Kassab Hardini, 50,000 Lebanese pilgrims travelled to Rome while thousands more attended celebrations in the Monastery of Kfifane. This canonization and the other recent one of St Rafqa in 2001, are viewed by Patriarch Sfeir as showing that God will not abandon his people and a great event for all Lebanese.[65] While the above spiritual renewal is not comparable to contemporary movements such as the Coptic revival since the mid-20th century, this focus on spirituality can provide solace for the Maronite community in this time of difficulty.

The social role of the church is also important in preserving Maronite identity. In the post war era, the Church has tried to maintain its presence throughout the country by repairing institutions and supporting the return of refugees in areas that have been depopulated of Christians. Aware of the economic plight of the country, the Church, particularly through the monastic orders, has continued its key role in education and

---

[65] 'Lebanese monk among 6 granted sainthood', *The Daily Star*, 17 May 2004.

health as well as providing land for affordable property. While the hierarchy has tried to provide for the needs of the community, some Maronites have criticised these efforts as inadequate considering the extent of resources that the Church possesses especially land and institutions.[66] Patriarch Sfeir also seeks to encourage Lebanese Christians, especially the youth, to resist the attractions of emigration. He welcomes initiatives that create jobs and eases the pressures on young Lebanese, urging them that 'the attachment to the homeland, especially in times of trial, is one of your first duties'.[67] It is clear that the Maronite Church has tried to address the post-war situation through spiritual renewal and social means—seen as acceptable activities by a church. However, it is the political role of the Maronite Church through the patriarchate—so significant in its past—that has received most attention both within the church and in Lebanon in general.

Patriarchal authority according to canon law

Before examining the political role of the Maronite patriarch in contemporary Lebanon, it is necessary to address the issue of patriarchal authority. The 1990 *Codex Canonum Ecclesiarum Orientalium*, the codification of canon law for the Eastern Catholic Churches is significant in defining the role of the patriarch. Regarding the patriarchal churches, Canon 55 states,

> According to the most ancient traditions of the Church, already recognised by the first ecumenical councils, the patriarchal institution has existed in the Church: For this reason a special honour is to be accorded to the patriarchs of the Eastern Churches, each of whom presides over his patriarchal church as father and head.[68]

Although the 1990 Code includes some constraints on patriarchal authority such as the role of the Vatican and the Holy Synod regarding amongst others, elections and the appointment of bishops, in general, it

---

[66] Boutros Labaki, 'The Christian Communities and the Economic and Social Situation in Lebanon' in Andrea Pacini (ed.), *Christian Communities in the Arab Middle East: The Challenge of the Future*, Oxford, 1998, 253.

[67] Patriarch Nasrallah Boutros Sfeir, Lent Message 2003.

[68] *Code of Canons of the Eastern Churches Latin-English Edition*, Washington, 1990, 25.

can be seen as confirming the legitimacy of the position of the patriarch within the church and the community. Regarding the patriarch, Marini asserts, 'He represents in his person the entire Maronite Church, and he is the principal representative and spokesman for the Maronite Church and for all Maronites everywhere'.[69] However, in the post-war era, there has been increased emphasis on the joint action of the patriarch and the Holy Synod. For example, the communiqués of the monthly meetings of the Council of Maronite Bishops presided by the patriarch, provide the views of the church hierarchy on national issues as well as church affairs. While not detracting from the office of patriarch, this ensures that any criticism is deflected from one individual and instead, responsibility is taken by all the bishops, thus indicating unity within the hierarchy. As Faris states, 'The patriarch neither functions in his church as a *little pope,* nor is he merely a first among equals in the Synod of Bishops'.[70] Consequently, the reform of canon law has not only reinforced the traditional leadership role of the patriarch but also helped provide the conditions needed to allow the church, in the person of the patriarch, to have an active political role in post-war Lebanon.

Political role of Patriarch Sfeir in post-war Lebanon

Under Patriarch Sfeir, the patriarchate has rediscovered its voice as the leader of the Maronite community. However, it is unclear whether this has developed into temporal authority as in the past. In the post-war era, the Maronite Church has been consistent in its call for the full implementation of the Taif Accord. However, the methods used to achieve this aim have varied depending on events in the country and the wider region. For most of the 1990s, the patriarch pursued a diplomatic approach; still speaking out against injustice such as the electoral laws, yet being careful not to intentionally cause any controversy for the church or the community. The views of the patriarch were given through the monthly communiqués of the bishops' meetings, sermons and messages at feast times. However by 2000, the political comments by the patriarch had become more pronounced. This change can be attributed partly due to the deteriorating

---

69 Francis J Marini, 'The Role of the Patriarch Outside the Middle East', *Journal of Maronite Studies* 5(1), 2001, www.mari.org/JMS/january01/The_Role_Of_The_Patriarch.htm.

70 Faris, *Eastern Catholic Churches: Constitution and Governance*, 218.

economic situation and the failure after ten years to implement many of the Taif provisions. The Israeli withdrawal from South Lebanon in May 2000 acted as a catalyst for opposition activists to increase their campaign against Syrian influence in Lebanon. Hence, the church hierarchy was keen to avoid being out of touch with popular opinion in the community as occurred in 1989 over support of Taif. Furthermore, the failure of the 2000 elections to provide a genuine representative parliament and the absence of influential Maronite figures in the cabinet, ensured a shift towards a more pro-active role for the patriarchate. Therefore, in September 2000, the monthly communiqué was used as an appeal to all Lebanese, listing complaints concerning elections, the economic crisis and calling for Lebanese sovereignty while retaining close relations with Syria. The contents of the communiqué were not new and had been said previously by Patriarch Sfeir and other clergy. However, it was the first time that they had been listed together and published as an official document.[71] The impact of the appeal was reviewed one year later in another communiqué which stated that instead of the concerns being considered, the authorities actually reacted against any consequent dialogue initiatives. However, it was acknowledged that the people had supported the appeal and thus, the church hierarchy reiterated their demands.[72] From the start of these appeals, patriarchal messages and especially the communiqués, have become substantially more politicised than previous ones. However, it is necessary to note that the hierarchy justified comments on national affairs from a theological approach. Furthermore, these issues were not addressed at the expense of exclusive church and spiritual matters.

Although the stance of the Maronite hierarchy on the Syrian presence in Lebanon has attracted most attention, they also provide opinions on a wide range of topics covering government actions, political participation, the economic situation, national unity and regional events. The repeated calls for the withdrawal of Syrian troops have always been put in the context of regaining sovereignty as outlined in the Taif Accord. The bishops reject the notion that the Syrian presence is necessary to ensure stability in Lebanon. 'When people say 'it's either the Syrian army or chaos', it is an argument that simply does not stand up'.[73] This campaign enjoyed limited success with the gradual redeployment of troops from Greater

[71] Communiqué September 2000, http://www.geocities.com/CapitolHill/Parliament/2587/declaration.html.

[72] Communiqué September 2001, www.bkerke.org.lb/commsept2001eng.html.

[73] 'Maronite-Shiite divide over Syrian presence in Lebanon' *Middle East Times*, 13 October 2000.

Beirut, Mount Lebanon and the north since June 2001. However, many Syrian troops remain in the Beqaa region and significantly, Syrian political influence over Lebanon is still strong. The bishops clearly identify examples of this influence. Regarding the upcoming 2004 presidential elections, they stated, 'It has become known that the Lebanese do not have the last say in the presidential elections and a lot of them have started to see it as a natural thing'.[74] Thus, the issue of sovereignty and the desired relationship with Syria are key themes in the communiqués. The hierarchy accepts that the two countries should be close but not at the expense of sovereignty. Therefore, they are consistent in their calls for the full implementation of the Taif Accord in order to achieve these aims.

Another major concern is the erosion of freedom and lack of respect for human rights in Lebanon. Stressing the history and identity of Lebanon, they argue 'What worth is Lebanon without freedom?'.[75] The patriarch has continually called for the release of political prisoners—from all communities not just individuals such as Samir Geagea.[76] Patriarch Sfeir has also been outspoken about the use of repression against protestors and opposition activists. During the Murr affair in 2002 when this politician was removed from his seat and his television station was closed, the bishops stated that 'measures are being taken to silence every free voice, although the constitution secures free speech'.[77] The patriarch is not afraid to highlight what he perceives as double standards even if it could potentially aggravate the religious divide e.g. the unequal treatment of protestors. Patriarch Sfeir is especially scathing about the inability of the government to solve the severe economic problems. In the July 2004 Communiqué, he stated, 'Officials do not seem concerned with the lack of job opportunities, exorbitant taxes, the corruption spread in the mobile and electricity sectors, the endless squandering, chaos in public departments and debts'.[78] The patriarch lends his support to various strikes and consistently speaks out for workers' rights, economic justice and tackling the crippling national debt. He stresses that it is the responsibility of the government to combat these issues especially unemployment—a major factor for emigration. 'Lebanon

---

[74] 'Maronite Patriarch calls on Syria to respect Lebanese sovereignty' *Middle East Times*, 23 June 2000.

[75] Communiqué May 2003, www.bkerke.org.lb/commmay2003.eng.html.

[76] 'After 10 years in jail, Geagea's supporters demand a full pardon', *The Daily Star*, 22 April 2004.

[77] Communiqué October 2002, www.bkerke.org.lb/commoct2002eng.html.

[78] 'Bishop's Council: Elections not in Lebanese hands', *The Daily Star*, 5 August 2004.

sinks day after day in the ocean of excessive debts, while his active forces emigrate abroad, maybe never to return'.[79] It is evident that the concern of the patriarch regarding the impact of the economic crisis on ordinary citizens extends to Lebanese from all communities—not just Maronites. Indeed, almost all of the issues raised by the patriarch, particularly those concerned with daily life, are stated on behalf of all Lebanese. As an example, the Final Communiqué of the Maronite Synod in 2003 asserted that 'the invitation of the Church to embrace the values of participation and liberty in order to restore to Lebanon all the components of its sovereignty, independence and autonomy of decision is addressed to all'.[80]

Regarding political participation, Patriarch Sfeir has encouraged Lebanese to take part in elections as part of their democratic duty. However, this has not deterred criticism of government conduct during elections. Concerning the 2000 parliamentary elections which were deemed to be relatively fair on the actual election days, the bishops stated that 'The results of the elections were known by the time election day arrived'.[81] Patriarch Sfeir has also made known his disapproval of efforts to agree a constitutional amendment to allow the extension of the term of President Lahoud.[82] Consequently, it is clear that the Maronite hierarchy believe it is vital that they speak out against the abuse of power which is prevalent in post-war Lebanon.

However, they have also been eager to clarify that their vision of a sovereign Lebanon is one of national unity and reconciliation where all Lebanese regardless of their sect can enjoy equal participation, representation and a decent standard of living. Regarding national reconciliation, the hierarchy acknowledges that terrible acts were committed by some Maronites during the civil war, just as occurred in other communities but urges all groups to look to the future together. Many public statements have been made stressing that the Maronite Church perceives Lebanon as a living example of Christian-Muslim dialogue and co-existence. 'Lebanon is the nation of freedoms and of religious diversity … it is the country of Islamic and Christian coexistence'.[83] The patriarch clearly believes that conviviality has always existed in Lebanon and can continue to be so if

---

[79] Communiqué September 2002, www.bkerke.org.lb/appeal3.html.

[80] *Final Communiqué of the First Session of the Patriarchal Synod*, 21 June 2003.

[81] Communiqué, September 2000.

[82] 'Four students arrested at demonstrations', *The Daily Star*, 15 March 2004.

[83] 'Crowds greet Lahoud on route to Diman', *The Daily Star*, 2 August 2004.

outside intervention recedes. Personal initiatives of the patriarch included an extremely symbolic visit—the first of a Maronite patriarch for 200 years—to the Chouf area, the scene of Christian-Druze conflict several times in the recent history of Mount Lebanon, including the 1860 Massacres and the 1983 Mountain War which left the area almost depopulated of Christians.[84] While not against deconfessionalism, he states that it first must be abolished from the soul before political deconfessionalism occurs. This reflects the Christian fear that its abolishment at the political level only, would allow the Muslim majority to exercise political power without being accompanied by a corresponding secularization process at all levels.

The patriarch has also been keen to emphasise the patriotic credentials of the Maronite Church. For example, the church rejoiced at the Israeli withdrawal from South Lebanon in May 2000 and welcomed the successful negotiations between Hizb'allah and Israel in 2004 which resulted in the release of some Lebanese prisoners.[85] Furthermore, Patriarch Sfeir is clearly aware of the regional environment that is the reality for the Maronite community. He has repeatedly condemned frequent violence in the Holy Land and Iraq which frequently has a direct impact on Christian communities in these countries. The patriarch reiterated the anti-war stance of the Pope regarding Iraq. This reflects the attentiveness of the patriarch to Christian fears that Middle East Christians could become scapegoats due to Muslim anger at the continual cycle of violence in the Holy Land and Iraq. Instead, the patriarch has stressed that the unity between the different communities illustrates that a clash of cultures or religions does not exist in Lebanon but instead all can live together peacefully.[86]

Another response of the patriarch to the lack of genuine political representation is the creation of a political grouping Qornet Shehwan (The Gathering) named after the monastery where it held its first meeting in April 2001. The impetus for its formation came from the 2000 communiqué calling for the withdrawal of Syrian troops. As the September 2001 statement noted, 'The knots in the tongues were untied, and people began to voice their convictions, albeit with caution.'[87] Deploring Maronite disunity that had harmed the community so greatly especially during the last years of the civil war, the patriarch was eager to encourage the

---

84 'Lebanon patriarch urges national reconciliation', *Middle East Times*, 10 August 2001.

85 Communiqué February 2004, www.bkerke.org.lb/commfeb2004eng.html.

86 Communiqué March 2003, www.bkerke.org.lb/commmareng.html.

87 Communiqué, September 2001.

opposition to unite not just within Maronite and Christian circles but also to expand to include other communities. As the leader of the entire Maronite community, Patriarch Sfeir could not be associated exclusively with one faction. Instead, a bishop was chosen to initially chair the group and acted as the representative of the patriarch. While the patriarch played an instrumental role in creating the conditions for the establishment of Qornet Shehwan, the group should not be regarded as the 'patriarch's political party' in the sense of the patriarch being actively involved in politics. Instead, the opposite is true. Qornet Shehwan was formed to take the ideas of the hierarchy into the political arena precisely because the Church believes its representatives cannot be directly involved in the actual political system. Furthermore, once their ideas enter the political process, the hierarchy actually loses control of them because they are often adopted by the politicians to fit into the political reality. Consequently, the views of Qornet Shehwan are not always identical to those of the patriarch. The Church is also against total unification of the opposition, preferring instead to work towards a situation where a variety of groups can express common principles as befits a democratic political system.

Qornet Shehwan can be categorised as an umbrella group of various politicians rather than a cohesive organised political party. Its members vary from former participants in pro-Syrian governments, those who adopt a policy of soft criticism and others who are more aggressive in their criticism of the current situation. It appears that the only issue which unites them is what they stand against—the Syrian presence. Even their means to oppose this differs greatly. Consequently, Qornet Shehwan cannot be viewed as an alternative government but instead a loose coalition of individuals. While the group includes non-Maronites, there has been little success in reaching out to Muslim politicians.

The record of Qornet Shehwan has been mixed so far. It has been successful in gaining publicity and making its views known—probably benefiting from its association with the patriarchate. However, it has also been beset with internal divisions. Their poor results in the 2004 municipal elections exposed disunity as they failed to organise effective alliances with other groups, thus affecting their ability to appeal as a national opposition. Furthermore, co-ordination between the patriarch and Qornet Shehwan has also been tested. Qornet Shehwan regarded the 2002 Metn by-election as an opportunity to confront the regime. Hence, they chose to support one of their members Gabriel Murr. The situation became extremely tense as he was running against the daughter of one of the most pro-Syrian politicians, the former Interior Minister, who happened to be his brother. Hence, Patriarch Sfeir regarded the contest as a family feud and accepted the compromise candidate for the disputed Greek Orthodox seat—the nephew of the deceased incumbent.[88] The success of Gabriel Murr, although short-lived, illustrated not only the strength of support Qornet Shehwan could attract when united, but also highlighted that the patriarch could not exercise temporal authority in the same manner as enjoyed by his predecessors. However in recent months, there appears to have been a rapprochement between Bkerke and Qornet Shehwan. Consequently, the case of Qornet Shehwan shows that Patriarch Sfeir, while keen to use his influence to assist opposition members to maximise their efforts against an unaccountable regime, is equally adamant that he will not overstep the boundaries of his office. Instead, he believes that by remaining aloof from this level of political activity, he can better serve not only the interests of his own community but all Lebanese.

Response to the political role of patriarch

In publicising their views on national matters, the Maronite hierarchy is aware that they are open to criticism. However, the patriarch states that his role as head and father of the community means that he must defend his people. Thus, like all spiritual chiefs, he is obliged to take positions on issues such as freedom, justice and human rights.[89] The 2003 Final Communiqué of the Maronite Synod also outlines the role the Church perceives for itself. 'The Church position is but a reminder of the rights of human beings and their dignity; a defense of freedoms and a warning against selfish passions; a call for the sovereignty, independence and free choice of the homeland'.[90]

In general, the response of the Maronite community and some other Christians has been favourable towards this proactive Church role. The majority accept that due to the absence of genuine representative Christian civil leaders, the patriarch is attempting to fill this vacuum. The fact that Patriarch Sfeir evidently has few personal political ambitions also

---

[88] 'Byzantine Politics', *Middle East International*, 31 May 2002.

[89] Interview, Patriarch Sfeir, Beirut April 2004.

[90] *Final Communiqué of the First Session of the Patriarchal Synod*, 21 June 2003.

attributes to their willingness to accept his involvement. The patriarch insists on providing general principles only rather than intricate detailed programmes. Furthermore, the history of the Maronite Church ensures that in times of crisis, the community expects the patriarch to defend their rights. Consequently, people treat him as an influential figure by telling him their grievances in expectation of finding a solution, handing over petitions to him and holding rallies at Bkerke. While many hope that the patriarch's endeavours to establish an effective democratic political system will be successful and allow political representation to return to civil leaders, others think that the patriarch should concentrate less on rhetoric and more on action. Yet others feel that Patriarch Sfeir should be less politically active because they are against the involvement of any religious officials—whether Christian or Muslim—in the political system.

The reaction of other communities has mostly been favourable. As has been seen, the Maronite patriarchate has generally been well-respected—some even go so far as to call the head of the Maronite church the Patriarch of Lebanon. Thus, Patriarch Sfeir hears the grievances of not just Maronites but also members of other communities.[91] As many of the stances taken by the patriarch are regarded as benefiting all Lebanese, this helps to defuse confessional conflict over his role. However, the communiqués calling for the withdrawal of the Syrian presence did result in a predictable inflammatory response. Several influential *ulema* (Muslim clerics) warned of the danger in blaming Syria for Lebanon's problems stressing that Syria guaranteed the security of Lebanon.[92] This reflects the widely held fear by Muslims that without the Syrian intervention, Lebanese Christians especially Maronites would revert to their political predominance of the pre-civil war era.

In general, the government response to the political activities of Patriarch Sfeir has been a combination of countermoves, exploiting divisions and working towards improving relations with Bkerke. The reaction to the communiqués regarding the Syrian withdrawal was once more predictable with President Lahoud accusing the bishops of provoking 'confessional, sectarian instincts which do not serve the nation's highest interests'.[93] The Maronites were also reminded by pro-Syrian figures

---

[91] Labaki, 'The Christian Communities and the Economic and Social Situation in Lebanon', 232.

[92] 'Maronite-Shiite divide over Syrian presence in Lebanon', *Middle East Times*, 13 October 2000.

[93] 'Syria hits back at Lebanese bishops', *BBC News*, 22 September 2000.

that Syria had actually entered Lebanon in 1976 to save the Christians.[94] Reconciliation initiatives between the Lebanese communities have been obstructed such as the arrest of opposition activists, immediately following the visits of the patriarch to the Chouf. The government has also tried to exploit divisions within the opposition by advocating good relations with Bkerke while targeting activists from groups such as the Lebanese Forces and the Free Patriotic Movement. The recognised influence and importance of the patriarchate also ensures that government figures, like many politicians (both pro-Syrian and from the opposition), endeavour to get close to the hierarchy in order to gain credibility and popularity. In particular, meetings between the patriarch and government ministers have increased in recent months. For example, during Easter 2004, Patriarch Sfeir received separate visits from President Lahoud and Prime Minister Hariri.[95] This rapprochement, especially between Bkerke and Damascus, can be seen in the context of increasingly tense United States-Syrian relations. Analysts suggest that the Syrian government has been keen to maintain favourable relations with Bkerke because the patriarch is considered one of the few leaders who can dampen anti-Syrian rhetoric among some Lebanese Christians. For example, *The Daily Star* suggested that by February 2004, such meetings were used for Damascus to illustrate that 'this particular sword of theirs had been temporarily changed into a ploughshare in appreciation for the patriarch's understanding in recent months while Syria faced the discomfort of US forces on its border'.[96] Certainly, there have been fewer calls for Lebanese sovereignty in some communiqués. However, it is evident from recent statements that the hierarchy still considers Syrian influence as impeding not only national reconciliation but also the revival of the Lebanese democratic system.

A new challenge—the growth of the Maronite diaspora

Although Lebanese emigration has been prevalent since the late 19th century, the vast increase in numbers (particularly Christians) since the beginning of the civil war, has opened new challenges and opportunities

---

[94] 'Maronite-Shiite divide over Syrian presence in Lebanon', *Middle East Times*, 13 October 2000.

[95] 'Sfeir is a popular man to visit at Easter time', *The Daily Star*, 15 April 2004.

[96] 'End of reign' in Beirut?', *The Daily Star*, 14 February 2004.

for the Maronite Church. The existence of many faithful outside of the existing patriarchal territory has raised questions regarding patriarchal authority and Maronite identity. The 1990 Code of Canons of the Eastern Churches confirmed the notion of patriarchal territory as geographic and thus, decisions regarding the appointment of Maronite bishops and the founding of eparchies outside of this area are taken by the Holy See. This has opened debate regarding the relations between the patriarchate and the diaspora. For example, one Maronite priest from the diaspora stated that although the patriarch is said to be the father of the entire Maronite Church, at present those outside the patriarchal territory feel more like stepchildren.[97] Aware of these issues, the Maronite Synod in 2003 examined as one of its major themes, the role of the church in the countries of expansion. At this and subsequent conferences, Patriarch Sfeir asserted that all who follow the Maronite rite and tradition are Maronites—whenever they were born or reside.[98]

Thus, the church can now be defined as a universal church although still with a special attachment to its spiritual homeland. Dioceses and churches have been established throughout the regions where the diaspora are concentrated. For example, the United States has two dioceses with over seventy churches and one seminary.[99] The church also perceives itself as providing a link between the Maronites of the diaspora and the homeland. Patriarch Sfeir encourages this by undertaking pastoral trips to the diaspora, receiving those visiting from abroad at Bkerke and supporting initiatives that help Maronites (especially from the second and third generations) to spend time in Lebanon. Through these efforts, it is hoped that not only the Maronite heritage will be preserved but their attachment to Lebanon will also be reinforced. Certainly, the patriarch, while accepting that many have established their future abroad, still hopes that if the situation in Lebanon was to improve, some would return to contribute their skills in rebuilding the country.

The Maronite Church also faces challenges in retaining links with its diaspora. Although Vatican II encourages the universal Catholic Church to preserve the heritage of the Eastern Churches and to provide appropriate pastoral care, assimilation to the Latin Church is still a major

---

[97] Marini, 'The Role of the Patriarch Outside the Middle East'.

[98] Opening Address of His Beatitude and Em. Nasrallah-Boutros Sfeir, 'The Maronite Church in its Worldwide Expansion', 4 March 2004, www.maronitesynod.org.

[99] *Opus Libani*, 'Maronite Dioceses', www.opuslibani.org.lb/newdioceses/ant/index.htm.

concern.[100] The dispersion of emigrés through different areas also creates difficulties in establishing Maronite parishes. In particular, religious education is vital to allow the diaspora to understand and appreciate their heritage—not just as Maronites but also as Lebanese. It is evident that Patriarch Sfeir is aware of these challenges, and therefore is attempting to use the resources of the church in Lebanon to retain crucial links with the Maronite diaspora.

Émigré lobby movements have also proved a challenge to the patriarchate. While keen to unite the diaspora, Patriarch Sfeir is wary of being associated with groups which are seen by some in Lebanon as supporting the interests of other countries such as the United States and Israel. This dilemma has placed the hierarchy in a delicate position as illustrated by the 2002 Los Angeles International Maronite Congress—a gathering that attracted figures from Lebanon and the diaspora representing a vast variety of views. The patriarch endorsed the conference but its final resolutions stated support for aspects of the US Congress *Syrian Accountability Act* (now been made law) which referred to Lebanon.[101] Although the patriarch and many other prominent figures denounced the endorsement of this law, the issue still raised controversy in Lebanon. His wariness of United States policies and their potential impact on Lebanon, has also driven his concern to avoid being identified with Lebanese activists—mainly Christian—who give the impression of being pro-American and anti-Syrian—a dangerous combination in the Arab world at present. Clearly the emerging role of the diaspora has implications not solely on church issues but also on the temporal authority of the patriarch. On one hand, it allows the patriarch to cement his position as the head of the Maronite community. Yet simultaneously, the involvement of some émigrés in political activities outside the sphere of the patriarch provides a challenge—mainly absent inside Lebanon—to his political leadership.

Conclusion

It is clear that the Maronite Patriarch is still a significant factor in the Maronite identity. Thus, in times of hardship, it is natural that the

---

[100] Labaki, *The Maronites in the United States*, 236.

[101] International Maronite Congress Resolution 2002, www.maronite.org/congress_date_ann.htm.

community will turn to the patriarch for leadership. Under Patriarch Sfeir, the patriarchate has been re-established as the main legitimate representative of the Maronite community and also as a respected national institution. It is evident that the present patriarch has used his position wisely and endeavoured to speak on behalf of all Lebanese, thus attempting to prevent any sectarian backlash to the political involvement of Christian religious leaders. The increased role of the Council of Bishops is also significant in ensuring group solidarity. However, as the figurehead of the community, the patriarch retains his traditional predominant role. Although successful at filling the Maronite leadership vacuum, this has not been transformed into credible temporal authority. While the redeployment of some Syrian troops can be viewed as a concession to the demands of the patriarch, further measures have been few and can be considered rewards for good behaviour. Reliant on his moral authority alone, Patriarch Sfeir can only advocate causes and reiterate his demands. Lacking the ability and willingness to force the government and others to fulfil his demands, the patriarch will continue to be a spokesperson for the Lebanese rather than a political activist. Consequently, it is clear that Patriarch Sfeir interprets his role as leader of the community as meaning that he must fill the present political vacuum until credible civil leaders emerge. Although the hierarchy always publicise their position on matters that affect the church and the country, the patriarchate in the 21st century is unlikely to revert to the temporal authority enjoyed in the past by his predecessors.

THE COPTIC ORTHODOX CHURCH: ORIGINS AND DEVELOPMENTS OF CHURCH MOBILISATION IN MODERN EGYPT

Nicolas Servas

For two years I had the chance of teaching French in a school run by the social services of the Coptic Evangelical Church. Although having some knowledge that the Copts were a minority, it quickly became obvious to my eyes that this Christian community was more apparent and dynamic than the term 'minority' would lead one to imagine.

This article is the continuation of my curiosity to understand why and how the Coptic Orthodox Church, Egypt's most ancient and important Christian denomination, has developed such visible services for Coptic Orthodox Egyptians.

To come up with a comprehensive explanation of the emergence of Coptic mobilisation, one must pay attention not only to discrimination, but also to the dynamic of the religious body itself. Whereas most scholars have concentrated on discrimination stemming from the State and Muslim Egyptians, I will put equal emphasis on the internal development of the Church and of the Coptic community.

The Copts: Egyptians with a distinctive sense of identity

Copts are traditional Christian Egyptians. According to the Coptic tradition, it is the disciple John Mark who brought Christianity to Egypt. From around AD 180, the patriarchate of Alexandria began having its own theological credo and traditions.[1] At the council of Chalcedon in AD 451, the Egyptian patriarch definitely opted for the monophysite dogma and broke up with the main current of contemporary Christianity.[2]

---

1 Anne Boud'hors, 'Ier-VIe siècle un christianisme triomphant', *Notre histoire*, 178 (2000), 33.

2 *Ibid.*, 36.

Today, Copts represent 6 to 7 percent out of a population of 70 millions, i.e. between 4 and 5 millions people. Although the Church hierarchy challenges this data and pretends representing 18 percent of the Egyptian population, the official numbers are likely to be right.[3]

Within the Egyptian population, how do the Copts perceive themselves and how are they perceived by their fellow Muslim citizens? My question here concerns the attributes of 'ethnic group' and 'minority' which are often used to describe the nature of the Christian community of Egypt.

The first condition for a people to form an ethnic group is its convergence around one or several of the following criteria: race; kinship; religion; language; social customs; regionalism; historical origins; and a population's experience within political institutions.[4] In addition to one or several of those markers, this group will fulfil all the following conditions: 1) Reproduce itself biologically; 2) Constitute a field of communication and interaction; 3) Identify itself, and being identified by others, as distinct from other groups of the same nature.[5]

A minority is any group of persons with a sense of cohesion who constitutes less than one-half of the population of a country.[6] The sense of cohesion will come from the same primordial variables as for ethnicity.[7]

Christian Egyptians are from the same race as Muslim Egyptians. They share together the same language, the same territory, and most of their social customs. Yet, other markers differentiate Copts from the Muslim majority: The identification to a different religion, distinct historical origins, a distinctive experience of Egyptian history, and the Coptic community is endogamous, as Christians barely mix with Muslims through marriages.[8] Consequently, due to its distinctive cultural markers

---

[3] The statistics of the Registrar General, which record a slower birth rate among Copts, and the censuses which record a slower growth of the community, are coherent. Moreover, the official statistics have been consistent since 1882: They show a regular decline in the Coptic population. Youssef Courbage and Philippe Fargues, *Christians and Jews under Islam*, London-New York, 1997, 181.

[4] Cynthia Enloe, *Ethnic Conflict and Political Development*, Boston, 1973, 38; Joseph Rothschild, *Ethnopolitics: A Conceptual Framework*, New York, 1981, 87-94; Ted Robert Gurr, *Minorities at Risk*, Washington, 1993, 38.

[5] Xavier de Planhol, *Minorités en Islam*, Paris, 1997, 15.

[6] *Ibid.*, 15.

[7] Mordechai Nisan, *Minorities in the Middle East*, Jefferson-London, 1991, 10-11.

[8] It can be argued that the great majority of Muslim Egyptians are descendants of Copts who converted to Islam. But the ancestors of those who are Christian today never married with Muslims, hence the endogamous character of the Christian community today.

and low representation in Egypt, the Coptic population can be referred as an ethnic group and a minority.

So, why do the great majority of Muslims and Copts, together with the head of the Coptic Church, reject the labels of 'ethnic group' and 'minority' for the Coptic population of Egypt?[9]

More than ethnic differentiation, it is the way a people perceives itself and is perceived by others, together with social and political constructions, which is the key to understanding group identities.[10] For the Coptic community has millennia of existence in the Nile valley and centuries of co-existence with Muslim people, the sentiment prevailing among Christian and Muslim Egyptians is that Copts are part and parcel of the Egyptian nation.[11] Hence the Copts' rejection of labels stressing their difference, as they assume they fully belong to the Egyptian nation.

Theories of communal mobilisation

Theorists of communal mobilisation agree that to become a political factor, a group needs a sense of identity.[12] However, the ties of identity alone are not sufficient to create the opportunity to mobilize this group socially. For that, the group must collectively suffer or benefit from systematic discriminatory treatment vis-à-vis other groups;[13] the group must have been the focus of political mobilisation and action in defence or promotion of self-defined interests.[14] A third factor, *modernity*, is neither

---

[9] A heated discussion took place in Egypt when the Ibn Khaldun Center and Minority Rights Group planned a conference, which comprised seminars on the 'Coptic minority'. The patriarch issued a statement rejecting the designation of Copts as a minority; Karim Al-Gawhari, 'Copts in the "Egyptian Fabric"', *Middle East Report* (July-September 1996), 21. There are obvious political reasons for rejecting such labels, i.e. the fear of being perceived and treated like a non-national group.

[10] X de Planhol, *Minorités en Islam*, 15; Airi Tamura, 'Ethnic Consciousness and its Transformation in the Course of Nation-Building', *The Muslim World*, vol. 75 (April 1985), 103, n. 2.

[11] Christiaan Van Nispen, 'Changes in Relations between Copts and Muslims (1952-1994) in the Light of the Historical Experience', in Nelly van Doorn-Harder & Kari Vogt (eds), *Between Desert and City: The Coptic Church Today*, Oslo, 1997, 22. About the national feelings of pope Shenouda, see John Watson, 'Signposts to Bibliography—Pope Shenouda III', in *Ibid.*, 243-253.

[12] R D MacLaurin(ed.), *The Political Role of Minority Groups in the Middle East*, New York, 1979, 4.

[13] T Gurr, *Minorities at Risk*, 6.

[14] *Ibid.*, 7.

indispensable, nor necessarily sufficient to form a communal group. Nevertheless, throughout history the consequences of modernity often fostered the raise of communal consciousness.[15]

As a group with 'transversal identities', Copts are integrated in some domains of the Egyptian society and polity, while they remain excluded and discriminated from others.[16] Copts reject the labels of 'ethnic' group or 'minority', but they have become a mobilized community, as they feel differently treated than other national groups with regard to religious rights and political representation.

But the existence of shared ties of identity is not sufficient to mobilise a group socially. For that, there must be *intracommunal integration*, i.e. the capacity by the group leaders to channel social mobilisation, to raise communal consciousness, and to tighten collective bonds;[17] and *mobilisation*, i.e. the ability of group leaders to propose new goals and fashion new strategies for the community, to be able to mobilize the community for reaching these goals, and to satisfy or deflect external demands.[18] Together with the absolute size of the minority, its cohesion and its mobilisation, relations with other forces inside or outside the country will be essential to exert influence.[19] Most disadvantaged groups will try to compensate their weakness by winning allies such as other disadvantaged groups or outside forces.[20]

If a first phase initiates co-operation among the cosmopolitan elements of a group, it is not followed automatically by actions among the majority. The communal elites loose their credibility in the eyes of their constituents; at the same time, relatively uncosmopolitan and lower-class persons grow more politicized and communally chauvinistic.[21] This model applies to the Coptic community, as clerics from a relatively

---

15 Colonial rulers sometimes encouraged minorities to take part actively in society, in order to dilute the power and the potential resistance of the majority. Such policies boosted minorities' consciousness and cohesiveness. Later, the entry to the consolidation phase of the postcolonial states in the 1970s was perceived as a threat to minority identity, hence the multiplication and radicalization of communal mobilizations in the same period. Finally, improved communications applied by the majority or alien cultures represent a threat of cultural invasion; R D MacLaurin, *The Political Role of Minority Groups in the Middle East*, 6 and 250-256; J Rothschild, *Ethnopolitics*, 3.

16 Joseph Maïla, 'The Arab Christians', 45.

17 C Enloe, *Ethnic Conflict*, 159 and 212.

18 *Ibid.*

19 R D MacLaurin, *The Political Role of Minority Groups in the Middle East*, 7.

20 T Gurr, *Minorities at Risk*, 37; Mac Laurin R. D., *ibid.*, 7.

21 C Enloe, *Ethnic Conflict*, 163.

uncosmopolitan and lower-class background replaced lay Copts from a cosmopolitan and wealthy background at the head of the Coptic community in the 1940s-1950s.[22]

In the context of communal mobilisation, religious groups bear characteristics which ease intracommunal development. First of all because any confessional group already is a social relationship with concentrated means of coercion. In the Middle East the imposition of the bond of *dhimma* to non-Muslim communities reinforced the potential for communal mobilisation of indigenous Christian minorities. Under the bond of *dhimma*, the *millet* under Ottoman rulers, Christian communities were free to organize and administrate their own religious and cultural affairs; at some point they were even responsible for their own legal and taxation matters. Such a statute, whose fundamental elements were still in force until the 19th century, still influences social, cultural and legal practices. Hence, the process of community mobilisation is made easier as the leaders of the community and the political authorities still have in mind the concept of community representation. Moreover, the communal mobilisation of a religious group is reinforced by the strong devotion of its members to their God, as well as to their community in which they seek and find psychological security.[23] Finally, the strong cultural ties which link a religious group to a certain universal community increase the possibility for the group leaders to get external support.[24]

The dynamics of the Coptic community mobilisation. Discriminations towards Christian Egyptians

Before outlining discrimination I shall remind that the situation of Christian Egyptians is very dynamic, as their status and daily life depend both on official and non-official political decisions, as well as on the events and ideas prevailing in the Egyptian society. Nevertheless, mentioning discrimination of the past 50 years is necessary to understand the rise of communal development and the emergence of the Coptic Orthodox Church as the sole representative of the Coptic Orthodox population.

---

[22] See my chapter on the *Cultural and Social Mobilization of the Community.*

[23] M Apostolov, *Religious Minorities, Nation States and Security*, 14.

[24] *Ibid.*, 11.

Cultural discrimination affecting the Christian Coptic religion

Because the sources of political legitimacy and identification in the majority of Middle Eastern countries are ethnic and religious, i.e. Arab people and Sunni Islam, the culture of the majority automatically assigns an inferior social status to different ethnic and religious groups.

According to the Egyptian Constitution, beliefs and religious practices other than Islam should be recognized and authorized. Article 46 of the Egyptian Constitution of September 1971 states that 'The State shall guarantee the freedom of belief and the freedom of practicing religious rights'.[25] Yet, clear historical reasons have made that Islam has been granted the status of official religion of the Egyptian State. As Article 2 of the Egyptian Constitution puts it: 'Islam is the Religion of the State'.[26] Because the Egyptian state represents itself as the defender of a single religion, Islam, it automatically assigns a lesser rank to other religious beliefs and practices present in Egypt.

In practice, this superiority in the Constitution set limits to the rights and possibilities for Christians to build churches. Furthermore, two decrees strictly regulate the building of churches: The Hamayouni Decree of 1856, which stipulates that church building requests have to be submitted to the Sultan by the Pope, today by the Pope to the President;[27] the 1934 Decree of Minister of Interior Al Ezabi Pasha with church-building requests to be subordinate to a number of conditions (the distance with the near-by mosques, the objections of Muslim neighbours, the distance with the nearest church of the same denomination, the number of Christians in the same area).[28]

These legal provisions officially term the Christian religion as inferior to the Islamic one, and restrict the religious rights of Christian Egyptians. Muslims do not have to comply to such obligations or request a permission from the President to build and restore their places of worship. Indeed, authorizations for permits for mosques are very easy to obtain; the informal agreement of local authorities suffices in some cases.[29]

---

25 Source: www.parliament.gov.eg (consulted 9 January 2003).

26 *Ibid.*

27 Saad Eddin Ibrahim, 'The Copts of Egypt', in *Minority Rights Group Report*, London, 1996, 11. President Moubarak recently delegated this power to local governors; 'Egypt's Copts After Kosheh', www.theestimate.com/public/01282000a.html, 28 January, 2000 (consulted 19 January 2003).

28 S E Ibrahim, 'The Copts of Egypt', 11.

29 *Ibid.*, 11.

Authorisations to build new churches are granted with parsimony. In the past, President Nasser had guaranteed Pope Kyrillos VI the right to build 25 churches a year. Indeed, in the whole decade of the 1960s, only 68 were authorized.[30] Again, when President Sadat visited Pope Shenouda in 1973, he promised to let 50 churches be built each year. This promise was never satisfied.[31] The Egyptian sociologist Saad Eddin Ibrahim found out that between 1981-1990 the Coptic Orthodox Church received only 10 permits to build churches and 26 permits for rebuilding.[32] This denial of religious facilities through harsh regulations and averse policies used to and still leads to conflicts between the authorities and the Coptic Church.

Since the Copts could not build enough churches to meet the growing needs of their community, they resorted to illegal constructions and the use of 'philanthropic' buildings as places of worship.[33] Unmistakably, this leads to conflicts between Muslim and Christian Egyptians. For the reason that Muslim neighbours can object the building and the repair of churches, Copts often rebuild them without having received an official permission. The conflicts which occurred in the Cairo suburb of Khankah in 1972,[34] in Shubra al-Kheima in 2001,[35] or in Assiut in 2002[36] are the result of this discriminatory treatment towards religions other than Islam in Egypt.

[30] T H Partrick, *Traditional Egyptian Christianity*, 172.

[31] S E Ibrahim, 'The Copts of Egypt', 18.

[32] *Ibid.*, 23.

[33] Partrick, 172; a committee set up by the People's Assembly in 1972 investigated Coptic grievances. It recorded 1442 churches in Egypt. At the same time, the Ministry of Interior had provided an estimate of 500 churches. If the numbers are right, the difference gives a gross idea of the number of illegal churches; Hamied Ansari, 'Sectarian Conflict in Egypt and the Political Expediency of Religion', *Middle East Journal*, vol. 38 (Summer 1984), 398.

[34] Muslim inhabitants of Khankah set fire to an illegal church; Hamied Ansari, 'Sectarian Conflict in Egypt and the Political Expediency of Religion', 400; Dina Al-Khawagah, 'Le développement communautaire copte: un mode de participation au politique ?', *Monde arabe Maghreb Machrek*, 135 (January-March 1992), 14.

[35] The governor ordered the demonlition of a newly renovated church. Although President Mubarak later ordered the reconstruction of the church, the Copts had to pay for it; 'Question copte, questions à l'Egypte', Kristianasen Wendy, *Le Monde Diplomatique*, Mai 2001.

[36] 'Egyptian governor orders the destruction of a newly renovated Coptic church', www.copts.net/asp?id=386, December 19 2002 (consulted 19 January 2003).

Cultural discrimination affecting Christian F

The status of official religion for Islam obliges the St
promote the Islamic religion through official policies.[37] In
the Islamic religion, Article 2 of the Constitution could be i
as the obligation for the state to use the *shari'a* as the principal sou
legislation, at least to conform its laws and domestic policies to Islamic law. Although Egyptian leaders, with the exception of President Sadat, opted for caring policies, other legal and political practices related to religious matters have contributed to the marginalization of Christian Egyptians.

In the field of education for instance, official programs overlooked the pluralism of Egyptian society. For a long time, history programs went deeply into the pre-Christian era then jumped to the Islamic era,[38] disregarding six centuries of national history dominated by Christian rulers and the Christian religion. In 2001, the Ministry of Education decided to introduce Coptic history in the schools' curricula, but fearing militant Islamism made that this decision has been enforced in primary schools only.[39]

Egyptian mass media oscillated between ignorance and hatred of the Christian predicament. From its outset in the 1960s and onwards, the state television service did not broadcast any programme dedicated to the Coptic Christian religion, whereas programmes on the Islamic religion abounded.[40] Today, sheikhs are given abundant air-time in radio and television programmes,[41] whereas priests do not. Verbal assaults targeting Christianity in general and Coptic Christianity occurred from time to time, more specifically during the 1980s and early 1990s, when Islamic programmes verbally assaulted the Coptic doctrine.[42] In the late years of

---

37 M Samaan and S Sukkary, 'The Copts and Muslims of Egypt', 141.

38 'Act, don't hide', Heggy Tarek, *Cairo Times*, 4-17 February 1999.

39 'Question copte, questions à l'Egypte', Wendy Kristianasen, *Le Monde Diplomatique*, Mai 2001. There are other examples of discrimination at schools, thus the imposition of the study of the Qur'an to all pupils in public schools, as result of the policy of fighting illiteracy; Y Courbage and P Fargues, *Christians and Jews under Islam*, 179.

40 Maurice Martin, 'The Renewal in Context: 1960-1990', in Nelly van Doorn-Harder & Kari Vogt (eds), *Between Desert and City: The Coptic Church Today*, Oslo, 1997, 18.

41 K Al-Gawhari, 'Copts in the 'Egyptian Fabric'', 22.

42 In the meantime the Egyptian market was saturated with books and tapes attacking the Copts, as well as the Christian creed and doctrines; S E Ibrahim, 'The Copts of Egypt', 26.

Cultural discrimination affecting Christian Egyptians

The status of official religion for Islam obliges the State to protect and promote the Islamic religion through official policies.[37] In the context of the Islamic religion, Article 2 of the Constitution could be interpreted as the obligation for the state to use the *shari'a* as the principal source of legislation, at least to conform its laws and domestic policies to Islamic laws. Although Egyptian leaders, with the exception of President Sadat, opted for caring policies, other legal and political practices related to religious matters have contributed to the marginalization of Christian Egyptians.

In the field of education for instance, official programs overlooked the pluralism of Egyptian society. For a long time, history programs went deeply into the pre-Christian era then jumped to the Islamic era,[38] disregarding six centuries of national history dominated by Christian rulers and the Christian religion. In 2001, the Ministry of Education decided to introduce Coptic history in the schools' curricula, but fearing militant Islamism made that this decision has been enforced in primary schools only.[39]

Egyptian mass media oscillated between ignorance and hatred of the Christian predicament. From its outset in the 1960s and onwards, the state television service did not broadcast any programme dedicated to the Coptic Christian religion, whereas programmes on the Islamic religion abounded.[40] Today, sheikhs are given abundant air-time in radio and television programmes,[41] whereas priests do not. Verbal assaults targeting Christianity in general and Coptic Christianity occurred from time to time, more specifically during the 1980s and early 1990s, when Islamic programmes verbally assaulted the Coptic doctrine.[42] In the late years of

---

[37] M Samaan and S Sukkary, 'The Copts and Muslims of Egypt', 141.

[38] 'Act, don't hide', Heggy Tarek, *Cairo Times*, 4-17 February 1999.

[39] 'Question copte, questions à l'Egypte', Wendy Kristianasen, *Le Monde Diplomatique*, Mai 2001. There are other examples of discrimination at schools, thus the imposition of the study of the Qur'an to all pupils in public schools, as result of the policy of fighting illiteracy; Y Courbage and P Fargues, *Christians and Jews under Islam*, 179.

[40] Maurice Martin, 'The Renewal in Context: 1960-1990', in Nelly van Doorn-Harder & Kari Vogt (eds), *Between Desert and City: The Coptic Church Today*, Oslo, 1997, 18.

[41] K Al-Gawhari, 'Copts in the 'Egyptian Fabric'', 22.

[42] In the meantime the Egyptian market was saturated with books and tapes attacking the Copts, as well as the Christian creed and doctrines; S E Ibrahim, 'The Copts of Egypt', 26.

Sadat's presidency, the President himself targeted the Church and Copts as being troublemakers and seditionists.[43]

Recently, the Copts have been allowed more visibility through the broadcasting of Christmas and Easter masses.[44] The official press has been given the task to stress co-existence by publishing Christmas messages of religious leaders, and interviews with Coptic personalities.[45] But policies of the past 50 years contributed to make Christian Egyptians feel different from their fellow Muslim citizens.They have been conducive to ignorance and misunderstanding of the other religion in a context of poverty and illiteracy.

Political discrimination

Two forms of political discrimination affect Christian Egyptians: The state interferes in the governance of the Church and the Copts have been under-represented in politics since the 1950s.

By interfering in the governance of the Coptic Church, the state intrudes in the internal affairs of a religious institution, which does not actually threaten the security of the country.

> —Although the Pope is elected by the representatives of the Coptic Church, their choice becomes official only after the approval of the President.The President also has the unofficial right to dismiss the pope, as President Sadat made use with Pope Shenouda III in 1981.[46]
>
> —Some land as well as build properties belonging to the Coptic Church are still administered by the state. After an internal conflict had occurred within the Church in 1957, Nasser decided to take over the *waqf* (estates and buildings donated to the Church) and to found a general body to supervise the

43 Ansari H, 'Sectarian Conflict and the Political Expediency of Religion', 404; Farah Nadia Ramsis, *Religious Strife in Egypt*, Montreux, 1986, 10-13.

44 'Question copte, questions à l'Egypte', Kristianasen Wendy, *Le Monde Diplomatique*, May 2001.

45 *Ibid.* In June 2001, an article of the independent *Al-Naaba* newspaper related the story of an ex-monk, who had had sexual intercourse with Coptic women.The Church complained and Copts demonstrated in Cairo.The Journalists Union decided to dismiss the chief redactor and to forbid the publication of the newspaper; 'Un numéro explosif', Abdel-Azim Sherin and Sabet Sabah, *Al-Ahram Hebdo*, 20-26 June 2001.

46 S E Ibrahim, 'The Copts of Egypt', 17.

Coptic *waqf*. This left the Coptic Lay Council without any role.[47] Some of these endowments started to be returned in 1998.[48]

—The 1957 Presidential Decree had substituted the Church's *waqf* with government's stocks. As the Coptic Lay Council complained, a new law restricted Church and monastic properties to 200 acres.[49]

The social and political under-representation of Christian Egyptians dates back to Nasser's presidency, when Coptic politicians almost disappeared from the political arena, influential Coptic families saw their power bases vanish, the state reoriented its foreign policy toward Arab and Islamic, rather than European and Western partners.

The scant representation of the Copts in the political field does not result from a deliberate policy of the successive governments. It is the consequence of the casting aside of political parties in 1953, more particularly of the Wafd which used to be the party where Coptic and Muslim politicians gathered for the commonwealth of the country. Another reason is the authoritarian nature of the regime, which relies upon military circles and has restricted the development of free associative and political activities. As Copts did not traditionally engage in the military forces, it ended up in the fact that the Revolutionary Command Council was made of Muslims only.[50] Since the state most powerful agents, the governors, are recruited almost exclusively from the military and security agencies, there is little chance for Christian Egyptians to get access to key political positions in Egypt. The last reason is the gradual removal of the Coptic elites due to President Nasser's agricultural reform and nationalizations.[51] Although nationalizations made no difference between Muslim and Coptic entrepreneurs, the fact that Coptic elites owned a large stake of the country's wealth affected Coptic Egyptians to a greater extent than Muslim Egyptians.[52]

---

47 *Ibid.*, 17.

48 'Encouraging signs', Saad Eddin Ibrahim, *Cairo Times*, 4-17 February 1999.

49 S E Ibrahim, 'The Copts of Egypt', 17.

50 M Heikal, *Autumn of Fury*, London, 1983, 154.

51 D Al-Khawaga, 'Le développement communautaire copte', 9-10.

52 S E Ibrahim, 'The Copts of Egypt', 15-16.

Although there is no openly discriminatory policy towards Christian Egyptians, the successive governments have neglected the problem: Nasser and his successors made no efforts in recruiting social and political leaders among educated Copts.[53] The rise of conservative Islam in the 1970s and its intrusion among state officials has made even a possible Coptic participation in politics more difficult.[54] Due to public negligence and prejudiced opinions, Christian Egyptians are rarely elected or selected for leadership positions:

> —There is only one major Coptic minister in the present government, Youssef Boutros-Ghali as Minister of Economy and Foreign Trade.
>
> —Neither does one find a single Coptic police chief, *nor* a Coptic mayor, *nor* a Coptic governor.[55] These officials are among the most powerful in Egypt.
>
> —Copts represent only 1.5 percent of the state employees.[56]
>
> —Copts are not fairly represented in the Parliament, where Coptic MPs represent much less than 6-7 percent, the actual percentage of the Coptic population in Egypt.[57] Although it is understandable that a Muslim majority identifies more easily with Muslim candidates, the party of the President and opposition parties are responsible of this indirect discrimination, as they seldom retain Coptic candidates.[58] Moreover, both the ruling party and opposition parties play the game of 'Coptic votes', which consists in addressing Coptic citizens as a whole, in order to get their votes. Thus, the NDP spread the rumours it would free Pope Shenouda before the 1984 elections, the

---

53 D Al-Khawaga, 'Les services sociaux dispensés par l'Eglise copte', n.1, 192.

54 'Encouraging signs', Saad Eddin Ibrahim, *Cairo Times*, 4-17 February 1999.

55 'Egypt's Copts After Kosheh', www.theestimate.com/public/01282000a.html, 28 January 2000 (consulted 19 January 2003).

56 'Question copte, questions à l'Egypte', Kristianasen Wendy, *Le Monde Diplomatique*, May 2001.

57 *Ibid*.

58 The NDP presented only two Coptic candidates at the parliamentary elections of November-December 1990; Iman Farag, 'La politique à l'égyptienne: lecture des élections législatives', *Monde arabe Maghreb-Machrek*, 133 (July-September 1991), 27. Nasser implemented the constitutional principle, still in use today, of appointing 10 individuals, mostly Copts; *ibid*., 26.

same year the New Wafd insinuated that Copts had joined the party.[59] Apart from retaliations and the search for Islamic votes, such practices increase the perception of Copts by others as a sectarian group.

As a consequence of this neglectful and malign political discrimination, Christian Egyptians have only a few representatives in the executives and legal spheres to express their concerns and defend their interests.

Discrimination in the wider society

Since President Moubarak's accession to power, the successive governments have taken a clear stance against any institutionalization of Islamic parties.[60] Notwithstanding, militant Islamism has been and remains a significant constituent of Egyptian society and politics. Today, Islamic parties represent themselves as a platform for the whole nation, but it is obvious that their religious political projects are all embracing. It remains ambiguous whether boundaries set by the Islamic law would allow Christians to redefine their cultural identity as differing from that of the majority, and to participate with all their rights in the administration and politics.[61] For

[59] S E Ibrahim, 'The Copts of Egypt', 20.

[60] D El-Khawaga, 'Le développement communautaire copte: un mode de participation au politique ?', 18.

[61] The issue of the non-Muslim in an Islamic state has been addressed by Muslim thinkers such as Yusuf al-Qaradawi, Muhammad Salim al-'Awwa, Tariq al-Bishri and others. Most of them agree to guarantee the protection of Christians from external aggression and internal oppression, to safeguard their property and honour, and to guarantee their freedom of religion. On the other side, Christians would have to pay the *jizya* as a substitute for the two religious obligations prescribed on Muslims (*jihad* and *zakkat)*, and to abide by the rules of the *shari'a*. Copts could be employed in the government, except in positions which are religious in nature, those include the positions of head of state, judge among Muslims, and leader of the armed forces. Christians would have to respect the feelings of Muslims by not flaunting their religious symbols, this also means not establishing a church in a Muslim city where none existed before; Yvonne Yazbeck Haddad, 'Christians in a Muslim State: The Recent Egyptian Debate', in Yvonne Yazbeck Haddad and Wadi Zaidan Haddad (eds), *Christian-Muslim Encounters*, Gainesville, 1995, 385-393. In practice, leaders of Islamic parties have sometimes defended Coptic candidates attacked on the basis of their religion. Political alliances between these leaders and Coptic politicians occurred as well; S Ismail, 'Confronting the Other: Identity, Culture, Politics, and Conservative Islamism in Egypt', *International Journal of Middle East Studies*, 30 (1998), 220, n. 7.

presently, the significant presence of militant Islamism in the society and its successes in informal politics make the Copts feel threaten in their Christian identity.

Political Islam was already existing in Egypt of the 1920s, but it is only after the 1967 defeat against Israel and under Sadat's presidency that it became increasingly powerful and visible. The rise of Islamic groups went along with the degradation of social and economic conditions, together with the President's encouraging of such currents in order to offset leftist and Nasserist rivals.[62]

Copts felt alienated by the society, which was increasingly going in the direction of conservative Islam. Although Islamic leaders expressed very disparate views with regard to the position of Christians in an Islamic State,[63] the general atmosphere was rather oppressive, with the persistence of anti-Christian rumours, imams subduing Egyptian Christians in Friday sermons,[64] sometimes leading to attacks on Coptic churches, shops, houses and people.[65]

Street violence

Street violence aimed at Copts because of their religious identity is a recent phenomenon which was first recorded in 1972, when Muslim villagers of Khankah burned an illegal church, and destroyed private property belonging to Copts.[66] Attacks went on in other parts of the country in the following 20 years, but they have been limited to Upper Egypt since.[67] Upper Egypt is the country's poorest region, the home of sporadic anti-government violence, and family vendettas. This tends to prove that social and economic factors greatly contribute turning minor clashes into fights. Street violence is a phenomenon limited in time and

---

62 Under Sadat's presidency, the parliament made moves to reaffirm that the *shari 'a* was the legal basis of the state. There was even an effort to introduce a law to formalise the death penalty for apostasy from Islam; H Ansari, 'Sectarian Conflict and the Political Expediency of Religion', 401; 'Egypt's Copts After Kosheh', www.theestimate.com/public/01282000a.html, January 28, 2000 (consulted 19 January 2003).

63 G Kepel, *The Prophet and Pharaoh*, London, 1985, 158-162 and 164-170.

64 Hamied Ansari, 413.

65 G Kepel, *The Prophet and Pharaoh*, 158-162 and 164-170.

66 H Ansari, 'Sectarian Conflict and the Political Expediency of Religion', 400.

67 Fights occurred in Cairo until the early 1990s; S E Ibrahim, 'The Copts of Egypt', 21.

space: the attacks occur in one place without spreading to other parts of the country at the same time. This feature makes understand that multiple motivations and actors are involved in the attacks, yet that the majority of Egyptian people do not support them.

Sectarian strife in the 1970s had been propagated by the authorities, as the political leadership had to contrive enemies of Egypt, in order to be able to eradicate all opposition forces. The massacre which occurred in the Cairo suburb of Al-Zawiyya al-Hamra in June 1981 resulted from such perverse State policies: The dispute that had started between Christians and Muslims in this vicinity had begun over a piece of land. Wishing to put an end to the activities of militant Islamists throughout Egypt, the government seized the opportunity and encouraged NDP militants to distribute provocative leaflets against Copts. After this had led to the massacre of 17 people, most of them Christians, the government gave all responsibility to radical Islamic groups and dealt heavy blows to them.[68] Today, government negligence put with mutual ignorance between the two communities continue producing clashes, as it occurred in Al-Kosheh, where twenty Copts, one Muslim and two unidentified people were killed in January 2000.[69]

On the other side, Islamic groups strove to demonstrate their ability to supplant the State. Radical Islamic groups were most often responsible for fuelling antagonism, through aggressive pamphlets and discourses, sometimes turning to physical violence as it occurred recently in the village of Al-Fiqriyya.[70]

Cultural and social mobilisation of the community

Notwithstanding, one should not assume that Coptic mobilisation began to emerge as from the 1970s, as a reaction to street violence. As chronology

68 G Kepel, *The Prophet and Pharaoh*, 164–170.

69 In the same village the killing of two Copts in August 1998 had not been properly investigated by the local authorities. On the contrary, hundreds of Copts were arrested, a roundup criticised by the local bishop, who was seized in turn; 'Egypt's Copts After El-Kosheh', www.theestimate.com/public/01282000a.html, January 28, 2000 (consulted 19 January 2003).

70 In February 1997 a radical Islamic group killed eight Copts. Physical aggressions led by radical Islamic groups occurred on several other occasions. 'Egypt's Copts After El-Kosheh'; www.theestimate.com/public/02112000.html, February 11, 2000 (consulted 19 January 2003).

shows it, the ideological seeds of communal mobilisation had already been planted in the late 19th century.

Western educated Copts were already advocating a community model at the end of the 19th century.[71] As early as 1874 prominent Coptic laymen were promoting the project of a Coptic Community Council (*majlis al-milli*), in which they would be in charge of the personal status, clerical affairs, education and social welfare of their fellow believers.[72] Although the laymen never reached their goal, they maintained their prerogatives and at least succeeded in promoting Coptic equality through their leading position in society and philanthropic institutions.

Modernity as the main incentive for the church's model of community development

Running parallel to the secular model, the religious model of mobilisation did not succeed at representing the Copts before the 1950s, when the secular elite lost both its wealth and authority. Historically, the clergy had always criticized any mobilisation for the sake of community interests, it perceived this kind of commitment as an alteration of the purely religious meaning of the Copts as 'sons of the Church'.[73] In the early 19th century Coptic religiosity consisted in the repetition of the cultural model,[74] monachism had almost disappeared,[75] the roles and hierarchy inside the Church were not exclusive and delimited.[76] The Church could have remained unaffected, but as Catholic and Protestant missions were establishing themselves in Egypt, as Syrian entrepreneurs and administrators were taking prominent positions in the state and the economy, as the Coptic elites were becoming more acculturated, the Church felt threatened in its religious identity.[77] So, it is the advent of modernity as an acculturing ethic that triggered the modernisation of the religious body.

---

71 M Apostolov, *Religious Minorities, Nation States and Security*, 43; D Al-Khawaga, 'Le développement communautaire copte', 7.

72 *Ibid.*

73 Dina Al-Khawaga, 'The Political Dynamics of the Copts: Giving the Community an Active Role', in Andrea Pacini (ed.), *Christian Communities in the Arab Middle East*, Oxford, 1998, n. 15, 182.

74 D Al-Khawaga, 'Le développement communautaire copte', 5.

75 *Ibid.*

76 *Ibid.*

77 *Ibid.*

Mobilisation around identity markers

From the late 19th century until the early 1920s, the Church hierarchy reaction focused on the construction of educational structures for its clergy. This phase began in 1893 with the opening of the Coptic Seminary, in order to improve the education of the clergy,[78] and confirmed in 1918 with the launching of the first Orthodox Sunday schools.[79] The attraction of all faithful back to the sphere of the Church was carried out in the same period through the opening of Orthodox schools and other welfare projects with a strong religious reference.[80] So, the primary concern of Church leaders was to defend Coptic religious identity against the effects of modern education, not to shelter the Copts from non existing discriminatory policies.[81]

In the 1920s-1930s, the parliamentary system, the national orientation of the state, and the better education of Christian Egyptians contributed to the economical, social and political integration of Christian Egyptians. Consequently, the Church kept discreet and accommodating when engaged in the defence of Coptic rights. But its internal renewal had made of it a dynamic institution with a strong potential for mobilisation.

Social and political discrimination increased intracommunal cohesiveness

The profound changes that affected the Egyptian society in the 1940s-1950s led to a feeling of disappointment for the majority of Christian Egyptians. A chain of political events beginning in 1936 led to the weakening of Coptic representation and influence in the state and society. From 1936, the royal family, minority parties and the Azhar hierarchy deliberately criticised the strong Coptic constituency of the Wafd, their main political opponent.[82] This led to the political reorientation of the Wafd

---

[78] After 14 centuries during which the Church did not have such a structure; D Al-Khawaga, 'The Political Dynamics of the Copts', 179.

[79] Dina El-Khawaga, 'Le développement communautaire copte: un mode de participation au politique?', 7-8. Ibrahim S E, 'The Copts of Egypt', 13.

[80] *Ibid.*, 179-180.

[81] Today, the safeguarding of a distinct Coptic identity remains one of the main concerns of the Church, it goes through historical and theological researches and publications, through the preservation and rebuilding of the architectural heritage; see Paul Balta, 'Les Coptes : exode, exil intérieur et renouveau', *Les cahiers de l'Orient*, 48 (1997), 16.

[82] D Al-Khawaga, 'Le développement communautaire copte', 10.

after the demission of its main figure, the Copt Makram Ubeid, in 1942;[83] in 1948 the party allied with the Muslim Brotherhood.[84] After 1952, the country came under the rule of army officers, among which Copts were non-existent, and political parties were eliminated. The nationalisation of the economy led to the impoverishment of the Coptic elite, which used to control large sectors of the agriculture, industry and services.[85]

As the Coptic youth could not find its bearings in politics and society anymore,[86] it engaged more actively in leadership positions within the Church. Between 1951 and 1970 a new generation of Church leaders engaged in religious education and social services.[87]

Organisation of the first social services by the Church

The development of social services for the community was an unprecedented event in the history of the Coptic Orthodox Church. The idea of developing social services first came from monks and priests who had been sent to religious and academic institutions in the West.[88]

The monk Makari al-Soriani, who had studied in Princeton, set up the first social projects of the Coptic Church directed toward the community.[89] Social services consisted in rural development, the improvement of work and living facilities, technical training, health and teaching.[90] They were mainly directed toward the lower middle class.[91] The funding came from protestant and ecumenical organizations.[92] With time these projects grew in importance and the new bishop Samuel was able to mobilise the Coptic Diaspora for financing larger agricultural projects, small businesses and make available grants for Coptic students.[93] The loosening of state control over economic and social actors between

---

83 *Ibid.*
84 A Pacini, 'Introduction', 16.
85 T H Partrick, *Traditional Egyptian Christianity*, 155.
86 D Al-Khawaga, 'Le développement communautaire copte', 13.
87 *Ibid.*
88 Al-Khawaga, 'Les services sociaux dispensés par l'Eglise copte', 191.
89 *Ibid.*, 189.
90 *Ibid.*, 198.
91 *Ibid.*, 203.
92 *Ibid.*, 198.
93 *Ibid.*, 204.

1970 and 1974 helped the Church continue developing its social services and relations with international partners.

The Church leadership took over the representation and protection of the community

The loosening of political control over society at the beginning of Sadat's era, was perceived by social and political forces as a suitable time to renegotiate their place in society and politics.[94] The establishment of the clergy as the nucleus of the community sphere, followed by the integration of all faithful in the community through social services, bestowed the new Church leaders with the image of a representative force able to mobilise the Copts and consequently to exert political pressure in behalf of the Christian community.[95]

The 1971 election of a leading actor of the Renewal, Pope Shenouda III, is the landmark for the advancement of community mobilisation under the Church's leadership. In order to curb discriminations emanating from both the State and the society, the Church leadership opted for a confrontational strategy. The prominent Coptic laymen who traditionally acted as intermediates between the Church and the state remained passive, creating a broader support from the Coptic population to the Church.

The conflict between the state and the Church started over the issue of church building, one of the most fundamental and at the same time most restricted needs of the Coptic community. It is in Khankah in May 1972 that the Church confronted the State for the first time. Khankah is a small city located north of Cairo, where an 'illegal' church was burned in May 1972. The police came to impose a ban, but Shenouda rallied some of his priests to go there and to protect the church by surrounding it.[96] For the first time, the clergymen, representatives of the Church, confronted the police, representatives of the state. The conclusion one can draw from this event is that the first reason for the Church to opt for a confrontational

---

[94] D Al-Khawaga, 'Le développement communautaire copte', 13.

[95] D Al-Khawaga, 'The Political Dynamics of the Copts', 188.

[96] H Ansari, 'Sectarian Conflict and the Political Expediency of Religion', 130.

strategy was not to gain more political rights for its adherents, yet to obtain the end of discrimination with regard to places of worship.[97]

With the increase of Islamic militancy directed against Christian Egyptians in the following ten years, the Coptic Church definitely opted for a confrontational policy. When fundamentalist Islamic groups attacked Coptic shops and individuals in March 1978, the Church announced a 40 days fast, hence mobilizing the entire community of believers.[98]

Role of the state in the making of the Church's leading position

It is the Coptic Church Renewal movement, with its identity and social activities, which turned the Church into the exclusive representative body of the Copts and the patriarch into their indisputable spokesman (1874-1972). But it is the damage caused to the wealth and influence of the Copts in the 1950s-1970s that led to the elimination of other forms of representation and triggered the confrontation for the defence of Coptic rights.[99]

For the presidency of Nasser, one has to consider the role of the State in the keeping off of challengers to the Church leadership. Apart from indirect economic and political discrimination, Nasser chose to intervene personally in Church's affairs and to give the primacy to the clergy in the century old conflict between lay and ecclesiastic leaders.

President Nasser opted for a direct and complying relation with the Coptic patriarch. As the Egyptian leader banned the corrupt patriarch Youssab in 1955, he also seized the opportunity to transfer the personal status responsibilities of the *majlis al-milli* (the Coptic lay council) to the government.[100] By 1960 Nasser had passed on the administration of Coptic *waqfs* to a special state committee, leaving the *majlis el-milli* with educational and building duties only.[101] In 1962 the president abolished the *majlis el-milli* and ordered the transfer of its remaining duties to the patriarch.[102] So, it is the political body itself, which put aside lay opposition forces and strengthened the Church authority.

---

[97] D Al-Khawagah, 'Le développement communautaire copte', 14.

[98] N R Farah, 'Religious Strife in Egypt', 122.

[99] Al-Khawaga, 'The Political Dynamics of the Copts', 185.

[100] T H Partrick, *Traditional Egyptian Christianity*, 156.

[101] *Ibid.*, 165.

[102] *Ibid.*

In this 'millet partnership'[103] developed between President Nasser and patriarch Kyrillos VI, the Egyptian leader ensured the security of Christian Egyptians and the status of Kyrillos VI as the Copts' legitimate representative.[104] In return, the president could count on the official support of the patriarch in its domestic and international policies. Kyrillos proposed the introduction of studies in socialism for the clergy,[105] he attacked the vestiges of colonialism in Africa, condemned the American involvement in Vietnam, voiced his support for the American civil rights movement and, in wake of the 1967 War, sent Church representatives to capitals worldwide to spread the Arab view on the conflict.[106]

In this context, pope Shenouda's choice to support President Moubarak and avoid clashes with the government, appears as fairly similar to the unofficial policy developed by the Church leadership in the 1950s and 1960s, one that aims at strengthening the Church spiritually and politically; and to help maintaining the national cohesion by preserving the state as a neutral arbiter. It is rather Sadat's period and the confrontational policy chosen by the president and the patriarch at that time which were exceptional, as the president himself threatened the national cohesion and the position of the state as a neutral arbiter.[107]

Spreading the Gospel and reinforcing the Church's domestic position

The field of 'international relations' of the Coptic Church is most revealing as the current Church leadership pursues objectives similar to its domestic guidelines: First, as a Christian religious body, the Church has to spread the Gospel and the Coptic doctrine worldwide. Moreover, as the Church

---

[103] P Sedra, 'Class Cleavages and Ethnic Conflict: Coptic Christian Communities in Modern Egyptian Politics', *Islam and Christian-Muslim Relations*, vol. 10, No. 2, 1999, 225.

[104] Thus, when administrative difficulties arose within the Coptic community, Kyrillos could intervene personally, often acquiring the state support by presidential decree; Watson J, 'Abba Kyrillos, Patriarch and Solitary', *Coptic Church Review*, vol. 17, Nos. 1 & 2 (Spring and Summer 1996), 60.

[105] T H Partrick, *Traditional Egyptian Christianity*, 165; Otto Meinardus, *Two Thousand Years of Coptic Christianity*, Cairo, 1999, 74.

[106] P Sedra, 'Class Cleavages and Ethnic Conflict', 225.

[107] M Heikal, *Autumn of Fury*, 220.

is also acting as the main representative of the Coptic community, it seeks to reinforce its position domestically through international awareness of the existence and struggle. The Church also supports the Egyptian government, which in return shall pay back with more independence for the religious body and more rights for the Copts. The unvarying guideline of this Coptic 'foreign policy' is to remain discreet and to avoid behaviours which could harm Egypt's position internationally, hence weaken the community domestically.

Affirming the Coptic credo worldwide and supporting the Church at home through relations with ecumenical organizations and foreign Churches

A good example of the Church's twofold oriented vision is illustrated by the early adhesion to ecumenical organizations such as the World Council of Churches and the All-African Council of Churches in the 1950s. This was done to affirm the Coptic heritage in the world of international Christian Churches; but Pope Kyrillos VI also had in mind the benefits he could enjoy from international recognition in case of a conflict with the Egyptian regime.[108] Pope Shenouda carried on with this approach and even expanded the contacts of the Coptic Church with ecumenical bodies abroad: The current patriarch has been one of the presidents of the World Council of Churches,[109] and one of the four presidents of the Middle East Council of Churches. Shenouda paid visits to the pope in Rome,[110] to the archbishop of Canterbury,[111] and to the Orthodox patriarchates of Damascus, Istanbul and Moscow.[112] In North America and Europe, the Coptic Church is a member of regional councils of Churches.

The sustained attention given to theological discussions with other Churches highlights the Coptic Church's desire to have its credo and traditions fully accepted by members of the world Christianity.[113] But, the patriarch's insistence on membership to regional and international organizations, together with his visits to religious leaders worldwide aim at

---

[108] D Al-Khawaga, 'Les services sociaux dispensés par l'Eglise copte', 194.
[109] O Meinardus, *Two Thousand Years of Coptic Christianity*, 7.
[110] *Ibid*.
[111] T H Partrick, *Traditional Egyptian Christianity*, 170-171.
[112] O Meinardus, *Two Thousand Years of Coptic Christianity*, 7.
[113] *Ibid*., 122-123.

developing an international attention to the Church's existence.[114] For in case of a conflict at home, the patriarch does not want to be left forgotten by foreign Churches and institutions,[115] as it occurred in the first months of his house arrest in September 1981.[116]

Africa as the main field for Coptic mission

The main field for Coptic mission in the past 50 years has been the African continent.[117] Despite its historical ties with Ethiopian Christianity and its presence along the Nile Valley,[118] the contemporary renewal of Coptic mission first took place in South Africa, soon to extend to Zambia, Zimbabwe, Kenya, Uganda, Tanzania, Namibia, Côte d'Ivoire and Congo.[119] Today, the Coptic Church supervises not only churches, but also social projects such as hospitals, schools and training centres. So, on the model of Western Churches, Coptic mission develops through pastoral work but also with the help of social, educational and medical activities.

Patriarchs Kyrillos and Shenouda have bestowed missionary activities in Africa with their approval and steady support: In 1962 Kyrillos opened a Department of African Studies in the Coptic Institute;[120] in 1976 Shenouda consecrated a new bishop for African Affairs;[121] furthermore the current patriarch has paid several visits to Coptic and independent Churches in Kenya, Zaire, South Africa and Zimbabwe.

Apart from genuine evangelising aims, what is the spur to such continuous efforts and how does the Church conceives its role in

---

[114] John Watson, 'Signposts to Bibliography—Pope Shenouda III', in Nelly van Doorn-Harder & Kari Vogt (eds), *Between Desert and City: The Coptic Church Today*, Oslo, 1997, 251.

[115] *Ibid.*, 250.

[116] After the Al-Zawiyya al-Hamra strife of June 1981 the Egyptian patriarch decided to boycott official celebrations. President reacted with resentment and force by putting Shenouda under house arrest; G Kepel, *The Prophet and Pharaoh*, 166-170.

[117] For an exhaustive record of the Coptic mission in Africa, see Bishop Antonius Marcos, *Come Across and Help Us ... The Story of the Coptic Orthodox Church in Africa in Our Present Time*, 1993 and 1996.

[118] 200,000 Copts live in Sudan where the Coptic Church has two archbishops; www.sudanupdate.org (reports, minorities, Coptic Christians), consulted 12 June 2003.

[119] J Watson, *Among the Copts*, 73-75.

[120] *Ibid.*, 73.

[121] J Watson, *Among the Copts*, 74.

Christian Africa? Decisions taken by the Church leadership such as the 1978 invitation of Antonius Marcos to independent Churches to meet in Cairo and to form an Organization of African Independent Churches,[122] or the seven days long visit of Pope Shenouda to the Kimbanguist Church with the declared intention to attract three million Kimbanguists,[123] clearly underlines the desire of the Coptic Church to establish itself as the main denomination in Africa. To achieve its objectives, the Coptic Church counts on its 'authenticity' as a traditional African Church; here the emphasis is put on the tradition of Coptic spirituality and theology, one supposed to be more mystical and eastern than institutional and western.[124]

Although Coptic evangelism in Africa is based upon pious foundations, there is an architecture made up of concrete religious and political aspirations that underpins the whole mission. These guidelines are Christian principles as taught by the Gospel, i.e. the whole concept of economic, social and political justice for individuals. These principles have political consequences as the Church struggles for the freedom of individuals, the liberation from foreign oppressive powers, and social justice.[125] Alone or together with African Churches the Coptic Church has promoted these values in discussions and official statements.[126] Nevertheless, the Church and the successive Egyptian governments do not ignore the concrete benefits they can draw from the application of these religious principles. For the Church, statements against European and American imperialisms in Africa and the Arab world also operate as means of rapprochement with the political power.[127] The government on its side understands the benefits it can draw from being supported

---

[122] *Ibid.*, 74.

[123] *Ibid.*, 75; the pope has also entertained the project of affiliating five million of Christians from Uganda; A Atiya, *A History of Eastern Christianity*, 120.

[124] J Watson, *Among the Copts*, 74-75. The author points out that with the decolonization of Africa, the Egyptian Church hoped to take the place of white missionaries in Africa. Apart from its emphasis on the tradition of Coptic doctrine and traditions, it could also count on Egypt's position as a leader of the non-aligned movement.

[125] Thus, the demand for the end of Portuguese occupation in Angola; or the steady support to the Palestinian cause; Kathryn Huenemann, 'Africa and Middle East Churches Consultation, June 18-23, 1974, in Cairo, Egypt', *Journal of Ecumenical Studies*, vol. 11, No. 4 (Fall 1974), 747; 'Il faut créer un lobby arabe opposé à Israël', *Al-Ahram Hebdo*, 3-9 January 2001.

[126] Hence, the Coptic Church and other African Churches demanded the respect of fundamental human rights by their respective national governments; Kathryn Huenemann, 'Africa and Middle East Churches Consultation, 18-23 June 1974, in Cairo, Egypt', 747.

[127] Kathryn Huenemann, 'Africa and Middle East Churches Consultation, June 18-23, 1974, in Cairo, Egypt', 747.

by a Christian institution in sub-Saharan Africa, and the Coptic Church indirectly contributes to increase Egypt's political sphere of influence. The successive governments have supported the Church through their implicit agreement of missionary activities and direct encouragements such as attendance at conferences and discussions.[128]

The mother Church of Alexandria and the Ethiopian Church

The political constituent that religious linkages sometimes trigger and accentuate, is well illustrated by the history of relations between the Coptic Church of Egypt and the Ethiopian Kingdom.

It is in the course of the 4th century that Ethiopia adhered to the monophysite dogma chosen by the Alexandrian patriarchate.[129] From then, Ethiopia became a diocese of the Egyptian Church[130] and the Ethiopian Church officially depended upon the Egyptian one. This relation of dependence was embodied in the institution of the *abun*, Ethiopia's bishop and head of Church, who had to be Egyptian and appointed by the Coptic patriarch.[131] In pre-modern times these strong religious ties strengthened the position of Christian Egyptians at home, thanks to the political significance of Ethiopia in the eyes of Egyptian rulers as these ones believed in the ability of the Ethiopian Kingdom to divert the river Nile.[132]

In the 19th and 20th centuries the rise of Ethiopian and Egyptian nationalisms affected the relation between the two national Churches and led to disputes on the issue of the choice and competence of the Egyptian *abun*, as well as on the nationality of the bishops who were to

---

[128] Hence, the presence of PM Hegazi and the messages addressed to African delegates by a representative of President Sadat at the Africa and Middle East Churches Consultation organized in Cairo by the Coptic Church; *Ibid.*

[129] Arnold H M Jones and Elizabeth Monroe, *A History of Ethiopia*, Oxford, 1965, 35-36.

[130] *Ibid.*

[131] Haggai Erlich, 'Identity and Church: Ethiopian-Egyptian Dialogue, 1924-1959', *International Journal of Middle East Studies* 32 (2000), 24.

[132] Low waters sometimes coincided with periods of religious persecutions in Egypt, it happened that they ended with the intercession of the Coptic patriarch; Bairu Tafla, 'The Fathers of Rivers: The Nile in Ethiopian Literature', in Haggai Erlich and Israel Gershoni, *The Nile*, Boulder-London, 2000, 161; Richard Pankhurst, 'Ethiopia's Alleged Control of the Nile', in Haggai Erlich and Israel Gershoni, *The Nile*, Boulder-London, 2000, 29-30.

serve in Ethiopia.[133] From the 1920s onward, King Haile Selassie led campaign to emancipate the Ethiopian Church from the ancient bond of affiliation. Himself and the Ethiopian population wanted the Egyptians to appoint an Ethiopian *abun*.[134] Although the Coptic Church authorities were intransigent on this last issue, they agreed to consecrate 5 Ethiopian bishops, a deal which already improved the situation between the two Churches.[135] In the period stretching from the late 1920s until the 1950s the Ethiopians continued pressing for the nomination of a national *abun*, a request that was firmly rejected by the Coptic Church clergy. Nevertheless, the support of the Egyptian government and Coptic laity, together with the more accommodating personality of patriarch Kyrillos VI, eventually conducted to the appointment of the Ethiopian Abuna Baselyos as head of the Ethiopian Church in 1959. By doing so, Kyrillos declared the Ethiopian Church autocephalous, thus put an end to the official dependence between the two Churches.[136]

Although the relation had been faltering for a long time, the 1959 separation represents a turning point: Decisions taken by the two sides after this date made the relation even more difficult.[137] After 1969 for example, Israeli handed in the keys of Deir al-Sultan to Ethiopians, this increased the resentment of Copts against Ethiopians.[138] In 1970 the Ethiopians got rid of the consecration of their patriarch by the Egyptian patriarch, the last remnant of their affiliation with the Egyptian Church.[139] In a kind of retaliation, the Coptic Church enabled the Eritrean diocese to secede from the Ethiopian Church in the 1990s, and Shenouda consecrated Abuna Filipos as patriarch of an autocephalous Eritrean Orthodox Church.[140] Today, the relationship between the two Churches is almost non existing.

---

[133] Haggai Erlich, 'Identity and Church', 26.

[134] Haggai Erlich, 'Egypt, Ethiopia, and the Abyssinian Crisis 1935-1936', in Haggai Erlich and Israel Gershoni, *The Nile*, 185.

[135] *Ibid.*, 195.

[136] Erlich, 'Identity and Church', 23. For more details on the century long process that led the separation of the two Churches: *ibid.*, 25-42.

[137] It is striking that the literature produced by the two Churches since 1959 either minimized the historical importance or emphasized the bad aspects of the relation. For example see Ayele Teklahaymanot, 'The Egyptian Metropolitans of the Ethiopian Church', *Orientalia Christiana Periodica*, vol. 54 (1988), 175-222.

[138] Hagai Erlich, 'Identity and Church', 42.

[139] *Ibid.*

[140] *Ibid.*

Together with the religious factor, political developments in the 1950s-1960s weakened the political leverage the Copts could enjoy in the past. Nasser's foreign policy choices emphasized Egypt's Arab and Islamic dimensions to the detriment of the historical link between Egypt and the countries of the Nile basin.[141] Obviously, this reorientation went along with the building of the High Dam, which Egyptian leaders believed to secure their country's water supplies.[142] Throughout the 1960s and 1970s, Egyptian leaders thought that their country had been definitely relieved from its dependence towards Nilotic countries and acted consequently in the orientation of Egypt's foreign policy.[143]

It is a natural event, the drop of water levels of Lake Nasser that triggered a renewed interest on Ethiopia among Egyptian officials.[144] In this context, Coptic intellectuals and the Church regained some influence on the question: It is the Copt Boutros Boutros-Ghali, the man behind the Egyptian-Ethiopian rapprochement of the mid-1980s,[145] and the Coptic Church who facilitated the first contacts and negotiations between Egypt and the African Nilotic countries in 1986-1987.[146] As a recent interview of the Eritrean president by an Egyptian journalist suggests it, Egyptian officials credit the Coptic Church with a substantial role to play in mediations between Egypt and Nilotic countries.[147]

---

[141] Haggai Erlich, review of *The Nile*, Collins Robert O., *The Middle East Journal*, vol. 57, No. 2 (Spring 2003), 352.

[142] H Erlich, 'Identity and Church', 38.

[143] However, the Egyptian leaders never completely overlooked Egypt's historical bond with the Nile valley and they enabled Coptic intellectuals to work on the subject. Coptic laymen such as Mirrit Boutros-Ghali, Murad Kamil and Zahir Riyad remained appreciative of the historic bond and encouraged Egypt to re-emphasize it. Under Boutros Boutros-Ghali's editorship, *Al-Siyasa al-Duwaliyya*, Egypt's most important platform of discussion on foreign policy, pursued a pro-African, pro-Ethiopian line; H Erlich, *The Cross and the River*, 194-197.

[144] *Ibid.*, 207.

[145] *Ibid.*

[146] D Al-Khawaga, 'Le développement communautaire copte', 18.

[147] 'President Issayas addresses the Egyptian Council for Foreign Affairs', *Eritrean Profile*, Dec 6, 2002.' Ahmed Idrees, Middle East News Agency: 'Tomorrow, you are intending to make a ceremonial to his Holiness, Pope Shenouda, on the occasion of his 31st year as pope. Excellency, do you believe that the Coptic Church could play a role as peace mediator between Eritrea and Ethiopia, given that the Ethnic background is the same Coptic. [...] Have you ever thought about the possibility that this ethnic culture can work on making peace between you? If the Azhar has got a role it can join effort with the Coptic Church?' President Issayas: 'The relation between the Orthodox Church in Eritrea, and the Coptic here in Egypt is more intimate than the relation between the Orthodox Church in Ethiopia and the Egyptian Coptic. [...] But I can say the possibility for playing a positive role is, at least, unseen in the horizon.'; http://www.shaebia.org/artman/publish/article_479.html, 6 December 2002 (consulted 15 August 2003).

Israel and the Deir es-Sultan issue: Theological viewpoints and political considerations

As for its relations with the State of Israel the Coptic Church follows an agenda made of theological viewpoints, political considerations, and material concerns.

The Coptic Church has its own theological agenda on Zionism and the Jewish people. On the basis of its own interpretation of the teachings of the Bible and Christian tradition, the majority of the Coptic leadership still considers the Jews guilty of the crucifixion of Jesus Christ.[148] Contemporary events such as military defeats and the occupation of Arab territories contributed to the amplification of anti-Semitic sentiments, thus the increased reference to Jews as 'murderers of God' among the Coptic clergy in the 1970s.[149]

Apart from its dismissive perception of the Jewish people, the Egyptian Church is genuinely worried by Israel's military and territorial aggressiveness, and has solicitude for Palestinian Arabs. The Church leadership consequently promotes a strong anti-Zionist line among African and Western Churches,[150] and among international ecumenical institutions.[151]

The third motive explaining Church hostility towards the Israeli government is the issue of Deir al-Sultan, a monastery adjacent to the Church of the Holy Sepulchre in Jerusalem. The monastery is said to have been occupied by Coptic and Ethiopian monks since the 5th century A.D., and has been a subject of disputes throughout history.[152] The most recent feud occurred in 1970 when Ethiopian monks, or the Israeli police according to the Egyptian monks, replaced the locks of two chapels.[153] The affair went up to the Israeli High Court of Justice, which ordered

---

[148] O Meinardus, *Two Thousand Years of Coptic Christianity*, 84.

[149] *Ibid.*

[150] Hence, the adoption of the following statement by the conferees of the 1974 African and Middle East Churches Consultation: 'The Church should continually state and clarify the fundamental distinction between Judaism as the religion of the Jewish people, and Zionism as a political ideology that adopted settler colonialism and racial discrimination as its basic policy in the Middle East. Christians should combat Zionism as well as any form of discrimination against Arabs and Jews'; K Huenemann 'Africa and Middle East Churches Consultation', 747.

[151] J Watson, *Among the Copts*, 46.

[152] See Stefan Wimmer, 'Le monastère Deir es-Sultan à Jérusalem', *Le Monde copte*, 23 (1993), 59-68.

[153] *Ibid.*, 61.

the Ethiopians to hand over the keys to the Copts, unless the Israeli government preferred to set up a commission to look into the question.[154] Since Golda Meir's government decided to use this prerogative and no agreement could be found until today, the Coptic bishop in Jerusalem and the leadership in Egypt have fought both domestically and internationally against the Israeli government.[155]

The Deir es-Sultan issue is symptomatic of the whole Church's attitude towards Israel. Apart from standing for the integrity of its real property in Jerusalem, the Church leadership's attacks on Zionism and Israel are actuated by:

— Solicitude for the Palestinian predicament in the occupied territories and for other Arab populations aggressed by Israel. As a Christian body the Coptic Church feels it is its duty to combat injustice, hence to stand up for the rights of Palestinian and Arab populations. In 1992 Shenouda declared that the Deir es-Sultan issue was not the principal reason for the retained attitude of the Church towards Israel, but the need for solidarity with the Palestinian people and protest against unjust policies of the Israeli government. That the Church leadership is highly committed is shown by Shenouda's announcement that the pilgrimage to Jerusalem will remain prohibited for Copts as long as a just peace does not take place in the region.[156] That such effort are intense and recognized by the Palestinian leadership is shown by the delegation that Yasser Arafat brought to Shenouda in November 1988 to receive congratulations for his efforts to create a Palestinian state and to achieve a just peace.[157]

—The necessity for a non-Muslim body to prevent accusations of betrayal coming from a predominantly Muslim society. The Coptic Church knows that in periods of political and economic strain, Muslim leaders and population tend to

[154] O Meinardus, *Two Thousand Years of Coptic Christianity*, 141.

[155] *Ibid.*, 141. The issue has been mentioned in negotiations between the Egyptian and Israeli governments, the Coptic Church also lobbied among other Churches, foreign governments and the United Nations; S Wimmer, 'Le monastère Deir es-Sultan à Jérusalem', 66; S Wimmer, 'Entretien avec sa Grâce l'Archevêque Amba Abraham le 11 mars 1992, Patriarcat copte de Jérusalem', *Le Monde copte*, 23 (1993), 69-72.

[156] Interview conducted for *Al-'alam al-yaum*, and reproduced in the Palestinian *An-Nahar* of 15/11/1992; S Wimmer, 'Le monastère Deir es-Sultan à Jérusalem', 67.

[157] T H Partrick, *Traditional Egyptian Christianity*, 179.

be more suspicious of Christian Egyptians.[158] As the main representative of the minority the Church seeks to avoid accusations and attacks, for that it wants to be perceived as a staunch Arab and Egyptian body towards Arab and Egyptian populations and governments. Shenouda's refusal of allowing Coptic pilgrims back to Jerusalem[159] is part of this strategy. The patriarch rebuked President Sadat, who had asked him to do so: 'The problems which separate Egypt from the rest of the Arab world will one day be resolved, and when that day comes I do not intend that the Copts should be branded as the traitors of the Arabs. I will not permit any pilgrimage to Jerusalem.'[160] In a more recent interview the Coptic bishop of Jerusalem declared that the pilgrimage remains prohibited because the coming of Copts would create problems for them at home.[161]

—The unspoken agreement, which entrusts the Church with the duty to put the stress on matters in which the government cannot itself be outspoken. In the 1980s and early 1990s the Coptic Church leadership fiercely attacked the Israeli government, a position the Egyptian government could not overtly stand up for at that time. Furthermore, Kyrillos and Shenouda's recurring declarations against Zionism and Israel's brutal policy in the Palestinian territories foster the government legitimacy towards the Egyptian population and Western governments.[162] The Church appears as an asset both domestically and internationally.

Discernment with the Coptic diaspora

The increase of Coptic emigration from the 1950s onwards led to the creation of Diaspora churches and Coptic organizations abroad. The

---

[158] At the beginning of the Crusades or during the French expedition of 1798-1801 Copts have been mishandled by Muslim rulers and populations; Tate Georges, 'VIIe-XIXe siècle, l'Eglise du silence', *Notre histoire*, 2000, 40-41.

[159] Before 1967 up to 50,000 Coptic pilgrims used to go to Jerusalem every year; M Heikal, *Autumn of Fury*, 220.

[160] *Ibid*.

[161] S Wimmer, 'Entretien avec sa Grâce l'Archevêque Amba Abraham', 71.

[162] Kathryn Huenemann, 'Africa and Middle East Churches Consultation, June 18-23, 1974, in Cairo, Egypt', *Journal of Ecumenical Studies*, vol. 11, No. 4 (Fall 1974), 747; 'Il faut créer un lobby arabe opposé à Israël'.

Church in Egypt pursues several objectives for its adherents living abroad. First, the Coptic hierarchy wishes to safeguard Diaspora churches and to insert them into the canonical framework of the Coptic Church.[163] The creation of bishoprics for these Coptic communities abroad and Shenouda's visits to these new Coptic churches in North America, Australia and Europe highlights the religious concern of keeping the faithful in the right canonical framework.[164] Second, the Church hierarchy does its best to limit the effects of the emigrate community discourse against the Egyptian government.[165] As some Diaspora organizations enjoy the benefits of security, as well as a financial and political base of support, they have been vigorously struggling for the rights of Copts in Egypt.[166] As the discourse of these emigrate organizations might damage the position of Copts at home, the Church tries to pacify them.[167] On the other hand, the Church will not completely bring them under its control, as it knows it can benefit from their financial and political resources. In a 1996 interview, a prominent cleric from the Coptic Church confessed: 'There is an unwritten argument between the two sides of the Atlantic. We are playing our role here perfectly. They are playing their role there perfectly. We do not communicate.'[168] Finally, Church leaders try to make use of the Diaspora for supporting the Coptic community at home. The organization of fund raising by Pope Shenouda is not only aimed at improving the community members' economic and social position, but also at alleviating the economic position of the Egyptian authorities, hence to ease the relation between the government and the community.[169]

---

[163] M Martin, 'The Renewal in Context', 20.

[164] *Ibid.*, 20.

[165] 'Question copte, questions à l'Egypte', Wendy Kristianasen, *Le Monde Diplomatique*, May 2001.

[166] For example the Coptic American Organization, see their website: www.copts.com. The head of the Coptic American Organization maintains that in recent years he has convinced the ex-American Secretary of State Warren Christopher and ex-Vice-President Al Gore to raise the issue of Coptic rights in their meetings with President Mubarak; P Sedra, 'Class Cleavages and Ethnic Conflict', 230; Khaled Elgindy, 'Diaspora troublemakers', *Cairo Times*, 4-17 February 1999.

[167] S E Ibrahim, 'The Copts of Egypt', 18.

[168] P Sedra, 'Class Cleavages and Ethnic Conflict', 231.

[169] D Al-Khawaga, 'Le développement communautaire copte', 18.

State concessions

Since the coming to power of President Moubarak, the Church leadership has opted for an unconditional support to the Egyptian government in its domestic and foreign policies.[170] The Church leadership has adopted an uncomplaining stance with regard to the issue of church building and repairing; it rejects any foreign government meddling in the solving of the Copts' domestic problems,[171] while it does encourage Copts to go voting for elections,[172] it does not overtly ask for a wider Coptic participation in politics.[173] With regard to international affairs, the Church uses ecumenical meetings and its relations with foreign Churches to make the promotion of official positions of the Egyptian government; it helps the government when it has the possibility to do so, thus when mediating between Egypt and African Nilotic countries, or when raising funds for easing the financial situation of Egypt. On several issues such as Israel and Palestine, the Church's own viewpoints genuinely match with those of the government. In this case, the Church will stress such issues in order to underline its loyalty to Egypt and its government.

In return, the state has yielded concessions to the Church. In 1985 a motion to adopt the *shari`a* into the Egyptian law was severely defeated before the Assembly;[174] the security of churches has been reinforced and the state has taken a clear stance against any institutionalization of Islamic parties; the Copts have been allowed more visibility in the society through the introduction of Coptic history in primary and secondary schools' curricula, through the broadcasting of Christmas and Easter masses[175] and the recent government's decision to observe Coptic Christmas as a national holiday.[176] More important in the context of community

---

[170] D Al-Khawaga, 'The Political Dynamics of the Copts', 173.

[171] 'Copts Reject US Meddling', www.sis.gov.eg/public/letter/html/text116.htm, 3-6 August 1997 (consulted 28 July 2003).

[172] D Al-Khawaga, 'Le développement communautaire copte: un mode de participation au politique ?', 18.

[173] In a January 2001 interview, Pope Shenouda suggests that the reason for the low participation of Copts to the last parliamentary elections might be linked to their failure at the precedent elections. Yet, the Coptic patriarch neither overtly complains, nor does he demand the government to intervene; 'Il faut créer un lobby arabe opposé à Israël', *Al-Ahram Hebdo*, 3-9 January 2001.

[174] T H Partrick, *Traditional Egyptian Christianity*, 173.

[175] 'Egyptian Muslims, Christians celebrate a new national holiday', *The Jordan Times*, 8 January 2003.

[176] *Ibid.*

leadership development, President Moubarak and the successive Egyptian governments continue dealing directly with the patriarch as the exclusive representative of the Coptic community.

The most basic obstacle to the assimilation of Copts is the way political legitimacy has been defined in Egypt in the past 50 years. Since the Islamic religion takes part in the definition of the state's identity, Christian Egyptians feel that their identity does not cope with the one of the polity and of the majority. Since the political system is authoritarian in nature and the elites have kept tight control over political participation, the majority of the population feels alienated, Christians and Muslims alike.

More opening of the polity and majority to cultural diversity would be the best option for the minority. But the possibility for more political and social opening seems very narrow in contemporary Egypt. The ruling class is still coming from the recently urbanized sections of society and its perception of inter-religious relations is based upon rural patterns. They treat the Coptic issue more in terms of domestic security and international credibility, than of national identity.[177]

For the moment, the Church appears as the best equipped and most active body engaged in the protection of Coptic interests. But does it look likely that this religious body will work towards the end of economic, social and political discrimination? Will it promote a strategy of defence of the political rights of the Christian of Egypt? Experience shows that religious minorities are satisfied with the achievement of practical religious demands, such as the respect of religious faith and customs, or the ability to construct facilities. In the Egyptian case, the most important concerns of the Coptic leadership have always been the return to the original prescripts of the Church and the priority of religion in the representations and actions of the faithful.[178] Thus, the mobilisation of the patriarch during the 1970s was not so much expressed in terms of political participation of the minority, rather as a reinforcement of the distinct religious identity of the Copts.[179] It follows that the Renewal movement should not be reduced to a community-oriented strategy. Since it does not conceive its task as political,[180] the Church seeks to increase its sphere

---

[177] D Al-Khawaga, 'Le développement communautaire copte', 15.

[178] T H Partrick, *Traditional Egyptian Christianity*, 177; D Al-Khawaga, 'The Political Dynamics of the Copts', 189.

[179] *Ibid.*, 176.

[180] Thus, the Church leadership does not interfere with the issue of Coptic freedom of press; A Sonbol, 'Society, Politics and Sectarian Strife', 278-279.

of influence but does not feel concerned with a militant assertion of the group's political interests.

Nevertheless, one should not minimize the achievements of thirty years of Coptic mobilisation. Based on its age-old experience of dealing with uneasy governments and society, the Church leadership follows a careful strategy which aims at guaranteeing religious freedom and security to its adherents. With the help of institutions based abroad, the actors of the Renewal have done their best to support the Coptic population, also in terms of welfare. The Church has also made a tactful use of its transnational linkages for improving the security of its adherents, as it has used them as a political leverage towards the government for reaching more equality for Coptic citizens.

Bibliography

Ansari, Hamied, 'Sectarian Conflict in Egypt and the Political Expediency of Religion', *Middle East Journal*, vol. 38 (Summer 1984), pp. 397-418.

Apostolov, Mario, *Religious Minorities, Nation States and Security*, Aldershot, 2001.

Atiya, Aziz S, *A History of Eastern Christianity*, London, 1968.

Ayalon, Ami, 'Egypt's Coptic Pandora's Box', in Bengio Ofra and Ben-Dor Gabriel (eds), *Minorities and the State in the Arab World*, Boulder-London, 1999, pp. 53-71.

Balta, Paul, 'Les Coptes: exode, exil intérieur et renouveau', *Les cahiers de l'Orient*, 48, (1997), pp. 13-17.

Ben-Dor Gabriel and Bengio Ofra, 'The State and Minorities Toward the Twenty-first century: An Overview', in Bengio Ofra and Ben-Dor Gabriel (eds), *Minorities and the State in the Arab World*, Boulder-London, 1999, pp. 191-205.

Boud'hors, Anne, 'Ier-VIe siècle un christianisme triomphant', *Notre histoire*, 178 (2000), pp. 32-36.

Carter, Barbara Lynn, *The Copts in Egyptian Politics*, Kent-Surry Hills, 1986.

Courbage, Youssef and Fargues, Philippe, *Christians and Jews under Islam*, London-New York, 1997.

Enloe, Cynthia, *Ethnic Conflict and Political Development*, Boston, 1973.

Erlich, Haggai, 'Identity and Church: Ethiopian-Egyptian Dialogue, 1924-1959', *International Journal of Middle East Studies*, 32 (2000), pp. 23-46.

Erlich, Haggai, *The Cross and the River*, Boulder-London, 2002.

Farag, Iman, 'La politique à l'égyptienne: lecture des élections législatives', *Monde arabe Maghreb-Machrek*, 133 (July-September 1991), pp. 19-33.

Farah, Nadia Ramsis, *Religious Strife in Egypt*, Montreux, 1986.

Al-Gawhari, Karim, 'Copts in the "Egyptian Fabric"', *Middle East Report* (July-September 1996), pp. 21-22.

Giannakos, S A (ed.), *Ethnic Conflict Religion, Identity and Politics*, Athens, 2002.

Gurr, Ted Robert, *Minorities at Risk*, Washington, 1993.

Heikal, Mohamed, *Autumn of Fury: The Assassination of Sadat*, London, 1983.

Huenemann, Kathryn, 'Africa and Middle East Churches Consultation, June 18-23, 1974, in Cairo, Egypt', *Journal of Ecumenical Studies*, vol. 11, No. 4 (Fall 1974), pp. 746-748.

Ibrahim, Saad Eddin, 'The Copts of Egypt', *Minority Rights Group Report*, London, 1996.

Irani, George Emile, 'Vatican: la diplomatie de la foi', *Politique internationale*, 54 (Winter 1991-1992), pp. 361-367.

Ismail, Salwa, 'Confronting the Other: Identity, Culture, Politics, and Conservative Islamism in Egypt', *International Journal of Middle East Studies*, 30 (1998), pp. 199-225.

Jones, Arnold H M, and Monroe, Elizabeth, *A History of Ethiopia*, Oxford, 1965.

Al-Khawaga, Dina, 'Le développement communautaire copte: un mode de participation au politique ?', *Monde arabe Maghreb Machrek*, 135 (January-March 1992), pp. 3-18.

Al-Khawaga, Dina, 'Les services sociaux dispensés par l'Eglise copte', in Kepel, G, *Exils et royaumes, les appartenances au monde arabo-musulman d'aujourd'hui*, Paris, 1994, pp. 189-212.

Al-Khawaga, Dina, 'The Political Dynamics of the Copts: Giving the Community an Active Role', Pacini Andrea (ed.), *Christian Communities in the Arab Middle East*, Oxford, 1998, pp. 172-190.

Kepel, Gilles, *The Prophet and Pharaoh: Muslim Extremism in Egypt*, London, 1985.

MacLaurin, R D (ed.), *The Political Role of Minority Groups in the Middle East*, New York, 1979.

Maïla, Joseph, 'The Arab Christians: From the Eastern Question to the Recent Political Situation of the Minorities', in Pacini, Andrea (ed.), *Christian Communities in the Arab Middle East*, Oxford, 1998, pp. 25-47.

Marcos, Antonius, *Come Across and Help Us... The Story of the Coptic Orthodox Church in Africa in Our Present Time*, ?, 1993 and 1996.

Martin, Maurice, 'The Renewal in Context: 1960-1990', in van Doorn-Harder, Nelly, and Vogt Kari (eds), *Between Desert and City: The Coptic Church Today*, Oslo, 1997, pp. 15-21.

Martin, Maurice, 'XXe siècle, une renaissance', *Notre histoire*, 178 (2000), pp. 49-51.

Meinardus, Otto F A, 'The Copts in Jerusalem and the Question of the Holy Places', in O'Mahony, Anthony, Göran Gunner and Kevork Hintlian, *The*

Christian Heritage in the Holy Land, London, 1995.

Meinardus, Otto F A, *Two Thousand Years of Coptic Christianity*, Cairo, 1999.

Nisan, Mordechai, *Minorities in the Middle East*, Jefferson-London, 1991.

Van Nispen, Christiaan, 'Changes in Relations between Copts and Muslims (1952-1994) in the Light of the Historical Experience', in van Doorn-Harder, Nelly, and Vogt Kari (eds), *Between Desert and City: The Coptic Church Today*, Oslo, 1997, pp. 22-34.

Pacini, Andrea, 'Introduction', in Pacini Andrea (ed.), *Christian Communities in the Arab Middle East*, Oxford, 1998.

Pankhurst, Richard, 'Ethiopia's Alleged Control of the Nile', in Erlich, Haggai, and Israel Gershoni, *The Nile*, Boulder-London, 2000, pp. 25-37.

Partrick, Theodore Hall, *Traditional Egyptian Christianity*, East Peoria, 1996.

Penanster, Alain de, 'Un pape de grand vent', *Politique internationale*, 54 (Winter 1991-1992), pp. 333-346.

Pennington, J D, 'The Copts in Modern Egypt', *Middle Eastern Studies*, vol. 18 (1982), pp. 158-179.

De Planhol, Xavier, *Minorités en Islam*, Paris, 1997.

Rothschild, Joseph, *Ethnopolitics: A Conceptual Framework*, New York, 1981.

Samaan, Makram, and Soheir Sukkary, 'The Copts and Muslims of Egypt', in Suad, J, and B L K Pillsbury (eds), *Muslim-Christian conflicts*, Boulder-Folkestone, 1978.

Sedra, Paul, 'Class Cleavages and Ethnic Conflict: Coptic Christian Communities in Modern Egyptian Politics', *Islam and Christian-Muslim Relations*, vol. 10, No. 2, 1999, pp. 219-235.

Sonbol, Amira, 'Society, Politics and Sectarian Strife', in Oweiss I M (ed.), *The Political Economy of Contemporary Egypt*, Washington, 1990, pp. 265-281.

Suad, Joseph, and Barbara L K Pillsbury, (eds), *Muslim-Christian conflicts*, Boulder-Folkestone, 1978.

Tafla, Bairu, 'The Fathers of Rivers: The Nile in Ethiopian Literature', in Erlich, Haggai, and Israel Gershoni, *The Nile*, Boulder-London, 2000, pp. 153-170.

Taklahaymanot, Ayele', 'The Egyptian Metropolitan of the Ethiopian Church', *Orientalia Christiana Periodica*, vol. 54, No. 1 (1988), pp. 175-222.

Tamura, Airi, 'Ethnic Consciousness and its Transformation in the Course of Nation-Building: The Muslim and the Copt in Egypt, 1906-1919', *The Muslim World*, vol. 75 (April 1985), pp. 102-114.

Tate, Georges, 'VIIe-XIXe, l'Eglise du silence', *Notre histoire*, 178 (2000), pp. 37-41.

Twite, Robin, 'Africa in Jerusalem—The Ethiopian Church', *Ariel*, 102 (1996), pp. 41-53.

Watson, John, 'Abba Kyrillos, Patriarch and Solitary', *Coptic Church Review*, vol. 17,

Nos. 1 & 2 (Spring and Summer 1996), pp. 5-46.

Watson, John, 'Signposts to Bibliography—Pope Shenouda III', in van Doorn-Harder, Nelly, and Vogt Kari (eds), *Between Desert and City: The Coptic Church Today*, Oslo, 1997, pp. 243-253.

Watson, John, *Among the Copts*, Brighton-Portland, 2000.

Wimmer, Stefan, 'Le monastère Deir es-Sultan à Jérusalem', *Le Monde copte*, 23 (1993), pp. 59-68.

Wimmer, Stefan, 'Entretien avec sa Grâce l'Archevêque Amba Abraham le 11 mars 1992, Patriarcat copte de Jérusalem', *Le Monde copte*, 23 (1993), pp. 69-72.

Yacoub, Joseph, *Au-delà des minorités*, Paris, 2000.

Yazbeck Haddad, Yvonne, 'Christians in a Muslim State: The Recent Egyptian Debate', in Yazbeck Haddad, Yvonne, and Wadi Zaidan Haddad (eds), *Christian-Muslim Encounters*, Gainesville, 1995, pp. 381-398.

Press articles

'A Christmas like no other', Tadros Mariz, *Al-Ahram Weekly*, January 2-8, 2003.

'Act, don't hide', Heggy Tarek, *Cairo Times*, February 4-17, 1999.

'Both sides of the fence', Rashed Dina, *Al-Ahram Weekly*, September 4-10, 2003.

'Egyptian Muslims, Christians celebrate a new national holiday', *The Jordan Times*, January 8, 2003.

'Encouraging signs', Ibrahim Saad Eddin, *Cairo Times*, February 4-17, 1999.

'Il faut créer un lobby arabe opposé à Israël', *Al-Ahram Hebdo*, January 3-9, 2001.

'Les Chrétiens égyptiens pourront enseigner l'arabe à l'école', Buccianti Alexandre, *Le Monde*, February 24, 2000.

'Living on the edge', Hammond Andrew, *Cairo Times*, February 4-17, 1999.

'Politics in the blood', Negus Steve, *Cairo Times*, February 4-17, 1999.

'Question copte, questions à l'Egypte', Kristianasen Wendy, *Le Monde Diplomatique*, Mai 2001.

'Un numéro explosif', Abdel-Azim Sherin and Sebet Sabah, *Al-Ahram Hebdo*, June 20-26, 2001.

Webpages

www.acpss.org/ereligion/95, 1995 (consulted January 19, 2003).

www.copts.com, , 1999 (consulted July 28, 2003).

www.copts.net/asp?id=386, December 19, 2002 (consulted January 19, 2003).

www.geocities.com/ccom_ctbi/CCOM_documents/Coyault_Protestantisme_Egyptien.htm, 2002 (consulted June 12, 2003).

www.parliament.gov.eg, (consulted January 9, 2003).

www.shaebia.org/artman/publish/article_479.html, December 6, 2002 (consulted August 15, 2003).

www.sis.gov.eg/public/letter/html/text116.htm, August 3-6, 1997 (consulted July 28, 2003).

www.sudanupdate.org (reports, minorities, Coptic Christians), ? (consulted June 12, 2003).

www.theestimate.com/public/01282000a.html, January 28, 2000 (consulted January, 19, 2003).

www.theestimate.com/public/02112000.html, February 11, 2000 (consulted January, 19, 2003).

PATRIARCHS AND POLITICS: THE CHALDEAN CATHOLIC CHURCH IN MODERN IRAQ

Anthony O'Mahony

THE CHALDEAN CHURCH UNTIL THE MID-19TH CENTURY[1]

The origins of the Chaldean Church go back many centuries.[2] In the 13th century, Catholic missionaries, Dominicans and Franciscans, had been active among the faithful of the Church of the East.[3] The first union of the Church of East with Rome was concluded at the Council of Florence. The Mediterranean island of Cyprus was home to a group of East Syriac Christians. On August 7 1445, following the acceptance of the creed before Archbishop Chrysoberges of Rhodes by Archbishop Timotheos of Tarsus (*Archiepiscopus Chalaeorum, qui in Cypro sunt*), union was established between the Church of the East and Rome. Timotheos petitioned the Lateran to allow him to take part in the Council of Florence, and a papal bull granted his request. Since then the term 'Chaldean' used by the pope, has referred to those East Syrians in union with Rome, though unfortunately the unwelcome efforts at latinization and the

---

1 On the historical background to Christianity in Iraq see the following studies, Anthony O'Mahony, 'Eastern Christianity in Modern Iraq', *Eastern Christianity: Studies in Modern History, religion and Politics*, (ed.) A O'Mahony, London, Melisende, 2004, 11-43; A O'Mahony, 'Syriac Christianity in the modern Middle East', *The Cambridge History of Christianity Eastern Christianity Vol. V*, (ed.) Michael Angold, Cambridge, Cambridge University Press, 2006, 511-535; Heleen Murre-van den Berg, 'Syriac Christianity', *The Blackwell Companion to Eastern Christianity*, (ed.) Ken Parry, Oxford, Blackwell, 2007, 249-268.

2 R Aubert, 'Iraq', *Dictionnaire d'Histoire et de Géographie Ecclésiastique*, Vol. 25, 1995, 1432-1440; H Suermann, 'Irak', *Lexikon für Theologie und Kirche*, Vol. 5, 1996, 578-580.

3 Leonhard Lemmens OFM, 'Relationes inter nationem Chaldaeorum et custodiam Terrae Sanctae, 1551-1629', *Archivium Franciscanum Historiam*, Vol. 19, 1926, 17-28; 'Notae criticae ad initia unionis Chaldaeorum ca. 1551-1629', *Antonianum*, Vol. 1, 1926, 205-218. See also for a later Franciscan- Chaldean encounter, Raimondo Sbardella, 'L'unione della chiesa caldea nell'opera del P. Tommaso Obicini da Novara', *Studia Orientalia Christiana Collectanea*, Vol. 5, 1960, 373-452.

problem of two hierarchies finally led to a collapse of this union in Cyprus.[4]

The common consensus is that it was Pope Eugene IV, in his Letter *Benedictus sit Deus* of 7 August 1445, [5] addressed to the 'Chaldean' Metropolitan Timothy of Tarsus and Cyprus, who made it known that from now on those members of the Eastern Syriac Church who had returned to Rome should no longer called 'Nestorians', as they were then known, but as 'Chaldeans'.[6] The expression used by the pontiff appears to indicate that the name already existed if not among the community themselves then in some circles. Scholars of the Chaldean Church would like to describe the origin of the choice of the name explained by the texts of the negotiations that preceded the letter of 1445. Perhaps these texts, as the well known Dominican historian Jean-Marie Fiey suggests, exist in the Roman archives, but, unfortunately, the published compendia of documents on the subject only give three later letters, those of Nicholas V in 1450 and 1453, but no text prior to the 1445 Letter.[7] In fact, the name 'Chaldean' appears to have been already used, but by whom, and with what meaning, we do not know with any precision.

Prior to 1445, some Westerners, Latin missionaries or travellers, had already begun to speak of 'Chaldeans'. A D von den Brincken[8] has noted that in the West in the Middle Ages the description 'sectae, generations, leges,

---

[4] Wilhem Baum and Dietmar WWinkler, *The Church of the East: a concise history*, London, RoutledgeCurzon, 2003, 112; Joseph Jacoub, 'La reprise à Chypre en 1445 du nom de "Chaldéens" par les fidèles de l'Église de l'Orient', *Istina*, Vol. XLIX, 2004, 378-390.

[5] For the debate around the origins of the term 'Chaldeans' the late Jean-Marie Fiey OP, suggests that it was in 1445 the names appears in the brief of Pope Eugenius IV formerly members of the Church of the East which sought union with Rome. Before that date, however, the use of the term to refer to Christians is hardly attested among Western writers before 1445 there are only three citations of the name 'Chaldean' for oriental Christians; but these show that the name meant 'Syriac speaker'. 'Chaldean' was also a usual term in early scholarship to denote Syriac. The conclusion he suggests is that the name 'Chaldean' originated in the West and derived from the name of the language which Syriac-speaking Christians used. J-M Fiey OP, 'Comment l'occident en vint à parler de "Chaldéens"?', *Bulletin of the John Rylands University Library of Manchester*, Vol. 78, 1996, 163-170.

[6] J D Mansi, *Sacrorum conciliorum nova et amplissima collectio* Vol. 31. B, Paris, 1901, col. 1755-8; J Hardouin, *Acta conciliorum et epistolae decretakes ac constiutiones Summorum Pontificum*, Paris, 1714-1715, Vol. ix. 1041; K J von Hefele and J Leclercq, *Histoire des conciles*, Letouzey, Paris, 1918, 1104-6, quoted in J-M Fiey, 'Comment l'occident en vint à parler de "Chaldéens"?', 168.

[7] Georg Hoffman SJ, *Epistolae pontificiae ad Concilium Florentinum spectantes*, Rome, Pontificum Institutum Orientalium Studiorum, 1946, Vol. iii, 127-40.

[8] A D von den Brincken, *Die Nationes Christianorum Orientalium im Verstäandnis der latinischen Historiographie: von der Mitte des 12 bis in die zweite Hälfte des 14* Jahrhunderts, Cologne, 1973, 300-301, quoted in J-M. Fiey, 'Comment l'occident en vint à parler de 'Chaldéens'?', 169.

nations, linguae' is given by the Latins for Eastern Christians. Among these examples, she found only three, all from the 13th century, which mentioned 'Chaldeans'. The others, the vast majority, continued to refer to members of the Church of the East as 'Nestorians'.[9] In what precise sense was the word 'Chaldean' then used? The first example is the Dominican Provincial of the Holy Land, Philip (1237), for whom the Chaldeans, with the Persians, the Medes and the Armenians, are under the jurisdiction of the 'Jacobite' Syrian Orthodox patriarch. This might be a reference to the Maphrianat of the Syrian Orthodox Church which was the juridical and ecclesial expression for the 'Persian provinces'. The Maphrianat was officially located at Tigrit (629-1152) and Mosul (1152-1859); since the middle of the 20th century it is now with the Syriac church of India.[10] The second example is from another Dominican, Ricoldo de Montecroce, who lived and preached in Mesopotamia, particularly in Mosul and Baghdad. He knew Arabic and met Patriarch Yahwalaha III.[11] For him the 'Chaldeans' were 'the Nestorians and the Jacobites'. A pilgrim, again from the 13th century, Burchard of Mont Sion, counted all the Oriental Christians, 'Nestorians, Jacobites, Medes and Persians' as Chaldeans. From this, A D von den Brincken concludes that 'The Chaldeans were those who spoke Syriac.' This term is not a specific idea, and is not clearly characterized.[12] Those from the Latin West appear to have chosen the name 'Chaldean' for linguistic reasons. The 'Chaldeans', along with the 'Jacobites' and sometimes others (Armenians, Medes, etc), are those who speak the Syriac language. Eugene IV, writing to the 'Chaldean' Metropolitan Timothy, speaks of *lingua tua chaldaea*.[13]

Joseph Habbi,[14] a Chaldean historian of the Church of the East,

---

9 In texts from the 12th century, A D von den Brincken, *Die Nationes Christianorum Orientalium im Verständnis der latinischen Historiographie*, 287-337, notes twenty references to the 'Nestorians' and only two for the 'Chaldeans'; J-M Fiey, 'Comment l'occident en vint à parler de "Chaldéens"?', 169.

10 Claude Sélis, *Les Syriens orthodoxes et catholiques*, Éditions Brepols, Tournai, 1988, 215-216. J-M Fiey, OP, 'Les dioceses du Maphrianat syrien, 629-1860', *Parole de l'Orient*, Vol. 5, 1974, 133-164, 331-393; Vol. 8, 1977/78, 347-378.

11 See the studies by Jean-Marie Mèrigoux, OP, 'Un précurseur du dialogue islamo-chrétien Frère Ricoldo (1243-1320)', *Revue thomiste*, no. 4, 1973, 609-621; 'L'Ouvrage d'un frère Prêcheur florentin en Orient à la fin du XIIIe siècle: le *Contra legum Sarracenorum* de Ricoldo da Monte di Croce', *Mémoire domenicane* (nouvelle série), Vol. 17, 1986, 1-144; 'Les grands religions de l'Orient à la fin du XIIIe siécle vues par Ricoldo da Monte de Croce, dans le monde de l'Islam' (thèse de doctorat, 1987); 'Ricoldo da Monte di Croce, frére prêcheur, +1320', *Dictionaire de Spiritualité*, 1988, col. 554-556.

12 J-M Fiey, 'Comment l'occident en vint à parler de "Chaldéens"?', 169.

13 Mansi, *Sacrorum conciliorum nova et amplissima collectio*, col. 1756.

14 Particularly in his studies J Habbi: 'Signification de l'Union chaldéenne de Mar Sulaqa avec

notes that Sulaqa, who would later be called the 'Chaldean Patriarch of Babylon',[15] the first patriarch created by Rome, was initially given the title 'Patriarch of Mosul' by Rome.[16] He succeeded Simon bar Mama, whom the Pope thought was dead, who was already the leader of the 'Patriarchal Church of Mosul, the Tigris island [Djazirat ibn 'Umar] and other cities and territories of the East'.[17] Habbi notes that later this 'local' title developed into a 'personal' title.[18]

It appears that Baron d'Avril[19] was right when he commented that the word 'Chaldean' came from the West, and it seems that it was purely because of the 'Chaldean/Syriac' language. The Roman Church is 'the Latin Church' for the same reason.

In the mid-15th century a tradition of hereditary patriarchal succession, passing from uncle to nephew, took effect in the Church of the East.[20] As a result, one family dominated the church, and untrained minors were being elected to the patriarchal throne. When such a patriarch was elected in 1552, a group of bishops refused to accept him and decided to seek union with Rome. They elected in 1552 the abbot of a monastery,

---

Rome en 1553', *L'Orient Syrien*, Vol. 9, 1966, 99-132 and 199-230; 'L'Unification de la hiérarchie chaldéenne dans la première moitié du XIX siècle, *Parole de l'Orient*, Vol. 2, 1971, 121-143 and 305-327.

15 Habbi attributes to 'Abdišo of Nisbis (d. 1318) the mention of the 'Patriarch of Babylon' with the note that 'he held the 5th place in the Church'. See *Signification de l'Union chaldéenne de Mar Sulaqa avec Rome en 1553*, p 129,

16 Habbi, *Signification de l'Union chaldéenne de Mar Sulaqa avec Rome en 1553*, 109, 220.

17 Habbi adds the text 'under the Chaldean nation'. Of the nine Latin original texts quoted following Giamil, dated between 1614 and 1617, eight have the title 'Patriarch of Babylon' and only one 'Patriarch of the Chaldeans', '*L'Unification de la hiérarchie chaldéenne dans la première moitié du XIX siècle*. 321

18 Habbi, '*L'Unification de la hiérarchie chaldéenne dans la première moitié du XIX siècle,* 322.

19 A D'Avril, *La Chaldée chrétienne*, Paris, 1892, 74. J-M Fiey, 'Comment l'occident en vint à parler de "Chaldéens"?', 170.

20 On the modern history of the Church of the East see the following studies: Heleen H L Murre-van den Berg, 'The Patriarch of the Church of the East from the fifteenth to Eighteenth Centuries', *Hogoye: Journal of Syriac Studies*, Vol. 2, no. 2, 1999; H L Murre-van den Berg , ' The Church of the East in the Sixteenth and Seventeenth Century: World Church or Ethnic Community?', *Redefining Christian Identity: Cultural Interaction in the Middle East since the Rise of Islam*, (ed.) J J Van Ginkel, H L Murre-van den Berg and T M van Lint, Orientalia Lovaniensia Analecta, Leuven, Vol. 134, 2005, 301-320; David Wilmhurst, 'The Ecclesiastical Organization of the Church of the East, 1318-1913', *Corpus Scriptorum Christianorum Orientalium*, Vol. 582, Subsidia 104, Leuven, 2000; J F Coakley, 'The Church of the East since 1914', *Bulletin of the John Rylands University Library of Manchester,* Vol. 78, 1996, 179-198; J F Coakley, 'The Patriarchal List of the Church of the East', *After Bardaisan: Studies on Continuity and Change in Syriac Christianity in Honour of Professor Han J. W. Drijvers*, (eds) G J Reinink and A C Klusgkist, Orientalia Lovaniensia Analecta, no. 89, Louvain, 1999, 65-83.

Sulaqa, as their own patriarch and sent him to Rome to arrange a union with the Catholic Church. In early 1553 Pope Julius III proclaimed him Patriarch Shimun VIII 'of the Chaldeans' and ordained him a bishop in St Peter's Basilica on 9 April 1553. The new patriarch returned to his homeland in late 1553 and began to initiate a series of reforms. But opposition, led by the rival patriarch in the Church of the East, was strong. Sulaqa was quickly captured by the Ottoman governor of Amadia (modern Diyarbakir), and was tortured and executed in January 1555.[21] Over the next two hundred years, there was much turmoil and changing of sides as the pro- and anti-Catholic parties struggled with one another until a settled Chaldean hierarchy developed.[22]

During the 18th century the Catholicos of the Church of the East, Mar Elias XII, made numerous contacts with the Roman Church without coming to complete union. He died in 1778.[23] It is known that from 1450 the Catholicossate of the Church of the East had been hereditary, passing from uncle to nephew or cousin. In 1776, Mar Elias XII had consecrated his nephew John Hormez as bishop and named him as guardian of the patriarchal throne with right of succession. On his uncle's death Hormez became Catholic and sent a profession of faith and a letter of submission to the Propaganda.[24]

The Congregation was mostly in favour of recognizing his patriarchate because it hoped it could thus attain union with the Holy See and the whole of the Church of the East. For a long time, however, the Catholic party was strongest at Diyarbakir and the leader of this Church had received a patriarchal title. Its last patriarch had resigned in 1780, but

---

[21] J Habbi, 'Signification de l'Union chaldéenne de Mar Sulaqa avec Rome en 1553', *L'Orient Syrien*, Vol. 9, 1966, 99-132 and 199-230; J M Vosté OP, 'Mar Johanan Soulaqa: premier patriarche des Chaldéens', *Angelicum* (Rome), Vol. 8, 1931, 187-234; Giuseppe Sorge, 'Giovanni Simone Sullaqa, Primo Patriarca dell' "Unione formale" della Chiesa caldea', *Annuarium Historiae Conciliorum*, Vol. 12, 1980, 427-440. Sulaqa is seen as a martyr for the unity of church under a Catholic banner, J-M Fiey, 'Martyrs sous les ottomans', *Analecta Bollandiana*, Vol. 101, 1983, 387-406.

[22] D Shammon, 'La Chiesa Assiro-Caldea', *Sacrae Congregationis de Propaganda Fide: Memoria Reurm, 1622-1972*, Rome-Freiburg-Vienna 1973, Vol. 2, 368-378; Giuseppe Beltami, *La chiesa nel secolo dell'unione*, Rome, Orientalia Christiana Analecta, no. 83, 1933.

[23] W de Vries SJ, 'Elias XIV. Letzer Nestorianischer Patriarch von Alquos', *Orientalia Christiana Periodica*, Vol. 26, 1960, 141-148. See also De Vries' further reflections on the Patriarchate of the Church of the East and the Holy See's relations with the Eastern Christians: 'Die Patriarchate der nichtkatholischen syrischen Kirchen' *Ostkirchliche Studien*, Vol. 33 1984, 3-45; 'La Santa Sede e I Patriarcati cattolici di Oriente', *Orientalia Christiana Periodica*, Vol. 27 1961, 313-361.

[24] Olivier Raquez, 'L'Église chaldéenne', Sacrae Congregationis de Propaganda Fide: *Memoria Reurm, 1622-1972*, Rome-Freiburg-Vienna, 1973, Vol. 3/Part 2, 29-39.

held on to the prestige of his see and to the 'old Catholic traditions' against the claims of former members of the Church of the East and that of the family of the Catholicos. Despite its desire to unify the Chaldean Church, the Propaganda was forced to play for time. On 18 February 1783, Hormez was named Archbishop of Mosul and Administrator of the Patriarchate of Babylon, but without jurisdiction over the Church of Diyarbakir.[25]

As the years passed with positive regard for Hormez' activity the Congregation decided, on 23 September 1801, to name him patriarch. This decision was not put into practice, as from then, the tone of relations with Rome changed considerably and Hormez was accused of various canonical 'irregularities', among which it was difficult to distinguish what was true or false. It is possible that Mar Elias XII's nephew was very close to his family and that, while governing the Church, he took greater account of private interests than of those of the whole Chaldean community. This attitude was particularly felt in the administration of property belonging to the ancient monastery of Rabban Hormez,[26] the former residence of the patriarchs of the Church of the East, emptied of monks from 1735 and which had become a source of revenue for the patriarchal family. To keep this family possession, he went as far as preventing anyone from becoming a monk. What is certain is that the whole question was infinitely complicated by the systematic opposition of the old Catholic party, led by Augustine Hindi, named Administrator of Diyarbakir in 1802 and consecrated bishop in 1804, and by the absolute incomprehension which must have reigned between Hormez and the members of the new religious Congregation of Saint Hormisdas who arrived to take possession of the monastery of Rabban Hormez in 1808 under the protection of Archbishop Augustine Hindi.[27] What is equally true, as Raquez reminds us, is that neither party hesitated to have recourse to the 'Muslim' civil power and to use brute force to achieve its aims.[28]

---

[25] Raquez, 'L'Église chaldéenne', 29.

[26] The monastery of Rabban Hormez is located like an eagle's nest on the mountain of Alqosh north of the city of Mosul. The monastery became the official residence of the patriarchs of the Church of the East between 1551 and 1804, although it served as the patriarchal burial site before the end of the fifteenth century. See the study by Stephane Bello, *La Congrégration de S. Hormidas et lÉglise chaldéenne dans la première moité du XIX e siècle*, Orientalia Christiana Analecta, Rome, no. 122, 1939.

[27] Stephane Bello, *La congregation de S. Hormisdas et l'Église chaldéenne dans la premiére moité du XIX e siècle*, Orientalia Christiana Analecta, Rome, no. 122, 1939.

[28] Raquez, 'L'Église chaldéenne', 30.

Whatever the truth, accusations against Hormez multiplied. The Propaganda, presided over by Quarantotto, found against him and removed from him his jurisdiction over Mosul and the administration of the patriarchate in 1812. The Archbishop of Diyarbakir, Augustine Hindi, was named Apostolic Administrator of the 'Chaldean nation' and thus his influenced reached over the whole of the patriarchate. The in-fighting in the Chaldean Church did not disappear, however, and led to a reversal of the situation when Pierre Alexandre Coupery was named Latin Bishop of Babylon and Apostolic Delegate to Baghdad in 1820.[29] The new delegate kept his distance from the opinions which had led Propaganda to deprive Hormez of his office. He pleaded the cause of the former bishop, who recovered his jurisdiction. He was finally elected patriarch on 12 August 1827 and was even honoured with the pallium, despite the bitter opposition of the monks of St Hormisdas. The letters of Coupery are full of interesting notes on the life of Chaldean Church, even though his judgements sometimes seem a little hasty and rather partisan; for example the way he depicts the situation of the Chaldeans with relation to the civil powers: 'The Muslims weigh down the Christians with an iron weight ... but the Christians increase their misery by their own fault; they accuse one another before the authorities who rejoice to have pretexts for demanding money.'[30] In his study of the Chaldean Church during this period, Raguez quotes Coupery's judgement on the monks of St Hormisdas: 'The monks of St Hormez deserve favour but wish to be too independent of the Ordinary. They would like to be directly dependent on the Holy See but this dependence would be illusory because of the distance which separates them.'[31] The Order was confirmed in 1830 by Propaganda.[32] The order took the Antonine Constitutions of the Syrian Maronite monks of Mount Lebanon and aimed, by the sanctification of every monk, for the sanctification of the souls of the faithful, through

[29] On the history of the Latin church, see Waad Al-Khazraji, 'L'oeuvre missionaire en Irak: Un apercu historique', *L'Afrique et l'Asie*, no. 157, 1988, 103-116; J M Vidal, 'La France at l'Archévêché latin de Babylone (Bagdad)', *Revue d'Histoire des Missions,* Vol. 10, no. 3, 1933, 321-371.

[30] Acta vol. 190 (1827), f. 463 quoted in Olivier Raquez, 'L'Église chaldéenne', 30-31.

[31] Acta vol. 190 (1827), f. 230, quoted in Olivier Raquez, 'L'Église chaldéenne', 31 On the value of the monastic order in the Chaldean Church the propaganda judged the following a decade earlier: "The Chaldean Church does not need monks dedicated to the contemplative life as much as it needs active people who, through their good life and labours can offer instruction and example to others. " Acta vol. 180 (1827), f. 180, in Raquez, 'L'Église chaldéenne', 31.

[32] Acta vol. 193 (1830), f. 208-223, in Raquez, 'L'Église chaldéenne', 31.

instruction, administering the sacraments and good works. In fact it would be for a long time the main centre for Chaldean religious education and most bishops would be trained there.

Patriarch Hormez died on 27 August 1838. To avoid possible disturbances and to cut short any attempt by the family of the dead patriarch to impose a candidate according to the former hereditary principle, Propaganda had already named an administrator with right of succession, Nicolas Isaïe di Giacobbe (Nikolas Eshaya 1838-1847), a former pupil of the Propaganda College in Rome. The Chaldean bishops had accepted this direct appointment without any show of opposition, but the hopes placed by the Congregation in Giacobbe would reveal themselves to be vain.[33] From 1843, the Congregation found itself obliged to ask Joseph Valerga[34] to carry out a complete inquiry into the behaviour of the patriarch. The report drawn up by Valerga is sombre reading who says 'the patriarch was immoral in every way.' Valerga suggested recalling him to Rome and appointing an episcopal administrator. Propaganda however contented itself with a severe admonition. This was fruitless, for in 1845 a new dossier as serious as the previous one was drawn up. Following pressure, Nicolas Isaïe was forced to resign in 1847.[35]

The Propaganda Archives studied by Raguez offer further information on the life of the Chaldean Church under the patriarchate of Nicolas Isaïe, such as these details about the life of the monastery of Saint Hormisdas. Relations between Patriarch Hormez and the monastery superiors were difficult. Many monastics became independent and were exclaustrated. According to a letter from Valerga, dated 4 November 1843, there were some thirty-three monks, of whom only four were priests.[36]

[33] Acta vol. 206 (1843), f. 475, in Raquez, 'L'Église chaldéenne', 32.

[34] Valerga was appointed the first Latin Patriarch of Jerusalem in 1847. S Manna, *Chiesa Latina e Chiese Orientali all epoca del Patriarca Giuseppe Valerga (1813-1872)*, Pontificio Istituto degli Studi Orientali, Naples-Rome, 1972; Pierre Duvignau, *Une vie au service de l'Église. S. B. Mgr Joseph Valerga, Patriarche Latin de Jérusalem, 1813-1872*, Imprimerie du Patriarcat Latin, Jerusalem, 1972.

[35] Acta vol. 211 (1848), f. 284, in Raquez, 'L'Église chaldéenne', 32. According to Propaganda archives at the same time, the behaviour of the Apostolic Delegate, Trioche, was hardly more satisfactory. From 1837, when he had attempted to give Patriarch Hormez an auxiliary, Pierre Georges di Natale, the Chaldean bishops had complained about him. The Apostolic Delegate in Mount Lebanon, Auvergne, should have gone to conduct an inquiry, but his death had intervened. Another Apostolic Delegate, Villardel, would arrive later. Trioche was recalled to Rome; he was allowed to return to the Church but with limited powers. Acta vol. 204 (1841), f. 224-248, in Raquez, 'L'Église chaldéenne', 32.

[36] Acta vol. 207 (1844), f. 150 in Raquez, 'L'Église chaldéenne', 32.

The visitor, however, judged that this small number could become a resurgence; in any case, the monastery should be encouraged. Despite the disagreements of the past, it offered great advantages for the Chaldean Church: all the Chaldean bishops and priests of any stature, with the exception of those trained at the Propaganda College in Rome, had come through the monastery. From the point of view of the Propaganda, better administration would give even more abundant fruit.[37]

THE CHALDEAN CHURCH UNDER THE PATRIARCHATE OF JOSEPH AUDO (1847-1878) AND HIS SUCCESSORS

In 1843, Valerga had suggested Joseph Audo, a former monk of St Hormisdas, as *procurator bishop* of the patriarchate.[38] An assessment of Audo is quoted by Raguez—'It is said of him that he has little attachment to the Holy See. This accusation is ill-founded, and I think comes from his tenacity with regard to oriental usages, and also from the fact that he has always been opposed to the slackening spirit which has, for a few years, started to make itself felt among the Chaldeans.'[39] Following the resignation of Giacobbe, Joseph Audo was appointed administrator of the patriarchal diocese and was followed by his appointment to the patriarchate on 26 December 1847.[40]

During the long patriarchate of Joseph Audo, relations between the Holy See and the Chaldean Church were made extremely difficult by the Malabar question.[41] Historically, the ancient patriarchal Chaldean Church had founded the Malabar Church, which remained closely linked to its mother-church.[42] This relationship of dependence had been confirmed in Rome on 7 March 1562 by Pius IV, when confirming

---

[37] Acta vol. 207 (1844), f. 150-151, in Raquez, 'L'Église chaldéenne', 32.

[38] Acta vol. 206 (1843), f. 491-492, in Raquez, 'L'Église chaldéenne', 33.

[39] Acta vol. 211 (1848), f. 278, in Raquez, 'L'Église chaldéenne', 33. See also Joseph Habbi unpublished study sets out Audo's ecclesiological Eastern Catholic culture: *Mar Joseph Audo et le pouvoir patriarchal: Étude historico-juridique*, Faculté de Droit de l'Université Pontificale Latran 1966.

[40] Acta vol. 211 (1848), f. 278, f. 284-285, in Raquez, 'L'Église chaldéenne', 33.

[41] J Habbi, 'Les Chaldéens et les Malabares au XIX eme siècle', *Oriens Christianus*, Vol. 64, 1980, 82-108.

[42] See the discussion in Jacob Kollaparambil, *The Babylonian Origin of the Southists among the St. Thomas Christians*, Orientalia Christiana Analecta 241, Pontificum Institutum Orientalium Studiorum, Rome, 1992.

the Chaldean patriarch. At the Diamper Synod in 1599, however, Latin Bishop Menezes had made the Malabars promise to never again accept a bishop who had not been appointed by Rome.[43] Apart from two or three attempts, not followed up because of Portuguese opposition, the Holy See governed the Malabars through the intermediary of Latin bishops, all the while allowing them a certain liturgical autonomy.[44] This situation caused a number of disagreements and even produced a Church gathered around a non-Catholic bishop sent by the Syrian Orthodox patriarch.[45]

More than once the Malabar Christians had attempted to come to the Chaldean Church.[46] Thus at the end of the 18th century they had sent a delegation to Mar John Hormez with the aim of getting a bishop. Hormez wrote about it to Rome from 1796, asking that his rights in this question be clarified. Not receiving any response, he ordained four Malabars, three priests and a bishop, Paul Abraham Pandari, and sent them back to their country, while suspending their jurisdiction until they were approved by Rome. The Congregation was in exile in Padua. It received this letter in 1799 and learned the news 'with sorrow'. Given the circumstances, Hormez was absolved from the situation into which he had inadvertently fallen and he was allowed to appoint Guriel as his vicar for the Malabar Chaldeans, limiting his jurisdiction to places where there was no Latin bishop or where Latin bishops could not exercise their jurisdiction. This directive could not be carried out because of the difficult circumstances of the Chaldean Church. Later still, in 1830, the Latin Apostolic Vicar of Malabar responded to the ritual needs of his subjects. Missals and rituals

---

43 P J Thaliath, *The Synod of Diamper*, Orientalia Christiana Analecta 152, Pontificum Institutum Orientalium Studiorum, 1958.

44 See the general history by the late E R Hambye, a Belgium Jesuit who was the leading historian of Syriac Christianity in India: *History of Christianity in India III: Eighteenth Century*, Bangalore, Church History Association of India, 1997; and C Th Paremmakal, *The Varthamanappusthakam. An Account of the History of the Malabar Church between the years 1773 and* 1786. Rendered into English with an introduction and notes by Pacid J Podipara, Orientalia Christiana Analecta 190, Pontificum Institutum Orientalium Studiorum, Rome, 1971. See also the important study by Dietmar Schon OP, on canonical jurisdiction, '"Jurisdiktion" und "Territorium" in der Syro-Malabarischen Kirche Indiens. Von der "Aussenmetropolie" der ostsyrischen Kirche bis zur Gewährhrung des portugiesischen patronatsrechts über die Syro-Malabarische Kirche im jahr 1600', *Ostkirchliche Studien*, Vol. 54, no. 1, 2005, 3-55.

45 B Dupuy, 'Aux origines de l'Église syrienne-orthodoxe de l'Inde', *Istina*, Vol. 36, 1991, 53-61. see also E R Hambye, 'A Syrian Orthodox Mission to Malabar in 1825-1826: Some remarks', *Orientalia Christiana Peridodica*, Vol. 34, 1968, 141-144.

46 The Chaldean Church and the Malabar had a long history of relations see, E R Hambye, 'Le métropolite chaldéen, Simon d' Âdâ, et ses aventures en Inde', *Parole de l'Orient*, Vol. VI-VII, 1975-1976, 493-513.

were too few. There was a lack of breviaries and manuscripts were used. It would be useful for a bishop, or at least a priest, of the Syriac rite to examine the entire Syriac liturgy and to instruct the Malabar priests. The intervention of the Latin Vicar was not followed up because the Congregation put the question to one side.[47]

[47] The quest for authenticity for Eastern Catholic church tradition in relation to the powerful Latin church was an important issue in the Chaldean Church under Audo. It continues to be an important contemporary issue. The wish also to give an authentic historical account of the Malabar Church was also the concern of Eugéne Cardinal Tisserant who dealt with the management of Eastern Christian affairs for the Holy See under three pontiffs Pius XI, Pius XII and John XXIII between 1936 and 1959. E R Hambye translated Tisserant's work from French into English, *Eastern Christianity in India: A History of the Syro-Malabar Church from the earliest time to the present*, by His Eminence Cardinal Eugene Tisserant. Authorized adaptation from the French by E R H, Calcutta-London-Westminster, Maryland, 1957. See E R Hambye, 'Eugene Cardinal Tisserant, 1884-1972: A Man of the Church', *Christian Orient*, Vol. 5, 1984, 78-81. Tisserant was also involved in the question of the Syriac liturgy for India see, Marie-Thérèse Desouche, 'Eugène Tisserant et l'Église syro-malabare: Le débat autour du pontifical de la nouvelle hiérarchie syro-malabare, lieu d'un changement paradigmatique de la politique de l'Église romaine envers les rites orientaux', *Le Cardinal Eugène Tisserant (1884-1972) Une grande figure de l'Église, Une grande figure française*, Institut Catholique et Université Toulouse-Le Mirail, Toulouse, 2003, 33-64. Tisserant was born in 1884, ordained priest in 1907; Tisserant was a great connoisseur of the Eastern Christian and Muslim world. He was polyglot and mastered Arabic, but also Hebrew, Syriac and Assyrian. During World War One, Tisserant was appointed to the 'Second Bureau' dealing with intelligence matters where he dealt with Middle Eastern concerns. In 1917, he was in Palestine as lieutenant of *spahis* and took part in the taking of Gaza at the side of the British, and he was present during the entry into Jerusalem in December 1917. In 1926, he supported the foundation of the Dominican Institute of Oriental Studies in Cairo and regularly stayed in the Orient. In 1936 he became head of the Congregation for Oriental Churches. Achille Silvestrini, ' Eugène Tisserant et La congregation pour l'Église Orientale', *Le Cardinal Eugène Tisserant (1884-1972) Une grande figure de l'Église, Une grande figure française*, Institut Catholique et Université Toulouse-Le Mirail, Toulouse, 2003, 101-115. The question of liturgy in the Syriac church in India is a still highly charged political-theological issue. Taking up these themes see the reflections on the work of Indian Eastern Catholic liturgical scholar Placid Podipara who worked to return 'authenticity' to the liturgy of the Malabar Church; E R Hambye, 'The Reverend Father Placid J. Podipara C.M.I, 1899-1985', *Orientalia Christiana Peridodica*, Vol. 52, 1986, 249-256; J Vellian, *The Malabar Church: Symposium in honor of Rev. Pacid J. Podipara* , Orientalia Christiana Analecta 186, Pontificum Institutum Orientalium Studiorum, Rome, 1970; J Madey, 'The Reform of the liturgy of the Syro-Malabar Church and the Holy See in Rome', *Ostkirchliche Studien*, Vol. 30, 1981, 130-168.

The question reappeared with urgency following the appointment of Joseph Audo to the patriarchal see. From 28 July 1849 he received two letters, which had also been sent to his predecessor, in the name of all the Catholic Chaldeans of Malabar, begging him to take interest in their cause and to send them a bishop.[48] Learning of this, the Apostolic Vicar of Malabar and all the missionaries opposed the project. In Mosul, Fr Marchi, superior of the Dominican mission, recommended the question to the patriarch in a letter of 6 January 1850. Fr Planchet, pro-delegate of Mesopotamia was not in favour. 'This cause is not in the interest of the Chaldeans, it has been brought up by a patriarch who has little support in his Church. There is also a lack of capable persons.'[49]

The situation became progressively more difficult. In Malabar, the opposition of the Latin clergy grew, as witnessed by the two letters of Fr Bernadion of Sta Teresa. In Mosul, on the other hand, the Chaldean clergy and the monks of St Hormisdas were so passionately in favour of the project that Fr Marchi thought it wise to write to the Congregation on 11 November 1856. He, and Delegate Planchet, thought that it would be wise to accept the initiatives of the patriarch. But the opposition of the missionaries continued and the Roman position hardened at the same time as that of Delegate Planchet. Audo came under much pressure from the Chaldeans and the Malabars while Rome, through the intermediary of Planchet, let him know that he had nothing to do with Malabar and should not get involved. In November 1859 Planchet was assassinated by the Kurds and was replaced on 25 April 1860 by Henri Amanton. He did not really succeed in being accepted by the local Christian community. A little after his arrival, braving Roman interdictions in canon law, Audo, on 30 September 1860, consecrated Thomas Rokkos bishop for Malabar. Amanton cried excommunication against the patriarch, which was beyond the delegates' power. Joseph Audo took advantage of this to make people understand that the Holy See approved of his actions. Called to Rome to justify his behaviour, he was once more ordered to leave Malabar alone, and was obliged to write to Bishop Rokkos and to pass on to him the order to return to his see in Basra.[50]

Rokkos submitted and left India. During his stay in Malabar, he had been excommunicated. Absolved by his patriarch, he believed himself

---

48 Joseph Habbi, 'La figure juridique de l'évêque dans l'histoire de l'Église assyro-chaldéenne', *Kanon*, Vol. 7, 1985, 195-212.

49 Raquez, 'L'Église chaldéenne', 34

50 Raquez, 'L'Église chaldéenne', 35

to be within the law but the apostolic delegate and Propaganda fought against him, and Pius IX himself sent a letter to the patriarch, *Nuper nobis*, dated 26 September 1862, on the subject. This insistence wounded Audo, who complained bitterly in a letter of 24 November 1862 to the cardinal, 'No-one can deny that if we had been treated with a little consideration, all these disagreements and schisms would not have come to pass and the Jacobites and Nestorians would not have appeared in Malabar.'[51] This was also the opinion of men as moderate as Benni, Syrian Archbishop of Mosul and future patriarch of that Church, and of the Syrian Bishop Joseph David, who admitted the Chaldean faults but also brought into the light the mistakes committed by the Delegation, the missionaries and the French consulate.[52] Whatever the case, the first Malabar question ended on 10 July 1864 with a letter from the patriarch to his clergy in which he demonstrated his total submission to Rome.

On 12 July 1867, Pius IX had published the Bull *Reversus*, in which he substantially changed the system of appointment of bishops and patriarchs in the Armenian Church, and reserved most of the rights of nomination to the Holy See.[53] He wished to extend these modifications to the other oriental Churches and a short time after the publication of *Reversus* he wrote to Audo to ask his opinion on the question. Without consulting his bishops, Audo replied that he saw no disadvantages. His response was ratified on 31 August 1869 when Pius IX published the Bull *Cum ecclesiastica disciplina*, by which he extended the *Reversus* legislation to the Chaldean Church.[54] At that point, Audo left for Rome with his bishops to take part in the Vatican Council. At that time, in early 1870, most of the eastern bishops and all the patriarchs, with the exception of the Armenian Patriarch Antoine Hassoun, were opposed to the extension of the rights of *Reversus* to the other oriental Churches. Influenced by them, or understanding the error he had made, Audo tried to retreat from his previous position. A concrete occasion presented itself. Before even publishing *Cum ecclesiastica disciplina* Pius IX, basing himself on the agreement in principle which Audo had sent

---

51 AO Acta vol. 2 (1965), f. 237 quoted in Raquez, 'L'Église chaldéenne', 35.

52 C Korolevskij, 'Benni (Benham)', *Dictionnaire d'Histoire et de Géographie ecclésiastique*, Vol. VII, 1352-1359; A O'Mahony, 'The Syrian Catholic Church: a study in history and ecclesiology', *Sobornost: Eastern Churches Review*, Vol. 28, 2006, 28-50.

53 John Whooley, 'The Armenian Catholic Church: a study in history and ecclesiology', *The Heythrop Journal: A Quarterly Review of Philosophy and Theology*, Vol. XLV, 2004, 416-434.

54 Constantin G Patelos, 'L'affaire du patrarche chaldéen Joseph Audo', *Vatican I et les évêques uniates: une étape éclairante de la politique romaine a l'égard des orientaux (1867-1870)*, Bibliothèque de la revue d'histoire ecclésiastique, 65, Louvain, 1981, 441-447.

him, had appointed two Chaldean bishops by the Bull, *Supremi Apostolatus*, of 22 March 1869, and instructed Audo to consecrate them. After some equivocation, however, he refused to do so. Pius IX immediately and energetically intervened. The patriarch had to submit. This submission, however, was forced. Back in his patriarchate, some years after the council, he went beyond the dispositions of *Cum ecclesiastica disciplina* and allowed himself to consecrate two bishops on 24 May 1874, and then two more on 25 July 1875, without any consultation with the Roman authorities.[55]

The ordinations were linked to the Malabar question. Audo had sent bishop Elie Mellous there and he had consecrated Philippe Jacques Ouraha bishop, also for Malabar. The Holy See would not accept such behaviour and after various more or less private admonishments, Pius IX published on 1 September 1876 his encyclical *Quae in Patriarchatu*, in which he recalled the events of the first Malabar crisis and announced ultimate sanctions: Audo had 40 days to submit; after this he would be excommunicated and suspended from his patriarchal jurisdiction. Audo submitted on 1 March 1877 and recalled his bishops from Malabar. The problem with the method of appointing bishops remained an unhappy point in relations between the Oriental Churches and the Roman authorities. The Armenian bishops led by Patriarch Hassoun were obliged to ask for several partial dispensations from the *Reversus* legislation. On 20 April 1877, Patriarch Audo asked for, and obtained, the extension of these disciplinary changes to his own Church. Bishop Mellous did not leave Malabar until 1882. He made his submission to Leo IX in 1889. Promoted to the see of Mardin, he died there in 1908. The Church which he founded in Malabar remained after his departure. Reduced to some 8,000, the Mellousians submitted to the patriarch of the Church of the East in 1907.[56]

Overtime the question of the Malabar hierarchy found a solution. Two apostolic vicariates were created in 1877 but their apostolic vicars were not yet of the Malabar rite. In 1895 the Malabar Chaldeans announced their plan to send a delegation to Rome with the idea of once again soliciting their rejoining the Chaldean Patriarchate, and Leo XIII consulted on 5 May 1895 with the Commission of Cardinals to bring the dissidents, so understood by Rome, back to the Catholic Church. Without agreeing to bring the Malabar Church back to the Chaldean Church, it

[55] Raquez, 'L'Église chaldéenne', 36.

[56] Raquez, 'L'Église chaldéenne', 37. See C Korolevskij, 'Audo (Joseph)', *Dictionnaire d'Histoire et de Géographie ecclésiastique*, Vol. V, 317-356, which gives a full description of Audo's life and career.

was decided to give Malabar its own hierarchy and Propaganda took it on itself to find out about future candidates for the episcopate. In 1896 the Malabar apostolic vicariates would number three and would receive titular holders of the Malabar rite. This initial emancipation from Latin Ordinaries would be crowned by the erection of a Malabar ecclesiastical province on 20 December 1923.

However, the question of the Chaldean Church at the First Vatican Council needs reviewing.[57] Audo had gone to the council with ten bishops and the monastic superior of St Hormisdas. On 25 January 1870, he made an important intervention, reacting deeply to the project of Latinising the Oriental discipline presented by the Commission for Oriental Churches and Missions. Declaring that he submitted himself in advance to the dogmatic decisions the council would take, he demanded respect for the Oriental disciplinary traditions. He himself had promised to keep and defend the privileges, customs and rites of the Oriental Churches during his episcopal consecration. The popes had recognized, approved and confirmed these rights and privileges. Justice and faithfulness demanded that no harm should be done to the safeguarding of the privileges of the patriarchal sees. If reform was necessary it could only be usefully done by national councils. It would be useful, therefore, to ask the pope and the council for authorization to draw up a new law conforming both to Vatican I and to the ancient Oriental discipline.[58] At the solemn session of 18 July 1870 at which the dogmatic constitution *Pastor Aeternus* was voted in, half the Chaldean bishops were absent, along with many other Oriental bishops, Patriarch Audo among them. He would not give his agreement to the new constitution until 29 July 1872 after much pressure, when he did so 'with the reservation of keeping all the rights, distinctions, favours, usages and traditions of which the ancient Oriental patriarchs enjoyed, general and particular, with no change or difference.'[59]

Aside from the patriarch, the other Chaldean members of the council were unremarkable. We should however note the comments of

[57] Constantin G Patelos, 'L'épiscopat chaldéen', *Vatican I et les évêques uniates: une étape éclairante de la politique romaine a l'égard des orientaux (1867-1870)*, 268-297.

[58] Raquez, 'L'Église chaldéenne', 38. On the sources of canon law for the Chaldean Church, see C Korolevskij, 'Classification et valeur des sources connues de la discipline chaldéenne', *Codificazione canonica orientate. Fonti, Fascicule VII, Studi storici sulle fonti del diritto canonico orientate*, Sacra Congregazione Orientale, Rome, 1932, 665-706; Jean Dauvillier, 'Droit Chaldéen', *Dictionnaire de Droit Canonique*, Vol. 13, 1942, col. 292-388.

[59] *Mansi*, vol. 53, 943; Raquez, 'L'Église chaldéenne', 37.

the Archbishop of Gesirah, Paul Hindi, on the plan for the missions. With bitterness, he raged against the discrimination which had been established between the Latin and Oriental bishops and demanded that the jurisdiction be conceded to the Oriental bishops over those who were missionaries in their dioceses. This request was taken up by several other Oriental bishops and would be examined further in 1894 at the patriarchal conferences held in Rome.

After Joseph Audo's death, the Chaldean community abandoned any claim to the Malabar Church and came into a new more peaceful phase. The patriarchate of Elie XIV Aboul-Yonan (1878-1894) was marked by a strong movement of conversions from the Church of the East. It was under his pontificate that the Dominicans opened a seminary for Chaldeans and Syrians at Mosul in 1882. At the time of the patriarchal conferences in 1894, Patriarch Elie XIV had been dead since 27 June. His successor, Audishu V, was only appointed on 28 October, and therefore could not take part in the conferences. His patriarchate was short and he died in 1899. Mar Emmanuel II succeeded Mar Audishu V in 1900. He died at Mosul on 23 July 1947. The beginnings of his reign were marked by many conversions from the Church of the East, but the 1914-18 war tested the Church considerably.[60]

The situation of the hierarchy in the modern history of the Chaldean Church had finally stabilized only on 5 July 1830, when Pope Pius VIII confirmed Metropolitan John Hormizd as head of all Chaldean Catholics, with the title of Patriarch of Babylon of the Chaldeans, with his see in Mosul.[61] The Chaldean Catholics suffered heavily from massacres during World War I when four bishops, many priests, and tens of thousands Chaldean Christians died. This period, in particular 1915, has been called the 'year of the sword'.[62] The location of the patriarchate shifted back and forth among several places over the centuries, but gained a measure of stability after it was established at Mosul in 1830.[63] In 1950 it moved to

---

60 Raquez, 'L'Église chaldéenne', 38-39.

61 J Habbi, 'L'Unification de la hiérarchie chaldéenne dans la première moitié du XIX siècle, *Parole de l'Orient*, Vol. 2, 1971, 121-143 and 305-327.

62 For a particularly important collection of documents from Catholic sources detailing these widespread massacres, see 'Documents sur les événements de Mardine, 1915-1920', *Collectanea: Studia Orientalia Christiana,* Nos. 29/30, 1996/97, 5-220.

63 Chaldean patriarchs from the nineteenth century until the election of Paul Cheikho in 1958 have been as follows: John Hormidd (1830-1838), Nikolas Eshaya (1838-1847), Joseph VI Audo (1848-1878), Eliya XIV [XIII] Abulyonan (1879-1894), Audishu V Khayyat (1895-1899), Joseph VI Emmanuel II Thoma (1900-1947), Joseph VII Ghanima (1947-1958).

its present location in Baghdad after substantial migration of Chaldean Catholics from northern Iraq to the city.

The 'Patriarch of Babylon'—this is the official name—has his seat in Baghdad. In the modern era two Chaldean patriarchs have navigated the community through difficult and challenging seas within which the Christians of the Middle East now chart: between minority and majority, between Christianity and Islam and in times of conflict and political upheaval. Paul Cheikho, who was elected patriarch at the time of the political upheavals of 1958 in Iraq. Born in 1906 in Alqosh in the north of Iraq and ordained in 1930, he became a bishop in 'Aqra in Iraqi Kurdistan in 1947 and transferred to Aleppo in 1957, when the newly established eparchy for the Chaldean community in Syria was created. Cheikho was elected patriarch for the Chaldeans in December 1958; he would have to care for his community through some very difficult periods in modern Iraqi history. During his near thirty-year tenure he led his church through three revolutions (1958, 1963, 1968), three regimes, the emergence of an oil driven economy, the Kurdish revolt and the long Iran-Iraq war.

Cheikho did all he could to adapt his church to difficult and changing times in organizational terms. However, he was deeply attached to Eastern Christian traditions, especially those associated with the Chaldean church and Syriac Christianity.[64] He supported a married clergy and, whilst bishop of 'Aqra, he would often petition Rome on the matter.[65] The Kurdish uprising brought new travails to the Christians in Iraq. Over the course of the fighting between the Iraqi army and the Kurds, many Christian villages and churches were destroyed. In June 1969 the monastery of Rabban Hormidz near Alqosh also fell victim to plundering.[66] In 1972 arose the question of seminary reform and the question of military service for priests and religious and in 1975 the Churches in Iraq had to deal with the nationalization of the school system which had a direct impact upon the Catholic school system. In 1984 during the Iraq-Iran war Cheikho led an ecumenical and interfaith delegation to the Vatican in witness to

---

64 'Les chaldéens' in J-P Valognes, *Vie et mort des chrétiens d'Orient,* Fayard, Paris, 1994, 406-449, 437. See also the comments by the Chaldean priest and scholar Joseph Habbi, 'Towards an open Church: The Chaldean Catholic Church', in *The Future of the Oriental Catholic Churches*, (eds) John Madey and Stanislaus Thomas Erackel, Tiruvalla (India), Santinilayam Publications, 1979, 217-246.

65 J-M Fiey OP, 'Prêtres mariés: quleques experiences', *Proche-Orient Chrétien*, Vol. 44, 1994, 299-300.

66 Baum and Winkler, *The Church of the East: a concise history*, 146.

the suffering of the Christian communities and Iraqi society. The number of Christian dead during the Iraq-Iran war was high estimated at some 60,000 killed, made prisoner or missing in action.[67]

Cheikho never abandoned a certain professed loyalty to the government; however, he was a powerful adversary when he thought that the rights of the Church were being challenged and he made assertive interventions when the government sought to impose the study of the Qur'an in Christian schools. In 1976, the government in effect nationalized Shi'ite organizations by suppressing their capacity to manage their religious properties and by transforming the imams into state employees who receive a salary from the state and are controlled by it. In 1981, the Ba'athist regime wanted to adopt similar measures toward the Christians, nationalizing their properties and turning their priests into state employees, thereby controlling through the ministry of the *waqfs* (religious property and endowments) all of the churches' functions. The Ba'athist government eventually backed down when faced with strong reactions from the bishops, but the threat was always present that these measures could be implemented. However, it was large scale and traumatic displacement of the Christians in the north of Iraq and their movement south into the large cities of Iraq that dominated his period of office. He constructed some 25 churches in Baghdad to service the needs of his Chaldean Catholic community.[68]

Mar Rouphael I Bidwid, Patriarch of Babylon for the Chaldean Catholics[69]

Bidawid[70] was born Raphael Yousif Warda on 17 April, 1922 at Mosul, Iraq. In his early years (aged11) he attended junior Chaldean seminary

---

[67] Vahram Petrosian, 'Assyrians in Iraq', *Iran and the Caucasus*, Vol. 10, no. 1 2006, 128.

[68] 'Iraq', *Proche Orient Chétien*, Vol. 39, 1989, 346.

[69] See also A O'Mahony, 'Christianity in Modern Iraq', *International Journal for the Study of the Christian Church*, Vol. 4, no 2, 2004, 121-142; 'The Chaldean Catholic Church: The Politics of Church-State Relations in Modern Iraq', *The Heythrop Journal: A Quarterly Review of Philosophy and Theology*, Vol. XLV, 2004, 435-450; 'The Life and Death of a Patriarch: Mar Rouphael I Bidwid, Patriarch of Babylon and the Chaldean Catholic Church in Iraq', *Sobornost*, Vol. 27, no. 1, 2005, 26-46.

[70] There are many versions of his name Bedawied, Badawid, Bidawid, however, the Syriac meaning of surname is the Son of David. Whilst many sources give him being born in Mosul 1922, his family certainly comes from a province in northern Iraq bordering Turkey. His family may well had emigrated to the relative safety. The 'year of the sword' (1915) had convinced Christians that they should move out of these areas dominated by the Turks and Kurds.

in Mosul administered by the Dominican mission;[71] and his secondary studies at the patriarchal seminary for the Chaldeans also in Mosul. He showed potential and was sent to study philosophy and theology in Rome. He spent most of the war years (1936-1947) studying in Rome at the Pontifical Urbaniana College, 'De Propaganda Fide'. In late 1944 he was ordained a priest. In the same year he completed a doctorate in Rome on the religious philosophy of the Muslim mystic, Al-Ghazali. Following this he gained a licence in Canon Law and Civil Law at the Lateran University. He completed his doctorate in theology on Patriarch Timotheos and the situation of the Christians during the 'Abbasid period, which was published at the Vatican in the prestigious series *Studi e Testi*, no. 187 as *Les letters du patriarche nestorien Timothée Ier* in 1956. On his return to Mosul in 1947 from Rome, he was appointed as the rector of the Chaldean seminary. Between 1948-1956 he was professor of philosophy and theology in the patriarchal Chaldean College at Mosul. Also between 1950-1956 he was chaplain responsible for the Christians working in the Iraq Petroleum Company from Kirkuk to the port city of Tripoli in north Lebanon. In 1956 he was appointed patriarchal vicar of the Chaldean diocese of Kirkuk, Arbil, and Sulaimaniya. Kirkuk was major centres for the Iraqi Petroleum Company, a city with a very diverse ethnic and linguistic mix—Syriac, Arabic, Turkish and Kurdish in addition to a large expatriate community. Kirkuk had a thriving Chaldean community that benefited from the oil industry. This was his first experience in acquiring the political skills needed by any bishop who would seek to shepherd his community in the modern Middle East.

From 1957 until 1966 he was bishop of the Chaldean Diocese of Amadia now redrawn and located in the Kurdish region of Iraq. His first test came with the 1958 revolution in Iraq, which was a violent affair. At the age of thirty-five he was one of the Catholic world's youngest bishops. He was responsible for one of the largest Chaldean dioceses covering a large area of Kurdistan, with well-established and prosperous Chaldean farming communities many of who were landowners. However, this was prior to the migration of Christians from the north to Baghdad; within the next few years his diocese would became the centre of the conflict between the Kurds and the government of Iraq. The task of the bishop in such a conflict demanded great political skill, for he had to maintain good relations with the Kurdish factions, without bringing himself into

---

[71] J-M Mérigoux, *Va à Ninive! Un dialogue avec l'Irak*, Éditions du Cerf, Paris, 2000, 445-475.

conflict with the government and not compromising the position of the Chaldean patriarchate in Baghdad. At this time the majority of the Chaldeans and members of the (Assyrian) Church of the East still lived in their historic heartlands in the north of Iraq. The Christian communities suffered greatly in the long and messy war of attrition between the Kurds and the Iraqi army. The conflict lasted up until till the agreement of Algiers between Iraq and Iran in 1975. During this period entire Chaldean and Assyrian villages were burned down and people were forced to emigrate to the safety of Mosul and Baghdad. To illustrate the point the number of Christians in northern Iraq has dwindled from 1 million to around 150,000 between 1961 and 1995.

It was during this period that Bidawid witnessed the destruction of his community in its historic context. Aware of the possible lost of their heritage he oversaw the cataloguing and transferring of the rich holdings of books and manuscripts of the bishopric to the patriarchal library in Mosul.[72] Passionate about the history of Eastern Christianity and particularly the Chaldean Church's relations with the West, he wrote numerous papers on the theme and translated the famous travel account by the Dominican Pére Lanza to Mosul in 1754 in the review *Al-Najm*. And whilst Chaldean bishop in Beirut he re-edited and re-issued two important works by Pére Eugène Manna, *Cours de langue araméenne selon les deux dialects syriaques et chaldïque* (1896) and *Vocabulaire Chaldéen-Arabe* (1900).[73]

In 1965 Bidawid was transferred to the Chaldean Diocese of Beirut (Lebanon) until his election as patriarch of the Chaldean Catholic Church in 1989. The first Chaldeans arrived in Lebanon at the end of the 19th centaury in 1895 to escape the persecutions of the Turks and Kurds. Their number increased after the first and second world wars, the Kurdish revolt and the Iran-Iraq war. They number some ten to twenty thousand a figure that fluctuated over this period. They have two parishes one in Beirut and one in Zahle.

Bidawid would spend 23 years at the head of the Chaldean Catholic Church in Lebanon during the difficult years of the civil war that witnessed Lebanese society and the different Christian political factions tear themselves apart. As leader of a relatively small Oriental Catholic community, he was aware of the power of the Maronite Church and

---

72 'Iraq', *Proche Orient Chétien*, Vol. 39, 1989, 346-347.

73 Joseph Habbi, 'Manuscrits arabes chrétiens en Iraq', *Parole de l'Orient*, Vol. 22, 1997, 361-380.

Maronite political parties who had created the modern state and who had dominated it since its creation in 1920 by the Maronite patriarch with the support of France. Bidawid with his political ability managed for almost nine tranquil years before the civil war to create a successful network in the Lebanon's pluralist society. He seems to have enjoyed a wide range of relations and friendships at all levels. The Chaldean church in the Lebanon provided a focus for Iraqi exiles, businessman and tourists regardless of their religious or political background.

He was one of the founders of the Council of Catholic Patriarchs and Bishops in Lebanon; he participated in several committees which included: the executive committee, the Catholic schools committee, the Committee for Communication, of which he was the first secretary and the Ecumenical Committee. He represented the Catholic Church in the fourth General Assembly of the Council of Churches of the Middle East in Cyprus. He was an advocate of the Catholic Church becoming a member of the Council of Churches of the Middle East. During his period in Lebanon he tried always to represent the best interest of the Chaldean Church, he was successful in fulfilling his dream of constructing a cathedral for the Chaldeans in Babda. It was also during this period that he was often caught up, often against his will, in the attempt by the Iraqi Ba'athist regime to court the Maronite Christian community. Both the Maronites and the Iraqi regime looked closely at the potential and the possibilities of exploiting the presence of a senior Iraqi Catholic bishop in the Lebanon. Bidawid maintained and used his Lebanese connections when required at the service of Iraqi Christianity.

The Chaldean Synod elected Bidawid patriarch on 21 May 1989 to succeed Paul Cheikho, and he received the *pallium* from Pope Paul II on 9 November 1989. He was enthroned as bishop at the patriarchal seminary at Doura, Baghdad, a ceremony, some 20-25,000 people attended. Bidawid was elected leader of the largest Christian community in Iraq after an eight-year war between Iraq and Iran. It was he who had to lead his community during difficult times—the Iraqi invasion of Kuwait, the defeat of Iraq by the coalition forces, the gruelling period of sanctions; economic reduction and the destruction of Iraqi society, a growth in Christian-Muslim tension, the Second Gulf War in 2003 and the removal of the Ba'ath party from power. Apart from Tariq Aziz, Bidawid was one of the few Christian personalities who had any real profile during this period. Like all the Christian patriarchs of the region, he often had to chart a course between the realities of political power, the growing hostile presence of Islamist radicalism and seeking to defend and promote the best interests of Christianity and the Chaldean Catholic Church in Iraq.

Sending the *pallium* to the new patriarch who had been in Rome for the *ad limina* visit of the Chaldean bishops, John Paul II recorded the history of the Chaldean church and its relations with Rome, mentioning the first *pallium* sent to first patriarch, Sulaqa, by Pope Julius III in 1553. The same patriarch died two years later as a martyr for the unity of the church, 'and here we are 436 years later, the successor of that martyred patriarch being presented in his turn to the successor of Peter to receive the sacred *pallium*.' John Paul II now asked the Chaldean church to do all it could to bring about a new civilization founded on love and respect for all.[74]

Due to emigration from the north there has been a changing geographic configuration of the Christian community.[75] In Baghdad alone, there were some 30 parishes with a total of 200,000-250,000, plus several further Iraqi dioceses Kirkuk, Arbil, Basra, Mosul, Alqosh, Amadia and Shamkan, Zakho and Dohuk. The Chaldean diaspora represents a significant element of the Church, with bishops and dioceses in Lebanon, Syria, Turkey, Israel and Jordan, Egypt, Iran, Australia and New Zealand, Europe, Caucasian republics(Armenian and Georgia), and North America. There are now almost thirty bishops. The church has also had to develop a flexible response to the number of Christian refugees in the region, for example Bidawid appointed a patriarchal vicar in 2002 to care for the 20,000 Chaldean Catholics in Jordan who lived in difficult circumstances. There had been 60,000 in 1991 after the First Gulf War.[76] In America a new eparchy was established in 2002 for some 35,000 new Chaldean arrivals, which supported the other Chaldean eparchy, which looked after some 100,000 Chaldean Catholics. It is estimated that now over two hundred thousand Chaldeans are resident in North America. This makes this one of the most important diasporas of the Chaldean Church. The patriarch of the Church of the East since leaving Tehran in the mid-1980s is also resident America. In total the Chaldeans have in Iraq, the Middle East and in the West over one hundred parishes. The permanent deaconate within

[74] *L'Osservatore Romano*, 10 November 1989.

[75] For a description of Christian village live in northern Iraq see the memoir by Éphrem-Isa Yousif, *Parfums d'enfance à Sanate. Un village chrétien au Kurdistan iraqien*, Paris Éditions l'Harmattan, 1993.

[76] 'Iraq' *Proche-Orient Chrétien,* Vol. 41, 1991, 376.

the tradition of Oriental Christian is a thriving model for the Chaldean Church particularly in North America.

The Chaldean Church in Iraq supported several educational institutions in particular the Babel College for philosophy and theology. In the early 1990s it was hoped to establish a Catholic University in Iraq (the influential Jesuit University in Baghdad was closed by the state in the 1960s)—in fact Babel College fitted this model. Since 1990 (and until late 2006 when it was forced to leave Baghdad) Babel College has undertaken the theological and philosophical formation of thousands of students of all denominations, including Chaldeans, Syrian Orthodox and Catholic, Armenians of both Churches, members of the Church of the East—an ecumenical form of the formation which has no parallel anywhere in the world. There was a minor and a senior seminary in Baghdad, open to the Latin rite and a dual rite seminary (Chaldean-Syrian Catholic) in Mosul. Under Chaldean direction there are two Journals; *Bayn al Nahrayn* ('Mesopotamia'), a cultural and historical journal; and *Najm al-Mashriq* ('Star of the Orient') published by the patriarchate since 1995. *Al-Fikr al Masihi* ('Christian Thought'), established in 1964 by the Syrian Catholics in Iraq, has now been taken over by the Dominican order reflecting the general culture of Christianity in Iraq. Journals became particularly important for theological formation, as the importing of literature from abroad has been difficult in recent times.[77] As private schools have been nationalized, Christian religious education was taught in state schools, provided it is requested by at least twenty-five percent of pupils. Catechism mostly taught in the churches, in spite of the lack of suitable educational centres and teachers. However, it is important to emphasize that an 'Institute of Catechism', attached to Babel College, was founded some years ago to train young teachers for Christian religious instruction. But the work of these institutes has been disrupted by the lack of security that has prevailed in Iraq since 2003.

The Iraqi church can be considered as a real mosaic of communities; however, ecumenism is very much alive in Iraq, where it is thought of as a natural coming together of all who share the common faith of Christ. It is from within this milieu that a great ecumenical stride was taken on 11 November 1994 when the patriarch of the Church of the East—the sister Church of the Chaldean Catholics—issued with

[77] Bärbel Dümler, 'Zur aktuellen Situation der Christen im Irak', *Ostkirchliche Studien*, 48, 1999, 107-143, here 115.

John Paul II a joint declaration on Christology.[78] This was followed by agreement, which allows for mutual admission to the Eucharist between the two Churches. In October 2001, the Pontifical Council for Promoting Christian Unity published two texts: 1. *Guidelines for Admission to the Eucharist between the Chaldean Church and the Assyrian Church in the East*; and 2. *Admission to the Eucharist in Situations of Pastoral Necessity*, the second being intended to clarify the meaning and application of the first. The mutualities associated with the admission to Eucharist are based on the official recognition, by the Congregation for the Doctrine of Faith on behalf of the Catholic Church, of the validity of an anaphora of Addai and Mari, traditionally used by the Church of the East, although it does not contain an explicit institution narrative.[79] This recognition is expected to have far-reaching pastoral and theological implications. The statement from the Vatican added that publishing guidelines for eucharistic sharing between the members of the Church of the East and Chaldean Catholics is particularly important because so many faithful from both Churches had emigrated from Iraq and the surrounding area.[80] Emigration continues to be a destructive reality that has affected all the Christian communities in the Middle East; however, it also creates an important, vital and growing expression of Oriental Christianity in the West.

The greatest challenge and the most important achievement of the bilateral and multilateral ecumenical theological dialogues that have taken place among Syriac Churches has been the opportunity for each Church to express its own theological tradition—be it Catholic, non-Chalcedonian or pre-Ephesian—and its self-understanding of its own theology, history, role in Christological disputes, sacraments, liturgy, and modern contribution to Christendom. Three main factors can be identified as being responsible for these developments: the ecumenical movement of the 20th century and the establishment (in 1948) of the World Council of Churches, the Second Vatican Council, and the large-scale emigration from the Middle East to Europe, the Americas and Australia, of Christians

---

[78] Gerald O'Collins SJ and Daniel Kendall, 'Overcoming Christological Differences', *The Heythrop Journal*, Vol. 37, 1996, 382-390; S Brock, 'The importance of the Syriac traditions in ecumenical dialogue on Christology', *Christian Orient*, Vol. 20, 1999, 189-197; S Brock, 'The Syriac Churches in Ecumenical Dialogue on Christology', *Eastern Christianity: Studies in Modern History, Religion and Politics*, 44-65.

[79] Frans Bouwen, 'Assyriens et Chaldéens: admission mutuelle à l'euchariste', *Proche-Orient Chrétien*, Vol. 51, 2001, 333-347 and S Brock, 'The Syriac Churches and Dialogue with the Catholic Church', *The Heythrop Journal*, Vol. XLV (2004), 435-450.

[80] *The Tablet*, 3 November 2001, 1580-1581.

from the non-Chalcedonian Churches, thus bringing these Churches into the direct consciousness of the Western Churches. In the case of several of the Syriac Churches, as in that of the Armenian Church, this large-scale emigration had been initiated by the widespread massacres in eastern Turkey, above all in 1915, 'the year of the sword', when huge numbers were either killed or displaced. In recent decades the political instability of the Middle East has led to further waves of emigration. Although this large-scale emigration has in general been disastrous from the point of view of the life of the indigenous Christian Churches in the Middle East, there have at least been other consequences: emigration to Western countries has provided the possibility of publication without censorship, and it has brought the existence of these non-Chalcedonian Churches more into the awareness of the Western Churches, thus providing an opportunity and incentive for theological dialogue.

One can identify three stages in the dialogue among the Syriac Churches and the Chalcedonian Orthodox and Roman Catholic Churches.[81] The first level is that of the dialogue between the Chalcedonian Eastern Orthodox Churches and non-Chalcedonian Oriental Orthodox Churches which began in 1964 and continues to the present. The second stage is that of the dialogue between the Roman Catholic Church and the non-Chalcedonian Oriental Orthodox Churches that began in 1971. The third is the multilateral dialogue among all churches of the Syriac tradition—pre-Ephesian, non-Chalcedonian, and Catholic—initiated and facilitated by the PRO ORIENTE Foundation in Vienna in 1994.

The first unofficial meeting at the PRO ORIENTE Foundation in 1971 resulted in a joint declaration between both Chalcedonian and the non- Chalcedonian churches known as the Vienna Christological Formula, the text of which has been received officially and is fundamental to all subsequent dialogue. The agreement on Christology states that Jesus Christ is

> ... perfect in His divinity and perfect in His humanity. His divinity was not separated from his humanity for a single moment, not for the twinkling of an eye; His humanity is one with His divinity without commixtion, without confusion,

[81] Sebastian Brock, 'The Syriac Churches in Ecumenical Dialogue on Christology', in A O'Mahony (ed.), *Eastern Christianity. Studies in Modern History, Religion, and Politics*, Melisende, London, 2004, 44-65, here 46-47.

> without division, without separation. We ... regard His mystery as inexhaustible and ineffable and for the human mind never fully comprehensible or expressible.[82]

Following the Vienna Formula, the next major breakthrough took place in 1984, with the joint declaration of Pope John Paul II and Syrian Orthodox Patriarch of Antioch and All the East Ignatius Zakka I Iwas.[83] Their declaration includes the statement that the schisms that arose in the 5th century 'in no way affect or touch the substance of their faith, since these arose only because of differences in terminology and culture and in the various formulae adopted by different theological schools to express the same matter.' The part of the declaration concerning Christology closely follows the language of the Vienna Formula. It is the recognition that the disagreement in Christology is one of terminology only and does not touch the substance of Christian doctrine

The Church of the East began its participation in the ecumenical discussion somewhat later than the Syrian Orthodox and Roman Catholic Churches.[84] Bilateral discussions between the Church of the East on the one hand and the Chaldean Catholic, Roman Catholic, and Syrian Orthodox churches on the other have achieved significant breakthroughs in consultations held throughout the 1990s. However, the Coptic Orthodox Church has asserted its authority over the other Oriental Orthodox Churches, preventing the Church of the East from participating in further official consultations with the Syrian Orthodox Church and in the Middle East Council of Churches, despite the support of the Roman Catholic Church.[85]

In 1984 an official meeting took place between the Patriarch Catholicos of the Church of the East, Mar Dinkha IV and Pope John Paul II. The application of the Church of the East to the Middle East Council of Churches (MECC) was given in 1985. The Coptic Orthodox Church

---

82 The full text of the Vienna Formula is available in PRO ORIENTE, *Syriac Dialogue 1*, Vienna, 1994, 27-28.

83 See Sebastian Brock, 'The Syriac Churches in Ecumenical Dialogue on Christology', 51-52. Originally printed in *L'Osservatore Romano*, 24 June, 1984.

84 Dietmar W Winkler, 'The Current Theological Dialogue with the Assyrian Church of the East', *Symposium Syriacum VII,* Orientalia Christiana Analecta 256, Rome, 1998, 158-173.

85 See Otto Meinardus, 'About heresies and the Syllabus Errorum of Pope Shenuda III', *Coptic Church Review*, Vol. 22, no. 4, 2001, 98-105 and the response by Sebastian Brock, ' " About heresies and the Syllabus Errorum of Pope Shenuda III": Some Comments on the Recent Article by Professor Meinardus', *Coptic Church Review*, Vol. 23, no. 4, 2002, 98-102.

was against the application and it was rejected. However, the matter of the Church of the East remained on the agenda of the MECC in 1992 and 1994. At a regional symposium of PRO ORIENTE held in the Wadi Natrun monastery in Egypt in 1991, a fierce debate erupted concerning the participation of the Church of the East in PRO ORIENTE consultations, in which the Coptic Orthodox Church did not wish to discuss the fine points of theological and terminological questions surrounding the Council of Ephesus, which had been called by Cyril and met in 431, and the removal of Nestorius from office (Nestorius was not in fact condemned at this council).[86] Nevertheless, the PRO ORIENTE foundation continued to discuss the involvement of the Church of the East in its activities.

In 1994 PRO ORIENTE initiated a dialogue between the Church of the East, the Syrian Orthodox Church, and the Eastern Catholic Churches of the Syriac tradition, including church officials and theologians representing sister churches in India. The event itself was of great significance even without a substantial Christological agreement.[87] A Common Declaration of Faith promulgated by Mar Dinkha IV and Pope John Paul II in the same year stated that the two churches had the same understanding concerning Christology and the Virgin Mary.[88] Following this declaration, the MECC decided to move forward with the inclusion of the Church of the East.

Despite the continuing opposition that the Coptic Orthodox Church had shown to any dialogue with or participation of the Church of the East in ecumenical affairs, in 1995 the two churches produced a draft Common Declaration on Christology. This document, which drew heavily on the Vienna Formula which the Coptic Church had formally accepted, as well as the Common Declaration of Faith, was quickly ratified by the synod of bishops of the Church of the East.[89] The Coptic Church synod subsequently rejected this document. The result of these developments has been essentially to halt any further official consultation between the Church of the East and the Syrian Orthodox Church. In meetings in 2002

[86] Sebastian Brock, 'The Syriac Churches in Ecumenical Dialogue on Christology', 53. The paper that set off the debate at this conference was by André de Halleux, 'Nestorius, histoire et doctrine', *Irénikon* 66 (1993), 38-51, 163-177; English translation without notes: Pro Oriente, *Syriac Dialogue 1*, Vienna, 1994, 200-215.

[87] Gerald O'Collins and Daniel Kendall, 'Overcoming Christological Differences', *The Heythrop Journal: A Quarterly Review of Philosophy and Theology*, Vol. 37, 1996, 382-390.

[88] Quoted in Brock, 'The Syriac Churches in Ecumenical Dialogue on Christology', 54-55.

[89] See Brock, 'The Syriac Churches in Ecumenical Dialogue on Christology', 55-58.

and 2004, the PRO ORIENTE Syriac Dialogues, now renamed 'Study Sessions', have focused to discuss matters other than Christology, such as liturgy and sacraments.

The Church of the East and the Chaldean Catholic Church have reached important agreements in many areas. Establishing closer relations was already an objective stated in the 1994 Common Christological Declaration between the pope and the catholicos patriarch, as discussed above. Representatives of the Chaldean Catholic Church were already participants in the 'Joint Commission for Theological Dialogue between the Roman Catholic Church and the Assyrian Church of the East', which Mar Dinkha IV and John Paul II initiated in 1984 and which provided a basis for the subsequent bilateral dialogue.[90]

In 1996, the patriarchs of the Church of the East and the Chaldean Catholic Church met to outline the course of the discussion for the future which rested in part on the clear goal: the restoration of full ecclesial unity of the Church of the East. In pursuit of this goal the two patriarchs stipulated that the entire common theological, patristic, liturgical, linguistic, cultural and historical inheritance of both churches should be the objects of study and reflection.[91] A 'Commission for Unity' was established with the task of creating a common catechism, a common institute for training priests, deacons, and catechists, as well as other important cultural and ecclesiastical joint projects.

In October 2001, Rome issued a document entitled 'Guidelines for Admission to the Eucharist between the Chaldean Church and the Church of the East'. This two-page document covered the conditions under which Chaldean Catholics in the diaspora are permitted to receive communion in a Church of the East, and the question of the validity of the eucharistic prayer of Addai and Mari, employed in the Church of the East. This eucharistic prayer does not contain the words of Jesus 'This is my body ... This is my blood,' in Western terminology called the 'words of institution'. Roman Catholic usage requires the presence of these two formulae for there to be a Eucharist. These words of institution were added to the eucharistic prayer employed in the Chaldean Catholic Church.

---

[90] Dietmar W Winkler, *Ostsyrisches Christentum. Untersuchungen zu Christologie, Ekklesiologie, und zu den ökumenischen Beziehungen der Assyrischen Kirche des Ostens*, Studien zur Orientalischen Kirchengeschichte 26, LIT Verlag, Münster, 2003, 146.

[91] Dietmar W Winkler, *Ostsyrisches Christentum. Untersuchungen zu Christologie, Ekklesiologie, und zu den ökumenischen Beziehungen der Assyrischen Kirche des Ostens*, Studien zur Orientalischen Kirchengeschichte 26, LIT Verlag, Münster, 2003, 155.

Scholars in the Catholic Church determined that the eucharistic prayer of Addai and Mari is ancient, and that this prayer without Jesus' words is a valid eucharistic prayer.[92] Pope John Paul II approved this determination early in 2001. This is a significant move for the Catholic Church, which for centuries taught that without these words in the eucharistic prayer there is no eucharistic sacrament.[93]

Despite these successes, and maybe because the speed and scale of change, the dialogue came to a sudden halt in 2005 due to division within the Church of the East about the implications of relations with the Catholic Church and the real possibility of 'full ecclesial unity'. Pope Benedict XVI and Catholicos-Patriarch Mar Dinkha IV of the 'Assyrian Church of the East' met in June 2007 in Rome to renew the dialogue. Cardinal Kasper in an interview after the visit of Mar Dinkha IV to Rome said these divisions in the Church of the East, 'cause difficulties, since they are improperly used by some Assyrian media to cast doubt on the Catholic Church and its true intentions toward the Assyrian Church.' What both churches have had to confront is that the two communities have been formed by a distinct identity and history, which to bring together now is just as traumatic as the original break. These difficulties have also to be set against the difficult modern history of Iraq and Christian displacement by war and conflict across the Middle East. The question of how Christianity should be configured in the post-Ba'athist settlement still struggles around Assyrian and Chaldean identity. Rome is aware of this acute dilemma and the recent meeting between the Pope and the Catholicos was initiated to give renewed heart to the communities involved as they seek reunion of the Church of the East.

The reunion of the great catholicos-patriarchate of the East from the Assyrian and Chaldean Churches in union with the papacy would be a profound and great moment in contemporary Christianity. Today with the significant growth in Christianity in Asia it should be recalled that it was the Church of the East which was in historical terms the great evangeliser. Until the 14th century, the Church of the East stretched over a very wide area,

---

[92] Guy Vanhoomissen SJ, 'Une Messe sans paroles de consecration? À propos de la validité de l'anaphore d'Addaï et Mari', *Nouvelle revue théologique*, Vol. 127, no. 1 2005, 36-46; M Smyth, 'Une avancée œcuménique et liturgique. La note romaine concernat l'Anaphore d'Addaï et Mari', *La Maison-Dieu*, no. 233, 2003, 137-154.

[93] Dietmar W Winkler, *Ostsyrisches Christentum. Untersuchungen zu Christologie, Ekklesiologie, und zu den ökumenischen Beziehungen der Assyrischen Kirche des Ostens*, Studien zur Orientalischen Kirchengeschichte 26, LIT Verlag, Münster, 2003, 158.

from the regions of the eastern bank of the Euphrates to South-East Asia. It is said to have had a total of some 250 dioceses and a thousand monasteries, distributed between Mesopotamia, Persia, Turkestan, the Gulf, India, Tibet, China and Mongolia. Only time will tell how this ecumenical dialogue will be received but its significance should not be under-estimated.

During the period of Cheikho and Bidawid, both patriarchs had to confront difficult political situations, war, emigration, economic sanctions and societal breakdown, as well as regime change, which engaged their communities to a point where survival was the key issue. With the establishment of the first Ba'athist government in 1963 and the second in 1968 (the latter including Saddam Hussein), the Christians hoped that the secular and pan-Arab ideology of the new party would give them more rights than was the case under more traditional Muslim rule. Ba'athist Iraq was theoretically a secular republic where citizenship prevails over religious and communitarian allegiances. The 1970 constitution recognized 'the legitimate rights of all minorities in the frame of the Iraqi unity'; this was followed by the recognition of the legal existence of the five main Christian communities with due legal rights. They were not granted any special political rights, but as long as they co-operated with the government, Christians benefited somewhat from the regime. They had no difficulty repairing or even building churches. At one time the regime considered supporting the Chaldean church in building the largest Christian cathedral in the Middle East; however, this was dropped after the First Gulf War ended in 1991. Religious ceremonies could be performed without excessive discretion and there were seminaries for the training of the clergy, which is not the case in some states in the region.

At all levels of political life, the participation of Christians has been very limited; hence the important rôle that the respective patriarchs and leaders of the different Christian communities have in the encounter between the political and religious in the public sphere. The Christians communities became involved in the Iraq-Iran war, as it was almost certain that if Iran won it would have lead to an Islamic Republic in Baghdad. This view was reinforced by the poor treatment that Christian prisoners of war received in Iran during the Iran-Iraq war, which for many removed any allusion they had about what their fate would be under an Islamic republic.[94] Shi'ite radicals aimed their most furious

[94] 'Les chrétiens d'Irak' in J-P Valognes, *Vie et mort des chrétiens d'Orient*, Fayard, Paris, 1994, 735-766.

attacks at the Ba'athist regime. They had traditionally exploited the fact that one of Saddam Hussein's chief lieutenants, Tariq Aziz, was a Christian. Indeed, Christian influence into what was considered 'Muslim' lands is an extremely sensitive issue and was used as a potent weapon against the Ba'ath Party. Occasionally Shi'ite radicals indulged in anti-Christian diatribes. Christians in Iraq were deeply suspicious of this strain of radical Shi'a opinion. The imposition of Islamic government and Shari'a (Islamic) law would bring to Iraqi—Christians feared—only political, religious and cultural marginalization isolation.[95]

It is worth noting that Christians had a high death toll proportionate to their numbers in the Iran-Iraq war. The reasons for this can only be speculated at; however, it has been suggested that Christian military units had a strong history of fighting prowess, especially the Assyrians;[96] that they were fighting the forces of the Islamic revolution in Iran, who if they had won the war against Ba'athist Iraq would have significantly weakened the position of Christians in society; and a willingness by commanders to place Christian units in difficult military situations; Christians units themselves wished to prove themselves vis-à-vis their Muslim colleagues. The losses to Mesopotamian Christendom from all denominations suffered during these times have been enormous. Thus an idea arose in Iraq that the Christians paid a tax in disproportionate amounts of blood for their rights and survival. Although there are official no statistics the numbers of graves in the Christian cemeteries and the number of single women showed that the community was severely affected. Joseph Jacoub estimates 100 officers and 40,000 killed during the conflict. Before 1991 it was estimated that the Christian population was 1,200,000 who represented eight percent of the country's population.[97]

Ultimately, the Christians of Iraq suffered in much the same way as their Muslim co-nationals did, under an extremely oppressive, totalitarian regime, one that did not tolerate any form of collective institution not under its direct control. In spite of the fact that religious freedom was

---

95 A Baram, 'Two Roads to Revolutionary Shi'ite Fundamentalism in Iraq', *Accounting for Fundamentalisms: The Dynamic Character of Movements*, (eds) Martin E Marty and R Scott Appleby, The University of Chicago Press, Chicago/London, 1994, 566.

96 Large numbers of Assyrians joined the British military in the interwar period and became a feared fighting force see David Omissi, 'Britain, Assyirans and the Iraq Levies, 1919-32', *Journal of Imperial and Commonwealth History*, Vol. 27, 1989, 301-322.

97 Joseph Jacoub, 'The Christians of Iraq: A Historical Perspective', *Journal of the Assyrian Academic Society*, Vol. 5, no. 2, 1991, 19-35, 19, 32.

enshrined in the constitution, religions were closely watched. All social and pastoral activities of the Church require a previous authorization; religious publications were subject to censorship; and the importation and dissemination of foreign books was strictly under control. All the dignitaries of the Church, bishops, or heads of Churches, had to obtain a formal agreement from the authorities before starting their new function.

The war between Iraq and Iran, followed by the Kuwait war and the difficult living conditions during the sanctions period contributed directly to the acceleration of Iraqi Christian emigration.[98] Other factors played a role in encouraging Christians in Iraq to emigrate. For instance, there was a more general pessimism regarding the future of Christians in the Middle East as a whole, as even the Christians of Lebanon, who were regarded as a model and a refuge, were perceived as having been defeated at the end of the Lebanese civil war.

In the thirty years leading up to the Gulf War in 1990, the Chaldeans had seen more than 50,000 of their population migrate to the United States. It is estimated that following the war, more than 150,000 Christians left Iraq for various destinations.[99] Today it is estimated that some 200,000 Chaldeans are resident in North America. The Assyrians now count more than 60 percent of their community in Europe, Australia, and the United States, with an important community in Chicago. The percentage of Christians leaving Iraq during the late sanctions period constituted some 30 percent of all Iraqis leaving the country, while they form only 3 to 5 percent of the total population. The rate of Christians leaving Iraq has intensified since April 2003 with one third leaving the country and the region.

Bidawid was an important figure in helping to define papal policy towards Iraq; and obviously as head of the largest Christian Church attempted to act as an intermediary between Rome and Baghdad.[100] He also brought senior Catholic figures to Iraq; Cardinal Silvestrini, Prefect of the Congregation of the Oriental Churches visited Iraq in May 1993;[101] and the Catholic patriarchs of the Oriental and Latin churches visited in May 1994.[102] Pope John Paul II was a dedicated opponent of the embargo, as well

[98] A O'Mahony, 'Iraq's Christians on the edge', *The Tablet* , 15 March 2003, 6-7.

[99] J Habbi, ' Les chrétiens en Irak', *Proche-Orient Chrétien,* Vol. 47, 1997, 323.

[100] 'Iraq: Le gouvernment et la mediation du saint-siège', *Proche-Orient Chrétien,* Vol. 43, 1993, 139.

[101] 'Iraq', *Proche-Orient Chrétien,* Vol. 43, 1993, 140-143.

[102] 'Iraq', *Proche-Orient Chrétien,* Vol. 45, 1995, 143-145.

as of military measures. In his opinion is that the weak it was the poor who pay for mistakes of others in power for which they are not responsible. From the beginning, he had condemned this form of economic sanctions.[103]

The pope used all available diplomatic contacts with the UN, US, Europe and with Saddam Hussein to bring about an end of sanctions. In the year 2000 John Paul II had wanted personally to visit Iraq. Bidawid tried right to last moment to clear the path for a papal visit to Iraq without success. Pope John Paul II has said that he wanted as part of a biblical pilgrimage to thc Middlc East to visit the site of the ancient Ur, birthplace of Abraham, the ruins of which are located in southern Iraq. However, a combination of United States diplomatic objections and the need for the Iraqi regime to work with the UN regarding security for the papal visit and the fear that the pope might say something which would have been unwelcome by the Ba'athist regime meant that the papal pilgrimage to Iraq did not take place. While the aborted visit of the pope to Iraq was not due to Islamist pressure, it may have resulted in part from the Iraqi government's unease about a papal visit to a predominantly Muslim country. In any case, Iraqi Christians were immensely disappointed.[104]

The collapse of the Ba'athist regime in March 2003 and the death of Bidawid in Beirut on 7 July 2003, at the age of 81 after a long illness created a new situation and context for the Chaldean Church in Iraq. Bidawid left his patriarchal see in Baghdad eight months before and was not present in Iraq when the allies invaded Iraq. In his final years, he was often away from Iraq, particularly for health reasons. This was much resented by many in the Church who complained that it lacked leadership when it most needed it. His funeral took place on 12 July in the Chaldean Cathedral in Beirut and was taken by Cardinal Daoud, the Syrian Catholic Prefect of the Congregation for Oriental Churches.

Election of new Patriarch Emmanuel III Delly

With the death of Bidawid in Beirut in July 2003, the Christian communities were in a difficult situation, especially as the largest

[103] See Jean Toulat, *Le pape contre la Guerre du Golfe—Jean-Paul II censure*, OEIL, Paris, 1991 on the early development of papal policy towards Iraq. It had been estimated that some 800,000 childrean died during the sanctions period quoted the head of Iraqi caritas, Bärbel Dümler, 'Zur aktuellen Situation der Christen im Irak', 130.

[104] 'Papal Pilgrimage to Iraq', *Eastern Churches Journal*, Vol. 6, no. 3, 1999, 261-267.

group—the Chaldeans—had no clear spokesman for their interests in a rapidly changing political situation, and especially as the bishops had not succeeded in electing a new patriarch soon after the death of Bidawid. The Chaldean bishops made representations to the Paul Bremer, the US Civil Administrator of Iraq. In a 'Declaration of the Chaldean Bishops on the Role of the Chaldeans in the New Iraq' (3 September 2003), they requested that new government should have a Chaldean representative who would speak for the interests of the community. The reasons they cited were that the Chaldeans are the third largest grouping in Iraqi society after the Arabs and Kurds, that Chaldeans are heavily represented in professional and administrative sphere of Iraqi society especially in the north and in Baghdad, that their presence in the culture life of the country was much greater then their numbers would suggest, and that at one time the Chaldean patriarch had represented the community in the Iraqi senate prior to the formation of the Ba'athist Republic of Iraq. The statement followed an early one issued in the name of the patriarchs and bishops in Iraq on 29 April 2003, requesting the guaranteeing the civil, religious and political rights to Christians.

The election of a new patriarch to the Chaldean Church proved to be a difficult affair. From 19 August 2003 onwards the synod of the Chaldean Church met in Baghdad to elect a new patriarch. As with most Eastern Catholic churches, the head of the Chaldean church is elected by the bishops, and then 'recognized' by the Holy See with the issuing of a *pallium*. However, John Paul II in his later years changed this practice for a concelebrated liturgy at St Peter's in Rome and expression of eucharistic ecclesiology. For nearly two weeks the bishops were cloistered in the Chaldean seminary of St Peter in the Doura quarter in Baghdad, but could not agree on a candidate. The debates, which took place at the synod, were difficult; however, very quickly the Chaldean bishop of Aleppo, Syria, Antoine Audo SJ, was confirmed at one of the more serious contenders. Set against him were the two Chaldean bishops serving the important diasporas in America, bishops Ibrahim Ibrahim and Sarhad Yawsip Jammo.[105] However these two candidates apparently encountered

[105] Sarhad Jammo was a leading scholar of the Chaldean tradition see his published doctoral thesis: *La structure de la Messe Chaldéenne du début jusqu'à l'Anaphore. Étude historique*, Orientalia Christiana Analecta 207, Pontificum Institutum Orientalium Studiorum, Rome, 1979; and his recent study on Chaldean identity, 'Al-Huwiyyah al-Khaldaniyyah fi l-watha'iq al-tar'khiyyah' [Chaldean Identity in Historical Documents], *Najm al-Mashriq*, no. 46, 2006, 187-92; no. 47, pp 314-318; no. 48, 455-465.

political difficulties as many bishops in synod had opposing views on the US-led invasion of Iraq. Accordingly Bishop Audo received 12 votes and Bishop Jammo 8 votes. A minimum of 14 votes was needed to secure the position of the next Chaldean patriarch under the code of canon law for the Eastern Churches. [106]

The question of who would lead the Chaldean Church in a new Iraq was a key question, because it was in fact a question about the character of the Church's future identity and mission. Hence the choice of Audo was interesting. Audo had many attributes in his favour, he was relatively young (57), [107] a biblical exegete, with a specialist knowledge of the Qur'an,[108] a doctorate from the Sorbonne in contemporary Muslim political thought,[109] and a supporter of a constructive dialogue with Islam. At the Asian Synod, which discussed the important relations between Christians and Muslims, Audo set out his vision, 'To survive and develop as living Churches in the Arab and Muslim world of the Middle East, Christian Arabs or Asians need a spiritual vision of their relation with Islam, seeing themselves as sent by Christ to be witnesses of love,' and that evangelization in those lands requires Christians to live 'within Islam, that is, to form an integral part of society, of the Arab and Muslim culture without complexes, but at the same time to be witnesses of the evangelical liberty in ways that go beyond this culture, seeking to read the language of the Qu'ran as a language of human relations.'[110] However, he had disadvantages, he was born in Syria, he was a Jesuit and hence too 'Latin' a formation, and of late his knowledge of Sourath, the Syriac dialect spoken by the Chaldeans of Iraq. But he was Chaldean bishop in Aleppo from were Cheikho had been before he was elected patriarch in 1958.

After much discussion the Chaldean bishops decided that the new patriarch should be elected from one of the bishops who had responsibly

[106] 'Les chaldéens n'ont toujours pas de patriarche', *La Croix*, 5 September 2003.

[107] Born in Aleppo in 1946 he entered the Jesuits in 1969, ordained a priest 1979. He commenced his academic formation with a 'licence de lettres arabes', University of Damascus, 1972; a doctoral these, Paris III, Sorbonne, 1979. He completed his philosophical and theological formation with biblical studies at the Pontifical Biblical Institute (Rome). He was for a time professor in biblical exegesis at Université Saint-Joseph and Université Saint-Esprit (Kaslik).

[108] 'Approches théologiques du récit de Joseph dans Gn. 37-50 et Coran sourate 12', *Proche Orient Chrétien*, Vol. 37, 1987, 268-281.

[109] On the Syiran Alawite and political thinker, *Zakî al-Arsouzî un arbe face a la modernité*, Université Saint-Joseph, Faculté des letters et des sciences humaines, Collection Hommes et Sociétés du proche-Orient, Dar el-Machreq, Beyrouth, 1988.

[110] Declaration at the Asian Synod, February, 2003.

for an Iraqi diocese. In December 2003 a retired bishop was elected to head the Chaldean Church after the Vatican intervened to break the deadlock. Pope John Paul II called the Chaldean bishops to Rome to continue their deliberations, from which Archbishop Emmanuel-Karim Delly, a 76 year-old was elected Patriarch of Babylon of the Chaldeans on 3 December 2003, taking the name Emmanuel III.[111]

On 3 December the same day the newly elected patriarch and bishops were received by the pope, during the audience the elected patriarch asked the pope for *Ecclesiastica communio* whilst the pope encouraged the bishops to safeguard unity.

> Respect brothers, always be developing unanimous harmony which has been shown in this synod. Unity of purpose allows for full development of ecclesial life. Harmony is even more necessary when we think about your country, which today more the ever needs to be recalled peace and calm order. Work to unite the strength of all believers in a respectful dialogue which at all levels will encourage the building of a stable and free society.

On the 5 December, the cardinal Ignace Moussa I Daoud and Patriarch Emmanuel III Delly concelebrated the divine liturgy using the Chaldean rite at the altar of the 'Chair' at the Basilica of St Peter's and members of the synod where present. During this celebration the cardinal prefect confirmed the *Ecclesiastica communio*.[112]

Patriarch E Delly III who had the baptismal name of Karim Geries Mourad Delly was born on 6 October 1927 at Telkaïf, in the region of Mosul. He entered the seminary in 1940, sent to Rome in 1945 and continued his studies. Ordained 21 December 1952, he gained a degree in philosophy, a doctorate in theology and canon law; his thesis was translated into Arabic and published in 1992. On his return to Iraq in 1960 he was secretary general to the patriarchate of Patriarch Cheikho. He was promoted to patriarchal vicar and bishop in 1962 and participated in the Second Vatican Council. As well as his responsibilities at the patriarchate, he taught canon law at the seminary and Babel College. On 19 October 2002 having attained 75 he presented his resignation to the patriarchal vicar, but the following 10 December 2002, Patriarch Bidwid named

[111] 'Mgr Delly, patriarche de transition', *La Croix*, 5 September 2003.
[112] *L'Osservatore Romano*, 16 December, 2003.

him patriarchal chancellor and made him responsible for church *waqfs* (religious endowments).

The new patriarch began his ministry 21 December at the Church of St Joseph in Baghdad in the presence of some 300 people including officials, representatives of other churches, Muslim dignitaries both Sunni and Shi'ite. He took the opportunity to appeal for the unity of all Christians in Iraq at a moment of such decisive importance for Iraqi society. His election was welcomed with mixed feelings in the Chaldean community. Everyone understood that it was a temporary solution given the age of the new patriarch, to re-unite the two opposing currents which emerged at the time of the election. On the other hand people recognized his courage that he had remained close to the people during the most difficult moments of the war; also he gave a certain continuity as he had often appeared at the head of the Church during the last few years because of the numerous absences of the former patriarch. It was also Delly who had gone to Iran on a number of occasions to comfort and pray with the number of Iraqi Christian prisoners of war, who might be considered some of the most forgotten of all, still held in Iran since the ending of the Gulf War. John Paul II had often intervened personally on their behalf with the Iranian government and it was his blessings that Delly also delivered.

The election of a new patriarch for the Chaldean Church came at a point when the Christians of Iraq hoped for a new political context which would see the community thrive. However, since the Allied intervention in Iraq in 2003 which lead to the overthrow of the Ba'athist regime in Baghdad, the Christian community has been troubled by an increasingly unstable security and political situation which has lead to the displacement of tens of thousands within the country and the region. This has led some Christians to push the establishment of a 'Christian enclave' in the Nineveh Plain. Others argue that this would undermine Iraq's traditional multi-faith fabric and could turn the Christian community into an ethnic 'Assyrian' minority locked in its own ghetto. To date the plan does not have the support of all Christians, especially the majority of the Chaldean episcopate, but increasing insecurity means that the idea is gaining currency, although the debate over such a solution risks creating a division among Christians. The current plan for the 'Nineveh Plains Autonomous Unit' was formally proposed by Assyrian and other Christian activists at a conference held in Baghdad in October 2003.

The autonomous region, which would be centred on one of the largest concentrations of Christians in the country, would also contain a larger number of other ethnic and religious groups within its area.

The idea for a Christian 'enclave' a has deep history as it was originally proposed for the Assyrians at the end of the First World War with the creation of the British mandate for Iraq. The Assyrians gathered in the north of the country with their Iraqi co-religionists after being displaced from the Hakkari region in the then new Turkish Republic. The Assyrian Christians were formed at the time into the 'Iraqi Levies', one of Britain's most feared, effective and loyal fighting forces in the imperial army. Betrayed by colonial politics of the period, the Assyrian state never materialised; left unprotected these Christians suffered in the famous massacre of 1933 when over 3,000 were slaughtered. This led to further exodus across the Middle East and into the lands of exile in the West.

Today the issue of how the Christian presence should be protected has become an important political issue that evokes deep passions. In January 2007, the senior Chaldean archbishop, Louis Sako of Kirkuk, expressed his fears about the idea: 'The Nineveh plain is largely surrounded by Arabs, and Christians would serve as a useful and undefended buffer zone between Arabs and Kurds.' According to the archbishop, the best solution is religious freedom: 'In my opinion it would be preferable to work at the constitutional level and each area to guarantee religious freedom and equal rights for believers of all faiths throughout the land, including Christians, who can be found everywhere.' The Vatican has not given any open support to the plan to create a Christian enclave, but the meeting between Pope Benedict XVI and President Bush on 8 June 2007 certainly had this as a discussion point in the context of the future of Christianity in Iraq.

Should the Assyrian and Chaldean Christian communities disappear from Iraq, it would mean the end of their Syriac language (close to that spoken by Jesus) and their customs, rites and culture. A unique part of Christian patrimony would disappear along with this 1st-century Church. The United States and the United Kingdom would have presided over the destruction of one of the world's oldest Christian communities. Its reverberations would be keenly felt beyond Iraq's borders. If the democratic project of Iraq ends in dismal failure for the Assyrian and Chaldean Christian, the future will be bleak for all the historic churches of the Middle East.

THE SYRIAN CATHOLIC CHURCH: MARTYRDOM, MISSION, IDENTITY AND ECUMENISM IN MODERN HISTORY[1]

John Flannery

Early Western contacts with Syriac Christianity

The city of Edessa, under Count Baldwin, became the first Latin state in the East during the First Crusade (1098-1144). Relations between the Syrian Church and the Crusaders were generally cordial. According to the statement of Patriarch Athanasius VII (in office 1138-1166), recorded in the Chronicle of Michael the Syrian,[2] 'the Franks ... never raised any difficulty on the subject of faith, nor attempted to arrive at a single formula between all the peoples and languages of the Christians, but considered all those who worshipped the Cross as Christians, without enquiry or examination.'[3] A newly-elected Syrian patriarch was consecrated in a Latin Church in 1129.[4]

---

1 The definitive history of the Syrian Catholic Church remains to be written. This article attempts a brief synthesis from a wide range of material, principally published in learned journals (that the majority of works cited are in French serves to indicate the close relationship between France and the Syrian Catholic Church from its inception). The author acknowledges a particular debt to the following: Jean Pierre Valognes, *Vie et mort des Chrétiens d'Orient: des origines à nos jours*, Paris, Fayard, 1994, Olivier Raquez, 'L'Eglise syrienne catholique' in *Sacrae Congregationis de Propaganda Fide: Memoria Rerum 1622-1972*, J Metzler (ed.) Rome-Frieburg-Vienna, 1973, v.3 Part 2, 1815-1972, 19-28 (also of value for an earlier period than that covered by Raquez is: Joseph Metzler, 'Die Syrisch-Katholische Kirche von Antiochen' in *Sacrae Congregationis de Propaganda Fide: Memoria Rerum 1622-1972*, J Metzler (ed.), Rome-Frieburg-Vienna, 1973 v. 2 (1700-1815), 368-378), and Claude Sélis, *Les Syriens orthodoxes et catholiques*, in the series *Fils d'Abraham*, Editions Brepols, Tournai, 1988. Sélis' work is particularly useful, being described by reviewers as both a 'mini-encyclopaedia' of Syrian Christianity, and a 'Syriac Summa'. Arising originally from pastoral concern for Syrian Christians he encountered in Brussels, this erudite and informative work was deemed worthy of a favourable review in *Le Monde* (14/7/1989), under the title 'Ces chretiens parlant comme le Christ ...'. In addition to maps, illustrations, linguistic information and an extensive bibliography relating to Syrian Christianity, the book has chapters on history, doctrine, an anthology of writings, sacred art, spiritual life, a sociological profile, and the organisation of the Syrian Churches.

2 Published, with a French translation, as: Michael the Syrian, *Chronicle*, J B Chabot (ed.), 4 vols. Paris, 1899-1924.

3 Quoted in Sélis 1988, 33

4 John XI. Sélis (1988, 213) gives the dates of his patriarchate as 1130-1137, as opposed to the earlier date suggested by Valognes (1994, 357).

It was in this atmosphere that the first tentative steps towards union were taken. The friendship between the Latin Patriarch of Antioch, Aimery of Limoges (*c.* 1142- *c.* 1196), and his Syrian counterpart, Michael the Syrian, no doubt owed a good deal to the political situation in which they found themselves. They did, however, have much in common: both were scholars, both had reservations over the theological orthodoxy of the Greeks, and neither approved of the Orthodox Patriarch of Antioch. In the circumstances, the fact that both claimed to be the true successor of St Peter in the Antiochene see appears to have been considered of little consequence, with Aimery on one occasion arranging for the Syrian patriarch to make a full ceremonial entry into the city. Later, in 1178, when visiting the city, Michael the Syrian received a formal invitation to attend the Third Lateran Council in the company of Aimery. He declined the invitation, although he did write a treatise against the Cathars for the consideration of the Council Fathers.[5]

Sélis considers that both sides benefited from their encounter, claiming that relations with the Latins explain at least in part the Syriac cultural renaissance of the 12th and 13th centuries, the time of Denys Bar Salibi, Michael the Syrian and Barhebraeus. Conversely, Syriac texts, especially those of Saint Ephrem, were translated into Latin and influenced Western thought. Thomas Aquinas had occasion to read Theodore of Mopsuestia, and Latin biblical exegesis of the 13th century owes something to Antiochene exegesis, characterised by its typological approach.[6]

Negotiations between Innocent IV[7] and the Syrian Patriarch Ignatius III were sufficiently advanced for the Syrian Church to be invited to the Council of Lyon in 1245 with a view to reconciling differences between the Churches. This enterprise failed due to Latin intransigence over the sensitive issue of ecclesial autonomy, although some years later, under the influence of the Dominicans, a Syrian patriarch accepted union with Rome in a purely personal capacity. If the policy of the Latin Church at the Council of Lyon was largely that of *reductio*, with union seen as

---

5 On Aimery of Limoges and his ecumenical endeavours, see the article in Bernard Hamilton, 'Aimery of Limoges, Latin Patriarch of Antioch (c.1142-c.1196) and the Unity of the Churches' in *East and West in the Crusader States. Context—Contacts—Confrontations, II, (Orientalia Lovaniensa Orientalia* no. 92), Krijnie Ciggaar and Herman Teule (eds), Lueven, Uitgeveru Peeters, 1999, 1-13.

6 Sélis. 1988, 32

7 For relations between Innocent IV and Eastern Christianity, see Wilhelm de Vries SJ.' Innozenz IV (1243-1254) unt der christiche Osten' in *OstKirchlichen Studien,* v. 12 (1963) 113-131.

the return of an erring, wayward Church to the authority of Rome, the Council of Ferrara-Florence-Rome (1438-1445) posited a different ecclesiology which saw union as a coming together of equals; although a certain emphasis on papal authority was hardly surprising in view of Eugene IV's continuing struggle with the schismatic Council of Basel.[8] Having achieved his goal of union with the Greeks in 1439 after fifteen months of closely-argued discussion (centered largely on the addition of the *filioque* clause to the Creed), the indefatigable Eugene IV then sought union with the other Eastern Churches. Acts of union were signed with the Armenians (1439), the Copts of Egypt (1442), the Syrians of Mesopotamia (represented by Abdala, bishop of Edessa) in 1444 with the Bull Multa et admirabilia (the Decree Pro Syris), and finally with the Chaldeans and the Maronites of Cyprus in 1445. Unfortunately, the official records of the discussions of the Council of Ferrara-Florence-Rome have not survived, and although three somewhat partisan accounts of the negotiations with the Greeks did survive, we have no knowledge of how agreement with the other Eastern Churches was reached.[9]

With the fall of the Byzantine empire, the Syrian Church was once again cut off from the West. In spite of sporadic contacts with Rome, it would be only in the 17th century that a 'Syrian Catholic Church' would emerge (while the term 'Syrian Orthodox' would be applied to the section of the Church which remained outside the Catholic Church: the term 'Orthodox' here is not understood in the strict sense of acceptance of the first seven ecumenical Councils and the primacy of the Patriarch of Constantinople, but is applied to all the ancient Eastern Churches).[10]

---

[8] The 'conciliar' movement, which asserted the authority of Church councils over the pope, triumphed at the Council of Basel (1431-1439). A minority of council members joined the pope at the Council of Union with the Greeks in Ferrara, effectively restoring papal prestige. The rump of the Council of Basel went on to depose Eugenius, declared conciliar authority a truth of Catholic faith, and elected an antipope, Felix V (1439). It would be nine years before Eugene IV forced the resignation of Felix, and the proceedings at Basel, invalid after the council's transfer to Ferrara, were brought to a close.

[9] For a scholarly study of the Council of Ferrara-Florence-Rome free of the polemic which characterises many earlier accounts see Joseph Gill SJ, *The Council of Florence,* The University Press, Cambridge, 1959. For a useful summary and analysis which relates Florence to the Council of Lyon see *Histoire des Conciles Oecuméniques* Alberigo *et al* Paris, Editions du Cerf 1994 tr. Jacques Mignon from the Italian original *Storia dei conclii ecumenici* Queriniana, Brescia 1990, 273-290.

[10] Sélis 1988, 36

For political and historical, at least as much as for theological reasons, the agreements of the ecumenical council were not accepted in the East. This failure to achieve union at the level of the hierarchy of East and West led to the adoption of entrenched positions on both sides which would last for centuries. Within the Latin Church, faced by the fragmentation of the West, the emergence of nation states and the Protestant Reformation, a strong centralising tendency developed which emphasised the importance of uniformity and obedience to the authority of the pope as essential for authentic ecclesial life.[11] From this perspective, union with the Eastern Churches could once again only be seen a 'return' to Rome. Such a view provided a theological and ecclesiological justification for a new approach, which entailed the sending of Roman Catholic missionaries to work among the 'dissidents' of other Churches. This selective approach, allowing groups to retain their liturgical and canonical traditions, together with a degree of autonomy, and which led to significant unions with sections of the Eastern churches rather than the full union between sister churches envisaged by Florence, has been described as 'uniatism'.[12]

Origins of the Syrian Catholic Church

In the view of Roberson, three principal models were followed by Rome and its missionaries to achieve union.[13] It would seem that the model whereby Catholic missionaries worked to create a sizeable pro-Catholic minority within a local church, and then attempted to secure the election

[11] See Ronald G Roberson, *The Eastern Christian Churches* Rome, Pontifical Oriental Institute, 1999, 193, n. 4. Corroboration of the emphasis on acceptance of papal primacy may be found in an account of the Augustinian mission to the Mandeans of Hawizah (1623-*c.* 1651), where it is presented as the most fundamental issue, rejection of which will prevent any kind of religious or military assistance (cf. Carlos Alonso OSA, *Los Mandeos y las misiones catolicas en la primera mitad del s. XVII* [Orientalia Christiana Analecta, 179], Rome, Pontificium Institutum Orientalium Studiorum, 1967, 16-17.)

[12] Robert F Taft SJ, Rector of the Pontifical Oriental College in Rome, discusses the origins of the term and surrounding issues in the text of his address 'Anamnesis, not Amnesia: the "Healing Memories" and the problem of "Uniatism"', www.utoronto.ca/stmikes/theology/taft-kelly2000htm.

[13] Roberson 1999, 193-4, does, however, stress that it is dangerous to generalise about the histories of these unions, some of which represented spontaneous pro-Catholic movements among the Orthodox. Taft *(op. cit.)* goes further, warning of the dangers of mythologising and polemic in this context, insisting that 'uniatism' was not a Catholic invention but part of the spirit of the times.

of bishops or even a patriarch with Catholic sympathies, was favoured in the Middle East. In the case of the Syrian Church, the action of Capuchin[14] and Jesuit missionaries was strongly reinforced by French diplomacy, especially during this period, in the figure of the French consul in Aleppo, François Picquet.[15] He was responsible for smoothing obstacles in the way of the establishment of the new Church, whose first steps would be protected by France. The Maronite Church in the Lebanon also took an active part in the enterprise, which was further favoured by the existence of three rivals for the Syrian patriarchate.

So it was that in 1656, André Aqidjan, a Syrian from Mardin converted to Catholicism, was consecrated as the first Syrian Catholic bishop by the Maronite patriarch. In 1662, thanks to the efforts of Picquet, he was officially recognised as patriarch by the Ottoman authorities, although it would be 1677 before his investiture by Rome. As Valognes points out, the fledgling Church was, from the first, strongly influenced by France as a result of the circumstances surrounding its birth (the new patriarch wrote to Louis XIV in 1663 to ask for his protection), and this situation would be exploited by its detractors.[16]

On the death of Aqidjan in 1677, French diplomacy put forward as his successor the Syrian Catholic Bishop of Jerusalem (who would become Patriarch Pierre IV Sahbadin). However, the opposing candidate put forward by the Syrian Orthodox Church, managed to gain recognition from the Ottoman authorities, and persecution aimed at the 'Patriarch of the French' and his followers led them to form even closer links with France against their adversaries. Pierre IV died in exile early in the 18th century,[17] and his successor, Isaac ben Jubair, was forced to take up residence

---

[14] See Denise Thiollet, 'Les capuchins et la Congregation de la Propagande (1624-1647)' in *Revue historique, no. 280 (1988)*, 397-393.

[15] On the involvement of Picquet in religious affairs, see the two articles by Georges Goyau: 'Le rôle religieux du consul François Picquet dans Alep 1652-1662' in *Revue d'histoire des missions* v. XII (1937), 161-198; and: 'Un précurseur: François Picquet consul de Loius XIV en Alep et evêque de Babylone', Collection Institut Français de Damas, Bibliothéque orientale, no. 2, P Geuthner, Paris, 1942. Picquet later joined the Carmelite Order, and was Prior of Grimault in Provence when he was appointed in 1674 to the bishopric of Isphahan, at the age of 48. It took him a full seven years to journey to Isphahan to take up the appointment, establishing residence in Hamadan, before his death soon after in 1685.

[16] Jean Pierre Valognes *Vie et Mort des Chrétiens d'Orient: des origines a nos jours*, Fayard, Paris, 1994 358.

[17] On the Syrian Catholic Church in 18th century Syria, see Pierre Chalfoun, 'L'Eglise Syrienne Catholique en Syrie au XVIII ème siècle' in *Parole de l'Orient*, v. 13, 1986, 165-182.

in the French embassy before being permanently exiled. With his death in 1721 the line of succession of Syrian Catholic patriarchs was broken until 1783. In the intervening period a number of bishops returned to the Church they had left, others were driven from their sees, and some found exile in the mountains of Lebanon. During the Lebanese exile the Syrian Catholic Church was free to reorganise, thanks to the support of France, the Maronite Church, and the Druze Emirs.[18] Events changed somewhat in its favour towards the end of the 18th century, when a number of Syrian Orthodox dignitaries and monasteries embraced Catholicism and union with Rome.

The patriarchate re-established

In 1774 the Archbishop of Aleppo, Ignace Michel Jarweh,[19] along with four other bishops, and together with a number of other clergy and laity, joined the Roman Church. Eight years later, on the death of the Syrian Orthodox Patriarch Gregory III, Jarweh was elected in his place. His election was approved by Rome, and he received the pallium at the end of 1782. The Syrian Orthodox, however, rejected his appointment and went on to elect Matthew, the Bishop of Mosul, fiercely persecuting the converts.[20] Jarweh was forced to flee to the Monastery of Our Lady at Charfeh, at Mount Lebanon, which served as his patriarchal residence, and from where he devoted himself to restoring the confidence of the small Syrian Catholic communities of Tur Abdin, Aleppo and Mosul. The line of Syrian Catholic patriarchs has since continued uninterrupted, although not without some difficulties following the death of Michael Jarweh in 1800.

Only five days after the death of Jarweh, the Syrian Catholic episcopate elected, albeit *in absentia*, Cyril Bennam, Archbishop of Mosul as patriarch. On Cyril's rapid abdication, Ignace Michel Daher was elected in his place, being confirmed in office by Rome in 1802. He soon experienced

---

18 Valognes, 358.

19 The patriarchs of the Syrian Catholic Church followed the practice of their Syrian Orthodox homologues in taking the name Ignatius as a sign of their link to the ancient Church of Antioch.

20 For an account of the patriarchate of Michael Jarweh and the Syrian Catholic Church see Pierre Chalfoun, 'L'Eglise syrienne catholique sous le gouvernement ottoman au XVIIIème siècle' in *Parole de l'Orient*, v. 9, 205-238.

problems at Charfeh, where he was accused of despoiling the monastery of its goods,[21] and asked permission to move the patriarchal seat to Aleppo, where he had been a curate before his elevation to the patriarchate. He resigned his position in 1810 and moved to Aleppo. The Apostolic Legate to the Lebanon, Gandolfi, advised the Propaganda of events.

The Congregation, while holding Daher's resignation technically invalid, accepted it nevertheless, since Daher had been accused of resigning in order to avoid the obligation to make restitution to the monastery of Charfeh. Ignace Simeon Hindi Zora, Archbishop of Damascus was elected patriarch in 1814 and confirmed in office by Rome in 1818. His patriarchate proved to be a time of dissension within the Syrian Catholic episcopate. In 1816 he demanded the removal of his predecessor, Daher, from Aleppo, accusing him of scandalous conduct. He also came into conflict with Pierre Jarweh, Archbishop of Jerusalem and nephew of the former patriarch, who objected to the election of another bishop, Homsi. Jarweh was also accused of being a troublemaker by Gandolfi, and had numerous differences with Bishop Jules Anthony Amedina. Raquez points out that the Acts of the Propaganda provide evidence that disputes between bishops and patriarchs were not new.[22] In this connection, Bishop Moses Sabbag, deposed by Michel Jarweh, is frequently mentioned in the records. Sabbag had protested his deposition since 1790, and complained to the Propaganda in 1801 and 1812, before he received judgement in his favour in 1818. The resignation of Ignace Simeon Hindi Zora was accepted by Gandolfi in 1817 and confirmed by the Propaganda in 1818. Meanwhile, the Bishop of Aleppo, Denis Michel Hadaja had been elected Patriarchal Vicar in 1817 and confirmed by Rome in 1818.

Returning to Syria in 1820 after a long journey to Europe, Pierre Jarweh visited Gandolfi and then called a Synod of four bishops. He was elected patriarch and took the name Ignace Pierre Jarweh. The Apostolic Legate advised the Propaganda immediately, but confirmation of his appointment was delayed while the case was closely examined, not only because of Jarweh's somewhat troubled past, but particularly on account

---

[21] This was not a trivial charge. In confirming the monastery of Our Lady of Deliverance for the perpetual use of the Syrian Catholic patriarchs, Paul V declared that anyone distraining or alienating the property of the monastery would be subject to excommunication *latae sententiae*, with absolution from this penalty reserved to the Pontiff. The relevant document is given in *Bullarium pontificium Sacrae Congregationis de Propaganda Fide ...*, Rome, Urban College 1840, vol. IV, 201-2.

[22] Raquez, 1973, 21.

of concerns relating to his travels in Europe, and especially to Britain, France's rival in faith and diplomacy.

Jarweh had in fact undertaken his long voyage in order to find funding for the printing of Syrian liturgical books 'free of error'. Seeking to obtain Syriac printing type from the British government, he came into contact with what the Congregation referred to as the 'Bible sect',[23] whom they suspected of being the mainstay of the Protestant missionary movement in the Middle East. Continuing to maintain his claim to the patriarchate, Jarweh was summoned to Rome in 1824. He sent a delegate instead, who was refused an audience with the Congregation. In 1826 the Propaganda declared his election invalid, stating that, in the circumstances, there was no point in his requesting the papal sanction required for the confirmation of all Syrian Catholic patriarchs.

Jarweh now appealed directly to the pope, with the written support of a number of Syrian clergy in his favour against the Vicar, Hadaja. Leo XII passed his request back to the Propaganda, asking them to give the complainant a hearing. While some came to the support of Jarweh by trying to show his good faith in his dealings with the Bible Society, others remained distrustful. Among the latter was the Maronite patriarch, who had waged war on the Protestant missionaries and succeeded in having them expelled from Lebanon.[24] Finally, however, pragmatic considerations would win the day for Jarweh. With the death of Hadaja, the Propaganda recognised the danger of leaving the Syrian Catholic Church without a leader, and after Jarweh had confirmed his Roman orthodoxy and repudiated the 'Bible sect', his appointment was finally confirmed and he received the pallium in 1828.

Jarweh should have been based at the monastery of Our Lady of Deliverance at Charfeh, as his uncle had been. In fact he spent most of his time at Aleppo, holding that See as well as Jerusalem. This caused difficulties with the Apostolic Legate as well as with his own bishops. It

---

[23] The organisation in question is The British and Foreign Bible Society. Founded in London in 1804, the Society was in fact a non-sectarian organisation devoted to the spread of Scripture 'without note or comment'. An account of the Society written in 1819 speaks of translations having already been made into a number of languages, including Syriac (in an excerpt from Samuel Leigh *Leigh's New Picture of London,* W Clowes, 1819, given at www.londonancestor.com/leighs/rel-bible.html). Apart from the Society, it is likely that only the major university presses would have held type-metal for printing Syriac.

[24] David Kerr treats of this in 'Maronites and Missionaries: a critical appraisal of the affair of As'ad al-Shidyaq (1825-1829)' in David Thomas & Clare Amos (eds), *A Faithful Presence, Essays for Kenneth Cragg* Melisende, London, 2003, 219-236. Raquez 1973 (p. 23) makes reference in particular to his Order of 1823 against the Bible movement.

should be noted, however, that there were genuine difficulties with respect to residence at Charfeh. Chosen originally as a place of refuge, the local population was not Syrian Catholic, and the monastery was far removed from any significant Syrian dioceses.

In spite of earlier suspicions of being in sympathy with them, Peter Jarweh, aided by French diplomats and the Congregation of the Propaganda, was able to mount strong resistance to the influx of Anglo-Saxon Protestant missionaries whose principal weapons were the distribution of Bibles in the local language and ecclesial separation for converts to Protestantism. Jarweh's response was the widespread distribution of missals in Syriac.[25] He created a seminary at the monastery at Charfeh, reorganised ecclesiastical structures and increased the number of bishops. Supported by Rome, Jarweh's Church generally fared better in the face of Protestant proselytism than the Syrian Orthodox: indeed, several Syrian Orthodox bishops were so inspired by Jarweh's dynamism that they converted to Catholicism.

In common with the other Eastern Churches now in union with Rome, the Syrian Catholics sought recognition from the Ottoman authorities. Their emancipation was progressive: in 1831 they were placed under the jurisdiction of an Armenian Catholic and allowed to worship in their own churches. In 1845, thanks once more to French diplomacy, Pierre Jarweh was unofficially delegated full responsibility for the civil affairs of his community, before full emancipation in 1866 was achieved with the help of the Melkite Church.[26]

The archives of the Propaganda provide some statistics for the Syrian Catholic Church in this period. In 1836 Jarweh wrote to the Congregation that of the eight bishops of his patriarchate, seven were 'converts from schism', while the eighth, Gabriel Homsi, born a Catholic, was 'neither competent nor of good conduct'. The Acts of the Propaganda of 1840 contain a report from the Apostolic Legate, Villardel, on each of the Syrian bishops, and in the records of 1852 we learn that five of the seven Catholic bishops had converted from the Syrian Orthodox Church in 1827. The Orthodox patriarch of the time had been sympathetic to Catholicism but the majority of his episcopate opposed union. The patriarch was prepared to wait until a majority were in favour, but in 1827

---

[25] It would be interesting to know if these were printed with type obtained from the Bible Society in London.

[26] Valognes, 368.

the bishops in favour of union were not prepared to wait and transferred their allegiance to Rome without waiting for the rest of their Church.

The Acts of 1852 also provide statistics for the two areas into which Syrian Catholic dioceses were divided, and the number of faithful in each. In Syria: Beirut (100), Tripoli (0), Emessa (one family), Aleppo (2,500), Nebk and Kariatim (1,500), Damascus (300). In Mesopotamia: Mosul and Baghdad (6000), Diarbekir and Mardin (3000), Mediat (70 families). A total of 13,400 faithful plus 71 families.[27]

The price of strong Roman support for the Syrian Catholic Church would be an increasing degree of 'latinisation'. The policy of assimilation applied to the Eastern Catholic Churches, which began with Pius IX, found a zealous supporter in Benoît Planchet, nominated Apostolic Pro-Delegate to the Syrian and Chaldean Catholic Churches in 1851, the year of Pierre Jarweh's death. The Apostolic Delegate for the Lebanon, Villardel, was also involved in the affairs of the Syrian Catholics, and had nominated Gabriel Homsi as Patriarchal Vicar. In the face of internal dissension, Rome decided to nominate another convert from the Orthodox Church. Although Antoun Samhiri, bishop of Mardin, was widely recognised as a man of exemplary character, the bishops in Syria objected to this appointment, and to the transfer of the patriarchal see to Mesopotamia. However with the death of the aged Homsi, Samhiri was unanimously elected by a Synod meeting at Charfeh in 1853 in the presence of Blanchet. His election approved by Rome, the patriarchal seat was transferred to Mardin, where he continued as patriarch until 1864.

The Synod of Charfeh which had elected Samhiri continued in session as a legislative Council. Planchet was successful in having a considerable number of latinising measures adopted. After the Acts of the Council were sent to Rome for translation into Latin and Italian, however, Patriarch Samhiri complained of a number of inaccuracies, possibly on the basis that the Council had shown insufficient respect for Syrian tradition. The matter remained unsettled, in spite of pressure from the Propaganda, with the Conciliar text still not approved when Samhiri died in 1864.[28]

Samhiri's patriarchate was marked by persecution of the Christians of Syria, including the sacking of the Christian quarter in Aleppo. In

---

[27] Raquez, 24.

[28] This account in Raquez 1973, 25, appears to contradict to some extent the suggestion put forward in Valognes, 1994, 359, that the Syrian Catholic Church was characterised by an attitude of submission in response to Roman demands.

response he undertook a long voyage to Europe, in order to raise funds for the support of the faithful. A part of the substantial donations he collected was applied to the immediate relief of those in need, with the rest being put on deposit with banks in Europe and Asia. The Propaganda was aware of the sums collected by Samhiri, and, in order to protect them, suspended the election of his successor as soon as news of Samhiri's illness was received. Rome designated the Bishop of Aleppo, Denis Georges Chelhot, as Vicar-in-charge of the patriarchate. An election was allowed in 1865, subject to two conditions. The bishops were required to formally accept the transfer of the patriarchal seat to Mardin, and a project to share Samhiri's inheritance between the various dioceses was to be put in place. In 1868 the Synod gathered at Aleppo with Chelhot as president, and succeeded in reaching real electoral agreement which took up again the decisions of the Synod of Charfeh, with some modifications.

Ignace Philippe Arquosse was elected patriarch in June of 1868 and his appointment ratified by the Holy See on the word of the Apostolic Pro-Delegate. The agreement reached at the Synod of Aleppo was submitted to Rome and closely scrutinised. The Propaganda wanted to insert a number of conditions, particularly in relation to the election of bishops, which would reflect the Bull *Reversurus*. This led to extremely strained relations, making publication of the Conciliar decisions impossible, and provoking mistrust of the Roman authorities which would last throughout the Vatican Council (1869-70). The patriarch did not take part in any of the solemn sessions of the Council, and only Bishops Benni and Jarkhi participated in the sitting which promulgated the doctrine of papal infallibility, voting in favour. Behnam Benni, Bishop of Mosul, played an active part in the Council, where he was elected to the Commission for the Eastern Churches and the Missions. While he had some criticisms of the *schema* produced by this Commission, as an erstwhile student at the College of the Propaganda he had been strongly influenced by Latin ideas, especially in the realm of discipline. In the debate on the Constitution *Pastor Aeternus*, on papal infallibility, he effectively acted as spokesman for the Curia in opposition to the Melkite Patriarch Youssef, who defended the distinctiveness and autonomy of the Eastern Churches.[29]

---

[29] On the Melkite patriarch, see the entry by Joseph Hajjar, 'Gregoire Youssef' in *Dictionnaire d'histoire et de géographie ecclesiastique*, v. 22, no. 126 (1987), 53-59.

The Archbishop of Aleppo, Georges Chelhot, succeeded Arquosse on his death in 1874 and was responsible for a number of important initiatives. In the liturgical sphere he ordered the publication of the Syrian Great Breviary, published in Mosul in seven volumes between 1886 and 1896. He also attempted, with limited success, to create a religious order to evangelise Syrian Orthodox villages, but his most important achievement was the Council held at Charfeh in 1888 which would give the Syrian Catholic Church its own lasting legal framework. The Council, under the presidency of the Apostolic Legate, Louis Piavi, drew largely on the decisions of other Eastern Catholic Councils, but made no reference to the two preceding Syrian Catholic Synods. With the accession to the papacy of Leo XIII the pressure for assimilation of the Eastern Catholic Churches eased, although the personal disposition of the pope[30] was not strongly reflected in the initiatives of the Curia, and especially those of the Propaganda. The decisions of the Council of Charfeh were strongly influenced by Roman Canon Law, and show little evidence of the respect for the individuality of the Eastern Churches which inspired the pope, and which would lead to the publication of the encyclical *Orientalium dignitas* in 1894.

During the patriarchate of Behnam Benni, who succeeded Chelhot on his death in 1891, a number of modifications were made to the decisions of the Council of Charfeh. The proceedings of the Council were finally approved and published by the Congregation in 1896, although a number of its articles would never be applied. Benni actively participated in the Patriarchal Councils held at the Vatican between 24 October-8 November. With the Armenian and Chaldean patriarchs absent, and the aged Maronite patriarch represented by his Vicar, Eli Huayek, Benni was able, in collaboration with the Melkite Patriarch, Youssef, to make his views known. As noted, these two had confronted each other over Roman primacy at the Vatican Council, where Benni had shown himself favourable to Roman influence on the question of Eastern discipline. Now, however, they found themselves united against the policy of latinisation being pursued by missionaries in the Near East, and demanded firm measures to bring this to an end. They were equally united over what they saw as the excessive and damaging interference of Apostolic Legates in the affairs of the Eastern Churches, a view shared by Eli Huayek. Benni also played a part in editing *Orientalium dignitas.*

---

[30] For an account of Leo XIII and his attitude to the Eastern Churches, see W de Vries SJ, 'Leo XIII und die Orientalen' in *Stimmen der Zeit*, no. 169 (1961), 375-379.

The 20th century

Benni died at Mosul in 1897, and the Bishop of Aleppo, Rahmani, was elected patriarch in the following year at an episcopal Synod at Mardin, taking the name Ignace Ephrem. Rahmani was born of modest origins at Mosul in 1848. He studied at the Dominican run Syro-Chaldean seminary in the same town, before completing his education at the college of the Propaganda in Rome. While maintaining good relations with the Holy See, and with France and Austria, he was able to remain in favour with the Ottoman authorities and to provide effective care for his community in both the civil and religious spheres. In order to be closer to his faithful, he left the remote and mountainous Mardin for Charfeh, near Beirut. He spent one year at Mosul (1910-1911), re-uniting factions which had divided the faithful, and assisted various initiatives by Rome and France aimed at facilitating both French and Catholic presence in the Near-East. During the First World War, he worked to protect his community from Turkish persecution.

He was recognised as a man of considerable culture, and throughout his patriarchate published a number of works from the printing press he had established at Charfeh,[31] particularly in the fields of history, liturgy and translation. Rahmani also left a number of institutions as a legacy to his Church. In 1902 he created a seminary for Syrian Catholic clergy at the Mount of Olives in Jerusalem, entrusting its management to the Benedictines. In the previous year he had founded the Congregation of Ephremite Sisters of the Mother of Mercy at Mardin and at Harissa-Daroun. The Order would disappear in the turmoil of the First World War, but was refounded at Harissa in 1958. The patriarchate of Rahmani was a generally propitious time for the Syrian Catholic Church, with a considerable increase in members, particularly from the Syrian Orthodox Church. In 1913 several Syrian Orthodox bishops converted to Catholicism. However, as Valognes points out, the indiscriminate suffering of all the Syriac communities in the First World War would serve to cruelly underline the absurdity of such inter-Christian proselytism.[32]

The end of the war found the Syrian Catholic Church in disarray. Some of its traditional centres, such as the region of Mardin, had been

---

[31] For titles of some his major works, see the entry 'Rahmani (Ignace Ephrem II)' in *Catholicisme: hier, aujourd'hui, demain,* Paris, Letouzey et Ané, 1948- , 443.

[32] Valognes, 359.

reduced to ruins. Others, such as Aleppo and Mosul were flooded by refugees, among whom was Gabriel Tappouni. A Syrian Catholic bishop, and future patriarch, Tappouni had been condemned to death by the Turkish authorities and narrowly escaped the noose. The patriarchal see was transferred to Beirut as a matter of necessity. In spite of these difficulties, however, the Church authorities were not deterred from launching a new wave of proselytism, encouraged as they were by Benedict XV and protected by the French Mandate in the Levant. Many Orthodox from the Syrian community in Iraq converted to Catholicism. In 1930, a schism in the Indian Malankara Church (under the jurisdiction of the Syrian Orthodox patriarch) gave rise to the Syro-Malankara Church, which shares the Syrian Catholic rite but has its own autonomous structure.

The period of the French Mandate was, for the Syrian Catholics, a period of socio-cultural advancement and ecclesial renewal. However, far from preparing for independence and supporting mounting Arab nationalism, the Syrian Catholic Church appeared to count on a permanent French presence in the region, and continued to strengthen ties with Rome. Gabriel Tappouni, who became patriarch on Rahmani's death in 1929, had accepted the cardinal's hat in 1935, thereby recognising, at least implicitly, this Roman office as superior to his position as Syrian Catholic patriarch.[33] His clergy and faithful appeared unmoved by this course of events, although the identical situation caused considerable turbulence in the Armenian Catholic Church.

When independence came, the policy of the Syrian Catholic Church forced it to re-centre in the Lebanon, the country where the spirit of the French Mandate would remain strongest. Of the four churches (Greek and Syrian) whose communities were divided between Syria and the Lebanon, only the Syrian Catholic Church had its patriarchal see at Beirut rather than Damascus. With strong personal ties to France, to whom he owed his elevation to the cardinatial purple, Gabriel Tappouni would continue to pursue, until his death in 1968, the ideal of an Eastern Christianity drawing from the wellsprings of both Western and Arab cultures. A seasoned Vatican hand, he had the ear of the Curia and was adept at handling the rivalries between Roman institutions. During the Second Vatican Council, he was the only Eastern Church dignitary with a seat on the Presidential Council. Thanks to his efforts, his Church enjoyed

[33] Valognes, 360.

an influence out of all proportion to its small membership, although it may be argued that he would leave it somewhat ill-prepared for the reality of Arab nationalism and Islamic resurgence.[34]

Ignace Antoine II Hayek would prove a worthy successor to Gabriel Tappouni.[35] Born in Aleppo, he undertook lengthy studies in Rome, ending with a degree in Canon Law. Returning as a parish priest to his hometown, his involvement with charitable organisations brought him into close contact with the impoverished workers and refugees of Aleppo's shantytowns. He was elected Archbishop of Aleppo in 1959, and took part in all the sessions of the Second Vatican Council before succeeding to the patriarchate in 1968. He published numerous works, including histories of the monasteries of St Ephrem Al-Raghem at Chbénié, and St Ephrem at Mardin. In addition to revising all the liturgical books used in the Syrian Catholic Rite, he was the moving force behind the construction of a new cathedral in Aleppo and, despite the war, both the Cathedral of the Annunciation and the Church of Saint Behnam in Beirut. During Hayek's patriarchate, the Monastery of Our Lady of Deliverance at Charfeh underwent major restoration, happily without losing any of its traditional character. He also had the foresight to establish Syrian Catholic missions in the USA, Canada, Australia, Venezuela and Sweden, as well as renewing the mission in Paris and restoring the Procurature in Rome. Having served his Church for thirty years, he resigned in 1998 at the age of eighty-eight, and was succeeded by Ignace Moussa I Daoud.

Born in the village of Maskané, near Homs (Syria), Daoud began his secondary education under the French Benedictines at the Seminary of St Ephrem and St Benedict in Jerusalem, and completed his studies at the monastery of Charfeh, to where the seminary had been transferred in 1948 following the Palestinian conflict. After ordination in 1954, he returned to his home diocese and exercised various ministries at Homs before being sent to study Canon Law at the Lateran University in Rome. Elected Bishop of Cairo in 1977, he served in that role for seventeen years and was responsible for a number of projects, including the construction of the Cathedral of Our Lady of the Rosary and a new wing at St Michael's School in Cairo, a Parish Centre at Heliopolis and a medical clinic. Daoud

34 So Valognes, 1994, 360.

35 The information presented here regarding the successors of Gabriel I Tappouni is largely drawn from the excellent Opus Libani website on the Oriental Churches at www.opuslibani.org.lb.

also taught Canon Law at the Al Maadi Coptic Catholic seminary, and at the Sakanini Institute of Philosophy and Theology in Cairo. He served as Consultor to the Commission for the Revision of Canon Law for fifteen years, and then as a member for a further five years. As well as heading the Commission for the translation of the Canon Law of the Eastern Churches from Latin into Arabic, he became a member of the Congregation for the Doctrine of the Faith. In 1994 he was translated to the diocese of Homs, before being elected patriarch of the Syrian Catholic Church in 1998 and enthroned in the Cathedral of Our Lady of the Annunciation in Beirut. During Daoud's visit to Rome shortly afterwards, the pope chose to renew an old tradition. Rather than presenting a pallium to the newly appointed patriarch, John Paul II said that in order to 'recognise the dignity of the patriarchal duty' there would be a eucharistic concelebration, on the basis that 'The Eucharist is by nature the symbol which best expresses full communion, of which it is, at the same time, the inexhaustible source'. The pope went on to say that 'this gesture, which will remain engraved in the memory of the faithful, will be repeated' whenever a new Eastern patriarch visits the Vatican.[36]

On being appointed Prefect for the Congregation for Oriental Churches[37] in 2000, he resigned from the patriarchate in 2001, being granted in the same year the title of patriarch *ad personam*, and created cardinal-bishop.

The current holder of the title of Patriarch of Antioch and all the East of the Syrians is Ignace Pierre VIII Abdel-Ahad. Born in 1930, at Aleppo, he was forced, like his predecessor, to leave Jerusalem and continue his studies at Charfeh as a consequence of the Arab-Israeli conflict. Ordained in 1954, he spent the next ten years at the seminary at Charfeh in the roles of bursar, teacher and administrator. During this period he re-edited the *Dalil Al-Hadi*, an Arabic missal and prayer-book. In 1965, he was appointed to the Parish of St Joseph, in Jerusalem, with particular

[36] The visit is reported in *Eastern Churches Journal: a Review of Eastern Christendom*, v. 6, no.1, Spring 1999, 289-290.

[37] The Congregation for the Oriental Churches, one of the offices of the Roman Curia, was established in 1862 as part of the Sacred Congregation for the Propagation of the Faith and became an autonomous institution during the pontificate of Benedict XV. It has the same role with regard to bishops, clergy, religious and faithful in the Oriental Catholic Churches that other Curial offices have in relation to the Latin Church. The Congregation for the Oriental Churches also oversees the Jesuit-directed Pontifical Oriental Institute in Rome, an important centre for Eastern Christian studies.

responsibility for the Syrian Catholic communities of Palestine and Jordan, a role he fulfilled with zeal and devotion, especially in connection with prisoners of war and refugees resulting from the tragic events of 1962 and 1973. He undertook a number of projects in the educational and welfare fields for the benefit of both his parishioners and pilgrims. These included a children's home and a hostel for pilgrims in Bethlehem, as well as the Church of Saint Thomas, a youth centre, and a pilgrim's hostel in Jerusalem. He was also responsible for the construction of a church and presbytery in Amman, Jordan. A good communicator, he speaks French, English and Italian, in addition to Arabic and Syriac. In 1996, he was elected Bishop of Jerusalem and the Holy Land by the Holy Synod of Syrian Catholic bishops. He was elected patriarch by the Synod meeting at Charfeh in mid-February 2001,[38] and formally sealed communion between himself and Pope John Paul II by concelebrating a liturgy at the Vatican on 8 June of the same year.[39]

Membership

It is not easy to gauge the number of Syrian Catholics who owe allegiance to the Patriarch of Antioch and all the East of the Syrians,[40] not least as many Syrian Catholics in the Diaspora, lacking a parish of their own rite, attend local Latin or Greek churches, while still considering themselves Syrians.

The difficulty is compounded by the relatively embryonic nature of hierarchical structures in territories outside the traditional centres of the Syrian Church. The figure of 175,000 given in the statistical summary presented to the first Congress of Eastern Catholic Patriarchs and Bishops,

---

[38] His visit to Rome to request communion with Pope John Paul II as recognition of his election as a Catholic patriarch is reported in *The Tablet* 23rd June 2001, 920.

[39] The liturgy and the later meeting of the pope and Syrian Catholic bishops is described briefly in *Eastern Churches Journal: a Review of Eastern Christendom*, v. 8, no.2, Summer 2001, 306-307.

[40] The Catholic Syro-Malankara Church, while sharing the Syrian Catholic rite has a completely separate hierarchical structure, and thus will be disregarded here.

held in the Lebanon in 1999,[41] appears somewhat inflated in view of the more conservative consensus estimate of something less than 150,000 put forward by Valognes.[42]

The main centre of the Syrian Catholic Church had formerly, been in Turkey, especially in the region of Tur Abdin (with the patriarchate installed at Mardin for most of the 19th century).[43] This presence is now little more than a memory, and the majority of the 2000 or so Syrian Catholics remaining in Turkey live in Istanbul. Iraq is now the country with the largest number of Syrian Catholics, some 40,000-60,000. A Syrian Orthodox presence had developed much earlier in Northern Mesopotamia, among those who rejected the teachings of Nestorius, and this presence was increased in the 7th century due to persecution under the Emperor Heraclius. After the massacres of the First World War, many Turkish Syrians fled to northern Iraq, especially to Mosul and the region to the west of the city.

Separated from their traditional church structures, many of these emigrants passed to Catholicism, and for this reason there are more Syrian Catholics than Syrian Orthodox in Iraq.

Under the regime of Saddam Hussein the nation's 800,000 Christians were allowed to practise their religion in approximate freedom, co-existing peacefully with their Muslim neighbours. Christians did, however, suffer disproportionate losses in the Iran-Iraq war of 1980-1988.[44] The political situation in Iraq post-Saddam has brought new challenges for Christians of all denominations living there.

Syrian Catholic churches were among those targeted by car bombings in Baghdad and Mosul on 1 August 2004 which killed 12

---

41 Details of the Congress and the statistics presented are given at the Opus Libani website referred to above. Notwithstanding the question of total members, the statistics provide a valuable source of information on a number of aspects of the Syrian Catholic Church. The difficulty of estimating numbers is clearly illustrated by the fact that another section of the Opus Libani site (on the history of the Syrian Catholic Church) agrees with Valogne's figure!

42 *Op. cit.*, 367-8.

43 A remarkable and highly evocative collection of photographs illustrating Syrian Christian presence in the Tur Abdin region appears on the website of the Montreal Syriac Catholic Youth Club: www.clubsyriaque.org/diapo11.html.

44 For possible causes, see A O'Mahony, 'Christianity in Modern Iraq', *International Journal for the Study of the Christian Church*, v. 4, no. 2, July 2004, 121-142, which offers a recent analysis of the situation of Christians in Iraq.

people and wounded others, both Christians and Muslims.[45] The bombings were immediately condemned by Christian and Muslim leaders alike[46] (although not by Sunni religious authorities in Iraq), but whether the attacks were the result of an increase in Islamic radicalism, long suppressed under Saddam, or the work of insurgents seeking to cause further destabilisation of an already fragile situation, they are likely to lead more and more Christians to flee Iraq and join communities in the diaspora.[47] A further blow to Christians in Baghdad came on the second day of Ramadan (Saturday 16 October) 2004,[48] when five churches were again the target of bombers. On this occasion, with the first explosion at 4.00 am local time and others soon after, no casualties were reported, but all the buildings suffered damage, and St George's Roman Catholic Church in the central district of Karrada was engulfed in flames and virtually gutted. In an interview, the acting bishop of the Syrian Catholic Church, Father Raphael Qutaimi, accepted that the explosions will no doubt push people to emigrate. He went on, however, to say '... this country has been ours for thousands of years. Our ancestors shed blood defending it. We mustn't leave it.' He is clear that the attacks are the work of foreigners, not Iraqi Muslims, and went on to say 'The foreigner is trying to create division and

---

45 The website www.iraq4u.com reproduces *The New York Times* article by Somini Sengupta and Ian Fisher which reports the incidents. See also the article by Liz Sly, 'Christians feel the tide has turned on safety' in *Chicago Tribune,* 3/08/2004, which quotes the AFP news agency report in which Iraq's national security adviser, Mouwafak al-Rubaie, implicates Abu Musab al-Zarqawi, the Jordanian terrorist accused of leading Al Qaeda in Iraq, in the bombings. Al-Zarqawi's motive is said to be that of driving a wedge between the Muslim and Christian communities.

46 See, for example, *The Joint Muslim-Christian Communiqué on Iraq Church Bombings* issued by the Middle East Council of Churches (MECC) and the International Islamic Forum for Dialogue on 2 August, at the website of the MECC at www.mecchurches.org.

47 In the immediate wake of the bombings, it is hardly surprising that attendance at the Syrian Catholic church in Baghdad fell by as much as 90 percent. Pascale Isho Warda, a Christian who is the interim government's Minister for Displacement and Migration, estimates that 15.000 Iraqi Christians have left the country in the three months following the August attacks (quoted in the article by Scheherezade Faramarzi of Associated Press, 'Iraq church bombings leave empty pews', in *Seattle Post -Intelligencer,* 16 October 2004).

48 Coincidentally, on the day before the attacks, Zarqawi's Tawhid wal Jihad (Unity and Holy War) group was declared a terrorist organisation by Washington and subjected to economic sanctions (reported in 'Iraqi Christians targeted in spate of bombings at Baghdad churches' on channelnewsasia.com: the article may be accessed at www.channelnewsasia.co/stories/afp_world/view/112009/1/.html.

emnity between Christians and Muslims. We must stand hand in hand and heart in heart and not give the outsider cause to divide us.'[49]

The other strongholds of Syrian Catholicism are in Syria and Lebanon, each with some 20,000 people.[50] Most of these are descendants of emigrants who left Turkey in the wake of the First World War, and grafted onto much older populations. At Aleppo, in Syria, there was already a Syrian Catholic community dating back to the foundation of the Church in the 17th. century, while in the Lebanon a Syrian Catholic presence was established in the 18th century, fleeing Ottoman persecution and transferring the patriarchal see to Charfeh for a time. Presence in Syria is divided between large towns (3000 in Damascus and 5000 in Homs), and in the Lebanon largely in Beirut. Elsewhere in the Middle East, Syrian Catholic presence is now very small and diminishing all the time, with some 2000 in Egypt and half that number in Israel-Jordan. Figures for the diaspora, largely in the Americas and Europe, are perhaps 50,000.

Institutions

Efforts to develop monastic life within the Syrian Catholic Church have met with little success. The three monasteries, Mar Moussa Al-Habchi near Nebek in Syria, Mar Semaan the Stylite near Aleppo, and Charfeh at Daroun-Harissa in the Lebanon, counted a total of only eight religious plus four postulants and four novices, according to the 1999 report to the Patriarchal Congress. Charfeh also serves as a seminary and residence for twelve seminarians studying at the Pontifical Theological Faculty at the Université Saint-Esprit de Kaslik (USEK) in Jounieh. There is a minor seminary at Aleppo. The only congregation of nuns, the Ephremite Sisters, Daughters of the Mother of Mercy, had thirteen professed members and four postulants in 1999. The motherhouse of the Order, near Charfeh, has charge of two Missions in Syria and an orphanage for young girls.

The Church has a total of eight schools in the Lebanon, Syria, and Egypt, in addition to a number of welfare projects and dispensaries divided between Iraq, the Lebanon, Syria and Egypt, and two hospices for pilgrims in the Holy Land.

---

[49] Qutaimi's interview is quoted in the American newspaper article referred to in note 43 above.

[50] In the absence of more recent data (unfortunately the report to the Patriarchal Conference of 1999 does not give a breakdown of numbers) the figures given by Valognes are cited here.

Liturgical life

Despite strong Roman influence on both its mentality and structures, the Syrian Catholic Church has nevertheless preserved an authentic Syro-Antiochene liturgy. Latin usage, agreed at the Synod of Charfeh in 1888, was limited to the administration of certain sacraments. From that time on, the rite of penance has followed that of the Roman Church, even though the Syrian Church has several. The rites for sickness and death, however, remain peculiar to the Syrian Church. The liturgical year largely follows the Roman calendar,[51]having imported a number of Latin feasts such as the Immaculate Conception and All Saints. Otherwise, the canonical customs and liturgical tradition of the ancient Syrian Church continue to hold sway.

In spite of the astonishingly rich legacy of liturgical texts possessed by the West Syrian Church,[52] both Syriac Orthodox and Syrian Catholics habitually use only two anaphoras (eucharistic prayers), that of St. James for great feasts, and that of the Twelve Apostles for ordinary Sundays.[53]

The Syrian Catholic rite differs from that of the Orthodox only in certain details. Where the Orthodox use only wine, the Catholics use wine and water, and only the Catholics include the *filioque* clause in the Creed.

Organisation

The spiritual leader of all Syrian Catholics throughout the world is the Patriarch of Antioch and all the East of the Syrians, currently His Beatitude Ignace Pierre VIII, with his patriarchal see in Beirut. The patriarch is chosen by a Synod and the appointment confirmed by Rome.[54]

---

[51] See Sélis, 188-196, for a summary of the liturgical year and a summary of the calendar of saints. References to more complete and detailed calendars are given on p. 194.

[52] Some seventy Eucharistic Prayers, according to Sélis (p. 181. Publication of Syriac anaphoras with a Latin translation on facing pages was begun under the editorship of A Raes in 1939 as *Anaphorae Syriacae*, and continues under the auspices of the Pontifical Institute for Eastern Studies, Rome).

[53] Sélis gives a description of the Eucharistic liturgy 184-188. The same chapter contains useful information on the origin of the West Syrian anaphoras and on the layout of Syrian churches.
The English text of a Syrian Catholic Eucharistic liturgy may be found at the site of the Syrian Catholic Eparchy of Newark, www.syrian-catholic.org.

[54] As Valognes points out (p. 360), this reservation of confirmation to Rome can be effectively interpreted as a nomination (so also Sélis, p. 211).

The Church comprises nine eparchies (dioceses),[55] mostly in the Middle East. Syria has four; Damascus, Homs and Emessa, Aleppo, and Hassaké, Iraq has Baghdad and Mosul, Egypt has the diocese of Cairo, and the Lebanon Beirut. Outside the territory of the patriarchate, the eparchy of Our Lady of Deliverance, Newark, established in 1995, serves Canada and the United States. There are also a total of twelve Titular Sees.

In addition, there are exarchates (provinces governed by a bishop subject to the authority of the patriarch, but with wider jurisdiction than diocesan bishops) for Iraq, Jerusalem and the Holy Land (including Jordan and Palestine), Sudan, Turkey, and Venezuela, and Syrian Catholic Missions in Brazil (Belo Horizonte), Australia (Concord, NSW), and France (Paris). The Patriarchal Procurature in Rome, founded at the beginning of last century, is responsible for relations with the Congregation for Eastern Churches, as well as assisting Syrian Catholic seminarians studying in Rome, and serving Syrian families in the locality.

Fourteen bishops (two retired) serve the nine dioceses, exarchates and missions, and are responsible for almost sixty parishes, with seventy-five priests and six deacons.

The future

A somewhat negative assessment of the Syrian Catholic Church, such as that of Valognes[56] may suggest that there is in fact little justification for it having an autonomous hierarchical structure, and that attachment to a neighbouring local Church is the logical course of events. It is true that the acceptance of a degree of latinisation has resulted in a loss of religious specificity, whereby the Syrian Orthodox Church may be seen as the truer repository of the ancient Syriac liturgical tradition. The vicissitudes of history have resulted in the majority of its faithful in the Middle East being in a country (Iraq) where it finds itself a 'foreign' Church in the presence of a 'national' Chaldean Catholic Church. In its birthplace, Turkey, it is not protected by the treaty of Lausanne and suffers the ill-will of local authorities as both a Church with a Syrian culture and one affiliated to

[55] Information here is drawn from the report to the Patriarchal Conference referred to above, supplemented in some details from *Catholic Dioceses of the Syrian Church in the World* at www.ca-catholics.net/dioceses/data/rites.htm, the Opus Libani site.

[56] Valognes (361-2) extends this to the entire Syriac tradition.

Rome, that is to say doubly foreign. In Syria it is still viewed with some distrust due to its earlier closeness to the mandatory power, and in the Lebanon has suffered greatly in the war.

Against this background, however, there are encouraging signs. While the hierarchy may indeed be stretched to provide pastoral care for its people in the diaspora,[57] the creation of new dioceses and exarchates, such as those of Newark and Venezuela respectively, indicates the importance given to it.

The existence of a group such as the Montreal Syriac Catholic Youth Club shows that the laity is also prepared to play an active part in meeting the challenges of being Syrian Catholics in the West. The group has some 250 members drawn from professionals and university students, and works to support the wider Syrian Catholic community through a variety of endeavours.

In the Middle East, the Syrian Catholic Church shoulders with other Churches of the region, the continuance of Christian witness,[58] often in difficult and dangerous circumstances, in the land where Christianity began In addition to sharing the sufferings of their Muslim neighbours, they are also actively involved in ecumenical initiatives. Chief among these is the Middle East Council of Churches (MECC),[59] which the Eastern Catholic Churches joined in 1990.[60] The MECC provides a meeting place for member Churches (Oriental and Eastern Orthodox, Catholic, and Protestant) in Arab countries, Turkey, Iran, Palestine/Israel and Cyprus, and promotes co-operation between them in religious education, service to the poor, interreligious understanding, and issues of justice and peace. The MECC model of co-operation between Churches where difficult

---

[57] The pressing need for the faithful in the diaspora, particularly in Canada, Venezuela and Australia, to have a more developed Church structure, was acknowledged by Patriarch Ignatius Moussa I Daoud at the audience with John Paul II on his visit to Rome referred to above (n. 39).

[58] A witness which would be rendered largely ineffective by the 'ghettoisation' of Iraqi Christians in 'safe havens' called for by some commentators in the West. Cf. the article in *The Tablet* by Michael Hirst (23/10/2004, p. 32), which refers to the article by Nina Shea, 'Canary in a Coal Mine', in the American *National Review*, 14/10/2004. Shea's article can be read in full at www.nationalreview.co/script/p.../shea200410140830.as.

[59] The MECC arose from the same initiatives which would lead to the establishment of the World Council of Churches, initiatives in which Eastern Christianity was central.

[60] In contrast to the situation in the World council of Churches, where the Catholic Church remains an involved observer, rather than member.

issues can be discussed in a fraternal aspect of mutual respect is remarkable and all too rare.[61]

---

[61] The well known difficulties in recent Catholic-Orthodox dialogue in Eastern Europe are detailed in Ronald G Roberson *The Eastern Churches: a brief summary*, Rome, Pontifical Eastern Institute, 1999, 189-236.

A concrete example of the Middle Eastern approach is the October 1996 meeting of Catholic and Orthodox Patriarchs at Charfeh to discuss the issues relating to mixed marriages, a common catechism, and first communion. Relaxing the harsh canonical proscriptions of both Catholic and Orthodox Churches, the new agreement allows the wife to retain membership of the Church to which she belongs, the marriage is to be held in the Church of the husband (with the participation of the minister of the wife, should he be present), and the baptism of children to be into the Church of the husband. Recognising a shared Antiochene heritage, a common catechism is to be produced (albeit one which recognises and respects differences in the teaching and liturgical praxis of each ecclesiastical tradition. In order to avoid problems of inter-communion, and in view of the fact that Orthodox children receive the Eucharist at baptism, the patriarchs resolved that first communion for Catholic children should also take place in a parish setting, rather than in school as had become the common practice. For further information on the joint agreement see www.opuslibani.org.lb/cpco/accordcatholique.html. It must be noted, however, that in spite of truly ground-breaking and theologically significant ecumenical advancements such as the joint statement of 1991 on the doctrine of Christ published by The Patriarch of the Church of the East and Pope John Paul II, and the 2001 agreement that inter-communion is permissible in certain circumstances between the Chaldean Church and the Church of the East, disputes such as that which lend to the continued exclusion of the Church of the East from the MECC on grounds of Christological difference can still cause disharmony between Oriental Churches.

On progress in overcoming Christological differences, see Gerald O'Collins and Daniel Kendall, 'Overcoming Christological Differences', *The Heythrop Journal: A Quarterly Review of Philosophy and Theology*, v. 37, 1996, 382-90; Sebastian Brock, 'The importance of the Syriac traditions in ecumenical dialogue on Christology', *Christian Orient* v. 20, 1999, 189-197; and S Brock 'The Syriac Churches in Ecumenical Dialogue on Christology', in A O'Mahony (ed.), *Eastern Christianity: Studies in Modern History, Religion and Politics,* Melisende, London, 2004, 44-65.

On the agreement on intercommunion, see Frans Bouwen, 'Assyriens et Chaldéens: admission mutuelle à l'eucharistie' *Proche-Orient Chrétien* (Jerusalem), v. 51, 2001, 333-47; Robert F Taft 'Mass without the Consecration? The Historic Agreement on the Eucharist between the Catholic Church and the Assyrian Church of the East, Promulgated 26 October 2001'. *Worship,* v. 77, no. 6 2003, 482-509.

For the impact of the agreement on Catholic theology, see Robert Murray SJ, 'Tradition and Sacred Texts' *International Journal of Systematic Theology,* v. 6, no. 1, 2004, 4-20.

On the background to the exclusion of the Church of the East from the MECC, see Otto Meinardus, 'About heresies and the *Syllabus Errorum* of Pope Shenuda III', *Coptic Church Review,* v. 22, no.4. 2001, 98-105 and the response by S Brock, ' "About heresies and the *Syllabus Errorum* of Pope Shenuda III". Some Comments on the Recent Article by Professor Meinardus', *Coptic Church Review,* v. 23, no. 4, 2002, 98-102.

The Syrian Catholic Church and others Churches of the region, perhaps working through MECC, may also be able to play a key bridge-building role between the cultures of East and West, something of which we certainly stand in need.[62]

[62] The significance for dialogue of non-Western Christianity, particularly in the context of Islam, is touched on by Adel Sidarus (himself a member of the Catholic Copt Church) in a paper presented to the opening conference of the European seminar, 'The Mediterranean-cooperation and (for) the construction of Europe' at a meeting of ICMICA-Pax Romana at Reggio Calabria in Italy, 21-23 May, 2004. The as yet unpublished paper is entitled 'Twenty propositions on Islamo-Christian dialogue in a Mediterranean context'.

HEBREW CATHOLIC THOUGHT, THEOLOGY AND POLITICS IN CONTEMPORARY ISRAEL

Leon Menzies Racionzer

The establishment of the State of Israel in 1948 created a unique situation in which Christians became a minority for the first time in nearly two millennia in a dominant Jewish majority.[1] The Arab-Israeli conflict in 1948 displaced some 60,000 Christians amongst an estimated 700,000 Palestinians who have never been allowed to return to their homeland.[2] Thereafter Latin and Eastern Catholics numbered slightly less than Orthodox Christians in the New State.[3] The State of Israel originated, as a 'secular state'; the Zionist movement was not primarily a religious

---

1 For a general survey, see Ian Lustick, *Arabs in the Jewish State. Israel's Control of a National Minority*, University of Texas Press, Austin, 1980. For the position of the Christian communities within the State of Israel and the historical background, see Ammon Kapeliouk, *Les arabes Chrétiens en Israël (1948-1957)*, Thèse de doctorat, Sorbonne, 1968; A Kapeliouk, 'L'État social, économique, cultural et juridique des Arabes chrétiennes en Israël', *Asian and African Studies* Vol. 5 (1969), 51-95; Anthony O'Mahony, 'Palestinian Christians: Religion, Politics and Society, c. 1800-1948', *Palestinian Christians: Religion, Politics and Society in the Holy Land*, (ed.) Anthony O'Mahony, London, 1999, 9-55; A O'Mahony. 'The Religious, Political and Social Status of the Christian Communities in Palestine, c. 1800-1930', *The Christian Heritage in the Holy Land*, eds. A O'Mahony, with G Gunner and K Hintlian, Scorpion Cavendish, London, 1995, 237-265; A O'Mahony. 'The Christian Communities of Jerusalem and the Holy Land: A Historical and Political Survey', *'The Christian Communities of Jerusalem and the Holy Land: Studies in History, Religion and Politics*, (ed.) A O'Mahony, University of Wales Press, Cardiff, 2003, 1-37.

2 Charles M Sennott, *The Body and The Blood*, Perseus Books Group 2001 25-26.

3 For a general description of the Christian communities in Jerusalem and the Middle East, see Frans Bouwen, 'The Churches in the Middle East' and 'The Churches in Jerusalem', Lawrence S Cunningham (ed.), *Ecumenism. Present Realitiesand Future Prospects*, University of Notre Dame Press, 1998, 25-36 and 37-49. On position of Christianity in Jerusalem, Israel, Palestine since 1948, see Bernard Sabella. 'Socio-economic Characteristics and Challenges to Palestinian Christians in the Holy Land' *Palestinian Christians. Religion, Politics and Society in the Holy Land, op. cit* 82-95 and 'Palestinian Christians: Realities and Hopes', *The Holy Land, Holy Lands, and Christian History: Studies in Church History*, Vol. 36 (2000), 373-397. Andrea Pacini. 'Socio- Political and Community Dynamics of Arab Christians in Jordan, Israel, and the Autonomous Palestinian Territories', *Christian Communities in the Middle East: The Challenge of the Future*, A Pacini (ed.), Clarendon Press, Oxford, 1998, 259-285.

impulse.[4] Some ultra religious Jews were anti-Zionist whilst other religious Jews were 'lukewarm' Zionists. However, the 1967 war created a shift in Zionism from being mainly secular to being an ideology with a predominantly religious character. 'Since then a strong component of successive Israeli governments has been the Jewish religious parties.'[5] Since 1967, there has also been 'a change in the character, content and outlook of the "religious" Jew in Israel.'[6]

Shortly after the establishment of the State of Israel a few Catholic thinkers saw the 'in-gathering' of the Jews in *Eretz-Israel* as the fulfilment of the Biblical prophecies, (Psalm 147:2) perhaps a naïve Zionism that had ironically more of a religious element than that of the original Jewish Zionists.[7]

Many of these Catholic thinkers, some of Jewish origin, endeavoured to create a Hebrew Catholic theology that would bear fruit as a community of Hebrew Catholics within Israel that would retain its Jewish identity.

---

[4] The main impulse in Zionism was the re-birth of a specifically Jewish nationalism as an alternative to Jews around the world either fighting a losing battle to be granted the rights of other citizens, or to bring about revolutionary change in the Jewish situation by changing the whole order in society through such as Socialism and Marxism but most of all as a reaction to the persecutions in Eastern Europe and the Russian Empire particularly. The leader of this political Zionism was Theodor Herzl who said of the first Zionist Congress in Basle in 1897 'At Basle I founded the Jewish State.' Cf. Martin Gilbert, *From The Ends of the Earth: the Jews in the Twentieth Century,* Cassell & Co, London, 2001 20-21 'Zionism [as a political movement) synthesized the two goals, liberation and unity, by aiming to free the Jews from hostile and oppressive alien rule and to re-establish Jewish unity by gathering Jewish exiles from the four corners of the world to the Jewish homeland.' Cf www.mfa.gov.il/mfa *Zionism,* Professor Benyamin Neuberger see also for a general description Raymond J Tourney, op 'La Terre Promise hier et aujourd'hui', *Proche-Orient Chrétien* (Jerusalem), Vol. 39, 1989, 35-59.

[5] See the work of the Anglican Palestinian theologian Canon Naim Ateek, 'Putting Christ at the Centre', *The Bible and the Land*, Lisa Loden, Peter Walker, Michael Wood (eds), Musalaha 2000, 55.

[6] Clive Jones, 'Ideo-Theology and the Jewish State: From Conflict to Concilliation?' *British Journal of Middle Eastern Studies,* Vol. 26, 1999, 9-26; Shmuel Sandler, 'Religios Zionism and the State: political accommodation and religious radicalism in Israel', *Religious Radicalism in the Greater Middle East,* Bruce Maddy-Weitzman and Efraim Inbar (eds.), Frank Cass, London, 1997, 133-154; and Mark Tessler, 'Religion and politics in the Jewish State of Israel', *Religious Resurgence and Politics in the Contemporary World*, Emile Sahiyeh (ed.), State University of New York Press, New York, 1990.

[7] It has been suggested by Revd John Sansour that this attitude may have gone some way in helping Israeli Jews commit injustices against the Arab population; cf. 'Hearing the Different Voices', *The Bible and the Land*, Lisa Loden, Peter Walker, Michael Wood, Musalaha (eds.), 2000, 140.

This paper will give the history of the emergence of these communities in Israel since 1948, biographical details and theological thought of some of the prominent Jewish-Catholic thinkers of whom some were founding members of the *Oeuvre de Saint Jacques l'Apôtre's* known as the *kehilla*,[8] and of the *Maison Saint Isaïe*, The House of Isaiah. It will compare their differing theologies of the Jews and Judaism, their vision for a Jewish Christian ecclesia and engage with the factors that militate against the growth of such an ecclesia. Finally it gives a brief history of the origins of the Latin patriarchate amidst Eastern-Rite churches and the politics of ecclesiology in contemporary Israel.

THE HISTORY OF THE EMERGENCE IN ISRAEL OF HEBREW CATHOLIC COMMUNITIES SINCE 1948

Two years after the founding of the State of Israel, Father Albert-Marie Avril, the Provincial of the Paris Dominican Province, wished to set up a centre for Jewish studies in the Jewish sector of Jerusalem [9] on similar lines to the Dominican centre for Islamic studies in Cairo.[10] The study centre, later known as The House of Isaiah, was not founded until two years after the founding of the Cairo house.

Father Bruno Hussar OP, who was born in Egypt of Hungarian Jewish parents, was regarded by the Provincial as the most suitable person to set up the centre for Jewish studies. But upon arrival in Jaffa in June of 1953 he found a ready-made group of Hebrew Catholics waiting for a priest. According to the American Catholic Historian of Christians in the

---

8 The word *kehilla* meaning community is singular meaning 'the community' but in fact there are four separate communities within the *Oeuvre.*

9 Prior to the Yum Kippur war in 1967 Jerusalem was divided into Jordanian and Israeli sectors: see Anthony O'Mahony, 'The Vatican, Palestinian Christians, Israel, and Jerusalem: Religion, Politics, Diplomacy, and Holy Places, 1945-1950', *Studies in Church History: The Holy Land, Holy Lands, and Christian History* Vol. 36 (2000), 358-359.

10 There was not wholehearted agreement within the province for the establishment of a centre for Jewish studies in Israel, but, with hindsight, it is this decision that may be seen as having sewn the seed for the creation of the Hebrew Catholic community in Israel. On the Dominican Institute for Islamic studies in Cairo, see Régis Morelon OP, 'L'IDEO du caire et ses intuitions', *Mémoire dominicaine: 'Les dominicains et les mondes musulmans'*, no.15 (2001), 137-216.

Holy Land, Thomas F Stransky,[11] the vast majority of the early Christian immigrants to the Holy Land were Catholic. These arrived as early as the mid to late nineteenth century originating from Western and Eastern Europe, North America, Ethiopia, Middle East and elsewhere.[12] He claims the main port of entry was Jaffa-Haifa where the first immigrants settled creating a community of mixed Jewish Catholic marriages resulting mainly from intermarriage in the lands of their origin. They were neither regarded as Jews or Christian Arabs.[13] They were therefore an isolated community, many having fled persecution elsewhere, welcoming the protection the Ottomans granted to 'imperfect' Muslims.[14] They had never had a priest and in view of their social and political position within the new State of Israel, had to express their Christian belief in a clandestine manner.[15] Having no place of worship of their own and being scattered throughout the population often living in non-Christian families, from whom their religious affiliation had to be kept secret,[16] they certainly could not be regarded as a community at that time.

Owing to these unique circumstances Bruno's[17] first priority was to bind these Jewish Catholics[18] together in a community (*kehilla*) that had its own place in which to worship and a common language, Hebrew. After overcoming several ecclesiastical and prejudicial hurdles a place was found and after several years of discussion and preparation with

---

[11] I interviewed Fr Tom Stransky on Wednesday 3 July 2002. Stransky is a Paulist Father then living in Tantur, the Ecumenical Institute for Theological Studies, Jerusalem-Bethlehem.

[12] For the history of this period see Thomas Stransky, 'Origins of Western Christian Missions in Jerusalem and the Holy Land', *Jerusalem in the Mind of the Western World,* Yehoshua Ben-arieh and Moshe Davis (eds) Praeger Publishers, Westport, Conn., 1997, 1-19.

[13] Christian Arabs comprise many different communities such as, to name only two, Orthodox or Catholic Melkite and Latin Catholic, their *lingua franca* was then, and still is, Arabic, a language that the immigrants would not speak hence increasing their isolation from the indigenous mainstream Christian communities.

[14] Christians under the Ottomans were given the status of *dhimmis* or protected people, they were granted protection for their lives and liberties and allowed to practice their own forms of worship subject to the payment of a *dhimmi* tax. Cf. Anthony O'Mahony, 'Palestinian Christians: Religion, Politics and Society c. 1800-1948', *Palestinian Christians: Religion and Politics and Society in the Holy Land,* Anthony O'Mahony (ed.), Melisende, London, 1999, 17-18.

[15] Hussar Bruno: *When the Cloud Lifted,* Veritas Publications 1989, 63.

[16] *Ibid*.

[17] I use this nomenclature because nobody ever referred to him as 'Father', to everybody he was known simply as Bruno.

[18] The vast majority were from Eastern Europe countries under communist domination, usually they were from mixed marriages with a Jewish husband and a Catholic mother. Hussar, *ibid.*, 65.

warm encouragement from Cardinal Tisserant, then prefect of the Sacred Congregation for the Oriental Churches, the creation of the *Oeuvre De Saint Jacques l'Apôtre's* was approved by the former Patriarch Albert Gori in 1955. The decision to found the *Oeuvre* was prompted not so much by the existence of those Jewish Catholics who had lived as *dhimmis* under the Ottomans but principally by the patriarchs' pastoral solicitude for the Catholics, apparently some several thousand of them at that time, who arrived in Israel as refugees or immigrants in the years following the Second World War and the creation of the State of Israel and who continued to arrive throughout the 1950s. They came also invariably from the countries of Eastern Europe and were either converted Jews or descendants of such converts or Catholic spouses in mixed marriages though in a few cases they had no connection at all with Jews and Judaism and were simply anxious to emigrate from their countries, now Communist or in the process of becoming so. The Patriarchate, especially in the person of the then vicar of Israel, Mgr Vergani, was conscious of its duty to those immigrants and fearing that because of differences of mentality and language, as well as of the complexity of the socio-political situation, they might not easily find their place within the normal parochial organisation, favoured the creation of a distinct framework within its jurisdiction specially designed to meet their needs. It was accepted that the pastoral centres envisaged would adopt Hebrew, as being the *lingua franca* for immigrants originating from a number of different countries with various vernaculars.[19]

Two co-workers of Bruno, Fr Yohanan Elihai, a 'Little Brother of Jesus', in conjunction with Fr Daniel OCD a few years later,[20] set about the translation of the liturgy into Hebrew and permission was given, thanks to Cardinal Tisserant's intervention with Pope Pius XII, for the Latin Mass to be said in Hebrew on the grounds that it was one of the three languages inscribed on Our Lord's Cross.[21] This was prior to the general rule that mass would be said worldwide in the vernacular.

The statutes of the Oeuvre approved on 11 February 1956, exhorts its members to acquire an understanding of the mystery of Israel. 'We insist

---

19 In fact the *Oeuvre* was granted permission by the patriarchate and the Vatican to have the liturgy in Hebrew as early as 1957. For the pioneering work of the French Jewish convert Priest, Jean-Roger Henné in creating a Hebrew Catholic culture, see Dominique Trimbur 'Les Assomptionistes de Jerusalem, les Juifs et le sionisme', *Tsafon: Revue d'études juives du Nord,* no. 48 (1999-2000), 71-111.

20 Elihai was a very early arrival in Israel, 1950/1. Bro. Daniel did not arrive until 1957.

21 Hussar, *ibid.*, 68.

upon a Biblical formation; we try to promote a Jewish Christian culture and spirituality in conformity with that culture … (We aim) to combat all forms of anti-Semitism, attempting to develop mutual understanding and friendly relations between the Catholic world and Israel.'

The majority of those who supported the creation of the Oeuvre seemed to have felt that, even though an open missionary drive among Israeli Jews would in the circumstances be unthinkable, they would welcome into their numbers any Jew who freely chooses baptism and enters into a covenantal relationship with the Catholic Church. It is the non-missionary nature of the *kehilla* that sets this group apart from all other Jewish believers and may explain why they and indeed the Catholic Church conflict less acrimoniously with Israeli society than do the Messianic Jewish Movement.[22]

A smaller number of the 'founding fathers' were (and still are) motivated by a much larger vision, which could be summed up as a desire to implant the Church within the Jewish people 'in such a way that Jews who become Christians should be able to preserve their national character in much the same way that members of any other people or nation are invited to do.'[23]

During the 1960s the *kehilla* thrived boasting some 2,000[24] members in the area of Jaffa and Haifa alone. The membership of the *kehillot* today is certainly very much smaller and the numbers of Jewish Catholics within it are very few. 'The attendance of Jewish people in

[22] This point is of particular relevance in distinguishing the *Kehilla* from the considerably larger Jewish Christian communities of Messianic Jews. These are Jews who have come to believe in Jesus through Protestantism, they are not recognised by the Israeli authorities as Christian and have alienated themselves from Israeli society by their missionary vocation. Various sources claim there are between 3,000 and 5,000 of them in Israel alone and many thousands in other countries (United States and France). They are not associated with any recognisable church and are perhaps most appropriately described as a religious movement, composed of faith groups that are mainly attended by ethnic/cultural Jews but there are among their numbers non-Jewish believers and non-Jewish spouses. There are other groups who actively seek the conversion of the Jews these are in the main linked to the Evangelical churches, among others Jews for Jesus and the movement of Christian Witness to Israel.

[23] David-Maria Hunter (D-MA. Jaeger), 'Holy land Christians: Hebrew-speaking communities', *The Tablet,* 7 January 1978, 5-7.

[24] Elihai Johanan: unpublished paper, *réponse à une demande du Patriarche au course du Synode,* Jerusalem, 15 October 1995, and cf. *Facts and Myths About the Messianic Congregations in Israel,* a survey conducted by Kai Kjaer-Hansen and Bodil F Skjott (United Christian Council in Israel 1999), 292.

the Catholic congregations does not exceed 50, out of a total number of 350 attending.'[25]

It was not until 1958 that Bruno's original mission got under way which meant Him moving from the community that he had founded in Jaffa to West Jerusalem where he was temporarily accommodated at the Ratisbonne Institute with the Fathers of Notre-Dame de Sion. In 1959 Brother Jacques Fontaine, a bible scholar joined him which meant the community was increased to two persons. In the same year accommodation was found and the centre was finally established under the patronage of an Old Testament prophet, Isaiah, who is celebrated in Jerusalem as Prophet and Martyr. From then on the centre was known as *Maison Saint Isaïe*, The House of Isaiah, and received canonical confirmation as such on 25 March 1960.[26] There were expectations of a high standard of intellectual and theological contribution to Hebrew Catholic formation and dialogue in Jerusalem with the establishment of The House of Isaiah but the two members of the community felt unable to fulfil the intellectual and theological expectations of the Paris Dominican Province.

It was a humble assessment of his own talents and those of Fontaine that prompted Bruno to approach Brother Marcel Dubois, (Jacques Dubois at the time) a highly qualified scholar and philosophy lecturer at Saulchoir. Dubois accepted an invitation to join the community for the purpose of fulfilling the theological and intellectual role. He joined on 20 May 1962. A fourth member, Brother Gabriel Grossman, an Austrian Jew, joined the community in 1967.[27] In spite of the great admiration the French Dominicans had for the success of the House of Isaiah the community never advanced beyond these four members.

The main task of the community was to study and understand the Jewish Spirit, the mystery of the election and it's meaning in order to help the Church rediscover its Jewish roots and allow 'the sap that flows from the olive tree to flow freely through it.'[28] Apart from studying

---

[25] These figures are based on information gathered from active members of the community in 1999 Kai Kjaer-Hansen and Bodil F Skjott, *ibid.*, 293-294. Diocesan official figures are between 250 and 400 but there are some who claim there are as many as 1,000.

[26] Hussar, *ibid.*, 73-78.

[27] Gabriel Grossman OP was responsible for the transaletion of the Rule of St Benedict into Modern Hebrew with Issac Jacob OSB, the prior at Tel Gamaliel in 1980. See Issac H Jacob, OSB, 'The Rule of Benedict: Bridge to Israel', *The American Benedictine Review* Vol. 45. no. 4. 1994, 399-406.

[28] An image taken by Hussar from the Apostle Paul (Romans 11), *When the Cloud Lifted*, 80. See also note 3 on 81.

theological and historical Hebrew Catholic relations it became a highly respected link between the Church, Judaism and the State of Israel. The respect it won from the Jewish establishment owes much to the singular desire of its members to understand the 'mysteries of Israel' without imposing Christian attitudes on its people, and without missionary intent. The House of Isaiah with others was responsible for many other activities and the establishment of many lasting foundations such as the 'Rainbow Group' and the 'Ecumenical Theological Research Fraternity', the ecumenical Hebrew Christian group that meet socially and for study. The fraternity has published in the region of 250 lectures on 35 different themes between 1966 and 2000.[29]

However, according to Dubois, because of a lack of interest and understanding of the Jewish people and the links of the Church with them on the part of younger Dominicans,[30] the House of Isaiah was disbanded in September 1997 at the provincial chapter of the provinces of Lyon and Paris. Only two of the original community are still living, Dubois, who continues to lecture in the Hebrew University, and Fontaine, who has retired from his work as a biblical tour guide[31] and now lives in retirement as chaplain to the Poor Clares.

III

Biographical details and theological thought of some of the Jewish Catholic thinkers

Bruno was the first pastor of the *kehilla* and the person who originally brought together the extremely heterogeneous mix of Jews and Jewish Catholics in Jaffa.[32] He was not an intellect seeing himself more as a man of action, an innovator, 'recognising in him the Jewish gene that causes the Jew to act first and question later.'[33] His simple belief that the way in which he lived his life, in obedience to the word of God, would do more to change the world than struggling, as some of his contemporaries did,

---

[29] The compendium of the Ecumenical Fraternity 1966-2000, Natali Posti ed. (The Ecumenical Theological Research Fraternity in Israel 2000.)

[30] An opinion of Dubois' given to the author in interviews with him in June and July 2000.

[31] Fr Jacques, a biblical scholar for many years conducted tours named appropriately 'The Bible on The Spot'.

[32] Hussar, *ibid.*, 78.

[33] Hussar, *ibid*,. 80-81.

to understand the meaning of the mystery of Israel, the election or the Holocaust.[34] He was concerned with actively living the life of the Gospels, which he did with openness to the existential pastoral realities.[35]

He was born in Egypt of non-practising Jewish Hungarian parents. He spoke French, English and Italian. His theology was, more or less, a narrative of his life. He saw himself as a meeting point of the three elements of his identity, Jewish and Christian but also of the Arab culture that influenced his earlier life. These three elements are brought together in the ultimate innovative fruit of his life, '*Neve Shalom*', the village of peace, a fundamentally non-denominational foundation,[36] but to Bruno those that live in peace and harmony, even in a worldly environment, are living the life of the Good News (Mat 5:9).[37]

Some in the local church later regarded Bruno as somewhat politically naïve. He was open to the Arabs, as his actions and life witness, but he was regarded by some of his own community as allowing himself to be used after the 1967 war when he agreed to attend the UN General Assembly as an adviser to the Israeli delegation.[38] Twenty years later in his autobiography he stresses that Zionism is not against the rights of Palestinian Arabs to a national existence in the same region,[39] and that as a result of the bloody struggles that have arisen a new aim of Zionism is now peace with the Arabs.[40] There is the same movement in Bruno's life to that of others concerned with Hebrew Catholic relations from an initial narrow concern with Hebrew Catholicism and a naive Zionism, to a wider concern for peace and harmony among the three 'Abrahamic' religions that constitute the plurality of contemporary Israel.

---

34 His autobiography, *When the Cloud Lifted*, illustrates this point.

35 In this he was supported by Rina Geftman, a Russian Jew, whose personality and thought were very similar to Bruno's. She shared the same traditional Catholic views as Dubois and was also driven by her perception of her Jewish roots that brought her close also to Fr Yohanan Elihai. She is the author of two books, *Guetteurs d'Aurore,* Paris, 1985 and *L' Offrande du Soir,* Paris, 1994. Geftman was influential in the *kehilla* and in *Maison Saint Isaïe* whilst still in Paris. Hussar, on his way back from the second Vatican Council, brought her from Paris to Jerusalem in 1966 where she died on 15 October 2001.

36 *Neve Shalom Newsletter* No 47, September 1996, 3.

37 Hussar, *ibid.*, 110.

38 Certainly in conversation with the author Fr Marcel Dubois made this comment and in Hussar's autobiographical work he refers to the difficulties he experienced in persuading his brethren, Dubois being one of them, that this was the right thing to do. Hussar *ibid.*, 94-95.

39 Hussar, *ibid.*, 97.

40 Hussar, *ibid.*, 123 on Arie Lova Eliat, 1972, see also Hussar, *ibid.*, 97 and the objectives of the 'Peace Now Movement' see note 7, Hussar, *ibid.*, 101, 'The Declaration of Independence'.

There is no better place to begin a comparison of the strong Hebrew Catholic personalities, who have all developed concepts and visions unique to themselves, than in the Carmelite monastery atop Mount Carmel in Haifa overlooking the Mediterranean. It may well be that on the site of the present-day monastery and near by church, Stella Maris, 'The Star of the Sea', the very first Jewish Christian/Catholic hermits lived, seeing themselves as the direct descendants of the prophet Elijah.[41]

The Carmelites are the only Catholic religious order founded in the Holy Land. At the request of the early hermits on Mount Carmel the Patriarch of Jerusalem, Albert Avogadro wrote a formula of life (between 1206-1214) for the lay hermits to follow. Various popes approved this formula of life until the group was transformed into a Religious Order, when in 1247 Pope Innocent IV approved the text as a Rule.

The first Carmelites, who did not view anyone in particular as their founder but saw Elijah as one of the founders of monastic life, lived in caves on Mt. Carmel for about a century. They were then forced to leave, in 1235, due to Islamic persecution that resulted, perhaps, from the *Qur'anic* prohibition of monasticism.[42]

Two members of this fraternity, Father Elias Friedman OCD and Father Oswald Rufeisen OCD, (popularly known as Brother Daniel), were both Jewish Catholics but from vastly different backgrounds, Rufeisen was very much involved with the *kehilla,* Friedman was not at all involved. Both of them were probably best known for their concerns about two different aspects of Jewish identity. Rufeisen sought to establish who was a Jew in the State of Israel; he was concerned with the identity of the *person* whereas Friedman was concerned with identifying *'the people'* of the election, the Hebrews who inherit the mark of the election in contemporary Israel and throughout the world today.

---

[41] Father Elias Friedman OCD in his *The Latin Hermits of Mount Carmel: A Study in Carmelite Origins*, Terestanum, Rome, 1979. He claims that this site had been a place of pilgrimage for Jews long before Christ, they came to worship at what was Elijah's 'School of the Prophets'. In 1150 AD Crusaders on a pilgrimage there found a small monastery housing Byzantine priests who claimed that when their predecessors first arrived they had found the site occupied by a community of Jewish Christians who were conducting a house of studies and who claimed to be the spiritual heirs of a Jewish monastic Order which had lived and studied there since the days of Elijah. It is back to these ancient times that the modern Catholic Monastic Order of Carmelites traces its origins.

[42] Elias Friedman, OCD, *The Latin Hermits of Mount Carmel: A Study in Carmelite Origins.* Terestanum, Rome, 1979, Collection: Institutum Historicum Teresianum Studia I; and, *El-Muhraqa: Here Elijah Raised His Altar,* Teresianum, Rome, 1986.

Elias Friedman was born to a South African Jewish family he was a Holocaust survivor who became a Catholic during the Second World War whilst serving in the South African Medical Corps as a doctor. He was ordained priest in 1953 living for over forty years as a Carmelite in Israel. He died on the feast of the Sacred Heart of Jesus, Friday 11 June 1999.

Deeply aware of the two great fears of the Jewish people; liquidation and assimilation, Friedman founded The Association of Hebrew Catholics (AHC) in1979[43] under the patronage of Miriam, Our Lady of the Miracle and St Teresa Benedicta of the Cross (Edith Stein), that works to establish an Israelite community in the Church to enable Jews to accept Christ and His Church without assimilation. The Association seeks to petition the Holy See to approve the establishment of an Israelite Community in the Church, such a community to serve as 'an eschatological sign of the times'.[44]

Friedman's views are diametrically opposed to that of the Polish Rufeisen. Friedman separates modern day Judaism that he calls Rabbinism, the religion of the Rabbis, from the religion of the Mosaic covenant that ended with the destruction of the temple in AD 70. He, although Jewish by birth, is deeply Catholic. He does not accept that the AHC should inherit any of the traditions and culture of modern day Judaism or Rabbinic Jewry. The AHC sees 'no assimilation' as meaning keeping the national, ethnic identity but becoming totally 'Catholic' in the Roman forms—theology, piety and culture. The *kehilla* in which Rufeisen was very much involved proposes 'no assimilation' as finding the right mode for Jewish Catholics to express their faith without necessarily taking on the Roman forms.

For Friedman the mark of the election since the destruction of the temple in 70 lies solely in the people not in their religion or beliefs.[45] He is particularly concerned then, to distinguish the identity of who are the people of the election. What people constitute the biblical Israel today? In the Old Testament, Friedman claims, the division of the twelve tribes constituted a moral schism in the people, ten tribes are lost only two remained, only a pious remnant returns from Babylon to rebuild Jerusalem.[46] Of that remnant a further split occurred when one

---

43 Although Lisa Loden in *Mishkan*, issue 29/1998 p72, refers to a branch (*sic*) in Israel, the author has been unable to find one although he has been told there are AHC sympathisers in Israel; the association is strongest in the United States of America and in South Africa.

44 Cf. Elias Friedman, *Jewish Identity*, Miriam Press, New York, 1987, 232.

45 Friedman, *ibid.*, 82.

46 Friedman, *ibid.*, 101.

group of Israelites, the Maccabees, remaining faithful to the Jewish Law repelled the Hellenists who tried to absorb Judaism into their world and impose a Greek-style religion and culture on them. It was a minority of this diminished remnant, who had remained faithful throughout many centuries that were set aside to believe in Jesus the Messiah. Friedman points out that, excepting for the geographical identification of Hebrews from Judah these people are not referred to in the Old Testament as Jews but as Hebrews or Israelites.[47] He claims it is the descendants of the elected Hebrews or Israelites (Ex 6:7) that posses and perpetuate the collective historic identity. Jewish identity (not Hebrew) comes from the 'elect people living under the law. From the time of Moses to Jesus, that was Mosaic Law. Following Jesus, the 'law' is the law of Christ. For Rabbinic Jews, who don't believe in Jesus, it is Rabbinic Law.

> 'They are Israelites; it was they who were adopted as children, the glory was theirs and the covenants; to them were given the Law and the worship of God and the promises.' (Rom 9:4).

Friedman points out that their importance far outweighs their inferior numbers. What he makes clear is that the intimate nature of the Church remains that of the faithful remnant. Those that founded the Church of Jerusalem in the New Dispensation are of the same faithful remnant as those that rebuilt the Temple and defended Judaism against the Hellenists. The disappearance of this category of the elect created an imbalance in the theological thinking on the nature of the Church. The correct balance could be re-established through recognition of 'the specific privileged role of a revived Church of Jerusalem'[48] It was this believing minority of the New Law that became the cultivated Olive Tree capable of receiving the Gentile in-grafting. Friedman avers that the majority that did not believe in the New Law continues to share in the sacred character of the tree and the believing minority has helped their survival and the maintenance of that sacred character.[49] He calls unbelievers and believers, in the New Law, two sections of Israel that will one day become one again so that all Israel will be saved.

---

[47] Friedman, *ibid.*, 50-54.

[48] Florival in *Service International de Documentation Judéo-Chrétienne* 3 (1970), 22-23, esp. 32, quoted by Friedman, *ibid.*, 102.

[49] Whilst this is not a theology of supersessionism it does verge on the suggestion that without those that believe in Christ the Jews of today might not exist.

In Friedman's analysis of the mark of the election a unique role in the history of salvation is given to the elect within the New Dispensation of the Church and he suggests a certain impediment in a purely Gentile Church. For it is the Israelites that must be gathered together,

> 'He will hoist a signal for the nations and assemble the outcasts of Israel; he will gather the scattered people of Judah from the Four Corners of the earth.' (Isa. 11:12)

Their religion is not the issue. In biblical terms and for such as the *Natorei Karta*,[50] Guardians of the City, for example, if the Messiah is to gather in the people of the election one must recognise who they are.[51] This is the paradox of the State of Israel. Is it a state for the elect of Israel only or a state for the new religion of post-Christic Rabbinism that includes converts not of the election but excludes those grafted in to the election, Christians? If it is a state for the elect can the mark of the elect be somehow removed?

For Friedman the question of 'Jewish Identity' that we have referred to here as 'the mark of the election', requires some serious

---

[50] These are an extremist sect comprising an alliance of all ultra-orthodox Jews some of whom are Hassidim they are strongly opposed to the existence of the State of Israel, they see it as a secular state that is gathering in to *Eretz Israel* Jews who, in the main, have rejected the traditional authority of the Rabbis in favour of ideologies such as socialism and nationalism. The majority of *Natorei Karta* regard 'the in gathering' of Western secular Jews as hastening the redemption. They cite rabbinical tradition that forbids any act that seeks to hasten the redemption. The Messiah must come first and it is He who 'will gather the scattered people of Judah from the Four Corners of the earth.' (Isa 11:12). They live in total separation from the Zionist Jewish community of Jerusalem seeing themselves as a totally '*different people*', not necessarily as Friedman's elect but as those loyal to the rabbinical law, even to the extent of joining in with Arab anti-Israeli demonstrations.

[51] The identification of who is a Jew, who is a Hebrew and who is a Jewish Christian or Hebrew Christian is such a complex problem that Robert Murray SJ does not offer a thesis on this subject rather he puts forward only a basis for discussion. Cf: 'Jews, Hebrews and Christians: Some Needed Distinctions' in *Novum Testamentum* XXIV, 3 (1982), 198. The basis for discussion is set out *ibid.*, in pp.194-208 stressing the valuable insights of earlier scholars but also pointing out the many remaining obscure areas that are filled out with further obscurities and variables. Whilst Friedman's book, *Jewish Identity*, is very skilfully argued it does not clarify the obscurity surrounding the period between the return from exile and Antiochus Epiphanus IV in the 2nd century BC. It is one thing to claim that those that founded the Church of Jerusalem in the New Dispensation are of the same faithful remnant as those that rebuilt the Temple and defended Judaism against the Hellenists, i.e. the Maccabees, but do we know who their descendants are today or who, out of the many factions that existed at the time of Jesus, they were in the first place?

consideration if a proper interpretation of the eschatology of salvation and the part that the in-gathering has to play in it, is to be properly understood.

The dilemma that faces the State of Israel is somewhat different. It is to understand its national identity and, perhaps less so, its destiny in theological terms. The two are inextricably entwined in the identity of the person. It was toward this identity that Rufeisen applied much effort, although not in the same intellectual manner as did Friedman toward identifying the 'elect of God'.

Rufeisen was born into a traditional Jewish Family in Poland. Whereas one might say Friedman was totally Catholic, born Jewish, Rufeisen always remained a Jew but became a Catholic. Ernest Seifter, Rufeisen's cousin, claimed that he was always an idealist, a revolutionary Zionist who never felt that he had left Judaism.[52]

Rufeisen joined the Zionist Youth Movement and, whilst serving as a police officer of the Germans in Mir, Poland, putting his own life at risk, saved the lives of hundreds of Jews. He famously challenged the Israeli government in the Supreme Court on the law of return when he had his application for automatic citizenship in December 1959 turned down as a consequence of 'the excluding clause' that excludes from automatic citizenship any Jews who have changed their *dat*, religion. Daniel's appeal to the Supreme Court against this decision attracted worldwide attention because it challenged modern Zionism to resolve the different understandings of the various factions of moderate secular Zionists, extreme secular Zionists of which Daniel was one, and the religious Zionists. Daniel's understanding of modern Zionism was extreme in that he thought it intended to divorce Jewish nationality from the Jewish religion. On June 12 1962 the Supreme Court upheld the 1959 decision thus establishing a union of religion and state so that even a non-believer claiming to be Jewish by origin is entitled to automatic citizenship but not a Jew who professes another religion.[53] The rabbinate ruled that Daniel should be given citizenship as a Jew; born to Jewish parents, his fate was with his people, regardless of any faith decisions he had made along the way.

---

[52] Nechama Tec, *The Lion's Den*, Oxford University Press, Oxford, 1990, 209-10.

[53] For details of the Supreme Court ruling see *Verdicts of the Supreme Court of Israel* (Heb.) (Abbreb. Verdicts), Government Printers, Jerusalem No 16 (1962), 2428-2455 also Fr Elias Friedman, *Jewish Identity*, 11-25, Miriam Press, New York, 1987, and Nechama Tec, *The Lion's Den*, 222-231.

The Supreme Court ruled that despite the halachic logic of the rabbinate's position it was not possible to be both a Catholic priest and a Jew. The extent to which Israel is a secular state is as a consequence compromised by the religious identity of its citizens.

Ideally, if Israel is a Jewish state, 'divinely ordained law should govern every aspect of life, everything from the privacy of the home, to the marketplace, to government, to matters of worship,'[54] similar in that respect to an Islamic state. If on the other hand it is a secular state there should be a clear differentiation between the Law of Torah and the State as is the case in the Greco-Roman Culture of the West. The Supreme Court ruling in Daniel's case makes Israel something of an anomaly as neither one thing nor the other.

Brother Daniel's motivation, apart from his personal desire to be recognised as a Jew, might also be seen as an effort to establish the abiding vision of the *Kehilla*; of implanting the Church within the Jewish people as opposed to Friedman's approach of establishing the elect within the Church.

Daniel saw himself as the spiritual guide and pastor to all non-Arab Christians in the Northern part of Israel, seeing them as marginalized by, what he regarded, as the Church's singular concern for Arab Christians. He was an uncompromising Zionist who attributed messianic significance to the return of the Jews to *Eretz Israel*; that might explain some of his actions such as cabling John Paul II requesting he did not meet Yasser Arafat[55] publicly for fear of damaging Hebrew Catholic relations with Jewish society in Israel.[56] This made it appear he was unsympathetic to the Palestinian people.

Daniel's unorthodox behaviour[57] and views, that expressed more his radical protest against the traditional Church and his desire to remain a Jew whilst also being a Catholic, priest and friar,[58] than any deep theological principle, should not overshadow the practical pastoral work[59] he instituted

---

[54] Ruth Langer, *Theological Studies* 64 (2003), 257. The Israeli political system does not allow for the separation of religion and state, so fundamental to most Western style liberal democracies.

[55] The Palestinian leader. He was the first president of the Palestinian Autonomy governing the West Bank and Gaza Strip. At the time of John Paul II's visit he was leader of the Palestinian Liberation Organsisation, (the PLO).

[56] Tec, *ibid.*, 243.

[57] Chapter 18 of 'The Lion's Den' gives an idea of Bro. Daniel's unorthodox Christian actions.

[58] When asked to leave his monastery and return to 'his people' he claimed he never left. Tec, *ibid.*, 211.

[59] Tec, *ibid.*, 235-237.

that is still carried on by his pastoral assistant Elisheva Hemker.[60] The theology of Daniel is his 'Jewish verticality'[61] a total openness to the *mitzvoth* expressed in his selfless pastoral work.

A factor that had a very strong influence on some of the thinkers, that tended to divide them rather than form a cohesive policy that would ultimately bring about a vibrant Catholic Jewish community, was what may be termed 'the French Catholic Cultural Divide.'[62] A divide perhaps due in part to a survival of some aspects of the historic conflict over *Action Française*.[63] Bruno had lived and worked as an engineer in Paris and later studied at Saulchoir. It was in Paris that he entered the Dominican Order. He may have been, to some extent, protected from early twentieth century debates and divisions among French Catholics on Judaism and inculturation by the very fact that he was not a French Catholic but he was Jewish. The divisions of these early years could not be more apparent than in the lives of

60 Tec, *ibid.*, 237. In 1991 Elisheva Hemker received the Mount Zion Award for her outstanding contribution to the enhancement of dialogue between Jews, Christians and Muslims.

61 An expression used frequently by Dubois in interviews with the author that refers to the unique uplifting of the Jewish heart and soul to God in a total obedience to the commandments, *mitzvoth*.

62 Aspects of this culture is possibly profoundly connected to the various writings on 'inculturation' and liturgical reform in France between the 1930s and 1960s coupled with a fascination with things Jewish after the Holocaust. There has also been perceived (not proved) a split in the French Church between 'anti-Semites' and 'philo-Semites' dating back to the Dreyfus affair at the end of the 19th century, but as Bruno illustrates, it persisted well into the mid-20th century; cf. Hussar's lecture at the Ecumenical Fraternity '20 years after *Nostra Aetate*' given on 18 May 1985.

63 During the first four decades of the twentieth century, the *Action Française*, tried to re-establish the French monarchy. Although its principle directors were atheist it had considerable intellectual influence among French Catholics. It promoted the idea that a return to French prosperity of the past required a return to France's past political form and religious practice. The Vatican became concerned over a considerable number of the clergy and particularly some bishops who sought the restoration of the monarchy. These clerics, who might be said to have not yet accepted the secularisation of the French Revolution and therefore rejected the republic, wanted to return to an ideal whereby the king was Catholic, the Church sovereign and everybody else, in particular the Jews, were denied any consideration within the political and social structure. Anti-Semitism to this day remains very strong among the tiny remnant of activists still surviving. *Action Française* can no longer be regarded as a movement in France, although their bi-weekly publication *L'Action* still exists, it is more an abiding spirit living on in some Catholic monarchist circles. There is considerable animosity between French Catholic traditionalists, who tend to be nostalgic monarchists and politically right wing, and French Catholic liberals who tend to be socialists. The divide has existed for a hundred years and was further exacerbated by the traditionalist's perception of liberalisation in Vatican II. The history of *Action Française* goes some way toward explaining the popularity among traditionalists of the French Archbishop Lefèvre's Tridentine movement, which may be seen as a return to the nostalgic past.

two gentile French Catholics living in Jerusalem today, one who is deeply concerned with the manner in which Christians of a Jewish background as well as gentile Christians can worship as Catholics in Israel fully inculturated with the Jewish majority and in the interests of Jewish Catholic relations, advocates a less overtly European or Latin mode of worship and traditional practice. The other who is very much a traditional Catholic but as such has a unique understanding of Jews and Judaism.

Both Fr Marcel Dubois OP and Fr Johanan Elihai are scholars and deeply intellectual but each affected in different ways by the French Cultural Divide.

Elihai's background would appear to have had a profound impact on his theological stance within the *kehilla* and his vision for its future. As a 'Little Brother of Jesus' he emulates the efforts of Charles de Foucauld toward simplicity, inculturation and marginality. But perhaps his life's experience as a worker-priest[64] may explain how he sees Hebrew Catholics in Israel as alienated from the traditional Church in a similar manner to the way in which the worker-priest movement viewed the French working class as alienated from the traditional Church in France.[65] Just as worker-priests set aside clerical garb[66] to be at one with the workers and to attract them back to the faith, so too Elihai would strip the *kehilla* of all vestige of what he sees as the traditional Church of Palestine in similar mould to that of France. The hallmark of the worker-priest movement was protest against the traditional Church in France, and against what it saw as its complicity in injustice.[67] To be truly at one with the Hebrew Catholics and the Jews he changed his name from Jean Leroy to Johanan Elihai.[68]

---

[64] Fr Jacques Loew OP founded the movement of Worker-Priests when he took up employment in the docks of Marseilles in 1941. He was followed by many others who sought to minister to France's secularised working class that he felt were marginalized from the traditional Church. The nature of their ministry disturbed the establishment because of its growing involvement in left wing politics and its abandonment of the traditional priestly life. Pius XII brought the movement to a halt in 1954. The author did not formally interview Elihai and therefore cannot say whether he was one of the protesters or whether he would have been old enough to continue work until John XXIII again discontinued it in 1959. As he retired from work as a print setter about ten years ago he would have obviously returned when Paul VI, in 1965, approved of the movement in a modified form.

[65] Collins, Peter SJ, 'The demise of the Worker Priest', *Newsletter of the Uniya Jesuit Social Justice Centre*, Autumn 1995, 12.

[66] Corley Felix, obituary of Fr Loew, *London Times*, 27 February 1999.

[67] Collins, *loc. cit.*

[68] Yves Teyssier d'Orfeuil, *Michel Sabbah: Paix sur Jérusalem. Propos d'un Eveque Palestinien*, Desclee de Brouwer, Paris, 2002, 71.

Elihai's linguistic skills would have made him a valuable employee in the multi-lingual milieu of Israel. Not only is he fluent in Hebrew but also in Arabic he also studied and is able to read Syriac.[69]

Elihai, first used a model for the *kehilla* based on the Syrian pre-Hellenisation rite. The Patristic tradition's devotion to Old Testament 'gentile/pagan' saints such as Melchisadek is something the Western Church has lost.[70] Elihai like all the members of the *kehilla* supports the role of Judaism in the continuing dynamic of Universal Salvation and presumably would wish to re-establish that which is lost. In his effort to create a Hebrew Christian rite, [71] along with Brother Daniel, he translated the liturgy into Hebrew and along with Sr. Maroussia, of Our Lady of Sion, he composed music based on that of the North African synagogue, rather than the Gregorian or polyphonic music of the traditional Church.

The Semitic ethos he has created as an alternative to the Greek ethos of the traditional Church is intended to replicate the culture and practice of the early Christians before Hellenisation,[72] but the majority of Hebrew Catholics in Israel are Western and Eastern European and therefore it has not become rooted in the pastoral reality. Elihai appears as one of those 'philo-semite' French Catholics profoundly affected by the

---

[69] Elihai is also the author of, among others, the great Hebrew-Arabic dictionary, and *Juifs et chretines d'hier et demain*, Frere Yohanan, Cerf, Paris 1990. He is also an expert in the field of the Arabic language used by the Palestinians.

[70] Robert Murray in *Symbols of Church and Kingdom A study in early Syriac tradition,* Cambridge University Press, Cambridge 1975. 49.

[71] It was Cardinal Tisserant, then prefect of the Church in the Orient, who suggested in 1956/7 utilising the Syrian rite in Hebrew. Cf. Elihau in his paper *Réponse à une demande du Patriarche au course du Synode*, Jerusalem, 15 October 1995.

[72] Any interpretation of the practice of the early Jewish Christianity prior to Hellenisation must rely to a large extent on individual assumptions. Since there was such diversity of practice and belief among Jewish factions prior to the Christ event it can never be positively established which of these Jews became believers in Jesus. Possibly believers came from several factions some of these would have had a strict adherence to Rabbinic Law, the Pharisees, others who saw the Temple as the centre of their religious focus, 'the establishment'. There were others, who rejected the establishment such as the Samaritans and the Qumran community. There would have been many different views about the method of worship, the calendar and if there was to be a continued adherence to pre-Christic tradition; which of the traditions was it to be? The only commonality that one may rely upon is that all the early Jewish Christians from whichever faction believed 'Jesus to be the Messiah and in a special relationship to God'. Cf. Robert Murray, 'Jewish Christianity', *A Dictionary of Biblical Interpretation,* London, 1990, 341-6.

horrors of the Holocaust (Shoah) to such an extent that they are attracted to Israel to identify with the Jews.[73]

Identifying with the Jews for Elihai means more than a personal identification. For him the Church too must identify by changing some if its practices and liturgy he speaks of the 'inculturation' of a Hebrew Catholic Church in Israeli society. In fact he speaks not of inculturation but of 'reculturation' a possible return to the *ecclesia circumcisione*.[74]

Dubois[75] stands in sharp contrast to the other founding fathers of the *kehilla* and particularly to Elihai.[76] He is profoundly a French Catholic who loves the Latin traditional Church.[77] He was brought up in a very conservative French Catholic milieu in the town of Tourcoing near Lille. To emphasise the conservative nature of his upbringing he adds '*the parish of Archbishop Lefèvre*.' At the age of eighteen he joined the Dominican Order and has lived his entire life since in the Scholastic and University tradition, a sharp contrast indeed to the 'popular' *milieu* from which Elihai and Daniel emerge.

There is good reason why when Dubois speaks, Israel listens. It is because he is not seen as anything other than a traditional Christian with a 'spontaneous preference for the Jewish people'.[78] Additionally he has a profound appreciation of Christianity's debt to Judaism that sees the Incarnation as a consequence of Judaism's abiding fidelity to the *Torah* and obedience to the *mitzvoth*.

John Paul II's sermon at Nazareth on the 25 March 2000 inspired him to see Mary the Mother of God in the light of this unique 'Jewish verticality':

---

[73] Some of the 'philo-Semite' French Catholics felt the French Church did not do enough to protect Jews at the time of the Vichy government. Dubois claims to be one of those and he said that many French Catholics felt a need to make reparation for this. Hussar makes a similar claim in his autobiography. Elihai's response to this was to immigrate to Israel (perhaps to make personal reparation) to what he saw as the traditional Church's failure.

[74] Elihai, *op. cit.*

[75] Quotes in italics in this section are from the transcripts of recorded interviews during the period 29 June–7 July 2002.

[76] Like Elihai, Dubois is an intellectual but he takes primarily, a philosophical and theological approach to the Bible compared to the philological approach of Elihai.

[77] He is, however, not right wing and is critical not of the traditional church but of 'the traditional French Catholic' He speaks of the *Action Française* as a strict adherence to French Catholic 'practice and tradition' i.e. adherence to the law with little or no faith in the giver of the law. He sees this as similar to a Judaic tendency in some quarters of what he calls 'secularised Judaism'—practice without faith.

[78] Rist Anna, 'An Interview with Pére Marcel Dubois OP', *New Blackfriars* Vol. 78 No. 914, March 1997, 187.

> 'Mary was never more Jewish than at the moment of the annunciation. She recognises the mitzvah and she opens the way of the new sacramentality. So we have before Christ, the time of the observance, the time of the law. Afterwards we have Jesus Christ as the sacrament. We touch God through Christ. At the moment of the annunciation there is a connection between before and after. It is precisely obedience to the word of God, the way that Mary begins the way of sacramentality. The new sacrament begins as a consequence of obedience to the mitzvoth so we must admire the Jews for that.'[79]

Dubois' understanding of the Jewish people has altered from his early 'spontaneous preference for the Jews',[80] that developed as an objection to the '*negative way they were spoken of by the sisters'* who taught him in high school, to a profound understanding of the 'Jewishness' that he now sees in Mary.

> 'Mary is the bridge between Judaism and Christianity. If only a large number of religious Jews could understand the Jewishness of Mary, they would then accept Jesus as the sacrament brought forth by the Torah.'

In this expression we might see a similarity to the importance Massignon[81] gives to Mary. Dubois never met Massignon but claims to have heard much of him from friends who knew him. Whilst both agree on the importance of Mary the manner by which each expresses their Mariology of the Jews is entirely different.

Dubois prays that one day the Jews will share his understanding of Mary as the obedient handmaid of the Lord but in the meantime he openly expresses his gratitude to the Jews for the obedience of Mary that

---

[79] Transcribed from recordings made by the author in his encounter with Fr Marcel Dubois in June-July 2002.

[80] Rist, *op. cit.*, 187.

[81] Louis Massignon was a renowned Christian Islamicist, a French Melkite priest and one time French diplomat much involved in efforts to internationalise Jerusalem both with the Holy See and the UN. He saw the division of Palestine as a victory of the State of Israel, a state that would turn non-Jews into secondclass citizens, for this reason he was anti-Zionist. See Anthony O'Mahony, 'Lé Pélerin de Jérusalem: Louis Massignon', *Palestinian Christians, Islam and The State of Israel,* Anthony O'Mahony (ed.), Melisende, London; 1999, 171-177. For the interpretation of Massignon's Mariology and attitude see, *op. cit.,* 172, 175-6.

results from Judaism's first principle of obedience to the word of God. Massignon on the other hand seems to be less tolerant than Dubois of the Jewish inability to accept Mary as the Mother of God, he openly expresses his incomprehension of the Jewish refusal to accept Mary as such. He too sees Mary's role as pivotal in salvation history, the bridge between Judaism and Christianity and also, like Jesus, one who renounces her own will to become the handmaid of the Lord. Massignon, described as 'the greatest Christian among Muslims and the greatest Muslim among Christians',[82] is not surprisingly influenced by the Islamic devotion to Miriam 'chosen among women' as Israel is chosen among the nations.

Whilst there may be a loose similarity in the Mariology of both Dubois and Massignon they were certainly poles apart, at least in Dubois' earlier time in Jerusalem, in their attitude toward Zionism. Massignon was anti-Zionist having the foresight to see the consequences of the displacement whereas Dubois had a major conversion from Zionism just over a decade ago.[83]

Dubois distinguishes between Jews and Gentiles thus:

> 'The Jewish mentality is made to know God in a unique way that a Gentile cannot appreciate'[84]

> 'A Christian reflecting on reality ... is soon amazed to discover that the heritage he shares with the Jews does not exist only in a book that can be read objectively ... This heritage involves the very attitude of Israel before its gifts and their giver, the very manner in which this people have received this book, preserved and transmitted it.'[85]

---

[82] Cf. the writings of Iranian Shi'a activist Ali Shari'ati, see Anthony O'Mahony, 'Mysticism and Politics: Louis Massignon, Shi'a Islam, Iran and 'Ali Shari'ati. A Muslim-Christian Encounter', *University Lectures in Islamic Studies* Vol. 2, London, 1998, 113-134, 130.

[83] The impressions given here are the result of several hours spent in his company, listening to his views on current affairs and to his reminiscing on his earlier views on Zionism and the Jewish people. He, in all humility, accuses himself of grave error with regard to his earlier Zionist-philo-semite approach based on biblical prophecy that had scant regard for the Muslim Arabs. He is at pains to make it known he recants much of his earlier anti-Arab attitudes. See also his personal letters to the author and the transcript of conversations with the author.

[84] One might compare this spiritual difference to the difference referred to by Elihai that relates to the way Jews understand existential happenings such as, for example, the Shoah. Bro Daniel too makes the same observation *cf.* Nechama Tec, *op. cit.*

[85] M Dubois 'Israel and Christian Self Understanding' *Voices from Jerusalem*, (ed.) David Burrell and Yehezkel Landau, Paulist Press, 1992, 75.

The foregoing is typical of his theological thought. It is this understanding that has done more to inform the Church on its 'new thinking'[86] regarding its encounter with Jews and Judaism than the ideas of other individuals.

His unique Christian understanding of Jews and Judaism has won him the Israeli Prize in 1996 and other awards for tolerance and understanding of Judaism's role in the continuing dynamic of Universal Salvation. Dubois is described as having an international reputation as being the most prominent Christian in dialogue with Jews in contemporary Israel,[87] but he does not wish to be known as a dialogue partner.[88] He prefers to be known as a philosopher and theologian who contemplates what Augustine calls the *intellectus spiritualis*. The 'spiritual meaning of Holy Writ that is the most important for faith.'[89] 'Seeking to understand the spiritual essence of Holy Writ goes beyond dialogue to become a genuine encounter with the mystery of Israel, of the election, of the promises and the economy of salvation after the incarnation.'[90] Inspired by Aquinas'[91] reference in *Summa Theologica* to Augustine's remark '*do not ask why God chose the Jews if you do not wish to be mistaken'*.[92] '*God may chose whom he wishes', and 'He has chosen the Jews; it is a fact'*. A lifetime's contemplation on the 'mystery of Israel', perhaps with too great an intensity, caused him to be blind to the existential reality and to 'forget at what price...' the State of Israel is founded '... this price is the fate of the Palestinians who inhabited that land.'[93]

The depth and sensitivity of his theological understanding of Jews and Judaism makes him more aware than any Jew or Christian of

---

[86] David Burrell describes him as 'a friend (and with regard to the Jewish Christian encounter) mentor' to John Paul II; cf. *The Cambridge Companion to Jesus*, (ed.) Marcus Bockmuehl, Cambridge University Press, Cambridge, 260.

[87] G Wigoder, *Christian Jewish Relations since WWII*, Manchester University Press, 1995, 133.

[88] He is critical of those 'self appointed dialogue partners who have tea with Jews to appease their own conscience so that they can claim to be in touch with the "other".'

[89] Dubois: 'Jews, Judaism and Israel in the Theology of St Augustine', *Immanuel* 22/23 (1989) 166.

[90] M Dubois, 'Israel and Christian Self Understanding', David Burrell and Yehezkel Landau (eds), *Voices from Jerusalem*, Paulist Press, 1992, 90.

[91] He is a Thomist scholar see: 'Mystical and Realistic Elements in the Exegesis and Hermeneutics of Thomas Aquinas', in *Creative Biblical Exegesis*, 39-53. And 'Thomas Aquinas on the place of Jews in the Divine Plan', *Immanuel*, 24-25 (1990), 241-266.

[92] Several times he repeats this in conversation with me.

[93] Cited by Alain Michel, *Désacords de Paix au-delà de la colére,* Paris, 2001, 342 (author's translation).

the grave disobedience to the *mitzvoth* and of his own earlier naivety. He says:

> 'I must tell you that … as a good Catholic I came here in 1962, sent by my superiors, as I was a friend of Father Bruno and I loved Judaism and my superiors thought it was a good thing to send me to Jerusalem. At this time we were so enthusiastic, we Christian people, about the people of Israel coming to the land of Israel. We were blind; we did not see enough the misery of the Palestinian people and so we were naively Zionist and perhaps … because there could be confusion between love of the people of Israel and the love of the State of Israel; it is not the same thing. In some way, I think that Netanyahu and Sharon have a scandalous attitude vis-à-vis the Palestinians; it is against the vocation of the Jewish people; it is against the Bible; they are unfaithful to their identity. So to think about the destiny of Israel, the vocation of Israel and the love of God for the Jewish people, the present day situation means they are unfaithful and the whole world is conscious of that by the way.'

Over the last 50 years of the Catholic Church it is this heterogeneous group of thinkers, along with others, who have been particularly influential in changing the Church's attitude toward the Jewish people. They were influential in compiling and pushing through the adoption of the Jewish text of *Nostra Aetate,* and, to a large extent, it was they who solidified the efforts of others to remove anti-Semitic attitudes and the teaching of contempt for the Jews within the Church. As important perhaps, they have created a theological space for a Catholic Jewish community that can retain its Jewish identity.

Having been successful in creating a theological space for Hebrew Christians within the Church there are remaining challenges, firstly to find the appropriate ecclesiological structure making existential space and secondly to find peace with the Arabs.

Some of them, possibly most of them, now accept that the Jewish State is a *de facto* reality, but, with hindsight, they regard the theology of biblical prophecies being fulfilled by a temporal state as misguided.[94]

---

[94] Dubois, in an interview with the author, admitted that the concept of Asher Ginsberg's cultural and spiritual centre in Israel would have been preferable, although this would not have saved the Jews in the Diaspora from the anti-Semitism they were experiencing.

Perhaps some of these 'immigrant thinkers' are only now able to see the moral, political and religious issues from an exclusively Middle Eastern perspective as did Massignon half a century earlier.[95]

As the foregoing illustrates there is much in the way of diverse opinion among the *kehilla* members regarding politics, ecclesiology and in religious practice, however, there is much that all hold in common. For example, all members of the *kehilla* are critical of the historical relations between the Church and the Jewish people and bringing about a radical change in relationship has certainly been one of their great successes. They aim to be fully integrated in the State of Israel. To exist within an Israeli milieu as part of the local indigenous Catholic Church, therefore Hebrew, the Israeli vernacular, must be the language, and Judaism the majority religion and culture. But it must be emphasised that it is Jewish, and 'part of the Universal Catholic Church united in faith with Catholics throughout the World'[96] not of any other Christian denomination or belief.

They realise that being a Christian minority in a Jewish environment links the community to the original church. There are parallels in the relationship that nurtures a profound appreciation among members of the Jewish roots of their faith and practice. There are varying degrees of this appreciation and of the extent of what there is of value to be inherited from the Jewish tradition.[97]

Whilst upholding the non-missionary stance, and avoiding overt missionary activity, there are few in the community that would fail to uphold the comment of Fr Cantalamessa, Pope John Paul II's in house preacher. 'To renounce the desire for the Jewish brothers that I love to arrive one day at recognition of Christ, the glory of Israel, would mean neither loving Christ nor the Jews. All of Christ's preaching and his call to conversion were aimed precisely at Jews.'[98] To be sure, Christians who know Christ and the Joy that comes from the knowledge of Him will

---

[95] Anthony O'Mahony, 'Lé Pélerin de Jérusalem', 175.

[96] David Mark Neuhaus SJ, '*Kehilla,* Church and Jewish people', *Mishkan* 29, Caspari Centre, 1998, 36/2002, 79.

[97] For trends in the theological encounter between Christianity and Judaism, see Dominique Cerbelaud, 'Bulletin d'études juives et judéo-chrétiennes: Jésus sur son horizon juif', *Revue des sciences philosphiques et théologiques,* Vol.84, 2000, 545-563; D Cerbelaud, 'Bulletin d'études juives at judéo-chrétiennes: Judéo-christainisme antique dialogue judéo-chrétien actuel', *Revue des sciences philosphiques et théologiques,* Vol. 86, 2002, 123-144.

[98] Cf: 'Should Catholics convert Jews?', *The Tablet,* 29 March 2003, 26 (partly paraphrased).

want to share that knowledge with all those that they love, for members of the *kehilla* particularly, that includes the Jews.[99]

In spite of this unexpressed desire for the Jews to convert to Jesus they are strictly non-missionary. This is the root cause of an increasing, albeit tenuous; trust that has developed between the Catholic Church and the Jewish people. However, this trust is fragile and there are some who are very conscious of the pain caused to the Jewish people by the canonisation of Edith Stein,[100] it is because of the dangers of such offence being given that the *kehilla* maintains a discreet, silent presence witnessing to the universal Catholic Church rather than to the Jewish people. It is this witness that has been responsible for the present day understanding of the Church with regard to its Jewish roots and the nature of contemporary Judaism and the Jewish people. The theological project is not only an engagement between individuals in this country that is governed by Jews, but it incorporates the larger engagement between Christianity and Judaism worldwide and is central to the fulfilment of the eschatological promise. The *kehilla* continues to pose questions about this engagement.

FACTORS MILITATING AGAINST THE GROWTH OF THE *KEHILLA*: ASSIMILATION AND EMIGRATION

Whilst a mission to convert the Jews is prohibited it is recognised that the growth of the *kehilla* is dependant either on conversions or being able to retain young people of Catholic origins within the community. In this respect there are deep-rooted problems. For example, a Christian child who is an Israeli citizen or the child of a Christian expatriate living in and around Jerusalem has the option of being educated in a Christian school usually run by one of the religious institutions or orders. Such a child will have a full understanding of the Universal Catholic Church and learns about the Jewish people from day to day encounters.[101] But not all the children of immigrant Jewish Catholics have the choice of attending

---

[99] On the contemporary image of Jesus, see Jean-Marie Delamire and Najib Zakka, *Jésus dans le literature arabe et hébraïicontemporaine,* Presses universitaires du Septenrion, Villeneuve-d'Ascq (Nord), 1998.

[100] David Neuhaus *Mishkan* 36/2002, 82.

[101] This is not the case with contemporary Jewish society, Jewish children attending the Jewish State schools learn very little if anything at all about Christianity.

a Catholic school or a Jewish State school, in Beer Sheeva, for example, the only schools that exist are Jewish schools. Therefore Catholic children of mixed families, practising often clandestinely,[102] and the children of Catholic expatriates are exposed to an education that teaches nothing about Christianity other than the negative aspects [103] of the historic relations between Jews and Christians, the identification of Christianity with the Holocaust, etc. These children, if they admit their faith, bear the burden of having to defend it, 'a burden often too much to bear.'[104] 'The teaching of contempt'[105] for the Jews may have been successfully removed from the history textbooks in France and elsewhere in Europe and North America, but the scars caused to Jews by that teaching emerges as a type of contemptuous teaching about Christians in the minds, hearts and textbooks of Israeli teachers and the children they teach.[106]

---

[102] Out of necessity because of the circumstances of their immigration or social situation.

[103] Elihai, 'The Christians', gives the example of a teacher speaking of the Exodus and the worship of idols asking the children, 'and who worships idols?' to be answered in chorus by the class.

[104] Elihai, *op. cit.*

[105] The title of a book (1956) by Jules Isaac who was a highly respected professor at the Lycée St Louis, Paris, where he became Inspector General of education in the field of history. He was the main architect of seven volumes of the history course used to this day in French schools. He was also the author of 'Jesus and Israel' (1948). The Papal Nuncio to France from 1944 to 1953 was Angelo Giuseppe Roncalli who, in 1958, became Pope John XXIII. Isaac met with him; it is widely held that his influence was an important factor in the Pope's desire to make a statement on the Jews in the Vatican II documents.

[106] Slowly small steps are being taken to rectify this. One such step is the establishment of an Institute for the Study of Christianity in the Hebrew University of Jerusalem. There are some indications that a reassessment of Christianity is taking place within Israeli society and culture. For example the recent visit by Pope John Paul II in March 2000 had a profound impact upon the public perception of Christianity among the Israeli population. Ron Kronish, a leading Israeli activist in Jewish-Christian dialogue commented on the Pope's visit, saying that the visit was a watershed. 'What particularly impressed me was what we call the great educational opportunity'. During the month before the Pope's visit and during the visit itself there was more about the Pope and Christianity on television and in the newspapers than during the last 30 years. 'The Pope gave a witness of humility, truth and openness of heart, thus showing Israeli society a face of the Church of which it was completely ignorant. It is for us to take up the baton and continue the Holy Father's witness.' Jean-Baptiste Gourion: Presentation for the meeting of presidents of Episcopal Conferences Jerusalem, January 2002. http://www.lpj.org/Nonviolence/Conf/Gourioneg.htm. The 'fundamental Agreement' between Israel and The Holy See, signed on 30 December 1993, included proposals for the correct presentation —in the education system and publicly controlled media—of Christ, Christianity and the Church but this proposal along with most of the Fundamental Agreement's proposals has not yet become law. David Jaeger, *The Tablet*, 19 July 2004 6-7.

Children in Beer Sheeva are therefore brought up entirely in the Jewish educational milieu. The community there consists of mainly new immigrants from Russia and North America, the only Christian Church being the *kehilla*.[107] They are exposed to the Jewish tradition of barmitzvah in school at the age of thirteen. This is a high point in the life of a Jewish child as indeed confirmation is in the life of a Christian child, but a Christian child, as a minority in a Jewish classroom, is inclined to feel left out when all of his colleagues are barmitzvah. There are some in the *kehilla* that would see no pastoral or theological dilemma in such a child being both barmitzvah and confirmed whilst others would insist on the child making a choice of one or the other. In such situations tolerant pastoral care is called for if the *kehilla* is to grow and ultimately produce its own Israeli Catholic community and priests.[108]

There is no doubt that Christians in Israel find themselves between two powerful factions, the Jewish State on the one hand, and powerful Muslim Arab tradition on the other. Since Christians suffer discrimination in both Palestine and Israel it is not surprising that Jewish Christians, who are seen as neither one thing nor the other, suffer even more. For this reason, many Jewish Christians hide their true identity as Christians and would not wish to be overt members of the *Kehilla*.

Added to this are the very different backgrounds and resultant differing opinions of the founders as to the ecclesiastical and liturgical needs of a heterogeneous community that mirrors the heterogeneous nature of the founders themselves. Cultural differences derived from the countries of origin such as Western and Eastern Europeans, the former Soviet Union but also from the Middle East, North Africa, Egypt, Ethiopia etc. are not to be underestimated. In addition one must have regard to the fact that many gain Israeli citizenship by declaring their Jewish identity. It is therefore necessary socially and in the work place to maintain at least the appearance of being Jewish.

There being no alternative for the education of Catholic children other than in a traditional Jewish Milieu along with various forms of conflict in a majority Jewish State emigration of young families or of

---

[107] Elihai, *op. cit.*, points out that the Beer Sheeva *kehilla* is the only one that is in itself an independent parish whereas all the others are subject to the local parish priest who is often not conversant with the objectives of the *kehilla* or fluent in Hebrew.

[108] Any failure to meet the pastoral needs of young people risks the very survival of the *kehilla* since many of the current members are an ageing community.

their children for the sake of their education is increasing considerably.[109] What is feared here also mirrors the fears of Judaism, annihilation and assimilation. Annihilation of Christians in The Holy Land by emigration or assimilation into Jewish society so that they become unrecognisable as Christians.[110]

Differing visions for a Jewish Christian ecclesia

Much has been made here of the heterogeneous nature and differing biographical cultures of both the founders and the contemporary members of the *kehilla* without much reference to what might be termed, the re-writing of history to suit contemporary political and theological thinking. There are some factions that assume, often on a questionable reading of history,[111] to have a proper grasp of the reality of the contemporary situation in Israel. Other factions would disagree with their understanding of that reality. We see therefore that even in understanding the *status quo* there is great diversity.

As will be apparent from the foregoing pages, life's experience and the *milieu* from which one emerges, perhaps have a greater influence on a person's theology, living in Israel, than it might have elsewhere in the

---

[109] There are many other reasons for the lack of young Catholics in the *kehilla* apart from education. Many well-educated Catholics find it difficult to get work because in the Arab or Israeli workplace they are immediately recognised by their names as Christian and discriminated against at job interview. In the last two decades particularly, the climate of intolerance within a culture and a political structure increasingly defined as Islamic on the Palestinian side and as religious Zionist on the Israeli side puts the Catholic Christian in a sort of no-mans land where mere presence evokes suspicion. Cf. Charles Sennott, *The Body and the Blood*, Perseus Books, 2001, 27.

[110] Bernard Sabella, a professor at Bethlehem University said that if the rate of decline continues the indigenous Christian community could disappear within two generations. Sennott, *op. cit.*, 23.

[111] Here I would refer not just to modern day thinkers, but also to the tradition of those as far back as the first and second century fathers. Their reading of the Old Testament, in some cases, views Scripture on typology and seems to render the OT redundant except as a source for proof texts foretelling the coming of Jesus. However, it is to this tradition that some members of the *kehilla* would seek to return whilst still wishing to uphold the validity of the covenant to the Jews and the authenticity of their reading of the bible. 'We cannot say anything about the Bible in this country in the face of those who know so very well the language and the original text and the rich Jewish tradition ...' Cf. Elihai, *op. cit.*

world where religious and political issues are less complex and acute.

On the political front, particularly since the six-day war of 1967, when Israel expanded its borders, and more so since the first *intifada* of 1987/8, what constitutes a just settlement that will bring about peace is not generally agreed. Although all do agree that the State of Israel is a significant factor, not all necessarily agree with Zionism. To what extent should this predominantly Arab Church express itself in Jewish society through the *kehilla*?

The extent to which Jewish tradition and practice might be integrated in the liturgy and life of the community varies. Should there be, for example, a celebration of the Jewish New Year (*Rosh Hashanah*) and Tabernacles (S*ukot*), and to what extent should these be incorporated in the liturgy. Should there be recognition of *Yom Kipur* with fasting, a day of adoration and prayer perhaps? Should *Shabbat* be recognised? Some members are opposed to taking over Jewish ritual and particularly the *Seder*. These feel an invitation to a Jewish family for this celebration would more appropriately witness to the Jewishness of the Jewish Christian community.[112] If introducing these feasts into the Hebrew Christian ecclesia is intended to acculturate it to Israeli society then it is worth noting that the Messianic Jews celebrate all of these feasts yet are more alienated in Jewish society than the *kehilla* and the Catholic Church. Some members may regard such introductions as Judaizing and not inculturation.

The issues concerning the adoption of Jewish tradition and practice raise the corollary issue of departure from the traditional liturgy of the Church. There are those who would not wish to depart at all and others who would seek the de-Hellenisation of the liturgy replacing what they regard as foreign elements with Hebraic-Syriac ones.[113] These

---

[112] Brother Daniel spent a great deal of time, in the homes of his many Jewish friends at these Jewish celebrations but not in the synagogue.

[113] Elihai and Bro. Daniel were very radical in this respect, seeking to re-write everything. Elihai first considered having the 'Chaldean' rite of the Oriental Catholic Church of the East as the basis for the Hebrew Christian Liturgy that would have had both Syriac and Hebraic elements. The Semitic *lingua franca* of Christians in northern Mesopotamia was Aramaic a dialect of the Syriac language of Edessa, which was the capital city of the Abgar dynasty that lasted from 132 BC to AD 244. It was the language spoken by Jesus. Syriac manuscripts containing all four Gospels were discovered at the end of the 19th century in the monastery of St Catherine on Mount Sanai that are considered to be derived from 2nd-century writings. The manner in which our knowledge of Christianity has been handed down to us owes as much to the Syriac language as it does to Greek or Latin. The original liturgical

questions must surely be very similar to those of the Jewish Christians in Jerusalem before the destruction of the temple.

The statutes of the *kehilla* are reasonably explicit on the spiritual and social activities of the community, on the work of the community and on its overall organisation. But they are somewhat lacking in defining its primary vocation and here we may see a reflection of Israel's own dilemma discussed earlier of self identity whether belonging is by nationality or by religion. Is the intention that it should be an Israeli Church or a Jewish Church? Should it have a modern Israeli Jewish identity or a religious identity? Should the emphasis be on the study of the Jewish Church or on the study of Jewish society in which lives the Catholic Jew? Also, there is to be considered that a concentration solely on what is going on in Israel, ignoring trends in the Diaspora, may result in an Israeli exclusivity that is alien to immigrants.

The *kehilla* consists of Jews and Gentiles.[114] What should the ideal relationship be between the two? Is it a place for Jews where Gentiles are also present or is it a place of unity where the barriers are completely eliminated? It is not uncommon for Gentiles to be made to feel different. There is, on the emotional level, a tendency for Jews to be seen as somewhat better within the *kehilla*.[115]

These questions by no means occupy the thoughts and minds of all members of the *kehilla,* in the main they are a praying community whose belief in Jesus the Messiah of Israel transcends all differences.

---

language was Syriac and remains so today for the Syrian rite Christians Cf. Robert Murray SJ, 'Syriac Studies Today', *Eastern Churches Review* (1), 1966-67. Elihai's vision of a return to the language and liturgical rite of the early Christians of Edessa, who were Jewish, may be interpreted as part of an expansion since the Second World War in Patristic studies particularly, but not exclusively, the writings of St Ephrem AD 306-373 and his contemporary Aphrahat AD 280-367.

[114] It is estimated that the total number of attendants in the congregation is 350 of which only 50 are Jewish. Kai Kjaer-Hansen and Bodil F Skjott, *op. cit.*, 294.

[115] Elihai, a gentile, refers to this in his response to the patriarch, but explains that it is not an expression of superiority but rather an honest attempt by Jews to explain how Jews 'feel' in certain circumstances that gentiles are culturally unable to understand. He cites the pope in conversation with Bro. Daniel with regard to a priest who did not understand certain things, the pope remarked 'Surely he is not Jewish'.

History of the origins of the Latin Patriarchate amidst eastern rite Churches

The *kehilla* exists within the jurisdiction of the Latin Patriarchate of Jerusalem. The existence of a Latin patriarchate amidst Eastern Rite churches in the Middle East is the legacy of the politics surrounding the patriarchates of Antioch and Jerusalem and the respective kingdoms at the time the crusaders entered Jerusalem in July 1099.[116] With hindsight this may be seen now as a pre-destined event designed to unite firstly the two lungs of Christianity and then from the platform of a united Christian Church approach dialogue with Judaism and Islam.

Before the Crusader's success in occupying Jerusalem the patriarchate was Orthodox and the Oriental titular Symeon of Jerusalem who had left Jerusalem for Cyprus in 1097 had died. The Crusaders replaced the titular with a Latin patriarch. Prior to this the only Latin presence in Jerusalem were two Benedictine communities, established c 1070, who were present there primarily for the spiritual direction and pastoral care to pilgrims from the West.

The structure of the new Latin Sees of Jerusalem and Antioch remained the same as the Orthodox sees. Most of the parish churches were brought into the new patriarchate[117] and some of the Orthodox clergy were even absorbed into the Latin episcopates, the patriarchs themselves did not have the autonomy enjoyed by their Orthodox predecessors instead they remained subject to papal authority.[118]

In 1187, almost two hundred years after the establishment of the Latin Patriarchate, the first Ayyubid Sultan, Saladin, attacked the Kingdom of Jerusalem causing the patriarch and many other clergy to flee to St Jean d'Acre where the kingdom was re-established around the city and from where they were reluctant to leave even half a century later when the Latins again regained temporary control of some of the Holy Places.[119] The

---

[116] Source for this and the following section is the *Catholic Encyclopaedia*; Bernard Hamilton, 'The Latin Church in the Crusader States' in K Ciggar, A Davids and H Teule (eds), *East and West in the Crusader States*, Louvain, 1996, 1-20.

[117] There were a few exceptions such as the Orthodox monasteries that were still in use and also the churches and monasteries belonging to other eastern Churches, Greek, Armenian and Syrian Jacobite. Any churches not brought into the Crusader Kingdom at the time remained Orthodox thereafter.

[118] Hamilton, *op. cit.*, 6 gives fuller details as to the reasons for this.

[119] Hamilton, *op. cit.*, 18-19.

political presence of the Latins ended when Nicholas of Hanapes, the last Latin Patriarch to reside in the Holy Land, was found dead in a ditch when the city capitulated on 11 July 1291 in the Mamluk conquest. From then on until the re-establishment of the patriarchate in 1847 there was only a titular patriarch with no real jurisdiction who resided in Rome using the Basilica of St Laurence Without the Walls as the patriarchal church.

The Catholic religious presence survived only in the Franciscan order that was favourably tolerated by the Mamluks following St Francis' dialogue with the sultan.[120] The Franciscans established a province and custody, in spite of resistance from the Greek Church, and although it was not formally agreed for more than a century afterwards, they became responsible for the Holy Places.[121] In the ensuing years there were many disputes between Greek Orthodox and Catholics and between different European nations, their jurisdictions over the ancient city and the Holy Places. All of these affected the continuity of the Latin rite and Roman tradition at different times causing the Franciscans at times to be removed and at others times reinstated but none of these need be dealt with in this paper. What is pertinent is that the Latin rite and Roman tradition prevailed.

In 1847 it was therefore not an establishment of a patriarchate in the Orthodox Eastern tradition that took place but a re-establishment of the patriarchate of the crusading Franks, in other words, re-established as it was in 1099, a Latin rite in the Roman tradition and not independent of Rome. Whilst the first official Latin patriarch, Daimbert, was claimed to be the lawful successor of the Orthodox patriarch his authority was more in keeping with a metropolitan in a western province[122] and throughout the early part of the twelfth century fears of a separation from Rome such as happened in the great schism of 1054 and that of 1130 caused there to be a steady stream of papal legates keeping an eye on the patriarch. Apart

---

[120] The history of the Franciscan Order records that St Francis, following the second general chapter in May of 1219, dispatched his brethren all over the Saracen empire with instructions to evangelise the infidels. He set sail himself with eleven colleagues on 21 June that year for the eye of the storm at Saint-Jean d'Acre. He is said to have witnessed and been horrified by the siege of Damietta where three thousand people, men, women and children died of thirst and starvation. But perhaps the most important achievement of his mission was that he was able to meet with the sultan and reside with him in dialogue for several days. Following the visit the sultan gave Francis safe passage to Jerusalem and ever since there has been a special relationship between the world of Islam and the Franciscan brethren.

[121] An agreement was concluded in 1313 between the King of Naples and the Mamluk Sultan of Egypt. Cf. Anthony O'Mahony, *op. cit.*, 99-100.

[122] Hamilton, *op. cit.*, 6.

from fears over a split with Rome there was also concern for the Holy Places so that more supervision from Rome was centred on Jerusalem than on the newly founded Latin Patriarchate of Antioch.

It was continued concerns for the Holy Places that caused Jerusalem once again to be chosen by Rome in 1847 for the re-establish the patriarchate in spite of the fact that the largest Latin parishes in the Middle East were sited in Lebanon. But there had been a great deal of aggression from the Greek Orthodox clergy who from as early as the thirteenth century had been hostile to the Latin presence and jurisdiction over the Holy Places. It was an escalation of this aggression in 1847 when the symbol of Catholic jurisdiction, the silver star over the Church of the Nativity in Bethlehem, was taken down that precipitated Pius IX's resolve to re-establish the Latin Patriarchate that today covers all of Israel, Palestine, Jordan and Cyprus.

The politics of ecclesiology

The re-emergence of Hebrew Catholicism in the Holy Land excites those who see in it a prophetic sign that heals the wounds of the great rupture between the Church of the Circumcision and the Church of the Gentiles. For them the resultant imbalance that saw the *Ecclesia ex Circumcisione* swallowed by the *Ecclesia ex Gentibus* in less than a century could again in modern times overwhelm this fragile shoot thus losing the benefits for all time of the Hebrew traditions and culture upon which the early Church was founded.

For over forty years those that fear the overcoming of this tender shoot, or at least restrictions to its full blossoming, have proposed ecclesial and liturgical changes for its well being within the Israeli milieu.[123] Cardinal Ratzinger writing to a member of the *kehilla* in 1992 says it is necessary that the Church be extended to cater for its original double structure that must shape the Church again from the inside.[124] The main proposals are intended to show the Israeli people that a Hebrew Christian Church of Israel participates in the life of the country, understands the culture and values of Judaism and also to help 'deepen [the Church's] understanding of

---

[123] Cf. Fr Johanan Elihai, unpublished paper, *réponse à une demande du Patriarche au course du Synode*, Jerusalem, 15 October 1995.

[124] Cf. Fr Johanan Elihai, *op. cit.*

itself'.[125] The criticisms that this 'movement for change'[126] make of Hebrew Catholicism's character in modern Israel, is that it does not show itself to be part of Israeli society. It appears foreign in its nationality, culture and language. In the opinion of some this is due to the continued use of the Roman liturgical style, symbols, and the ecclesial structure. The symbol of the cross particularly serves only as a reminder to Israeli society of the horrors inflicted upon them under this sign[127] and the statues of saints are perceived as idols that Christians worship.[128]

Cardinal Daoud, Prefect of the Sacred Congregation for the Oriental Churches is reported[129] to have observed at the meeting on the future of Christians in the Holy Land, Vatican City, 13 December 2001, that the character of the *kehillot* are that the Church is not actually very visible and has no voice within the ethnic-cultural majority but he asks 'What in practice would be the 'ecclesial structure' best adapted to resolving the problem?'

This movement for change seem to consider that many of the issues of inculturation and relations between the Catholic Church and Israel would be resolved if there were established a separate jurisdiction for Hebrew speaking Catholics in Israel directly dependent on Rome and independent of the predominantly Arab Latin Patriarchate. In the past the patriarch has not ignored the requests for more autonomy and authority for the *kehilla*. Since 1999 the patriarchal vicar[130] to the *kehilla*

---

[125] The words of Cardinal Martini in 1984. Cf. Elihai, *op. cit.*

[126] What I refer to, as a movement for change is only a small number of the *kehilla* members in Israel supported by only a few sympathetic voices in Rome and the French church. The members are not united with regard to ecclesial change, liturgical form etc.

[127] Edward Flannery in the foreword to his book *The Anguish of the Jews*, Macmillan, New York, 1965, tells of how he was walking down the Park Avenue in New York in the company of a young Jewish couple. Behind them was a large, brightly lit cross, which is raised over the Grand Central building every Christmas. Turning round suddenly the young woman, never being hostile towards the Christians whatsoever, said: 'This cross makes me shudder, makes me sense some evil presence.' He writes that the symbol that is to Christians one of common love was for this Jewish woman a symbol of fear and a curse. Her reaction of terror followed what she knew about the great pain that her people suffered through twenty centuries because of the Christians.

[128] Elihai, *op. cit.*

[129] See the well-informed American Jesuit, counsellor for international affairs to the United States Conference of Catholic Bishops, Drew Christiansen, 'A Campaign to Divide the Church in the Holy Land', *America*, 19 May 2003.

[130] The Abbot of Abu Gosh, Dom Jean-Baptiste Gourion has been patriarchal vicar since 1990 until his appointment as Auxiliary Bishop with special responsibility for Hebrew Speaking Israeli Catholics in 2003.

has been an invited member of the assembly of Catholic Ordinaries[131] of the Holy Land. But this issue has become an extremely complex mix of ecclesiastical and secular politics.[132]

Ironically the 'Roman' intervention, part of this movement for change, claims to be motivated not by issues of inculturation but by pastoral concern for the growing numbers of non-Arab Catholics among Israel's immigrant population of whom many are temporary residents who do not speak Hebrew. Such concern could well be the final blow that destroys the re-emergence of the *ecclesia circumcisione*.

The largest immigrant group is Russian, of which an estimated 250,000 to 400,000 are listed as 'non-Jewish'. Of these, only 27,000 to 30,000 acknowledge being Christian, and for the most part these are Orthodox.[133] If the intention were to set up a Church of Israel, a Hebrew speaking Church, that supplants the fledgling Hebrew Catholic Church, the *kehilla,* a jurisdiction that is primarily concerned with non-Arabs and non-Jews, the gentile imbalance already existing in the *kehilla* would once again overpower the *ecclesia circumcisione.*

Linked to this movement for change there have been vigorous attacks on the patriarch, Michel Sabbah, in the French Catholic press by some French churchmen who have supported the idea. These attacks would not appear to be out of solicitude for the pastoral care of the non-Arab immigrant population since immigrant Christians of varying ethnicity and nationality are already well served by chaplains speaking the language of their countries of origin. Nor is it conceivable that the strong support by some in the Israeli government for the establishment of a church within the Jewish State does not have a wider political agenda.

Michel Sabbah is the first Palestinian cleric to rise in the Catholic hierarchy and to be named patriarch.[134] He has spoken out for Palestinian rights and national aspirations and against the Israeli occupation and human rights violations. He has also demonstrated his concern for Catholics within the State of Israel. His ministry is to be admired for he is the first patriarch to be seen to speak for all Christians in the Holy Land. As the leading Catholic churchman in Israel his views are taken seriously throughout, not only the Catholic but also to a large extent, the Christian

[131] This gave greater authority and autonomy to the Patriarchal Vicar in matters concerning Hebrew speaking Catholics in the Holy Land.

[132] Drew Christiansen, 'A Campaign to Divide the Church in the Holy Land', *America*, 19 May 2003.

[133] *Ibid.*

[134] The Latin Patriarchate was re-established in 1847 when Giuseppe Valerga was appointed to the see, since then there have been seven European Patriarchs until 1987 when His Beatitude Michel Sabbah, a Palestinian Arab originating from Nazareth was appointed. His appointment

world. Some in the Israeli government may regard his current position that straddles the geo-political and ethnic divide as too powerful from a public relations point of view. Therefore, the motives of those in the Israeli government in there support for what effectively would divide the Church in the Holy Land would seem to be to undermine the Patriarch who has been portrayed by some as the 'Islamic Patriarch'[135] who, if the patriarchate were divided, would no longer be regarded as the head of a united Church in the Holy Land speaking for all Christians.[136] The supporters of the move in the French church for a separate jurisdiction as proposed by the Roman faction was perhaps unwittingly playing into the hands of a government that is not averse to interfering in ecclesiastical appointments.[137] Perhaps also it would be counterproductive to the other bridge building objectives of Pope John Paul II. The Church is concerned not only to build bridges between Catholic and Jew but also between Jew and Arab the present patriarchal structure that straddles the geographical boundary is ideally suited to do the latter. Further, a Hebrew Catholic community within that structure fostering the vision of Cardinal Tisserant by using the Syrian rite may also begin to bridge the gap between the two lungs, East and West, of the Church. Patriarch Sabbah's achievements in being seen as a spokesman for all Christians in the Holy Land is surely a first step in that direction.

The reality of the situation however, is that any person who expresses criticism of Israeli policies tends to be accused of anti-Semitism[138] even if they go out of their way to create an environment that encourages

---

has been controversial not only in some Hebrew Christian quarters but also to Jews because the perception is that an Arab patriarch is biased in favour of the Palestinians. European patriarchs have not raised the same objections on account of their being seen as ethnically neutral in the Holy Land.

[135] Ambassador Gadi Golan, head of the Israeli Foreign Ministry's Department of Interreligious Affairs, declared that the establishment of 'a Catholic church in Israel' would make it clear that Michel Sabbah is 'the Islamic patriarch'. Quoted by Drew Christiansen, 'A Campaign to Divide the Church in the Holy Land', *America*, 19 May 2003.

[136] Drew Christiansen, *ibid*. Michel Sabbah has been seen as not only speaking for Catholics but has successfully united all Christians in the Holy land so that his influence around the world is very considerable. He is fully aware, as is the Israeli government that he speaks to all Christians around the world. In his Christmas message 2003 he comments, 'These questions might also be of interest to our brothers and sisters in the different Churches around the world.'

[137] In the mid nineties the government tried to prevent the appointment of what they considered a pro-Palestinian as the Melkite archbishop of Akko. Cf. Drew Christiansen, 'A Campaign to Divide the Church in the Holy Land', *America*, 19 May 2003.

[138] The worldwide Catholic Church teaches that dialogue with the Jewish people is distinct from the political options adopted by the State of Israel. Cf. the Patriarch's Christmas message 23 December 2003, *Independent Catholic News*. http://www.indcatholicnews.com/latgrt.html.

mutual understanding and respect for Jews as they are, and dialogue with them as a fundamental Christian priority.[139] The Patriarch's efforts in this respect seem to have gone unnoticed, his condemnation of both violence and of the provocative situations that lead to violence[140] are seen as supportive of the violence of the Palestinians in spite of his continual condemnation of all violence. He states, 'Terrorism is illogical, irrational and unacceptable as a means of resolving conflict.'[141] Ironically his anti-violence stance[142] and dialogue with the Israelis,[143] alienates him from the very Arabs that the Israelis accuse him of supporting.

The issue of inculturation of the *kehilla* into Israeli society whilst keeping it within the Universal Church so that it might shape it again from the inside, could not be more appropriately served than by the appointment of the first Jewish Bishop[144] in the Holy Land since James the Apostle. Jean Baptiste Gourion was appointed auxiliary bishop to the patriarch with special responsibility for Hebrew-speaking Israeli Catholics on the 14 August 2003 and consecrated by the patriarch on the 9 November 2003. (However, he died soon after in 2004.) Perhaps we can regard this appointment as a rejection by the Vatican of the criticisms of Patriarch Michel Sabbah and of the Latin Patriarchate of Jerusalem as the dominant Catholic ecclesiastical voice in Jerusalem and in the Holy Land. Perhaps too it is a prophetic move in nurturing the rebirth of the *ecclesia circumcisione* through which the two lungs of the Church may be re-united and into which will be gathered all the elect of God as well as those grafted in.

---

139 The diocesan synod of 2000 led by Sabbah introduced all this and more in its General Pastoral Plan.

140 The Patriarch's Christmas message 23 December 2003, *Independent Catholic News*. http://www.indcatholicnews.com/latgrt.html.

141 Michel Sabbah, 'Seek Peace and Pursue It: Questions and answers on Justice and peace in the Holy Land' (September 1998), n. 15.

142 Michel Sabbah led a delegation of Christian clerics to the spiritual leader of the militant Hamas movement, Sheikh Ahmed Yassin, on 10 August 2002 in a bid to stop suicide bombings against Israeli targets. Cf. *Independent Catholic News*, Jerusalem, 12 August 2002.

143 On 23 March 1998 in preparation for the Pope's 2000 visit Patriarch Sabbah met with Israel's chief Ashkenazi rabbi, Meir Lau, and the chief Sephardi rabbi, Eliyahu Bakshi-Doron to discuss issues ranging from the Holocaust to the status of Jerusalem's holy sites. While the two sides disagreed in several areas, all participants agreed that the meeting itself was a positive development. Cf. *Daily Catholic*, world news, 25 March 1998.

144 Gourion is the first Catholic Jewish bishop, the first Jewish bishop in Jerusalem was the Anglican bishop Michael Solomon Alexander appointed on 7 November 7 1841. see Gershon Nerel, 'Hebrew Christian Associations in Ottoman Jerusalem: Jewish Yeshua—Believers Facing Church and Synagogue', *Revue des Études juives*, 161 (2002), 431-457.

PALESTINIAN CHRISTIANS: THEOLOGY AND POLITICS IN THE HOLY LAND

Leonard Marsh

I want to look briefly at the following issues. Firstly, who are Palestinian Christians? Secondly, to say something about Palestinian Christian response to the creation of the State of Israel and their theological contribution to the dilemmas of Palestinian Christian experience; thirdly, to ask about ecumenical opportunities and responses in recent times; and fourthly, to comment on the relationship of Palestinian Christianity to Islam and Muslim-Christian relations; and finally to look at the prospects and challenges for the future of this minority in Palestinian society.

Firstly, who are Palestinian Christians? Palestinian Christianity, albeit a small minority within the Palestinian population overall, is an indigenous expression of Christianity which lives a rich and complex reality both in the Holy Land and aboard in the extensive Palestinian diaspora. It has great strengths and weaknesses representing the capacity of Christianity to 'inculturate' itself in different cultures and languages. The varieties of liturgies to be heard in the Church of the Holy Sepulchre are a witness to the conflicts and fragmentation among the Christian churches. The variety of Christian experience is remarkable; Palestinian Arab and Greek Orthodox churches, Oriental Orthodox churches represented by Armenians, Syrians, Copts, and Ethiopians. The Latin and Eastern Catholic Churches are part of this kaleidoscope—Anglican, Protestant, and various evangelical churches are of course more recent. Other groups, such as Messianic Jews, are also part of the complex phenomenon that is Palestinian Christianity.

How can Palestinian Christianity be characterised? It can be said to contain eastern, western, Orthodox, Catholic and Protestant, indigenous, expatriate, theologically liberal and theologically conservative elements; worship that is strongly liturgical but also of a much freer kind, traditional and modern. Geographically, Palestinian Christianity is represented in the

Gaza Strip and the West Bank in at least fifteen different localities. Many are concentrated in the urban centres of Bethlehem, Jerusalem and Ramallah. Dr Bernard Sabella, professor of Sociology at Bethlehem University, estimates the total number of indigenous Palestinian Christians as just over fifty thousand, distributed as follows: 52 percent Greek Orthodox, 30 percent Latin, 5 percent Greek Catholics, 5 percent Protestant, 3 percent Syriacs, 3 percent Armenians, 0.5 percent Copts, 0.5 percent Ethiopians and 0.2 percent Maronites.[1]

I want to speak now about Palestinian Christianity and its relationship to Palestinian nationalism. At the time of the Balfour Declaration, and the period of the British Mandate over Palestine, 1920-1948, the drive toward Palestinian national identity intensified. This sense of national identity was partly focused as a result of religious factors. As Rashid Khalidi points out, although Muslims and Christians had somewhat different conceptions as to what makes Palestine a Holy Land, and also differed regarding its boundaries and extent, they shared a similar general idea of the country as a unit and as being special and holy. The jurisdictions of the Latin and Greek Orthodox patriachates, and the Protestant Episcopate of Jerusalem, which covered Palestine entirely, reinforced this sense of identity, even when administrative units changed.[2] The British mandate over Palestine ended of course on the 14th of May, 1948, and the State of Israel was immediately proclaimed, and Arab forces entered Palestine. The extent of the defeat of the Arabs allowed the new Israeli state to expand its boundaries almost at once. The impact of what Palestinians refer to as *Al-Nakba*, The Catastrophe, is exemplified by the experiences of the Palestinian Christian writer, Father Elias Chacour. Father Chacour is a Greek Catholic priest who chronicles his personal experience of being forced as a child from a village in Galilee destroyed by Israeli troops in 1948, in two important books, *Blood Brothers*[3] and *We Belong to the Land*.[4] Father Chacour was trained for the Greek Catholic priesthood in Nazareth and St Sulpice in Paris, and was ordained in 1965. He has a degree in Biblical Studies including the Talmud from the Hebrew

---

1 Bernard Sabella, 'Socio-Economic Characteristics and Challenges to Palestinian Christians in the Holy Land', in *Christians in the Holy Land*, M Prior and W Taylor (eds.), World of Islam Festival Trust, London, 1995.

2 Rashid Khalidi, *Palestinian Identity*, Columbia University Press, New York, 1997, 150.

3 Elias Chacour, *Blood Brothers*, Chosen Books, Grand Rapids, Michigan, 1984.

4 Elias Chacour, *We Belong to the Land*, Harper, San Francisco, 1990.

University in Jerusalem. The title, *Blood Brothers*, is significant in that it stresses the Semitic unity of Arabs and Jews. Father Chacour does have sympathy for a Jewish Israel but contrasts the hopes and aspirations of pre-Holocaust Zionism with the brutality and oppression he himself has experienced as a Palestinian. *Blood Brothers* is a reflective autobiography that relates his growing radicalisation as a Palestinian Christian activist. Father Chacour's conviction that Palestinians have a right to live in Israel on the basis of equality, even if Zionists believe they have the right to the land to the exclusion of others by the authority of Scripture, was enhanced by his pastorate of the Melkite Church in Ibillin in the Galilee. He witnessed and documented the oppression of Palestinians in this community.

Another contemporary Christian thinker from the Holy Land is Canon Naim Ateek, a Palestinian Anglican theologian. He sees the 1967 Six-day War as a crucial moment in the history of the Israeli state. Many Jews and many Western Christians according to him, perceived the occupation of Gaza along with parts of Syria and Egypt as a sign of God's purposeful and powerful intervention on the side of Israel and against the Arabs.

Canon Ateek believes that after 1967 Palestinians faced a Zionism that was less based on secular ideology than on religious zealotry. This development has been important in the growth of a specifically Palestinian Christian response to the nationalist question.

Palestinian Christians in the main, initially did not support the eruption of the first Intifada in the refugee camps beginning in the Gaza Strip in December 1987. This situation changed, however, when on 9 February, 1988, Khalid Tarazi, a Christian boy from Gaza, died after interrogation following his arrest by the Israelis. Daphne Tsimhoni, a senior researcher at Ben Gurion University in Israel, identifies this event as symbolizing the common fate of Christians with their Muslim counterparts in Palestine.[5] Tsimhoni notes the contribution of Palestinian Christians in bringing the Palestinian cause to Western public opinion, including Dr Hannah Aswari, prominent delegate to the Madrid peace talks. She observes that such contributions are not meant to represent the Christian but rather the national cause. The Latin patriarch, Michael Sabbah, and the Greek Catholic Archbishop, Lufti Laham, and the retired Anglican bishop Samir Kafity, organised the collective effort of

---

[5] Tsimhoni, Daphne, *Christian Communities in Jerusalem and the West Bank since 1948*, Praeger, Westport, Connecticut, 1993, 168.

Jerusalem churches supporting the Palestinian national cause. In April, 1989, they issued a joint statement against injustice and the oppression of the Palestinian people: 'In Jerusalem, the West Bank, and in Gaza, our people are experiencing in their daily lives constant deprivation of their fundamental rights because of arbitrary actions deliberately taken by the authorities. Our people are often subjected to unprovoked harassment and hardship. We are particularly concerned by the tragic and unnecessary loss of Palestinian lives, especially among minors. Unarmed and innocent people are being killed through the unwarranted use of firearms, and hundreds are wounded from the excessive use of force. We protest against the frequent shootings and incidents in the vicinity of holy places. We also protest the practice of mass administrative arrests and the continuing detention of adults and minors without trial. We further condemn the use of all forms of collective punishment, including the demolition of homes, and depriving whole communities of basic services such as water and electricity.'[6]

Such joint statements continue to be made at Christian festivals and special occasions. This identification with the Palestinian national cause, and the society in which Palestinian Christians live in Israel/Palestine, is a paramount factor in the development of a Palestinian indigenous theology.

Palestinian Christians have had to address the critical issue of Biblical interpretation. All theology needs to engage with interpretation of the Bible, but Palestinian Christians need to address the central issue of the Bible and the land. This is because, as Michael Prior points out, the Bible at face value provides not only a moral framework which transposes Jewish claims into a divinely sanctioned legitimacy, but postulates the taking and possession of the promised land, and the forcible expulsion of the indigenous population, as the fulfilment of a Biblical mandate.[7]

It is important to appreciate that this question of the Bible and the promise of land is not just the concern of writers such as Canon Ateek, who might characterize himself as a liberation theologian, it also is a concern of the hierarchies of the church in Palestine. Latin Patriarch Sabbah wrote a pastoral letter in November 1993, titled 'Reading the Bible today in the land of the Bible.' In this, Patriarch Sabbah notes that we have to struggle

---

[6] *Ibid.*, 169.

[7] Michael Prior, *Zionism and the State of Israel: A Moral Inquiry*, Routledge, London, 1999.

in order to maintain and build peace with justice. The word of God in the Bible is a difficult and delicate task, and the matters to be tackled are related to our daily lives. They even concern our very national and personal identity as believers because unilateral, partial interpretations run the risk, for some people, of bringing into question their presence and permanence in this land, which is their homeland. Patriarch Sabbah points out that, for Palestinian Christians, the Bible is an integral part of their faith and religious heritage, whether this is meditated upon individually or realized in the community, in liturgies and prayer groups, etc. The fundamental questions raised in these prayer and reading groups have been numerous. These questions persist now: how is the Old Testament to be understood? What is the relationship between the Old and New Testaments? The Bible narration includes stories of violence which have a striking resemblance to our present history, which are attributed to God. How are these to be understood? And what is the relationship between ancient Biblical history and our contemporary history? Is Biblical Israel to be identified with the State of Israel? What is the meaning of the promises, the election, the covenant, and in particular the promise and gift of the land to Abraham and to his descendants? Does the Bible justify current political claims made on its behalf? Could we be victims of our own salvation history, which seems to favour the Jewish people and condemn us? Is that truly the will of God to which we must inexorably bow down, demanding that we deprive ourselves in favour of another people with no possibility of appeal or discussion? Many Jews in Israel have differing views. Some of them, by what they say and sincerely believe, seem to confirm the fears and anguish of the Palestinians. They maintain that God has given the land to them alone; such implies their title and exclusive ownership of the whole of the Promised Land.

Some Christians would say the same thing. Certain fundamentalist Christians will go so far as to seek to directly link all of present history with the fulfilment of specific Biblical prophecy. They even accuse those Christians who do not ascribe to this idea as being unbiblical and not true believers.

Michel Sabbah, the Latin Patriarch of Jerusalem roots his pastoral letter in the Decree on Divine Revelation from the documents of the Second Vatican Council. In this Decree, it is asserted that the Bible is the divine and human Word revealed to a community. Its message is divine, spiritual, and eternal, but it comes to us clothed in linguistic, literary, cultural, historical and geographical terms which are human. Sabbah says that we cannot ask of the Bible what it is unable to give. He presents the Bible as a matter of progressive revelation, as noted at the Second Vatican Council, and notes the importance and value, for Palestinian Christians as well as anyone else, of Biblical criticism in understanding the meaning and value of the Bible.[8]

Canon Naim Ateek is perhaps the most well-known exponent of what might be called a Palestinian Christian Liberation Theology. He recognises that the Biblical text represents a major challenge to such a theology. For Palestinians, the Bible itself is not a source of strength, offering an encouragement to faith and the gift of salvation. Rather, some Jews and many Christians have used the Bible in a way to validate injustice and inequality. Understood in a 'literal' way, the Bible appears to Palestinians to enslave them and undermine their hopes for a national homeland. Ateek provocatively asks the question, when Christians recite the Benedictus, including the words 'Blessed be the God of Israel,' what does this mean? Which Israel is being referred to? What redemption is being promised, and to whom?

How can Palestinian Christians appreciate the Bible? Conflicting issues in the Biblical text pose the question: is God partial to the Jews, and is the God of the Bible a God of justice and peace? Ateek believes it is necessary to undertake a process of contextualisation in relation to the Bible. An awareness of what Palestinians face in approaching the Biblical text seems to be what Ateek refers to here. According to Ateek, such a perspective is a necessary preliminary task in any process of interpretation. At the same time he is also keen to be faithful to the Biblical message.[9]

Canon Ateek and Patriarch Sabbah both believe that the Bible can only be understood for Christians in the light of Jesus Christ. Not surprisingly, Ateek has a preference for the prophetic strand in the Hebrew Scriptures, and this is put in the context of a belief in a God who has a commitment to the underprivileged, the disadvantaged, and the vulnerable. This is a theology of hope and compassion.

Ateek observes that Eastern Christians have experienced a heavy price historically because they share the name 'Christian' with Western

---

[8] Michel Sabbah, the Latin Patriarch of Jerusalem, Pastoral Letter— 'In pulchritudine pacis': 'Reading the Bible Today in the Land of the Bible'. November, 1993.

[9] NaimAteek, *Justice and only Justice: A Palestinian Theology of Liberation*, Orbis, Maryknoll, New York, 1989.

Crusaders of a previous epoch. Living as a minority among different countries in the Middle East, the task of Palestinian Christians, according to Ateek, is to realise a two-dimensional ministry entailing elements of prophecy and non-violence. Most Arab Christians are united by a common faith even though some church hierarchies are preoccupied with past differences. Ateek sees the theological implication of his exegesis as a matter of faith in an inclusive God of truth, justice and peace, choosing to regard the Incarnation as the basis for God's involvement in the world and the church being the conscience of the nation.

In evaluating Canon Ateek's approach, it ought to be acknowledged that its strength lies in the placing of emphasis on forgiveness in a Christ-centred hermeneutic. Kenneth Cragg, a leading scholar of Arab Christianity, sees this as the distinctive contribution that Palestinian Christianity can bring to the intractable history of the Israeli-Palestinian conflict.

Sabeel is a Palestinian Christian organisation devoted to liberation theology in the Palestinian context. The first Sabeel newsletter, from 1994, places the impetus of the centre initially with pastoral concerns experienced by clergy working with the people at the grass roots and listening to their cries. Although at first this was largely a response to physical suffering, there was a growing awareness that this suffering was being aggravated by religious argument in the political conflict. Sabeel began to raise profound theological questions, such as where is God in all of this? Why does God allow the confiscation of Palestinian land? Why does God allow the occupation and the oppression of our people?

Sabeel also began to deal with the reflection on Biblical text, particularly the question of how the Old Testament has been used to justify or rationalise the suffering of Palestinians. A committee of clergy and lay theologians came together to explore how liberation theology could be practically applied to the experience of Palestinian Christians.

The early work of this committee resulted in an international conference in 1990 held at the Tantur Ecumenical Theological Centre situated between Jerusalem and Bethlehem. The conference looked at such issues as Palestinian Christian identity; power, justice and the Bible; women; faith and the Intifada. Workshops were held on topics including holy land Christians and survival; reclaiming our identity and redefining ourselves; Biblical justice, among others. The work of the first conference was published through an editorial team of Naim Ateek, Mark Ellis, a

Jewish American writer, and Rosemary Radford-Reuther, the resulting work entitled *Faith and the Intifada*,[10] lead to a permanent centre being established for the organisation, Sabeel.

Another international conference was held on the campus at Bethlehem University on 15 February, 1998. The work of this conference was published as *Holy Land, Hollow Jubilee*, edited by Naim Ateek and Michael Prior.[11] The theme of the conference was the challenge of jubilee: what does God require? Its aim was to look at the 50 years since the founding of the State of Israel, and evaluate this history and learn from it. Sessions concerned a range of issues including religious fundamentalism, Christian-Muslim relations, Jubilee as a Biblical tradition, the Bible and Zionism, human rights and pilgrimage alternatives. Although primarily a theological conference, participants were transported to a number of sites on the West Bank, where they were able to witness first-hand the reality of checkpoints, destroyed villages, and confiscated land. The late Edward Said, the internationally known Palestinian academic, who was raised as a Protestant Christian, addressed the conference. Professor Said drew an analogy between the Palestinian movement and opposition to apartheid in South Africa, and called for a sustained campaign in universities and churches in order to demonstrate what was—and is—a public and moral cause. Without such a sustained campaign, Said was pessimistic about the Palestinian situation.

In their newsletters, Sabeel provides commentaries and reflections on the perspective of liberation theology in Palestine and contemporary political developments.

In May 2000, four months before the second Intifada began, Sabeel issued the Jerusalem Sabeel document, *Principles for a Just Peace in Palestine and Israel*. This document sets out the theological, political and moral basis for a peace with justice in the Israeli/Palestinian conflict. It calls for a Palestinian state to be established on the West Bank including East Jerusalem as well as the Gaza Strip. It affirms the great injustice that has been done to the Palestinian people, and a call for this to be acknowledged by Israel; allowing the right of return for refugees and reparations to be made, as the only basis for a settlement based on the establishment of two sovereign and fully democratic states.

---

[10] Marc Ellis, and Rosemary Radford Reuther (eds), *Faith and the Intifada*. Orbis, Maryknoll, 1985.

[11] Naim Ateek, and Michael Prior (eds), *Holy Land, Hollow Jubilee,* Melisende, London 1999.

In February 2002, Sabeel organized a conference entitled Speaking Truth, Seeking Justice, inviting 250 delegates from 21 countries. The political context of this conference was the continuation of the second Intifada and the election of Ariel Sharon as Israeli prime minister. Corresponding with the Friends of Sabeel in North America, Sabeel immediately expressed sorrow and outrage at the September 11 tragedy in the US, noting that now is the time to work with more determination to deal with the root causes that create violence, a violence that is consuming our world. Naim Ateek has sought to understand but not to justify the phenomenon of suicide bombers. He believes that as these individuals have been driven into profound despair and the utmost isolation, their desire to hit back by any means possible has intensified. Ateek rejects the concept of a God that seeks to justify such actions—as some have interpreted the story of Joshua in the Old Testament. He points out that God's justice is not devoid of mercy.[12]

The fifth International Sabeel Conference, Challenging Christian Zionism, was held in Jerusalem in April 2004. Over five hundred delegates took part from over thirty countries. Because of the difficulties experienced by Palestinian Christians in attending the conference due to the lack of freedom of movement, the conference moved about. One day was spent in Ramallah at the Friends Boys School, later the delegates were received by President Yasser Arafat. Both Jewish and Muslim, as well as Christian scholars explored the implications of the union of theology and politics that is Christian Zionism. Speakers included Marc Ellis, the Jewish liberation theologian, and Michael Prior, the Catholic Biblical scholar. Rosemary Radford Ruether, now Carpenter Professor of Feminist Theology at the graduate Theological Union in Berkeley, California, addressed the more diffuse sense in which Christian Zionism has influenced main stream churches in assuming that Israel's right to the land excludes Palestinians from their rights and even threatens their existence. A forthcoming book will be published from these papers. The sensitivity of the present religious and political situation in Israel-Palestine is perhaps reflected in the fact that Dr Rowan Williams, Archbishop of Canterbury, was due to attend and address the conference. In the end he did not attend in person, but sent his Ecumenical Secretary to give his address.

Recently, in a reflection on the new security fence that Israel continues to construct, Ateek observes that where there is injustice in one

---

[12] Naim Ateek, 'Suicide Bombers', in *Cornerstone*, Issue 25, Summer, 2002.

form or another, humans resort to building walls separating neighbours and enemies. Ateek believes that the building of this wall is Israel's way of realising empire. He contrasts this with the vision in the Book of Revelation wherein the choice for Christians and all people of faith is between empire and 'the new Jerusalem' where the community has its defence and security in God.[13] Naim Ateek gave the Chichester Cathedral Lecture on the 24 May 2004, and again he returned to the theme of peace. He strongly emphasized that a political Jewish ideology, and a religious Jewish Zionist, as well as a Christian Zionist theology, obstructs the way to peace and security.

I'd like to say a few words now about ecumenical relations. The disunity of the church has nowhere been more apparent than in the Holy Land, where the churches historically have been aware of their territorial and other rights, and are particularly zealous in their defence. The conflicts that have arisen have been especially damaging to the Christian cause. At the level of ordinary Christians, I think it is true to say that a large measure of mutual respect already exists. Inter-church marriages among Christians are not uncommon. It is, however, at the level of the church hierarchies that problems are most acute. Although co-operation among the churches has increased during the periods of the Intifadas, a great deal of further work needs to be done in this area. At the level of theological dialogue, co-operation or even discussion is hard to find.

It surely is a great irony that the gospel that is about forgiveness and reconciliation between God and humanity, and among human beings, can be used as a source for conflict. I suppose there will always be a tension between being a Christian—a member of a church which is called to transcend that which separates human beings—and being part of a typical human 'society' which tends to defend its own identity by setting itself up against other societies.

A source of contention among the Holy Land churches is the willingness of certain churches, and individuals, to sell land in particularly sensitive areas.

Now I would like to comment on Christian-Muslim relations in Israel/Palestine. Kenneth Cragg, in his seminal work, *The Arab Christian*,[14] entitles his last chapter, 'A Future With Islam?' He observes that there can be

---

[13] Naim Ateek, 'Walls of Separation', in *Cornerstone*, Issue 29, Summer, 2003.

[14] Kenneth Cragg, *The Arab Christian*, Mowbray, London, 1992.

no future for Arab Christianity without Islam. In fact, as far as Palestinian Christianity is concerned, there have been good relations with Islam.

A number of factors have contributed to these positive relations. The modern history of Palestine and the Arab-Israeli conflict have affected the entire population, Christian and Muslim alike, with their experience of loss and dispersal. At least since the 19th century, the contribution of Christian institutions in the areas of health and education and other social needs have continued irrespective of religion. Islam respects the importance and centrality of Jerusalem, Bethlehem and Nazareth to Christianity. The urban nature of the Christian population, and living in mixed neighbourhoods, has enhanced the openness and neighbourly relations between Christians and Muslims. Christians do take pride in their national and religious roots; it has never been the case that being a good Christian need detract one from being a nationalist Palestinian.

The history of good Christian-Muslim relations seems to be confirmed by research done in the early 90s at Bethlehem University among students.[15] Not only did they perceive each other favourably, but they felt they had a lot in common. Having said this, it's perhaps necessary to note a small caveat. Daphne Tsimhoni asserts that the isolation of Christians as a minority within the Palestinian Arab national movement has existed since the movement's inception.[16] This dilemma has been obscured because of the Israeli occupation of Jerusalem and the West Bank, but the Intifada has brought this into the open. Tsimhoni's view of the situation would tend to be supported by Said K Aburish in his book, *The Forgotten Faithful.*[17] Based on a series of interviews conducted after the first *Intifada*, many interviewees reported a growing antagonism towards Christians based on the attempt to redefine Palestinian identity in Islamic terms. This book's methodology is anecdotal, but supported by Arburish's insistence that despite intentions of those in leadership positions to promote harmony among Christians and Muslims, mutual suspicions remain. The role radical Islamicists play when secular nationalism is perceived as having failed in achieving its goals increases Christian apprehension.

---

[15] Jeanne Kattan, 'A Study of Muslim and Christian Students' attitude to each other at Bethlehem University', in *Christians in the Holy Land*, Michael Prior and William Taylor (eds), The World of Islam Festival Trust, London, 1995.

[16] Daphne Tsimhoni, *Christian Communities in Jerusalem and the West Bank since 1948*, Praeger, Westport, Connecticut, 1993, 182.

[17] Said K Aburiah, *The Forgotten Faithful*, Quartet Books, London, 1993. 77-95.

Whilst those outside the conflict may have important things to contribute, Canon Ateek notes that Palestinian Christians should look to themselves and their own experience, especially regarding Christian-Muslim relations, perhaps before anyone else.[18]

Now I would like to reflect on prospects and challenges for the future. An important consequence of the conflict since the establishment of the State of Israel has been the emigration of a considerable number of Palestinians.

Christians have shared in this emigration in disproportionate numbers. Michael Prior observes the difficulty emigration poses for the Christian community. He says that recent surveys in Israel have shown that the intention to emigrate is three times higher among Christians as opposed to Muslims. This evidence compounds the fact that 7 percent of the 714,000 who were made refugees in 1948 were Christians. Since the occupation of the West Bank and Gaza in 1967, nearly 40 percent of Palestinian Christians have left the country.[19]

An additional factor undermining the situation for Palestinian Christians is Christians are a minority not just in relation to Muslims but also to the Jewish majority which identifies itself with the Israeli state. Andrea Pacini notes that although the Arab Christian legal position is guaranteed by the state, Arab Christians are not in practice integrated into Israeli society. Nor do they enjoy equal opportunities in social and political life. High unemployment, and an inordinately low number of university students among Arabs in Israel, further adds to the general disillusionment with the Israeli state among Arab Christians.[20]

A further factor depleting the strength of Palestinian Christians, in proportion with the Muslim population, has been a lower birth rate among Christians. Muslims are recorded as having a 4.7 rate of children per family compared to 2.4 for Christians.

In a statistical analysis, Bernard Saballa has noted that Palestinian leave because of the lack of educational and economic opportunities.

---

[18] Naim Ateek, 'Who is the Church? A Christian Theology of the Holy Land', in *The Christian Heritage in the Holy Land*, Anthony O'Mahony, with Göran Gunner and K Hintlian (eds), London, Scorpion, 1995, 316.

[19] Michael Prior, 'The Future of the Christian Community in the Holy Land', in *The Month* (April 1, 1996), 141.

[20] Andrea Pacini, 'Socio-Political and Community Dynamics of Arab Christians in Jordan, Israel and the Autonomous Palestinian Regions', in, *Christian Communities in the Arab Middle East*, Andrea Pacini (ed.), Clarendon Press, Oxford, 1998, 272.

Palestinian Christians are particularly vulnerable because they tend to occupy more middle class occupations and have a higher educational achievement. Saballa contends that Islamic radicalism per se has not brought about Palestinian Christian emigration. But the Christian emigration had lead to an ageing of the Christian population left behind with a high median age of 30 years, which tends to weaken the social position of churches in society.[21]

The challenges for the future arc thc following:

Palestinians have found it extremely difficult to build the civil society that is necessary for the construction of the state. The question remains, can Palestinians through their institutions, in terms of health and education, contribute to the construction and maintenance of a civil society necessary for the realisation of a Palestinian homeland. The death of Arafat, and the election of Mahmoud Abbas as President of the Palestinian Authority, in January 2005, is seen by some as an opportunity for more 'moderate' elements to bring their influence to bear on the Palestinian political situation. How realistic this will prove to be, remains to be seen.

There are also challenges for Western Christians. There has been a pervasive theological tradition that identifies Jewish history in the Old Testament as part of the Christian revelation. Christian Zionism, a perverse manifestation of this tradition, has had the effect of isolating Palestinian Christians in their own society, linking them potentially—in the minds of their fellow Palestinians—with Western hostility to the Palestinian cause and with support for Zionism. Western Christians need to make themselves more aware and critical through engagement with Palestinian Christian thinking, and realise the extent to which Palestinians have had to suffer under the impact of Western Christian anxieties regarding its own anti-Semitic history, especially since the Holocaust has intensified Western guilt in this area.

Perhaps, however, Palestinian Christians' greatest contribution could be to bring to bear not just their own claims for justice, but also what they

---

[21] Bernard Sabella, 'Socio-Economic Characteristics and Challenges to Palestinian Christians in the Holy Land', in *Palestinian Christians, Religion, Politics and Society in the Holy Land*, Anthony O'Mahony (ed.), Melisende, London, 1999, 92.

have to offer in terms of reconciliation and forgiveness. In an intractable situation, where the legacy of the past hangs so heavily, this disinherited and dwindling Palestinian Christian community survives as a prophetic sign that reconciliation and renewal only can occur when enemies can forgive and be forgiven.

THE GREEK ORTHODOX PATRIARCHATE OF JERUSALEM: CHURCH-STATE RELATIONS IN THE HOLY LAND BETWEEN THE PALESTINIAN-ISRAELI CONFLICT

Sotiris Roussos

The centuries-long history of the Greek Orthodox Patriarchate under Islamic rule led to the formation of a co-optation attitude in Church-state relations among the members of the Greek Orthodox upper-clergy.[1] The Patriarchate co-operated closely with state policies in political, social and economic spheres in exchange of Church autonomy in its internal matters.[2] The *millet* system of the Ottoman empire institutionalised this behaviour, which became the main guideline of the Patriarchate's policy towards the state.

This policy enabled the patriarchate to face Western European influence in the Holy Places maintaining its predominance among the Churches in the Holy Land. In the 19th century, the Greek Orthodox Patriarchate was in the midst of Russo-Turkish antagonism in the Levant. In the struggle for control of the Holy Places, the patriarchate managed to exploit Greek-*Phanariotes* connection with central Ottoman administration

---

1 See my previous studies *Greece and the Arab Middle East: The Greek Orthodox communities in Egypt, Palestine and Syria, 1919-1940* Ph.D School of Oriental & African Studies, University of London, 1994; 'The Greek Orthodox Patriarchate and Community in Jerusalem', A O'Mahony, Kevork Hintlian and G Gunner (eds), *The Christian Heritage in The Holy Land*, Scorpion, London, 1995, 211-224; 'The Greek Orthodox Patriarchate and Community in Jerusalem: Church, State and Identity', A O'Mahony (ed.), *The Christians communities in Jerusalem and the Holy Land: Studies in History, Religion and Politics*, University of Wales Press, Cardiff, 2003, 38-56; 'Patriarchs, Notables and Diplomats: The Greek Orthodox Patriarchate of Jerusalem in the modern period', A O'Mahony (ed.), *Eastern Christianity: Studies in Modern History, Religion and Politics,* Melisende, London, 2003, pp.372-387; 'The Greek Orthodox community in Jerusalem in international politics: international solutions for Jerusalem and the Greek Orthodox community in the nineteenth and twentieth centuries', Lee I Levine (ed.), *Jerusalem: Its Sanctity and Centrality to Judaism, Christianity and Islam*, Continuum, New York and London, 1997, pp.482-495; 'The Patriarchate of Jerusalem in the Greek-Palestinian-Israeli Triangle', *One in Christ: A Catholic Ecumenical Review*, Vol. 39, no. 3 2004, 15-25.

2 P Ramet, 'Autocephaly and National Identity', in P Ramet (ed.), *Eastern Christianity and Politics in the Twentieth Century*, Duke University Press, Durham and London, 1988 14-15.

and to enlist Ottoman support as well as the Ottoman suspicion for Russian plans in the Near East.

After the two world wars the creation of the state of Israel and the Arab-Israeli conflict changed the situation. Nation-states replaced multi-ethnic empires. The Palestinian struggle for self-determination and statehood included now the antagonism between laity and Greek upper-clergy. For those of the Greek Orthodox Palestinians who participated in the national struggle, nationalising the hierarchy and the Church land became part of the national agenda.[3]

Post 1967 discontinuities

The 1967 Arab-Israeli war and the Israeli occupation of East Jerusalem, West Bank and Gaza Strip created a new situation. The Patriarchate followed the well known path of closely co-operating with state policy in order to maintain its prevailing position in the Holy Places. However the structure, aims and methods of the Israeli state apparatus were different from those faced by the patriarchate in the past.

The patriarchate had now to deal with a state policy of certain intentions, priorities and plans. It was clear from the beginning that the State of Israel would do everything to promote the Jewish character of the city and consequently would take every step to facilitate Jewish pilgrimage and protect Jewish Holy Places which were ignored during the Ottoman and Mandate arrangements of the status quo.[4] On the other hand Israeli authorities tried to re-assure the interested parties and international organisations over their commitment to the rights and privileges of the various Christian Churches in the Holy Places. It was probably understood that any confrontation over the Holy Places status quo would inevitably lead to a Christian front both inside and outside Israel.

As for the Arab Orthodox community, the period after 1967 possessed similar characteristics regarding nation-building and national vis-à-vis communal identification with those of the Mandate period.

---

[3] Daphne Tsimhoni, 'The Greek Orthodox Patriarchate of Jerusalem during the Formative Years of the British Mandate in Palestine', *Asian and African Studies* (Haifa), Vol. 12, 1978, 77-122; A O'Mahony, 'Palestinian-Arab Orthodox Christians: Religion, Politics and Church-State Relations in Jerusalem', *Chronos*, No. 3, 2000, 61-91.

[4] M Dumper, 'Church-State Relations in Jerusalem since 1948', in *The Christian Heritage in The Holy Land*, 272-273.

Under Israeli occupation and turbulent relations with Arab regimes, the Palestinians and more importantly Christian Palestinians re-defined their position raising the banner of 'secular' nationalism over communal identification and sectarianism. Middle class Christian Palestinians became leading advocates of nationalism, secularisation and radicalisation of the Palestinian national struggle. In general the political terminology, slogans and methods of the post-1967 Palestinian groups indicate a break with domination by the traditional elites. Several leaders of militant leftist groups were middle class Christian Palestinians. They also acquired command positions in the inner councils of the Palestinian national movement.[5]

Israeli occupation led to the social and economic dislocation of the Christian Palestinians and the Orthodox Palestinians, in particular. In his most interesting study on the Palestinian Christian demography, Bernard Sabella demonstrated how vulnerable the Palestinian Christians are to emigration pressure. Until 1991, the estimated number of Christians who have emigrated reached 18,000 or 40 percent of the Christian population in the West Bank including East Jerusalem.[6] In 1922 more than half of Jerusalem's population were Christians whereas, in 1991, they constituted only ten per cent of the population in roughly the same territory.[7] In Israel the Christians were estimated, in 1949, at 21.3 percent of the non-Jewish population but by 1990 they were about 12 percent.[8]

In 1996, there were 26,473 Greek Orthodox Palestinians out of approximately 50,000 Christians in East Jerusalem, West Bank and Gaza. In 1992 the total faithful of the Patriarchate of Jerusalem were estimated at 145,000 in the Occupied Territories, Israel and Jordan.[9] Greek Orthodox Palestinians, as the whole of the Palestinian Christian community, fit the model of a migrant community. High educational qualifications acquired in Western schools, relatively high living standards and ties with relatives abroad are the main characteristics of Christian Palestinians. Moreover,

---

[5] Don Peretz, 'Palestinian Social Stratification: The Political Implications', *Journal of Palestine Studies*, vol.VII, no. 1, Autumn 1977, 70-71.

[6] Bernard Sabella, ' Palestinian Christian Emigration from the Holy Land', *Proche-Orient Chrétien* (Jerusalem), XLI, 1991, 75.

[7] N B Williams Jr., 'In Mideast. A Christian Exodus', *Los Angeles Times*, 10 August 1991.

[8] S Geraisy, 'Socio-Demographic Characteristics: Reality, Problems and Aspirations within Israel', in Michael Prior and William Taylor (eds), *Christians in the Holy Land*, WIFT, London, 1993, 47-48.

[9] Y Courbage, P Fargues, *Chrétiens et Juifs dans l'Islam arabe et turc*, Paris, Fayard 1992, 328.

Church institutions can employ only 26.5 per cent of them and Christian unemployment reaches almost 35 per cent of heads of households.[10]

The Protection of the Holy Places Law made, as Michael Dumper noted, no explicit reference to Status Quo arrangements and brought confusion and insecurity in Churches' leaderships.[11] Moreover, Likud policy of altering the character of Jerusalem by promoting the Judaic character of the city prompted extremist settler groups to seize houses in the East Jerusalem and the Old City. The illegal seizure of the St John Hospices in Jerusalem by settlers of Ateret Kohanim extremist group in 1990 was part of that endeavour. That incident marked the first break of the co-opting with state tradition of the Church. The late Patriarch Diodoros came to direct confrontation with the settlers and the Israeli government and this was the first time that the Patriarchate searched for alternative alliances in Greece, the European Union and the region, including the European Parliament and Syria.[12]

During the Oslo process

The Oslo Process complicated the matter for the Jerusalem Patriarchate and its strategy towards the state. The formation of the Palestinian Authority as a would-be-state created new facts on the ground. Major issues such as land sales or leasing have surpassed the symbolic patterns of Palestinian nationalism and become part of the negotiations' agenda. The land in Abu Ghneim/Har Homa is a case in point. The large Israeli settlement in this area very near to East Jerusalem became one of the major issues of criticism by the Palestinian Authority against Israeli settlement policies, which create facts on the ground and as such violate the Oslo Accords.

According to Arab Palestinian press part of the land in Abu Ghneim belonged to the Greek Orthodox Patriarchate, which sold or leased it to the Israeli state and business. Notwithstanding the accuracy of these press accusations, it is safe to argue that the Patriarchate and its land

---

[10] B Sabella, 'Palestinian Christian Emigration from the Holy Land', 76.

[11] In June 1967 the Israeli Knesset passed 'The Protection of the Holy Places Law'; see Michael Dumper, *The Politics of Jerusalem since 1967*, New York, Columbia University Press, 1997, 161-165.

[12] 'Brief Account of the St John Hospice's capture by fanatical Israelis', *Nea Sion*, vol. 83, 1991, 141-155 [in Greek].

were brought again into the centre of not only the national struggle but of the negotiations process. Although there are no details concerning the size of land sales and the circumstances under which these land sales have taken place, if there were any at all, the perception that the Patriarchate is selling large plots of land to Israelis was very strong among the Arab Orthodox community.

In 1998 Israeli sources saw also an intensification of the Palestinian Orthodox movement activity against the Greek character of the Patriarchate. Most significantly they noticed that there was a Palestinian Authority involvement in the establishment of a united front of the Arab Orthodox faithful living in Israel, the West Bank, Gaza and Jordan.[13] The same sources maintained that the Palestinian Authority and main figures of PLO mainstream politics such as Marwan Barghouti and Ramzi Khuri were behind this attempt of a unified Arab Orthodox front.

Despite sometimes fierce criticism by the Palestinian press, the Palestinian Authority and the former Chairman Arafat personally dealt with the matter in a rather discreet manner. The Palestinian side did not wish to be misunderstood by a most friendly government, namely Greece, on this issue. Secondly, an open conflict between the Palestinian Authority and the ancient Jerusalemite Christian Church institution might spoil its unifying image as the representative of all Palestinians, Christians and Muslims. Most importantly, an open controversy with the patriarchate could have presented Arafat and the Palestinian negotiators with considerable problems during the final status talks on Jerusalem and the political control over the Holy Shrines. However Arafat found indirect ways to send his message of disapproval to the patriarchate.[14]

Moreover, the Oslo Process presented the Orthodox Church with the issue of the international guarantees for the Status Quo in the Holy Places. The signing of the *Fundamental Agreement between the Holy See and the State of Israel* on December 30, 1993 had an alarming effect on the Greek Orthodox Patriarchate in Jerusalem, the Church of Greece and the Greek Government alike. The main anxiety of the Orthodox Church was that the Vatican would exploit the agreement in order to encroach the Patriarchate's rights over the Holy Places.

---

[13] 'The PA's attempts to take over Christian Churches & Communities in Jerusalem', *Israel Report*, September/October 1993, www.cdn-icej.ca/isreport/attempts.html.

[14] Suleiman al-Akawi, 'The Orthodox Patriarchate and the Peace Prize', *An Nahar*, 18 October 1995.

The then Metropolitan of Dimitrias and presently Archbishop of the Church of Greece, Christodoulos claimed in an article of his, in July 1994, that according to unnamed Middle-Eastern sources an agreement between Israel and the Palestinians on the Holy Places was imminent. This agreement would have provided for Saudi control over the Muslim Holy Places and Vatican's control over the Christian ones.[15] The Metropolitan of Dimitrias hinted also the conspiracy atmosphere created by the secrecy and obscurity of the negotiations between the two parties. There was a widespread view in the Greek press that Israel had come to some kind of arrangement with the Holy See, which would be detrimental to the preponderant role of the Greek Orthodox Patriarchate in the Holy Land.[16]

During the same period there were widespread discussions and proposals among Palestinian and Israeli intellectuals as to the future of Jerusalem and of the Holy Places, which attempted to map out the character of the city and ways of co-existence between the three monotheistic religions.[17] In most of the plans proposed the issue of the religious communities is treated with a sort of constructive ambiguity. Emphasis was given to freedom of access and prayer and the preservation of what is considered cultural heritage, whereas there only few references to the preservation of the Status Quo, which it is seen mainly as a remnant of the Ottoman and British administrative and foreign policy needs mainly as a useful experience for modeling the city's administration.

Moreover the Madrid Peace Conference reopened the issue of the Holy Places as the third constituent element of the question of Jerusalem, the other two being the sovereignty over the city and the physical planning of it.[18] The end result of this process could have been a broad re-negotiation of the terms and references of the Status Quo system in the Holy Places. Such a process sent shivers to the Greek Orthodox Patriarchate and woke up its darkest fears, which were fuelled by the negotiations between Israel

---

[15] Metropolitan of Dimitrias, Christodoulos, 'The Vatican and the Holy Places', *To Vema*, 17 July 1994 [in Greek].

[16] S Alexiou, 'Give and Take by the Vatican', *To Vema*, 24 July 1994 [in Greek].

[17] G Baskin, R Twite (eds), *The Future of Jerusalem. Proceedings of the First Israeli-Palestinian International Academic Seminar on the Future of Jerusalem*, Israel/Palestine Center for Research and Information, Jerusalem 1993 and *Jerusalem. Religious Aspects*, Palestinian Academic Society for the Study of International Affairs, Jerusalem 1995.

[18] Y Reiter, M Eordegian, M Abu Khalaf, 'Between Divine and Human: The Complexity of Holy Places in Jerusalem', in Moshe Ma'oz, S Nusseibeh (eds), *Jerusalem: Points of Friction-And Beyond*, Kluwer Law International, The Hague, 2000, 107.

and the Holy See in the same period. It seems that cautiousness over the outcome of these negotiations was shared by circles wider than the Greek Orthodox Church, who wished to see more concerned nations and Churches to be taken into account in safeguarding the city's unique religious character.[19]

The Greek Foreign Ministry sensed the changes in the international and regional arena. Though it did not seem to share conspiracy theories, the Greek Government showed its interest on preserving the rights of the Greek Orthodox Patriarchate. The unilateral declarations of both Greece and Israel with which they normalised their diplomatic relations on May 21, 1990 essentially recognise the right of the Greek Government to have a special interest on the Greek Orthodox presence in the Holy Places and a say on any future arrangement concerning the religious Status Quo and the rights and privileges of the Patriarchate.

The Greek Foreign Minister Karolos Papoulias wrote a letter to his Israeli counterpart expressing the concern of the Greek public opinion worldwide regarding negotiations held between the Vatican and Israel over the Holy Places. The Greek Foreign Ministry expressed fears that the Greek Orthodox views were not taken into consideration since neither the Patriarchate nor the Greek government had been invited to participate to such discussions.[20] The Israeli government responded through its Embassy in Athens reassuring the rights of the Greek Orthodox Patriarchate '... according to the religious Status Quo'.[21]

The issue of the Holy Places and the rights of the religious communities resurfaced with the agreement between the Holy See and the PLO in 1999 as well as with the approaching final status negotiations in 1999-2000. The agreement that came after more than two years of negotiations with the PLO helped the Vatican to promote its vision for a special status for the Holy City. Chairman Arafat did not object to such a possibility as in any case he was agreeing to something he did not at that time have and thus there was no possibility to uphold and implement.[22]

From 1947 onwards the Patriarchate of Jerusalem has been deeply concerned over any sort of international control or international custody

---

[19] Y Reiter, 'Religious Issues and Holy Places in Jerusalem—Towards a Permanent Solution', in *Jerusalem. Religious Aspects*, Palestinian Academic Society for the Study of International Affairs, Jerusalem 1995, 64.

[20] *To Vema tis Kyriakes*, 7 August 1994 [in Greek].

[21] *Ibid.*, 14 August 1994.

[22] M Benvenisti, 'The Theology of an Agreement', *Ha'aretz*, 17 February 2000.

of the Holy Places preferring to deal bilaterally with the sovereign or occupying power. Following this line even from 1967 the Patriarchate would have preferred bilateral agreements or concordats with Israel and after Oslo with the PLO. However the Church gave no official reply when the Israeli government had, parallel to the agreement with the Vatican, proposed a similar agreement to the patriarchate.[23]

The patriarchal election of 2001

The major break, however, with the tradition of 'co-optation for internal autonomy' came with the patriarchal election after the death of the late Patriarch Diodoros in February 2001. The elections were more or less in accordance with the traditional typology. Personal feuds and shifting alliances around certain prelates and excessive lobbying in Athens, Constantinople, Tel Aviv, Ramallah and Amman is a familiar pattern of patriarchal elections.

Equally familiar were recurring political controversies. The alleged leasing of church property to foreign investment firms including Israeli companies, a conflict between certain segments of the Arab Orthodox and the Greek upper clergy over equitable representation in church property and welfare administration and allegations of corruption and bribery perpetrated by members of Greek clergy, customarily surface prior to elections.[24]

The regional situation had profoundly changed since the 1980s with the Peace Process and the formation of the Palestinian Authority. The *locum tenens* had now to submit the list of the candidates to three ruling powers, Jordan, the Palestinian Authority and Israel and seek for their formal approval. After the collapse of the Taba talks and the eruption of violence all interested parties, namely Israel, the Palestinian leadership and the Arab Orthodox were particularly concerned about the outcome of the patriarchal elections. In the international arena, also, the collapse of

---

[23] Archbishop Timothy, Secretary of the Greek Orthodox Patriarchate of Jerusalem in the 1990s, stated that there was such invitation by the Israeli government. Comments made at the Conference 'Greek Orthodox Church in the Modern Era' held on 3 March 2003, by the Program of Modern Greek Studies of the University of Haifa, Israel.

[24] S Ma'ayeh, 'Jerusalem: Orthodox clergy prepares for election showdown', *The Jordan Times*, 30 May 2001.

the Cold War format allowed religious institutions and religious legitimacy to play an active role in international politics.[25]

The Arab Orthodox community was not unified behind common goals. Three main groupings can be discerned: first, well established professionals and notables mainly in Jordan who pressed for the arabisation of the patriarchate, second, Palestinian middle class professionals, priests, intellectuals, activists or not, aspiring to Palestinian national goals[26] and close to the Palestinian Authority, who asked for a compromise—better education, communal welfare and higher Arab representation in the Church—and third, the poorer strata, disillusioned with the political situation and ready to forget their communal Greek Orthodox identity.[27] With such a split Arab Orthodox community both the PA and Jordan kept a very discreet and very low profile policy, sending however the message that they wished to see a better stance for the Arab Orthodox community from that in the period of late Diodoros.

The Israeli Government of Ariel Sharon could not afford to see a 'pro-Palestinian' patriarch at such a critical moment in the region. Israel would like to avoid the arabisation of the Greek Orthodox patriarchate, which would follow the example of the Latin patriarchate and most importantly they feared possible Palestinian control over the patriarchate's property. Last but not least they would like to prevent any kind of non-Greek i.e. Russian interference, in the patriarchate.[28]

On this line it was decided to interfere in the internal affairs of the patriarchate by erasing from the candidates' list five prelates, including Metropolitan Eirinaios, who was eventually elected patriarch. It was the first time from the 19th century onwards that the sovereign or occupying power intervened directly and essentially in the patriarchal election and it constituted a major break with the tradition of church-state relations in the Holy Land. This kind of precedent was reminiscent of the attitude of the Turkish government to the patriarchate of Constantinople which

---

[25] J Fox, 'The Influence of Religious Legitimacy on Grievance Formation by Ethno-Religious Minorities', *Journal of Peace Research*, vol. 36, no. 3, May 1999, 292.

[26] Letter of the Chairman of the Arab Orthodox Benevolent Society in Beit Jala, Dr Simon Araj to the Orthodox Peace Fellowship webmail.earlham.edu/archive/opf-1/April-2002/msg00060.html.

[27] R Panzer, 'Die Politische Identifikation griechisch-orthodoxer Christen im Vorderen Orient', *Orient*, Vol. 39, (1998), 240.

[28] G Kalokairinos, 'Behind the scenes in Jerusalem', *Kathimerini*, 22 July 2001 [in Greek].

could mark the beginning of direct and heavy involvement of the sovereign power in Church affairs.[29]

The dangers emanating from such a decision were almost immediately visible. It could create a very dangerous precedent of state intervention into the heart of Church functions and lead to schism inside the Church. The majority of the Synod refused to accept it and sought help from Jordan. At the same time leading Arab Orthodox figures from both Jordan and the Palestinian Authority expressed their desire to conduct the election of the Patriarch according to the Jordanian Law of 1958, ignoring the decision of the Israeli government.[30]

Meanwhile there was immense lobbying in Jerusalem and Athens. This lobbying was fruitful in bringing the support of the up to that point rather inactive Greek government and of the Church of Greece. The Archbishop of Athens and all Greece send discreet but clear messages to the Israeli authorities that such an action would not be allowed to go on without an outcry from the Orthodox faithful.[31] At the same time there was considerable mobilisation of the Greek Orthodox Church and communities in North America particularly in the USA.[32] The universal importance of the issue has been clearly understood in the USA and this is the main reason why major American Jewish organisations distanced themselves from current Israeli policies and advised the government in favour of non-interference in internal Church affairs.

Lobbying was also effective in forming an alliance of various parts of the Israeli policy-making and eventually succeeded to avert the decision. The Israeli Ministry of Justice approved the list of candidates without erasing any of them. However the Israeli government did not formally acknowledge the election of Patriarch Eirinaios.

Notwithstanding state interference in Church affairs and the insistence of the Israeli government in withholding the patriarch's official recognition the patriarchate has not yet decided to break with its state co-optation tradition and to take the path of resistance. Patriarch Eirinaios

---

[29] Statements by V Feidas, Professor in the Theology School of the University of Athens in B I Korahaes, 'Plan to conquer the Holy Places', *Estia*, 24 July 2001 [in Greek].

[30] *Al-Quds*, Wafa (Official Palestine News Agency), 8 January 2002.

[31] *Imerisia*, 4 August 2001.

[32] The pressure by this communities continues for the recognition of the Patriarch by the Israeli government. Resolution-Recognising the Patriarch of Jerusalem of the Executive Board of the National Council of Churches in the USA, 11 October 2002, www.wfn.org/2002/10/msg00137.html.

immediately and boldly refused to recognise the Palestinian Archimandrite Attala Hannah as spokesman of the patriarchate. In a lecture at the Arab League think tank 'The Zayed Center for Co-ordination and Follow-up', in Abu Dhabi on 19 June 2003, Hannah had allegedly supported all forms of Palestinian resistance including suicide attacks.[33]

Arab press attributed the dismissal of Hannah to unbearable Israeli pressure on Patriarch Eirinaios connecting the issue with that of his formal recognition by the Israeli government and uncertified copies of Israeli Ministry of Religious Affairs letter to the patriarch concerning this issue were distributed in websites.[34] The patriarch's decision regarding Attala Hannah was part of the general pattern of patriarchate's policy of non-interference in the Palestinian-Israeli conflict.

Nonetheless, the patriarchate was willing to re-define its attitude towards the other Churches. In January 2003 the Greek Orthodox Patriarchate had for the first time taken the decisive step to send a representative in the Week of Prayer for Christian Unity in Jerusalem. The chief secretary of the patriarchate, Archbishop Aristarchos, stated the Church participated in this Week of Prayer 'with reservation, but perhaps this is already a positive change in our attitude'.[35]

The patriarchate was also concerned over possible seizure of its property for purposes of the Israeli security fence or of by-pass roads, for the settlements. In October 2003 the Israeli army demolished 120 newly built houses of the Arab Orthodox Housing Project in Beit Sahour allegedly to build by-pass road for the surrounding settlements. The land belongs to the Greek Orthodox Church and was leased to the Housing Project.[36] Such incidents were reminiscent of the seizure of the St John Hospice incident in 1990.[37]

---

[33] See www.gulfnews.com/Articles/, 20 June 2003 and www.zccf.org.ae/LECTURES/A2_lectures/231.htm.

[34] *Al-Hayat*, *Al-Ahram* 16 July 2002, see also www.sabeel.org/reports/attalah/letter.htm.

[35] *Ecumenical News International*, 24 February 2003.

[36] B Wing, 'Housing Demolitions', 6 October 2002 www.zmag.org/content/.

[37] 'Press Release from the Greek Orthodox Patriarchate concerning the Housing project of Beit Sahour', 15 October 2002, www.al-bushra.org/hedchrch/greek.html.

Some general observations

We discussed here two major breaks with the tradition of church-state relations regarding the Greek Orthodox patriarchate in Jerusalem, the Vatican-Israel and the Vatican-PLO agreements and the handling of the last patriarchal election. It was evident that the centuries old close co-operation policy was not enough to secure the autonomy of its internal affairs from either political priorities of the state actor or even from certain typical thinking within the process of Israeli decision-making.

The alternatives presented to the patriarchate were, firstly, to rely heavily on the Greek diplomatic assistance and on the lobbying of the archbishop of Athens in favour of such assistance. The policy of enlisting the patriarchate in bilateral Greek-Israeli relations might be successful in short and medium term but it reduces the universal importance of this religious institution for the Orthodox faithful worldwide.

The second possible option for the patriarchate is to become an interest group in the Israeli, Palestinian and Jordanian politics following the assumption that a particular state policy decision is the result of competition, coalition building and compromise between governmental and non-governmental actors. In such a strategy it is imperative for the patriarchate to build or attach itself in transnational networks oriented around common strategies that serve the patriarchate's role and interest.

The third option for the patriarchate would be to advocate religious legitimisation of the Palestinian national struggle. In many cases when a mutually beneficially social contract between a religious elite and the state is broken then this religious elite may become a 'resistance' elite. However, in the case of the patriarchate, the Greek religious elite could not raise the banner of Palestinian nationalism for the simple reason that this may have been the beginning of the end for the Greek character of the patriarchate. Moreover it could also expose the Greek Orthodox Christian presence to the dangers of the growing political Islam.

The fourth and most important option derives from the central role of the Greek Orthodox patriarchate in Jerusalem as the Custodian of two thirds of the Christian Holy Shrines and the Church with the largest community of faithful in historic Palestine and particularly in Jerusalem. In any political settlement, non-governmental centuries old institutions, such as the Greek Orthodox patriarchate in Jerusalem, with no affiliation to either the State of Israel or the Palestinian Authority, but manned and operating across the line can be instrumental in building cross-line connections and preserve the City's unity by using their rich experience in dealing with the matters on the ground and in this sense to be channels of peace. Every state actor in and outside the region has every strategic interest to facilitate such channels.

ARAB ORTHODOX CHRISTIANS OF JERUSALEM AND PALESTINE IN THE INTER-WAR PERIOD: A STUDY IN RELIGIOUS AND POLITICAL IDENTITY AND CHURCH-STATE RELATIONS

Helen Bryer

Introduction

> It was a perfectly glorious day, cold, bright sun and not a cloud ... At 12 o'clock the C-in-C entered the Jaffa Gate accompanied and followed by the various people according to arrangement...with a crowd of local dignitaries, Syriac, Arab, Abyssinian, Coptic, Roman Catholic, Greek, Armenian, Austrian and other church dignitaries all beautifully got up with all their jewels...The moment when we walked in under the Jaffa Gate, the C-in-C as Chief of a victorious army after 600 years, was not one to be forgotten.[1]

So began the British administration of Palestine in December 1917. Wyndham Deedes' description of Allenby's entry into Jerusalem showed a powerful awareness of the beauty, history and religious significance of the land and city he had just entered. These ideas provided the backdrop to all British action in Palestine, always at the back of the minds of so many British men and women who lived in, worked in and visited the Holy City. Within this context, they had to deal with a unique political situation; of promises to Jews and Arabs that could not be kept and growing internal tension, erupting with increasing regularity into disorder and violence. This study does not aim to revisit the complex and controversial political debates that have raged ever since, still without widely accepted solution. It approaches from a new angle, illuminating wider sensibilities at work on British policy in Palestine and the empire, by throwing light upon British attitudes to one small but relatively powerful Jerusalem community, the Arab Orthodox Christians. The period from 1917 to the mid 1930s

[1] Oxford, St Antony's Middle East Centre Archive, GB165-0079, Brigadier-General Sir W H Deedes to Rose Deedes, 11/12/17.

is particularly worthy of attention as British attitudes to Palestine and its people were still very much evolving and policy was being formulated, both in the Administration and by missionaries and the Church of England. The Orthodox Church was also readjusting to new circumstances; a new governing power, the near disappearance of the Russian Church as a political power in Jerusalem following the Russian revolution, and the impact of growing Arab nationalism upon its congregation.[2]

The Christians of Palestine could not easily be overlooked by the British, in political, social or religious terms. In 1922, Christians comprised approximately 9.6 per cent of the Palestinian population, the majority in a few significant centres, but, chiefly due to relatively high levels of education, they enjoyed disproportionate influence.[3] In 1931, 73 per cent of male Christians in Jerusalem were literate, compared with just 24 per cent of Muslim men, and 48 per cent of women, compared with just 4 per cent of Muslim women.[4] The majority of Palestinian Christians were Arab Orthodox, under the Greek Orthodox Patriarchate of Jerusalem, making up over 45 per cent of the Christian community of Palestine in 1922 (in the first British census). It is upon this, the largest of the communities, that this study primarily focuses. The other communities represented in Jerusalem included the Latins (Roman Catholics), Armenian Orthodox, Armenian Catholics, Chaldean Catholics, Syrian Catholics, Greek Catholics, Maronites and the Syrian Orthodox, and a number of other even smaller communities who did not enjoy official recognition, but nevertheless had congregations in the city, such as the Anglican Church or the Ethiopian Church. The largest concentration of Christians in Palestine was in the Jerusalem district (an administrative area including the towns of Jerusalem, Bethlehem, Ramallah and the surrounding villages), largely due to the presence of the Holy Places in Jerusalem and Bethlehem.[5] As the centre of political and religious life, this district provides the most interesting and significant arena within which to explore the relations between communities.

---

2 Sotiris Roussos, 'The Greek Orthodox Patriarchate and Community of Jerusalem' in Anthony O'Mahony (ed.), *The Christian Heritage in the Holy Land*, London, 1995, 218.

3 Doreen Ingrams (ed.), *Palestine Papers, 1917-22: Seeds of Conflict*, London, 1972, 105; See also London, Public Record Office (P.R.O.), CAB27/222, January 1923, 4.

4 Anthony O'Mahony, *Palestinian Christians: Religion, Politics and Society in the Holy Land*, London, 1999, 39.

5 Anthony O'Mahony (ed.), *The Christian Heritage in the Holy Land*, London, 1995, 257, 263-4.

From 1917, particularly after 1922, the British endeavoured to ensure that all churches felt that their rights were being upheld; a near impossible task but one that dominated Mandatory-Orthodox relations during this period.[6] Quarrels, many of them centuries old, were commonplace amongst and within the Churches, particularly regarding ownership and control of the Holy Places. Under the Ottomans, rivalries had been exacerbated by Muslim concepts of ownership and the ruler's right to allocate buildings at will. In the 19th century, the rights of the respective churches had been more or less laid down in the Imperial Regulations of 1875, whose contents came to be known as 'the Status Quo'.[7] From then on disputes focused upon interpretation of this Status Quo; a dilemma that occupied the time and energy of many a British official. Even within the Orthodox Church great disputes arose, mostly centred on the ongoing tension between the Greek hierarchy and Arab pastoral clergy and laity.These erupted into crises at various times through the Mandate period, and resolution of such troubles was a grave concern of the Administration.[8]

The interaction between and within these Christian communities has been the subject of detailed and perceptive historical study, and a certain proportion of this work has touched on Orthodox relations with the British authorities.[9] Much remains unexplored, however, and no full in depth study exists of British attitudes to these communities. Attitudes were formed through a combination of personal, social and cultural assumptions, combined with experiences and knowledge acquired in Palestine. The role the British saw themselves playing was also affected by their own position and purpose within the country. Officials tended to be most concerned with maintenance of peace and good diplomatic relations with all, while Churchmen and missionaries could focus more upon their avowed aim of rejuvenating the Eastern Churches. All were constantly responding to new circumstances, knowledge and wider

---

[6] Ronald Storrs, *Orientations*, London, 1937, especially 278-284, 297; Edward Keith-Roach, *Pasha of Jerusalem: Memoirs of a district commissioner under the British Mandate*, London, 1994, especially 152-163.

[7] L G A Cust, *The Status Quo in the Holy Places*, Jerusalem, 1980.

[8] Sotiris Roussos, 'The Greek Orthodox Patriarchate and Community of Jerusalem' in (ed.) Anthony O'Mahony, *The Christian Heritage in the Holy Land,* London, 1995, 219-220.

[9] Anthony O'Mahony, 'The Religious, Political and Social Status of the Christian Communities in Palestine', in Anthony O'Mahony (ed.), *The Christian Heritage in the Holy Land*, London, 1995; Sotiris Roussos, 'The Greek Orthodox Patriarchate and Community of Jerusalem' in Anthony O'Mahony (ed.), *The Christian Heritage in the Holy Land,* London, 1995.

considerations, while these very responses reflected more profound beliefs and preconceptions stemming from personal backgrounds, and social and cultural assumptions and values.

Within this matrix of concerns, the Orthodox Arabs were an interesting, or even disturbing, paradox to many Westerners, in the need to reconcile their alien 'Arabness' with their common Christianity. A fascination with all things Arab was widespread amongst the British in the Middle East at this time, often with greater sympathy and respect for these people and their way of life than for those of the Jews. This grew out of a long tradition of interest in the East, as well as from more personal experiences in Palestine and the surrounding region.[10,11] Such sympathies did not always count in the Arabs' favour, however; when they failed to live up to the expectations of their British observers, profound disappointment and disillusionment could follow, on both sides. Moreover, while notions of the East and 'the Arab' were clearly extremely important in forming Westerners preconceptions of Palestine, they do not go far enough to explain the images the vast majority of British people had of that country. Because Palestine was not just another Middle Eastern country; it was the Holy Land, and Jerusalem was the Holy City.

Interest in Palestine had grown in many countries during the 19th century. In England, it was of particular interest in light of a growing interest in the life of Christ, amongst theologians, the clergy and the laity.[12] Most significantly perhaps, from the middle of the century it became possible for a greater range and number of people to visit Palestine, particularly within the middle classes.[13] By the early 20th century, the craze for so-called 'Biblical tourism' had died down somewhat, but powerful images of the Holy Land remained. It was from 19th century books and art work, and from the Bible itself, that most British men and women of the early 20th century continued to draw their knowledge of Palestine

---

[10] ESCO Foundation for Palestine Inc., *Palestine: A study of Jewish, Arab and British Policies*, New Haven, Conn., 1947; Frances Newton, *Fifty Years in Palestine,* London, 1948, 130; St Antony's, GB165-0099, 26/10/19.

[11] Edward Keith-Roach, *Pasha of Jerusalem: Memoirs of a district commissioner under the British Mandate,* London, 1994,151; See also St Antony's, GB165-0031.

[12] Sarah Kochav, 'The search for a Protestant Holy Sepulchre', *Journal of Ecclesiastical History,* 46(2), (1995).

[13] Timothy Larsen, *Contested Christianity: The Political and Social Contexts of Victorian Theology*, London, 2004, 37. William Hepworth Dixon, *The Holy Land*, vol. 1, 1865; Thomas Nelson & Sons Ltd., *The Holy Land*, London, 1855; R Hichens, *The Holy Land*, London, 1898; Naomi Shepherd, *The Zealous Intruders: The Western Rediscovery of Palestine*, San Francisco, 1987.

and Jerusalem. Travellers and even soldiers used their Bibles as guide books to explore the country.[14] A common feeling was expressed in newsreels of the time that nothing changed in Palestine, and this allowed visitors to feel even closer to the Biblical stories. One reel even considered new technology in Galilee in the light of how Jesus would have seen it.[15]

All British travellers and residents in Palestine shared something of this common heritage, yet the diversity of their first impressions of Jerusalem is striking. Many writers and visitors still revelled in the history and romance, as well as the religious significance, of the many ancient biblical sites in modern Palestine.[16] Others were more negative; after centuries of European depictions of these Biblical scenes, often set in luscious green Italian hills or even in familiar English scenery, the bare, dry desert of the Middle East could be disappointing, even disillusioning. Mark Twain, in his 1867 book *The Innocents Abroad* epitomized this cynical attitude to the sites he visited in Palestine, and set something of a trend for further negative interpretations of what European visitors found there.[17] Many continued to find the rugged mountains and biblical scenery enchanting, but were disappointed by Jerusalem and its inhabitants. The Holy City was, to many, depressingly run down and many a traveller commented on the smell of the open drains (admittedly a problem gradually resolved by the British administration).[18] Moreover, the politics of the city was usually at best petty and mundane, and at worst vicious and even violent. This was in many ways the most important context for our inquiries here; it was the contrast between expectations of the Holy Land and the Holy City and the reality of the politics and conflicts that took place within them, not least amongst the various Christian communities, that could be so disappointing. This was eloquently summarised by a pilgrim named H.V. Morton, in 1934, in his thoughts on Palestine: 'From our earliest years it begins to form in our minds, side by side with Fairyland, so that it is

---

[14] Major Vivian Gilbert, *The Romance of the Last Crusade—With Allenby to Jerusalem,* London, 1924, 180; also John Finley, *A Pilgrim in Palestine After Its Deliverance*, London, 1919, vii.

[15] Pathé Newsreels: from http://www.britishpathe.com/index.html: 2863.04, Jerusalem, 1920-1939; 873.08, Gallilee, 26/11/1931; also Donald Maxwell, *A Painter in Palestine*, London, 1921, 84.

[16] Edward Keith-Roach, *Pasha of Jerusalem: Memoirs of a district commissioner under the British Mandate*, London, 1994; Ronald Storrs, *Orientations*, London, 1937, 297.

[17] Timothy Larsen, *Contested Christianity: The Political and Social Contexts of Victorian Theology*, London, 2004, 30.

[18] Frances Newton, *Fifty Years in Palestine,* London, 1948, 130.

often difficult to tell where one begins and the other ends. Therefore, the Palestine of reality is always to conflict with the imaginary Palestine, so violently at times that many people cannot relinquish this Palestine of the imagination without a feeling of bereavement'.[19]

This significance of Palestine's position as the Holy Land in the eyes of the British has most often been assessed in relation to British attitudes to the Jews and Zionism.[20] Of greater interest to this study is the extent to which the British saw themselves as a conquering Christian power. Officially, strict neutrality was to be maintained at all times and chief administrators refused to be portrayed as Christian liberators, yet individuals often proved far harder to convince. This is best seen in the debates surrounding the conquest of Jerusalem in December 1917. The symbolism of the Holy Land was not a decisive factor in the decision to invade Palestine, but it was undoubtedly an issue much on the minds of the overwhelming majority of British men or women involved. The taking of the city provided a valuable morale boost to many within the army and the Allies. It was a proud victory in a war that had been much dominated by the tragedies of the Western front and repeated losses in the East.[21] Yet it was celebrated with joy disproportionate to its obvious political and strategic value. In many portrayals of the time, this was no ordinary campaign; this was a battle for the return of the Holy City to the hands of a Christian ruler after centuries of what was widely perceived as tyrannical Ottoman rule. It seemed natural to many, soldiers and the press back in Britain, to speak of it as a crusade.[22] There is evidence of the Christians of Palestine hoping for particular benefits from their fellow Christians, the British, after years of second rate minority status under the Ottomans.[23]

---

19 HV Morton, *In The Steps Of The Master*, London, 1934, 112.

20 M Vereté, 'The Balfour Declaration and Its Makers', *Middle Eastern Studies*, 6, (1970), 48-76, especially 60-64; Naomi Shepherd, *Ploughing Sand: British Rule In Palestine,* London, 1999, 43-45; I Friedman, *The Question of Palestine, 1914-1918: British-Jewish-Arab Relations*, London, 1973, 283.

21 Anthony Bruce, *The Last Crusade: The Palestine campaign in WWI*, London, 2002, 1-2, 165.

22 Elizabeth Siberry, 'Images of the Crusades' in J Riley-Smith (ed.), *The Oxford Illustrated History of the Crusades,* Oxford, 1995, 383; Major Vivian Gilbert, *The Romance of the Last Crusade—With Allenby to Jerusalem,* London, 1924.

23 Daphne Tsimhoni, 'The Status of the Arab Christians under the British Mandate in Palestine, *Middle Eastern Studies*, 20, 4 (1984), 166-92, 166; P Valognes, *Vie et Mort des Chretiens d'orient: des origines à nos jours*, Paris, 1994, 570.

It is essential to recognise, however, that policy makers and military leaders did not take Palestine because it was the Holy Land and those who took control had no intention of ruling it as a conquering Christian power. For General Allenby and many officials, the importance of the Palestine campaign was to be seen in strictly strategic terms. Allenby banned the terminology of crusading within the army and the press.[24] A report written for the Foreign Office in October 1917 stated that Bishop MacInnes appeared 'to regard our invasion of Palestine somewhat in the light of a Crusade … This is a natural enough attitude on the part of a Christian Bishop, but it does not take into account the question of military and political expediency by which we must be guided.'[25] The conquest of Palestine was at the time hailed by many as a key strategic victory, and it did have its strategic merits, but the significance of the move has been exaggerated; even at the time many were already well aware of the potential problems it might cause Britain.[26] A number of historians have even argued, like Segev, that 'occupying Palestine brought them [the British] no strategic benefit …, despite their assumptions that it did'.[27] Segev goes too far here, focusing almost exclusively on what others have termed the 'emotional' reasons for interest in the country. He implies that decision makers were so blinkered by their desire to take Palestine that they constructed a strategic justification for their actions. Shepherd's argument is somewhat more subtle and more convincing; she ties in emotional considerations with recognition of the vital role Palestine was seen to play in the geopolitical struggles of the region.[28]

The complex feelings British people had about the Arabs, the Holy Land, Islam, Zionism, and Oriental Christianity itself formed the backdrop to British expectations and preconceptions about Palestine and its people. The direct impact of these ideas and beliefs upon British policy and administration was limited, it is argued, because the Administration was in general governed by a fairly pragmatic outlook in its relations with the

---

[24] P.R.O., CAB27/23: 21/1/18; See also Elizabeth Siberry, 'Images of the Crusades' in J Riley-Smith (ed.), *The Oxford Illustrated History of the Crusades,* Oxford, 1995, 383.

[25] P.R.O., FO141/773: 15/10/17.

[26] Anthony Bruce, *The Last Crusade: The Palestine campaign in WWI*, London, 2002, 2; P.R.O., CAB27/222: 27/6/23; Feb 1923; 16/2/23.

[27] Tom Segev, *One Palestine, Complete: Jews and Arabs under the British Mandate,* Jerusalem, 1999 (trans. London 2000), 4.

[28] Naomi Shepherd, *Ploughing Sand: British Rule In Palestine*, London, 1999.

Christian communities.[29] This is not to underestimate the significance and power of expectations, preconceptions and established values and beliefs; decisions were formed within that context and they had far more impact that many officials of the time would have acknowledged. Ultimately, however, the British Administration, in its relations with the Orthodox Church, was reacting far more to political and practical circumstances than it was guided by the beliefs and prejudices of its individual members. From a different perspective, records of the Anglican Church and the Church Missionary Society trace many of the same reactions to the Orthodox as expressed by lay people, but in some ways they go further. The Anglican Church expressed interest in forging closer relations with the Orthodox Church, while both Bishopric and Missionaries were deeply concerned about the state of the Orthodox Church.

The role of the British in Palestine was always ambiguous and a matter of contention. Even amongst those who saw the conquest of Palestine as a crusade, there was a degree of uncertainty as to who or what they believed they were freeing. An official memorandum in February 1923 argued that the Mandate could not be given up because the Turks would take Palestine back and then 'We [would] stand for all time as the Christian Power which, having rescued the Holy Land from the Turks, lacked the strength or the courage to guard what it had won'.[30] To the majority it seems that what mattered was the land itself; it was important to them that the Christian Holy Places and the Biblical lands should be back in Christian hands, but they seem to have paid far less attention to their fellow Christians, who were hoping for so much. As we will see, the dealings of the British with the Christian communities of Jerusalem were often far from a simple reflection of common Christianity, representing instead a clash of expectations, realities and differing values.

'A faith of centuries'

British attitudes towards the Orthodox Christians of Jerusalem were to a large degree defined by their own expectations, preconceptions and

---

[29] Gabriel Sheffer, 'The images of Arabs and Jews as a factor in British policy towards Palestine', *Zionism*, 1,1 (1980), 105-28, 105; Segev is much less sympathetic: Tom Segev, *One Palestine, Complete: Jews and Arabs under the British Mandate*, Jerusalem, 1999 (trans. London 2000), 9.

[30] P.R.O., CAB 27/222, Memo. 16/2/23.

value systems. An interesting paradox had to be faced in looking at the Orthodox and other Eastern Christians; on one hand their Christianity was more ancient and traditional in form than that of the Anglicans, but on the other hand it was exotic and to many it seemed improper. By no means all the British in Jerusalem were Anglican or even Christian and it is noticeable that the Jewish officials who have left memoirs paid less attention to the Christians and their Churches than the Christian British. However, their relations with the Orthodox in a social context were not all that different; in fact, social relations between the Orthodox and the British were very limited and a mutual faith (if it could even be seen to be that similar) was not enough to override other social and racial considerations. Yet the fascination of many Britons in Palestine with Eastern Christianity is extremely evident in the overwhelming majority of their writings. The focus tended to be on the Orthodox as the biggest and most powerful community. Much attention was paid to Orthodox services, particularly those in Holy Week and at Easter, and to the Christian Holy Places; responses to these events and sites are revealing. They reflect something of the Britons' understanding of their own faith, as well as revealing more of the way British people related to Palestine and its people.

This concern with Orthodoxy was nothing new, but from 1917 far greater numbers of British people were coming into contact with it as they arrived in Palestine; often also their first experience of the Orient. A few Britons had a deep appreciation of the Orthodox services; one young woman described her experiences on Good Friday in Bethlehem in the late 1920s:

> It seemed that I was no longer on earth, but at the Gates of Heaven. A spirit of intense prayer pervaded the whole atmosphere. Little children stood with their lighted candles in an attitude of the deepest reverence … Alas, I did not understand the service in Greek, but it did not matter; for it seemed as if the Angels hovered in the air, and the Mighty Presence of God brooded over that great throng, till the whole building was wrapped in a spirit of Holy Worship.[31]

To some, the ancient nature of the traditions of the Church was an added attraction. In defending the Orthodox Church, Estelle Blyth, daughter of the bishop, argued that that those Westerners who questioned

---

[31] Theodora Eyton-Jones, *Under Eastern Roofs*, London, 1931, 61.

the appropriateness of the Holy Fire ceremony should remember that, 'it has been held this way, year by year, for centuries in just this way; that Crusaders and pilgrims believed in it then just as pilgrims and people do now, and surely custom and the faith of centuries do count for something in the world, even if manifested in a form not understood by the West'.[32]

Blyth was responding to a common protestant sensibility amongst Britons in Palestine at this time, a tendency to view the Orthodox rites and services as 'pagan' or even 'barbaric'. This was intended as the harsh criticism it appears to be, but one that also incorporated the idea of the thrill of barbarism. Miss Emery, a school teacher in Jerusalem in the 1920s, found the Holy Fire ceremony 'very exciting, but of course utterly Pagan'. Evidently for her the nature of the service was not entirely negative, although it seems to have been in sharp contrast with her own conception of the Christian faith. She described the moment when the Fire appeared as 'one of the most thrilling moments I have known'.[33] The strength of Orthodox belief in the veracity of the Holy Places provided further contrast with the often more cynical outlook of many British Christians.[34] This contrast between the denominations was central to, and chief cause of ambiguity within, British attitudes to the Orthodox. The ancient Churches were felt, especially by those who came to know them best, as just as valid as, if not more so than, the Anglican Church, yet it could certainly not be admitted by many (on a conscious or even a subconscious level) that the Anglican Church did not represent an improvement on these old traditions. This tied in with more general assumptions of the superiority of the British political and imperial systems. It is striking that the language employed to describe the Orthodox was the same used across the empire to describe various supposedly lesser races or societies.

Notions of 'the Orient' played an integral part in these discussions. Sir Ronald Storrs, Governor of Jerusalem, described his first Orthodox

---

[32] Estelle Blyth, *When We Lived in Jerusalem*, London, 1926, especially 46, 316; H V Morton, *In The Steps Of The Master*, London, 1934, 331-4.

[33] 'Pagan' see St Antony's GB165-0099; C R Ashbee, *A Palestine Notebook, 1918-1923*, London, 1923; 'barbaric' see Revd H G Harding, *The Land of Promise*, London, 1919, 55; H C Luke, *Prophets, Priests and Patriarchs: Sketches of the sects of Palestine and Syria*, London, 1927, 13, 28; Hichens, *The Holy Land*, London, 1898; Ronald Storrs, *Orientations*, London, 1937, 25; 'bogus' see St Antony's, GB165-0093.

[34] Revd H T F Duckworth, *The Church of the Holy Sepulchre*, London, 1922; Sarah Kochav, 'The search for a Protestant Holy Sepulchre', *Journal of Ecclesiastical History*, 46(2), (1995); Mary Berenson, *Modern Pilgrimage*, New York, London, 1933.

liturgy as 'an unforgettable experience of the undisciplined Oriental pageantry'. It was certainly felt by many that Eastern Christianity was well-suited to the Eastern character and temperament. Storrs himself felt that 'Syrians and Near Easterns should be either Latin or Orthodox' not Protestant.[35] He even suggested that 'nothing seemed to denationalize an Arab, a Copt or an Armenian like becoming a Protestant'.[36] The more emotional attitude to faith was a significant, and often positive, attribute of Eastern Christianity, which, it was felt, the Anglicans lacked. 'The Anglicans, of course, are more respectable. There is a certain uprightness about their hard starched white collars; but as soon as you get them on religion all their better nature gets atrophied. They become their collars'.[37] The use of terms such as pagan could even take on new meanings in this context, as they become romanticized and exoticised by notions of the East. Ashbee who so hated the Holy Sepulchre for its 'paganism' preferred Islam; yet described the Dome of the Rock as 'that great pagan, oriental, imaginative building'.[38] In general, the 'Oriental aesthetic' evidently fitted most comfortably with the eastern religion of Islam, but could be reconciled with Eastern Christianity by those who did not feel it as a threat to their own faith and manner of worship.[39]

Criticisms of the Church, then, did not just grow up because it was 'different'; these differences could be disliked, but by others could be embraced. There were further issues that left many Britons disillusioned with the Orthodox, although the boundaries between these and concerns of superstition could become very blurred. A common accusation against the Orthodox Church was that it was too materialistic. This was partly a reflection of the contrast between the extravagance of Orthodox robes, decorations and style of liturgy, but also a sign of deeper dissatisfaction with the way the Church was run. Dennis Doyle, working for Reuter's in the 1930s, wrote that the Holy Sepulchre was 'all dreadfully commercial and irreligious' with candle sellers and monks wanting alms.[40] Another observer

---

[35] Ronald Storrs, *Orientations*, London, 1937, 335.

[36] Ronald Storrs, *Orientations*, London, 1937, 410.

[37] C R Ashbee, *A Palestine Notebook, 1918-1923*, London, 1923, 1; Theodora Eyton-Jones, *Under Eastern Roofs*, London, 1931, 51.

[38] C R Ashbee, *A Palestine Notebook, 1918-1923*, London, 1923, 7.

[39] For appreciation of the 'oriental aesthetic' see Robert Byron, *Road to Oxiana,* London, 1937.

[40] St Antony's, GB165-0093.

described it as 'a display of wealth and barbaric splendour'.[41] Much further criticism of the Churches referred to the constant tensions, bickering and argument between and within them. Estelle Blyth was disillusioned to see 'how unlovely a thing Christianity can be when inflamed and scarred by strife, by the lust of place and money, by jealousies racial and political; when you see Church arrayed against Church, Moslem against Jew, Jew against Gentile.'[42]

MAINTAINING THE STATUS QUO: THE BRITISH ADMINISTRATION

The majority of interaction between British and Orthodox took the form of political manoeuvring, diplomacy and practical day-to-day administration, first by the army and Military Administration, and from 1920 by the Civil Administration. It generally revolved around mediating in these disputes. A better understanding of British perceptions of the Orthodox within these contexts, as well as the extent to which these ideas had an impact upon the actions of the Administration with regard to the Orthodox community illuminates a range of wider influences on Mandatory policy. It is clear that, although they were predominantly Christian and even at times described themselves as 'a Christian Administration', the British did not favour the Christians above other communities.[43] Indeed, a sense of pride in the ability of the British to work equally with all communities of Jerusalem is evident in much official and unofficial writing of the time.[44] The British Administration was guided by other priorities and desires, including carefully defined and often unquestioned notions of British justice and government, while their actions were frequently delineated by immediate concerns of international politics, the requirements of basic maintenance of law and order and the conditions of the Mandate itself.[45] These ideas tie into the wider debate as to the motives behind British policy making and administrative action; they can provide no definitive

---

[41] Revd H G Harding, *The Land of Promise*, London, 1919, 55.

[42] Estelle Blyth, *When We Lived in Jerusalem*, London, 1926, 45.

[43] P.R.O., CAB27/23: 25/1/18; P.R.O., FO141/773: 18/7/17; L G A Cust, *The Status Quo in the Holy Places*, Jerusalem, 1980, 13.

[44] Ronald Storrs, *Orientations*, London, 1937, 311; Edward Keith-Roach, *Pasha of Jerusalem: Memoirs of a district commissioner under the British Mandate*, London, 1994, 102.

[45] Mandate for Palestine, 24 July 1922, *Parliamentary Accounts and Papers / State Papers*, vol. 25 (13/2/1923-16/11/1923), 421-429.

answer, but a greater understanding of British dealings with the Orthodox sheds light upon wider policy making decisions. It is argued here that, with regard to their responsibilities towards the Orthodox Church, the British generally acted in what they believed to be the best interests of the Church, as long as this did not compromise the best interests of the British Government and wider British imperial concerns.

The British had to believe they were the best people to be ruling Palestine; the need to see themselves as 'neutral' and benevolent, to justify British rule and to maintain their national honour were of great importance to the British officials in Palestine.[46] The Christian communities in many ways represented the most difficult context within which to assert this 'superiority'. These people were Christian, often well educated and as capable as any British officials; it was essential to the continuation of British rule that those in the administration not only asserted but truly believed that they were, nevertheless, still the best people for the job. This was all the more problematic as a disproportionately high number of Christian Arabs worked in most government departments compared to the number of Muslims, in fact they often outnumbered them, which was remarkable considering the relative population sizes. In June 1921, 1049 Christian Arabs held government posts, compared with just 584 Muslims, and eighty four of the 145 Arabs in the Senior Service were Christian. This was due to the far higher levels of education amongst Christian Arabs than amongst their Muslim compatriots and cannot be seen as a sign of the British favouring their fellow Christians. Indeed, British policy was to increase the numbers of Muslims in such positions, although there was little success, as Muslim education was not improved rapidly enough.[47] It appears that the appointment of Arabs, whether Christian or Muslim, was often resented by British officials; the fact that these people were not British was seen as a challenge to the security and value of their own positions. It was a particular problem in senior posts, as few British officials at this time relished the idea of an Arab superior, of any religion.[48]

Belief in the advantages of British rule can also be seen in the comparisons many British writers drew between British rule and that of

---

46 P.R.O., CAB27/222, 27/6/23; Pathé newsreel from http://www.britishpathe.com/index.html: 991.08.

47 B Wasserstein, *The British in Palestine: The Mandatory Govt and the Arab-Jewish Conflict, 1917-29* Oxford, 2nd ed., 1991, 169.

48 *Ibid.*

the Ottomans. In writings on the Status Quo in the Holy Places, Cust, a former district officer of Jerusalem, asserts that 'a fundamental reason for the present state of affairs is that, except for limited periods, the Holy Places were for thirteen centuries under the dominion of a non-Christian power from whom concessions were obtainable by diplomatic pressure or other influences', whereas after the First World War 'the Peace found the Holy Places once more under the control of a Christian Power, not, as in the days of the Crusades under the shadow of a perpetual menace, but sheltered in the world wide dominion of Great Britain'.[49] The implications here of Ottoman corruption contrast starkly with the justice of the British, Christian, administration. In this context, it is increasingly clear why the hopes the Christian communities held for benefits under a new Christian administration were not realised. Any improvements Christians found in contrast with others groups tended to be as a result of the removal of Muslim privileges, notably the use of Islamic law as common law, rather than an introduction of specific advantages for the Christian communities.[50] For the British, the common faith was less important than the notion of British justice and fair government. In some ways this was not so much a case of justice for its own sake as the need for Britain to be seen to be a fair and just ruler in international eyes; this was key to the continued good reputation of British rule and most importantly, to their own sense of the legitimacy of their presence in Palestine.

The Administration was also very reluctant to become involved in the affairs of any particular church or community. It was felt to be against the principles of British government and it was easier to avoid accusations of improper government by simply avoiding confrontational situations. This proved a short-sighted policy, eventually impossible to sustain, but it prevented the British from becoming more involved in the affairs of the Orthodox Church. It was clearly stated in a key report by Bertram and Young on the affairs of the Orthodox Patriarchate in 1926 that 'nothing could be more repugnant to the instincts of any Government, constituted on the basis of British traditions, than that it should be asked to intervene in the internal affairs of any religious community under its rule'.[51] Yet in

---

[49] L G A Cust, *The Status Quo in the Holy Places*, Jerusalem, 1980, 5.

[50] Ruth Kark, 'Missions and Architecture: Colonial and Post-Colonial Views—The Case of Palestine', in E Tejirian and R Spector Simon (eds), *Altruism and Imperialism: Western Cultural and Religious Missions in the Middle East*, New York, 2002, 53.

[51] Bertram and Young; Palestine Commission, *The Orthodox Patriarchate of Jerusalem Commission's Report on certain controversies, 1926*, OUP, London, 1928, 122; See P.R.O., FO371/4153.

practice the government was involved in a whole range of disputes and other issues arising over the next decades; the Bertram-Young report itself was a sign of Government involvement in an internal dispute between Greek Patriarchate and Arab clergy and laity over the election of the next Patriarch. The danger of friction and conflict created a strong feeling, running through the official documentation and correspondence of the time, that the British were playing a very delicate balancing game, which could, at any moment, come crashing down around them. The old ways were not the best, they were merely the least dangerous.

The main pressure upon the British in their relations with the Orthodox Church was the real and almost constant threat of discord and disorder, particularly in such a fragile political climate. It was essential that small issues were not allowed to erupt into much bigger problems. Great concern was caused by the internal disputes between the Christian Churches and within the Orthodox Church itself, bearing in mind the wider context of political turmoil that made these conflicts all the more dangerous. Ongoing disputes as to ownership rights in the Holy Sepulchre and the Church of the Nativity did not tend to spill over into violence, but they certainly contributed to the tense atmosphere that could culminate in such an eruption. Correspondence regarding these claims seems almost incredibly extensive, considering the apparent pettiness of many of the complaints. We find, for example, pages and pages of letters referring to a dispute over the cleaning of the windows of the Church of the Nativity, as no denomination wished any other to be allowed to clean the windows. In the end, the only possible solution appeared to be to get a British official to do the job instead.[52] That the British administration took the complaints so seriously in official terms, while remaining more cynical in private, demonstrates the importance they accorded the return of peace and concord.[53] Those responsible for policing the Christian festivals prepared detailed notes on managing the crowds and disruptions and they had far more trouble from the Christian Festivals than those of the Jews or Muslims.[54]

The strength of emotion behind these conflicts comes through very clearly in various anecdotes recited by the officials involved in solving

---

[52] St Antony's, GB165-0161-19-2, Report and Additional Notes.

[53] P.R.O., CAB27/23: 25/1/18; Also St Antony's, GB165-0117; GB165-0001.

[54] St Antony's, GB165-0117.

the disputes. Keith-Roach described one such incident in the Church of the Nativity in Bethlehem, a rare but by no means solitary case:

> One year, I was asked to go urgently to the grotto. There I found a mess of blood on the floor, hangings pulled down, vestments strewn about and two dishevelled priests, a Greek monk and a Franciscan friar, breathing heavily and looking much the worse for wear. Each held tenaciously to a brass candlestick that had been snatched off the altar and used as a weapon. Each accused the other of overstepping his legitimate time for holding Mass.[55]

The contrast with the sedate Anglicans, not involved in such conflicts, exacerbated the feeling that the British were above such petty wrangling. The Anglicans made no claim of ownership because they had never had any such right, not because of some innate superiority, but the contrast was powerful nevertheless.[56] An amusing, but telling example of the sense of the efficiency and value of British rule can be seen in a description of the Holy Fire ceremony, in which it was believed that Holy Fire came down miraculously from heaven. In the past, people waiting many hours for the arrival of the Fire (it could come at any time due to its miraculous nature) had been crushed in the crowd; 'However, the British now ruled Palestine, and the Government had decreed that the fire must appear punctually at twelve noon'![57] In this, the sense of the semi-pagan nature of this tradition combined with a sense of the genuine danger of the surging crowd. Alongside requirements of preventing crowd violence, genuine concern for the rights of the Orthodox to free worship is also apparent in official documents; Storrs wrote in a memo of 1918:

> I presume that it is no part of the Military Administration to decide upon the intrinsic merits of miraculous manifestations, and that, in accordance with the Commander-in-Chief's general instructions re. non-interference and the maintenance of the status quo in such matters, it is not desirable that we should explicitly or implicitly prevent the services being held.

---

[55] Edward Keith-Roach, *Pasha of Jerusalem: Memoirs of a district commissioner under the British Mandate*, London, 1994, 156-7.

[56] Ronald Storrs, *Orientations*, London, 1937, 409.

[57] St Antony's, GB165-0099, autobiography.

> The effect, indeed, upon the Christian population would be deplorable if we did.[58]

Disputes *within* the Orthodox Church could also be extremely disruptive; although usually less violent, they were no less dangerous in their long-term consequences. The depth of the British response to various crises within the Orthodox Patriarchate demonstrates how seriously they had to be taken, despite the avowed dislike of government intervention. Key reports throughout the Mandate period probed the complex history of the Church and looked for precedents and guidance in dealing with the disputes. The tone of documents referring to these events is very telling. Official correspondence and reports reflect a very precise and careful attempt at an 'objective' understanding of the historical context.[59] Unofficial comments generally remain respectful, but the writers are often astounded and despairing at the depths of hostility expressed.

There was a particular fear, especially from the later 1920s onwards, that disputes within the Church would contribute to the development of wider Arab nationalism.[60] The Bertram-Young report shows an awareness of and sympathy for the many young Arab Orthodox, attached to their Church but also to their nation and people, while their Church was run by 'aliens', in stark contrast with the Arab Patriarchate in Antioch. 'It was often necessary deliberately to remind oneself and the company that we were not discussing a question of racial politics but a question of religion.'[61] Many Arab Orthodox Christians were involved in, often deeply committed to, the growing Palestinian nationalist movement, although the dual identity of Arab and Christian could prove difficult for even the

---

[58] Cambridge, Pembroke College, Ronald Storrs' Papers, Reel 6.

[59] Bertram and Luke, *The Orthodox Patriarchate of Jerusalem: Report of the Commission*, 1921; Bertram and Young, Palestine Commission, *The Orthodox Patriarchate of Jerusalem Commission's Report on certain controversies, 1926,* London, 1928; L G A Cust, *The Status Quo in the Holy Places*, Jerusalem, 1980.

[60] Daphne Tsimhoni, 'The Status of the Arab Christians under the British Mandate in Palestine, *Middle Eastern Studies*, 20, 4 (1984), 166-92; Anthony O'Mahony, 'Palestinian-Arab Orthodox Christians: Religion, Politics and Church-State relations in Jerusalem, c.1908-1925', *Chronos*, 3 (2000), 61-92, especially 61-3; Albert Hourani 'The Arab Awakening: Forty years after' in *The Emergence of the Modern Middle East*, London, 1981, 214-215.

[61] Bertram and Young, Palestine Commission, *The Orthodox Patriarchate of Jerusalem Commission's Report on certain controversies, 1926*, London, 1928, 107-8; Ronald Storrs, *Orientations,* London, 1937, 404.

most committed nationalists to reconcile.[62] Educator, writer and leading figure of Jerusalem society, Al Sakakini, was the most famous example; he despaired that 'No matter how much I do to revive this nation... as long as I am not a Muslim, I am nought.' But many others found their own, sometimes more simple, solutions to the dilemma; the poet Wadi al-Bustani wrote the following:

> Yes, I am a Christian
> Ask yesterday and ask tomorrow,
> But I am an Arab
> Who loves Mohammed.[63]

This feeling was widespread and it was clear that to antagonise the Arab Orthodox in their relations with the Greek Patriarchate, could spark off far more wide-reaching consequences. The Government's failure to resolve the conflicts within the Church led to anger from the Orthodox Arab Congress at the Administration's supposed bias towards the Patriarchate.[64] The reluctance to confirm the new Patriarch in 1938 was explained in this context, as to confirm the Patriarch could 'drag this issue into the nationalist dispute and only enflame opinion.'[65]

Political concerns regarding the Church were massively exacerbated by the interest of various foreign parties. International pressure came in part through the League of Nations, on whose behalf Britain held the Mandate, and more specifically from a number of other parties interested in the Christian Holy Places and rights of the various Christian communities of Palestine. The attention Britain paid to these concerns demonstrates the power such fears had in influencing the direction and nature of British policy. On his way to Palestine to become High Commissioner, for example, Herbert Samuel's meetings were with the French Prime Minister, the King of Italy, Pope Benedict XV and Cardinal Gaspari, the Papal Secretary of State.[66] These are representative of some of the key outside powers who took an interest in Christian affairs in

---

62 Qustandi Shomali, 'Palestinian Christians: Politics, Press and Religious Identity, 1900-48' in Anthony O'Mahony (ed.), *The Christian Heritage in the Holy Land*, London, 1995, 230-233; Kenneth Cragg, *The Arab Christian*, Louisville, 1991, 13.

63 Quoted in Anthony O'Mahony, *op. cit.*, 21.

64 P.R.O., FO371/21886, Faraj.

65 P.R.O., GB165-0161-19-2: 28/4/38.

66 Daphne Tsimhoni, 'The Status of the Arab Christians under the British Mandate in Palestine, *Middle Eastern Studies*, 20, 4 (1984) 166-92, 168.

Jerusalem. The Vatican, of course, kept a keen eye on events in Jerusalem and was quick to object any unfair treatment of Catholics therein, yet in many ways it was the French who really saw themselves as protectors of the Catholics of the Holy Land.[67] They were prepared to make concessions and compromises in return for greater rights for the Catholics of Jerusalem, even suggesting in 1921 that a French Catholic chair the Holy Places Commission in return for border concessions in Northern Palestine. In fact, the British concluded that 'the post would be most suitably filled by an Englishman of judicial experience, and so far as possible world-wide reputation'.[68] In another early dispute, concern was expressed as to the nationalities of the various guards at the Christian Holy Places as this was 'bound to lead to fresh claims being put forward by various nations and give constant cause for friction' and in the end only British military police were used.[69] The conviction that the British were the best people to be ruling Palestine was reinforced by repeated requests, from various interested parties within the Churches, for the British to solve disputes or resolve other complex situations.

The Orthodox patriarchate also enjoyed international support. By the time Britain entered Palestine, Russia was effectively out of the picture, following the Bolshevik Revolution, but, with the consolation of the Greek State after the First World War, Greece continued to take a strong, even growing, interest in the Patriarchate of Jerusalem's affairs.[70] This kind of pressure meant that in order to retain the Mandate, and British honour, the administration had to tread carefully in order not to upset one of the rival parties and its international representatives. The British particularly resented any attempt by other powers to interfere directly with the internal affairs of the Christian communities, and specifically the Orthodox Church. The main culprit was the Greek government.[71] The greatest dispute arose over the financial problems the patriarchate was facing throughout the 1920s, an internal struggle that was internationalised by the offer of a loan from the National Bank of Greece. The administration was prompt in its decision that this would be totally unacceptable, on the grounds that it

---

[67] Albert M Hyamson, *Palestine under the Mandate*, London, 1950, 26; Cambridge, Pembroke College, Ronald Storrs' Papers, Reel 7.

[68] P.R.O., CO733/13.

[69] P.R.O., CAB27/23 January 1918.

[70] Sotiris Roussos, 'The Greek Orthodox Patriarchate and Community of Jerusalem' in Anthony O'Mahony (ed.), *The Christian Heritage in the Holy Land*, London, 1995, 211-224.

[71] P.R.O., FO371/21886-E940.

would 'subject the patriarchate and the whole of its financial administration to a foreign government'.[72] The Bertram-Luke report of 1921, the result of the government's investigation, was an extremely methodical document, assessing the historic and legal claims of all sides and looking for alternative sources of jurisdiction, preferably within the Church. They argued that the patriarchate could effectively do whatever it wanted, as long as there was no 'foreign political control of whatever nature over the internal affairs of the Orthodox Church in Palestine'.[73]

This determination to prevent foreign governments intervening in internal Church affairs was due chiefly to a feeling of threat or challenge to British supremacy. The Administration was positively eager for the Ethiopian government to play a part in the affairs of the Ethiopian Church, because this did not entail the same political significance or risk as when the Greek government took any action with regard to the Greek Church. A 1921 memo from Herbert Samuel to Churchill specifically recommends, for example, that 'an authoritative representative of the Abyssinian Govt should proceed to Jerusalem without loss of time to settle the dispute' between the Abbot and one of his monks.[74] The friendly relations the British enjoyed with Haile Selassie at the time, not to mention the influence they held within that country, ensured much closer cooperation between the two states in affairs in Palestine. British prestige had to be maintained in international terms, just as it did in social and political terms internally. Retaining the say in who could become involved in internal Palestinian affairs and who could not was as central to the British government's international standing as it was to Britain's sense of control within Palestine itself.

This study does not aim to address in detail the impact of British policy upon the Orthodox Church, but it is illuminating to assess briefly what was achieved, if only to compare it with the asserted aims of the Mandate and the Administration. The Orthodox retained their rights as defined within the Status Quo of 1757, but in the context of the changing times of the 1920s and 1930s, this was not of much benefit to those within the Church. The internal crises the Church faced cannot be blamed on the British alone, but British reluctance to get involved did become so extreme as to be seriously counter-productive.[75] After the death

[72] Bertram and Luke, *The Orthodox Patriarchate of Jerusalem: Report of the Commission, 1921,* 35.

[73] Bertram and Luke, *The Orthodox Patriarchate of Jerusalem: Report of the Commission, 1921,* 37.

[74] P.R.O., CO733/2.

[75] P.R.O., FO371/21886: 30/11/37.

of Patriarch Damianos in 1931, a new patriarch was not officially elected until 1938, following deadlocks in discussion between the Arab clergy and the Synod. In spite of a real sense of urgency, evident in correspondence of 1935 a new Ordinance was not finally passed through as law until 1938.[76] Even then hostility and tensions remained, fuelled by and fuelling the nationalist conflict. It is futile to question what more the British could or should have done; it is more useful to recognise why they did what they did. The sense that Jerusalem could remain as it was, with modifications but no fundamental alterations or modernisation, was widespread, but did not fit with the swiftly changing times. Honest attempts to impart justice, in whatever form they perceived this to take, for the sake of Palestine as well as the empire, and the desire to maintain peace and order all contributed to the confusing and at times contradictory policies of the British towards the Orthodox of Jerusalem.

On a more positive note, the British did demonstrate, in their relations with the Orthodox Church, a genuine desire to solve the problems they were faced with, not just for the sake of personal and national honour, but for the sake of Palestine and its people. This can be seen in preparations made by officials in 1947, aware they would soon leave Palestine, for a handover to whoever was next to run Palestine; at that time they could not be sure who that was, but there was a feeling of wishing the country the best of luck in the future, as well as a residual sense of pride and responsibility. An official called James Pollock specifically left a document outlining certain aspects of British relations with the Orthodox, as 'a permanent record of what took place under British stewardship in the Holy Places [and] in the hope that it may be of use to whatever authority is finally charged with the preservation of the Status Quo'[77]

'The reconciling ministry': The Anglican Church

The other significant body representing Britain in Palestine to the Orthodox Christians was the Anglican Church. Attitudes amongst the British laity and secular authority were to some degree reflected in the

---

[76] St Antony's, GB165-0161-19-2: 10/8/35.

[77] St Antony's, GB165-0231; on failure of Mandate, see W Roger Louis, *Imperialism at Bay, 1941-5,* Oxford, 1981.

relations of the Anglican Church and the Orthodox. These relations reveal much about the Anglican Church and its priorities, as well as providing a different perspective on wider British and imperial concerns. Considering the regularity with which many Anglicans referred to Orthodox ceremonies and beliefs as pagan or superstitious, it may seem surprising that the two Churches enjoyed such close relations at this time. Great efforts were made to bring the two Churches ever closer and the Anglican Church and missionaries (Anglicans and others) wished to 'reinvigorate' the Orthodox Church, in Palestine and elsewhere. This stemmed from a deep respect on the Anglican side for the other, older church and from a genuine desire for greater ecumenical understanding. A 'revival' of the Orthodox Church was also seen as a vital step in bringing Christianity to the Muslim population of Palestine. Moreover, it seems it was far easier for the Orthodox to achieve this with the Anglicans than with other churches with older and more vested interests in Jerusalem and its Holy Places, with whom they were always in disagreement. This is not to argue that those in the Anglican Church had none of preconceptions that the British laity held, but that more effort was made to understand and work with the Orthodox. Indeed, those 'within' the Church were not so very different from those here classed as laity or within the secular authority; as we have seen, most of the British in Palestine were heavily influenced in their attitudes and actions by their own Christian beliefs.

The Anglican Church had established its presence in Jerusalem in 1842 and in 1881 the Jerusalem Bishopric Fund, later the Jerusalem and East Mission Fund was set up for the maintenance and development of the work of the diocese.[78] Alongside the Bishopric, the missionary presence in Palestine grew massively from the end of the First World War.[79] The largest body, and the focus of this study, was the Anglican Church Missionary Society, which was closely linked to the Bishopric and the Jerusalem and East Mission. The United Free Church of Scotland, the London Jews Society and some freelance missionaries also worked in Palestine at this time, but their focus was upon conversion of the Jews and they had far less to do with the Orthodox Church.[80] With the departure of the Turks

78 Kenneth Cragg, 'Being Made Disciples—The Middle East' in *The Church Mission Society and World Christianity, 1799-1999*, K Ward and B Stanley (eds), Cambridge, 2000, 120-136.

79 St Antony's, G3PP6-11.

80 J H Proctor, 'Scottish missionaries and the struggle for Palestine, 1917-48' *Middle Eastern Studies*, (7/1/1997).

and the cessation of hostilities, missionaries could gradually build upon the very limited relief work they had been able to carry out throughout the war. They could also resume and extend some of their more long-term work, which had all but ceased since 1914. The Mandate did not in any way show favour towards the missionaries' attempts at conversion, in fact often viewing them as something of a nuisance, but the strict respect for all religious beliefs, which the British so prided themselves upon, meant security and greater confidence amongst missionaries.[81] The more practical missionary work was indeed seen as a very useful complement to the government's own projects, as the government could not provide enough schools and hospitals for the population of Palestine, and the missionaries were useful allies in achieving these goals.

The Anglican and Orthodox Churches had traditionally enjoyed good relations, but Anglican-Orthodox relations in Jerusalem were particularly strong during the early Mandate period.[82] The Anglicans in Jerusalem had always accepted a lesser status than that enjoyed by the Orthodox; when the Anglican bishopric was established in Jerusalem in 1842 it was held by the bishop *in* Jerusalem not *of* Jerusalem. This was simply because the bishop *of* Jerusalem already existed in the Orthodox patriarch, and the Anglicans did not try to supersede the Orthodox claim to this title. The strengthening of efforts to unite the two denominations further was partly a result of a growing Anglican presence. However, it has been convincingly argued that this closeness was greatly strengthened in the early 20th century by an Anglican desire to gain recognition of their orders by the Orthodox, following the condemnation of Anglican orders by Rome in 1896.[83] In this sense, close Anglican—Orthodox relations were by no means a Jerusalem phenomenon, but were part of a wider picture of ecumenical efforts in many countries across the globe. This is evident in letters and instructions from Lambeth Palace to the bishop in Jerusalem, and in events taking place elsewhere. In 1923, a concerted effort was made towards strengthening such ties, with representatives of the Anglican Church pursuing discussions in various parts of the world.[84]

---

[81] G Hewitt, *Problems of success: a history of the CMS, 1910-42*, vol 1, London, 1971, 362.

[82] M Tanner, 'The Church of England and its relationship with the Roman Catholic and Orthodox worlds', *Sobornost*, 19: 2 (1997), 9-22.

[83] C Davey, 'Anglicans and Eastern Christendom', *Sobornost,* 7: 2 (1985), 6-17.

[84] St Antony's, GB165-0161-19-1: 19/2/23; St Antony's, GB165-0161-19-1: Report, 1927; Theodora Eyton-Jones, *Under Eastern Roofs*, London, 1931, especially xi, 9, 80.

It is not surprising that within the context of Jerusalem, the Anglicans expressed more concern than the self-proclaimed neutral Mandatory Administration, for the rights of the native Christians within the Mandate. The Church's response to the Palestine Commission Report pointed out that the commissioners 'curiously ignore the fourth, fifth and sixth-century period when Palestine was predominantly a Christian country, contenting themselves with concealing that period under the vague phrase 'Roman and Byzantine rule', which does less justice to oriental Christianity and its historical services to and claims on the country.' The report was given credit, however, for avoiding the 'common error of regarding the Palestine problem as one between Muslim and Jew and ignoring the Christian interest, whether indigenous or foreign'.[85] The Anglican Church certainly did not aim for political or judicial power of its own and no objection was ever made to the fact that the Anglican Church was not a millet and did not have its own courts.[86] They wished to ensure the rights of Arab Anglicans and Hebrew Christians were protected through the civil courts, but nothing more.[87] Moreover, whilst the Anglican Church always took a considerable interest in local Church politics, there was a particularly strong feeling that it was not for the Anglican Church, or its members, to get directly involved. When this convention was broken it could cause considerable concern, as not just unethical, but potentially disruptive.[88]

Relations between the Orthodox Church and British missionaries, particularly the evangelicals, were not always as good as between the two Churches, but improved throughout this period. Indeed, by 1932 one missionary believed that 'the days of a virtual antagonism between the bulk of the evangelical missionary forces and the ancient Churches of the Near East have passed.'[89] There were a number of freelance missionaries, both British and American, 'whose zeal, not always matched by wisdom, caused considerable embarrassment to the more responsible missionary bodies'. In fact, even the most zealous British evangelicals tended to pale

85 'Palestine Commission Report', *International Review of Missions*, vol. 26 (1937), 467; St Antony's, GB165-0161-17- 3: 8/3/22 and 17/3/22.

86 St Antony's, GB165-0161-17-3: 24/5/23.

87 St Antony's, GB165-0161-18-5.

88 St Antony's, GB165-0161-19-2: 28/9/31: Bishop MacInnes was concerned at Anglican clergy, especially Canon Douglas, interfering in election of Greek Patriarch.

89 'Ten Years in the Middle East', *International Review of Missions*, vol. 21 (1932).

in comparison with many of the American missionaries who began to enter Palestine at this time.[90]

Alongside this respect for the political rights of the Orthodox Church lay a far more profound and unusual desire to bring the churches closer together in worship and work. The annual service in St George's commemorating the liberation of Jerusalem of 1917 included all the Christian prelates of the city and was a matter of great pride to many British officials as well as Churchmen.[91] Going still further, fascinating correspondence tells of the discussions that were taking place in the 1920s and 1930s between senior Orthodox and Anglican clergy as to the possibilities of intercommunion between the two Churches. In a letter of 1921, Bishop MacInnes described 'a very remarkable and wholly unexpected suggestion' from Archbishop Themelis on the possibility of the Archbishop's receiving Communion from MacInnes. The main condition was that the service took place in the chapel of Abraham in the Holy Sepulchre, not in the Anglican Cathedral of St George's, but it would have represented a dramatic step in ecumenical relations.[92] This development, as with so many of these ideas, never reached the final stages, but the discussions were extensive and earnest; many on both sides were strongly committed to bringing the two Churches closer together. A booklet was produced as late as the early 1930s considering in detail possible 'Terms of Intercommunion'.[93] Similar discussions were taking place elsewhere; in Belgrade Patriarch Dmitri of Serbia had allowed some Anglicans to take communion in December 1927, although this did not set a true precedent as he had not first asked permission of his Synod or the Archbishop of Canterbury.[94] Nevertheless, clearly the developments in Jerusalem were not taking place in a vacuum.

Another issue that received much attention from the Bishopric was that of conversion. The Anglican Church, including the CMS, was quite clear that it was not aiming to convert Orthodox Christians to

---

[90] St Antony's, GB165-0161-19-1: 8/5/23 and 5/6/23.

[91] H C Luke, *Prophets, Priests and Patriarchs: Sketches of the sects of Palestine and Syria,* London, 1927, 8; Vicount Samuel, *Memoirs,* Bristol, 1945, 166.

[92] St Antony's, GB165-0161-19-1: 1/11/21.

[93] St Antony's, GB165-0161-19-2: 'Terms of Intercommunion'; Theologians still dispute whether the two Churches could be 'in communion' see Timothy Ware, *The Orthodox Church*, Harmondsworth, 1963, 319; Hugh Wybrew, 'Anglican-Orthodox dialogue: its past, its present and its future', *Sobornost*, 15:1 (1993), 7-19.

[94] St Antony's, GB165-0161-19-1: Report, 1927.

Anglicanism. Only a small proportion of missionaries went against this line, and the overwhelming majority of them were American; the attitude of these few often caused considerable embarrassment and frustration to the majority.[95] The prevailing attitude amongst British churchmen and missionaries was summed up in a letter of 1922, written by a member of the Jerusalem and East Mission staff, Donald Carr; 'I quite agree that we do not want to proselytise among the Eastern Churches.'[96] Indeed, not only would they not go out looking for converts, but Church leaders showed a considerable reluctance in allowing conversions of non-Anglican Christians to Anglicanism. The Church would allow a few individuals to convert if they could not 'with a safe conscience continue in their own communions', but any attempt by a whole congregation to switch to Anglicanism was 'invariably refused, courteously but firmly'.[97] Priests were equally reluctant to baptise the children of non-Anglican parents.[98] This reluctance to allow Orthodox to become Anglicans stemmed from a whole variety of causes, not least a sincere belief among many that the Churches should be working together and not competing. After all, they all shared the same God and the same ultimate aim (as the missionaries saw it) of spreading the word of God.

The key concern of Anglicans in many areas of the world, not least in Palestine, was to use the Eastern Churches to help convert the Muslim population. The CMS in particular stated conversion of Muslims as their primary aim in statements of policy in 1918 and, officially at least, this policy did not change into the 1930s.[99] It was considered essential to get the Orthodox Church involved, as it was felt that Arab priests and other Arab Christians would be far more effective in bringing the Christian message to their fellow Arabs.[100]

> Has not the Providence of God a purpose for this larger Christian community? How far, we may ask, is the Spirit of Jesus incarnate in the great Oriental Churches, or able through them to reach the unshepherded multitude of Moslems and

[95] St Antony's, GB165-0161-19-1: 8/5/23 and 5/6/23.

[96] St Antony's, GB165-0161-20-1.

[97] S A Morrison, *The Way of Partnership with the CMS in England and Palestine*, London, 1936, 27-8.

[98] St Antony's, GB165-0161-17-1, 3; A L Tibawi, *British Interests in Palestine, 1800-1901*, Oxford, 1961, 254; Birmingham University, Church Missionary Society Archive, G3PL15: 9/6/22.

[99] Birmingham University, Church Missionary Society Archive, G3PP6-5.

[100] St Antony's, GB165-0161-19-1: Biskersteth.

> Jews? And what is the high calling of the Anglican Church in regard to them? May it not be at once the privilege and responsibility of this small community to lead them to a deeper spiritual experience, to a renewed zeal for evangelism and to a more commanding desire for unity with one another in and through the one Lord Christ?[101]

Many of the questions raised in these circumstances were arising in various other contexts around the world at the time. The following quotation comes from a missionary in Ceylon, yet its words reflect the very ideas expressed by so many missionaries in Palestine at the same time. 'Christianity often comes to the East in too western a garb and the foreign aspect must be preventing many from accepting the message'.[102] The Orthodox Church seemed the perfect way to bridge this divide.

To place this question in a wider context: the role of the Anglican Church and of British missionaries of all denominations in contributing to a British sense of identity, and contributing more widely within the British Empire, have long been the subject of heated debate, amongst contemporaries and historians. Indeed, questions of the impact of missionary work on the spread and interaction of cultures remain highly pertinent today. The most recent and most comprehensive contribution to the debate, from Andrew Porter, has shown that missionaries of the 19th century were not merely imperial agents, and were not responsible for the extent of cultural domination that has so often been attributed to them.[103] No equivalent work has yet assessed the part played by missionaries in Britain's 20th century imperial concerns, but many of the key issues raised by Porter can be applied, albeit carefully, to early 20th century Palestine. The British missionaries in Palestine were not there as part of a self-conscious attempt to impose Western civilisation upon the unsuspecting East. As we see in their relations with the Orthodox, their actions stemmed from a far more complex set of concerns, beliefs and aims. Moreover, this is clearly not just a question of motive but also of impact. In Palestine, missionary education provided many of the leaders of Arab Nationalism, and explains why so many leading figures in the

---

[101] S A Morrison, *The Way of Partnership with the CMS in England and Palestine*, London, 1936, 26.
[102] Anon., *International Review of Missions*, vol. 13 (1924), 55.
[103] Andrew Porter, in *Introduction to Post-Colonial Theory*, Peter Childs, and Patrick Williams (eds), New York, 1997, especially 320.

movement were Christian despite the ambiguous relationship between Arab Nationalism, Islam and Christianity.[104]

In the early 1920s, missionaries in Palestine were fired up with hopes of great conversions of the Muslim population, but by the mid 1930s this hope was fading fast. The missionaries believed that one fundamental obstruction was the state of the Orthodox Church and its lack of enthusiasm or ability for proselytisation. One missionary complained that 'one has to deplore an entire lack of missionary spirit among the native Christians. The Eastern Church, at least in Palestine, has no sense of mission to the Moslems around her, no belief in the power of her message or of her Master to change their hearts'.[105] Seeing this as a major failing, many Anglican churchmen and particularly the missionaries desired to revive and reinvigorate the Orthodox Church in Jerusalem. The Patriarchate itself was strongly criticised and put under pressure for reform, because Arabs were never allowed to enter the ranks of the upper clergy in the Orthodox Patriarchate and provision for their training was minimal. In 1923, Bishop MacInnes pointed out the urgent need for a theological college for 'native or Arab 'Greeks'' claiming that 'the poverty-stricken, superstitious and absolutely uneducated native priests of Palestine are a living reproach to these ecclesiastical dignitaries from Greece'. He believed that 'native-born' priests should receive higher ecclesiastical positions and denounced the fact that not all the Greek bishops could even speak Arabic. He also described Greek fears of an increase in Latin control of the Holy Places as 'a magnificent opening' to push the Orthodox Church towards reform, if they wanted the 'continued support and help' of the bishop and the sympathy of British and American Anglicans.[106] There was even a suggestion of using non-Greek Orthodox countries to help or encourage the patriarchate to reform. This plan was dropped due to the risk the Arabs would play the countries off against one another and that the Greeks would 'shift the responsibility for the Arab flock' but keep control of the Holy Places.[107]

The patriarchate never met the conditions the Bishop wished to impose and in the end there was little the Anglicans could do in this regard. The patriarchate was powerful and stubborn; compromise withinits

---

[104] George Antonius, *The Arab Awakening: the story of the Arab national movement*, London, 1938.
[105] Revd H G Harding, *The Land of Promise*, London, 1919, 62.
[106] St Antony's, GB165-0161-19-2, MacInnes to Archbishop 1923.
[107] St Antony's, GB165-0161-19-2, Personal comments by staff, 1935.

ranks could not be found. Instead, the real impact of the Anglican Church, particularly the missionaries, came through the missionary schools. These aimed to provide a 'Christian education' for Christians of any church and to introduce non-Christians to Christ.[108] It was hoped the schools would contribute greatly to the reinvigoration of the Orthodox Church, as a new generation of Christians could grow up who would understand their own faith. These were to become some of the new priests, as well as a far better educated laity. In the early 1920s, Arab parish priests, according to one missionary, 'failed to teach and shepherd the illiterate masses, whose religious thought hardly differed from that of their Moslem neighbours'[109] The schools were felt, by the British but also the Jerusalem elite of Christian, Muslim and Jewish communities, to provide an excellent education. These schools were one of the very rare places where children of all faiths mixed freely, and this was felt to relax the tensions that otherwise dominated the city. One missionary spoke of the Hebrew Christians and Arab evangelist old boys of Bishop Gobat School 'In their common loyalty to Him [Christ] the difference of race had raised no barrier to a friendship which was firmly established on a basis of equality and mutual respect, and formed a tribute to the reconciling ministry of a Christian school'.[110] The educated elite produced were not, however, necessarily a Christian elite. There was a fear that attempts to avoid open proselytism to the non-Christian and non-Anglican pupils could result in a diminished focus on Christianity, or risk a 'Churchless' Christianity, whereby the Christian pupils would not learn what distinguished their own Church from the others.[111]

The failure to convert Muslims to Christianity was very disheartening for many missionaries, particularly those who had seen the Mandate as their one chance to win back the Holy Land for a reinvigorated Christianity. Others felt that the education and health care they had provided was valuable enough to justify their efforts. The Orthodox Church had not reached the standards to which the Anglicans had hoped it would aspire, but many remained optimistic regarding the future of the

[108] S A Morrison, *The Way of Partnership with the CMS in England and Palestine*, London, 1936, 17-18.

[109] S A Morrison, *op. cit.*, 27-8; see Revd H G Harding, *The Land of Promise*, London, 1919, 58.

[110] S A Morrison, *op. cit.*, 34; See *International Review of Missions,* vol. 19 (1930); Birmingham University, Church Missionary Society Archive, G3P/1919, 8.

[111] Winifred A Coate, 'The function of secondary schools in Palestine in relation to the growth of the Church', *International Review of Mission*, vol. 25, 1936, especially 186.

Orthodox Church. Reverend Harding, for all his criticisms, held out hopes for it; 'Her light is dim, but it has not gone out, and by the mercy of God it may yet burn with a brighter radiance than ever'.[112]

Conclusion

'Thus my memory leaves her, in the peace of eventide; still the Holy City—the Holy City still.'[113] Years of political turmoil, administrative and political failure, even the deeper sense of the humiliation of the empire as the British left Palestine in 1948, could not destroy this persistent image of the Holy City, as described by District Commissioner Keith-Roach on his departure from Jerusalem. Preconceptions about the land and its people had had a greater influence upon the British in Palestine than, at times, they would have cared to admit. We have seen how the Orthodox Christians were viewed and how this affected British policy and administration, as well the complex role the Church of England and Anglican missionaries played in the imperial enterprise. Even after the end of the Mandate, the Orthodox Christians continued to fascinate Western residents, visitors and missionaries in Palestine, although contact was never again on the same scale as it had been during those years. The departure of the British was soon followed by the flight of Palestinians during the first and subsequent Arab-Israeli wars. Since then, the majority of Palestinian Christians have left the country; their better education and Western contacts have enabled them to emigrate in far larger numbers than their Islamic neighbours.

Inevitably, while answering certain questions regarding the British and the Orthodox in Palestine, this study also opens up a number of new and exciting possibilities for further exploration. The contrast between British attitudes to the Orthodox and to the Muslims has been but briefly touched upon, and would shed further light on the way in which each was perceived and why such perceptions arose. The attitudes of other Western powers to the Orthodox would doubtlessly have similarly illuminating results. In particular, those of American travellers and missionaries could provide interesting insights into the differences in

---

[112] Revd H G Harding, *The Land of Promise*, London, 1919, 62; also Birmingham University, Church Missionary Society Archive, G3pP8-8.

[113] Edward Keith-Roach, *Pasha of Jerusalem: Memoirs of a district commissioner under the British Mandate*, London, 1994, 228.

American and British mentalities regarding religion, and regarding 'the East'. Whilst the overarching questions of the nature of the Mandate and Orientalism will continue to be debated, we have seen here the attraction of the exotic—perhaps to the historian as much as to the subject of the historical study—and the power of religion, its traditions, values and beliefs, as a vital influence upon the decision makers and other players in the great experiment that was the British Mandate in Palestine.

THE ARMENIAN CATHOLIC CHURCH: A MODERN HISTORY UNTIL THE SYNOD OF ROME OF 1928

John Whooley

This paper attempts to relate a complicated history by beginning at what some would hold as the Armenian Catholic Church's real inception, that is to say, in the 18th century, it being understood as one of the consequences of the Latin Catholic Reformation. Paradoxically, for others, the creation of an Armenian Catholic patriarchate at that time was only one significant step in the long though perhaps at times slender association with Catholicism, or at least with that Chalcedonian position that had been officially rejected by the Armenian Apostolic Church. It is this earlier period, prior to the Reformation in Europe, which forms the second part of the paper. A study is then made of the eventual emancipation of the Armenian Catholic community within the Ottoman polity. The dominant figure in the following period was to be Mgr Andon Hassoun whose close allegiance to Rome led to serious internal commotion, indeed, schism, as many saw the papacy's centralising policy of the time as undermining Armenian tradition and expectation. The final period in this study is first given to the somewhat calmer years that followed Hassoun's demise, though once more the community was to suffer schism on the very eve of the Great War. It concludes with the Synod held in Rome in 1928 called to deal as effectively as possible with the dramatic change of circumstances that had resulted from that world conflict.

The origins and development of the Armenian Catholic Church in the Ottoman empire

To attempt to describe the history of the Armenian Catholic Church, the year 1742 may be used as a convenient *point de départ*, though this does not necessarily imply any definitive date for the appearance of Armenian

Catholicism on the stage of ecclesiastical history. It was in that year, on 26 December, that Pope Benedict XIV (1740-1758) placed the pallium on the shoulders of Archbishop Abraham Ardzivian (1679-1749)[1] who, two years before in Aleppo, Syria, had been elected for the second time (the first occasion being in 1721) Catholicos of Sis by a vocal group of Armenians, clerical and lay, a group that had strong Catholic sympathies.[2] These sympathies had been fostered by Latin Catholic missionaries active in a number of areas in the Ottoman empire, and especially so among the Armenian population. The missionaries were able so to work due to the support of ambassadors at the Sublime Porte in Constantinople, representing certain of the Great Powers of Europe, primarily those of France and Austria-Hungary.

As is well known, the Armenians were already Christian, virtually all of whom were members of their own national Church, a body that today is often termed the Armenian Apostolic Church, and, for convenience, we shall largely keep to that title throughout this work, despite a certain anachronism in so doing.[3]

The Church in question had been established by St Gregory the Illuminator in the early 4th century—the seventeen hundredth anniversary of the official conversion of the state of Armenia was widely celebrated in 2001. By tradition, however, it is understood that Christianity was first

---

1 For details of the life of Abraham Ardzivian, cf. Tournebize, 'Abraham (Apraham) II', *Dictionnaire Historique, Géographique et Ecclésiastique*, Paris, Vol. I, 183-186.

2 'Des sympathies individuelles à l'égard de Rome subsistèrent et se renouvelèrent à divers moments chez les Arméniens du Proche-Orient' (Charles de Clercq, *Histoire des Conciles d'après les Documents Originaux*, Tome XI, *Conciles des Orientaux Catholiques*, Letouzey & Ane, Paris, 503). For a disdainful view on this matter: 'The Armenians of the southern provinces of Turkey, whose minds were still impressed with the memory of the Cilician kingdom, were more inclined to lean towards Roman Catholicism. They were even bold enough, with the co-operation of two bishops and a few priests, to establish a Catholic patriarchal see in Cilicia. The first incumbent was the bishop Abraham Ardzivian (1740), who hastened to appear before Pope Benedict XIV in the capacity of supreme Patriarch of the Armenians. The pope, indeed, was aware of the value to be placed on his pretensions, but he did nothing to discourage them; for he saw therein an opportunity of realizing his plans in the East. Accordingly he gave his sanction to the establishment of an Armeno-Catholic patriarchate which was officially subject to the Roman Curia (1742).' Malachia Ormanian *The Church of Armenia: Her History, Doctrine, Rule, Discipline, Liturgy, Literature and Existing Condition* (English translation of *L'Eglise arménienne ...*, Leroux, Paris, 1910), A R Mowbray, London, first English edition 1912, second revised English edition 1955, 68-69. For further information on Ardzivian and his particular circumstances, cf. Le Clercq, *Histoire des Conciles*, Tome XI, 503-504.

3 The term 'Gregorian' is also used, but appears not to be in official favour. It is understood that it was first introduced by the Russian government shortly after the conquest of eastern Armenia in 1828.

introduced into Armenia by the apostles Thaddeus and Bartholomew. Thus any missionary work instigated by other Christian denominations among the Armenians, if it led to an abandonment of what was regarded as a sacred inheritance, an inheritance understood in both spiritual and national terms, and one which so often had involved much suffering for its very maintenance, such work would lead to and did cause serious conflict.[4]

Despite papal support, or possibly because of it, the bold design for the new Catholic leader, Ardzivian, to take up residence in the Ottoman capital was to be thwarted. The seat of the Armenian Apostolic patriarch, whose power was no mean matter in the body politic of the empire, was there located, and would not brook the activity of a rival Armenian hierarch and, moreover, one in union with Rome. Besides, this new hierarch, who was now termed by the Holy See 'Patriarch of the Armenian Catholics and Catholicos of Cilicia', had absolutely no legal standing in the eyes of the Sublime Porte.[5] The latter, in the probably correct belief that further disruption in the Armenian community of the capital would ensue—and there had already been much conflict over the question of conversions to the Catholic Church—made it be known that disembarkation would be unwelcome. Neither was he welcome in Aleppo itself, where once again the Apostolic party was dominant and where already a recently-elected patriarch was installed and naturally hostile to a romanophile claimant.[6] Fortunately for the new Catholic patriarch, Maronite help enabled him to find refuge in the Holy Saviour monastery at Kreym in the Lebanon. It was, however, to be at Bzommar in the same region that his successors, from 1750 until 1867, were to make their home and where, over the years, a new ecclesiastical complex was to be created. Since 1928, this has once again been the seat of the Armenian Catholic patriarchs, the current patriarch being Nerses Peter XIX Tarmouni, the name 'Peter' (or 'Bedros')

---

4 Though many would hold that Ardzivian was the first of a new line of patriarchs, others may see the matter differently: Mesrob Terzian in *Le Patriarcat de Cilicie et les Arméniens Catholiques (1740-1812)*, La Photo-Presse, Beyrouth, 1955, speaks of 'restauration' (p. v) or 'reconstitution' (p. vi) rather than of the patriarchate as being 'new'.

5 '... they have a great horror for those amongst them that change to the Roman religion.' Lady Mary Wortley Montagu, *Embassy to Constantinople*, Christopher Pick (ed.), London, Melbourne, Auckland, Johannesburg, 1988, 194. 'This circumstance was owing to the unhappy (Stephanus's) being turned papist, and wishing him (Emin) to be in the same way of thinking; but could by no means prevail on him to become a turn-coat like himself.' Joseph Emin, *Life and Adventures of Joseph Emin, an Armenian 1726-1809*, Baptist Mission Press, Calcutta, 1918, 32.

6 The Catholicoses of Sis, due to local circumstances, often had their residence at Aleppo.

being always included in the title of the holders of the See, as a sign of their union with Rome. He was elected in 1999, succeeding Peter XVIII Kasparian who had resigned in that year.[7]

We may ask ourselves, at this juncture, as to wherein lay the power of the Armenian Apostolic patriarchate that it was able to contribute to the distancing of the Armenian Catholic hierarch from that place where the latter's flock was most populous, that is to say, in Constantinople itself. Naturally, the basis of such power had been laid down by the Ottoman state itself, with what is known as the *millet* system, the form of which the Ottoman dynasty had adopted and adapted from previous Muslim imperial administrations.[8] This was the simple device of equating a particular religion with a particular 'nation' (in Turkish *millet*).

There were, however, clusters within these *millets*: those Christians who supported Chalcedonian Christology, for example, were placed under the jurisdiction of the Ecumenical Patriarchate, already long established in the capital; while all those who adhered to the non-Chalcedonian Christological position were placed under the Armenian patriarchate, itself created, it is usually understood, in 1461 by Mehmet II, the conqueror of Constantinople. Thus within the Turkish orbit, all Coptic and Syrian Orthodox, though keeping their own religious heads, as well as all Armenians, technically, came within the jurisdiction of the Armenian patriarchate.[9] These jurisdictions had grown as the Ottoman empire had expanded.[10]

---

[7] The immediate successors of Patriarch Ardzivian Bedros I prior to the transfer of the See to Constantinople: Hagop Bedros II (1750-1753); Michael Bedros III (1754-1780); Basil II Bedros IV (1780-1787); Krikor XI Bedros V (1788-1812); Krikor XII Bedros VI (1812-1841); Hagop V Holas Ankuratsi Bedros VII (1841-1843); Krikor XIV Astvadzatourian Bedros VIII (1844-1865). The reason for double titles is not necessarily clarified by examining the patriarchal lists of either Etchmiadzin or of Sis. Nor is it clarified by Tournebize who gives the above details (*DHGE*, 338-339). The system seems to have been discontinued with Hassoun and his successors. Undoubtedly, it would have been a cause of irritation to the Apostolic Church. Tcholakian makes no mention of these double titles. There are slight date differences in his list (*L'Église Arménienne Catholique en Turquie*, Ohan Matbaacılık Ltd, Istanbul, 1998, 17.)

[8] Umayyads of Damascus, 'Abbasids of Baghdad, Mamluks of Cairo.

[9] According to Artinian, the Chaldeans also found themselves so placed, as did Ethiopian and Georgian subjects. It is not clear why the last named were not within the jurisdiction of the Greek patriarch. cf. Vartin Artinian *The Armenian Constitutional System in the Ottoman Empire, 1839-1863: A Study of its Historical Development*, Istanbul, 1988, 11. There was also a 'millet' for the Jewish community, the Grand Rabbi acting as 'milletbaği', or 'ethnarch'.

[10] 'By the end of the first quarter of the 19th century the Armenian patriarch exercised jurisdiction over fifty dioceses throughout the Ottoman empire which were governed through the agency of subordinate ecclesiastics'. *Ibid.*, 17.

As regards the Armenians, this growth was to be of such an extent that the traditional status of Etchmiadzin, the generally acknowledged spiritual and ecclesiastically authoritative centre for most Armenians, came to be somewhat overshadowed by the musculature of the Constantinopolitan patriarchate. It should be understood, however, that the relocation of this spiritual centre from Cilicia to Etchmiadzin occurred only in 1441, after an absence of some 500 years, and even then not with general accord, as the survival of the Catholicosate of Cilicia attests, both in its Apostolic manifestation and, dare it be said, much later, as we have seen, in its Catholic manifestation.[11]

The patriarchs of Constantinople, both Greek and Armenian, were directly responsible to the Sublime Porte for the behaviour of these many Christians throughout the empire and, having the rank of Pasha, could have easy recourse to the secular arm of the state to deal with any problematic individuals or groups. And certainly such recourse was often to be made by the Armenian ecclesiastical authorities, particularly during the eighteenth and early 19th centuries when a number of Armenians changed their spiritual allegiance to that of Rome. We may note here that it was not till the latter century that Protestant missionaries arrived in the empire, where they, too, gained converts among the Armenians, causing some further disruption in the *millet*, though for a much briefer

[11] It is generally accepted that the Catholicate now established at Etchmiadzin has moved ten times since the 4th century. According to Hratch Tchilingirian 'The Catholicos and the Hierarchical Sees of the Armenian Church' in Anthony O'Mahony (ed.), *Eastern Christianity: Studies in Modern History, Religion and Politics*, Melisende, London, 2004, 40. n. 4., the moves were as follows: from Etchmiadzin to Dvin (484-931); to Aghtamar (931-944); to Arghina (944-992); to Ani (992-1065); to Dzamendav (1066-1072); to Shughri-Karmirvank (1105-1116); to Dzovk (1116); Hromkla (1147-1292); to Sis (1293-1441); and finally back to Etchmiadzin (1441-present): n.b. the years 1072-1105 are not dealt with. There are variations in other lists: Cf. Terzian, *Le Patriarcat de Cilicie* [8.]. As regards the Catholicos of Sis, '(he) still governs a small branch of the Armenian Church, in full communion with the rest, according to a treaty of peace and amity signed by the incumbents of the two sees A.D. 1651.' (Smith and Dwight, *Missionary Researches in Armenia. Including a Journey through Asia Minor and into Georgia and Persia*, George Wightman, London, 1834, 40.) However, Tekeyan, in challenging the claim of the Catholicos of Etchmiadzin to be the legitimate successor to St Gregory, states that even the Apostolic encumbents of Sis still do not accept that claim, '... jusqu'à ces derniers temps encore, anathématisaient le Catholicos d'Etchmiadzin, à chaque nouvelle election.' (*Le Patriarcat Arménien Catholique de Cilicie*, 63.) Such matters may have been influenced by the fact of Soviet domination of Armenia at that time.

period. Any official steps taken by the patriarchate against their proselytism became illegal by 1850.[12]

Though there was this adoption of Catholicism, overtly or covertly, those who took such a step were, by law, still subject to the Armenian Apostolic Church and her administration. Thus they could be refused, for example, the rites of baptism, marriage or burial, as well as travel or other mundane but necessary documents. This could cause serious hardship for the social life of individuals and entire families.[13] In addition, certain *firmans* were issued from time to time forbidding conversions from one *millet* to another, so as to maintain strict order among Ottoman subjects.[14] Conversion to Islam was, however, continually encouraged.

Terzian states that throughout the Ottoman empire during the 17th century there was barely any distinction between those Armenians who were inclined to Catholicism and those who were not. They frequented the same churches and depended on the same hierarchs '...qui parfois étaient unis au Saint-Siège.'[15] There was as yet no great matter for any partizanship. Clement Galanus, the Italian Theatine missionary who

---

[12] For a history of the development of Protestantism among the Armenians of the Ottoman empire, cf. Leon Arpee, *A History of Armenian Christianity from the Beginning to Our Own Time*, New York, The Armenian Mission Society of America Inc., 1946; in addition, Arpee, *The Armenian Awakening. A History of the Armenian Church, 1820-1860*, University of Chicago Press, Chicago, and Fisher Unwin, London, 1909.

[13] 'Their numbers at the capital and in other places were considerable; they were, as a body, more intelligent than their countrymen; among them were men to whom uncommon wealth and official station gave great influence; and European sympathy was altogether on their side. Still they were everywhere obliged to rank as a part of the flock of the patriarch. They could have no churches of their own; their priests could not wear the clerical garb nor be known as such, except under the shadow of European influence; and at baptisms, marriages, and burials, they were obliged to call upon the Armenian clergy, and pay them the accustomed fees. Such, very nearly, was their situation even at Angora, where they amounted to many thousands while the Armenians were only a few hundred.' (Eli Smith and H G O Dwight, *Missionary Researches in Armenia*, 60-61).

[14] One such *firman* was issued by Ahmed III (Sultan 1703-1730) in 1722, which applied itself particularly to those who wished to convert to the Catholic Church. Just over a century later, we may note: 'More than five years after the official recognition of the Armenian Catholics in Ottoman Turkey as an additional millet, hostility between the two communities was not over. According to an imperial rescript dated 27 July/24 August 1835 and which I came across in the state archives, Armenians were prohibited from converting to Catholicism, and Catholics from joining the Armenian Church as of the aforementioned date, in order to bring an end to the conflict between the Armenians and Catholics in Istanbul. At subsequent dates similar legal measures were taken by the Ottoman government on many subsequent occasions as testified by documentary evidence.' Pars Tuğlacı, *Istanbul Ermeni Kiliseleri,* 287. Tuğlacı gives the reference for the document of 1835, but not for the others.

[15] *Le Patriarcat de Cilicie*, 17.

had had substantial experience of the Armenians in Georgia and who had published a grammar and logic of the language in Constantinople, where he had opened a college, described the position of the Armenian Church as being 'neither Catholic nor schismatic.'[16]

A number of the patriarchs were certainly more than sympathetic to Rome, including Khatchadour I (1642-1643) who was much influenced by Galanus. On this patriarch's deposition, however, the Theatine's attempts to promote another Catholic sympathiser to the See, aroused the fury of the successful candidate, Tavit I. In consequence, Galanus and a number of his followers were forced to flee the empire in 1645.[17]

This incident could perhaps be seen as the first open breach between the two tendencies, though it was not till towards the end of the century that that breach reached serious proportions. It could be argued that contemporary developments in the Armenian community in Poland, most especially at Lviv where Catholic influence, begun by Galanus, had become paramount and had led to 'defections' to Rome, including that of Archbishop Torosowicz, must have alerted the suspicions of concerned Apostolic prelates elsewhere. Likewise, Armenians in Transylvania, through the efforts of the missionary, Oxynde Vrzarian, were brought into union with Rome between 1684 and 1690.[18] Latin missionary activities in Isfahan and Baghdad were also claiming success among a number of Armenians. A Latin bishopric was established in the former city in 1632, a city that had very particular significance for Armenians, as the Armenian presence there was the result of the ruthless but successful policy of Shah Abbas at the beginning of the century.[19]

---

[16] Galanus, *Conciliationis Ecclesiae Armenae cum Romana*, Rome, 1650, II, t. l., 57-58: 'Elle n'est pas toute catholique, elle n'est pas toute orthodoxe; mais c'est une Église mélangée des deux. Ce qui vient à dire: une Église dans laquelle s'affrontent deux conceptions et deux convictions ecclésiologiques chacune d'elles ayant ses adhérents'. (cf. Tcholakian, *L'Église Arménienne*, 7).

[17] On his arrival in Rome, Galanus was given charge of the Armenians at the Urbanum. Later (1663), he and Louis Pidou were sent to the Armenian community in Lviv (Leopolis) where they opened a college. Thus began the process of the reunion of a portion of that community with the Holy See (Cf. 'Galano, Clemente', *New Catholic Encyclopedia*, Vol. 6, 242).

[18] *Le Patriarcat de Cilicie*: *anent* Poland, 35-36; *anent* Transylvania, 37-38.

[19] For a description of Latin missionary activity among the Armenians in Persia at this time, especially by the Capuchins, whose great mentor was the 'Éminence grise', Fr. Joseph du Tremblay, councillor to Richelieu, see Francis Richard, 'Missionnaires françaises en Arménie au XVIIe siècle', *Arménie entre Orient et Occident*, 196-202. Also Vazken Ghougassian, *The Emergence of the Armenian Diocese of New Julfa in the Seventeenth Century*, Scholars Press, Atlanta, Georgia, 1998, Ch. 7: The Opposition of the Diocese of New Julfa to Catholic Missionary Expansion, 125-156.

In the meantime, two movements that were solely Armenian in origin had developed. These were inspired by a resolve to revive Armenian monasticism along the lines of Latin religious Orders. Such an ambition had become manifest at an earlier period with the 'Unitors' and the Friars of Saint Bartholomew, whose histories we will be outlining in the second part of this paper. This new inspiration, however, specified that all the monks had to be Armenian. Though this too had been a specification of the 'Unitors', the preponderant influence of the Latin Dominicans could not in the long run but affect the ethos of that Order. Despite some of the negative consequences of these earlier experiences, a western monastic structure was still thought to be more efficient and more likely to succeed than the traditional Armenian mode, especially considering the dangers that Armenian culture in general was facing, often due to disastrous political circumstances. It was not simply a question of spiritual growth and influence, but also of cultural salvation and dissemination.

This last matter was of particular concern for Mkhitar Sebastatsi (1676-1749) who had been much influenced by Khatchatour Arakelian, another distinguished but discerning convert to Rome. Mkhitar was to found his religious community in Constantinople in 1701, he and his followers calling themselves the '*Adoptive Sons of the Blessed Virgin Mary and the Teachers of Penitence*'. Due to opposition from the Apostolic Church and the continual dangers of state interference, they left shortly thereafter for Modon in the Morea, establishing a monastery there in 1703. However, the Venetians lost the region to the Turks in 1715, forcing the monks to take refuge in Venice itself. Two years later, the Order finally settled on the island of San Lazzaro in the Venetian lagoon, where they are still to be found today. Another branch was eventually to settle in Vienna. The contributions made by these two centres of the Mekhitarists, as they came to be called, and their role in helping to salvage so much of their national culture, especially in historical and linguistic works, is generally appreciated by all their fellow Armenians, no matter their religious affiliation.[20]

[20] Ormanian on the Mekhitarists: 'Mkhitar had to yield to the demands of the Roman Curia in order to be able to devote himself without restraint to his work of intellectual culture; he wisely abstained from being a party to the work of proselytism. Such a line of conduct, which was in keeping with national interests, had become traditional among his congregation during the course of the eighteenth century; but later other opinions took root in their midst. Nevertheless, it is a grateful task to pay homage to the Mkhitarists of Venice and Vienna for the great services they have rendered to the nation by enriching so profusely the Armenian language and literature.' Malachia Ormanian *The Church of Armenia*, 68; these 'other opinions'

The second Order to be recognised by Rome was that of the Antonians, founded it is believed by the four Mouradian brothers, at approximately the same time as the Mekhitarists, though others believe that Ardzivian was more directly responsible for its foundation. The brothers had established themselves at the monastery of the Holy Saviour, Lebanon, mentioned previously, and to which they had fled from the intercommunal conflicts in Aleppo. Though by no means as prestigious as the Mekhitarists, the Order's missionary work in the Ottoman empire was nevertheless not inconsiderable.[21]

However, the Antonians were to be decimated in the 1870s, when disputes concerning the attitudes and proceedings both of Rome and the then Armenian Catholic patriarch, Andon Hassoun, became critical.[22] The most famous casualty of these conflicts was the gifted Malachia Ormanian,[23]

---

seem to have been more associated with Vienna than Venice. From other evidence, it would appear that Mkhitar handled the Curia with patience and intelligence, eventually achieving exactly what he had aimed to do. Cf. M Nurikhan (tr. John McQuillan), *The Life and Times of the Servant of God Abbot Mekhitar: Founder of the Mekhitarist Fathers*, Venice, Mekhitarist Press, 1915. Among many unhesitatingly positive appraisals of the Mekhitarists may be found that of H Pasdermadjian, *Histoire de l'Arménie: Depuis les Origines jusqu'au Traité de Lausanne*, Librairie Orientale H Samuelian, Paris, 1971, 265-268.

21 Date of founding: 1705. 'An attempt to join their group to the Mechitarists of Venice failed, and the congregation adopted (1752) the Rule of St Anthony after the manner of the Maronite Antonines. Clement XIII approved the Constitutions in 1761. The monks never exceeded 60 and their number declined after they went into schism during the politico-religious troubles (1869-1880) under the rule of the Armenian patriarch and Cardinal Anthony Hassoun (1809-84). The former library of these Antonines is conserved in the Armenian Institute at Bzommar.' 'Armenian Antonines', El-Hayek, *New Catholic Encyclopedia*, Vol. I, 646.

22 These disputes largely concerned themselves with the vexed question of the safeguarding of Armenian traditions as opposed to changes wished for by the more centralised papal authority at Rome. Tournebize is quite clear that it was with the election of Placid Kasanjian as their Abbot General in 1864 that matters deteriorated. This was to be '... le prélude des plus regretables déviations au point de vue religieux, tant de la part du supérieur que d'une grande partie de la congrégation.' ('Antonins Arméniens', *DHGE*, 868). Cf. in general 867-870. Also, Gregorio Petrowicz: 'Origine dei Monaci Antoniani Armeni', *Bazmavep*, Vol. CXLIII, No. 1-2, 1985, 143-148.

23 'As to Ormanian himself, you know that he was a convert from Roman Catholicism. He was a very ambitious man. He admits this quite openly in his autobiography. He wanted to be (and in fact he became) a patriarch and then a catholicos. Any criticism of any prevailing custom on his part would make him suspect in the eyes of the people of Constantinople as a "romanizer" (there was a strong feeling against the Roman Catholics then) and this would frustrate his projects. Indeed, in spite of his extreme caution and loudly proclaimed protestations of faithfulness to the Armenian Church he was still called "cut- tail", in order to throw doubt on the sincerity of his conversion.' Roberta Ervine (ed. and tr.), *The Unpublished Writings of Tiran Nersoyan, I: Early Correspondence (1924-1944)*, St Nerses Armenian Seminary, New Rochelle, New York, 2002, 43-44. We note that 'cut-tail' was a derogatory term given to all those who had joined the Roman fold, but who still insisted on keeping the Armenian rite.

who, along with others, transferred his allegiance from the Catholic fold to that of the Apostolic. Eventually, he himself even became the Apostolic Patriarch of Constantinople (1896-1908) and was to prove a severe critic of Rome.[24]

The arrival of Archbishop Ardzivian had been welcomed by the Mouradian brothers who, as we have seen, had already established themselves at Kreim. However, it appears that the ultimate aims of the Antonians (or perhaps 'proto-Antonians') were somewhat different from those of the Archbishop. [25] Hence, eventually, the Order of the Armenian Antonian Monks and what was to become the Congregation of Patriarchal Clergy of Bzommar, the former consisting of clergy who wished to be more independent of patriarchal control, became quite distinct. The transfer of the Antonian novitiate to Rome in 1761 would have contributed to the demarcation. Eventually, partly in response to this setback, Krikor XI Bedros V (1788-1812) established a seminary at Bzommar, but only in 1810. The position of his successor, Krikor XII Bedros VI (1812-1840), was strengthened numerically when a number of priests arrived, refugees from the persecution of 1828.

According to Tournebize, it was Patriarch Krikor XIV Bedros VIII (1844-1865) who established this congregation of missionaries at Bzommar. These men were 'soon exercising a fruitful apostolate, particularly in Cilicia where the American Protestants were extremely active.'[26] Hence there appears to be a considerable time lapse between these two temporal points. This could be explained by considering that Bedros VIII believed that those priests trained at or attached to Bzommar

---

[24] Interestingly, Ormanian barely mentions the Antonians to which he himself had belonged. It is to Abraham Attar that he gives the credit for their foundation. *The Armenian Church,* 68.

[25] '... autres étaient les intérêts de l'Ordre, autres les besoins apostoliques de l'évêque, qui restait évêque des Arméniens catholiques d'Alep, et tendait vers un titre plus étendu: celui de catholicos-patriarche pour ceux-ci; ce qui eut lieu canoniquement, lorsque son élection comme tel, opérée à Alep, fut approuvée par le pape Benoit XIV... Dès lors la scission en deux instituts devenait une nécessité.' Mécérian, 323.

[26] '... qui exercèrent bientôt un fructueux apostolat, particulièrement en Cilicie, où les protestants américains se montraient fort actifs.' (*DHGE*, 339.). Their activity largely remained within the jurisdictional boundaries of the patriarchate at that time: Cilicia, Syria, Mesopotamia and Egypt. After the two jurisdictions of Bzommar and Constantinople were united shortly after the death of Bedros VIII, their field of activity was widened. At the time of his death, there were ten dioceses attached to Bzommar: Egypt, Aleppo, Mardin, Amid (Tigranakirt-Diyarbakir), Sivas, Tokat, Malatia (Melitene), Marash, Adana, and Caeserea *(Ibid.)*.

should be given a more formal recognition and perhaps thus afford him greater control.[27]

A number of the converts won by the Latin missionaries belonged to what is known from the second half of the 18th century, as the Amira class, the highest stratum of Armenian society.[28] Some of these were bankers *(sarrafs)*, whilst others held positions of substance within the administration of the empire and have been described as 'salaried' amiras.[29] Because of their wealth and influence, such persons were a sore loss to the Apostolic Church, both financially and psychologically. The taunt made by some Apostolic hierarchs and others against what they regarded as 'renegades' who had betrayed both their faith and their very identity as Armenians—strongly denied by those so accused—was that they had in effect become 'franks': 'foreigners' in the Turkish understanding of that word.

Such a taunt against these converts could lead to serious consequences, as their loyalty to the Ottoman state could be, and was indeed in a number of instances, put in question, arousing Ottoman wrath: fines, confiscation of property, condemnation to the galleys, or even death. The martyrdom of the married priest Der Komitas Keumurgian in 1707 is a particularly painful reminder of these inter-communal disputes and violence.[30]

Another significant case concerned the distinguished Duzian family, responsible for the Ottoman mint. Not only were severe fines, confiscation and exile inflicted, but some members of the family were summarily and publicly executed in 1819, the whole affair originally instigated by the Grand Vezir, Halet Effendi, who was in debt to the family. The last great persecution of Armenian Catholics under similar circumstances took place a decade later under the shadow of the Russian threat to the empire as well as the humiliation suffered by Turkey with the loss of Greece. These circumstances were to lead, as we shall see, to an unexpected consequence for the beleaguered community. It has to be

---

27 The Order is still active; its clergy are meant to be at the disposal of the patriarch who sends them wherever he thinks fit. Today they are to be found quite far-flung, for example in parishes in Russia, California and Argentina.

28 During the previous 200 years this social group had been known as 'Hocas' or 'Celebis'.

29 For a detailed description of the social position and influence of the Amiras, cf. Artinian, *The Armenian Constitutional System*, 19-24.

30 He was to be beatified by Pope Pius XI in 1929.

borne in mind, however, that Apostolic fury was sometimes in reaction to insults delivered by 'fanatical and indiscrete Catholics'.[31]

Early relations between Armenia and the Catholic Church

It need hardly be said that the Armenian Church had been in contact with the Church of Rome long before the problems and disturbances that have just been touched upon. Indeed, according to some accounts, St Gregory himself, having accomplished so much in Armenia, travelled to Rome to embrace and confer with Pope St Sylvester (pope 314-335). That such a meeting took place, however, is regarded today, by most Apostolic and many Catholic commentators, as apocryphal.[32] Both sides, it may readily be understood, had much to gain or lose from its veracity or otherwise.[33]

It should be borne in mind that at the Council of Dvin (506-507) the Armenian Church had condemned the decrees of the Council of Chalcedon, held a half-century before in 451, while a second Council of Dvin in 551 had formally rejected the decrees, thereby creating a definite

---

[31] Terzian, *Le Patriarcat,* 19. To these may be added, among other matters, the activities of the French ambassador Charles de Feriol who was involved in the infamous kidnapping of the Apostolic patriarch, Avediq, an opponent of the Catholic movement. Avediq was to spend the rest of his life in France. Cf. Frazee, 'The Formation of the Armenian Catholic Community in the Ottoman Empire', *Eastern Churches Review,* VII, 2, 1975, 149-163.

[32] 'There was a later legend based on a pseudographic document of the 13th century that Gregory the Illuminator had met with Pope Sylvester. Despite the use of this story by Armenians and the papacy as late as the twentieth century, the account must be rejected as spurious.' Charles A Frazee, 'The Christian Church in Cilician Armenia: Its Relations with Rome and Constantinople to 1198', *Church History,* vol. 45, 1976, 166-184, cf. 169, n. 11. Pius IX refers categorically to the matter in his encyclical, *Quartus supra,* 29, (6 January 1873): 'the Enlightener ... received his power from the Apostolic See. He came to the See in person, undeterred by the length and great hardship of the journey.'

[33] As mentioned earlier, Saints Thaddeus and Bartholomew were, by tradition, the first to introduce Christianity into Armenia. A number of names are associated with that faith during the period that intervened between the apostles' arrival and martyrdom and the creation of the National Church by St Gregory the Illuminator with the support of King Trdat III, whom he had converted. Some of these are given by Ormanian in Appendix I of *The Church of Armenia,* 195. Cf. also Tournebize: 'Cependant l'évangélisation des provinces soit occidentales, soit méridionales de la Grande Arménie avant le IIIe siècle, n'est pas invraisemblable' (*DHGE.,* 294). Cf. also H F B Lynch's general comments in *Armenia, Travels and Studies* 2 vols., Khayats Oriental Reprints, New York, 1990 (first published London and New York, Longmans, Green and Co, 1901; reprinted Khayats, 1965), cf. Vol. I, 279-281.

schism.[34] This decision was to prove a watershed in it relations with the great Churches that lay to the west of the Armenian heartlands, those of Constantinople and Rome which themselves were to remain in union with one another for a further half a thousand years.

It should also be recollected, however, that the Armenian Kingdom had been divided by treaty not long before Chalcedon, that is to say divided between the imperial powers of Rome and Persia in 387 AD. This meant that numbers of Armenians now found themselves under the jurisdiction of the Bishop of Constantinople, whose pre-eminence, after that of Rome, had been recognized shortly beforehand at the First Council of Constantinople of 381.[35] It is probable that the Armenian bishops in Byzantine Armenia had been able to be present at Chalcedon. It is not unlikely that they and their flocks had accepted its decrees, one of which had conferred patriarchal powers on the Bishop of 'New Rome'. The bishops of Persian Armenia, the much larger portion of the division,

---

[34] There appears to be some confusion among a number of authors as to when and where the decrees of Chalcedon were actually condemned: Tournebize gives the date of the Second Council of Dvin as 554 (*DHGE*, 303), whilst Rondot speaks of the Armenian 'secession' as being already confirmed in 491 by the Synod of Vagharchapat (Pierre Rondot *Les Chrétiens d'Orient* Paris, J Peyronnet, 1955, 174.). On the other hand, Tiran Nersoyan appears to place the matter one half century later than Tournebize: 'During the first decade of the seventh century ... a powerful Armenian prince by the name of Sembat Bagratuni, who had a very high and privileged position in the Persian court, was instrumental in compelling the bishops of the Church to denounce the Council of Chalcedon for the first time in a Synod, after having his candidate elected to the throne of the Catholicate in April, 607 AD.' Nersoyan, 'Laity in the Administration of the Armenian Church', in Nerses Vrej Nersessian (ed.), *Armenian Church Historical Studies: Matters of Doctrine and Administration,* St Vartan Press, New York, 1996, 102.

[35] 'Convinced Chalcedonian Armenians (of whom there were many in the western provinces of historical Armenia) had been advocating the same for centuries.' Aristeides Papadakis, in collaboration with John Meyendorff, *The Christian East and the Rise of the Papacy: the Church 1071-1453 A.D.*, St Vladimir's Press, Crestwood, New York, 1994, 116. This is à propos the Byzantine-Armenian unity talks held in the twelfth century. Cf. V A Arutjunova-Fidanjian: 'The Ethno-Confessional Self-Awareness of Armenian Chalcedonians', *Revue des Études Arméniennes*, Tome XXI, 1988-1989. Simeon Vailhe: 'Si je me suis étendu quelque peu sur ces réorganisations administratives, qui paraissent au premier abord d'ordre purement politique, c'est parce qu'elles éclairent du même coup l'histoire religieuse de l'*Armenia minor.* Romaines ou Byzantines, les deux provinces d'*Armenia prima* et d'*Armenia secunda* reconnaissent la juridiction du métropolitain de Césarée ou celle du patriarche de Constantinople; les fidèles des divers évêchés de ces provinces, hellénisés pour la plupart, ne peuvent aucunement être rangés parmi les tenants de l'Église arménienne proprement dite. Il importe donc de distinguer avec soin—et dès le début—ces deux contrées, pour ne pas attribuer à l'Arménie autonome ou Grande-Arménie les faits religieux qui appartiennent à l'Arménie romaine.' *Formation de l'Église Arménienne:* 1—Les Origines de l'Arménie et l'Introduction du Christianisme, *Échos d'Orient,* Tome XVI, 1913, 119.

were, on the contrary, prevented from attending due to severe political and religious pressure from their Zoroastrian rulers.[36] Cowe states, however, that Armenian bishops from the Roman portion were indeed present and that their names are recorded. The bishops in Persian Armenia could not even have been invited, as they were beyond the bounds of the empire.[37]

> '... as animosity between the Greeks and Armenians increased in the following centuries, so did the determination of the national church to hold firm to Cyril of Alexandria's phrase at Ephesus, 'Jesus Christ is the one nature incarnate of the Word of God'. In the opinion of the imperial church, the Armenian position was considered Monophysite, while the Armenians argued that the Greeks and Latins were Nestorians.' (Charles Frazee, 'The Christian Church ...' p. 166.)

The probability that there had been an Armenian presence at Chalcedon is of some significance. An argument often stressed by the Armenian Catholic Church is that there has always been, among the Armenians, a strand of Chalcedonianism and that they themselves are the inheritors of that particular strand.[38] Even though there had been a breach over the Fourth Ecumenical Council, '... adherents of Chalcedon remained numerous, especially in the western provinces of Armenia, as evidenced by the pro-Chalcedonian *Narratio de Rebus Armeniae* (8th c.)...western Armenian bishops disregarded (the Catholicoses') injunctions and continued to attend Byzantine Church councils.'[39]

---

[36] '... it is likely that Armenian opposition to Chalcedon arose not so much from doctrinal dissent from a council where they had not been present as from hostility towards the subordination of Armenia to the ecclesiastical jurisdiction of Constantinople.' J M Hussey, *The Orthodox Church in the Byzantine Empire*, Clarendon Press, Oxford, 1986, 15.

[37] Cowe's information was given verbally at UCLA (2003). He is Narekatsi Professor of Armenian Studies.

[38] It may be mentioned here that more than grave doubt has long been cast upon the so-called 'monophysitism' of the Oriental Churches in general, a doctrine the implications of which they resolutely deny. '... in 725/6 the Council of Mantzikert proclaimed the union of the Armenian and Syrian churches, while maintaining their rejection of extreme Monophysitism.' 'Armenian Church' in *The Oxford Dictionary of Byzantium* 3 vols, Oxford University Press, New York and Oxford, 1991, 179.

[39] *The Oxford Dictionary of Byzantium*, 179. The article continues, 'After the new partition of Armenia in 591, the Emperor Maurice even succeeded in installing a rival *katholicos* at Awan near Erevan, thus creating a schism that lasted some twenty years.' Later, '... the Council of Ani in 969 again condemned Chalcedonianism and its adherents in Armenia.' For some insight into the confusion and conflict between these two opposing positions, confer Peter Cowe 'An Armenian Job Fragment from Sinai and its Implications' in *Oriens Christianus*, Band 76, 1992, 123-157.

Hence, it has been further argued, the Armenian Catholic Church, though understood to have been, in a sense, formally established, or re-established, in 1742, it cannot rightfully be considered a so-called 'uniate' Church, and not simply because of either the phenomenological or the derogatory implications of that term. If a 'uniate' Church is taken to be, by one simple definition at any rate, where a minority, coming from a 'mother-church', 'unites' or 'reunites' itself with the See of Peter, then such a definition cannot strictly be applicable to those Armenian Chalcedonian communities that are understood to have survived one way or the other in various places through the centuries. On the contrary, the Armenian Catholic Church understands itself as part and inheritor of that tradition which has never considered itself, dare it be said, 'outside' the Church Universal—in the Church of Rome's sense of that term, or, indeed, the Byzantine/Greek sense of that term.

However, most adherents of the Armenian Catholic Church recognize that the Armenian nation's isolation, surrounded and almost submerged as it was by an Islamic sea,[40] wherein the people struggled just to survive as a Christian entity, led to a strong identification of that nation with the Armenian Apostolic Church to which the vast majority of Armenians had always adhered and still do.[41]

Leaving aside the question of Armenian Chalcedonianism, important though it be, it may safely be said that, apart from individual pilgrims to the tombs of Peter and Paul in Rome,[42] and some evidence that a number of monks and bishops travelled elsewhere in the West, for example, as far as Ireland and Iceland,[43] it was only in the medieval period, and thus

---

[40] For a swift overview of this matter of near submersion, cf. Edmond Schütz 'Armenia: A Christian Enclave in the Islamic Near East in the Middle Ages' in M Gervers and Ramzi Jibran Bikhazi, *Conversion and Continuity: Indigenous Christian Communities in Islamic Lands: Eighth to Eighteenth Centuries*, Pontifical Institute of Medieval Studies, Toronto, 1990.

[41] '... l'Arménie doit à son Église les fondements de sa culture et la préservation de sa langue et, pour une large part, la conservation du sens national au milieu d'immenses épreuves.' (Rondot, *Les Chrétiens d'Orient*, 51).

[42] '... monks sometimes settled there as part of the general emigration of Christian Orientals to the West after the Islamic conquest ...' Frazee, 'The Christian Church', 169.

[43] Cf. Gerard Dédéyan, 'Les Arméniens en Occident fin Xe-au début XIe siècle', *Orient et Occident au Xe siècle*, Dijon-Paris, 1980. A relevant section of this may be found in the Bulletin de l'Éparchie des Arméniens Catholiques de France: *L'Église Arménienne*, Série Nouvelle No. 6, 2ème Trimestre, 1992. 'Gregoire de Tours nous apprend qu'en 591, l'évêque Simon, victime des guerres perso-arméniennes, était venu se réfugier dans son diocèse. Au VIIe siècle, des religieux arméniens vont en Irlande, où les barbares n'ont pas réussi à entamer la culture romaine, et fondent l'important monastère de Cell Achid (note 5). Au debut du VIIIe siècle,

after the 'formal' division of the Roman and Byzantine ecclesiastical worlds, that opportunity arose for a more active communication to be established between the Church of Rome as such and the Armenian Church, and with possible Catholic sympathisers within her ranks.[44]

Of no small interest, in this context, was the spread throughout Europe of the cult of Saint Blaise, an Armenian Bishop of Sebaste, possible evidence of a sympathy that might have become general in western circles of the time to the Armenian situation and predicament.[45] It is not clear, however, whether the majority of Armenians had themselves such a fervent devotion to him. European sympathy may also be found in the literary works of the period.[46]

As forces from Europe moved in the late 11th century to rescue the Holy Places from the 'infidel'—spurred on no doubt by simply more than anger at the destruction of the tomb of Christ in 1009 by the probably unbalanced Caliph Hakim—and then to organise of necessity various political structures 'outremer' to maintain their initial success in that intention, they seem to have found a Christian people in the region more willing to aid them than the Greeks. The latter had been cause of much aggravation to the Armenians: '... relations between the separated eastern Churches and the Franks contrasted favourably with the injudicious and intolerant treatment which the former had often received from the Orthodox Church.'[47]

Léon l'Isaurien, le premier empereur iconoclaste, envoie le supérieur du couvent arménien de Tathev chercher des livres de controverse à Rome (note 6),' 11 of the said Bulletin. (Note 5: Françoise Henry, *La sculpture irlandaise*, Paris, 1933, 133.) (Note 6: Stéphanos Orbélian, *Histoire de la Siounie* édition Chahnazarian, 2 vols, Paris, 1859, t. I, 179-180.)

[44] '... there is not a single document extant to show that there was ever any official correspondence between the two churches during the first Christian millenium *(sic)*'. Frazee, 'The Christian Church', 169.

[45] St Blaise (Vlas) of Sebaste (Sivas, in modern Turkey) was martyred early in the 4th century, during the persecution of the Emperor Licinius. His cult had begun to spread in Europe as early as the 8th century and received much impetus as a result of the Crusades; he was to be canonised during the First Council of Lyons (1245). Clearly, and perhaps significantly, he predates the Chalcedonian controversy. He is one of the fourteen Auxiliary Saints, his feast being celebrated in the Western Church on 3 February. Cf. Armand Tchouhadjian, *Saint Blaise Éveque de Sebaste. Un Saint d'Arménie en Occident*, Dupli-Print, Paris, 2000.

[46] Cf. Kohar Karagozian, 'Arménie et Arméniens dans la littérature médiévale française', *Arménie entre Orient et Occident*, 78-81.

[47] J M Hussey, *The Orthodox Church*, 174. 'With the annexation of Ani in 1045 the last remaining kingdom of Armenia had fallen to Byzantium. It no doubt seemed undesirable to Orthodoxy to have an independent non-Chalcedonian Church within the Empire and, however unwise

It was through Cilicia, above all, that such contacts and influence became so noticeable.[48] Here, a little before, two fiefdoms, 'baronies', had been created by Armenian refugees displaced by the Seljuk invasions of Greater Armenia, the plateau heartland of the nation. A century later, these having been united, the resulting fusion was now to be raised to the status of a Kingdom in 1198[49] by the authority of the Holy Roman emperor, Henry VI. It is said that the crown given to Levon I on that occasion was a gift from the pope himself.[50] Levon was anointed by the Catholicos at the same ceremony on January 6, the second most important day in the Armenian ecclesiastical calendar. Thus the ceremony combined both Latin

---

from the political angle, Byzantine religious policy towards the Armenians was in accordance with usual practice ... It was probably with conformity in mind that in 1048 Constantine IX invited Peter I, Catholicos of the Armenian Church, to Constantinople. The meeting in 1048 was amicable but negative in result and subsequent relations were to deteriorate as attacks on the monophysites were intensified later on during Constantine X's reign. The Armenian Church had always been the symbol of its people's nationalism. Annexation and dispersal could not extinguish this spirit, as the successful establishment of Lesser Armenia in south-east Asia Minor was soon to demonstrate. (Hussey here refers to Sirapie Der Nersessian, *Armenia and the Byzantine Empire* [Cambridge, Mass., 1945], for a brief account of the Armenian point of view.) It was unfortunate that Byzantium's 11th-century ecclesiastical policy towards Armenia should have exacerbated the long-standing antagonism between Greek and Armenian, provoking endless friction in Asia Minor just at a time when a united front against Turkic invaders was needed.' (Hussey, 130-131) 'The usual Byzantine policy in the eleventh century was to treat the Armenians as untrustworthy subjects, ready to renounce their allegiance to Constantinople whenever an opportunity presented itself, as well as heretical Christians, hence fit objects for either persecution or conversion.' Frazee, 'Christian Church', 167.

[48] 'Malgré certaines désillusions ultérieures, les Arméniens ont considéré les Francs arrivant en Orient, dans le cadre de la Première Croisade, comme des libérateurs tant de leur people que du tombeau du Christ.' Gérard Dédéyan, 'Le Rôle Complémentaire des Frères Pahlawuni Grigor III, Catholicos, et Saint Nerses Snorhali, Coadjuteur, dans le Rapprochement avec les Latins, à l'Epoque de la Chute d'Edesse (v. 1139-v.1150)', *Revue des Etudes Arméniennes,* tome XXIII, 1992, 238. 'Apparently, the Cilician aristocracy was the only native Christian element in Syria with whom the Frankish nobility were willing to intermarry. Arguably, the same amiable climate was also in the end responsible for the introduction of Latin feudal law, dress, and even knighthood, at the royal court of Cilicia.' Aristeides Papadakis, John Meyendorff, *The Christian East and the Rise of the Papacy: The Church 1071-1453*, St Vladimir's Press, Crestwood, New York, 1994, 117. Earlier, we are informed that '... Latin toleration did not mean integration but condescension. The multiplicity of native Christian confessions was transformed by the Franks into a caste of native inferiors. To put it otherwise, under the Franks, the Jacobites and all former *dhimmis*—non-Muslim clients of the Muslim state—became *dhimmis* of the crusader kingdom.' *Ibid.*, 112.

[49] The year 1199 is sometimes given for the Coronation at Tarsus (cf. David Marshall Lang, *Armenia. Cradle of Civilization*, Allen and Unwin, London, 1970, 203). Most authors, though, give 1198 for this significant event.

[50] Celestine III (1191-1198), or Innocent III (1198-1216).

and Armenian elements, though the former could be said to have been the dominant and might be seen by some contemporaries as boding ill for the kingdom.[51]

A number of the Catholicoses who had established their See in the area, first at Hromkla on the Euphrates in 1125[52] and then, in 1292, at Sis, the kingdom's capital, were distinctly eirenic in their relationship with the Roman Church. The prelates of the Pahlawuni dynasty, founded by Catholicos Gregory II, Vkaiasser—the Martyrophile (1065-1105)—were particularly remarkable in this respect.[53] We may mention here a figure well known in the West, Nerses of Lambron (1152/3-1198) who followed in the tolerant steps of his great-uncle, Nerses Clayetzi, or 'Shnorhali' (the Graceful) (1166-1173), though the latter was more immediately concerned with union with the Greek Church.[54] It was to be at the Councils of Sis in 1307 and Adana in 1316 that the Armenians of Cilicia finally accepted formal union with Rome, though not all of their fellow countrymen were by any means agreeable to this decision, as was to be proved in the following and final decades of the Cilician kingdom.[55]

Suspicion of amicable contacts with either Latins or Greeks was not confined to a certain number of the Armenians of Cilicia: such contacts were especially viewed with hostility in Greater Armenia. The monasteries, in particular, were conservative in their outlook and had far reaching influence on the population. Such conservatism was inimical to any influence that was felt to be a threat to the integrity of Armenian

---

[51] For a detailed treatment of the kingdom: Frazee, 'Church and State in the Kingdom of Cilician Armenia, 1198-1375', *Byzantine Studies/Études Byzantines*, Vol. 3, Part 2 (1976), 30-58. Cf. also Boghos Levon Zekiyan and Azat Bozoyan, 'Le Relazioni con il Papato e le Prime Crociate (VII-XII secolo)', *Roma-Armenia*, 117-136; from the same publication: Mutafian, 'L'Armenia Cosmopolita, (XIII-XIV secolo)', 137-159. For a general history of the region, including the Armenian Kingdom itself, cf. Claude Mutafian, *La Cilicie au Carrefour des Empires*, 2 vols., Société d'Édition 'Les Belles Lettres', Paris, 1988.

[52] The Catholicos Gregory III had previously been at Dzovk near Lake Kharput. Hromkla was to be sacked by the Mamluks in 1292.

[53] For a brief outline of the genesis of this ecclesiastical dynasty, see Frazee, 'The Christian Church', 167.

[54] (54) Cf. Gerard Dédéyan, 'Le Role Complémentaire ...', 237-252. Cf. also: Dédéyan, *Les pouvoirs arméniens dans le Proche-Orient Méditerranéen (1068-1144),* thèse d'État dactylographiée, 4 vols, Paris, 1998.

[55] May, 1307: '... a Church council was called and presided over by the King of Cilicia, Leo III, whose dogmatic views were imposed on an unwilling synod in order to court favour with the Pope of Rome.' Tiran Nersoyan, *Laity*, 102. Furthermore, '... the stiff opposition to union even led to violence, and the assassination of the last six pro-Latin catholicoi.' Papadakis, *The Christian East*, 118.

tradition. 'In the centuries that followed … a real division of interest appeared between the conservatives based in the old homeland and the more liberal Cilicians, a separation which lasts to this very day in the two hierarchies still found within the Armenian Church.'[56]

An earlier division had occurred in 1113. According to Terzian, the schism that arose at that time within the Armenian Church, led by Tavit of Aghtamar,[57] though it made the task of union with Rome more complicated, did not affect the legitimate Catholicos '… qui se maintint dans l'unité catholique …'[58] However, the creation of the Armenian patriarchate of Jerusalem in 1311, and with the necessary approval of the Mamluk authorities, was in reaction to the concern that the Catholicos of Sis was too close in belief and sentiment to the Church of Rome.

It is interesting to note that to protect the autonomy of the Cilician patriarchate from the claims of the Latin patriarchate of Antioch, the former was finally to be made directly dependent on the Holy See (Apostolic Letter, March 1, 1239). This had already been granted by Pope Innocent III in 1202, but had been withdrawn in 1238 by Gregory IX who was not supportive of the idea of having two religious heads in the same region and had been taking heed of the continuing claims of Antioch. However, Hetoum I (1226-1270) and his queen, Isabelle, successfully appealed to the pope by claiming that the independence of the Cilician See dated back to St Gregory the Illuminator himself who, furthermore, had made a 'pacte d'union' with St Sylvester.[59]

The Franciscans were active in Cilicia; indeed, to such an extent that one of the Armenian kings, Hetum II, took the Franciscan habit

---

[56] Frazee, 'The Christian Church', 170. 'Chez les Arméniens de Transcaucasie, c'est l'esprit conservateur, isolationniste et sectaire qui s'est de plus en plus renforcé, et quelques monastères riches et actifs ont eté les porte-drapeau de cet esprit. On s'est habitué à en donner surtout quatre: Haghbat et Sanahine au nord du lac de Sévan; Tathève et Orodn dans le sud du même lac, en Siounie.' Jean Mécérian, *Histoire et Institutions de l'Église Arménienne*, Imprimerie Catholique, Beirut, 1965, 101.

[57] Gregory III Pahlavouni (1113-1166) was only eighteen when elected, and furthermore made priest, bishop and catholicos on the same day. This had come about by the unexpected death of his cousin, Catholicos Barsegh, who himself had succeeded his great uncle, Gregory II, in 1105. In reaction to this, Tavit, the Archbishop of Aghtamar, had himself declared Catholicos by a synod that he had summoned. (Cf. Frazee, 'The Christian Church', 172.)

[58] *Le Patriarcat*, 10. He continues, '… les patriarches déclarèrent souvent la soumission de l'église arménienne à la chaire de S. Pierre personellement dans leurs relations épistolaires ou avec les évêques aux synodes d'union …', whilst Tavit's successors '… restèrent, semble-t-il, toujours anti-chalcédoniens jusqu'à la disparition de leur siège dans le lac de Van (1895).'

[59] Terzian, *Le Patriarcat…*, 9.

himself. However, a number of the friars seem to have had a tendency to be fairly hard-lined in their attitude to Oriental Christians, preferring greater uniformity to Roman ways, a policy that appears not to have altered even in the 19th century, or possibly later.[60] This does not seem to have been the case as regards the Dominicans, at least not to the same degree.

Following the decision of Pope John XXII in 1318 to divide the field of Asia among the friars for the purpose of mission, the Order of Preachers had penetrated Greater Armenia shortly thereafter. Here, and especially under the early and crucial leadership of Bartolomeo da Poggia,[61] they were to exercise great influence over a number of Armenian monasteries. They were to help form the 'Brothers of Unity of St Gregory' known generally, as 'Unitors'—an Armenian monastic order the members of which desired not only that Roman influence should trigger a spiritual renewal within the Apostolic Church, but also that union with the See of Peter be the ultimate goal.[62] To help in this matter, translations were made of such works as the *Imitation of Christ* and certain works of St Thomas Aquinas.

According to Terzian, the Unitors founded some fifty monasteries in some five dioceses. In these communities it was customary to use the

---

[60] Long standing conflicts between Franciscans, Greeks and Armenians over guardianship of religious sites in Jerusalem and elsewhere in the Holy Land is well known. This may have led to a greater lack of sympathy for non-Latin ways. An example of tension between Franciscans and Armenian Catholics in the first half of the nineteenth century is related by Tekeyan. Though Patriarch Krikor Bedros VI was generally on good terms with members of the Order, nevertheless he had '… plus d'une fois, l'occasion de se plaindre de leurs efforts de faire passer les Arméniens Catholiques au Rite Latin. Plus d'une fois aussi, le Saint-Siège dut intervenir pour défendre aux Missionnaires Latins de tels manèges, qui se faisaient le plus souvent à l'occasion de mariages entre personnes de rites différents' (*Le Patriarcat Arménien,* 10).

[61] Bartolomeo da Poggia (d. 1313) is often termed 'of Bologna' (cf. Tournebize, 'Arménie', *DHGE*, XVII, 318. Cf. also Mécérian, *Histoire et Institutions de l'Église Arménienne*, 294-295 where he gives an explanation for this confusion). Bartolomeo was already a bishop when he arrived in the region and established himself at Maragha, in the vicinity of Lake Ourmia. On his reputation becoming widespread, two Armenian monks came to visit: Hovhannes and Hakobos of the Monastery of Grna. They spent two years with him, learning Latin and acquainting themselves with western theology. Bartolomeo, who had in the meantime learnt Armenian, was himself invited to Grna by Hovhannes who eventually formed the *Miabanoghq*. In what is called the *Encyclical Letter of John of Grna*, he names those who were sympathetic to this new influence from the West.

[62] Hovhannes, in his *Encyclical Letter,* also speaks of their enthusiastic activity in this respect, '… nous nous mîmes tous à prêcher dans toute l'Arménie la nécessité de s'unir à l'Église de Rome pour le salut des âmes … et plus nous traduisîmes des livres du latin, plus nos esprits reçurent de lumières et plus manifestement parurent les défauts de notre nation. A la pensée donc, qu'auparavant il ne nous était rien resté de la foi chrétienne hormis le nom, nous étions ébahis et confus et nous n'avons plus rien à dire' (Mécérian, *Histoire et Institutions de l'Église Arménienne*, 296).

Latin rite translated into Armenian.[63] Yet according to Ormanian: 'The earliest missionaries ... had conceived the idea of introducing the Latin rituals, translated into Armenian; but they were obliged to give up the project on account of the strenuous opposition which it excited.'[64] No date is given by Ormanian for this change of policy.

Such Latin enterprises were eventually and perhaps inevitably to meet hostility from the Apostolic Church, most especially in Greater Armenia, in that the growth of 'latinisation'—'romanisation', both theologically and culturally, was seen to be a threat to the very essence of the Church and of the Armenian people.[65] In other words, that it would lead to absorption and loss of identity—and this after so much difficulty and suffering to maintain that identity. According to Mécérian, the 'Unitors', though gifted with both knowlege and virtue, were over zealous in their activities, causing legitimate Armenian susceptibilities to be wounded.[66] Understandably, it was this anxiety that continued to fuel hostility, the residue of which may still be found even into the modern period.

Also to be considered for the understanding of the demise of these enterprises was the matter of further Muslim infiltration and conquest. In addition, in 1349 the advent of the Black Death took its toll on the region, followed by the incursions of Timur (1336-1405) which devastated Greater Armenia. The Cilician kingdom itself was finally to succumb to the Mamluks in 1375. As we have noted, remnants of missionary activity did survive in the former region, though matters appear unclear as regards the latter. There is also, as we have seen, evidence of a continuing sympathy for

---

63 *Le Patriarcat*, 40.

64 *The Armenian Church*, 184.

65 Their zeal in their relations both with the 'schismatics' and the Muslims—the word 'persécutions' is employed by Tournebize (*ibid.*, *DHGE,* 318)—ended finally in their dispersion and collapse (1330-1794). By the 18th century, only the diocese of Nakhitchevan had survived and ten monasteries (cf. Terzian 40). According to Frazee, the last of these monasteries was abandoned in 1745, in which year also the archbishop, Domenico Salviani, fled to Rome. Shortly thereafter, as warfare remained constant in the region, virtually all surviving Armenian Catholics, much reduced in numbers, made their way to Smyrna, led by one of their priests, Tomas Issaverdens. Here they seem to have been eventually absorbed into the Latin community, as that rite was the one most familiar to them.

66 'Ceux-ci, doués de science et de virtu, mais égarés par leur zèle excessif, avaient blessé certaines légitimes susceptibilités des Arméniens,' *Histoire et Institutions de l'Église Arménienne*, 102. For further information on the 'Unitors', cf. R Loenertz, *La Société des Frères Pérégrinants, Étude sur l'Orient Dominicain*, Instituto Storico Domenicano, S Sabina, Rome, 1937, 141-150. For a concise study of the foundation and work of the *Fratres Unitores*, and the *Fratres Perigrinantes*, who had been instrumental in their foundation, cf. Frazee, 'The Catholic Missions to Azerbaijan and Nakhichevan', *Diakonia*, IX, 3, (1977), 251-260.

Rome in Cilicia; at least, that hostility that has sometimes been associated with Greater Armenia was not to the fore there.

As already indicated, a number of monks were to be found among those Armenians who at various times sought refuge in Europe from marauding peoples from the east. These monks now began to arrive in some quantity, obliged to leave as Mamluk raids became more persistant and successful. They were to found monasteries in Italy, Poland and the Balkans.

One group of such monks were the Armenian Friars of Saint Bartholomew, a group which were to exist in Italy from 1307 till 1650. It was in Genoa in the former year that they founded a convent dedicated to St Bartholomew and which provided the name for their religious Congregation. They were to spead rapidly throughout the peninsular, thus affording a partial explanation for the many Armenian echoes detectable in Italy today. In 1356, though holding St Basil as their patron, they adopted the rule of St Augustine with the Constitutions of the Order of Preachers. This development was approved by the Holy See, thus recognising the monks as now forming a new Armenian congregation '*citra mare consistentium*' ('*en deçà des mers'*—'on this side of the seas'), that is to say, they were to be found neither in Cilicia nor in Greater Armenia, but in Europe. This was meant to distinguish them, not always successfully, from the 'Unitors' who, as we have already seen, were also associated with the Dominicans. In contrast, the 'Unitors' were '*au-delà des mers*'—'beyond the seas'.

From the beginning, the Congregation admitted Italians which policy eventually led to a lessening of its Armenian ethos.[67] In addition, the increasing difficulty of finding recruits from the Armenian homelands contributed to the Congregation's demise in the middle of the 17th century.[68]

---

[67] 'Contrairement à ce que nous observons chez les Frères Uniteurs et dans la congrégation des Mekhitharistes, les frères de St Barthélémy de Gênes—et celà, semble-t-il, dès le début—avaient ouvert leurs portes toutes larges à des candidats non-arméniens. Ce système finit par transformer peu à peu la congrégation d'arménienne en italienne.' Marc-Antoine van den Oudenrijn, 'Les Constitutions des Frères Arméniens de Saint Basile en Italie', *Orientalia Christiana Analecta,* 126, 10.

[68] Most of the above information concerning the Friars of St Bartholomew has been taken from Mécérian, *Histoire et Institutions de l'Église Arménienne*, 332-333. Mécérian lists the following cities as having convents of these friars: Ancona, Rimini, Bologna, Florence, Milan, Naples, Perugia, Pisa, Rome, Salerno, Siena, and Venice. Apart from Poland and the Balkans, where other monks had settled, at least one monastery was to be founded in the Crimea.

That union with Rome that was at least partially achieved during the period of the Cilician kingdom appeared to have ceased, at least on a formal level, with the latter's disappearance. There was to be another attempt at union with the Armenians at the Council of Florence (1438-1445). An act of union was indeed signed (22 November 1439), but which, like most such agreements at that Council, proved short-lived, almost all Armenian prelates either refusing to recognise the agreement or simply ignoring it.[69]

It was to be the Council of Trent and the Catholic Reformation, two centuries later, that would enthuse new Orders, new missionaries, to penetrate the most recent Muslim polity of the region—the Ottoman empire—and to make contact, once again, on any substantial level with the Armenian Apostolic Church. The papacy was now to make this a priority.[70] Of the new Orders that were to pursue this matter within Ottoman domains, the Jesuits, the Theatines and the Capuchins were to be the most active in the period immediately subsequent to Trent. Many other Orders and Congregations, male and female, were to arrive in the 19th century.

Armenian Catholic emancipation

Having touched on these earlier contacts, many of which were ephemeral and intangible in their effects, let us now return to the more, in a sense, sharply-defined Armenian Catholic community in Constantinople with which we began. As we do so, we bear in mind that there were also other such communities, though by no means as prestigious. According to Terzian,

---

[69] The Council produced the decree, 'De Armenis', which concerned itself with the sacraments. The text of this decree may be found in Norman P Tanner, *Decrees of the Ecumenical Councils*, 2 vols. Sheed & Ward, London; Georgetown University Press, Washington DC, Vol. 1, 534-559. For further information on the Armenians at Florence: Joseph Gill, *The Council of Florence*, AMS Press, New York, 1982 (originally published Cambridge University Press, Cambridge, 1959), 305-310. For a general description of the events at Florence, as seen within the wider context of 'uniatism': Hajjar, *Les Chrétiens Uniates du Proche-Orient,* 194-200.

[70] 'Avec Grégoire XIII, la papauté se tourne décidément vers l'Orient chrétien. Les initiatives romaines … marquent un tournant capital dans l'histoire de l'Unité chrétienne. D'aucuns ont vu dans cette impulsion orientale de la papauté un désir de combler le vide causé par la sécession protestante. En tout cas, les démarches enterprises par les pontifes romains dénotent une préoccupation fondamentale et une ligne de conduite précise visant à reconquérir les vielles chrétientés orientales avant qu'elles ne s'allient avec les églises réformées' (Joseph Hajjar, *Les Chrétiens Uniates du Proche-Orient*, Editions du Seuil, Paris, 1962, 205-206).

the principal centres in the 18th century, apart from Constantinople, were Ankara, Aleppo, Mardin, Erzeroum and Akhelzkha.[71]

The Constantinopolitan community, as we have indicated, was largely the fruit of Latin missionary activity, but it was also due in time to the labour of those Armenian clergy who were ex-alumni of the Urbanum in Rome.[72] These were often affected by a certain 'Romanitas' and therefore more likely to be closely allied to most Latin clergy and their penchant for 'latinisation' in the internal struggles that so marked the Catholic community as it grew in numbers and influence.[73] There was usually also a strong sense of personal attachment to the papacy by those educated in Rome.

However, there was at least one notable exception to this pattern at that time and one who, as we have mentioned, had exercised no small influence on the gifted Mkhitar. That is to say that, while remaining faithful to Rome he was yet willing to advocate a more nuanced approach than that normally pursued by the Congregation of Propaganda Fide itself.[74]

Khatchatour Arakelian (1666-1740) made serious attempts to reach a compromise whereby it would have been possible for converts to receive the sacraments in the patriarchal churches.[75] As we have noted earlier, these converts were not permitted by the state to have churches of their own, nor was it always possible or desirable to attend Latin places of worship. The question that Arakelian and others now raised was none other than the sensitive matter of 'communicatio in sacris'.[76] In the negotiations conducted by Arakelian it was agreed that, in order

---

[71] *Le Patriarcat*, 25. Alkhelzkha is now in present-day Georgia.

[72] The college was founded in 1627 by Urban VIII (1623-1644).

[73] '... the rival interests of their clergy, as they happened to have been educated at Rome or Venice, produced no inconsiderable degree of strife in the community.' Artinian, *The Armenian Constitutional System*, 39.

[74] Gregory XVI (1621-1623), had established the Roman curial Congregation of Propaganda Fide in 1622. It concerned itself with the work of missionaries in those areas where no hierarchical structures were to be found or where such structures were not perhaps on a firm footing. It was responsible for the creation of an Apostolic Vicariate in Constantinople in 1653.

[75] Before these particular developments in Constantinople, we have evidence of the trust that Pope Innocent XII had in Arakelian's diplomatic skills, as well as even the sensitivity of Propaganda. On being sent on a mission to the Etchmiadzin Catholicos, Nahapet I of Edessa, in 1698: 'La congrégation de la Propagande avait tracé au délégué une ligne de conduite, aussi libérale que prudente, touchant les ménagements à garder à l'égard du catholicos, le maintien de son autorité, la conservation du rite et des anciens usages religieux arméniens ...' Tournebize, 'Araqélian, Khatchatour', *DHGE*, Vol. 1, 1436.

[76] There was also the related question of permitting secret conversions under certain circumstances.

to facilitate this, the condemnations both of Chalcedon and Pope Leo the Great, which normally featured in the Armenian ordination rite of those days, would be abandoned. Thus it was hoped that some tranquility would be forthcoming.

Well-intentioned though they were, Arakelian's efforts had the consequence of making even more public the rivalries and disputes between the two tendencies.[77] Opposition from certain quarters on both sides refused to countenance the compromise solution and attitudes became more entrenched. Regrettably, converts were not always understood sympathetically by their fellow Catholics of the Latin rite, even though it was clearly evident that Armenian Catholics had found themselves in a somewhat anomalous position, a position that could spell extreme danger.

The situation soon deteriorated when the patriarchate took the first steps in the persecution of those who seemed to to be in its eyes the cause of dividing the Community. In consequence, there was almost continual pressure during the first fifteen years of the 18th century on those Armenians of Constantinople who had Catholic inclinations.[78] As we have already indicated, further persecution was to occur at other times and in other localities.[79]

However, the Holy See does not appear to have been continually opposed to such tolerant views as those supported by Arakelian and later by the Mekhitarists. Frazee recalls Propaganda Fide's response, to the difficult question as to whether clandestine conversions were permissable or not. This response, made, after some deliberation, on 9 July 1723, left such matters to the discretion of qualified persons of the locality: 'Oriental converts were simply told to consult the opinion of "theologians, doctors, and missionaries who have lived in those areas for a long time." '[80]

---

[77] Terzian, *Le Patriarcat*, 17-18.

[78] It was with the election of the gifted Patriarch Hovhannes IX Golod in 1715 that a more sensitive approach was taken by the Apostolic Church, at least, as has been remarked, until he was severely provoked by Propaganda Fide. He reigned until 1741. As to Arakelian, having been forced to quit Ottoman territory shortly after the execution of Der Komitas in 1707, he was given charge of the mission at the church of the Holy Cross at Venice under the jurisdiction of the patriarch of that city. In 1719, he was sent as Apostolic Visitor to Transylvania and Belgrade by the Holy See to correct '... les erreurs et les abus introduits dans la discipline et le rite.' (Terzian, 38.)

[79] *Ibid.* Terzian gives some details of these persecutions: 18.

[80] Charles A Frazee, *Catholics and Sultans: the Church and the Ottoman Empire 1453-1923*, Cambridge University Press, London, 1983, 182.

Another solution offered to ameliorate the situation had been that papal ratifcation of the election of Abraham Ardzivian presented earlier. Some felt, however, that this creation of a separate Catholic hierarchy would only exacerbate differences rather than remove them. They favoured a more diplomatic approach and not one that appeared to them to involve so blunt a demarcation. There is some evidence that this school of thought may still be active today. As to the thorny question of 'communicatio in sacris' it was not to be solved till 1830, an event that will be described in due course,

Some twenty years later, virtually the same proposal that had been put forward by Arakelian was mooted once more, only on this occasion by the Apostolic authorities themselves. It was met with enthusiasm by many Armenian Catholics. The Rome of Benedict XIII (1649-1730; pope from 1724), however, was distinctly hostile: '... participation in false worship conducted by heretical ministers ... opened the door to scandal, indifference and danger to faith.'[81] The decree that was issued on this matter by Propaganda Fide on 9 July 1729, not unnaturally provoked no small fury at the patriarchate, and the Armenian Catholics found themselves in further difficulties. Thus we already find a change of heart since the previous papacy, that of Innocent XIII (1721-1724), when it had been decided that such sensitive matters were to be left, as we have seen, to the judgment of those in authority in the region concerned. It may readily be imagined that such an open-ended response from the papacy, which at heart meant matters could be left to the conscience of the individual, would lead to further difficulties and contradictions, thus laying the path, in this instance, to a less tolerant approach.

Despite these difficulties, the community in Constantinople continued to wax and, with the example of the developments in Aleppo surrounding the person of Ardzivian to give some encouragement, there had been a growing desire for an Armenian ecclesiastic to lead and to speak for its own special needs.[82]

We have here to remind ourselves that with the termination of the Latin occupation of Constantinople in 1261, Latin patriarchal vicars were appointed to minister to the Latins who remained and for those

---

[81] *Ibid.*, 183.

[82] We are informed by Tournebize that Arakelian, when first sent from Rome to Constantinople after ordination, received the title, 'nonce apostolique auprès des Arméniens.' 'Araqélian, Khatchatour', *DHGE*, Vol. 1, 1436.

who were later to settle in the city, usually for commercial reasons. This system continued to be maintained after the metropolis finally fell into Turkish hands in 1453.[83]

Later, as the Ottoman empire's strength declined, the Capitulations that had been originally and condescendingly granted to foreigners who wished to have dealings with the empire gradually took on the character of privileged legal 'enclaves' within the State.[84] This development likewise caused the Latin vicars to gain prestige proportionately. It was under their spiritual supervision that Armenian converts and their families now fell. These Latin vicars, however, were loath to encourage the creation of a separate Armenian jurisdiction, one reason being the loss of control over a group much larger than their own Latin flock and the concomitant loss of revenue that would ensue.[85]

Added to this was the prospect, thought worthy of pursuit by many, of truly 'latinising' that Catholic community. Even among many Armenian Catholics themselves, this idea seems to have been welcomed. Admiration for western thought, methods and progress led naturally to emulation. The self-confidence of the Latin Church as to its superior theology, language and style was impressive. In addition, for a number

---

[83] Cf. Ludwik Biskupski, *L'Origine et l'Historique de la Représentation Officielle du Saint-Siège en Turquie (1204-1967)*, Umit Basimevi, Istanbul, 1968. Cf. Giuseppe M Croce, 'I Rappresentanti Pontifici a Costantinopoli (1814-1922). Tra Missione e Diplomazia'. *Roma-Armenia*, 349-351. Despite its title, the author also gives information on the period 1204 to 1814.

[84] Concerning these Capitulations: 'The general tenor of these treaties was exemplified in the Treaty of 1503 between Sultan Bayezid II and Venice. This treaty provided that a Venetian consul would reside in Istanbul, grant permission to Venetians to travel in the empire, and settle all disputes between them. Similar treaties were signed with France in 1535, 1604, and 1673.' (Artinian, *The Armenian Constitutional System in the Ottoman Empire, 1839-1863,* 31)

[85] Indeed, so great were the numbers of Armenians moving over to Rome, that the term 'Catholic' was reserved specifically for them by the Ottoman authorities and remained so until at least the late nineteenth century (cf. Pars Tuğlacı, *Istanbul Ermeni Kiliseleri-Armenian Churches of Istanbul*, Pars Yayin Ltd., Istanbul, 1991, 287). Latin Catholics were termed either as 'Latins' (as they still are in Istanbul and elsewhere in Turkey and the Middle East today) or as 'Franks'. According to Frazee, there were eight thousand such 'Catholics' in the capital by 1700. By 1720 this number had increased to twenty thousand, if the Latin patriarchal vicar, Mauri, was correct in his estimation (cf. Frazee, *Catholics and Sultans*, 182). Despite fluctuations over the next fifty years or so, due to the effects of persecution, the number by 1783 was still twenty thousand as reported by the Patriarchal Vicar Francis Frachia (cf. Frazee, 'The Formation of the Armenian Catholic Community in the Ottoman Empire', *Eastern Churches Review*, VII, 2, [1975], 149-163: 'This number compared to 7,800 Latin Catholics and 300 Ragusans shows the importance of the Armenians to Catholicism in Constantinople', [159]). There were at that time, according to Frachia, and quoted by Frazee, one hundred and fifty thousand Armenians in the capital.

of Oriental Christians, greater protection might be expected from the Europeans, if a closer adoption of their rite and culture were pursued.[86]

Due to continuing tension, however, and that generated by those who opposed total 'latinisation', Rome was eventually moved to grant the community a Ritual Vicar in 1745, the first to hold that position being Athanasius Merassian. According to Frazee, he was not to receive episcopal ordination, as titular bishop of Hromkla, until 1758, as Latin opposition persisted.[87] He was then allowed to ordain clergy for his own community, but was not given a specific geographical area in which to exercise his jurisdiction. There was the further stipulation that he and his successors were still to be subject to the Latin Vicars, perhaps as a result of the former having been allowed to be elected by the community itself, both clergy and lay. Such a procedure was close to the heart of Armenian tradition, but was possibly viewed with some hesitation by Rome, so that complete autonomy was not thought advisable. Alas, total harmony with their Latin colleagues was not always to be in evidence. Merassian, going to Rome, attempted to free himself from this tutelage, but without success. Resigning in 1778, he was succeeded by Anton Miserlian.[88]

There were also problems with the geographically remote Armenian Catholic patriarch, Michael Bedros III Kasbarian (1753-1780). He claimed jurisdiction over all Armenian Catholics, wherever they were, this claim seemingly of no great interest to the Catholics of the capital. The patriarch was none too pleased with the appointment of an Armenian Ritual Vicar and sought clarification from the Holy See as to what were the limits of his own jurisdiction. He himself arrived in Rome in April 1759, but left dissatisfied as the Ritual Vicar was confirmed in office. Whilst Propaganda Fide did clarify the patriarch's own jurisdiction as being Cilicia, Anatolia, Cappadocia, and Syria, and even though the pope added Mesopotamia for good measure, nevertheless that dissatisfaction remained with Kasbarian and his immediate successors.

---

[86] '...il y avait parmi les Catholiques Arméniens un fort courant à embrasser le rite Latin, surtout pendant les périodes de persécutions; les Latins, en effet, étaient indépendents du Patrik schismatique, duquel dépendaient les Arméniens Catholiques, et jouissaient de la protection immédiate des Puissances Catholiques, la France et l'Autriche.' (Tekeyan, *Le Patriarcat Arménien Catholique de Cilicie au Temps de Grégoire Pierre VI [1812-1840]*, 10.)

[87] *Catholics and Sultans*, 184. Mgr Tcholakian makes no mention of this in his treatment of the Ritual Vicars: *L'Église Arménienne Catholique en Turquie,* 18-19.

[88] Cf. Frazee, 'The Formation of the Armenian Catholic Community', 159. For two conflicting lists of holders of this post, one containing five, the other seven names, cf. Tcholakian, *ibid.*, 19.

The year 1830 has already been referred to, and it was in that year that, unexpectedly, a new *millet* was created by the Ottoman authorities, that of the 'Katolik *Millet*', or 'Catholic Nation'. It is a question of no small import as to how such a development occurred, since it involved an almost seismic shift in the Ottoman polity, untouched in this respect for almost four hundred years.

Despite the success in exterminating the Janissary corps in June 1826,[89] the enormous problems faced by the reforming sultan, Mahmoud II (1808-1839) in the next few years, first with the defeat of his fleet at Navarino (18 October 1827) by the French and British in support of the Greek struggle for independence, and then by the continuing encroachments of Russia—the Russian army was even within sight of the capital on 20 August 1829—had made the Armenian Catholics, as mentioned above, once again accused of disloyalty, easy victims of his suspicion and rage. It was particularly those in the capital who were originally from Angora (Ankara) that met the brunt of this new persecution. These had the reputation of being the most conservative in their convictions, indeed possibly forming the most fanatical element of the Catholics. They had aligned themselves a few years earlier to those who were opposed to the attempted compromise known as 'The Invitation to Fraternal Love' (*Hraver Siro*), promulgated on 20 April 1820. Though largely the work of seven Armenian Catholic priests, five of whom were of the Venetian branch of the Mkhitarists,[90] the 'Invitation' had been drawn up in collaboration with the apostolic amiras, Balian and Bezjian, and with the blessing of Boghos I Krikorian, patriarch of Constantinople. By this it was once more proposed that the condemnation of Leo the Great and the Council of Chalcedon would be removed from the Book of Ordination, as well as the removal of three saints from the reformed liturgical calendar of Catholicos Simon (1763-1780), saints who had been particularly opposed to the Chalcedonian position (John of Orotn, and Krikor and Movses of Tathev). In return, the Catholics would accept the jurisdiction of Boghos.

---

[89] The massacre of the Janissaries in 1826—they had mutinied once again—was, it appears, a necessary prelude for radical changes to be accomplished. It came to be known as the 'Auspicious Incident'. Mahmoud's predecessor, Selim III (1789-1807), who had introduced the 'Nizam-i Cedid' (New Order) in an attempt to reform the outdated Ottoman system, had met serious opposition from the Janissaries. Finally, he was to be deposed and murdered.

[90] Tournebize, *DHGE,* 334.

The Armenian Ritual Vicar, Missirlian, was not in favour of this development,[91] nor, once more, were the Armenian ex-alumni of the Urbanum. Regrettably, due, it is understood, to the malicious or unthinking action of a Catholic shoemaker from Angora, reflecting the feelings of his fellows, a riot ensued at the patriarchate by those Apostolic Armenians who felt that their beliefs had been betrayed.[92] Thus the well-known antagonism of the Angora party to any reasonable attempt at compromise may have aroused the lasting hostility of the sultan against this particular section of the Armenian Catholic community.

Mahmoud, however, now facing certain defeat at the hands of Russia, to the east and to the west, appealed to France and Austria for arbitration. These powers at the request of Pope Leo XII (1823-1829) took the opportunity to have inserted among the clauses of the Treaty of Adrianople, signed on September 14, 1829, provision for the emancipation of the Armenian Catholic community from the authority of the Apostolic patriarchate.[93]

Thus within a year or two, the Armenian Catholic community experienced a complete reversal of fortune, though, alas, the relief and optimism were comparatively short-lived: internal conflict was soon to be the order of the day. However, in the meantime, the establishment of the Catholic *millet* gave the community legal recognition and protection by the Ottoman state. Not only were places of worship permitted,[94] the Armenian Catholic community was now also able to convene its own National Assembly of Representatives. The first such convention was held on 15/27 February 1830, consisting of ninety lay notables and six priests. On that occasion, they

---

[91] According to both lists, this was during Missirlian's second term of office (1806-1824).

[92] For a particular version of this affair, cf. Artinian, *The Armenian Constitutional System*, 35-37. Artinian also describes two similar attempts at reconciliation just prior to this, the first in 1810, the second in 1817 (34-35).

[93] Tournebize, 'Arménie', *DHGE*, XXVI, 335; Mécérian, *Histoire et Institutions de l'Église Arménienne,* 136. Pius IX refers directly to this in *Quartus supra*, 20, though in stronger terms: 'The Ottoman emperor, at the insistence of Leo XII and Pius VIII, and relying on the support of the Catholic rulers of Austria and France, recognized the distinction which exists between Catholics and heretics; therefore, he removed Catholics from the civil power of the latter, decreeing that Catholics should have their own head or prefect.' The question of 'insistence' may not have been appreciated by the Porte at the time of the encyclical's publication. The idea of such a 'millet' was not entirely novel. Just over a century before, the then French ambassador, Pierre des Alleurs, in an attempt to solve the mounting tension in the Armenian community, had approached the Porte with that very suggestion, '... but the Ottoman Authorities, fresh from a victory over the Russians, were in no mood to grant concessions which would enhance the position of Christians in Ottoman lands.' Frazee, *Catholics and Sultans*, 181.

[94] Cf. Tcholakian, *L'Église Arménienne*, for considerable detail concerning these places of worship in Constantinople.

elected, by secret ballot, Mgr Andon Nouridjian, to be their new spiritual and civic leader. By the Brief *'Quod Iambu'* (6 July 1830), Pius VIII ratified the election and announced the creation of an Armenian Archbishopric of Constantinople, thus abolishing the system of Ritual Vicars. Archbishop Nouridjian's jurisdiction was to cover all those areas that did not yet have their legitimate pastors, that is to say, areas not under the control of the Catholic patriarch who still resided in the Lebanon.[95]

Unfortunately, when it was disclosed that Nouridjian was in fact an Austrian citizen, the Porte refused to grant him the necessary Berat, or Imperial Diploma, of formal recognition.[96] The Assembly was therefore obliged to meet a second time (18/31 December 1830) to elect another person as 'Patrik' ('ethnarch' or 'Imperial patriarch'). A priest, Father Hagop Tchoukourian—and this was the pattern to be followed—was chosen and was recognised as 'Patrik' when the Porte issued the Berat on January 5, 1831, which event may be understood as the formal and final establishment of the Catholic *millet*.[97]

---

[95] 'Les bulles de fondation du siège (of Constantinople in 1830) et de nomination du premier titulaire, Antoine Nouridjian, précisent que la juridiction du nouvel archevêque s'étendra sur tous les territoires de l'empire ottoman où les Arméniens dépendaient jusqu'alors du vicaire apostolique latin, c'est-à-dire où les autres évêques arméniens catholiques n'exerçaient aucune autorité et où, par conséquent, de nouveaux évêchés pourraient être érigés comme suffragants de Constantinople.' De Clercq, *Histoire des Conciles*, 504.

[96] The disclosure, it has been said, was made by Apostolic 'conspirators'! Frazee gives quite a different account of this matter. He also names Hagop Manuelian as the first 'patrik' for the Catholic 'millet' rather than Tchoukourian (*Catholics and Sultans*, 259-260). Likewise Tekeyan mentions Manuelian to have been the first (*Le Patriarcat Arménien Catholique de Cilicie*, 50). The two versions are correct, however, as both in fact refer to the same person: his father was Manuel. Of greater interest was the fact that some four years before his election, he had been nominated by the eirenic Amira Harutyiun Bezdjian to the Vicariat of the Apostolic Patriarchate to be the instrument of communication between the Apostolic patriarch and his Armenian Catholic 'subjects', a post that earned him the opposition of a number of Angorites at his election. Even though he himself had been exiled at the time of the 1828 persecution, nevertheless his preceeding connections with the Apostolic Church must have acted against him. The unfortunate role played by the patriarch, Garabet III, at the time had led to the infamous forced march of Catholic Angorites in winter from the capital to their place of origin resulting in hundreds of casualties, mostly children. This must still have been fresh in the minds of the survivors who had only recently been allowed to return, that is to say in January, 1830. (Cf. Frazee, 'The Formation of the Armenian Catholic Community', 162.)

[97] Apparently, technically, the actual title, 'patrik', was not granted to the holder of the post till 1835. As regards the Protestant community: 'An Imperial Trade, secured by the British Ambassador, Sir Stratford Canning, afterward Lord Stratford de Radcliffe, November 15, 1847, granted the Protestant community the right of freedom of conscience. By an Imperial Firman of November 27, 1850, the community's legal status as a "Nation" was permanently confirmed.' Arpee, *A History of Armenian Christianity*, 269.

Thus was brought into being a dual system whereby Mgr Nouridjian was recognised by the community, and by the Holy See, as its spiritual head, whilst Fr Tchoukourian was recognised by the Porte as its civic head.[98] It was to be Fr Tchoukourian alone who could have official contact with the Porte, and thus all Catholics of the non-Latin rites—Armenians, Melkites, Syrians, Maronites and Chaldeans[99]—had to

---

[98] He was assisted, it would seem, by a Nazır, Hagop Chelebi Duz, and a select group of ten notables. Originally, the Nazir, or 'Prince Temporel', had been elected by the Assembly precisely for this purpose (cf. Tcholakian, 25-26). It is uncertain as to why he was immediately superseded by the need for a different civic head, unless the 'Patrik' was expected by the Porte to be a 'religious' of some description. Such a mould, if it were so, was to be broken with the appearance of the Protestant 'millet'. The first head, or 'askabed', of the Armenian-led Protestant millet, Stepan Seropian, was none other than the brother of a former Armenian patriarch, Hagopus, a cause of no small embarrassment. He had been acting as Protestant 'Agent' to the Porte since 1847. Cf. Vahan Tootikian, *The Armenian Evangelical Church*, Detroit, Michigan, Armenian Heritage Committee, 1982, 42-43.

[99] '...par l'ordre du gouvernement, les catholiques durent nommer, pour les affaires temporelles, un patrik, seul intermédiaire officiel entre la Porte et les catholiques, soit arméniens, soit des autres races indigènes.' Tournebize, *DHGE*, XXXI, 339. This arrangement regarding the other Oriental Catholics was confirmed by the Ottoman government in 1839, despite Rome's continuing opposition: cf. Tcholakian, *L'Eglise Arménienne*, 119, n. 85. However, matters did not always run smoothly. According to a Protestant missionary, the Revd Mr Bird of Beirut, after having given a resumé of the genesis and history of the 'papal Greeks of Syria', continues: 'When it was at first reported that the Sultan intended to appoint a common head of the three sects of popish converts, viz. the Armenians, Greeks and Syrians, and that this head was for the present an Armenian, the Greeks expressed their determination sooner to return to their mother church than to yield obedience to a chief from their Armenian brethren, and so they still remain, as it appears, nominally unknown at Constantinople.' (Quoted in Smith and Dwight, *Missionary Researches in Armenia*, 62, n.†.] According to Rondot (*Les Chrétiens d'Orient*, 81-82), the Ottoman government was eventually to recognise the various Catholic patriarchs as 'patriks' or 'civil' leaders of their respective communities as follows: Greek-Catholic in 1848; Chaldean in 1861; Syrian-Catholic in 1866; Coptic-Catholic in 1898. As regards those Latin Catholics who were Ottoman subjects, their somewhat unique position among non-Muslim communities is described by Marmara, *Précis Historique de la Communauté latine de Constantinople et de son Église*, Anadolu Ofset, Istanbul, 2003, 49-54. Never given the status of 'millet', the Magnifica Comunità di Pera (or Confrérie de Sainte-Anne), established immediately after the Turkish conquest, and thus replacing the government of the Genoese podestà, was to represent the interests of this group. In the 19th century, the Comunità evolved into the Latin Ottoman Chancellery which survived until 1927. Georges Varthaliti was a Director, or 'Latin Consul', from 1843 to 1866 to be succeeded by his son, Othon. 'The Director's duties were the same as those of the patriarchs in the *millets*: to serve as intermediary between the government and the Latins, to act as judge in cases of dispute between Latins, and to issue certificates of nationality in matters of birth, marriage, death and foreign travel. For practical purposes, the state of relations between him and the patriarchal vicar and between him and the French ambassador determined his usefulness' (Frazee, *Catholics and Sultans*, 224.)

have recourse through him for any formal dealings with the government, and this would include not only the archbishop-primate, but also the patriarch-catholicos at Bzommar.[100]

According to De Clercq, on the death of Nouridjian in 1838, Gregory XVI (1831-1846) nominated Paul Marouchian as his successor, thereby ignoring the Armenian laity's wish to present their own candidates. What should be noted, and of vital importance, is that Mgr Tcholakian quite contradicts this statement concerning the election of Marouchian. The archbishop claims, on the contrary, that Marouchian was indeed elected by the National Assembly on 2 February 1838, and was consequently recognized by the pope as the new holder of the See.[101] In addition, Tcholakian gives the names of those involved in that particular election.[102] We may note further the heavy preponderance of lay representation within the Assembly: sixty lay notables and only two priests (the 'patrik' and his vicar). We may not wonder that the attempted removal, later, by Pius IX of such strong lay participation in the task of electing primates and the supervision of church property was to be the cause of serious friction and, indeed, schism.

Anton Hassoun (1809-1884) and troubled years

Whatever be the case concerning the elevation of Mourachian, there is no uncertainty that in 1842, the pope decided to choose for himself Marouchian's coadjutor with the right of succession. The person so chosen,

---

[100] 'C'est à ce chef civil, que le Patriarche dut recourir plusieurs fois, pour obtenir des Firmans permettant la construction de nouvelles églises dans les Missions du Patriarcat.' Tekeyan, *Le Patriarcat Arménien Catholique de Cilicie au Temps de Grégoire Pierre VI (1812-1840),* 11. Though at any religious function of note within the Armenian Catholic community both the archbishop-primate and the 'patrik' were expected to be present, seated on separate thrones within the sanctuary, such harmony on one level was not always borne out on others, nor did the new arrangement prevent conflict with the patriarch-catholicos. The places for two such thrones, facing each other in the sanctuary are still to be seen at St Saviour's, the former Armenian Catholic patriarchal church in Istanbul. As a gesture of good will, part of the cost of furnishing this church was met by the philanthropist, Harutiun Amira Bezjian, the leading layman of the Apostolic community at that time.

[101] That Marouchian was elected directly by Pope Gregory XVI is also the position of Patelos. Cf. *Vatican I et les Évêques Uniates*, Editions Nauwelaerts, Louvain, 1981, 236. Cf. also Tournebize, 'Arménie', *DHGE* XXXI, 339.

[102] Details of the election, including the names of forty-nine of the participants, are to be found in Tcholakian, *L'Église Arménienne Catholique en Turquie,* 32-33.

Andon Hassoun, was to prove one of the most controversial figures in the following decades in the development and direction of the Armenian Catholic Church. So pointed was this move by the papacy that Hassoun was obliged to go secretly to Rome itself for his consecration in order to avoid difficulties anticipated in Constantinople.[103]

Hassoun was to be elected the nation's representative or 'patrik' on 25 July 1845, and thus before he succeeded Marouchian as archbishop. This is evidence that, at least for a time, he did have the confidence of the community at large. However, such confidence was soon dissipated when it was learnt that he had become archbishop, or rather, specifically, that he had been automatically elevated to the see. Marouchian had died shortly after the accession of Pius IX (1792-1878) to the papal throne in June 1846. Presumably, there had been no wide public knowledge of Hassoun having been made coadjutor a few years earlier, or perhaps there had been little understanding of the significance of that term. Consequently, no small discontent arose among the faithful; his succession provoked '…nouvelles remonstrances de la part des grandes familles arméniennes de la ville'.[104] Such moves were not in accord with Armenian tradition. Furthermore, he was forced to resign from his position as 'patrik' on 18 November 1848, as the *millet* could not accept that one and the same ecclesiastic should have two functions.[105]

However, some years later, in order to bring some control into what he considered to be too volatile a system, the pope, despite this setback, pressed the French government to persuade the sultan to recognise Hassoun once again as 'patrik'. The Porte's frustration in attempting to coerce the *millet* to elect a suitable candidate to replace the Antonian,

---

[103] 'En 1838, à la mort de Nouridjian, les laïques arméniens influents de Constantinople manifestèrent au Saint-Siège leur désir de désigner des candidats au siège primatial vacant. Mais, le 9 avril, Grégoire XVI nomma Paul Marouchian; puis, devant les intrigues croissantes des laïques, qui auraient également voulu que le primat reçut le titre de patriarche, il lui donna, en 1842, comme coadjuteur avec droit de succession un personage qui jouera un rôle de premiére importance dans l'histoire de l'Église arménienne unie: Antoine Hassun. Celui-ci se rendit en secret à Rome pour recevoir la consécration épiscopale, en sorte que les laïques furent mis devant le fait accompli.' *Histoire des Conciles,* 504.

[104] De Clercq, *Conciles,* 504. It is worthy of attention that De Clercq already speaks here of the 'intrigues croissantes des laïques'. The word 'intrigues' (or 'intrighi dei laici') is often to be found in the writings of those who opposed any attempt to uphold traditional procedures in the face of that papal resolve that came to manifest itself in the second half of the 19th century.

[105] 'Mgr Hassoun fut contraint de démissionner, la Communauté, fidèle à ses traditions, n'acceptant pas qu'un même ecclésiastique cumulât deux charges.' Tcholakian, *L'Église,* 38.

Fr Gagonian, who had himself resigned from the post on 10 December 1860,[106] finally permitted Hassoun to assume the duties of civic head after his election as patriarch of Cilicia in 1866. Thus was terminated that dual system of internal government that had found little favour with the Holy See, as disagreements were not infrequent between archbishop and 'patrik'. When Hassoun was elected to the patriarchate itself, all powers, civic and spiritual, were then to be concentrated in his hands alone.[107] This development was not greeted sympathetically by many in the *millet*.

In response to a certain turmoil that had now arisen in Constantinople, Pius IX sent the titular archbishop of Side, Innocent Ferrieri, to investigate the general situation at first hand.[108] In consequence, and after consultation with Hassoun, it was recommended that new bishoprics be erected to the number of six. On 30 April 1850,[109] this was accomplished with five dioceses created within Ottoman territory (Angora, Artvin, Bursa, Erzerum, and Trebizond) and one in Persia (Isfahan). At the same time, the names of those who were to hold the sees were announced. It would seem that the new pope was not in favour of lay involvement or intervention in the form of presentation of candidates.[110]

However, the consecration of these new bishops was not easy to accomplish, for the sultan was not willing to accommodate himself to this development.[111] The Ottoman authorities felt aggrieved, for

---

[106] Of the seven elected 'patriks', from 1830 to 1860, the first two died at their post, whilst the remaining five resigned. Cf. Tcholakian, *ibid.*, 38. That so many resignations occurred might indicate the difficulties that were involved in holding this post.

[107] 'Ainsi Mgr Hassoun fusionnera non seulement le pouvoir spirituel et temporel du Siège Primatial, mais aussi les deux obédiences religieuses du Catholicossat de Cilicie et du Siège Primatial d'Istanbul.' Tcholakian, *ibid.*, 39. According to Tournebize, however, this possession of both spiritual and secular powers occurred in 1857. There appears to be some confusion as regards the *berat* of 1857. (Cf. Tcholakian, *ibid.*, 37-38.) It could be that no *berat* had been granted Hassoun by the Porte when he became archbishop in 1846 due to the manner of his appointment and/or the influence of his opponents at Court. What Tournebize takes to be Hassoun's restoration as 'patrik' could have simply been his formal recognition as bishop, in other words as an official within the government system. Indeed, from Tcholakian's list of 'patriks', as already noted, Fr Gagonian resigned from this role only in December, 1860. (*L'Église*, 10)

[108] De Clercq, *Conciles*, 505.

[109] A few months, we may note, before the restoration of the English Catholic Hierarchy, 29 September 1850. The reaction of the sultan and the Porte was not dissimilar to that of the then prime minister, Lord John Russell, with his charge of 'Papal Aggression'.

[110] 'Pie IX ne voulut admettre aucune intervention laïque dans la présentation des candidats; le 30 avril, il érigea les six sièges et en nomma lui-même les titulaires'. De Clercq, *Conciles,* 505.

[111] *Ibid.*, 505-506.

they regarded bishops in general as officers of the imperial machinery and therefore not to be chosen without their agreement, nor was the establishment of new dioceses without prior consultation seen in an amicable light. In consequence, the new bishops were refused permission to take up their responsibilities until French pressure eventually gained their recognition.[112]

Pius IX, following this success and knowing of the support he would continue to receive from Napoleon III, now began to pursue more energetically the task of introducing what he considered to be reforms needed for the Armenian Catholic Church. The manner of electing bishops could not, he believed, be left in hands other than those of the rightful ecclesiastical authorities. In pursuance of this, he issued in 1853 the instruction '*Licet*' whereby he reserved to himself the right to choose, if he thought fit, a person other than the candidates formally presented to him for selection to a vacant see. Yet it does appear from an Instruction issued in the same year by Propaganda that some lay participation would still be tolerated.[113]

Leaving aside the question of the election of Mourachian, which appears to be a matter of dispute, (though the testimony of Tcholakian, the present Armenian Catholic archbishop of Istanbul, appears to carry some weight), let us rather concern ourselves, at this juncture, with the appointment of Hassoun as coadjutor. We may ask what had caused Rome so to act, presumably knowing that by so doing she appeared to be deliberately flouting what was held to be so dear by Armenians in general, thus triggering the first stage of a series of dissensions within the community.

It seems that it might have been to pre-empt the possible effects of the *Hatt-ı Sherif Gülhane* ('*Noble Rescript of the Rose Chamber*') granted by Sultan Abdul Mejid (1839—1861) in the first year of his reign. This was

---

[112] 'Il fallut que l'ambassadeur de Napoléon III intervint pour faire délivrer aux évêques les firmans impériaux.' Tournebize, 'Armenie', *DHGE* XXXI, 340.

[113] 'Une instruction de la Congrégation de la Propagande, le 20 août 1853, régla la question de l'élection des évêques de la province ecclésiastique de Constantinople: le chef civil de la nation arménienne devait réunir une assemblée composée en nombre égal de clercs, séculiers et réguliers (s'il s'en trouvait dans le diocèse), et de laïques, qui devait désigner de six à douze candidats, les réguliers ne pouvant être proposés que dans la proportion d'un tiers; les évêques recommanderaient ensuite au Saint-Siège trois candidats, dont un régulier (s'il en était présenté), ou feraient réunir une nouvelle assemblée s'ils estimaient qu'il n'y avait pas trois candidats dignes d'être recommandés; le Saint-Siège devait élire l'évêque.' (De Clercq, 505-506).

to be the beginning of a series of reforms that came to mark the period known as 'Tanzimat' ('reorganisation' or 'reform'), a period that concluded in 1876 with the accession of Abdulhamid II who had no particular care for such matters. It is generally understood that these reforms were encouraged by the European powers, so as to prevent further Russian interference in the internal affairs of the Ottoman empire.[114]

The Rescript of 1839 guaranteed, among other matters, 'the life, liberty, and property of all the Sultan's subjects'.[115] This gave, at least officially, protection of an individual nature to those subjects, thereby allowing them, should they wish, to be more vocal within their own communities and not liable to be victimised by the whims of their own leaders. Almost inevitably, this would lead to greater democratisation within communal affairs. Thus prerogatives formerly possessed only by leading personalities of the community, such as the amiras, could now be extended to other interested ranks in the *millet*, and especially so to the *esnafs*, or artisans, who had long felt frustration at their exclusion from the governing body of the community. Being grouped into guilds that had become more confident with their economic success, they felt their time had come to participate in the direction of communal affairs. This would also include the question of greater lay involvement in the election of bishops.

In the light of these developments, it could be argued that what might be interpreted as the machinations of the Papacy in regard to the consecration of Hassoun as co-ajutor was possibly a policy meant to avoid the danger of too much democratisation being involved in the future selection of Catholic prelates. This policy was bound to be problematic for the Armenian Catholic Assembly.

Causing further concern to the Catholic Assembly had been that sudden creation of six new dioceses in 1850. Seemingly, Mgr Hassoun had advised Ferrieri and the newly elected Pius IX so to do, in order to strengthen the ecclesiastical 'party' in the face of the powerful lay preponderance within the Catholic community and which held sway in

---

[114] Particular Russian interest in the Ottoman and Persian empires may safely be dated to the reign of Peter the Great (1689-1725) and this interest was further stimulated by the visit of the Armenian hero and adventurer, Israel Ori (d. 1711) who wished to recruit the Tsar's aid for the liberation of Ori's own people. As for Peter: 'En qualité d'empereur chrétien, défenseur du peuple arménien opprimé, il «accepta»—et ses successeurs diront de même—de s'intéresser à ce probleme' (Mécérian, *Histoire et Institutions de l'Église Arménienne*, 121).

[115] Bournoutian, George A, *A History of the Armenian People*, Vol. II, *1500 A.D. to the Present*, Mazda Publishers Inc., Costa Mesa, California, 1994, second printing, 17.

the Assembly. Up to that point, the Armenian Catholic Archdiocese of Constantinople had had no suffragan sees. The almost cavalier disregard for what the Assembly understood as its prerogative in having some influence on the establishment of new sees and on who should occupy such sees was cause for much misgiving. There had been no consultation whatsoever with the *millet*, and, in the Ottoman context, such an event must have seemed shocking.[116]

It is clear that Hassoun was a most faithful devoté of Rome, showing a constant and absolute fidelity to the Holy See. Indeed, later, he was to be the sole Oriental patriarch willing to vote for papal infallibility at the Vatican Council. This and his earlier support for the Bull *Reversurus* earned him even more serious opposition from sections of his own community who resented his continual deference to Rome to the detriment of what was seen to be essential features of Armenian church tradition.[117]

Furthermore, his apparent subservience was in stark contrast to the rebellious Audo, the Chaldean patriarch, who refused to allow that same Bull to be implemented as far as his own flock was concerned[118]

---

[116] One of the points of tension between what we may term the two poles of the community lay in the field of education where, according to Tournebize, the laity wished to deprive the primate of his supervision of the schools. Those who had this in mind, and who were accused of freemasonry, were condemned in 1850 both by the primate and by Rome (*DHGE*, XXXI, 34). The encyclical *Neminem vestrum* (2 February 1854) was an attempt to calm the growing discontent, including, in section 5, the assurance to all and sundry that concerning their educational establishments the Mekhitarists of Venice have 'sent Us a splendid profession of Catholic faith and doctrine.' It appears that the question of 'communicatio in sacris' was still alive and the Holy See much exercised about it.

[117] 'Antoine Hassun, archevêque primat de Constantinople depuis 1846 et plus tard patriarche, est la figure centrale de cette époque: il fait preuve d'une fidélité constante et absolue au Saint-Siège, qu'il met cependent timidement en garde contre des mesures trop hâtives; il est le seul patriarche oriental à voter l'infaillibilité pontificale au concile du Vatican. La bulle *Reversurus* et l'infaillibilité sont les deux occasions d'une opposition contre lui, qui tourne au schisme…' De Clercq, *Conciles,* 499.

[118] 'Dans cette période, Rome développe une ferme politique centralisatrice en donnant tout son appui à Mgr. Hassoun qui, aux yeux d'une grande partie du clergé arménien, devient le symbole même des envies de centralisation romaines.' Maurizio Russo, '"Armenia Missio". Le Manuel du Bon Missionnaire Jésuite. Outils et Méthodes pour la Conversion des Arméniens de l'Empire Ottoman' in Gilbert Meynier and Maurizio Russo (eds), *L'Europe et la Méditerranée*, L'Harmattan, Paris, Presses universitaires de Nancy, Nancy, 1999, 266. 'Joseph Audo, patriarche chaldéen de 1847 à 1878, est d'un tempérament bien different d'Hassun: énergique et personnel, il ne craint pas la révolte ouverte contre le Saint-Siège, spécialement lorsque Pie IX étend les dispositions de la bulle *Reversurus* à son Église' (De Clercq, *Conciles*, 499-500).

and who, it seems, remained self-contained even in the face of a personal scolding from the pope. Such independence of mind would have been inconceivable to his Armenian counterpart, despite his own undoubted strength of character.

It could be said that as far as the Armenian Catholic Church was concerned battle lines were now being well and truly drawn between those who supported Hassoun's position on the one hand and those who were enfuriated by his ready agreement for what they considered to be continuing Roman intrusions into community prerogatives.

Despite these difficulties and tensions, it should continually be borne in mind that Pius and his successors were adamant in their defence of the various oriental liturgies, that no unnecessary changes be made to them, that any tendencies to 'latinisation' be kept at bay. In this, they were clearly in the tradition of Benedict XIV.[119]

Evidence that Pius IX was taking serious interest in the Oriental Churches can be seen in the special commission established by him in Propaganda Fide in 1862 that was to be devoted to their affairs.[120] However, as Frazee points out, the letter of foundation for this commission contained the following: 'The Holy See demands one thing only, that in these rites

[119] Benedict XIV (1740-1758) had been particularly concerned for the Italo-Greeks as well as for the eastern-rite colleges in Rome. Furthermore, he pronounced against the transference of the faithful, for whatever reason, from any Oriental rite to that of the Roman. However, transferring from the latter to the former, was even more strongly prohibited, for, as Frazee informs us (*Catholics and Sultans,* 158-159), there was still the understanding that the Latin-rite was superior to any other: 'In the document *Esti pastoralis* (the Pope) spoke of the Latin rite as enjoying *praestantia,* a 'primacy' over the ancient Oriental churches.' This belief is reiterated in section 20 of his encyclical *Allatae sunt* (July 26, 1755) which claims that the Latin rite should be preferred above all other rites. Nevertheless, the document cautions missionaries not to be blindly over-zealous in their desire to win Christians from the Orthodox and Oriental folds, thus causing further antagonism. The missionaries must not make them give up their own rite. Frazee: 'It is surprising that this pope, so well versed in Eastern Christianity and honestly concerned about its future, saw no contradiction between what he wrote and the Maronite synod of al-Luwayzah, which he sponsored, and which sought to bring that church into complete conformity with Latin practice even on small details' (*Catholics and Sultans*, 159).

[120] The Apostolic Constitution *Romani Pontifices* (6 January 1862). De Clerq: 'D'autre part, le Saint-Siège prête une attention de plus en plus suivie aux affaires de rite oriental: une section spéciale de ce nom est créée, en 1862, dans le sein de la Congrégation de la Propagande et reçoit son secrétaire propre; elle est sans doute pour beaucoup dans les mesures que prend Pie IX pendant les années qui suivent' (*Conciles*, 499).

nothing be introduced which would be contrary to the Catholic faith, dangerous for souls or opposed to virtue.'[121]

A further document of the same year (*Amantissimus*: 8 April 1862) affirmed the legitimacy of having a diversity of rites in the worship of the Church, thus clearly rejecting the position of those who sought uniformity in liturgical expression, especially of such persons as Dom Guérenger (1805-1875). The latter's influence had ensured that various local rites in France had been superseded by that of the Roman. Despite the Benedictine's ultramontanism, that influence was unable to convince the papacy that the same principle should be applied to the Oriental Churches.[122]

In the early days of the disagreements that began to envelope the Armenian Catholic community in Constantinople, the Armenian Catholic patriarch, Krikor Bedros VIII Asdvadzadourian (1843-1866), felt that he too, like the Assembly, had been ignored. Even with the negotiations for the establishment of the Catholic *millet*, the patriarchate had been excluded, much to its chagrin. The creation of new bishoprics under Mgr Hassoun's jurisdiction now prompted the Catholic Catholicos, in his turn, to call a synod of his own bishops in 1851 in order, it is thought, to extend his own sphere of influence.[123] This was actually to be the first Armenian Catholic Synod since the 'formal establishment' of the Church

---

[121] *Catholics and Sultans,* 232. Cf. Adrian Fortescue, *The Uniate Eastern Churches The Byzantium Rite in Italy, Sicily, Syria and Egypt*, Burns, Oates and Washbourne, London, 1923, Introductory chapter: 'Concerning Uniates in General', 1-44. Towards the end of his reign, Pius IX had cause for alarm about changes being introduced in the Greek-Ruthenian rite, by a self-appointed administrator of the diocese of Chelm. In condemnation, he issued the encyclical *Omnem sollicitudines* (13 May 1874).

[122] Referring it appears to yet another encyclical on the matter, Patelos: 'Pie IX ... était bien décidé à respecter les liturgies orientales, et son encyclique du 6 avril 1863 (Note 167), affirmant la légitime diversité des rites, tranchait sur l'opinion courante, défendue encore d'un ton catégorique par dom Guérenger, d'après laquelle l'unité de l'Église devait avoir pour corollaire normal l'uniformité liturgique.', *Vatican I*, 126. (Note 167: Texte dans Gerhard Schneemann, ed. vols 1-6, Theodor Granderath, ed. vol. 7 *Acta et decreta sacrorum conciliorum recetiorum, collectio Lacensis* ... 7 vols., Herder, Freiburg, 1870-1890, t. II, col.558 et ss.).

[123] For further details concerning Krikor Bedros VIII and this particular matter, De Clercq, *Conciles*, 50. For a description of the early struggles over jurisdiction between the first archbishop-primate in Constantinople and Patriarch Krikor Bedros VI—and which clearly places the blame on the ambition of the former, thus throwing a different light on the *raison d'être* of the Council of Bzommar—cf. Tekeyan, *Le Patriarcat Arménien Catholique de Cilicie,* 51-55. There was also dispute over the use of the term 'catholicos' by the patriarchs in the Lebanon: Tekeyan, 57-61.

in 1742.[124] Six bishops participated with the patriarch—those of Adana, Mardin, Amasya, Marash, Kayseri, and Alexandria in Egypt.[125]

The creation of five new bishoprics at the Synod of Bzommar was an event of some magnitude, as the Holy See was not privy to this decision. Three of these dioceses were clearly in the patriarch's own territory—Baghdad, Damascus and Killis. However, the other two, Sivas and Tokat, were on the frontier zones of the Constantinopolitan orbit and could be interpreted as an ambitious ploy to challenge that orbit. There was also the question as to whether this flush of bishops was altogether necessary. Ankara, Tokat, Sivas and Diyarbakir had reasonable numbers of Armenian Catholics, but others, possibly not.[126] This spirit of independence was not entirely appreciated in Rome. Nor was it seen in good part by the Ottomans who often made it difficult for these new prelates to visit their flocks on a regular basis, forcing them to rest for the most part within the confines of Bzommar.

According to De Clercq, however, the patriarchs had actually been given the right to erect dioceses when they thought fit. On 9 July 1759, Propaganda Fide had given them permission to do so, 'dans la mesure des nécessités'.[127] Whether this proviso was justly appreciated in this particular case is perhaps open to question. However, by another decree, that of 22 April 1769, Tokat had indeed been placed within the patriarch's jurisdiction.

De Clercq has pointed out how influential the 1736 Maronite Synod of Mount Lebanon (otherwise known as 'al-Luwyzah') was on the direction and decisions of Bzommar. This was largely due to the

---

[124] There had been, however, the Synod of Lvov of 1689, but with only one Armenian bishop present, Vartan Hunanian, he of the said city, patron of Arakelian, and successor to the controversial Nicholas Torosowicz (d. 1681). The proceedings had been presided over by the Nuncio to the Polish court, Mgr Cantelmi. On this occasion, at Bzommar, no Latin emmissary was involved.

[125] The Synod issued 200 canons under 12 chapters. The substance of those chapters may be found in De Clercq, *Conciles*, 508-518.

[126] Sivas and Tokat were often combined both before and after the schism. There appear to be certain anomalies as regards a number of these bishoprics which are difficult to disentangle; cf. Tcholakian, *L'Eglise*, 59-63.

[127] 'Un décret de la Congrégaton de la Propagande, du 30 avril 1759, limita l'autorité du patriarche de Cilicie à l'Arménie Mineure, à la Cappodoce et à la Syrie.; une décision du 9 juillet lui permit d'ériger des diocèses dans la mesure des nécessités; un décret du 20 juillet 1760 ajouta au patriarcat la Mésopotamie; un autre, du 22 avril 1769, y joignit les régions de Tokat et de Perkenik en Asie Mineure.' (*Ibid.*, 503-504.)

fact that no less a person than Abraham Ardzivian had been invited to participate.[128] That he was able so to do indicates something of the esteem in which he was held by the Maronites, and explains their willingness to give refuge to him once again after it had proved impossible to establish himself at Constantinople.

It was, however, with the election, already referred to, on 18 September 1866, of Archbishop Hassoun himself as no less than the Catholicos of Cilicia (taking the name Andon Bedros IX) that matters began to go seriously awry. To begin with, his election to that office by eight bishops of the Cilician jurisdiction, an election, we may notice, presided over by the then Latin Patriarch of Jerusalem, the forceful Mgr Valerga, who had conveyed the Holy See's strong wish to unite the two jurisdictions without further ado—was thereby seen by many Armenian Catholics as yet further interference by Rome. The latter had sought, as she had done before (and was to do later), to rationalise an uneasy situation, but, at the same time, seeming to ignore the sensitivities of the communities concerned.

Furthermore, the Bull *Reversuru'*, of the following year (12 July 1867), not only confirmed the election and the amalgamation of the two jurisdictions, but also established that the seat of the catholicosate was henceforth to be in Constantinople itself.[129] Thus from the point of view both of the Holy See and of Mgr Hassoun, the inconvenience of having two jurisdictions, often at odds, would be resolved, whilst the relocation of the catholicosate from the periphery of imperial affairs to the administrative heart of the empire, where it was felt it should have been a century before, would enable it to be more effective and influential. It was there, as we have gathered, that the largest and most prestigious Armenian Catholic

---

[128] 'Le concile maronite du Mont-Liban tenu en 1736, qui avait toujours joui d'une grande faveur chez les Arméniens catholiques, du fait que leur premier patriarche en avait signé les actes, servit de source aux canons de Bzommar. La plupart du temps, les textes maronites ont été servilement copiés. Quelques interpolations ou canons originaux concernent des situations particulières à l'Église d'Arménie ou ajoutent le témoignage des anciens textes arméniens, et même d'auteurs latins modernes.' (*Ibid.*, 507). Also present at that first Maronite synod had been Joseph Assemani (1687-1768), the Orientalist, who on that occasion '… used his influence to bring his countrymen into closer connection with Rome.' (*The Oxford Dictionary of the Christian Church*, Third Edition, 1997, 115.)

[129] The Latin text of *'Reversurus'* may be found in Mansi, *Synodi Orientales, 1806-1867*, doc. no. 26, 1025-1032.

community was to be found. In addition, the *millet's* representative to the Porte had necessarily to reside in the capital.

Such decisions simply left the communities concerned with a *fait accompli* to which many did not take kindly. There had been, in all these developments, no lay representation, no rank and file clergy involvement. This, too, had been engineered with the obvious acquiescence of Mgr Hassoun who, being somewhat authoritarian by temperament, found it difficult to collaborate with so independent-minded a body as the National Assembly. The new catholicos-primate was therefore viewed by many of his co-religionists as betraying the Armenian inheritance yet further and thereby conforming himself to that caricature whereby, as has already been pointed out, Armenian Catholics were often described by their co-nationals as 'cut-tails'.

Those bishops gathered in Rome to witness Hassoun receiving the pallium and to be the first to understand the import of the Bull were not able to reach any consensus as to how the Armenian Catholic Church was to order its house in future, for it was not only with the question of amalgamation that the Bull *Reversurus* had caused misgivings. There was also the sensitive matter of episcopal elections. The pope, '… usant de son droit souverain',[130] decreed that the laity and the ordinary clergy could only bear witness to the personal qualities of those candidates for the episcopate that had already been chosen by the synod of bishops. In addition, the pope retained the right to choose someone apart from those being presented by the synod for any particular see. As regards the election of new patriarchs, they could only be elected by the bishops. Furthermore, they could not be enthroned or exercise any of their patriarchal functions prior to their being confirmed by the pope, nor before they had received the pallium. There was also the injunction that no major decisions concerning ecclesiastical property could be executed without the permission of the Holy See.

Frazee describes shortly and bluntly the total effect that the Bull would have not only on the Armenian Catholic Church but also on Eastern Christians not in union with Rome: '… Pius issued the decree *Reversurus* for Armenian Catholics which, more than any other previous display of Roman authority, frightened the Orthodox hierarchy in the East, since it

[130] Tournebize, 'Armenie', *DHGE* XXXI, 340.

effectively removed the administrative autonomy of that church.' It was also meant as 'a model for other Eastern Catholic churches'.[131]

Elsewhere Frazee comments, '*Reversurus* attempted to rewrite the agreement between East and West made at the Council of Florence. In this regard it was a dangerous document, destroying the balance between Western and Eastern traditions, and placing one more hurdle in the way of church unity.'[132]

Not surprisingly, opposition was fast and furious. According to Tournebize, this was encouraged by the adversaries to papal infallibility as well as by certain unnamed powers hostile to the traditional French protectorate of the Catholic Church in the region.[133] In an attempt to find a solution to the serious predicament in which the Church now found itself, Mgr Hassoun summoned a National Synod to meet in July, 1869.[134]

The Antonian monks, led by their abbot, Placid Kasandjian, were to be the most vocal of those opposed to Mgr Hassoun and to '*Reversurus*'. The Synod heard their complaints, as well as the viewpoints of those in favour of the new dispensation. Reference was especially made to the document's categorical refusal to allow anyone not in episcopal orders to be involved in the election of bishops and patriarchs, and where the prime role of the oriental patriarchs appeared to be merely that of representatives of papal authority in their particular territories. Further, there was the imposition of the visit *ad limina apostolorum*, as well as the submission of

---

[131] *Catholics and Sultans*, 233.

[132] *Ibid.*, 274.

[133] *Arménie*, 340. It may be interesting to note that the position and influence of Mgr Valerga in the region was of some concern to France as he was of Sardinian nationality.

[134] Viewing, on Friday, 4 July 1869, what must have been an impressive procession of Armenian Catholic prelates as they accompanied relics of St Gregory the Illuminator (granted them at the pope's request from the church of San Gregorio Armeno in Naples) to the new cathedral of Sainte-Marie in Pera, it would have been difficult to imagine that in reality there was any serious dispute among them. Apart from Hassoun, there were nine archbishops, two abbots (of the Venetian Mekhitarists and of the Antonians), and six bishops. One of the six secretaries was no less a person than Ormanian. The following day the synod commenced. Cf. Tcholakian, *L'Église*, 309-311. Cf. also Anatolio Latino, *Gli Armeni e Zeitun*, Bernado Seeber, Firenze, 1899, 272, who adds the Abbot of the Viennese Mekhitarists to the list. Latino continues, with little sympathy for the point of view of Hassoun's critics: 'Ma poichè non mancano mai i perturbatori ed i perversi che creano disordini nelle umana società, si formò tosto un partito contro il nuovo patriarca. Lo accusarono di aver violati i diritti di alcuni; minacciarono di non più prestargli obbedienza; dissero che il Papa non può restringere i diritti degli Orientali, che questi non sono obbligati ad obbedirgli in punti di disiplina, ecc.; mentre la giurisdizione del sommo pontefice su tutta la chiesa universale, anche nei punti di disciplina, trovasi affermata nelle definizioni dei due concilii ecumenici, fiorentino e vaticano.'

reports on the state of their jurisdictions, obligations that all Latin bishops were already accustomed to perform.

These developments seem to reflect the adoption of a more inflexible attitude on the part of the Roman authorities towards the Oriental Churches. Patelos suggests that there was a strong inclination to impose the discipline of the Latin rite on those Churches, an inclination stemming from a desire for greater centralisation. Not that this would affect liturgical celebrations, for these were protected, as we have seen, by the Holy See itself. Rather did the concern lie with the structures and institutions of those Churches that were felt to harbour a tendency to schism.[135] Patelos in his treatment of the Commission for the Oriental Churches and the Missions that was established to help prepare for the Vatican Council summoned by Pius IX states clearly that such sentiments dominated the Commission[136] and that part of the task it set itself was to apply wherever possible the disciplinary measures of the Council of Trent to the Oriental Churches.[137] The heavy-handed approach of Mgr Pluym (1808-1874), the vicar apostolic in Constantinople, to ensure that the desire of the Holy See be implemented, only exacerbated the tense situation.[138]

As no compromise was forthcoming between the two parties in the Synod, despite seventy-nine sessions on the matter, the patriarch suspended the proceedings. The prelates were now preparing to leave for Rome to attend the Vatican Council, and it was hoped that the coming interlude would provide time for calmer reconsideration.

---

[135] '... les courants centralisateurs conduisaient à l'idée d'appliquer la discipline latine chez les Orientaux, puisque leur législation était si mal connue. Cette conception a été renforcée par l'idée que l'attachement des Orientaux à leurs antiques structures et institutions cachait une tendance au schisme, et qu'il fallait donc bien arriver à changer graduellement l'ancienne discipline.' Patelos, *Vatican I et les Eveques Uniates*, 127.

[136] '... la tâche essentielle de la commission consister à étudier ce qui, dans les décrets disciplinaires du concile de Trente, pouvait être appliqué dans les Églises unies d'Orient.' *Ibid.*, 128.

[137] 'La composition de la commission pour les Églises orientales et les Missions...reflète le climat et les idées regnant à cette époque à Rome sur l'Orient. C'est dans ce climat que se sont déroulées les délibérations de la commission.' *Ibid.*, 126.

[138] 'Mgr. Pluym (1808-1874) fut nommé vicaire général du patriarcat latin de Constantinople et délégué apostolique pour les rites orientaux avec le titre d'archevêque titulaire de Thyane. Son nom fut directement lié à la crise arménienne qui éclata à Constantinople contre l'application de la bulle *Reversurus*. Ignorant les traditions et la sensibilité orientales, il essayé d'appliquer, sans aucune souplesse ni compréhension de la situation locale, les directives de la Propagande et, de ce fait, il contribua au schisme au sein de l'Église arménienne.' *Ibid.*, 395-396.

During the Council,[139] the so-called 'dissidents' sent representatives to Rome to express their loyalty to the Holy See, but also to seek a revision of the import of *Reversurus*. Abbot Kasanjian, a participant at the Council, was naturally supportive of their views, but that support was not pleasing to the papal authorities. Those authorities then went so far as to place an 'injunction' on the Antonian monastery in Rome. Its denizens, however, claimed Ottoman protection—they were Ottoman citizens and the appropriate flag had always been displayed.[140] As a further response, Kasanjian and two of his episcopal colleagues, slipping away by night, returned to their sees, convinced, along with a powerful section of the Armenian Catholic community, that their Church was being drained of its autonomy, an autonomy that had seemingly been protected under previous papacies.

This matter appeared to become more urgent as there was an ever- growing possibility that the Council would indeed eventually pass a decree supporting papal infallibility.[141] According to Frazee, Hassoun and eleven Armenian bishops finally signed for the promulgation of such a definition.[142] Many other Eastern Catholic prelates did not, leaving Rome, not in the same charged frame of mind as Kasanjian, but simply to avoid voting 'non placet'—they had no further serious intent.

What could be said to have exacerbated the problem between the two factions in the Armenian Catholic community was the growing consciousness of the Armenian people in general of their past history and achievements. This to some extent was the fruit of the gradual influence of the 18th-century European Enlightenment. Causing some discomfort

---

[139] The Council was opened on 8 December 1869, and formally suspended on 20 October 1870.

[140] It was not unusual for Ottoman diplomats, a number of whom were Armenian, to pay visits to the monastery. The Ottoman flag also flew over the island of San Lazarro.

[141] Sensing that a schism was a strong possibility, Pius IX had acted quickly to a Declaration of Faith (6 February 1870) published in Constantinople by the disaffected clergy and laity. An Apostolic letter, *Non sine gravissimo*, was issued on 24 February, and a second letter, *Quo impensore*, on 20 May of the same year, thus during the very Council itself. A day by day description by an Anglican observer of the atmosphere in Rome and the development of the proceedings of the Council, though with a great deal of wry comment, is be found in the Revd Thomas Mozley's. *Letters from Rome on the Occasion of the Oecumenical Council, 1869-1870*, 2 Vols., Longmans, Green, London, 1891. Mozley was the correspondent for *The Times*, and specially appointed for the event. He deals specifically with the Armenian problem, not without some glee, in the second volume, 185, 191 and 192.

[142] *Sultans and Catholics*, 236.

to the more independent party within the Catholic fold, as opposed to the party sympathetic to what had become the more focused intentions of Rome, were the events that were happening contemporaneously within the much larger Armenian Apostolic *millet*.[143]

This was the steady growth towards a more formal constitutional system within the *millet*, a process encouraged by the ambiance created by 'Tanzimat' to which reference has already been made. The process itself had been given further ratification by yet another proclamation of Abdul Mejid, that of the *Hatt-i Hümayun* ('The Imperial Rescript') of February 1856. This had received international confirmation at the Congress of Paris on 30 March of the same year. Turkey, one of the final victors of the Crimean War (1853-1856), was here welcomed, and possibly largely so due to the Rescript, as an equal member of the Concert of Europe.

The practical consequence of this process had begun some fifteen years earlier when, by order of a *firman* of 1841, which itself was the fruit of the *Gülhane* Rescript of 1839, a council of laymen was elected to help control the affairs of the *millet*, so that they were not entirely in the hands of the amiras. This step was not successful, for the council '... became nothing but a centre of continuous intrigue and controversy. The patriarch was transformed into an obedient instrument in its hands.'[144] The *esnafs*, though they now represented a powerful financial constituency within the community, had, as we have mentioned earlier, no say in decisions that affected that community. Their recourse to the sultan concerning this omission effected a change in 1844 whereby the patriarch was able to elect fourteen *esnaf* representatives from their guilds out of the total of thirty members that sat on the Supreme Council.[145]

An important milestone in the process of democratisation for the Armenian Apostolic *millet* was reached with the establishment in 1847 of a Civil Council, a development confirmed by a *firman*, dated 9

---

143 'Political consciousness within the Armenian Catholic community was growing at the time when Pope Pius IX was attempting to appropriate to himself all the decision-making privileges of the Eastern churches. It was not long before a clash occurred'(Frazee, *Catholics and Sultans*, 264).

144 Salahi Ramsdan Sonyel, *The Ottoman Armenians. Victims of Great Power Diplomacy*, K Rustem & Brother, London, 1987, 18.

145 *Ibid*. For a detailed examination of the *esnafs*, cf. Artinian, *The Armenian Constitutional System in the Ottoman Empire, 1839-1863*. 24-29. Of particular interest was the invitation of Patriarch Golod, over a century before, for leaders of the *esnafs* to participate in the election of a new Catholicos for Etchmiadzin that took place in Constantinople in 1725 (28).

March 1847.[146] The Council consisted of twenty members elected by the aforementioned *esnafs*. Although the patriarch held the presidency of this body, as he did of the Spiritual Council, also established in that year, he could not make a decision without the agreement of its members. Indeed, Patriarch Madteos II was heavily criticised the following year for attempting to conceal a certain financial transaction. Concerning the election of his successor in 1848, it was the people who wished to pronounce on the matter *'en souverain'*.[147] Despite these advances, '… they in no way satisfied the aspirations of the *Jeune Arménie*, or the liberal and educated party who continued to work and agitate for a more popular and democratic form of administration.'[148]

Another contributing factor to the movement for greater democratisation within the Armenian *millet* was the influence of Protestantism. As Artinian points out, '…the predominant lay control, which was the essence of the organization of the Protestant community, furnished an example to the Armenian nationals.' With copies of the Protestant constitution in circulation, '… the central administration of the Armenian *millet* came to realize that increased lay participation in *millet* affairs would be imperative to prevent more defections to Protestantism.'[149]

In the meantime, according to Tuğlacı, a Legislative Assembly had been established in 1849 by that Assembly of Representatives that had come into being with the Catholic *millet* almost twenty years before. This new body consisted of twenty-five members and was presided over by the 'Patrik'. Having drawn up a statute for its own community, they presented it to the Sultan who approved it by *firman* on 23 December 1849. It was titled, *Nizamname-i Meclis-i Millet-i Katolikan* ('Statute of the Assembly of the Catholic Community').[150] However, the spiralling conflict that marked the following fifteen years must have made this Statute of little effect, the final fusion of the roles of 'patrik' and 'patriarch' presumably altering its import irrevocably.

---

[146] Sonyel, *The Ottoman Armenians*, 18.

[147] Tournebize, *DHGE*, XXVIII, 336.

[148] *Ibid.* Nevertheless, the decline of Amira influence is clearly demonstrated by comparing the membership of the first Civil Council of 1847 with that of 1855: the former comprised nine Amiras, ten *esnaf* representatives and the 'logothete' (acting as both chairman and secretary); Only two Amiras were to be found on the Council of 1855. (Artinian, *The Armenian Constitutional System in the Ottoman Empire,* 75-77.)

[149] *The Armenian Constitutional System in the Ottoman Empire*, 44.

One of the important effects of the reform of the *Hatt-ı Hümayun* of 1856, apart from the abolition of the poll tax, the *jizre*, would have been a further curtailment of the powers of the 'patriks'. This was certainly the case with the Armenian Apostolic *millet*, achieved by giving an official stamp of approval to the process of democratisation now underway, and by expecting, and not simply encouraging, further lay representation. This process was then meant to be enshrined in a written constitution to protect the rights of all concerned. Such a document, the Armenian National Constitution (*Nizamname-i Millet-i Ermeniye*) of 1860, was finally approved by the Ottoman government in 1863 after the latter had made a number of alterations and additions to the original. The Constitution substantially placed the control of the *millet* in the hands of the new economic power in the community—the *esnafs*—and allowed representation to be made even from the provinces. By this means in every diocese the bishop was to be chosen by local councils, laymen forming six sevenths of the membership. This was not welcomed by those in the community who had benefited from their previous privileged status, the conservative aristocracy,[151] but was so by the new liberal middle-class.

The promulgation of the Constitution[152] was, in a sense, very much in tune with Armenian tradition, for it continued the principle of lay participation in the affairs and administration of the Armenian Church, though in the present case the constituency was far wider. What may be understood as the foundation of this principle may be seen as dating from the time of Gregory the Illuminator himself, but not followed in exactly that manner throughout the centuries that followed: 'The first bishop of the Church was elected by a gathering of princes, provincial governors, military chiefs, and prominent freemen. No clergy are mentioned as having

---

[150] *Istanbul Ermeni Kiliseleri*, 287. A copy of the text is provided on 368-369 (Document 101). A question of interest arises here as to the manner of the election of this Legislative Assembly. It remains unclear as to whether Catholic *esnafs* had any say in these developments, as their co-nationals appear to have done in the Apostolic equivalent of 1847.

[151] 'Certaines hautes personnalités chrétiennes de Constantinople, prélats orthodoxes et financiers arméniens, bénéficiaires des privilèges et prébendes de l'antique régime, accueillent d'ailleurs mal cette évolution libérale et ce projet de réforme démocratique des communautés: ce sont des Chrétiens qui mèneront l'agitation la plus vive contre l''auguste écrit''. (The latter refers to the 'Imperial Rescript') (Pierre Rondot, *Les Chrétiens d'Orient*, 85.) As to the 'National Constitution of the Armenians in the Turkish Empire', a copy of the text may be found in Lynch, *Armenia. Travels and Studies*, Vol. 2, Appendix 1, 445-467.

[152] It is generally understood that the Armenian Constitution formed the basis of the Ottoman Constitution of 1876, the one proclaimed reluctantly by the then new Sultan, Abdulhamid II. Details of the Constitution are given in Sonyel, *The Ottoman Armenians,* 21-22.

taken part or even as having been present in the electoral meeting. This does not mean that there were no clergymen in the country, but rather that they had no part in the events that led to the conversion of the king and inaugurated the greatest event in the history of the nation.'[153]

Despite the laity's interest and participation in the life of their Church, there was a clear demarcation between the secular and the sacred aspects of that Church, and it was to the former that the laity generally applied themselves. It was along similar lines that many Armenian Catholics understood their involvement in their own Chuch's affairs. Even from a simple human point of view the loss of the ability to so participate meant loss of face before their fellow Armenians whose accusations of Rome's ultimate lack of respect for Armenian custom was only too clearly being demonstrated. The proclamation of the Rescript was therefore to have serious effect on the expectations of Armenian Catholics as indeed it did on all the Christian minorities in the empire.[154]

The development of greater rather than less lay representation and participation, in both the spiritual and secular domains of the Apostolic *millet*, was in stark contrast to the apparent designs of Rome to spirit away certain traditional processes familiar to, and beloved by the Armenian community, and which were still active within the 'Katolik *millet*'[155] itself. The contrast between the achievement embodied in the Armenian National Constitution and the import of *Reversurus,* though only four years apart, must indeed have seemed momentous.

In addition, such processes had now received the complete sanction of the Ottoman State, and to oppose those processes must therefore have

---

[153] Nersoyan, *Laity*. 99. Cf. Artinian, *The Armenian Constitutional System*, 19: 'Clerical exclusiveness has been alien to the Armenian church.'

[154] 'La publication du *Hatti-Houmayyoum* du février 1856 et sa confirmation internationale par le congrès de Paris le 30 mars suivant, sont à la base de la régénération des Églises uniates et en général du christianisme oriental contemporain au Proche-Orient. Les chrétiens de l'empire ottoman ont en effet trouvé dans les dispositions libérales de ce firman à leur égard une situation politique favourable, même si les tracasseries administratives locales étaient frequentes et si l'hostilité non dissimulée des musulmans allait parfois jusqu'à l'émeute.' (Patelos: *Vatican I*, 378).

[155] An example of lay participation in Church decisions in the Crimea, just prior to the Council of Florence, and a participation not inimical to Rome: 'On 12 May 1439 a kind of synod of the Armenians, composed of the Bishop Malachus with twenty-one priests, two monks and fourteen laymen, agreed at a meeting with a committee of the local Italian officials to send an envoy to the Pope whether or not their patriarch assented, though they stipulated too for an interval of three months while a messenger went to him to seek his approval.' (Gill, *The Council of Florence*, 305.)

been cause for an undercurrent of dissatisfaction to be present in that State's views of, and dealings with, the Holy See. The influence of France and its continuing support of the papacy in the Orient, and therefore of Hassoun himself, meant that the Ottoman authorities were somewhat hampered in their wish to have the Catholic *millet* arranged in the same manner as its apostolic equivalent. However, it is clear that this was not the case in the earlier period of Pio Nono's reign when designs to re-establish the Latin patriarchate of Jerusalem met the approval of the sultan. On 3 October 1847, not only was it announced that the patriarchate had been formally restored, but also that diplomatic relations with the Ottoman authorities had been resumed.[156]

Serious opposition to Mgr Hassoun and to what has commonly been described as the papal government's ultramontane style, continued unabated, despite Rome's appeals and admonitions. Finally, according to Latino, on 2 November 1870, the pope, through the special offices of the Constantinopolitan Apostolic Vicar, Mgr Pluym, declared that the Antonian Abbot, as well as three bishops and a forty five other clergy, both secular and religious, had all incurred canonical penalties.[157] But the loss of prestige suffered by France, due to her recent defeat at the hands of Prussia, meant a temporary weakening of support for Mgr Hassoun

---

[156] 'Les 3 octobre 1847, Pie IX annonça un succès politique: la reprise des relations diplomatiques avec le gouvernement ottoman qui autorisait le rétablissement d'un patriarcat latin à Jerusalem, dont le titulaire, Mgr Valerga, aurait des pouvoirs étendus sur tous les catholiques de l'Empire. Il faut noter que les autorités turques étaient arrivées à cette position parce qu'elles «supportaient de plus en plus impatiemment la politique des ambassadeurs d'Angleterre, de Russie et surtout de France, qui sous prétexte de protéger leurs coreligionnaires, travaillaient souvent à favoriser les intérêts temporels de leurs gouvernments.»' (note 95, R Aubert, *Le pontificat de Pie IX [1846-1878]* Tournai, Desclée, 1952 21-22, Patelos, *Vatican I et les Eveques Uniates*, 107-108). Though it is not altogether clear as to when relations between the Ottoman empire and the Holy See had been broken, the Latin patriarchal vicar, as a step in furthering relations, though not on any formal diplomatic level, was to be given the office and title of Apostolic Delegate in 1868. cf. *Roma-Armenia,* 349. For the reasons behind this development in the policy of the Holy See as regards both the Ottoman empire and the Oriental Catholics, cf. Del Zanna, *Roma e l'Oriente. Leone XIII e l'Impero Ottomano (1878-1903)*, Guerini e Associati, Milano, 2003, 91-99. The date given here is 1867 with the Pontifical Brief, *Iam inde*. We may note the importance, in the late 1870s, of Mgr Stepanos Azarian in these matters, but also the fear felt in Rome that if he, as an Oriental Catholic, were to be the Delegate, he might prove too independent. Shortly thereafter, in 1881, he was to be elected to the Armenian Catholic patriarchate.

[157] *Gli Armeni e Zeitun*, 273. According to Ciril Korolovskij, the forty five clergy in question consisted of eighteen Antonian monks, twelve Mekhitarists of Venice, two ex-alumni of Propaganda, eight secular priests and five missionaries of the Bzommar congregation ('Armena, Chiesa', *Enciclopedia Italiana*, Istituto Giovanni Treccani, Milano, 1929, Vol. IV, 428.)

and his party at the Porte.[158] Indeed, even before the disaster at Sedan (1 September 1870), it is said that Napoleon III, for a number of reasons, had become irritated with the pope and had instructed his Ambassador to press the Ottoman government for the recognition of the minority, though rebellious, faction. The latter took advantage and obtained the withdrawal of the patriarch's *berat* of appointment, choosing instead Bishop Bahdiarian as their leader. Thus a schism was now in place. In response to this, the Nuncio to Spain, Alessandro Franchi, was sent to negotiate with the Grand Vizier, Ali Pasha, who seemed sympathetic to the papal cause. The sudden death of the Ottoman minister, however, meant in effect the continuance and strengthening of the secessionist group.

Their new leader, by also entitling himself Bedros IX—thereby, effacing, as it were, the 'cartouche' of Mgr Hassoun—was perhaps meaning to indicate thereby that despite both his excommunication and his illicit consecration of four new bishops, the situation was not meant to be definitive.[159] For the point of contention that concerned the anti-Hassounite party, as they continually pointed out, was one of discipline rather than one of doctrine. Their opponents, on the other hand, supported the view that the pope's prerogatives included supervision of both doctrinal and disciplinary matters throughout the Universal Church.

The Porte was either not accommodating in extending the *berat* to Bishop Bahdiarian as 'Patrik' or the 'neo-schismatics' themselves,[160] wishing for a return to the dual principle of previous days, chose, in a separate election held in May 1871, Bishop Kupelian, one of the above four,

---

[158] The ability of the Great Powers to intervene on behalf of the missionaries was sometimes limited by the lack of any exact legal instrument by which to do so: 'Le problème est que *le bras sèculier* auquel les missionnaires peuvent recourir, la diplomatie francaise, est décidément moins influent de ce qu'on croit normalement. Les diplomates n'ont pas toujours l'instrument légal pour intervenir, car le Protectorat plus qu'un droit est une tradition politique. Il est donc déterminé par le poids politique conjoncturel de la nation protectrice.' Russo, 'Armenia Missio', 274.

[159] On 11 March 1871, the pope, by the Apostolic letter, *Ubi prima*, had declared excommunicate Mgr Bahdiarian and all those who had elected him Patriarch. Kupelian, who was to be elected 'Patrik' the following May, had already been excommunicated on the authority of the Apostolic Delegate for Mesopotamia, for encouraging the schismatical movement in the Diyarbakir region. It appears that further condemnations emanated from Rome on 14 June 1872.

[160] The term was used by Pius IX to describe those had challenged Hassoun and himself and had created a separate hierarchy.

for that post and was recognised as such by the Porte.[161] Thus Bahdiarian acted for spiritual affairs and Kupelian for the breakaway community's relations with the State. It was the latter personality who, with the aid of the secular arm, was able to intensify pressure on those who wished to remain loyal to Hassoun whose banishment was finally engineered in July 1872. In the meanwhile more churches and other properties were sequestrated for their use.

Probably due to the confused dynastic situation that marked the year 1876,[162] Mgr Hassoun was enabled to return Constantinople, and that with the blessing of the ageing Pius. Though he was once again afforded recognition by the Porte, opposition remained as sharp as ever. Consequently, Leo XIII (1878-1903) recalled him to Rome, presumably reluctantly, and granted him the Red Hat in 1880.[163] The following year,

---

[161] It is sometimes stated that the election took place in May, 1872, though to leave such an election so late would be puzzling. F-H Kruger supports 1871 ('Hassoun', *La Grande Encyclopedia*, H Lamirault et Cie, Paris, no date, Vol. 19, 907) as does Cyril Korolevskij ('Armena,Chiesa', *Enciclopedia Italiana*, Vol. IV, 423-429). Of no small interest, however, may be the following from the same article by Kruger: 'Lorsque le patriarche (Hassoun) se rendit à Rome pour le concile de 1870, les mécontents constituèrent l'Église catholique arménienne orientale, que la Porte, sur l'avis de l'ambassadeur français, reconnut ainsi que le nouveau patriarche, Ovham Koupélian, élu en mai 1871. Ce schisme, englobant un tiers environ des arméniens unis, dura jusq'en mars 1879; alors, le sultan, sollicité par l'Autriche et par la France mieux informée, extorqua sa démission à Koupélian.'

[162] Sultan Abdulaziz had been deposed by the Young Ottomans in May 1876. His nephew Murat assumed power, but shortly thereafter was declared unfit due to a nervous breakdown. It was Murat's younger brother, Abdulhamid, who succeeded him that same year.

[163] Though it is often understood that he was the first Oriental to receive the Red Hat since John Bessarion (1403-1472) (cf. *Catholics and Sultans*, 269), it appears that Michael Lewykyj (1815-1858), Archbishop of Lemburg/Lvov received the same distinction in 1856, the first Ukrainian-rite prelate to be so honoured. Cf. Owen Chadwick, *A History of the Popes. 1830-1914*, Clarendon Press, Oxford, 1998, 117. Cf. also Attwater, *The Christian Churches of the East.* Vol.1, *Churches in Communion with Rome*, Thomas More Books, St Helens, Lancashire, 1961, 76. Also his footnote: 'Very few Orientals have been made cardinals. The office is radically in relation to the local church at Rome: that is why they are called 'Cardinals of the Holy Roman Church.' After a somewhat tumultuous life, Cardinal Hassoun was to die peacefully in Rome in 1884. Apart from contributing to the foundation of the Armenian College in that city in 1881, a further legacy of the Cardinal to the Armenian Catholic Church was to be the Congregation of the Armenian Sisters of the Immaculate Conception, which, in conjunction with Mother Serpouhe Hadji-Andonian, he had founded in 1847 '... à l'instar des filles de la Charité.' (Tournebize, *DHGE*, 351) These sisters are still active in education in a number of places throughout the diaspora as well as, more recently, in Armenia itself.

Stepanos Azarian was elected patriarch and was accorded recognition by both the pope and the Ottoman government.[164]

Fortune, though, had by now changed for the 'neo-schismatics'. The defeat of Turkey at the hands of Russia in 1878, the Treaty of San Stefano and the Conference of Berlin, as well as the closure of the Ottoman parliament by an exasperated Abdulhamid, spelled a gradual loss of interest and support for the movement.[165] The French Republican government, whatever its views on and treatment of the Catholic Church at home, wished to maintain its influence in the Orient by acting as the protector of Catholic interests in that region and therefore had turned decidedly in favour of Rome's point of view. In addition, Pope Leo was altogether more conciliatory than his predecessor. Finally, Kupelian and most of his companions sought and received pardon from the Holy See in March, 1879, the former, significantly, requesting a personal audience with the pope to affect his reconciliation. This was granted him the following month, on April 18, though with all the Curial cardinals present.[166] Later, between 1880 and 1881, Bahdiarian and even Abbot Kasanjian were finally reconciled. The schism was at an end,[167] but the loss of many of

[164] According to Tournebize, Hassoun's successor, Azarian '... poursuivit non sans succès l'œuvre de réconciliation, grâce à quelques adoucissements apportés par Pie IX (1877-1878) et par Léon XIII (1887) à la bulle *Reversurus*.' ('Antonins', *DHGE*, 870.) What these 'sweeteners' might have been is not made clear, though the more nuanced approach of Leo's pontificate helped to lessen hostility, for he abandoned 'il disegno del suo predecessore di sopprimere ovunque ogni autonomia nella scelta dei vescovi di tutti le chiese orientali' (Korolevskij, 'Armena, Chiesa', 428). Russo, however, states categorically that 'En 1879, Rome accepte en même temps de renoncer au "*Reversurus*" et de remplacer Mgr. Hassoun, qui, en 1880, est obligé d'abandonner sa charge de patriarche.' ('Armenia Missio', 266) It remains uncertain as to whether Rome actually ever 'renounced' the Bull as such; rather, it would seem, was it gradually placed to one side. We may note here that Russo also informs us that the Ottoman government, at the behest of a number of influential Armenian Catholics, had 'annulled' the Papal Bull as early as 1872 *(ibid.)*. As to the exact significance of the date 1887, given by Tournebize, it has not yet been identified. There was, however, the encyclical of Pius IX, *Quartus supra*, (6 January 1873), already referred to, that endeavored to answer objections to '*Reversurus*', but it is difficult to interpret its general tone as being an aid to the process of reconciliation.

[165] It would appear that the defeat of Turkey by Russia in 1878, '... favorisa l'extinction du schisme' (Tournebize, 'Arménie', *DHGE* 342).

[166] 'Il sacerdote Cupelian parti per Roma, fece ammenda del suo passato, fu nominato vescovo ordinante, ed ora vive in quella città nell'ospizio di San Biagio degli Armeni', Latino, *Gli Armeni e Zeitun*, 273.

[167] However, it was not until 1887 that the last church still in the hands of a number of 'neo-schismatics' was finally returned to the Catholic party (cf. Korolevskij, 'Armena, Chiesa', 428). It appears, though, that other properties remained in their hands. This seems to be evidence that discontent was still current and indeed, as we shall see, would manifest itself with the opportunity that the Young Turk *coup d'état* of 1908 was to present.

the Antonians, especially Ormanian, was a grievous embarrassment. The Order never recovered.

Calm—tension—catastrophe

Despite the growth of revolutionary movements towards the end of the century[168] and the sufferings that the Armenian people had to endure under the Hamidian regime (1876-1908), or indeed due to these very factors, the Catholic authorities maintained a low profile, preferring to make no move that was thought might further aggravate the situation.[169] There was in addition, perhaps, a certain sense of exhaustion after the turmoil of the Hassoun years.[170]

However, the internal affairs of the Catholic community were not neglected, for in 1888, prior to the worst excesses of the regime, the Armenian Catholic bishops decided on a new constitution dealing, yet once again, with the election of prelates, and by so doing were still tacitly rejecting Pius IX's *Reversurus*. The attempt in Rome in 1867 to create a common legislation for the united ecclesiastical jurisdictions that had come into being in that year with the implementation of the Bull was now to be repeated. In addition, compromises that were willing to be

---

[168] The 'Armenakans' were founded in 1885 (Van); the 'Hunchaks' in1887 (Geneva); the 'Dashnaks' in 1890 (Tiflis); the 'Ramgavars' in 1908 (Cairo) and reconstituted in 1921 (Constantinople). These had been created partly through the perceived failure of the implementation of Clause 61 of the Congress of Berlin of 1878, which itself had been an alteration of Clause 16 of the Treaty of San Stefano that had concluded the Russo-Turkish War, 1877-1878. Cf. Nalbandian, *The Armenian Revolutionary Movement: The Development of Armenian Political Parties through the Nineteenth Century*, University of California Press, Berkeley and Los Angeles, 1963.

[169] Unlike the Apostolic patriarch, Khoren Ashegian, who, in the summer of 1890, was forced by a number of his faithful to march to Yildiz, the residence of Abdulhamid II, where a riot ensued and arrests made. In 1896, also in the capital, the Ottoman Bank was seized by an armed group of Armenians who wished to bring to the notice of the Great Powers the events unfolding in Anatolia. There were disastrous consequences for many of their co-nationals in the city as well as in the provinces. There is no evidence that Armenian Catholics were involved in either of these affairs. Korolevskij on Patriarch Azarian à propos this question: 'Molto prudente e stimatissimo dal sultano 'Abd ul-Hamīd, seppe impedire ai proprî correligionarî di partecipare ai movimenti insurrezionali delle società segrete armene, e così salvò in gran parte il suo popolo dalla strage nel 1896.' ('Armena, Chiesa', 428).

[170] According to Tcholakian's list (*L'Église Arménienne*, 51), the following are the Catholicos-Patriarchs of Cilicia who were to succeed Hassoun and who concern us at present: Stepanos Bedros X Azarian (1881-1899); Boghos Bedros XI Emmanuelian (1899-1904); Boghos Bedros XII Sabbaghian (1904-1909); Boghos Bedros XIII Terzian (1910-1931).

made by Leo XIII regarding that controversial document had managed to create an atmosphere conducive to reconciliation.[171] It was hoped that a regulation that would satisfy those who continued to be vehemently opposed to the papal document, and who appear still to have had some control of certain properties, though not of the churches themselves, could be, at the same time, recognised by the Porte as the official constitution of the Armenian Catholic *millet* itself, a constitution that had long been demanded by the Porte.

The Regulation of 1888 consisted of ten chapters, containing seventy-four articles. Of importance was the ruling that five episcopal candidates could be presented by a general assembly to the Synod of bishops when a patriarchal vacancy occurred. This assembly was to consist of at least sixty persons of which eight would be clerics. The new patriarch would be enthroned immediately on his election. Confirmation and the pallium would then be sought from the Holy See, and the necessary *berat* from the Porte. In addition, the patriarch himself could nominate bishops, choosing one of the three candidates presented by the local community, though his choice had to be in accord with the Synod of bishops. The

---

[171] Leo XIII and his interest in Eastern Christianity: The Apostolic Letter, '*Praeclara gratulationis*' (June 20, 1894) was an invitation to Orthodox and other Eastern Christians to come into full union with the Roman Church. Though eirenic in tone, it generally received the same negative response as previous and similar communications. Cf Giorgio Del Zanna: *Roma e l'Oriente.* 318-321. Cf. also Joseph Hajjar, *Le Vatican—la France et le Catholicisme Oriental (1878-1914). Diplomatie st Histoire de l'Église*, Editions Beauchesne, Paris, 1979, 17-79. Meetings were held in Rome, from 24 October to 28 November, 1894, for heads of Eastern Catholic Churches 'on ways to improve the condition of their churches' (Frazee, *Catholics and Sultans*, 237). These meetings were to bear fruit with '*Orientalium dignitas*' (30 November 1894), a document that stressed 'the importance to the universal church of the Oriental communities, and the security which they enjoyed because of their union with the papacy' (*Catholics and Sultans*, 236-237). It is of interest to note that the Armenian Catholic Patriarch, Azarian, was prevented by the Sublime Porte from attending. The reasons for this are discussed in Del Zanna: *Roma e l'Oriente*, 321-323. Those actually present, apart from various Latin prelates, were the Melkite patriarch, Youssef, and the Syrian patriarch, Behnam Benni. Due to advanced age, the Maronite patriarch was represented by his vicar, Mgr Huayek. The Chaldean patriarchate was vacant at the time. Also of note are the various establishments and scholarly publications encouraged by Leo XIII: the Armenian College in Rome itself, as well as a revival of the Greek College in the same city (only 'natives' might now enrol); Capucin schools in the East; the French Assumptionist college at Kadıköy, Constantinople; St Anne's seminary for Melkites in Jerusalem; a Coptic Catholic college in Cairo. Publications: *Revue de l'Orient Chrétien, Revue des Églises d'Orient, Échos d'Orient, Bessarione, Oriens christanus.* However, with Pius X, 'a shift in Roman policy occurred', his interests being westwards. 'The Eastern Catholic Churches were of interest only to the extent that they might show any independence from Roman direction.' *Catholics and Sultans*, 238.

latter was also the highest tribunal of the Community and to which any shortcomings of bishops or even of the patriarch could be referred.

As regards the direction of schools, hospitals and cemeteries, there was to be a central administrative council consisting of two ecclesiastics and ten laymen. This body would supervise various sub-councils, each responsible for one of the above concerns. This also applied to the administration of church buildings; they were to be the responsibility of the community. The patriarch was discouraged from involving himself in any administrative details.

By article 60 of the Regulation, the National Assembly was to consist of forty-two members from Constantinople, eight of whom, as we have noted, were to be clerics, as well as a number of delegates from the provinces.

The Sublime Porte proved accomodating to the constitution, approving it on 2 May 1888. Though put into effect immediately, it was understood that it would be submitted for formal acceptance at the council that Patriarch Azarian was expected to summon as soon as it was convenient to do so. Thus would be concluded the work begun in Rome in 1867.[172] The whole matter, however, proved unacceptable to the Roman authorities, though it was not openly condemned. It would seem that the Holy See, rather than adopting draconian measures, was now attempting to approach the Armenian Catholic 'problem' with greater caution, as well as hoping to avoid irritating the Ottoman authorities. Azarian, himself, had come to find the constitution unacceptable, but whether this was due to Roman pressure or to his own judgment remains unclear.

Finally, a National Synod was summoned to meet at Chalcedon. It opened on 27 June 1890, and was to last three months. The patriarch presided and twelve bishops were present. However, the choice of venue (present-day Kadıköy) must have seemed provocative to the Apostolic hierarchy.

The articles or canons are to be found under chapters which themselves are arranged under four headings: The Faith: seventeen chapters; The Sacraments: thirteen chapters; Worship: thirteen chapters; The Hierarchy: nine chapters. Much evidence is found of the influence of the conference of 1867, especially as regards the schemas themselves. Though approbation for the decisions of Chalcedon was sought from the Holy See, the matter was held in suspense, as the National Synod was seen

[172] Further details concerning the Constitution or Regulation of 1888 may be found in De Clercq, *Conciles*, 717-719.

as being tied in part to the Regulation of 1888.[173]

On the death of Patriarch Azarian at the beginning of 1899, the Armenian Catholic prelates assembled in the capital to elect his successor. Before doing so, however, they consecrated three new bishops for vacant sees and transferred the Bishop of Marash, Turkian, to the diocese of Aleppo. They then proceeded to bring under control the financial affairs of the patriarchate; these had become chaotic during Azarian's time in office.[174] Thirty-three resolutions were agreed and all eleven bishops present signed, as did the patriarchal vicar, Arpiarian, and the patriarchal secretary.[175]

It was only after this business had been completed that the prelates elected Boghos Emmanuelian of Cappadocian Caesarea as Patrarch under the name Boghos Bedros XI. He had been one of the five candidates presented by the Armenian electoral assembly. Rome confirmed the appointment in December of the same year, thus again turning a blind eye, apparently, to the fact that lay representation had been involved.

That comparative calm that had descended on the Armenian Catholic community after the extraordinarily intemperate period associated with Mgr Hassoun, a calm that Pope Leo XIII had perhaps been loathe to disturb unduly, was to be severely disrupted yet again. With the Young Turk Revolution of 1908 causing the collapse of the Hamidian regime, and the general excitement and hope that that provoked through all communities, Muslim, Jewish and Christian, of the major cities, especially with the restoration of the 1876 Constitution, the holding of elections and the reopening of parliament, tensions in Armenian Catholic circles over the question of election of prelates and the administration of church property now rose to the surface. The consequent disturbances led to the resignation of Patriarch Sabbaghian (1904-1909) whose health had thereby

---

[173] For a detailed examination of the canons of the Council, confer De Clercq, *Conciles*, 719-752. For the general background of the Council and for the character of Azarian, who appears to have won the respect of Abdulhamid himself, cf. Hajjar, *Le Vatican—La France,* 178-181. For a bitter attack on Azarian for his role as the sultan's plenipotentiary to Leo XIII, cf. Petrosian, 'On the Circular-Letter Entitled 'Return to Armenia' of the Armenian Catholic Patriarch Hovhannes Petros' in Hagopian, *A Critical Examination of Armenian Catholic Communities in Transcaucasia: Their Late Origins, Historical Development and Contemporary Status*, St Vartan Press, New York, 1994, 83-86.

[174] Of particular concern was the lack of accountability for the use of funds sent from abroad, above all those given by the Association of the Propaganda of the Faith based in Lyon.

[175] For details of these resolutions, De Clercq, *Conciles,* 753-754.

been seriously affected. The Holy See appointed the Bishop of Alexandria, Bedros Koyounian, as administrator.

The National Assembly prevaricated in their task of presenting the required five candidates, but finally Terzian, Bishop of Adana, was elected in April 1910. This choice was apparently due to two considerations, the first being the suffering undergone by his diocese during the events in Cilicia of 1909, and the second, the belief that in his thinking he was less susceptible to Roman influence than Koyounian.[176] Shortly thereafter, the new patriarch, with the title Boghos Bedros XIII, along with his predecessor and seven bishops then present in Constantinople, authorised the publication of the decrees of the Council of Chalcedon of 1890, declaring them to be the norm until such times as the Holy See should say otherwise.

In the meantime Koyounian, whilst in Rome, had persuaded Pius X (1903-1914) that a new synod should be called.[177] To that effect, the Latin text of Chalcedon, with the observations made by Propaganda Fide, was delivered to John Naslian, rector of the Armenian College in the city, who now found himself responsible for almost all the preparatory work. Noticeable were some serious changes recommended by a number of Latin theologians who had been requested to examine the decrees.[178]

Preparations for the synod were well underway when Patriarch Terzian arrived, receiving the pallium on 1 May 1911. He took the opportunity to explain to the pope the cause of the continuing malaise, largely due to what was considered to be the intransigence of the laity. This had resulted among other matters, in the continuing vacancy of no less than nine dioceses. The pope then took it upon himself to cut the Gordian knot, choosing persons acceptable to the patriarch to fill those same vacancies.[179] He also summoned by letter all the bishops to the synod in Rome, to resolve once and for all the Church's difficulties. Those bishops not within the patriarchal jurisdiction were to have a deliberative role: Lvov, Venice, and Vienna.

---

[176] Tournebize: 'Plusieurs des laïques l'acclamèrent parce qu'ils s'imaginaient que Mgr. Terzian n'était point uni au Saint- Siège ... Ils lui prêtaient une figure plus ou moins modernisante, plus arménienne que catholique,' 'Armenie', *DHGE*, 343.

[177] According to Rizkallah, one of the reasons for calling the synod was to study 'la situation créée en Turquie par les Jeunes Turcs' (Salim Rizkallah, *Le Bienheureux Ignace Maloyan, Archevêque arménien catholique, Martyr de la foi à Mardine, 1869-1915*, Bzommar, 2001, 12).

[178] The names of these theologians are given by De Clercq, *Conciles,* 881.

[179] The new bishops' names are given *ibid.*, 882.

On 31 August, the patriarch announced that the Synod would begin on 15 October of that year. This was made public to his community by means of a pastoral letter dated 8 September,[180] which meant, it would seem, that the bishops might be enabled to leave for Rome without too much time for any planned opposition. Taking all these matters into consideration, those who had believed in the patriarch's 'independent spirit' now realised that they had deluded themselves; he was very much for the Roman option: 'Ils se trompaient fort.'[181]

The Synod duly opened on the arranged date. A sermon in Italian was given by the Jesuit, Galletti, the first of a number so given by various Latin priests throughout the proceedings. The profession of faith was made according to that of Urban VIII, as well as the anti-Modernist oath of Pius X that had come into effect on 1 September of the previous year. Thirteen bishops were present, others being prevented by the Ottoman government from attending, due to influence from the opposing party. However, contrary influences persuaded the government to relent, so that a number of detained prelates were able eventually to participate in the proceedings. Finally, apart from Terzian himself, a total of eighteen bishops were to be present, with only six absent.[182] One thousand and nine canons under twelve chapters were finally agreed upon, covering all manner of matters.[183]

As for the delicate matter of lay participation in the affairs of the Church, particularly as regards the appointment of prelates, significantly, nothing clear was stated. However, on 12 December, the Council Fathers addressed two letters to the Armenian nation '… proclaiming the exclusive rights of the Church and stressing that only a certain amount of intervention by the laity could be tolerated in episcopal elections or in the administration of the goods of the Church. This precision to a certain degree made up for the silence of the Council on this subject.'[184]

It was declared that the next Council would be held in 1921. Propaganda Fide approved the decrees on 14 September 1913. Indeed up

[180] According to De Clercq, 'On voulait agir quelque peu par surprise et sans longs delais', *ibid.*

[181] Tournebize, 'Armenie', *DHGE*, 343.

[182] The absentees: Pascal Djamdjian of Bursa; Michel Katchadurian of Malatia; the former patriarch, Sabbaghian; the Abbot of Venice and two titular bishops. (*Conciles,* 883, n. 5.)

[183] Details of the canons are to be found in *Conciles*, 885-937.

[184] '… proclamant les droits exclusifs de l'Église et soulignant qu'une certain intervention des laïques pouvait seulement être tolérée dans les élections épiscopales et dans la gestion des biens ecclésiastiques. Cette dernière précision comblait, dans une certaine mesure, le silence du concile à ce sujet.' (*Ibid.,* 937.)

to that time, it was to be '... le seul concile arménien qui soit approuvé par le Saint-Siège'.[185] On 8 December of the same year, following one of that Council's decisions, the patriarch proclaimed that the Gregorian calendar was henceforth to be obligatory everywhere, '... ce qui souleva de nouveaux incidents.'[186]

In the meantime, in October, and in reaction to these developments, the National Assembly in Constantinople voted to remove the patriarch. On his return to Constantinople on 5 January 1912, Terzian found great opposition, the patriarchal residence itself being locked against him. As Tournebize remarks, this was as grave a division as that in the days of Hassoun with the sole difference that now opposition to the patriarch was almost exclusively led by the laity.[187]

On 31 March the Ottoman authorities announced that they, too, no longer approved of Terzian, as he had presided over a synod outside Ottoman territory, and, furthermore, had also been involved in consecrating bishops without their consent.[188] He was therefore no longer to be recognised as civil head of the nation.

The National Assembly then chose a 'locum tenens', Bishop Hatchadourian, and, though Rome suspended him from office, only a revision of Ottoman policy would allow a restoration of Patriarch Terzian. This did not occur, however, as the First World War soon altered matters dramatically, and these intra-communal affairs and tensions, so much the cause of passionate exchange, faded before the overwhelming tragedy that befell the Armenian population, whether Apostolic, Catholic, or Protestant.[189]

After the conflagration,[190] being still in exile, Terzian's positon vis-à-vis his flock in Turkey continued to remain ambiguous. In consequence, and after the resignation of the papal *locum tenens*, Mgr Sageghian, in the

---

[185] Tournebize, 'Armenie', *DHGE* XXXI, 343.

[186] *Conciles,* 938.

[187] 'Arménie', *DHGE* XXXI, 343. '... la révolte, cette fois, était presque exclusivement limitée aux laïques.' According to Korolevskij, only two priests were involved in the schism; he does not mention Bishop Hatchadourian. Indeed, he points out that the new schism '... non poté effetuarsi per mancanza di capi spirituali.' ('Armenia, Chiesa', 428). For a contemporary treatment of these events, cf. Janin, 'Déposition du patriarche' in *Chronique des Églises Orientales, Échos d'Orient,* Tome XV, 1912, 260-261.

[188] This animosity may partly have been caused by the fact that the synod had been held in the capital of the nation then at war with the Ottomans over Tripolitania-Libya.

[189] Constantinople, however, being more in the Western eye, suffered somewhat less.

[190] During the world conflict, Pope Benedict XV (1914-1922) was to do much to aid the eastern Christian communities in the Ottoman empire, a recognition of which may be seen today in

summer of 1921, Jean Naslian, bishop of Trebizond, was then named to succeed him in that post.[191]

A further synod was held in Rome, from 8 May until 1 July, 1928. This was at the invitation of, and was to be presided over by, Cardinal Sincero, Prefect of the Oriental Congregation. It was here that the Armenian Catholic Church reorganised itself, attempting to adapt to new realities. And harsh was the reckoning. According to Frazee's figures,[192] it is believed that of the 140,000 faithful on the eve of the Great War, 100,000 perished, including seven bishops, 130 priests, and 47 nuns.[193]

---

the statue raised in his honour by public subscription in the courtyard of the Latin Cathedral of Saint-Ésprit in Istanbul. Prince Abdulmecit, the future and last caliph, was present at its inauguration on 11 December 1921 (Cf. Marmara, *Précis Historique*, 119). In Rome itself, Benedict was to establish the Sacred Congregation for the Oriental Church on 1 May 1917, with himself as prefect. In addition, he founded the Pontifical Institute for Eastern Studies. As regards the new Code of Canon Law which came into effect in 1917, it was not to concern itself with Oriental Catholics, though, as Frazee points out, '... Canon cclvii placed all persons, discipline and rites of Eastern Catholics under the jurisdiction of the Sacred Congregation for the Oriental Church—all of this done in a way which recognized no inconsistency in Rome's position.' (*Catholics and Sultans*, 238. Cf. *Codex juris canonici* [Rome, 1919], C. 257, para.1).

[191] On 12 August the National Assembly met and themselves voted for Naslian, thirty out of thirty five votes being accorded him: 'Le vote de l'Assemblée était donc la consecration officielle de la politique pontificale.' (*Échos d'Orient*, Tome XXIV, 1921, 481). Whether this result was due to the competence of Naslian both in the eyes of Rome and of others, or whether this was evidence of that exhaustion mentioned earlier, or a combination of these two factors, remains uncertain. Whatever be the case, some resentment was still in evidence, for Terzian did not regain all his rights until 16 April 1928: 'À Istanbul, les fidèles n'ont pas totalement disparu, mais les querelles d'autrefois, qui ne sont pas oubliées, empêchent le retour de Mgr Terzian'. Valognes, *Vie et Mort des Chrétiens d'Orient*, 497.

[192] *Catholics and Sultans*, 273. According to Ormanian, Armenian Catholics prior to the First World War numbered 128,400; he also gives their distribution. In contrast, the Apostolic Church claimed 3,472,000, whilst Protestant Armenians numbered 49,900. *The Armenian Church*, 209. Of note: the Apostolic Church had 3,909 parishes with 3,788 churches. Figures given for 1954 in the same work and applied to all Armenians, including the diaspora: Apostolic Church—3,674,757; Armenian Catholics—51,349; Armenian Protestants—29,667. Apostolic parishes—446; churches—417 (Appendix III, 212).

[193] The names of the seven bishops are given by De Clercq in *Conciles*, 938. On 7 October 2001, Pope John Paul beatified one of these, Archbishop Ignadios Maloyan of Mardin who had been murdered in June, 1915 (Cf. Salim Rizkallah, *Le Bienheureux Ignace Maloyan*). 'Signalons encore ... la lettre d'adieu adressé par l'archevêque arménien catholique de Mardin à son clergé et à son people avant d'être mis à mort ...': *Échos d'Orient* No.123 Juillet-Sept. 1921 378, review by G Rieutort of articles in *Pazmaveb*, Venice Jan.-Mar. 1921. Further details of the Armenian Catholic Church on the eve of the First World War are to be found in the Article 'Arménie' by Tournebize in *DHGE*, XXXVI, 368-371. Statistics are also given for the Apostolic Church: XXXV, 367-368. According to Mécérian, from the end of the 19th century until the fateful year of 1915, there existed diocesan institutes for

There were thirty-seven sessions, with eight prelates participating.[194] One of the major decisions of the Synod was to re-establish the patriarchate in its former home in the Lebanon, whilst Constantinople reverted to being an archdiocese, with the titular bishop Hovsep Rokossian as the holder of the see. This was formally declared by a decree of the Oriental Congregation on 23 June 1928. The patriarch remained administrator of the diocese of Isfahan. Aleppo and Alexandria continued as before.[195] Thus was set the scene for that period of recuperation that was to last till a somewhat different upheaval was to occur when the Second Vatican Council was to begin its sessions in the autumn of 1962.

Conclusion

One cannot but be struck by the extraordinary loyalty and perseverance shown by many of those Armenians who had converted to or identified themselves with Catholicism. The suffering they endured, prior to the establishment of the Catholic *millet* in 1830, is proof positive of their commitment to their new allegiance. One must bear in mind, though, that often that allegiance was not always understood as 'new', but rather as a continuation of a Chalcedonian tradition within the Armenian

---

women at Angora, Trebizond and Marash. Only five members of the last named survived, arriving in Aleppo in 1922 in the company of Mgr Avedis Arpiarian, who later became patriarch (*Histoire et Institutions de l'Église Arménienne,* 220). Tournebize, however, mentions only two such institutes: the 'Congregation of the Immaculate Conception of Angora', founded by Mgr Chichemanian in 1859 in imitation of the Congregation of the same title founded by Mgr Hassoun in Constantinople in 1843; the 'Congregation of the Assumption', founded by Mgr Paul Marmarian on 21 June 1887, being restored after the Great War by Mgr Naslian, (*DHGE,* 351). It is understood, however, that any surviving members of these congregations eventually became part of the strongest, that founded by Hassoun and which is still active today.

[194] Bishops present in Rome for 1928: Naslian, Keklikian of Adana, and Bahabanian of Angora, refugees outside their dioceses; Cuzian of Alexandria; George Kordikian, bishop of Aleppo since 31 January of that year; Koyounian and Rokossian, titular bishops. Also present, Theodorowicz of Lvov. 'Le patriarcat arménien se trouvait ainsi singulièrement réduit en évêques, en prêtres et en fidèles.' De Clercq, *Conciles*, 939. Curiously, he gives no further details on the synod of 1928.

[195] According to De Clercq, Jacques Nessimian was appointed to Mardin, but this must have been in a titular capacity, as Tcholakian states that there has been no resident bishop there since 1928, probably, indeed, since 1915 (*L'Église Arménienne,* 63). We may note here that to serve the diaspora today, the Armenian Catholic Church has a number of eparchies and exarchates.

world, or at least as a return to the original state of affairs before the dismemberment caused by Chalcedon.

For many, however, that loyalty was twinned with a number of factors dear to their heart. Not only were their language and liturgy of great worth, but also customary lay involvement in matters affecting the community at large, and which necessarily included the Church, was understood to be quite natural. It would seem that some awareness of this state of mind was occasionally in evidence and sympathetically treated by the Holy See, at least up to end of the Napoleonic period. However, the greater emphasis on centralization that became characteristic of the papacy as the 19th century progressed,[196] welcomed by many, but not altogether by others, was to be the cause of serious conflict within the Armenian Catholic Church.

Thus, not only was there the continuing and debilitating animosity between the Apostolic and Catholic Churches that had to be contended with, but, in addition, the struggle within the Armenian Catholic community itself on whether to compromise with the Holy See or whether to defend to the last that which gave it its very own particular stamp was to cause grievous wounds.[197] This struggle between two quite opposing views of church government began to poison the spiritual and moral well-being of that Christian witness the Church was called to bear. How the situation would have developed if the Great War had not caused the mayhem that it did is a matter about which it might be difficult to speculate. However, at the conclusion of hostilities, and up

---

[196] It could be said that Pope Gregory XVI (1831-1846) had set the tone. 'During his pontificate he created more than seventy dioceses and named nearly two hundred missionary bishops.' (Richard Whinder, 'Gregory XVI—a much-maligned Pope', *Catholic Life,* April, 2003, 10). 'Gregory's missionary activity did much to promote the influence of the papacy around the world. Wherever the Pope created new dioceses—for example in the former colonies of South America—he ensured that Rome itself would appoint the bishops, without the interference of the former colonial powers. Where secular interference was inevitable—for example in France—he did his best to ensure that the candidates were at least chosen for pastoral, and not political, reasons' (*ibid.*, 11). It is of note that it was as Bartolomeo Capellari that Gregory had charge of the negotiations with the Sublime Porte for the establishment of the Catholic 'millet' a year before his election to the papacy.

[197] 'Si les relations des Arméniens Catholiques avec les Arméniens Grégoriens sont caractérisées par l'hostilité et la méfiance, les difficultés ne sont pas moindres du côté des rapports avec la hiérarchie romaine. Il n'est pas sans intérêt de rappeler que la période, peut-être la plus trouble dans l'histoire des relations avec le Saint-Siège est représentée par la deuxième moitié du XIXe siècle' (Russo, 'Armenia Missio.', 266).

to 1928, somewhat incredibly, there was still to be some serious conflict in what was to become the former capital over the direction of the affairs of the Armenian Catholic community there. The decision of the Rome Synod to remove the patriarchate to its former seat brought that dispute to an abrupt end.[198]

[198] Cf. *Echos d'Orient*, Vol. XXVI, no. 148, 1927, 459-461; Vol. XXVII, no. 151, 1928, 328-330; Vol. XXVII, no. 152, 1928, 477-478.

ANTIOCH AND CANTERBURY: THE SYRIAN ORTHODOX CHURCH AND THE CHURCH OF ENGLAND, A STUDY IN ECUMENICAL RELATIONS IN THE EARLY 20TH CENTURY

William Taylor

This paper recounts the history of relations during the first third of the 20th century between the Syrian Orthodox Church and the Church of England, especially through the relationships and exchanges between the see of Canterbury and the patriarchal see of Antioch for the Syrian Orthodox. These relations did not, of course, take place in a vacuum, and it is important to place this story in the bigger political narrative of the time. Britain was a significant player in the vicissitudes of the Near East during this period, and it was natural that the Church of England should sometimes have been seen (rightly or wrongly) as being in a position of influence with the British government. This was also the case, of course, with British Imperial power in India at this time. Syrian Orthodoxy has a significant presence in Kerala in the south west of India, and there had been a complex earlier relationship between Syrian Orthodox patriarchs of Antioch and the British authorities in India, especially during the patriarchate of Peter III, now referred to in Syrian tradition as Peter IV. Relations between the Church of England and other churches, especially the Roman Catholic Church, also had a significant impact on the latitude individual archbishops of Canterbury felt they had in their dealings with Syrian Orthodoxy. A clear example of this is the reaction of Archbishop Davidson in the Babha case, which is given in detail below.

The narrative is a frustrating one. There are cases of helpful new initiatives and careful theological research on both sides of this relationship. Very often, these initiatives came to very little, as the Churches often seemed to lack the resources or the will to build on the foundations of earlier work. Changes of archbishops and patriarchs also had a significant impact on the ability of either Church to work strategically and thoroughly at sustained closer relations. This can be seen clearly in the change of patriarch from Abd-al-Messih II to Abdallah in 1906, and again to Elias

III in 1916. A more dramatic example of this can be seen in the change of archbishop from Randall Davidson to Cosmo Gordon Lang in 1928. In this sense, the narrative is 'stop-start' in itself, and often exacerbated by external political factors—not least the First World War and the continuing Kurdish question. The Lambeth Conferences could have been in a position to give stability and breadth to these exchanges, arranged as they were on a Communion-wide basis. Again, the office of the archbishop of Canterbury at the time can be seen to have a great impact on the content of the Lambeth Conferences' treatment of Oriental Orthodoxy in general, and Syrian Orthodoxy in particular.

There is something arbitrary in the choice of dates for this study. In the latter half of the 19th century there were important and sustained contacts between the two churches during the long patriachate of Peter III/IV. Patriarch Peter III/IV's contact with Archbishops Tait and Benson, is a study in itself, and there is a history yet to be told of relations between the two Churches since this narrative ends. The narrative is an important one, because all the potential pitfalls in relations between Occidental and Oriental Churches can be seen in microcosm in this vignette. One of the most poignant expressions of these pitfalls came from the Syrian Orthodox Bishop Mar Severius in 1928 when he wrote to Archbishop Davidson: 'The ordinary expressions "I will try" and "I am sorry" and "I regret" intimidate me. I regret very much that our Church cannot engage the attention of the Episcopal Church.' As we shall see, when Mar Severius succeeded to the patriarchate in 1932 as Ignatius Ephrem I Barsoum, he was to direct his considerable intellect and energies in other directions. The continuation of the narrative is yet to be told.

Randall Davidson and the patriarchate of Antioch

With the accession of Randall Davidson to the primacy in 1903, a more informed period of Syrian-Anglican relations began. He had been prepared, through his work at Lambeth under Tait, and through his close involvement with the Lambeth Conferences of 1878, 1888 and 1897, for a more systematic contact with all the Orthodox churches. He wrote to the patriarch of Constantinople on the day of his own enthronement on 12 February, 1903, 'It was our duty on three occasions to act as one of the secretaries of the Lambeth Conferences, and we can therefore speak from long experience of the entire goodwill of our brethren in all quarters of the globe to the Orthodox Eastern Church in all its branches'.[1]

This 'long experience' of the Orthodox Churches was much more than any of his predecessors could claim. Unlike them, he was aware of the existence of the Syrian Orthodox, and aware of the existence of a society (however nominal) whose principal aim it was to further their interests. Davidson's major pre-occupation in his contacts with the Oriental churches was, of course, the Assyrians.[2] Benson had established the Archbishop of Canterbury's Mission to the Assyrians in 1886 and the first fifteen years of the 20th century were to see that Mission overtaken by political events and its eventual collapse. The same political circumstances were to engulf the Armenians in the Ottoman empire, [3] leaving only the Syrian Orthodox as a cohesive Christian community in Anatolia. Anglican relations with the Syrian Orthodox were thus to take on a significance which they had hitherto not possessed.

Shortly after Davidson's accession to Canterbury, the whole issue of the formal relationship between the two churches was raised in a specific incident.

Dr Bhabha was a Syrian Orthodox priest ordained as such in India, but with a Presbyterian background and upbringing. He came to London in 1903 with the intention of working as a priest in the Church of England. In this intention, he had the support of the Syrian Orthodox bishop in Jerusalem, Jemis Elias. Bhabha arrived in London bearing a letter from him, which stated, 'he has my permission to communicate and officiate in the Church of England.'[4]

This incident was to force Davidson into a sharp examination of the state of the relationship between the two churches. Early in 1904, he wrote to the Bishop of London presenting, as he saw it, the issues raised by the case:

> 'I can hardly doubt that an English Bishop would consent to his so communicating. His officiating as an ordained priest is another matter altogether. It raises questions of extreme difficulty—eg.—Where is he to officiate? If it is the English liturgy he uses he must hold an Archbishop's licence … If it is

---

[1] G K Bell, *Randall Davidson*, 2 Vols., London, 1935, Vol. 1, 417.

[2] See *Randall Davidson*, Vol. II, ch. LXXV.

[3] See *Randall Davidson*, Vol. 1, ch. XXXIII.

[4] Davidson, 112, f. 205-6.

> not the English liturgy that he uses, then the Act of Uniformity is being violated.'[5]

Other spectres were being raised by this Syrian case. Raising a fear which was present in the Church of England at the end of the 19th century, Davidson went on:

> 'Why should not some extremist belonging to the unwise section of the clergy claim that a Roman priest should celebrate the Mass in Latin on the analogy of the precedent set by Dr Bhabha's Syrian service?'[6]

Bhabha's application had the support not only of the Syrian Bishop in Jerusalem, but also of the Syrian Orthodox Metropolitan, Dionysius, from the Church in India. Dionysius seems to have encouraged Davidson to look to ways of improving and making more systematic Anglican-Syrian Orthodox exchange. He wrote to Davidson in support of Bhabha, but also went on to suggest three specific ways in which the framework of Anglican-Syrian relations could be strengthened,

> 1.'Firstly, that a Syrian priest should be stationed in England to represent the orthodoxy of the Syrian church.
> 2.Secondly, that high church clergymen should undertake occasional tours through the churches of Malabar.
> 3.Thirdly, that educational establishments of the Syrian Orthodox should be improved under high church supervision.[7]

Davidson considered these suggestions, and looked anxiously over his shoulder at the effect which any decision might have in Anglican relations with other churches. Bhabha in the meantime had written to various Anglican bishops asking for employment; all of which requests eventually came back to Davidson. Two years later, he was ready to act. He wrote, forbidding any Anglican bishops to employ Bhabha, and rejecting Bhabha's repeated requests. Writing to Bhabha himself, he closed the matter, 'Either you are an Anglican priest or you are not.'[8]

---

5 Letter of Davidson to the Bishop of London, 21 January 1904 (Davidson 112. f.209).

6 *Ibid.*

7 Letter of Mar Dionysius to Davidson, 8 February 1904. (Davidson 112. f.214-20).

8 Letter of Davidson to Bhabha, 14 March 1906 (Davidson 112, f. 268).

Davidson appears to have been influenced during this period by the re-opening of an old wound between the CMS and the Syrians.

CMS

The short experiment between the CMS and the Syrians at Kottayam in South India between 1810 and 1836 had left both participants bitter. The cases of litigation and counter-litigation had dragged on in interminable fashion.

H E Fox of the CMS had written to Davidson in 1903 referring to a Syrian Orthodox litigation in India, where the Syrians were demanding from the CMS, 'payment of certain trust funds'.[9] Fox drew to the archbishop's attention the fact that CMS were considering their own litigation against the Syrians.[10] This exchange was heightened in 1902-03 by the publication in India of a 31 page document setting out the case of the Syrians in their dispute with the CMS.[11] Property related to the seminary of Kottayam was being claimed by both sides. The Syrian case lay in their assertion that the terms of co-operation had been broken by the CMS in their active proselytising amongst the Syrian Orthodox, and the creation of 'Anglican Syrians' in 1836. CMS were now to introduce the same allegation in their published pamphlet in 1904.[12] Attention was drawn to the case of René Villate, a priest of the Protestant Episcopal Church of the United States of America, who had been consecrated by Syrian Orthodox bishops in Colombo in 1892 as Mar Timotheus. Mar Timotheus had in turn consecrated

H M Marsh-Edwards in Cardiff in 1903 as 'Bishop of Caerlon'. CMS, introducing these new elements, were to claim that the Syrian Church, and not the Anglicans, had been responsible for the more flagrant proselytism. The bitterness of this pamphleteering war cannot but have influenced Davidson in the decisions he eventually took in the Bhabha case, and, to a lesser degree, in his perceptions of the Syrian Church as

---

9 Letter of 30 January 1903 (Davidson 83, f.378).

10 For the details of the proposed litigation, see Davidson papers 83, ff. 379-87.

11 See E M Philip, *A Letter to the Secretary of the Corresponding Committee of the CMS*, Kottayam, 1902.

12 *A Statement of the Anglican Episcopate—Proselytising by the Jacobite Metropolitan of Malabar and disorderly consecrations.* (Madras 1904).

a whole. The Patriarch 'Abd-al-Masih was to make representations to Davidson at this same time.

Patriarch Abd-al-Masih II

'Abd-al-Masih had attempted to initiate contact with the Church of England while Frederick Temple was archbishop of Canterbury. His requests repeatedly fell on deaf ears. The American Congregational Missionary in Mardin, A N Andrus, wrote to Davidson in 1903 pointing this out. Andrus first made reference to the fact that Temple had not responded to the patriarch's letters (see Chapter IV, note 23) and then went on to make reference to the last initiative of the Syrian Patriarchate Education Society, 'In the fall of 1895, two young men were on their way to Deir Zaafaran in Mardin and had reached Aleppo, when they turned back from there, and since then nothing has been done looking to the assistance of the patriarch in any direction'. Andrus was aware of the sensitiveness of such contact taking place, and refers to the political context in this way, 'The patriarch would be glad to renew correspondence ... only to do so directly would excite the suspicion of the government already too sensitive.'[13]

Davidson, in response, exhibited seriousness of purpose in attempting to get expert advice on the Syrians in Turkey. He was at least prepared to consider the possibility. As we have seen, 'Abd-al-Masih's request for permission to visit India was turned down. But in the process, the patriarch had enlisted the help of the Foreign Office. The Foreign Office had, in turn, informed the archbishop of these developments. Davidson immediately sought to ascertain the facts, and after doing so, replied to the requests which Archbishop Temple had ignored over a period of five years. Two months after the initial requests, Davidson wrote declining any assistance, 'I fear that it would be impossible for us to hold out any hope at present of being able to send emissaries to help the members of the church, because of the work which is at present being carried out amongst the Assyrians.'[14]

---

[13] Letter of A N Andrus to Davidson, 22 June 1903, (Davidson 83, f.409).
[14] Letter of Davidson to A N Andrus, 1 August 1903, (Davidson 83, f.434).

'Abd-al-Masih was deposed in 1906,[15] and was succeeded by 'Abd-Allah Sattuf as patriarch, which was to provide an opportunity for renewal of contact between the patriarchate of Antioch and Canterbury.

'Abd-Allah and R T Davidson

'Abdallah Sattuf (the former Mar Gregorious, Bishop of Jerusalem) was consecrated as patriarch on 28 August 1906. A N Andrus attended the consecration, and after a formal meeting with him, wrote to Davidson:

> 'I had an audience with him, and he wished me to re-open, on his behalf and in his stead, correspondence with Your Grace in regard to the possibility of extending financial aid for the school which was opened last fall'.

Andrus then went on to give an account of the school in Mardin itself, which must have been of interest not only to Davidson, but also to the Syrian Patriarchate Education Society who had sponsored the work:

> The Patriarch has publicly committed himself to the support of this school and I am happy to say that it has re-opened this fall with a larger number of scholars. The purpose of this school is to train up a better educated corpus of monks, priests and deacons, so as to improve both the spiritual and intellectual standards of the lower orders in the church.
>
> We are heartily in sympathy with the Patriarch in the effort he is making at his entrance upon his new office, and are lending to him our moral support in assisting him in providing a teacher and text books for the school'.

Andrus was clearly aware of the erstwhile support of the Syrian Patriarchate Education Society in some detail since he then went on to mention the printing press, also supported by the society, 'He is also having one of the printing presses removed to the city in order to

---

[15] Details of the deposition are difficult to trace, and disputed. See L W Brown, *Indian Christians of St Thomas*, Cambridge, 1983, 151-3, and A S Atiya, *op. cit.,* 372f. A Fortescue cynically suggests, 'It cost Sattuf much intrigue and £T.350 to secure his own election', *The Lesser Eastern Churches*, CTS, 1913, 338.

procure government permission to work it.' The presses had created some difficulties for the Syrian Orthodox with the authorities, and Andrus is enlightening on the situation, 'I would like to bespeak the renewed interest in such undertaking of the friends who so liberally furnished the means for the purchase, transportation and erection at the Deir of the two fine printing presses which the government so soon put under seal.' Andrus concluded by referring to 'Abd-Allah's planned visit to India, and his efforts to secure permission to travel:

> 'I hope he will be successful with the Sultan, as the previous Patriarch was not, and he will have the honour of conferring with Your Grace at Lambeth … It seems to me that with the consecration of this Patriarch the psychological moment has come for entering on relations with this Church with a view to help it on its way in the struggle upward to a plane spiritually, ethically, and intellectually.'[16]

The letter of Andrus reveals a detailed knowledge of the operations and support of the Syrian Patriarchate Education Society, and seems to be in sympathy with its aims. From the tone of his correspondence, it is very difficult to construe the aggressive Protestant proselytism of which the Syrians so bitterly and so regularly complained. He presented the case for support for the Syrian Orthodox to Davidson in better and more detailed way than others had done. And the request was a repeat of one made three years earlier, but with the added incentive of a new patriarch. It is thus all the more surprising that Davidson's response delivered on 1 December 1906, was a very definite and unelaborated negative.

London

As we have noted, Ignatius 'Abd-Allah visited London in 1908, on his way to India. Unlike his predecessor, 'Abd-al-Masih, he was granted the necessary permission by the sultan to make the journey. He arrived in October 1908, and shortly after his arrival, Elizabeth Finn wrote to the archbishop outlining his mission:

---

16 Letter of A N Andrus to Davidson, 21 October 1906 (Assyrian Mission Papers, Box VII, 1899-1906).

> 'He is carrying on in Mesopotamia the school for boys opened by the former Patriarch, with aid of the Syrian Patriarchate Education Committee which was formed with the approval of His Grace Archbishop Tait. That Committee was also enabled to provide two fine printing presses with type, and will we hope be able still further to aid the Syrian Patriarch in his efforts for the good of his people.'[17]

It is still hoped to enlist Davidson's formal support in creating something akin to the Mission to the Assyrians. Publicity for the patriarch was thus built up in London by those who supported his case, publicity not only for the proposed work, but also for the patriarch himself. Considerable interest was built up in the person of the patriarch and the church he represented.

F N Heazall wrote a helpful and accurate memorandum to the archbishop concerning the patriarch himself.

He wrote:

> 'Mar Ignatius 'Abdallah was at one time Bishop of Diyarbakir. He joined the Latin Obedience owing to persecution from the late Patriarch (Jacobite), who was deposed a few years ago. This last succeeded the old Patriarch Peter III who visited England in 1874-5. Peter III sent Mar Ignatius to London again in 1888. These men above mentioned are Jacobite ,and nominally monophysite. This body through its representatives in Mesopotamia has more than once made a request to the Archbishop of Canterbury for help on the lines of the Assyrian mission.'[18]

Heazall, however, assumes that the work and existence of the Education Society are at an end, since he added a description of Elizabeth Finn saying, 'she was at one time secretary of a small society which used to aid the Jacobites in education and gave the patriarch two printing presses, which were confiscated by the Turkish government.'[19]

'Abd-Allah's visit which was, in fact, his third visit and his first as patriarch) was much more prominent, in terms of diplomatic activity,

---

[17] Letter of E A Finn to Davidson, 14 October 1908, (Davidson 150, f.330).

[18] Memorandum of F N Heazall, 24 October 1908, (Davidson 150, f.335).

[19] *Ibid.*

that either of his two previous ones. He is recorded, during his time in London, as having had two audiences with the king, four interviews with the archbishop of Canterbury, and an interview with Lord Morley, the Foreign Secretary. He arrived in December 1908, and stayed until August 1909. His visit gave the Syrian Patriarchate Education Society the impetus to produce a pamphlet appealing for funds,[20] and outlining the history of the society to date. It produced a grander and more organised picture than was in fact the case. The funds of the society at that date were a mere £150.18*s*.9*d*, and they were raised by the appeal to £166.9*s*.9*d*.[21]

The patriarch seems to have been aware of the lack of resources of the Society, and in his public pronouncements placed no great emphasis on the collection of funds. Writing to Davidson in June 1909, he stated, 'I came to your great city with two-fold intentions, the first for the purpose of presenting my homage to his exalted Majesty King Edward the Seventh and the second for the honour of greeting Your Grace and the Bishops'. And, almost as an afterthought, he added, 'I had intended also to appeal to your helping hand for the promotion of printing, and the care of orphans in my country.'[22]

He wrote in the same letter that he had not intended to stay so long in Britain, but had done so because of illness. Davidson, for his part, was clear in his response. He wrote in August to the Bishop of Calcutta explaining the patriarch's visit, 'He has had two interviews with the King.[23] He also has seen Lord Morley. I gather that he hopes in India to collect some funds for his own flock for the benefit of the suffering people in Mesopotamia ... although it is clear, and I think he understands this, that we cannot accept definite responsibility for helping him to meet these particular needs.'[24]

In August 1909, when the Patriarch 'Abd-Allah left for India, the funds of the society stood at £166.11*s*.8*d*.[25] In the same year, the society made a further appeal for funds. Their appeal stated:

---

[20] As already noted, the Syrian Patriarchate Education Society produced *The Ancient Syrian Church in Mesopotamia* in 1908.

[21] See the letters of E A Finn to Davidson of 31 March 1909, and 16 June 1909, respectively (Davidson 299. f.55, 61).

[22] Letter to the Patriarch 'Abd-Allah to Davidson, 14 June 1909 (Davidson 299, ff.57-59).

[23] The audiences with the king were on 23 December 1908, and 23 July 1909.

[24] Letter of Davidson to the Bishop of Calcutta, 6 August 1909 (Davidson 299, f. 78).

[25] Memorandum of Captain Heath, RN, on the funds of the Society, 17 August 1909 (Davidson 299, f.89).

> 'The Syrian Patriarchate Education Fund was formed in1874, to help the late Patriarch to open schools of which there were none. Her Majesty Queen Victoria gave £80 donation. With funds then raised schools were opened, to which the present Patriarch has added four, for girls and women. There are 15, now at a standstill for want of money to pay the teachers. £30 will maintain a school for a year. The children are intelligent and eager to learn.
>
> *Printing:* In 1876, these Christians had no printed books at all. To copy a psalter takes months, to copy a Bible, a lifetime. Friends enabled the Committee to send two printing presses and some type, but during Kurdish raids sad havoc was made with the type. Type of various sizes is urgently needed.
>
> *Clergy and Teachers:* A very pressing need is means for educating clergy and teachers. Many of the clergy cannot read their service books, but learn to repeat the prayers by heart. The church has no endowments. It is chiefly supported by offerings in kind, of the simple and God-fearing people. A parish priest may have £5 a year, and a Bishop perhaps £40. With all this, it is astonishing how much the people know of the Bible. Old and New Testament are read in the Churches. The Patriarch knows his Bible by heart, and has, like his people, a most retentive memory. It is now hoped that his friends here, who now hear of the pitiful condition of this primitive people will come forward with liberal aid'.[26]

As we have seen, the funds of the society stood at £166.11*s*.8*d* in August 1909, when the Patriarch 'Abd-Allah left London. It still stood at £166.11*s*.8*d* on 16 December 1914[27] when it was withdrawn from the account and paid to the Reverend Dr A N Andrus. The account was then closed. As Aziz Atiya states, 'the material resources of the project in England were unequal to the goodwill of its mission.'[28]

The political difficulties which had arisen from the Syrians in Turkey, as symbolised by the confiscation of the presses, were clearly on

---

26 General Appeal for funds, March 1909 (Davidson 299. f.31)

27 The account was kept at Coutts & Co., The Strand. It was opened on 31 October 1888, and closed on 16 December 1914 (information from the archivist of Coutts Bank).

28 A S Atiya, *op. cit.*, 217.

'Abd-Allah's own agenda for discussion in London. The Foreign Office, however, was anxious to avoid the potential embarrassment of an anti-Turkish stance, and in Abd-Allah's two audiences with the king, it had been emphasised that no political subject should be raised. Those who had been involved with the work of the Syrian Patriarchate Education Society were anxious to see the patriarch and have detailed accounts of the latest situation, O H Parry among them.[29] In accordance with the wishes of the British government and the archbishop, the articulated concerns during the patriarch's visit remained strictly ecclesiastical.

Only by inference can anything other than strictly ecclesiastical concerns be discovered. In their printed booklet of 1908, the Syrian Patriarchate Education Society alluded to the political sensitivities of working in the Tur 'Abdin area of Turkey, 'The Turkish Government willingly allows the Syrian and other Christian churches under their rule to establish schools for their people if they can afford to do so. But schools established and carried on by foreigners have been regarded with jealousy for political and other reasons.'[30] Political events of 1895 and the following years had made the position of Christian minorities in Turkey far more difficult. The Ottoman empire was undergoing its own political upheavals,[31] The sultan, Abdul Hamid II, was in his final years, and much greater sensitivity was needed in foreign dealings with Christian minorities. The Syrian Patriarchate Education Society reveal a far greater subtlety in their dealings with the Syrians in Turkey than had previously been the case. They wrote, 'Present events in Asia Minor serve to show the delicate position which the Syrian people and church occupy … None of them have been involved in political intrigues, which in the case of other communities have brought destruction on innocent fellow Christians.'[32] And having clarified the Syrian Orthodox position within Turkey, the society went on in justification of the work it had done:

> 'The Syrian Patriarch Education Committee is anxious to further the Patriarch's good work in every possible way—while at the same time using every care to avoid giving cause for any

[29] Parry wrote to Davidson saying he would like to see the patriarch but could not 'because Mrs Finn hates me like poison, and I don't know quite how to go there.' Letter of O H Parry, 20 November 1908 (Davidson 150, f.349).

[30] *The Ancient Syrian Church in Mesopotamia*, 1908, 13.

[31] See Lord Kinross, *The Ottoman Centuries*, New York, 1977, 569-81.

[32] *The Ancient Syrian Church*, 15.

> idea that foreign interference in Turkish affairs, ecclesiastical or civil, is being attempted by the English friends, who desire to aid the Syrian Patriarch and church in their legitimate efforts to obtain sound education for their people.'[33]

LAMBETH 1908

The Lambeth Conference had taken place earlier in the same year, and some movement had been seen in the position of Anglican relations with Syrians. New initiatives had been taken, which the patriarch was directly to experience during his visit. It is therefore appropriate to look in some detail at the significance of the Lambeth Conference of 1908.

The Sub-Committee appointed to deal specifically with the Oriental churches began its report thus:

> 'Your Committee have taken into consideration the consideration of the ancient and separate churches of the East, and desire to reaffirm their conviction that our position in the East involves real obligations in regard to the churches which, whatever their short-comings, have at least stood alone in the maintenance of our Holy Faith in many lands; and thus under much obloquy and amid many persecutions.'[34]

The Anglican Communion as represented at the Lambeth Conference was clearly aware of the inter-relationship between the existence of British Imperial power and the existence of the Anglican Church. Against much high church opposition, and Anglican bishop in Jerusalem had been appointed, and an Anglican Church in the Middle East was beginning to come into existence. Nor could the Conference have been unaware of the seeming political advantages for the Oriental Churches in forming liaisons within the Church of England. The archbishop of Canterbury himself was widely perceived as exercising real political power by the majority of Oriental Orthodox churches.

On the theological level, the Conference made an attempt at rapprochement:

---

[33] *Ibid.*

[34] 'Report of the Committee appointed to consider the relation of the Anglican Communion to the Eastern Churches'—*The Five Lambeth Conferences* (SPCK, 1920), pp.167-70.

> 'It has been contended that the monophysite heresy has no longer any real hold amongst the Syrian Jacobites, and that it is even less vigorous in the Coptic Church. Similar statements have been made with regard to the Syrian Churches in South India. These struggling Christian Churches, each an all of which have often turned towards us for help, have a real claim upon our love and sympathy.'[35]

Having thus set the scene for closer co-operation in the future, the Committee went on to make its specific recommendations, all of which were to greatly influence the future course of events:

> 'In view of these facts, your Committee are of the opinion that steps should be taken to ascertain the doctrinal position of the separate churches of the East, with a view to possible intercommunion; and that this could best be done by the appointment of commissions to examine the doctrinal position of each of them, and, for example, to suggest some carefully and sympathetically framed statement of the Faith as to Our Lord's Person … And they are of the opinion that, in the event of such doctrinal agreement being obtained, it would be right for any church of the Anglican Communion to admit individual communicant members of those Churches to communicate with us when they are deprived of the means of grace through isolation and, conversely, for our communicants to communicate on special occasions with these churches, even when not deprived of this means of grace through isolation.'[36]

The resolutions are quoted in full because they were to directly influence the course of Anglican-Syrian relations for the next twenty years.

The Lambeth Conference had taken place in the summer of 1908, and in the winter of the same year, the Patriarch 'Abd-Allah made his visit to London. Resolutions 63-65 of the Conference had recommended closer co-operation between the two churches, and the opportunity of his visit was taken to effect a formal interchange. In December 1908, the patriarch had a formal interview with the Bishop of Salisbury, John Wordsworth,

---

35 *Ibid.*

36 *Ibid.*

which resulted in their conversation being published.[37] In the printed record of their exchange, he was asked if he had studied Resolutions 63, 64 and 65 of the Lambeth Conference, and he responded,'I quite approve of them. I am quite prepared to do what in me lies to further the object contemplated in them.'[38] When he was asked if he had studied the English Formularies, he replied:

> 'I have studied your formularies and find no difference between them and our own belief. I have discovered nothing in your Book of Common Prayer which is contrary to the faith as set forth in the gospels and the rest of the New Testament. We do not ask you to change your customs … in your language, you write from left to right, and we write from right to left, but there is no essential difference in the Faith.'[39]

The Lambeth Conference had recommended the production of a joint statement of faith. In the *Interview at the Palace*, the statement of faith is included as an appendix containing twenty articles of faith. Mutual assent was given, and rapid steps appeared to be being made in a movement towards inter-communion. As already noted, the patriarch 'Abd-Allah stayed in Britain ten months, leaving in August 1909. From the promising beginning in January 1909, events took an entirely different turn by the time 'Abd-Allah left. *The Daily News* of 23 August 1909, reported his visit thus:

> 'Unfortunately, there was no practical outcome of the efforts made during the Patriarch's stay to promote a closer union between the Eastern and Anglican Churches. In accordance with a resolution of the Pan-Anglican Congress, the Patriarch was approached, and had a series of interview upon the subject with the Bishop of Salisbury, who endeavoured to draw up a species of catechism for the information of the Lambeth Committee of Bishops. The language difficulty, however, seems to have proved fatal to any understand, His Holiness

[37] Published as *Interview at the Palace, Salisbury, 21st December 1908, between H. H. Mar Ignatius Abdallah II, Patriarch of the Jacobite Syrians, and the Bishop of Salisburyt (Dr John Wordsworth) in reference to Resolutions 63-65 of the Lambeth Conference of 1908* (Bennett Bros., Salisbury, January 1909).

[38] *Op. cit.*, 7.

[39] *Ibid.*

> subsequently repudiating entirely the Protestant character of the answers attributed to him by his English interpreter.'[40]

'Abd-Allah rejected the synthesis of views which was represented by the printed statement. He was not, however, willing to suspend negotiations entirely, because he went on to say, 'I myself am most anxious for a rapprochement between the two churches, if it can be accomplished without the sacrifice of any vital doctrine. We are entirely at one with the High Church party, but the attitude of Low Churchmen is a great obstacle.'[41]

The Chairman of the Eastern Churches Committee, Dr John Wordsworth, was to continue to attempt negotiations with 'Abd-Allah but less than a year later was forced to write to the archbishop:

> 'As regards the Jacobite Syrians, while we have had an interesting interview with the Patriarch Abdallah II and several of our body have seen him privately on more than one occasion, we think that at present the complications of his position in South India make it very difficult to suppose that he could give any enthusiastic statement as to his church's creed, which might not be at once attacked by some prominent person of his communion. We have, therefore, thought it wise to suspend our intercourse with him for the present.'[42]

Communication with 'Abd-Allah thus faltered and these specific negotiations were not to be continued until the 1920's. Political circumstances played a part in the ability of either church to pursue negotiations. It is therefore appropriate to turn to a presentation of the political context of the negotiations.

The political context, 1908-1914

As we have seen, Syrian Christians in the Ottoman empire were not immune to the violence which had befallen the Armenians since 1895. John Joseph[43] has documented some of the hardships which befell the

---

40 *The Daily News,* 23 August 1909.

41 *Ibid.*

42 Letter of the Bishop of Salisbury to Davidson, 8 July 1910 (LC.79: 200).

people of the Tur 'Abdin and Mardin during these years. 'Abd-Allah himself alluded to them in his interview with the Bishop of Salisbury in which he referred to the circumstances of his election, 'I was then appointed Bishop of Diyarbakir and was elected patriarch in 1895. I did not, however, enter upon my office, as another Bishop, 'Abd-el-Messih, was irregularly nominated, and held office for ten years. The numbers of bishops are twenty four, and the population in Turkey is 250,000 souls.'[44] In response to a question asking if any circumstances had occurred to make intercourse with England difficult during this period, he gave this information, 'The intrusion of 'Abd-el-Messih and the Kurdish raids in 1895-6; these completely prevented the employment of the press between the years 1895 and 1906. Barely a couple of months ago, there occurred another severe Kurdish raid, and, since that, a famine.'[45]

The presses which had been provided by the Syrian Patriarchate Education Society functioned, during this period, as a kind of barometer to gauge the stability (or otherwise) of the community. 'Abd-Allah went on, 'The authorities were allowed the use of one of the presses, and great havoc was wrought upon our types.'[46]

Discerning developments in the life of minority communities in the Ottoman empire requires 'reading into' seemingly neutral statements, other, more serious elements. Direct references to political events are rare. One such development did, however, occur. In January 1911, a 'Pastor' of the Old Syrian Church, Abdul-Messih wrote to Davidson with a covering letter from A N Andrus. In it, the Syrian priest referred directly to political events:

> 'We are a church in the Vilayet of Diyarbakir and near to Ras-al-Airn. We number about 120 houses of Syrians, poor and plundered because we were sacked during the Rebellion of Ibrahim Pasha.[47] During his rule, we possessed an ancient church bearing the name of St John, as history testifies. Its ruins are still standing, and Syriac writing is still found upon stones and sarcophagi. In the year 1887, our congregation repaired it at

---

[43] See Chapter IV, note 4.

[44] *Interview at the Palace,* 5.

[45] *Interview at the Palace,* 6.

[46] *Ibid.*

[47] This refers to a rebellion led by the Kurdish Ibrahim Pasha. For details of the rebellion, see H Arfa, *The Kurds, an Historical and Political Study*, London 1966, 25.

an expense of £1,200. We occupied the church and conducted services in it for about fifteen years. In the year 1902, Khaleel Agha[48] destroyed the church and built upon the premises houses, stores and store-houses and used them for eight years, down to the time of our release from this oppression and advance towards freedom. Then we complained to the government of this violence, and it gave us lying promises day after day for two years—the Constitution in these parts being but a name and without reality. It came to pass that this year the Vali visited ... and commanded that on payment to Khaleel Agha, the premises could be regained ... And now, we are in need of quite a sum to erect the church and a school and inasmuch as we with difficulty support our pastor and primary school, owing to our losses and poverty, we therefore have knocked at the door of God's mercy and of the pity of Your Highness, because we are near to one another in doctrine and ritual, and are constantly in ecclesiastical communication with one another.'[49]

The letter is quoted in detail because it lays out the entire difficulties which the Syrian Orthodox and other Christian minorities regularly experienced in the Ottoman empire. The letter, in this sense, is in no way exceptional. It does indicate, however, the extent to which consciousness of the Anglican-Syrian exchanges had gone. The comments which the leaders of this small community had made were supported by Andrus, who wrote, 'I can testify to the accuracy of the statements presented and also to the need they are in for assistance in their noble purpose, and their worthiness to receive it. Permit me to add my plea to theirs that you aid them to restore their church and erect a small school building'.[50] Andrus, ever indefatigable in presenting the case of the Syrians, and appealing form formal Anglican support, went on, speaking of the Patriarch 'Abd-Allah's visit to London, 'We had hoped that by his visit to London something would have been done in the way of aiding the Orthodox Syrian Church to establish a theological school in Deir-el-

48 Presumably a local Kurdish Agha, see M M Van Bruinessen, *Agha, Sheikh, and State*, Schonhooven, 1978.

49 Letter of 'Abd-el-Messih, Elias and Samuel to Davidson, 1 January 1911 (Assyrian Mission Papers, Box 13, 1911-1917).

50 Letter of Andrus to Davidson, 8 February 1911 (Assyrian Mission Papers, Box 13, 1911-17).

Zafaran.'[51] The presentation of the case for formal Anglican support for the Syrians in Turkey had regularly been put to Davidson from the beginning of his primacy until 1911. Efforts to have such a formal mission created reached their peak in 1913, with the formal recommendation that the Archbishop of Canterbury's Mission to the Assyrians should be extended to include the West Syrians.

1913, The extension of the Assyrian mission

As we have seen, requests to Davidson to provide formal support for the Syrians continually fell on deaf ears, despite the fact that the Lambeth Conference of 1908 had urged the Anglican Communion to take a real responsibility for the affairs of the Syrian Church in the Middle East. In 1913, these efforts to create such a mission were intensified. As the Assyrians moved increasingly away from reliance on British support, and towards support from the Russian Orthodox Church, the directors of the mission were urged to concentrate their support elsewhere. Advice from Consular officials was in line with this. In 1913, Henry C Hony, the British Vice-Consul in Mosul, wrote to Davidson suggesting this:

> 'The Archbishop of Canterbury's Mission to the Nestorians has had ideas of sending a similar mission to the Jacobites. If Mar Shimum eventually throws in his lot with the Russians, as seems possible, the Archbishop of Canterbury's Mission will very likely be compelled to withdraw, and should this be the case it is certainly hoped that they will turn their attention to the Jacobites. They would, I think, find it a more grateful task; moreover, the Jacobites are a well-to-do community, and would bear the greater part of the expense themselves; they only want Englishmen as organisers and teachers'.[52]

Davidson did not immediately respond, and later in the year, he was visited at Lambeth by the priest Ephraim Stephan Barsoum (later to become patriarch). Patriarch 'Abd-Allah wrote to Davidson commending

---

51 *Ibid.*

52 Letter of Henry C Hony, Vice-Consul in Mosul, 20 February 1913 (Assyrian Mission Papers, Box 13, 1911-1917).

him, and explaining that he was on a mission seeking support for the Syrian schools and presses.[53] Davidson saw Barsoum in October at Lambeth, and later wrote this of the interview, 'He did not impress me as a strong man, and he was thus more obviously begging than many of his type. I think I was civil to him, and I desired him to convey messages of fraternal regard to the patriarch, but the interview did not come to much'.[54] Davidson's response came in December 1913, when he wrote to Barsoum in French declining any help from the Church of England.[55] A J Mason suggested, however, that W A Wigram could be sent to the Syrians as 'ecclesiastical consul to the Jacobites'.[56]

Davidson was emphatic in response that no formal support could be given, and wrote to Sir Eyre Crowe at the Foreign Office explaining his reason for refusing support:

> 'The Archbishop of Canterbury and the Council of the Mission to the Assyrian Christians retain a very keen interest in all that affects the well-being of the Syrian Jacobites. It would not, however, be possible to include in the work of the Assyrian Mission to the so-called Nestorians direct mission work—educational or other—on behalf of the Jacobite Christians. The two tasks would necessarily be independent of one another, and the Archbishop desires me to assure you that he is not losing sight of the matter, and that he would be ready to take advantage of any suitable opportunity which might arise for practically furthering any efforts made on behalf of the Jacobites with a view to promoting their progress and well-being—both educational and religious.'[57]

Davidson's assertion that work with the Syrian Orthodox in Turkey must be considered only as a separate undertaking from the work

---

53 See the letter of 'Abd-Allah to Davidson, 22 June 1913 (Assyrian Mission Papers, Box 13, 1911-17).

54 Memorandum of Davidson, 16th October 1913 (Assyrian Mission Papers, Box 13, 1911-17).

55 See letter of Davidson to Barsoum, 5 December 1913, (Assyrian Mission Papers, Box 13, 1911-17).

56 Memorandum to Davidson of 15 December 1913 (Assyrian Mission Papers, Box 13, 1911-17).

57 Letter to Davidson to Sir Eyre Crowe (Assistant Under-Secretary of State for Foreign Affairs represented Britain at the 1919 Peace Conference), 24 December 1913 (Assyrian Mission Papers, Box 13, 1911-17).

with the Assyrians was an accurate assessment. Geographically separate, confessionally diverse, the two churches would have been unlikely to consent to being included under one mission umbrella. Less convincing is Davidson's assertion that the matter was not being lost sight of. He wrote shortly before the First World War, and the events of the war were to overtake all Christian communities in the Ottoman empire. The collapse of Ottoman imperial power and the subsequent events were to make contact with minorities within the Turkish lands impossible.[58] Anglican contact with the Syrian Orthodox ceased, and was only to be resumed in 1919.

THE POLITICAL CONTEXT 1919-1924

During the period in which the British and Ottoman empires were at war, no contact was possible between the Anglican and Syrian Orthodox Churches.

The Archbishop's Mission to the Assyrians had formally ceased operations at the beginning of the war, and it was thus left to the Syrian Orthodox to initiate any further contact. The Paris Peace Conference of 1919 provided the opportunity for such renewed contact between the Church of England and the new Syrian Orthodox patriarch.

Patriarch 'Abd-Allah Sattuf had died during the war, in 1916, and was succeeded by the Patriarch Elias III Shakar. The new patriarch, seizing the opportunity of gaining the support of the victorious Allied Powers, delegated Severius Barsoum, archbishop of Syria, as his representative at the Conference.[59] All the Christian minorities of Anatolia were represented at the Conference, and had been given high hopes of varying degrees of autonomy by the Allies. The Assyrians had been 'assured' of British support; the Armenians of Allied support. Barsoum, representing the cause of the Syrian Orthodox came to London and put forward their requests in an interview with the press on 4 February 1920, 'I have been sent here by the Patriarch of Antioch, who resides at Mardin in Mesopotamia, to draw the attention of the Allies to what my half million co-religionists have

---

[58] For an account of the political developments, see Lord Kinross, *The Ottoman Centuries,* 595-609. See also FO.608/85, files 3472-3481 for a detailed account of Syrian Orthodox losses during the war.

[59] Mar Severius Barsoum was the former Ephraim Stephan Barsoum, and future patriarch. Barsoum was apparently regarded at the Conference as championing the Arab cause—see J Joseph, *Muslim-Christian Relations,* 1010f.

suffered under the Turk. I have seen M. Poincaré in Paris, and I hope, during my stay in London to lay my case before the heads of the Foreign and India Offices.'[60] Barsoum went on to elaborate exactly in what points the British authorities could be of help:

> 'Firstly, remove the Turk entirely from Mesopotamia. Secondly, after removing the Turk, do not leave the Kurd in his place. "The Kurd", he said epigrammatically, "is a a savage Turk. The Turk is a civilised Kurd". Thirdly, the Armenians, English people must remember, are not the only victims of the Turk. Orthodox Syrians and Chaldaeans have also suffered. Indeed, one hundred-thousand of his own people have perished as a result of the Turkish massacres.'[61]

Having thus presented the case for British help to the Syrian Orthodox, Barsoum went on to elaborate on the potential gains for Britain of such a course of action. The journalist interviewing Barsoum reported him thus:

> 'As to Mesopotamia, he thinks that the British are making a mistake in extending their control over only one part of it and leaving the Turk still in the North. "Baghdad", he said, "is the heart of Mesopotamia, and he who holds the heart should hold the whole." Its possibilities from the point of view of riches he thinks are immense, and will far exceed anything that Egypt can possibly provide.'[62]

Barsoum, during his stay in London, was in regular communication with Davidson and, through him, requested an audience with the King in order to lay the Syrian Orthodox case before him.[63] The request was refused. Barsoum's request for British protection for the Syrian Orthodox in the defeated Ottoman empire appeared to have been heard sympathetically by Davidson. He had earlier written to the archbishop of York of his concern for the Syrian Orthodox position:

---

[60] *Morning Post,* 4 February 1920.

[61] *Ibid.*

[62] *Ibid.*

[63] For details of the request, see Davidson 299, f.116.

> 'I do not think we can allow the session to end without raising a grave debate on the possibility of Turkey being allowed to resume control over the Christian populations, Armenian, Assyrian, and others. In the rush of great events, people have lost sight of the unutterable horrors of Turkish cruelty to the Armenians, and at present opinion is drifting in the direction of letting the Turk resume control throughout the Turkish Empire. Of course, the difficulties are immense. America has miserably failed us and appears unwilling to accept any responsibility by Mandate or otherwise. France cares nothing for any interests except French interests, so at least it seems to me, and I may learn that there is very grave fear that French weight may be thrown into letting the Turks alone. All this being so, I feel rather bound to raise the question by an actual resolution in the House of Lords to the effect that the Turk must not in our opinion be allowed to have power to recommence the hideous misrule of barbarity of the past.'[64]

After Barsoum's arrival in February 1920, interest in the Syrian Orthodox situation in Turkey was once more generated. British agents in the Middle East had already drawn attention to their plight, and their analysis varied. [65] A report to the General Staff Intelligence gave an account of a meeting in Mardin of minority groups in the area. The meeting took place in the Kurdish Aghas's house in April 1919. The Kurds were represented, and spoke of the need for Kurdish autonomy; the Syrian Catholics spoke of their wish to see an Allied Protectorate. And, according to Mgr Gabriel Tapponi, (the Syrian Catholic archbishop of Mardin), the Syrian Orthodox, 'were not molested by the Turks during the massacres, and propaganda is now being carried out among them in support of Turkish rule.'[66]

A Syrian Catholic archbishop cannot be said to be an impartial observer, but the degree of divergence between his analysis and the statements of Barsoum in Paris and London is large. Tapponi went on with the prediction, 'The Midyat Jacobites at present lean either to Catholicism

---

64 Letter of Davidson to Cosmo Gordon Lang, Archbishop of York, 6 December 1919 (Lang 190. f.98).

65 For details of the British reporting on the condition of the Syrian Orthodox, see FO. 608/85, files 3472-3481.

66 Report of B T Buckley to General Staff Intelligence, 22 May 1919, (FO.608/85, file no. 365).

or Protestantism, and the purely Jacobite religion is likely to disappear entirely in this region in time'.[67]

Davidson, however, inclined towards acceptance of the statistics and views put forward by Barsoum and conveyed to the archbishop by various people who considered themselves informed. W A Wigram wrote to the archbishop on Barsoum's arrival, 'Mar Severius has political work to do, in that he seeks political protection for his whole nation.'[68]

Barsoum may have exaggerated the afflictions of the Syrians, for he appears to have told A H Finn, the son of Elizabeth Finn, that 90,000 Syrian Christians had been massacred during the war.[69] And Athelstan Riley had expanded on the aims of Barsoum, by his assertion that, 'he really wants material help—but so do all nations and churches'.[70] The sought-after help, material or political, was not forthcoming. Other preoccupations pressed on Davidson, not least the preparations for the Lambeth Conference of 1920. The appeal from the Syrian Orthodox for support was, however, to continue. The Paris Peace Conference of 1919-20 was followed by an Imperial Conference in London of 1921. The Patriarch Elias III was to appeal to Davidson during this Conference for help of specific kind:

> 'during this horrible and abominable war that caused the calamity of all the Christians of Turkey, my community also living in the Eastern part of Asia; that is, the provinces of Bitlis, Siirt, and Kharpoot and dependencies in Mesopotamia; the provinces of Diarbakir, Mardin, its dependencies and Urfa were, like the Armenians, deported and hundred thousands of them died of misery or were murdered. 166 of our churches and convents situated in these provinces were sacked and destroyed. Last year, October 1919, our Bishop of Syria, Severius A Barsoum, was delegated from our Patriarchate and requested by me to submit that case to the Parish Conference and to Your Grace to be dealt with; which he did, and it was kindly promised on March 12th 1920, by His Majesty's Secretary of State for Foreign Affairs on behalf of the President of the Supreme Council and by Mr Eric Phipps directed by Early

---

67 *Ibid.*

68 Letter of W A Wigram to Davidson, 25 February 1920 (Davidson 299. f.118).

69 See letter of A H Finn to Davidson, 4 February 1920 (Davidson 299. f.111).

70 Letter of Athelstan Riley to Davidson, 12 February 1920 (Davidson 299. f.115).

> Curzon of Kedleston, in reply to his letters of 8th March that the interests of our nation will not be lost sight of when the moment for their consideration arrives.'[71]

Having thus set the scene for a specific request for assistance, the patriarch then went on to be politically explicit:

> 'Now we apply to you and ask your kind help and mediation at the London Conference.
> 1. First, to protect our rights and have an indemnity taken for us by those who caused us unlegally such a great loss and damage.
> 2. Second, to restore our churches and convents with all belonging to it *(sic)*.
> 3. Third, to assure, for the future, our security in the Turkish territory.'[72]

The patriarch's perception of the archbishop of Canterbury was clearly that of a person who held real political power; or if not holding political power directly, with certain access to it. His three stated requests are thus to be understood in that light. The patriarch went on to describe the present situation of the Syrian Orthodox remaining in Turkish territory in his attempt to influence Davidson. He wrote:

> 'The ancient Syrians extremely suffered the time of the Christians' deportation (sic), our schools and churches are destroyed, and our children remain in ignorance, especially the orphans, and there are also thousands of widows living in conditions undescribable. We unfortunately cannot provide for an feed all those people. That is a great pity for the ancient Syrians who were the authors of civilisation and those arts and antiquities adorn the museums of Europe today'.[73]

Eastern Anatolia was in upheaval at the time of writing, and the patriarch himself was forced to move to Constantinople, from where he wrote. Yet again, the hopes raised for the Syrians by the suggestion

---

71 Letter to Patriarch Elias III to Davidson, 16 February 1921 (Davidson 299. f.121-2).
72 *Ibid.*
73 *Ibid.*

of British support in their predicament, were to be dashed. Both civil and ecclesiastical authorities began to withdrawn from any articulated commitments. Davidson, who had contemplated raising the issue in the House of Lords, wrote in reply to the patriarch's requests, offering nothing:

> 'Nothing would give me greater satisfaction than to know that our government is able to meet the wishes your letter expresses, and I am transmitting it to the Conference now sitting in London, for the consideration of its members ...
>
> Whatever influence I possess would be always in favour of our Nation doing all that is in its power for the strengthening of the life of the Christian peoples of the East. Unhappily, the conditions limiting what is possible have become graver and more anxious since the date to which Your Beatitude refers, and I know that any Government may now find difficulties in doing all that it would desire to do on the lines originally planned, or at least foreshadowed.'[74]

Davidson's Chaplain, G K A Bell, did, however, write to Sir Maurice Hankey (one of the senior British representatives) asking him to lay the case before the Conference. Hankey responded by offering to distribute the information to the delegates.[75]

No more is heard of these proposals, and the correspondence between the archbishop and patriarch now changed in character. From the articulation of stated political aims, a new concentration on matters more strictly ecclesiastical emerged. The political question was left aside. Mar Severius was to make one more attempt in 1927 to influence political opinion. He undertook another journey to Britain, and, in addition, the USA.[76] The unfruitful nature of the discussions, and the lack of any concrete outcome is powerfully expressed in a letter written by Mar Severius at the end of his mission. He wrote to Davidson:

> 'The ordinary expressions "I will try", and "I am sorry", and "I regret" intimidate me. I regret very much that our church

---

[74] Letter to Davidson to the Patriarch Elias III, 2 March 1921 (Davidson 299. f.124).

[75] For the details of this correspondence, see Davidson 299. ff. 123-7.

[76] For the details, see the Douglas correspondence (J A Douglas 70, 50-80) in Lambeth Palace Library.

> cannot engage the attention of the Episcopal Church and my three missions in 1913, 1920 and 1927 have been unsuccessful … I have to explain that if the Episcopal Church would like to make sincere relations with Eastern Churches it will have to make a fund to pay the expenses of the eastern prelates to the conferences or to London, in comfortable way to their dignities and to help them in fact—not in words, in their needs; and to explain to them clearly its conditions, lifting the uncertainty.'[77]

The refusal of British authorities both ecclesiastical and civil, to deal directly with the political questions raised by the Syrian Orthodox must be seen in the general context of British wariness of the 'minorities issue' within the emerging Kemalist Turkish nation. This, coupled with a hyper-sensitivity to foreign inference or criticism from the part of the new Turkish government created an atmosphere of mutual suspicion, if not hostility. Contemporary Turkish perceptions of this question may be summarised thus, 'The Archbishop of Canterbury and the Bishops of London and Manchester and their brethren were always ready to preach a crusade against Turkey and Islam'.[78] And the influence of returned missionaries was treated with equal suspicion, and it was suspected that facts were grossly distorted. 'The missionaries … were filled with pleas for the oppressed Christians and denunciations of their Turkish oppressors. There was thus gradually developed, under the aegis of our churches, a powerful anti-Turkish opinion'.[79] In this atmosphere of mutual distrust and caution, the political arena seemed too fraught with danger and misapprehension for any church to enter. An awareness of this fact is shown in the Report of the Lambeth Conference of 1920:

> 'The present moment, when under the draft Turkish Treaty, the West Syrians remain under Turkish rule is not specially suitable for endeavouring to establish closer relations with them; but we suggest that the recently appointed Eastern Churches Committee should watch for any suitable opportunity of doing so, and that when such opportunity arises, the above considerations will greatly diminish any doctrinal difficulties. In

---

77 Letter of Mar Severius to Davidson, 19 May 1928 (J A Douglas, 70: 60).

78 Felix Valyi, *Revolutions in Islam*, London 1925, 31.

79 E Alexander Powell, *The Struggle for Power in Moslem Asia*, New York 1925, 120.

> the meantime, a greater desideratum is a better knowledge of the Jacobite liturgical books, which are mostly in manuscript.'[80]

From the political, the focus of activity was to shift to the more strictly ecclesiastical, to which consideration we now turn.[81]

The Eastern Churches Committee and intercommunion

At the archbishop's request, the Eastern Churches Committee was set up in 1919 under the chairmanship of Bishop Gore. Its brief was the monitoring and furthering of contacts with the Orthodox churches, both Chalcedonian and non-Chalcedonian. It emphatically had no political brief, and differed from the earlier Syrian Patriarchate Education Society in having a much wider brief, and in having no access, or even the pretence of access, to funds.[82] The newly formed Committee's first major task was the opening of correspondence on Intercommunion, which had been initiated by the Patriarch Elias III.

In 1921, the patriarch approached the Anglican chaplain in Constantinople, R F Borough, asking him to enquire as to the terms on which intercommunion could be established between the Anglican Church and his own Church.[83] In particular, the patriarch was interested to know the conditions for intercommunion for Syrian Orthodox living in Britain and the USA who had no access to a priest of their own church. Borough referred this question to the committee, which met in June 1921, to consider the issue, and produced the following statement. On the Syrian Orthodox Church and its relations with the Church of England, the Committee stated:

> 'It is now a small body widely dispersed from Mosul to Beyrout and Jerusalem, numbering at most 100,000 after the late terrible massacres. The Patriarchal seat was at Diyarbakir until recent years. The condition of the "Jacobites" is very depressed. There

---

80 *Conference of Bishops of the Anglican Communion—Report of the 1920 Lambeth Conference* (SPCK 1920), 150f.

81 The wider political context is dealt with in G K A Bell, *Randall Davidson*, Vol. II, ch. LXVIII.

82 See G K A Bell, *Randall Davidson*, Vol. II, 1104. The earlier Anglican and Eastern Churches Union had been set up in 1906.

83 See G K A Bell, *Documents on Christian Unity (Third Series) 1930-48* (1948), 52-7.

> was serious consideration at one time as to the sending of an Archbishop's Mission, after the pattern of that to the Assyrians, to this church; the request for such a mission was made as recently as 1913.'[84]

Having thus outlined the background to the correspondence, the Committee went on to state what particular recommendations could be made to further the practical moves to intercommunion.

> 'The Lambeth Conference of 1908 passed resolutions (63, 64, 65) which were renewed in 1920 (22,23) whereby while recording its uncertainty as to the doctrinal position of this church and the other three with which it is in communion, recommended that on their acceptance of some carefully framed statement of the Faith as to Our Lord's Person to the satisfaction of a commission to be appointed by the Archbishop of Canterbury, and on the approval of the Metropolitans and Presiding Bishops of the Anglican Churches, mutual communion should be sanctioned with them in emergency and on special occasions.
>
> Further than that, however, and in view of our relations with the Eastern Orthodox Churches, the Lambeth Conference of 1908, and apparently that of 1920, were not prepared to go.'[85]

The conditions of the Anglican acceptance had thus been laid out, together with the authority for any action—the Lambeth Conferences of 1908 and 1920. The Committee then went on to make clear what conditions the Syrian Orthodox would be expected to fulfil before the negotiations could proceed.

> 'We, therefore, recommend that the Archbishop of Canterbury be advised to authorise Mr Borough to inform Mar Ingatius that on the totality of the Bishops of the Syrian Orthodox Church declaring that:
>
> They affirm the christological statements of the Athanasian Creed.
>
> They affirm not the validity of, but the doctrines defined by the

---

[84] Report of a meeting of the Eastern Churches Committee, 16 June 1921 (Davidson 299. ff. 128-30).

[85] *Ibid.*

> ecumenical councils: The members of that church be admitted in emergency to communion, and vice versa, and that on other special occasions representatives of both churches be declared free with Episcopal permission to communicate at each other's altars, but that full intercommunion should be postponed until terms of Dogmatic Union be arranged.'[86]

The Committee then went on to authorise Borough to convey these terms to the patriarch. Davidson himself gave the Committee's views his validation, and asked his chaplain, G K A Bell, to prepare a memorandum for him on the background to the negotiation.[87] The thoroughness with which Davidson researched the details of this more strictly ecclesiastical exchange with the Syrian Orthodox contrasts interestingly with the way in which the political issue was often sidestepped. A response was delayed, since in the meantime, the patriarch left Constantinople for Jerusalem.[88]

The requested statement of belief on the Nature of Christ was then formulated by J A Douglas, Chairman of the Separated Churches Sub-Committee and sent to the patriarch in April 1922.[89] The question asked whether the second person of the Trinity took mortal flesh of the Virgin Mary, whether manhood and Deity became indivisibly one in the Incarnation, and whether the Deity and the manhood retained their 'proper qualities'.

No grand scheme of dogmatic union was conceived as a result of these negotiations, and as Douglas was to point out, 'the assurance from them (the Jacobites) is needed for a very limited purpose, namely, simply for economic acts of charity, and not as a basis for dogmatic union'.[90]

The patriarch's response to the 'questionnaire' was swift. He replied on 5 May 1922, with his explanation that, according to Syrian belief, the second person of the Trinity took mortal flesh from the Virgin Mary, that manhood and Deity were fused, but in the fusion manhood retained the properties of manhood and Deity of Deity.[91]

---

86 *Ibid*.

87 Each stage of the negotiations was carefully documented by Bell, and set out in his memorandum, 'Mar Ignatius and the West Syrian Church' (Davidson 299, ff. 144-46).

88 See the letter of R F Borough, 17 March 1922 (Davidson 299, f.141).

89 The questions are set out in Bell, *Documents on Christian Unity*, 52f. and in Davidson 299, ff. 161,165, 166.

90 Letter of J A Douglas to Davidson, 4 April 1922 (Davidson 299, f.162).

91 See Bell, *op. cit.*, 53 and Davidson 299, f.179.

At this stage, Davidson informed the Ecumenical Patriarch of these exchanges, since discussions were also proceeding with the Greek Church and the archbishop was anxious not to prejudice the discussions. He wrote to Meletios, the Ecumenical Patriarch describing the course of the exchanges in detail, and citing the Lambeth Conferences of 1908 and 1920 as his authority. He began the letter, 'friendly relations have existed for some time between the archbishops of Canterbury and the Syrian Jacobite Patriarchs of Antioch.'[92] He also wrote on the same day to the Patriarch Elias III informing him of his permission given to clergy of his own church to administer the sacraments to members of the Syrian Orthodox Church when deprived of that means of grace through isolation.[93]

By this stage, however, the patriarch Elias had begun to withdraw from what may have been perceived of as too hasty a progression. He wrote in September 1922, to Davidson, laying out the conditions for reception of communion clearly. He wrote that it was necessary for the communicant to confess his sins to the priest, and that it was impossible for him to sanction any arrangement alone, as the necessary authority must come from a council of the bishops and metropolitans of the whole Syrian Church.

1924–1928

The proposed meeting of Bishops was a virtual impossibility in the Near East of 1922. The Turkish Peace Treaty was yet to be concluded, and the patriarch himself was moving continuously. He had moved (as we have noted) from Deir el-Zafaran to Constantinople, and from Constantinople to Jerusalem. In December, he moved from Jerusalem to Aleppo, and by April 1923, was in Urfa.[94] Accounting for this constant movement and in an analysis of the situation, the Anglican chaplain in Constantinople, Borough, wrote, 'It was fear of the Turk which made him hesitate, as they have given no excuse whatever for ill-treatment. Anything like a meeting

[92] Letter of Davidson to Meletios II, 20 June 1922 (Davidson 299, f. 189).

[93] See Bell, *op. cit.*, 53-6, and Davidson 299, f.195.

[94] See the letters of R F Borough to Davidson (Davidson 299, f. 270, and 273.

of Bishops is out of the question as it would at once be called sedifious and imprisonments would follow.'[95]

Even after the concluding of the Treaty of Lausanne, the situation in the area was little better. Still no meeting of the bishops had been possible, and still the patriarch had no fixed base. A 'mission' of the Protestant Episcopal Church of the United States of America was sent from February to March 1924, and a gloomy picture of the area is painted by the American priest, W C Emhardt, 'I am afraid I cannot get to Mardin. The Turks are driving all Christians out of the district. I understand that they are concentrating troops at Urfa for a demonstration against Mosul. I knew before leaving America that they would have to have some foreign war, in order to break the threatened revolution in Constantinople.'[96] The mission was a failure, and was overcome by the political upheaval in the Near East. Turkish suspicion of all Christian minorities remained too strong for any community to risk an open identification with foreigners. The population exchanges had taken place of Greek Orthodox for Turkish Muslims, and Christians of all churches remained suspect to the Turkish authorities. The Lausanne Treaty had been concluded, and in it only three minorities were recognised within the new Turkish republic—Jews, Greeks, and Armenians. These minorities thus retained the right to practise, teach, and publish in their own languages, and to run schools. And according to a domestic interpretation of the Treaty, the minorities not mentioned in the Treaty were simply not recognised as existing.[97] Numerically, the Aramaic-speaking Syrian Orthodox in Turkey represented no threat to the emerging Turkish state, and had never been involved in secessionist activities, but their neighbours, the Kurds, represented a major threat to Kemalist Turkey. By their non-appearance in the Lausanne Treaty, the Kurdish threat was contained in the eyes of the Turkish authorities. The Syrian Orthodox thus fell into the same conditions. The Kurdish Revolt of 1925 further compromised the Syrian Orthodox to the authorities in Ankara.[98] Patriarch Elias III was expelled from Deir-el-Zafaran, and was forced south of the so-called 'Brussels Line' delineating Turkish from Iraqi

[95] Letter or R F Borough to Davidson, 3 April 1923 (Davidson 299, f.274), Lambeth was suspicious in the eyes of the Turks because of support for the Ecumenical Patriarchate in 1923. The Turkish newspaper *Hakimiet Millie* spoke of 'intrigues' (Davidson 299, f.275).

[96] Letter of W C Emhardt to G K A Bell, 2 March 1924 (Davidson 299, f.283–4).

[97] See *Christian Minorities of Turkey*, Churches Committee on Migrant Workers in Europe, Bruxelles, 1979, 40–8.

[98] See J Joseph, *Muslim-Christian Relations*, 101-3.

territory. A British observer at the time clearly thought that the Syrian Orthodox who remained in Turkish territory were in serious threat of extinction. He wrote of the Tur 'Abdin,

> 'Unluckily for the Jacobites, this region is on Turkish territory; and they have been subjected, since February 1924, to a renewal of the persecution they underwent during the War. It would be tragic, indeed, were this interesting survival, with its venerable language, customs and liturgy, to be extinguished.'[99]

The Syrian Orthodox, sensing that they were being abandoned by those who held political power in the Near East, had turned to anyone whom they thought could influence events. Borough wrote of one such initiative which had been contemplated. He wrote to Davidson informing him that the Syrian Chorepiscopos in Istanbul had made a definite suggestion that, 'Mar Ignatius should apply to the pope for help, financial and diplomatic. This, of course, would be meant to lead to his submission and the formation of another uniate church.'[100]

Such an initiative would indeed have been drastic, and it seems not to have been taken. The situation, however remained bleak for the Syrian Orthodox and for the patriarch himself. After his expulsion from Deir el-Zafaran, the situation became even less clear, and the Anglican authorities could come to no clear conclusion on which side of the 'Brussels Line' represented a better future for the Syrians. Davidson's Chaplain wrote at the end of 1925:

> The Patriarch has been prevented by the Turks for many months from receiving any communications whatsoever and from leaving his post. Neither Syrians in Jerusalem, nor in the Northern parts of Syria can get in touch with him although they have tried again and again. One cannot of course say what the result of the League's decision with reference to the boundary may have upon this virtual confinement of the Syrian Patriarch.'[101]

---

[99] H C Luke, *Mosul and its Minorities* (1925), 113. See also H A Foster, *The Making of Modern Iraq* (1936), 164–8.

[100] Letter of Borough to Davidson, 6 May 1924 (Davidson 299, f. 285).

[101] Letter of Davidson's Chaplain to the Bishop of Travancore and Cochin, 10 December 1925 (Davidson 299, f. 290).

The events of 1924-25 had thus overtaken the strictly ecclesiastical exchange between the Anglicans and Syrian Orthodox on the question of inter-communion. It had, however, not died. The patriarch was still, in theory, waiting for the opportunity to hold a synod of his bishops, in order to sanction the proposals.

In 1927, the proposals were again under discussion, and the Eastern Churches Committee produced a memorandum on the state of the discussions with the patriarch.[102] The memorandum had been produced in response to a questionnaire which had been submitted by the Patriarch Elias to the Eastern Churches Committee on the nature of Anglican belief. The memorandum is detailed, and gives the provenance of the discussions, going back to the Lambeth Conference of 1908. The provenance is described in a list of twenty-five developments, most of which we have already noted. Not already noted was the fact that the patriarch wrote to the Eastern Churches Committee in 1926 that he, 'could not enter on correspondence with the archbishop even on church matters without it being interpreted by the government as a political affairs.'[103] The questionnaire of the patriarch was then submitted on 14 June 1926, and after the draft of the answers had been formulated, members of the Eastern Churches Committee met the patriarch in Jerusalem on 14 March 1927. The questionnaire was, at that meeting, the formal discussion, with the presentation of the Anglican answers. The questionnaire itself deals with the Anglican belief concerning the departed, the Resurrection and Ascension of Christ, the doctrine of purgatory, reception of communion, the Holy Spirit and the creedal 'Filioque' clause, the Virgin Mary and saints, the ordination ceremonies, and the nature of church union. The questionnaire is framed in eight questions and answers, the eighth of which deals with church union. In response to the question:

> 'What do we have in mind when we discuss "Union"?', the Eastern Churches Committee answered, 'The Union which Anglicans desire may be illustrated by the Union existing between that Church of Egypt, sometimes known as the Coptic, the Syrian Orthodox Church, sometimes known as the Jacobite, whereby the faithful of either church may resort to the ministry of the other for sacraments and the two Churches know each

---

[102] See Davidson 299, ff. 294-309.

[103] Davidson 299, f.296.

> other as equal sister churches but whereby neither has right nor power to constrain the other or to interfere in its affairs.'[104]

The Eastern Churches Committee, in producing their formal response to the patriarch's questionnaire, had gone further than Davidson was prepared to go. When the details of the exchange were presented to him, he wrote, 'The matter of formal as distinct from occasional intercommunion was, I think never raised.'[105]

The long-awaited Synod took place later in 1927 and the bishops discussed the proposals for intercommunion. J A Douglas wrote to Davidson saying, 'Mar Ignatius held a Synod of his Bishops … and he is now prepared to go forward in the matter of economic intercommunion.'[106]

The decision was the result of almost twenty years of negotiations, at times sporadic, at times systematic, since the Lambeth Conference of 1908. Davidson's primacy thus saw positive moves forward in the establishing of formal Syrian Orthodox-Anglican relations. Under the patriarchate of Elias III and Davidson, the two churches came nearer to establishing formal and systematic relations than at any time in their history. But Davidson was nearing the end of his time at Lambeth, and the final request which came to him in 1928 for the setting up of a formal mission to the Syrian Orthodox was deflected from Canterbury into the Anglican Communion. Any mission to be set up, he wrote, 'must be not of any one Archbishop, but the whole Anglican Communion.'[107]

Davidson resigned in November 1928, and was succeeded by Cosmo Gordon Lang. The systematic and effective work of the last twenty years now came to an end. As was so often the case with a change of primate at Lambeth, continuity was lacking. The primacy of Lang and the short primacy of William Temple show little interest in, and even less involvement with, the Syrian Orthodox, either in the Middle East or in India.

---

[104] Eastern Churches Committee, Correspondence with Mar Ignatius Elias III (Davidson 299, f. 308).

[105] Letter of Davidson to Eastern Churches Committee, 13 July 1927 (Davidson 299, f. 310).

[106] Letter of J A Douglas to Davidson, 16 August 1927 (Davidson 299, f.323).

[107] Letter of Davidson to Patriarch Elias III, 1 June 1928 (Assyrian Mission Papers, Box 17).

Postscript

After the accession of Cosmo Gordon Lang to the primacy, the relationship between Syrian Orthodox Church in both India and the Near East and the Church of England practically ceased. The careful and detailed work of the twenty-five years of Davidson's primacy in the field of Syrian Orthodox-Anglican relations was not built upon. This was in spite of the fact that shortly after his accession, Lang made a journey to the Near East, and called on the Orthodox patriarch in Jerusalem, and made the first ever visit by an archbishop of Canterbury to the Ecumenical Patriarch. Lang himself said of the visit that it had, 'some measure of importance not only in my own life, but in the long-drawn efforts to strengthen the ties between the Anglican and Orthodox Churches.'[108] Relations with the Chalcedonian Orthodox had been vastly improved towards the end of Davidson's primacy by the decision of the Oecumenical Partriarchate that Anglican orders had the same validity as the Roman, Old Catholic, and Armenian Churches. But with the non-Chalcedonian Churches, relations were hampered by a far more complicated political situation in the Near East.

The Armenian events of 1895-1918 had seriously complicated a lot of all the remaining Christian minorities of Turkey. The perceived disloyalty of the Armenians in allying themselves with Turkey's opponents had implicated all other Christian groups and exacerbated a situation already charged with mutual distrust.[109] The situation of the Assyrians under the British Mandate in Iraq was also fraught with tension. The Assyrians had been invited to form the 'Assyrian levies' by the British to fight against the rebellious Kurds. That this course of action was neither in the long term best interest of the Assyrians nor of any of the remaining Christian minorities within the emerging Kemalist Turkey has been drawn attention to by John Joseph.[110] Simultaneously, the Greek Orthodox minority in Anatolia had been expelled and exchanged for Turkish-speaking Muslims

---

[108] J G Lockhart, *Cosmo Gordon Lang*, London, 1949, 326.

[109] A classic statement of the Turkish sensitivity of this issue is to be found in Kamuran Gurun, *The Armenian File*, London, 1985. There is a great deal of literature on the period, and this emotive issue is dealt with in most of it in a less and objective way. In that period, fact is difficult to disentangle from propaganda, of either side. A balanced presentation is given by Christopher J Walker, *Armenia: The Survival of a Nation*, London 1980.

[110] John Joseph, *The Nestorians and their Muslim Neighbours*, Princeton, 1961, 173.

within the Greek territories. The Greek Orthodox population in Turkey dwindled to approximately 100,000 scattered around Istanbul.[111] In Turkey, therefore the Greek Orthodox were politically compromised, the Assyrians had been driven out, and the Armenians dwindled to a community centred on Istanbul. Only the Syrian Orthodox thus survived as a homogenous Christian entity in Anatolia.

Many Syrian Orthodox had fled from Turkey into Syria during the Armenian disturbances, and with the removal of the patriarchal seat from Deir-el-Zafaran into Syria, many more Syrian Orthodox left,[112] settling mainly in North-East Syria, the Jazira. The main 'waves' of migration took place in 1922 and 1924,[113] and the Syrian Orthodox rapidly began to settle in their newly-found home.[114] At the same time, they were careful to distinguish themselves from those of their co-religionists, (Armenians, Greeks and Assyrians), who had sought foreign intervention as the solution to their problems. Syrian Orthodox had also fled to Iraq, where the Arabic-speaking leadership distances themselves from any move to look to European powers for help, at the same time pointing out that they had no intention of requesting any form of autonomy. The far-sighted leader who emphasised this policy of support for the Arab cause was the new Syria Orthodox patriarch, Ignatius Ephrem I Barsoum.

The Patriarch Elias III Ignatius, who had concluded the negotiations with Archbishop Davidson, and had been patriarch at the time of the enforced removal from Deir-el-Zafaran to Homs in Syria, died an old man in February 1932. *The Times* said of him in an obituary on 20 February 1932:

> 'Though by Jacobite standards a highly cultured and erudite man and possessed of no small practical insight and ability, he had had few contacts with Europeans and belonged altogether to the old static order of the Ottoman regime. The Great War and its aftermath, which drove him and those of his people whose homes were in the present Turkish dominions into the

---

[111] On the 'exchange of populations', see R Brenton Betts, *Christians in the Arab East*, London, 1979, 110.

[112] See U Bjoklund, *North to Another Country*, Stockholm, 1981, 26f.

[113] For an account of the general migration of Syrian Orthodox from Turkey to Syria, Lebanon and Iraq, and more recently, to Europe, see G Yonan, *Assyrer Heute*, Hamburg, 1978.

[114] R Boghossian points out that between 1920 and 1940, the Syria Orthodox had established many schools in the area, in all their main centres, *La Haute-Djezireh*, Aleppo, 1952, 52.

> Mosul Vilayet, found him incapable of facing his troubles. But according to his lights, he did his best.'

The Patriarch Elias III died in India, where he had gone in an attempt to resolve a dispute which had arisen about the validity of ordinations preformed by the deposed Patriarch 'Abd-el-Messih.'[115]

The new patriarch, Ignatius Ephrem I Barsoum, was an entirely different man. Sophisticated, politically astute, and erudite, he was not anxious to create any ties with 'Christian' European powers which would compromised him with the new Syrian government. He was a member of the Arab academy in Damascus, and a scholar of international repute in both Arabic and Syriac.[116] Relations with the Syrian Orthodox in the Near East were thus to take on a different character for those from within the Church of England who had an interest. The patriarchate was now resident in Syria, and with a patriarchate who was anxious to demonstrate not only his loyalty to the emerging Syrian nation, but also to demonstrate the harmony of the Syrian Orthodox with Arabic language and culture. The remaining Syrian Orthodox in Turkey took on an increasingly isdated character. All the above political factors, coupled with a new primate at Lambeth and a new patriarch in Syria, the former with no great interest in the Eastern churches and the latter who had had less than satisfactory experiences in dealing with Anglicans, meant a decisive turning point in ecclesiastical exchange between the two churches. From the 'high water mark' of the Davidson period, exchanges now reached 'a low water mark'.

An invitation went out from the Committee responsible for inviting non-Anglicans to the Lambeth Conference of 1930 to the patriarchate in Syria. Replying on behalf of the patriarch, Mar Severius Barsoum (the later patriarch) wrote, 'The Syrian Orthodox are not willing to send a representative to the Lambeth Conference'.[117] Nor did he express any great interest in the deliberations of the Conference. The Syrian Orthodox are dealt with in a passing way in the Report of the Conference, and no new initiatives were planned.[118]

---

[115] See L W Brown, *Indian Christians*, pp 155f.

[116] See J Joseph, *Muslim-Christian Relations*, 115.

[117] Letter of Severius Barsoum to Lang, 9 June 1930 (Lambeth Palace Library, LC.153: 129).

[118] See the *Report of the Lambeth Conference 1930* (SPCK, 1930) 147.

One major concern to which the Conference was asked to address its attention was the emerging problem of the *episcope vagantes*. In July 1930, the 'commissary in England to His Holiness the Patriarch of Antioch', Dr Bhabha, wrote a letter to the organising Committee of the Conference drawing the delegates' attention to the claims of Frederick Lloyd, who claimed to be a Syrian archbishop of the 'Western Orthodox or American Catholic' Church.[119] It was rumoured that Lloyd was to apply to the Conference for Anglican recognition of his church. Anxious to expose his false claims to have an association with the Syrian Orthodox Church, Bhaba wrote, 'Mar Severius Barsoum saw him in America and denounced Lloyd to his face as a pretender, and falsely claiming to be a member of the Syrian Church.'[120]

Lloyd apparently came to London from his native American and administered ordination to four men.

The affair, however, was not to end there. Other *episcopi vagantes* were to spring up, all claiming connections with the Syrian Orthodox Church through the René Vilatte 'succession'.[121] In 1925, Stephen Theodosius de Nemeth, a Hungarian priest of the Orthodox Church had left his Church in protest at the extension of the authority of the Serbian patriarch to Budapest.[122] On 23 September 1934, Nemeth was consecrated as Mar Theodosius, 'Archbishop of the Hungarian Greek Oriental Orthodox Church' by the Patriarch Ephrem I Barsoum. This would have been of no concern whatsoever to Archbishop Lang and the hierarchy of the Church of England, had not 'Stephen B. Foyta, Archepiscopal Counsellor' to Mar Theodosius written to Lang, seeking recognition.[123] Canon J A Douglas, advising Lang on behalf of the newly formed Church of England Council on Foreign Relations, counselled writing to the patriarch to ascertain whether or not Nemeth's claims were genuine. This was done, but no response from the patriarch was

[119] See P F Anson, *Bishops at Large*, London, 1965, 253-9. The 'connection' between Peter III and the *episcope vagantes* is discussed on 36.

[120] Letter of Bhabha to Lambeth, 12 July 1930 (Lang 101, f.216). See also LC. 153: 295, where the letter is also reproduced.

[121] There is a large literature on the Vilatte 'succession'. Claiming that his orders ultimately came from Patriarch Peter III, the Syrian Orthodox consistently rejected his claims. See A J McDonald, *Episcopi Vagantes in Church History*, London, 1945, P F Anson, *op. cit.* and The *Catholicate of the West* (bound volume of pamphlets dealing with the question between 1954-64) in Lambeth Palace Library.

[122] For the details of the background to the dispute, see Anson, *op. cit.*, 512f.

[123] See the letter of Stephen B Foyta to Lang, 28 March 1937 (Lang 151. f.284).

forthcoming. Douglas' conclusion was that Nemeth should be treated, in the official response of the Church of England, as one of the *episcopi vagantes.*[124] The affair was about to its conclusion when yet another claim arose when Frederick Harrington, of 324 Hornsey Road, claimed the title of 'Metropolitan of the One Holy Orthodox Catholic Church', having been consecrated by Vilatte in Chicago in 1915. On 10 December 1938, the patriarchal denunciation of all thee individuals was delivered in a formal declaration. The Patriarch Ephrem I Barsoum delivered his *démenti* through Lambeth, and denounced, 'all the sects claiming succession through Vilatte' and distancing the Syrian Orthodox church from their claims.[125]

As can be seen from the above incidents, the Syrian Orthodox Patriarch Ephrem I Barsoum was now no longer willing to involve himself and his church in any negotiations with Western churches which would compromise him in the eyes of the national authorities where his people lived, Syria, Turkey or Iraq. The concern articulated remained, therefore, strictly ecclesiastical, and left no room for possible political misinterpretation. From the Syrian point of view, sustained and detailed negotiations with the Anglican Church were neither possible nor desirable.[126]

Conclusion

The story which has been told, of Syrian Orthodox-Anglican relations between 1874 and 1928, is an erratic one. At times, the exchange is full of promise and mutual enrichment, at other times, it is full of deception and disillusionment. It coincides with the late eighteenth and early 19th century increase of British power in the Near East and India. That the contacts should wane in the 1930s with the beginning of British decline in the Near East and the rise of Arab nationalism after the disillusionment of the First World War is no accident. As already stated, ecclesiastical exchange never takes place in a hermetic environment.

---

124 Douglas' correspondence with Lang is in Lang 151, ff. 284-304.

125 The Patriarchal *démenti* is in the Headlam Papers in Lambeth Palace Library (MS.2638, f.348), See also Anson, *op.cit.*, 241.

126 Some isolated pockets of Syrian Orthodox-Anglican co-operation remained in India. An *Indian Liturgy* was produced in 1922, based on the Syrian rite and intended for use by both Anglicans and Syrians. It was sanctioned by the Bishop of Bombay in 1933. It was only used, however, in the Chapel of an Anglican-Syrian Ashram at Poona. See *The Indian Liturgy*, revised ed., Bombay, 1948.

Contacts between Archibald Tait and the Patriarch Peter III were the real beginning of any sustained contact. All the instances of contact between patriarch and archbishop prior to this are sporadic and isolated. With the exception of India, it is only during this period that the beginnings of mutual knowledge were initiated. The earlier Indian exchange, represented *par excellence* by the CMS-Syria Orthodox venture at Kottayam of 1816-36 was hampered from the Anglican perspective by only being a contact between one specific form of the Church of England. CMS represented only one aspect of the Anglican Church in its more evangelistic, biblicist, and Protestant character. Had the 'mission of help' been balanced by representatives of less hard-line Protestants, the venture would have been on a more solid footing. As it was, the evangelical party had the ascendancy in the Church of England at the time, and it was not until the 1840's that the 'Tractarian' or High Church party began to exercise an increasing influence. Furthermore, the hierarchy of the Church of England, especially the archbishops of Canterbury, were never fully informed or aware of the exchange.

The individual missions and visits of the mid-19th century were hampered by the same disadvantage. The missions were always dependent on individual enthusiasm backed by particular societies with limited and specific aims. This was true of the expeditions of Ainsworth, Southgate and Badger, tangential though their interest in the Syrian Orthodox church was. The Church of England clearly never viewed these contacts as sufficiently important for the hierarchy to place the missions on a more official footing.

The only such mission to be created during the period under consideration was the Archbishop's Mission to the Assyrians in 1886, under Archbishop Benson. And, as we have seen, it was during the same period that repeated requests came to successive archbishops of Canterbury from successive patriarchs of Antioch for some such similar formal mission. That it was never created may be regarded as fortuitous. Despite the fact that the authorities of the Archbishop's Mission continually stressed that theirs was a non-political mission, when the Assyrians raised their opposition to Turkish authority, the fact that they had for so long been connected formally to a Mission of a foreign church and power cannot have helped them. Protestant missions especially were viewed with suspicion by the Ottoman authorities, as a thinly-veiled disguise for expansionist ambitions on the part of foreign governments. CMS, for example, saw the British occupation of Egypt in 1882 as providential. As Tibawi has stated:

> 'Protestant missions had made sufficiently clear their attitude towards the legitimate Government and the territorial integrity of the state in which they resided and worked. Not only did they publicly declare their intention of subverting its established religion, not only did they openly pray for the extinction of the state, and the absorption of its own territories by their own governments, but pending the achievement of these ambitions, they claimed special privileges and exemptions, and with these very claims they accused the Ottoman authorities of intolerance, fanaticism, and bigotry'.[127]

Similarly, even though the Syrian Orthodox suffered greatly in the period of 1895-1914, the fact that they were spared the full blast of those events may partly be attributable to the fact that they never created formal alliances with any foreign churches or governments.

During the primacy of Davidson, the Church of England came closer to an official and formal connection with the Syrian Orthodox Church than had previously been the case. But, as we have seen, the character of the exchange varied. Prior to 1914, the exchanges often moved towards formal political intervention, although never reaching that point in actuality. The mortal danger which this policy represented for Christians of the Near East became increasingly apparent to both sides of the exchange during this period.

As Joseph had stated:

> 'Christians of the Middle East have found themselves in the uncomfortable position of being the so-religionists of peoples and nations who were considered to be the rivals, if not the enemies, of the Muslim state. They have suffered from that position in the past and continue to feel ill at ease from it at the present'.[128]

---

[127] A L Tabawi, *American Interests in Syria 1800-1901*, 256f. See also his 'Unpublished letters on Protestant Missions in Palestine', in *Muslim World*, Vol. 67, No. 4 (1977), 258-65.

[128] J Joseph, *Muslim Christian Relations*, 120.

The story of relations between the Syrian Orthodox Church and the Church of England between 1874 and 1928 is only a small, and overlooked, aspect of this wider context of religious, cultural, and political exchange. It is to be hoped that this study has contributed to a greater understanding of the importance of all such exchanges.

Bibliography

Unpublished and Primary Sources

Lambeth Palace Library: Tait Papers, Benson Papers, Frederick Temple Papers,

Davidson Papers, Lang Papers, Lambeth Conference Papers, Manuscript Series, J. A. Douglas Papers.

Archives of the Kerala United Theological Seminary, Trivandrum, Kerala: Papers on CMS-Syrian Orthodox Seminary at Kottayam.

SPCK Archives, London: Report of Proceedings Papers.

USPG Archives, London: Missionary Reports 1870-95. Letters of G. Curtis.

Royal Geographical Society Archives: Papers on the Ainsworth and Rassam Euphrates Expedition.

CMS Archives, London: Papers related to the CMS Mediterranean Mission. (These papers will be re-opened as a Special Collection in Birmingham University along with papers related to the Kottayam Seminary).

Universitäts Bibliothek, Bonn: Goussen, 86, Shhima.

Public Records Office, Foreign Office Files, Turkey (FO. 78), India Office, Fort St. George Records.

Theses: Perry, Robert F., 'European Explorations in Turkish Kurdistan, 1800-1842' (Masters thesis, American University of Beirut, 1965).

Published and Secondary Sources

Agur, C M — *Church History of Travancore*: Madras, 1903.

Ainsworth, W F — *Travels in Asia Minor*: London, 1842.

Personal Narrative of the Euphrates Expedition: London, 1888.

Claims of the Christian Aborigines of the Turkish Empire: London, 1843.

'An Anglican Syrian' — *The Malabar Syrian Church and the See of Antioch*: Kottayam, 1928.

Anderson, R — *Missions of the American Board to Oriental Churches*: 2 Vols., New York, 1872.

Andrus, A N — 'Report from Mardin' in *Missionary Herald* (1875).
'Obituary of Peter III' in *Missionary Herald* (1895).

Anson, P F — *Bishops at Large*: London 1965.

Aprem, Mar (formerly Geoge Mooken) — *The Chaldean Syrian Church in India*: Trichur, 1977.

Arfa, Hassan — *The Kurds in historical and political study*: London, 1966.

Atiya, A S — *A History of Eastern Christianity*: London, 1968.

Badger, G P — *The Nestorians and their Rituals*: 2 Vols., London, 1852.

Bell, G K A — *Randall Davidson*: 2 Vols., London 1935.
Documents on Christian Unity, 1920-24: London, 1924.

Benson, A C — Life of E. W. Benson: 2 Vols., London 1899.

Betts, R B — *Christians in the Arab East*: London 1979.

Björklund, Ulf — *North to Another Country: The Formation of a Suryoyo Community in Sweden*: Stockholm, 1981.

Brant, James — 'Journey through a part of Armenia and Asia Minor' in *Journal of the Royal Geographical Society*: Vol. VI, (1836).

Brown, L. W. — *The Indian Christians of St Thomas*: C.V.P. revised Ed., 1982.

Bruinessen, M M Van — *Agha, Sheikh, and State*: Schonhooven, 1978.

Buchanan, C — *Christian Researches in Asia*: (2nd ed.), Cambridge, 1811.

Carpenter, S C — *Church and People, 1789-1889*: London 1959.

Cheriyan, P — *The Malabar Syrians and the Church Missionary Society 1816-1840*: Kottayam, 1935.

Christian Minorities of Turkey: Churches Committee on Migrant Workers in Europe, Bruxelles, 1979.

Curson, R — *Visits to Monasteries in the Levant*: London, 1849.

Dark, S — *The Lambeth Conferences*: London, 1930.

Dauphin, C — 'The Rediscovery of the Nestorian Churches of the Hakkiari' in *Eastern Churches Review*, 1973.

Davidson, R T and Benham, W — *Life of Archibald Campbell Tait*: 2 Vols., London, 1891.

Davis, R — *Aleppo and Devonshire Square*: London, 1967.

Deighton, H S — *'The Impact of Egypt on Britain' in Political and Social Change in Modern Egypt* (ed. P. M. Holt): London, 1968.

Dölapönü, Hanna	*Tarihte Mardin*: Istanbul, 1972.
Douglas, J A	*Relations of the Anglican Churches with the Eastern Orthodox*: London, 1921.
Edwards D L	*Leaders of the Church of England, 1828-1914*: London, 1971.
Etheridge, J W	*The Syrian Churches*: London, 1846.
Fiey, J M	'Proto-histoire chrétienne du Hakkiari Turc' in *L'Orient Syrien*, Vol. 9, (1964).
Finn, Elizabeth A	*Reminiscences of Mrs Finn*: London 1929.
Fortescue, A	*The Lesser Eastern Churches*: London, 1913.
Foster, H A	*The Making of Modern Iraq*: London, 1936,
Frazee, C	*Catholics and Sultans*: London, 1983.
Geddes, M	*History of the Church of Malabar*: London, 1694.
Gibbs, M E	*The Anglican Church in India, 1600-1970*: Delhi, 1972
Gürün, K	*The Armenian File*: London, 1985.
Hajjar, J	*L'Apostalat des missionares latins dans le Proche-Orient selon les directives romaines*: Jerusalem, 1956.
Heber, R	*Narrative of a Journey throught he Provinces of India, From Calcutta to Bombay 1824-25*: London, 1828.
Hunt, W S	*The Anglican Church in Travancore and Cochin, 1816-1916*: Kottayan, 1933.
Joseph, J	*The Nestorians and their Muslin Neighbours: Princeton, 1961.*
	Muslim-Christian Relations and Inter-Christian Rivalries in the Middle East: New York, 1983.
Kawerau, P	*Amerika und die orientalischen Kirchen*: Berlin, 1958
Keay, F E	*History of the Syrian Church in India*: Madras, 1938.
Kerr, R H	*Report to Lord W. Bentinck on the State of the Christians Inhabiting the Kingdom of Cochin and Travancore*: London, 1813.
King, H S	*Missionary Enterprise in the East*: London, 1873.
Kinross, Lord	*The Ottoman Centuries*: New York, 1977.
La Croze, V	*Histoire du christianisme des Indes*: 2 Vols., The Hague, 1723.
Laird, M A	*Bishop Heber in Northern India*: London, 1971.
Lash, W	'Treasurers New and Old' in the *Star of the East* (Vol. I-II. 1939-41): Sasthamkotta, 1941.
Lockhart, J G	*Cosmo Gordon Lang*: London, 1949.

Luke, H C	*Mosul and its Minorities*: London, 1925.
Macuch, R	*Geschichte der Spät und Neusyrischen Literatur*: Berlin, 1976.
McDonald, A J	*Episcopi Vagantes in Church History*: London, 1945.
Parry, O H	*Six Months in a Syrian Monastery*: London, 1895.
	'The Ancient Syrian Church in Mesopotamia and Extracts from the letters and reports of O. H. Parry', pamphlet printed in 1892.
Penny, F	*The Church in Madras*: 3 Vols., London, 1912.
Perry, W A	*The Third Lambeth Conference, 1888*. (Privately Printed, 1891).
Powell, E Alexander	*The Struggle for Power in Moslem Asia*: New York, 1925.
Reed, G S	*La Mission de l'Archevêque de Cantorbéry Auprès des Assyriens*: Paris, 1968.
	Report of the 1920 Lambeth Conference: London, 1920.
Rich, C J	*Narrative of a Residence in Koordistan*: 2 Vols., London, 1836.
Richards, W J	'The Indian Christians of St Thomas' in *Church Missionary Intelligencer*, March, 1895.
Richter, J	*A History of Protestant Missions in the Near East*: London, 1910.
Runciman, S	*The Great Church in Captivity*: London, 1968.
Sadadi, A	'Rihlat al-Mutran (al Batriark ba'da'ithen) Abdallah Sadadi ila Istanbul wa London wa Malibar al-Hind' (English translation—'The Journey of Bishop (later Patriarch) Abdallah Sadadi to Istanbul and London and India') in *Magallat al-Batriarkiyal*: Damascus, nos. 42-49, February—September, 1985.
Saka, I	*Kanisati al-Suryaniyah*: Damascus, 1985.
Sertoglu, M	*Süryanoi Türklerinin*: Istanbul, 1974.
Shaw, P E	*American Contacts with the Eastern Churches, 1820-70*: Chicago, 1937.
	The Early Tractarians and the Eastern Church: Chicago, 1930.
Simsir, Bilâl N	*British Documents on Ottoman Armenians*: 2 Vols., Ankara, 1983.
Smith, G	*Bishop Heber*: London, 1895.
Southgate, H	*Narrative of a Tour through Armenian Kurdistan, Persia, and Mesopotamia*: 2 Vols., London, 1840.
Stanley, A P	*The Eastern Church*: London, 1869.

Stephenson, A M — *Anglicanism and the Lambeth Conferences*: London, 1978.

Stock, E — *History of the Church Missionary Society*: 3 Vols., London, 1899.

Sykes, M — *The Caliph's Last Heritage*: London, 1915.

Dar ul-Islam: London, 1924.

Taylor, T — *Life of Heber*. London, 1836.

Frederick Temple (ed. Sandford) 2 Vols., London, 1906.

Tibawi, A L — *A Modern History of Syria*: London, 1969.

American Interests in Syria, 1800-1901: London, 1966.

'Unpublished letters on Protestant Missions in Palestine' in *Muslim World*, Vol. 67, No. 4 (1977).

Tisserant, E — *Eastern Christianity in India*: London.

Valyi, F — *Revolutions in Islam*: London, 1925.

Verghese, P — (ed.) *Die Syrischen Kirchen in Indien*: Stuttgart, 1974.

Vithayathil, V J — *The Origin and Progress of the Syro-Malabar Hierarchy*: Kottayam, 1980.

Walker, C J — *Armenia: The Survival of a Nation*: London, 1980.

Warkworth, Lord — *Notes from a Diary in Asiatic Turkey*: London, 1896.

Waterfield, R E — *Christians in Persia*: London, 1973.

Whitehouse, T — *Lingerings of Light in a Dark Land*: London, 1873.

Winslow, Festing, Athavale and Rutcliff — 'The Rule of the Jacobite Patriarch over the Christians of St Thomas' in *Church Missionary Intelligencer* (January, 1875).

Yonan, G — *Assyrer Heute, Kultur, Sprache, National-Bewegung Der Aramaisch—sprechenden Christen im Nahen Osten*: Hamburg, 1978.

Abbreviations

RGS	Royal Geographical Society
SPCK	Society for the Promotion of Christian Knowledge
SPG	Society for the Propagation of the Gospel
CMS	Church Missionary Society
FO	Foreign Office
LC	Lambeth Conference

BETWEEN EASTERN AND WESTERN CHRISTENDOM: THE BENEDICTINES, FRANCE AND THE SYRIAN CATHOLIC CHURCH IN JERUSALEM*

Dominique Trimbur

Despite particularly difficult political circumstances across the decades, the network of French institutions in the Holy Land is characterised by its tenacity and longevity. The great majority of the institutions founded, for the most part, in the second half of the 19th century still exists. Only two of these institutions have disappeared—one, the convent of Marie Réparatrice sisters, after its complete destruction in the course of the Israeli-Arab war of 1948. The current Benedictine presence, at the abbey of Sainte-Marie de la Résurrection in Abu Ghosh, almost entirely obliterates the memory of the other, a former Benedictine foundation, existing between 1899 and the middle of the 1950s.

In an earlier study, we examined the founding of this establishment, trying to discover how matters were divided between religion and politics in a new French, Catholic, establishment in Ottoman Palestine.[1] Because of this emphasis, we could only sketchily describe a project nowadays almost fallen from memory, the Syrian-Catholic seminary run by the French Benedictines. Conversely, its Greek-Catholic (Melkite) counterpart at Sainte-Anne's is still in everyone's mind, the fruit of an early meeting between Eastern and Western Christianity which was carried forward in

* A French version of this article appeared under the title: 'Vie et mort d'un séminaire syrien-catholique—L'établissement bénédictin de Jérusalem', in *Proche-Orient chrétien*, 52, 3-4, 2002, 303-352. One should note that the Benedictine monks in Israel at present come from the Abbey of Bec-Hellouin (Congregation of Monte-Oliveto), whereas the first Benedictines of the modern area belonged to the Congregation of Subiaco.

1 'Religion et politique en Palestine: le cas de la France à Abou Ghosh', in Dominique Trimbur/Ran Aaronsohn (eds), *De Bonaparte à Balfour—La France, l'Europe occidentale et la Palestine, 1799-1917*, 'Mélanges' collection of the French Research Centre in Jerusalem, vol. 3, CNRS-Éditions, Paris, 2001, 265-293.

the periodical *Proche Orient Chrétien* ('Christian Near East') published by the White Fathers.

The present paper will not be a matter of nostalgia. Beyond the purely political aspect, it is our ambition to paint a picture, however briefly and incompletely, of the achievements of the Benedictines in the Holy Land. By calling to mind their varied activities, it will be possible to establish their contribution to that meeting of East and West which Pope Leo XIII had wished for in his own time. To take a longer view is also to try to establish the validity of the motives and other factors which had prevailed from the creation of this Benedictine foundation. In fact, in such a foundation, two different approaches coexisted, the political and the religious. Its birth and its continuance depended on a good relationship between two essentially different systems of thought. It is to the recollection of this harmony that we shall first set ourselves. We shall mention the convergence between the two approaches in the first part. But, as we shall indicate in the second part, while the two approaches could accommodate each other in a common concern, they could also fall out of harmony, which in turn led unavoidably to the calling into question and, finally, the disappearance of the project.

I. Forces for harmony

a. France and the Benedictines in the restoration of a Benedictine presence in Palestine 1899-1901

It was the French authorities who provided the basis for re-establishing the Benedictine presence in the Holy Land at the end of the 19th century. It was, in fact, because France had possessed since 1873, through a gift from the sultan, a Crusader church and since then had looked for a community to establish there, that France concluded an agreement with the French branch of the Order of Saint Benedict.

But it was also because France did not know to what ends exactly to put this church, leaving it unoccupied for 25 years, that religion came into the matter. This focusing of attention was due to the priest of the Parish of Saint-Léger Vauban, wherein stood the Abbey of la Pierre qui Vire. In course of a pilgrimage the Priest noted that the site was vacant and he organised a meeting between representatives of the State and the Church. As a result, Abbot Moreau was at the source of the convergence between the Republic and the monks, between the French Foreign Ministry and the Benedictines.[2] On both sides, the negotiation and the subsequent agreement, reflected long-term as well as immediate demands. This resulted in a making use of religion by politics but also a making use of politics by religion.

On the Republic's side, it was a matter of enhancing the value of a church that was an eloquent testimony to the greatness of the Latin kingdom of Jerusalem. But beneath this concern for the Republic there also lay the possibility of taking over the heritage of the Frankish kingdom, and so of supporting the Republic's own claim to be *the* protector of Oriental Catholics. This would strengthen an overtly *francophone*, if not actually French, atmosphere in the local Catholicism. With this purpose in view, the French administration had, since the beginning of the 1890s, studied the possibility of restoration works.[3] The significance of the building was not only aesthetic; its importance was also acknowledged 'from the point of view of our political interests'.[4] The French representative in Jerusalem called for immediate action in the interest of 'our good reputation in the Holy Land'.[5] After twenty years of neglect, the French government showed a serious interest in the fate of the church, especially because the political context had changed. International rivalry and the exacerbation of differing interests were at their peak and the Holy Land seemed to have definitely emerged from the somnolence that characterised it in earlier centuries. One could see the growing investment by traditionally rival Powers (Italy, Russia), but especially by countries only recently present in this field (Germany). Thus, France had to prove her firmness and to put up a definite response to the audacity of the other nations.

For that purpose, the spiritual could, and had to, put itself at the service of the temporal. The allocation of French ownership to a religious community could not be decided without deep reflection. It would become a responsibility for France, but also for the religious community,

---

2 Abbé Adolphe Moreau, *Mémoire sur les fouilles d'Abou-Gosch (Palestine)*, Sens, 1906 with, in the introduction, the memory of his intervention from 1893 onwards.

3 Archives of the French Foreign Ministry, Paris, (hereafter MAE, Paris), Affaires diverses politiques—Secours religieux, 27—1891, note for the Minister, grants for the institutions in the Orient, 28 July 1891.

4 *Ibid.*, Affaires diverses politiques Turquie, 26 Jérusalem 1882-1892, note for the Minister, restoration of the church of Abu Ghosh, December 1891.

5 *Ibid.*, Nouvelle Série, Lieux Saints 86 Basilique d'Abou Ghosh I 1899-1901, letter from the French Consulate general in Jerusalem (28) to the MAE, 1 July 1899, Auzépy.

which had to merit a highly patriotic mission entrusted to it by its country of origin. In the case of Abu Ghosh, the new foundation had also to be contiguous with the historical tradition. As the Marquis de Vogüé put it:

> 'In the unchangeable East, where nothing changes, the same sites keep to the same purposes, as if they were consecrated by tradition and by the custom of the centuries.'[6]

With the very first discussions between France and the Benedictines, from the beginning of 1899, the primacy of the political approach clearly appeared. In the French diplomats' eyes, the religious became 'new collaborators in the work we have undertaken.'[7] This aspect of the links between the French authorities and the monks prevailed during the negotiations. French official perception of the issues became progressively more focussed. The matter in question became part of the theory of establishments in the Holy Land: they were French arms in the region.[8] It was this, for instance, that appeared in the legal framework that was chosen for the collaboration between France and the religious. Since these Congregations, under the force of the anticlerical laws of 1880, had 'placed themselves [...] in an irregular situation with respect to the Government of the Republic, we shall not know how to negotiate officially with their representatives'. To deal with this obstacle an ingenious solution was found. Since official negotiations were impossible in Paris itself, unofficial talks in Jerusalem could be considered.[9]

Furthermore, Paris had to find a community that brought sure guarantees. This had to do with the outlook of people destined to be standard-bearers for France. In this context, the writings of the Benedictines presented an eloquent testimony of what these religious supported, in the nationalistic mentality of those days, as well as, in the

---

6 Quoted in *Les anciens monastères bénédictins en Orient*, Lille-Paris, Desclée-De Brouwer et Cie, 1912, 13.

7 Archives of the French Foreign Ministry, Nantes (later: MAE, Nantes), Jérusalem—Domaines nationaux Abou Gosch II July 1899-1912, 50, letter from the French Consulate general in Jerusalem (373) to the Congregation of Subiaco, 28 July 1899, Auzépy (draft).

8 When the first part of the Assumptionist establishment of Notre-Dame de France was inaugurated, in 1888, the French Consul used a military image in placing the French houses at the outposts of the struggle (*Échos de Notre-Dame de France*, NR. 1 July 1888).

9 MAE, Nantes, Jérusalem—Domaines nationaux Abou Gosch II July 1899-1912, 50, letter from the MAE (Midi, 29) to the French Consulate general in Jerusalem, 5 October 1899, Delcassé.

specific context of the Holy Land, the heritage of the Crusaders.[10] Further, the community in question had in fact to be genuinely French, and the agreement foreseen for the church at Abu Ghosh had to enshrine the principle that a majority of the Benedictines who settled there would be French; they, and not the very Italian Congregation of the Primitive Observance, should be granted rights.[11] As the French ambassador to the Holy See summed it up, the basilica should be allocated to a French Congregation, composed of French people, and the church handed over to French individuals.[12]

The agreement was signed by Dom Bernard Drouhin, representing the Benedictines in Jerusalem, and by the French Consul Ernest Auzépy on 12 August 1901. The French character of the new foundation was guaranteed, as well as that of all the buildings that would be part of it. In all these details the preoccupation of Paris is explained by the local context, more than ever dominated by international rivalries. As the Political section of the French Foreign Ministry put it, this arrangement presented two advantages:

> '1°—[...] to ensure the restoration and maintenance of a building of historical interest, with no expenses for the State, while adding to our national prestige in Palestine.
> 2°—[...] to bring about the re-entry into our sphere of influence in the East of a famous and important Order, while forestalling attempts to involve it in policies opposed to those of France.'[13]

According to the Ministry, from this perspective, it was a matter of avoiding a tendency observed in other establishments. As recourse was increasingly made to recruiting monks from within the

---

[10] *Ibid.*, letter from D Drouhin, OSB, to Auzépy, 11 September 1899: 'In this surprising concourse of circumstances, there is for us, Mr Consul, a very precious encouragement: we would gladly say, with our generous Crusaders of the eleventh and twelfth century: God wants it, God wants it! especially as our consciences and our hearts give their testimony that, like them, we are only looking for the greatness of our dear France and the extension of God's reign, which for individuals and for peoples is the real, the unique source of civilisation and happiness.'

[11] *Ibid.*, letter from the MAE (Midi, 30) to the French Consulate general in Jerusalem, 28 March 1901.

[12] MAE, Paris, Nouvelle Série, Lieux Saints 86 Basilique d'Abou Gosch I 1899-1901, letter from the French Embassy to the Holy See (73) to the MAE, 31 March 1901, Nisard.

[13] *Ibid.*, note for the Minister, 18 September 1899, Eventual concession to the Benedictines of the custody of the shrine of Abu Ghosh near Jerusalem.

local population,[14] any development should be resisted that could lead to the settlement of foundations calling themselves French, but led by or filled with non-French-speaking monks.[15] From this point of view, the political approach is unyielding. But it is two-faceted: the French wish to be assured of the French character on the part of the religious was accompanied by a sense of urgency. While it was quite logical that French monks should reinforce the efforts of the Republic, the Foreign Ministry wished, even so, to sign an agreement with a partner whose legitimacy and legal character were acknowledged. This explains the signing of the agreement before the coming into effect of the Law on Associations of 1st August 1901—a law whose main aim was to prohibit every religious Congregation, such as the one with which France was preparing to conclude an agreement.

A foundation directed against France's rivals in Palestine

The Benedictine foundation could also appear to be a further aspect of the French reaction to Wilhelm II's visit to Jerusalem, in October-November 1898. Such an idea existed from that date, and France decided to use the same weapons as Germany.[16] The designation, in July 1899, of German Benedictines to occupy the reputed site of the Dormition[17] was a weighty argument in favour of their French counterparts.

---

[14] MAE, Nantes, Jérusalem—Domaines nationaux Abou Gosch II July 1899-1912, 50, letter from the French Embassy to the Holy See to the MAE, 8 July 1901, Nisard.

[15] As Consul Auzépy wrote: 'I believe this would be an error, and a serious one, to deliver freely a shrine of the value of which we speak now, to a foreign community that would, without a doubt, be ready to profit from such a favour to take advantage, as against our countrymen, of the claim to be a 'French' community in order to urge their generosity towards new foundations in Judea, projects that would all carry a great risk, it is clear of being motivated far from our own aims and of soon forming themselves into hostile centres, preoccupied only with withdrawing from our tutelage and with fighting our influence' (MAE, Paris, Nouvelle Série, Lieux Saints 86 Basilique d'Abou Gosch I 1899-1901, letter from the French Consulate general in Jerusalem [4] to the MAE, 2 February 1901).

[16] On the French behaviour in this matter, see our article 'Intrusion of the "Erbfeind"—French Views on Germans in Palestine 1898-1910', in Thomas Hummel, Kevork Hintlian, Ulf Carmesund, *Patterns of the Past, Prospects for the Future, The Christian Heritage in the Holy Land*, London, Melisende Press, 1999, 238-256.

[17] MAE, Nantes, Jérusalem, A, 28 Lieux saints, Cession de la Dormition, letter from the MAE (Midi-23) to the French Consulate general in Jerusalem, 25 July 1899. See Oliver Kohler, 'Mehr als Anhängsel ... Das Grundstück "Dormition" und die katholische Dimension des 31. Oktober 1898', in Karl-Heinz Ronecker, Jens Nieper, Thorsten Neubert-Preine (eds), *Dem Erlöser der Welt zur Ehre—Festschrift zum hundertjährigen Jubiläum der Einweihung der evangelischen Erlöserkirche in Jerusalem*, Leipzig, Evangelische Verlagsanstalt, 1998, 136-153.

But the matter did not relate only to Palestine; the Quai d'Orsay was anxious to widen the discussion. At a time when France was herself engaged in intense anticlerical discussions, it was a matter, from her point a view, of making the monastic orders really French. Two birds could thus be killed with one stone: to obtain an extra advantage in Palestine and to confirm French preponderance at the Vatican.[18] This was possible thanks to a wide-ranging policy—as when, for instance, certain dignitaries refused to follow papal directives favourable to France. And as when Cardinal Ledochowski, former Bishop of Posen, and Prefect of Propaganda, was reluctant to establish French Benedictines in Jerusalem, despite being requested to do so by Leo XIII. In order to act against such opposition, Paris did not hesitate to exert pressure, obtaining from the pope a *motu proprio*, a Pontifical act that could overrule any resistance at a lower level.[19] Similarly in Jerusalem; Ludovico Piavi, the Latin patriarch, was seen as an old adversary of France and was perceived to be wholly under German influence.

In the same way, when the talks between the French Government and the Benedictines fell behind, France used the German argument in order to accelerate the solution. A favourable outcome for France and for the Benedictines was all the more urgent since 'the German Benedictines, supported by their government, proclaim loudly, for the month of September, the laying of the foundation stone for the shrine of the Dormition.'[20]

The Syrian-Catholic seminary

The initiatives of France's rivals were numerous and made necessary new French advances and supplementary projects in the name of the new community. For instance, the German Benedictines were already interested in the idea of a Syrian-Catholic seminary. This already old idea was revived at the time of the negotiations between the French Foreign

---

18 MAE, Paris, Nouvelle Série, Lieux Saints 86 Basilique d'Abou Gosch I 1899–1901, letter from the French Embassy to the Holy See (143) to the MAE, 19 August 1899, Navenne.

19 *Ibid.*, telegram from the French Embassy to the Holy See (82) to the MAE, 31 October 1899, Navenne.

20 *Ibid.*, letter from the French Embassy to the Holy See (145) to the MAE, 20 July 1900, Navenne.

Ministry and the French Benedictines. France was then approached by the Syrian-Catholic Patriarch, himself jealous of the benefits granted by France to the Melkites via the seminary of Sainte-Anne, run by the White Fathers. Under such circumstances, Paris could only see with satisfaction a French client calling for still more attention.[21] The Syriac request, at first merely on record, was afterwards taken up actively when the German Benedictines made their appearance. Why shouldn't the French Benedictines put themselves at the service of their country in this context also?

The acquisition by the religious of a plot on the Mount of Scandal, next to the Mount of Olives, by the end of 1900, was the first step in the new project. Its significance was made even clearer by the fact that it occurred at the very same time as the laying of the foundation-stone of the Abbey of the Dormition by the German Benedictines. Logically, Paris brought its diplomacy to bear in order to obtain the rights to the site from the Vatican. The stakes were high, since, beyond Jerusalem, the whole of Syria would be affected. The seminary in question would send there the priests whom it had trained, who 'in the future would be an important element in developing our interest.' Furthermore, the very idea was attractive since the Primate of the Benedictine Order was putting all his weight into the balance in order to impose a German solution,[22] helped as he was yet again by the Prefect of Propaganda, the German (by nationality) Ledochowski.[23] The final decision dated only from the end of July 1901 and was favourable to France, thanks to the help of Pope Leo XIII, but especially to the senior Vatican Cardinal and Secretary of State Rampolla, closely collaborating with Cardinal Langénieux, former Pontifical Legate to the 1893 Eucharistic Congress in Jerusalem. Paris had, however, taken precautions beforehand, following the precedent of Abu Ghosh. The community installed must be French, as must its dependent

[21] MAE, Nantes, Jérusalem, A, 129 Syriens catholiques, letter from the French Consulate in Beirut to the MAE, 7 June 1899, Sercey. About the relations between Paris and the Syrian-Catholic church, see Joseph Hajjar, *Le Vatican, la France et le Catholicisme oriental (1878-1914)*, Beauchesne, Paris, 1979, 167-173 and 377-384.

[22] MAE, Nantes, Jerusalem, A, 82 Bénédictins séminaire syrien catholique, letter from the MAE to the French Consulate in Jerusalem, 1 May 1901.

[23] *Ibid.*, letter from the MAE (16) to the French Consulate general in Jerusalem, 2 July 1901. France had a fixation about the claimed germanophile attitude of the highest prelates at the Vatican, such that Ledochowski passed in Rome for a militant germanophile. (see Claude Prudhomme, *Stratégie missionnaire du Saint-Siège sous Léon XIII (1878-1903)—Centralisation romaine et défis culturels*, École française de Rome, Rome, 1994, 151-153).

houses.[24] Since the seminary of the Mount of Scandal would be in the name of these Benedictines, the French future of this new house of studies was guaranteed.

Furthermore, the success of this operation also meant growing prestige for France; its role as protecting power for the Oriental Christians was supported by the Syrian-Catholics. At the point of time when her protectorate was strengthened at the international level through the *diktat* imposed upon the Ottoman empire, the treaty of Mytilenes of 12 November 1901, France finally succeeded, further, in having the new foundation registered on the list of officially protected French establishments.[25] The new foundation thus came to be perceived as a permanent element of French influence.

The Benedictines as zealous auxiliaries of France

In both these matters—the allocation to the Benedictines of the care of the church of Abu Ghosh and the development of the Syrian-Catholic seminary—what was the attitude of the Benedictines themselves?

Generally speaking, it appears that the religious adopted the spirit of that period. To their eyes, the French reputation was more important than any reluctance that could strengthen the French anticlerical policy in Paris. Dom Drouhin, initiator of the contacts and agent on the ground, showed a patriotic urgency from the beginning.[26] The Benedictines were at the service of France, a proud heir of the Crusader tradition. Therefore it was worth while submitting themselves to 'a Minister who is so much preoccupied with French interest' and 'to foresee and neutralise, from the point of view of French Catholic influence, the impending establishment of

---

[24] In order 'to prevent any confusion with the German branch of the same Order established in Palestine.' (MAE, Paris, PAAP 240 Doulcet, 4 Protectorat religieux 1890-1907, Religious Congregations settled in Palestine according to the date of their installation, and MAE, Nantes, Jérusalem, A, 82 Bénédictins séminaire syrien catholique, letter from the MAE [17] to the French Consulate General in Jerusalem, 18 July 1901).

[25] Bernardin Collin, OFM, *Le problème juridique des Lieux Saints*, Centre d'études orientales, Sirey, Cairo-Paris, 1956, 167, and MAE, Paris, NS-Protectorat catholique, 30, dossier général, 1899-1903, letter from the French Embassy to the Holy See (233) to the MAE, 1 December 1901, Nisard.

[26] MAE, Nantes, Jérusalem, Domaines nationaux Abou Gosch II July 1899-1912, 50, letter from Subiaco Congregation to the French Consulate in Jerusalem, 28 July 1899, D Bernard Drouhin.

rival Benedictine projects'.[27] This submission could only serve 'the work of extending the noble influence of France',[28] since the religious themselves wanted to be at 'the centre of the French Syrian Rite project'.[29] This pro-French eagerness grew progressively as the German threat materialised. As Dom Drouhin wrote, just as the allocation of the seminary on the Mount of Scandal to the French Benedictines was negotiated:

> 'The mission of France and its foreign ambition, under the name of Protectorate, must be to attract and unite all parties under one French direction, strong it is true, but also wide and secure. It has been clearly perceived in Paris that our projects on the Mount of Olives [...] were the best means of opposing the projects of our political adversaries.'[30]

The Benedictines' patriotism was even more wholehearted once they had acquired the concession of the Mount of Olives. It was considered as a 'truly French' success against the Primate of the Benedictine Order, 'a person in league with German interests'.[31] The co-operation between France and the disciples of Saint Benedict was satisfactory on a Palestinian level, since it allowed them to play an important role within the local population by obtaining a prestigious responsibility;[32] but it was also valuable on the level of international politics. The Benedictines were not looking merely to a local victory; their achievement would make sense only in terms of its strengthening of the French position in the Ottoman empire. Dom Drouhin in consequence soon afterwards expressed this view when he greeted the 'fine victory won by French diplomacy' with the Treaty of Mytilene.[33]

---

[27] *Ibid.*, Report presented to the French Foreign Ministry about the agreement relating to Abu Goch *[sic]*, Draft from Reverend Abbot General, April-June 1901, D Bernard Drouhin.

[28] MAE, Paris, NS-Lieux Saints 86 Basilique d'Abou Gosch I 1899-1901, letter from the French Consulate in Jerusalem (5) to the MAE, 1st February 1900, Auzépy.

[29] *Ibid.*, letter from D Drouhin to Maurice Horric de Beaucaire (official of the Quai d'Orsay), 1 April 1900.

[30] *Ibid.*, letter from the French Consulate in Jerusalem (20) to the MAE, 20 July 1901, with an appendix: letter from D Drouhin to Auzépy, 16 July 1901.

[31] *Ibid.*, letter from D Drouhin to Beaucaire, 25 August 1901.

[32] *Ibid.*, 'for all Oriental people, who are nothing but great children, a material gift is the main way to achieve respect, esteem, trust.'

[33] *Ibid.*, PAAP 012 Beaucaire, 1 Lettres particulières reçues et envoyées, 1898-1907, letter from D Drouhin to Beaucaire, 8 December 1901.

b. For God and France: the activity of the French Benedictines in Palestine

The acceptance of the political approach by the religious was not only the result of a nationalism common to the French whether diplomats or religious. It was also possible in that acceptance of the political approach had its counterpart in the corresponding demands of the religious.

Certainly, this new mission also reflected concerns about circumstances that were less favourable. In fact, like the other religious congregations, the Benedictines were at the time looking for shelter abroad that would provide a refuge following a very probable expulsion from France. They perceived clearly the radicalisation of French politics beneath the first anticlerical measures since 1880, which must have made them fear the worst. For had not the negotiations with the Quai d'Orsay been hastened, to be complete before the coming into force of the Law on Associations? In practical terms it was thanks to this law that the new Benedictine foundation experienced a promising start, in that it led to the arrival of personnel. For the Benedictines, the foundation and development of a new mission was also in tune with the spirit of the times, leading to foundations in foreign parts. Expression *par excellence* of the vocation of a religious congregation, the new Benedictine foundation in Abu Ghosh/ Jerusalem reflected furthermore the wish to carry on an active apostolate. In parallel with French efforts in the framework of an early cultural policy, according directly with Pope Leo XIII's desire to improve the training of the Oriental clergy, and accepting the request of the Syrian-Catholic Patriarch Rahmani, the Benedictines threw themselves into unfamiliar activity. After financial difficulties and some delay, the seminary of the Mount of Olives opened in 1903, bringing back together a small number of students (four) from Syria. If the preliminaries were not as easy as expected, the outlook seemed promising, or at least reasonable:

> 'The French language constitutes from now onwards the basis for our teaching, since our Syrians should conduct their study in French, as do the Greek Melkites at Ste Anne's. [...]
> Our seminary opened only three months ago. Nevertheless we see that our students have made noticeable progress, which is a good omen for the future. They already express themselves with some fluency in French.'[34]

---

[34] MAE, Nantes, Jérusalem, A, 82 Bénédictins séminaire syrien catholique, letter from D Benoît Gariador to Auguste Boppe (French Consul in Jerusalem), 21 November 1903, with a letter from D Gariador to the MAE, 20 November 1903, report on the seminary's opening.

The comparison with the foundation at Saint Anne's, held by the White Fathers, was present everywhere. It appeared during the preliminary negotiations for the title to the Syrian-Catholic seminary and at the foundation's official opening, but still more in the context of the practical running of the establishment. The numbers of students were certainly not to be compared and for the White Fathers the education of the Melkite clergy was the main activity, in parallel with the care of the national church of Saint Anne. But the Benedictines also soon concentrated on their educational activity, somewhat neglecting the custody of the Abu Ghosh basilica, for which they had been specially chosen by France. This new orientation, with the neglect of a church that was certainly beautiful but located far from Jerusalem and in the middle of a completely Moslem village, aroused some irritation on the part of the French diplomats.[35] But the spread of French culture which the Benedictines brought about quickly overtook the preoccupation with prestige. The material and spiritual building of the seminary met with approval from the different French Consuls in Jerusalem at its various stages:[36]

> 'Our Protectorate is therefore trying out a new way, which will be that of the future, and against which no fierce and jealous rivalry from other nations will be able to do anything, since the latter will also lack what will characterise our French action: the gift of oneself without superiority or a second thought for greed or domination. Yes, M. le Comte, these various Oriental rites raised up by the French Apostolate and thereby attached to our dear France by all the fibres of their religion and their nationality, beyond the fact that they are the real and noble object of a French Protectorate in the Orient, these rites will comfort us a thousand times from the arrogant disdain of a few Italians or a few Germans.'[37]

---

[35] Abu Ghosh becoming a recreation centre for the staff and students of the Syrian-Catholic seminary.

[36] Consul Boppe, departing for Jerusalem, received these instructions from his Minister: 'You will take care of the development of this new foundation that may provide a means of exerting influence on one of the Oriental rites that offer the most interest for us.' (MAE, Paris, PAAP 240 Doulcet, 4 Protectorat religieux, letter from Delcassé to Boppe, 14 October 1902). Whereas the works to enlarge the seminary were supported by the Consuls following (MAE, Nantes, Jérusalem, A, 82 Bénédictins séminaire syrien catholique, letters from the French Consulate in Jerusalem [101 and 102] to the French Embassy at the Sublime Porte, 15 July 1913).

[37] MAE, Paris, PAAP Beaucaire, 1 Lettres particulières reçues et envoyées, 1898-1907, letter from D Drouhin to Beaucaire, 30 May 1903.

The object of the struggle was not only political. A strong religious approach underlay it, which allowed it to benefit from the Vatican's material support.[38] Since the project for the Oriental seminaries appeared to be successful and met with enthusiasm from the Oriental prelates: the latter, agreeing with the pope, saw in such institutions a practical way to train their successors, in a modern spirit and at the lowest cost.[39] The outlook was soon promising, arousing the continuous attention of the Vatican, and requiring firm control of student recruitment, following the example of Saint Anne's.[40] In its stride, before World War I, the foundation accounted each year for an average of a dozen students; but there was still more to be done in commissioning the seminary, notably the building of a church, to start in 1906.[41]

Furthermore, the prospect of expansion necessitated the setting up of a stable teaching staff, which underlay the question both of recruiting French Benedictines dedicated to Jerusalem and the deed of foundation itself. This last item related at once to its public status, soon to include the matter of raising it to the status of an abbey;[42] as well as to its internal status, since until then the new foundation depended on the French province of the Subiaco Congregation as a whole and in turn on the goodwill of the abbots of its constituent monasteries.

Despite relatively modest results, the Syrian-Catholic seminary fulfilled its function from two points of view, religious and political. From the religious point of view, it allowed the small Syrian-Catholic community

---

[38] This support concerned the acquisition of a plot on the Mount of Olives (MAE, Nantes, Jérusalem—Domaines nationaux Abou Gosch II July 1899-1912, 50, letter from the MAE [Midi, 30] to the French Consulate in Jerusalem, 28 March 1901), and later complementary assistance (as shown by the book of gifts kept at the archives of the Subiaco Curia Generale, convent of Sant Ambrogio, Rome—later: Subiaco).

[39] Therefore, from 1904 onwards D Benoît Gariador was approached by the Syrian Patriarch regarding the establishment of a new seminary, this time in Syria itself (Subiaco, file 207 a, Gerusalemme Abou Gosch, correspondence with the Curia Generale, letter from D Gariador to the Abbot General, 4 November 1904).

[40] *Ibid.*, letter from D Gariador to the Abbot General, 22 August 1905, insisting on the difficulties of this task: 'It would doubtless be preferable for us to conduct the selection of the students ourselves, as do the White Fathers for theirs. But for us this is practically impossible since the main centre for the Syrians lies in Mesopotamia and it takes one month to travel from Beirut to Baghdad for instance.'

[41] *Ibid.*, letter from D Gariador to the Abbot General, 16 September 1906. Plans were settled, but the seminary would have at its disposal nothing more than a chapel.

[42] This question apparently was of a wholly political nature: the creation of a French Benedictine abbey would be achieved before the raising of the German Benedictine monastery at the Dormition (*ibid.*, letter from D Gariador to the Abbot General, 2 January 1905).

of Jerusalem to find a definite place there: after several years looking for a base in Jerusalem,[43] it obtained in this way effective roots and a mediation towards Rome and France that offered stability and permanence. The construction of a chapel in 1903,[44] and then a pilgrims' hospice bound it solidly to the Benedictine Order ... and to France.[45] In the political field, the Syrian-Catholic seminary was fully integrated into the network of French institutions in Palestine, thanks to its contribution to the spread of the spirit of France.[46] A *firman* was requested in its favour even before the money had been raised for its construction,[47] while the Benedictines who would have to work there would have the benefit of the traditional exemption from military service granted to French religious abroad.[48]

In this situation, there was genuine agreement between the political and the religious approaches. Thanks to this favourable situation, the disciples of Saint Benedict could devote themselves fully to the establishment of the 'Syrian mission of the Benedictines in the Orient'. The latter, supplied with a newsletter of the same title, did not consist only in the activities already mentioned, the custody of Abu Ghosh and the administration of the seminary of the Mount of Olives. It also involved the revival of the Catholic tradition in the Orient, with a bias towards the history of the Crusader architecture in the Latin Kingdom of Jerusalem,[49] the Benedictine heritage in the Holy Land.[50] To this small

---

43 MAE, Nantes, Jérusalem A, 129 Syriens catholiques, letter from the Syrian Patriarch in Antioch to Charles Ledoulx (French Consul in Jerusalem), 22 May 1897, and letter from Sarkis, Syrian-Catholic Vicar in Jerusalem, to Auzépy, 12 June 1900.

44 *Échos de Notre-Dame de France*, NR. 122, November 1903, 185-186. This chapel was completed in 1930 by the consecration of a church in Bethlehem (Subiaco, file 207 a, Gerusalemme Abou Gosch, Varia, correspondence, Jerusalem 1904-1930, letter from D Chibas-Lassalle to the Abbot General, 11 June 1930).

45 MAE, Nantes, Jérusalem A, 82 Bénédictins séminaire syrien catholique, letter from the French Consulate in Jerusalem (75) to the French Embassy at the Sublime Porte, 23 December 1902.

46 Raymond Koechlin, ' Les œuvres françaises de Jérusalem ', in *Le Journal des Débats*, 21 March 1904 (III).

47 MAE, Nantes, Jérusalem A, 82 Bénédictins séminaire syrien catholique, letter from Ledoulx, Constantinople, to Auguste Boppe (French Consul General in Jérusalem), 8 December 1902.

48 *Ibid.*, letter from D Gariador to Boppe, 28 March 1903, and letter from the French Consulate General in Jerusalem (36) to the MAE, 28 March 1903.

49 With the publication of a booklet on the Abu Ghosh church (Subiaco, file 207 a, Gerusalemme Abou Gosch, Correspondence Ab. Gen. 1910-1950, letter from D Chibas-Lassalle to the Abbot General, 13 December 1919).

50 D Gariador, *Les anciens monastères bénédictins en Orient*, *op. cit.*

scale scholarly activity had just been added a further contribution to the encounter between Oriental and Western Churches and to the revival of the Syrian-Catholic Church, with the publication of its liturgy.[51]

It was in the name of this double approach that the Benedictines were expelled from Palestine in 1914. Sharing the fate of the other French religious in the Holy Land, they had first seen several of their colleagues leave, the younger ones in response to the French general mobilisation.[52] The remaining religious, who no longer had either the human or the material means to pursue their activities, were at length deported and then formally expelled from the Ottoman empire in December 1914. Whereas the church of Abu Ghosh was relatively respected, becoming a shelter for some neutral religious authorised to live in Palestine, the seminary of the Mount of Olives was requisitioned to become a depot for the Ottoman army. Once in Europe, some of the French Benedictines from Jerusalem gave their lives for their country; while others nourished the hope of a rapid return to the Holy City, to continue their apostolic work there.[53] This hope was entertained also by the French Foreign Ministry which continued to pay subsidies to the French establishments in Palestine, despite the fact that their buildings were no longer occupied, with the aim of seeing them take up the French and Catholic torch after the conflict.[54]

The revival after the First World War

It was in the name of the double approach, political and religious, that the Benedictines returned to Palestine after the conflict. Having long

---

[51] Subiaco, file 207 a, Gerusalemme Abou Gosch, Correspondance Ab. Gen. 1910-1950, letter from D Gariador to the Abbot General, 10 February 1914. This effort lead after World War I to the publication of a *Recueil des chants liturgiques du Rit Syrien* (MAE, Paris, Levant 1918-1940, Palestine, 31, religion musulmane, établissements français, letter from the MAE-Europe to D Chibas-Lassalle, 22 November 1923).

[52] Subiaco, file 207 a, Gerusalemme Abou Gosch, Correspondance Ab. Gen. 1910-1950, letter from D Gariador to the Abbot General, 31 August 1914.

[53] Subiaco, file 207 a, Gerusalemme Abou Gosch, Correspondance Ab. Gen. 1910-1950, letter from D Gariador, then in Vitailles (Benedictine monastery in southern France), to the Abbot General, 31 July 1916.

[54] MAE, Paris, Guerre 1914-1918, Turquie, 961, allocations aux établissements religieux, 1914-1915, grants to reserve for the French establishments that must probably still function in Turkey. Concerning the details, see our article 'Le destin des institutions chrétiennes européennes de Jérusalem pendant la Première guerre mondiale', in *Mélanges de Science Religieuse*, NR. 4, October-December 2001, 3-29.

prepared for this return,[55] the Benedictines were from the start faced with the difficulties of returning;[56] once installed, they could not avoid noticing the scale of the damage. Even so, this was not enough to make them abandon their mission. After some setbacks, they were able to take up their work again, proclaiming their patriotism in a way strongly reminiscent of their declarations at the time of the foundation twenty years earlier. This patriotism was even strengthened, some time later, by a painful episode in the history of the Benedictine presence in the Holy Land. This was a kind of historical revenge—which recalled the rivalry at its beginning and the destiny of the French monks at the end of 1914—the eviction of the German Benedictines from the Dormition and their temporary replacement by their francophone Belgian colleagues from the abbey of Maredsous.[57] The arrival of new monks was also a challenge, since the latter were active, dynamic and well educated, having spent some time at the college of Sant-Anselmo in Rome.[58]

This new turn of events was also for the Benedictines an opportunity to re-establish their stability. This concern involved in the first place the situation of the foundation and of the Congregation in relation to the French Republic. In fact, since the religious had taken part in the fighting of World War I as soldiers or medical orderlies despite their rejection by France itself, it seemed possible for them to return to

---

[55] As early as 1915 the Benedictine Procurator declared, thanking the French Foreign Ministry for its generosity: 'Once it is possible, we shall go to take up again with courage our place in Jerusalem, and there continue to promote French influence.' (MAE, Paris, Guerre 1914-1918, Turquie, 961, allocations aux établissements religieux, 1914-1915, letter from D Bernard Etcheverry to the Political Directorate of the MAE, 2 November 1915.)

[56] Whereas the Benedictine Procurator expressed his impatience for a return once Jerusalem was taken, on 9 December 1917 (*ibid.*, 963, allocations aux établissements religieux, 1917-1918, letter from D Bernard Etcheverry to the Political direction of the MAE, 13 December 1917), the declaration of martial law by Allenby hindered such a rapid arrival for all Palestine religious; whereas the MAE tried to accelerate this movement in the name of France's overriding interest (*ibid.*, telegram from the MAE [113] to François Georges-Picot [French High-Commissioner in Palestine and Syria], 22 March 1918, Margerie).

[57] See Bernard Lorent, OSB, *L'affaire de la Dormition (1918-1920)*, Rome, degree thesis at Pontificia Università Gregoriana, Faculty of church history, 1992; or Nikolaus Egender, OSB, 'Belgische Benediktiner in der Dormitio in Jerusalem 1918-1920, in *Erbe und Auftrag*, 77, 2001, 155-164.

[58] Sant-Anselmo being the Benedictine university in Rome, which the French Benedictines never attended. See D Denis Huerre, *Enquête sur la Pierre-qui-Vire*, volume II: *Les fondations*, La Pierre-qui-Vire, 1975, appendices: Monastère de Saint Benoît et Saint Ephrem—Jérusalem, 202 seq. Thanks to D Huerre who was kind enough to let me use this unpublished study.

their French fold and to obtain the recognition denied to them until then as a consequence of the anticlerical laws of 1901, 1903 and 1905. Such an authorisation would be a not only much desired, or even deserved, rehabilitation; it would also allow the 'Syrian mission' to begin again, through confirming its lines of support, in the opening of 'two recruiting centres for our work in the Orient.'[59] From this point of view, there were some chances of success, as shown by the welcome given to this request.[60] Furthermore, the French High-Commission in Syria, in the hands of supporters of France's colonial policy and of favourably-inclined Catholic officials, showed generally speaking great goodwill towards the French Catholic institutions in the Levant. It thus provided for the cost of restoring the Syrian-Catholic seminary. This goodwill reflected the policy of the '*bleu horizon*' Parliament, promising a political majority in favour of the future of Catholicism in France.[61] It required that the Benedictines in Jerusalem should be equal to the task.[62] Following this, the French authorities maintained their support for religious grappling with the problems of the British administration;[63] they also still considered

---

[59] Subiaco, file 207 a, Gerusalemme Abou Gosch, Correspondence Ab. Gen. 1910-1950, letter from D Chibas-Lassalle to the Abbot General, 3 August 1919. The matter concerned every community in Jerusalem, the authorisation of the Congregations being a central point of the French political debate (Maurice Barrès, *Faut-il autoriser les congrégations?*, Plon, Paris, 1924).

[60] MAE, Paris, Turquie, Affaires religieuses, Établissements religieux, 122, 1920-1921, letter from the French High-Commission in Beirut (169) to the MAE, 23 April 1920, Gouraud: 'I consider my duty to call the benevolent attention of Your Excellency to this request. In welcoming it, the country would discharge a debt of gratitude towards good Frenchmen who, having widely shed their blood in its service, try in a distant land to make it better known and loved.'

[61] 'In France the political horizon had become clearer since last elections. It would be a mistake, and a great mistake, not to take advantage of this lull.' (Subiaco, file 207 a, Gerusalemme Abou Gosch, Correspondence Ab. Gen. 1910-1950, letter from D Chibas-Lassalle to the Abbot General, 13 December 1919).

[62] 'I would like—whatever may happen—all the Capitular Fathers to be as convinced as we all are here [...] of the need to give the Seminary a new impetus and a first rate importance. Everything around us here tells us loudly that there is a real urgency to do so: be it the ardent emulation from similar institutions, which are reorganising as quickly and as well as possible; be it the great sympathy, the encouragement, and the really generous help coming from official and officious France. We have offered it our hand, and it has freely given, against a promise from our side that we would relaunch and develop the Project as soon as possible. It is a matter then of keeping one's word' (*ibid.*, letter from D Chibas-Lassalle to the Abbot General, 3 August 1919).

[63] MAE, Levant 1918-1940, Palestine, 31, religion musulmane, établissements français, letter from the French Consulate in Jerusalem (10) to the MAE-Levant, 10 March 1927, Alphonse Doire: concerning difficulties of D Lannes in re-entering Palestine with a colleague, D Maur Massé, who was to take over the direction of Abu Ghosh. According to Doire, one must perceive there a systematic British ill-will towards the French religious.

the Syrian seminary as one of the most significant centres of the French presence in Palestine.[64]

It was equally a matter of settling the status of the Jerusalem project within the Congregation. This would be brought about, first, through a sufficient and guaranteed recruitment, of good quality.[65] It would be reinforced by decisions about the fate of the foundation being determined by consensus within the Congregation. This question, looked into notably at the Chapter of the French Province in 1925, to which we shall return, did not lead to any decision.[66]

The need for the status of the Jerusalem foundation to be made clear was even more fundamental since there were prospects for expansion, which would eventually have practical consequences. In fact, the harmonious interaction between the religious and the French diplomats, concerned with Catholic progress on the one hand and French progress on the other, was crowned by a development dating to the turn of the 1930's. Since 1917, the year of the creation of the Sacred Congregation for the Oriental Church, Rome's Oriental policy had been reinvigorated after having been somewhat neglected by Pius X. Placed under the authority of the new Congregation, the Syrian-Catholic seminary of Jerusalem became the focus of close attention by Mgr Tappouni, Patriarch of this Rite from 1929 onwards. The Patriarch, perceiving the weakness of his own seminary, located in Charfet, in the Lebanon, took advantage of a journey to Palestine to put forward the idea of involving the Benedictines in Charfet. The reaction of the Jerusalem religious to the discussion about their possible involvement was interesting. In fact, although they set conditions, they wanted the matter to be settled as soon as possible.

---

64 *Ibid.*, Turquie, Affaires religieuses, Protectorat, 117, dossier général, July 1925-1929, letter from the MAE to the French representatives in Tehran, Isfahan, Tauris, Cairo, Alexandria, Port Said, Suez, Athens, Baghdad, Mosul, Jerusalem, Haifa, Sofia, Roustchouk, Constantinople, Saloniki, Addis Ababa, 8 January 1927: the seminary has in common with several other establishments that it is again possible to demand the liturgical honours due to the French Consul.

65 D Chibas-Lassalle wrote: 'When I learned that Father Ernest would be sent to us, a German citizen—and a full-blooded one moreover—I wrote to the Rme Father and to D Bernard to cancel the arrangements. At this time, to admit a Boche into the Community would provoke a great commotion in Jerusalem, where all the houses have hastened to be free of elements too undesirable that could still exist.' (Subiaco, file 207 a, Gerusalemme Abou Gosch, Correspondence Ab. Gen. 1910-1950, letter from D Chibas-Lassalle to the Abbot General, 13 December 1919.)

66 The Capitular Fathers expressed themselves in favour of the foundation's independence, but this was not viable without having settled the question of recruiting the establishment (*ibid.*, letter from D Gariador to the 'Révérendissimes Pères capitulaires', 13 October 1925).

If, thirty years earlier, it had been a matter of progressing more quickly than the German Benedictines, in the present the danger lay elsewhere. To take in hand the management of the Charfet seminary meant not only advancing on to new ground for the French Benedictines, but also putting down roots in a region dependent on Beirut ... and on the French religious already based there.

> 'Owing to the official intrigues of the Beirut Jesuits, to the rivalry of the Lazarists and the Dominicans, and to the opposition from the other Oriental Rites, it is important to put the work in hand immediately, in order to say to all these opponents or rivals and to the general public: "The Benedictines have begun."'[67]

The stakes were still higher in that the project represented a possible further step along the road to the reunion of the Churches, ultimate aim of the Benedictine presence. In fact, Tappouni had in mind the creation of a Syrian-Benedictine Province, 'a direct reconstitution of the former French Benedictine Province of Palestine, [that was] so glorious in Charlemagne's days and during the following centuries, and to which the first French Protectorate owed its existence'.[68] It was this ambition which inclined the French Province in favour of Tappouni's project.[69] This project, so far as it was made public, took on a considerable importance. The proposals for the Jerusalem seminary remained confidential; the one in Charfet looked more promising; located not far away from a Syrian-Catholic population, it should allow activity on a large scale. 'A round figure of 80 religious could be foreseen in 15 years.'[70]

Viewed as combined with the Jerusalem foundation (this latter becoming a minor seminary, Charfet a major), Charfet should resolve the material difficulties prevailing up to that time. Disposing of its own resources, it would benefit from the support of the Holy See and of the

---

[67] *Ibid.*, Correspondence, Jerusalem, 1929-1934, letter from D Chibas-Lassalle, then in Bétharram, to the Abbot General, 15 October 1929.

[68] MAE, Nantes, Jérusalem A, 82 Bénédictins séminaire syrien catholique, letter from D Drouhin to Auzépy, 6 December 1900. The similarity in the tone of this letter written in 1900 and the tone at the end of the 1930's is striking and eloquent.

[69] Subiaco, file 207 a, Gerusalemme Abou Gosch, Correspondence, Jerusalem, 1929-1934, note on a meeting of the French Province, on 27 October 1929 (D Chibas-Lassalle, then in Paris, was present).

[70] *Ibid.*, letter from D Chibas-Lassalle, Betharram, to the Abbot General, 11 November 1929.

French High-Commission in Syria and the Lebanon, and provide for the needs of 'Jerusalem'. Beyond that, the Benedictines would be freed from basic problems, since the religious would have charge of the training and moral formation of the students, while the temporal administration would remain with the Syrians. Also settled would be the insistent question of recruitment thanks to 'a providential and unexpected solution, and the happiest outcome for the French Province, which would be from then on unburdened, since indigenous recruitment, made possible and normal, would dispense the Province from providing new students for our Palestine houses.' The matter was definitely attractive, as summed up by Dom Chibas-Lassalle:

> 'At a higher level of considerations, it would be a great honour, for our Province and our Congregation, to introduce the Benedictine life into an Eastern Church; to deserve the favour of the Holy See, in responding to the invitation which Pope Pius XI had recently addressed to several religious orders with similar initiatives in view ... '[71]

In order to follow up this proposal, two Jerusalem monks were immediately sent to Charfet. And after some months of negotiations the Jerusalem Benedictines took charge of the management of this seminary, 'jewel' of the Syrian Rite. The matter was concluded despite the anticipated obstacles,[72] and this was only a first step.[73] The first results were satisfactory, even if, for canonical reasons, the establishment of the Syrian-Benedictine Province was delayed.[74]

Reflecting the demands of a religious approach, the handing over of the Charfet seminary to the French Benedictines agreed, point by point, with the political approach. Emanating from a community

---

[71] D Chibas-Lassalle here refers to the Encyclical *Rerum Orientalium* (8 September 1928), asking the clergy to become more engaged in Oriental affairs.

[72] Subiaco, file 207 a, Gerusalemme Abou Gosch, Affaires diverses, correspondence, Jerusalem 1904-1930, letter from D Chibas-Lassalle to the Abbot General, 24 May 1930: 'The Jesuits have recently moved heaven and earth in order to hinder it.'

[73] *Ibid.*, 'According to [Tappouni] and the bishops, our settling at Charfet is only a beginning; the important thing is the foundation of the Syrian-Benedictine Province.'

[74] *Ibid.*, Correspondence, Jerusalem, 1929-1934, letter from D Chibas-Lassalle to the Abbot General, 3 March 1933. A concrete project existed (*ibid.*, Correspondence, Jerusalem, 1934-1949, letter from Mgr Tappouni to the Abbot General, 4 April 1934), but such a Syrian-Benedictine Province would never see the light.

that was particularly bound to France, the project answered the deepest wishes of those in charge in Paris and of the French Mandate authorities. It therefore met with 'the favour of the Government, since the monastic work would take place in Syria, in French Mandate territory.'[75] As it was undertaken by Tappouni, who kept up very good relations with the French High-Commission, the High Commission fully supported this work, at once both traditional and new. By creating a bond between Syria and Palestine by means of a religious community and an Eastern Church, it could only exert a beneficial influence on the interests of France and therefore it deserved French assistance.[76] In the same way, the project met with approval from the French foreign Ministry especially from Louis Canet, Counsellor for religious affairs, who saw no contradiction between this further undertaking and the 1901 convention between France and the Benedictines.[77] Some years later the Benedictines drew credit from seeing themselves associated in a small way with the elevation as Cardinal of the Patriarch of Antioch. As Dom. Chibas-Lassalle wrote to him, using the same words as the French High-Commissioner: 'Your nomination is a triumph for us.'[78] In the same vein, France could only applaud the nomination of Dom Chibas-Lassalle, who had master-minded this project,

---

[75] *Ibid.*, letter from D Chibas-Lassalle, Bétharram, to the Abbot General, 11 November 1929.

[76] MAE, Nantes, Service des Œuvres françaises à l'Étranger (SOFE), série D, 173 Palestine 1929/1932, letter from the High-Commission of the Republic in Syria and Lebanon to the MAE-Levant, 30 August 1930, Hoppenot.

[77] This concerned especially the composition of the seminary, that would probably be incompatible with having a French majority: 'In Paris I saw Mr. Canet at length who applauds our settlement in Charfet, like all the others, Marx [official of the Service for French cultural Institutions abroad—Service des œuvres françaises à l'étranger, SOFE], Mgr Lagier [head of the *Œuvre d'Orient*], etc. Concerning the citizenship of the Superiors and of the majority of the religious in our Palestine houses, he does not advise touching the text of the agreement [...]. This agreement is a strength and a precious guarantee for us (legal authorisation in France, etc.). The position of France in Syria is not defined. There is nothing urgent and we must doubtless wait over a number of years for the conclusion of a treaty and a de facto legal position for our indigenous personnel. Only then shall we see whether there is room to insert an additional note, while retaining the text of the Agreement in its integrity. [...]This is also the opinion of Mr. L[éon] Bérard [French senator] and of L[ouis] Massignon [orientalist, professor at the *Collège de France* and counsellor at the MAE].' (Subiaco, Affaires diverses, correspondance, Jérusalem 1904-1930, letter from D Chibas-Lassalle, then at the Abbey of Belloc, to the Abbot General, 31 July 1930).

[78] *Ibid.*, Correspondance, Jérusalem, 1934-1949, letter from D Chibas-Lassalle to the Abbot General, 4 December 1935.

as Apostolic Commissioner for the Lebanese monks, and honour him by awarding him, at Canet's request, the *Légion d'honneur.*[79]

In Lebanon, as in Jerusalem, France maintained its support for the Benedictines during the years following. Aware of their financial difficulties, Paris was committed to making their task easier. For instance, at the request of the Consul Amédée Outrey,[80] and outside any judicial framework, France authorised the listing of the Abu Ghosh basilica as a Historical Monument (*Monument historique*) in September 1938.[81] In other respects, too, the Benedictines continued to be the concern of France, even in the most delicate situations, as when the seminary received funds from the Vichy regime up to the end of World War II, although the building was rented by the British.[82] Whereas Free France, replacing Vichy France at Jerusalem from July 1941 onwards, also went out of its way to help the Benedictine mission.[83]

As we have just seen, the Syrian-Catholic seminary in Jerusalem, with its extension in the Lebanon from 1930 onwards, reflected an enduring compatibility between two distinct approaches. On the one hand political, aiming to maintain an institution that had contributed to French prestige, and encouraging it to this end by giving way to its own requirements. On the other hand religious, responding to a spiritual vocation and, also, to the Vatican's political line which profited from the priorities of French foreign policy in order to serve its own ends and to escape from the harassment of the Hexagon's internal politics. Nonetheless, such an institution walked a narrow path between these two approaches; and it could not escape being affected when the one prevented the other

---

79 *Ibid.*, letter from Mgr Tappouni to the Abbot General, 12 December 1936.

80 MAE, Paris, PAAP 130 Outrey, 29, Jérusalem Correspondance (dépêches) 1938, letter from the French Consulate General in Jerusalem (22) to the MAE, 22 April 1938, Outrey.

81 Archives of the Heritage Directorate (Ministry of Culture), Paris, procès-verbaux de la Commission des monuments historiques 80/15/20. Proceedings of the Commission for Historical Monuments, session of 8 July 1938 (the decree concerning Abu Ghosh is dated 5 September 1938). Such a decision was exceptional since the church, although belonging to France, was not located on Metropolitan territory.

82 MAE, Paris, Guerre 1939-1945, Vichy, série E Levant, 151 Palestine, Intérêts français, dispatch note from the French Embassy in Madrid [Spain being in charge of French interests in Palestine after May 1941, after the French Vichy Consul had been expelled from Jerusalem] (182) to the MAE-Levant, 7 April 1943.

83 Archives nationales, Paris, private papers of René Cassin (Commissioner for Public Instruction, on a tour of the Middle-East), 382 AP 59 dossier 3 Syrie, Liban, Palestine, letter from the National Commissioner for Justice and Public Instruction (JU 754) to the National Commissioner for Finance, 21 April 1942.

from being completely realised, as happened, in this specific case, where the religious approach progressively prevailed.

II. Discordant approaches

As in the case of many French Catholic institutions in the Holy Land, the Benedictine presence in Palestine showed religion becoming an instrument of politics.[84] This held good so long as the political approach did not restrain the religious one. Conversely, it is also possible to speak of politics becoming an instrument of religion.

The Benedictines: more Catholic than French? Limited differences.

This dichotomy, entirely relative, made itself felt through the resurfacing of differences going back to the first negotiations between the Republic and the Benedictines, in 1899-1900. In consequence of their criticism that France perceived the Protectorate too much in French terms and not enough in Catholic,[85] the Benedictines were suspicious when France applied pressure on the subject of the precise status of the community to which Abu Ghosh and its dependencies should return. If the Benedictines accepted heavy demands in respect of national property, which the church building was, they could not passively allow the same criteria to apply to the future Syrian-Catholic seminary on the Mount of Scandal.[86] This was made clear by the Subiaco General Chapter, in July 1901.[87] The divergences resulted from isolated difficulties, when the religious found it difficult to adapt to a context beset by international rivalries, in which they could not avoid becoming tools of power

[84] 'Travels, official receptions, speeches, everything became a pretext to confront the adversary and, *nolens volens*, a religious foundation itself gained a strong nationalistic touch, accentuated without even wishing it.' (D Denis Huerre, *Enquête sur la Pierre-qui-Vire*, *op. cit.*, 174).

[85] *Échos de Notre-Dame de France*, NR. 99, 15 November 1901.

[86] MAE, Nantes, Jérusalem—Domaines nationaux Abou Gosch II July 1899-1912, 50, letter from the French Consulate in Jerusalem (20) to the MAE, 20 July 1901.

[87] Debates took place between Italian and French monks, the latter yielding in order to avoid a withdrawal of the French proposal (Dom Huerre, *op. cit.*).

politics[88] and where they were the subjects of criticism by the very State which had commissioned them.[89]

Fundamental divergences

Further divergences were due to the presence of completely differing perspectives. Both France and the Benedictines had indeed been anxious to make a 'Catholic and French' response to the German offensive, illustrated by Wilhelm II's visit and its consequences. But this response proved limited and short-term, the restoration of the status quo lasting only until the next acquisition of privileges by Germany. Thus, the allocation of Abu Ghosh to the French Benedictines, settling in principle the issue raised by the allocation of the Dormition site to their German counterparts, established a state of affairs that was immediately called into question by the possible allocation of the Syrian seminary to the German Benedictines. In this context, the French Benedictines were prepared to play the game, but for them the stakes had a higher significance.

It was a matter, first, of restoring a Benedictine tradition. As it was perceived at that time, the Congregations were considered as the successors of a prestigious past, Frankish and Catholic. If Abu Ghosh had never known a Benedictine presence, it was otherwise for the Mount of Olives.

Consequently, the Benedictine mission went beyond the very pragmatic politics of Paris to embrace a wider dimension. The negotiations carried on with France and, through them, the search for a community which could hold the custody of Abu Ghosh offered an opportunity for action. In this respect, a shift of initiative may be discerned.

The initiative of the religious and French action in their favour

What was the aim of the religious, and consequently of the missions they gave to France? For them, there was no question of a temporary

---

88 *Un moine—Dom Théodore Andrieu, OSB. (1834-1923)*, Albi, w.d., with a description of Jerusalem where 'one does not belong to oneself any more. The new connections with the religious and political authorities impose themselves at once on the newcomers.' (21).

89 For instance, Consul Boppe wrote to the Departement that the Benedictine project after several years was 'quite defective' (MAE, Paris, NS-Turquie politique intérieure, 131 Palestine 1898-1907, letter from the French Consulate general in Jerusalem 96 to the MAE, 17 August 1903, Boppe).

settlement in Palestine but rather of a lasting foundation. Consequently, an embarrassment appeared on their side when France became insistent about the future status of the foundation. For the Benedictines, the aim was to become in the end autonomous in relation to the centre, that is in relation to the politics of Paris.

Furthermore, the Benedictines supported the 'Oriental policy' of Pope Leo XIII, aiming at the unity of Christians.[90] Their mission in Palestine should not be only to take care of an ancient church, where the site itself seemed cramped. Lost there, in the midst of a Moslem environment, they felt that they could not flourish. Soon they recognised that the Syrian seminary could become theirs; and, just as soon, their activity focussed on Jerusalem: acquisition of land, the start of building a convent, the setting up of the seminary. This expansion of what at the beginning had been only a 'useful complement to the settlement of the French religious at Abu Ghosh',[91] became their main concern. The custody of the medieval basilica was relegated to the background, to the great displeasure of Paris.[92] Nevertheless, the French officials felt constrained by the fact that the matter had gone too far and that the stakes were too high to get side-tracked by obstacles that might harm the realisation of the project. From 1902, the ability of the head of the Jerusalem Benedictines, Dom Gariador, was certainly criticised by Consul Boppe,[93] but this did not prevent his requesting a *firman* for the foundation.[94]

---

90 Claude Soetens, *Le Congrès eucharistique international de Jérusalem (1893) dans le cadre de la politique orientale du Pape Léon XIII*, Bibliothèque de l'Université catholique de Louvain-Éditions Nauwelaerts, Louvain, 1977. See also Giorgio del Zanna, *Rome e l'Oriente, Leone XIII e l'Impero romano (1878-1903)*, Guerini, Milan, 2003.

91 MAE, Nantes, Jérusalem, A, 82 Bénédictins séminaire syrien catholique, letter from the MAE (9) to the French Consulate General in Jerusalem, 1st May 1901, and Domaines nationaux Abou Gosch II July 1899-1912, 50, letter from the French Consulate General in Jerusalem (373) to the Congregation of Subiaco, 28 July 1899, Auzépy (draft).

92 Consul Auzépy wrote on 17 July 1901 (*ibid.*): 'what everybody knows here, is that in the mind of our Benedictine the Abu Ghosh foundation is now relegated to the background, that it will be nothing but a house of retreat, or even rest, and that the Mount of Olives establishment will become the real seat of future projects [...], those for which no effort and no sacrifice will be neglected.'

93 MAE, Nantes, Jérusalem, A, 82 Bénédictins séminaire syrien catholique, letter from the French Consulate General in Jerusalem (44) to the MAE, 9 December 1902, Boppe, and MAE, Paris, PAAP 240 Doulcet, 14. Correspondance, letter from Boppe to Jean Doulcet (official at the Quai d'Orsay), 16 December 1902.

94 MAE, Nantes, Jérusalem, A, 82 Bénédictins séminaire syrien catholique, letter from the French Consulate General in Jerusalem (70) to the French Embassy at the Sublime Porte, 9 December 1902.

The reversal was clearly seen in the engagement of the French diplomatic apparatus for the benefit of the French Benedictines. Through a combination of well understood interests, France took up and realised the wish of a modest parish priest from the Département de l'Yonne, the Abbé Moreau. The working-out took place in Paris, at the Vatican, in Jerusalem and Constantinople, and officials offered their skills to the religious, with a formula that allowed official negotiation, even though in contravention of the current republican legislation. As part of the same approach, the Minister put in place an unusual procedure in order to spread the assets entrusted to the Benedictines. For, in Ottoman and Moslem Palestine, the growth of Christian institutions was problematic. Therefore, to facilitate the establishment of new foundations, despite the difficulties, the Powers had recourse to stratagems; for instance the acquisition of sites in the first place by individuals, who then passed them on to the communities.[95] For Abu Ghosh, as for Sainte-Anne, this solution was not precisely applicable, since the site of each foundation was national property. This being so, the respective Consuls involved themselves personally and acquired the sites. On each occasion it was the Benedictines who signalled to the diplomat about the opportunity to purchase. The Consul informed the department, and the diplomat was mandated by the minister to buy. The situation was the same with the works required before the installation of the religious. A financial undertaking by France was requested in order to meet the expenses involved. If the Government had sometimes to remind the Benedictines of their peculiarly French undertaking, the Benedictines themselves regularly reminded their supporting authorities of their promise to pay an official grant.[96]

Furthermore, even though the 1901 agreement obliged them to restore the church building, the religious focussed at first on what appeared to be two secondary projects, the Abu Ghosh convent and the Syrian-Catholic seminary.[97] This failure to meet their primary obligation

---

[95] The most eloquent case was that of Count Amédée de Piellat, patron of the French Catholics in Palestine (see Zvi Shilony, 'Un mécène catholique: le comte de Piellat et les communautés françaises de Terre sainte', in Dominique Trimbur/Ran Aaronsohn (dir.), *De Bonaparte à Balfour*, *op. cit.*, 241-263).

[96] MAE, Nantes, Jérusalem—Domaines nationaux Abou Gosch March 1901-1912, 51, letter from D Drouhin to Auzépy, 30 September 1901.

[97] Consul Boppe had to write, in the Autumn of 1903, that the restoration works on the basilica had not yet begun (MAE, Paris, NS-Lieux Saints 87 Basilique d'Abou Ghosh II 1902-1907, letter from the French Consulate in Jerusalem [112] to the MAE, 12 October 1903).

was due to the monks concentrating on their purely religious aim. The medieval church, located wholly in a Moslem area, could not be of great use in this respect. Their vocation and the task included in the agreement signed with France excluded a mission among non-Christians.

The focus of the religious on their religious task was more obvious later. And even though it later became the guiding thread, the religious approach was itself plural. For instance certain Jerusalem religious, resident there for several decades, wondered about the precise aim of the Benedictine presence. Beyond the fact that the church of Abu Ghosh hardly seemed to fascinate the newcomers, the troubled beginnings of the Syrian seminary seemed to indicate that the Benedictines had merely taken advantage of an opportunity to make a foundation in the Holy Land. From this point of view, the seminary was simply a pretext and it was to be expected that the religious would not develop the Syrian mission on a large scale.[98] These pessimistic forecasts did not however materialise, since, as mentioned, the Jerusalem Benedictines devoted themselves to their task of training the Syrian-Catholic clergy, to the great satisfaction of France. Nevertheless, a rift soon appeared within the Benedictine family, with the emergence of two divergent approaches. On the one hand was found the enthusiasm and the exclusivism of the Benedictines who made up the nucleus of the Syrian mission: Fathers Bernard Drouhin (founder and negotiator with France), Benoît Gariador (his associate and successor, raised in 1907 to the rank of Abbot Visitor to the Oriental monks), Anselme Chibas-Lassalle (his successor), and Alexandre Lannes (who spent the major part of his monastic life in Abu Ghosh). On the other hand we find pragmatism, rationality, and a far less developed enthusiasm for the Syrian mission on the part of the French Province, particularly on the part of the Abbots of the monasteries which it comprised.

The problem of the recruitment of Benedictines

This dichotomy appeared for instance in the problem of recruiting for the mission. As already seen, the agreement establishing the Benedictine foundation was signed between France and the French Province. It was

---

[98] Archives of the White Fathers, Rome, second period, file 34, lettres de confrères de Jérusalem au Procureur de Rome, letter from Fr. Féderlin (head of Sainte-Anne seminary) to Fr. Burtin (bursar), 11 October 1903.

not, then, a matter of an arrangement between a particular monastery and the Republic, and a *modus vivendi* indicated that the Syrian mission depended on the French Province as a whole. Accordingly, the abbots were ready to supply monks to support the new foundation.[99] This undertaking reflected the religious and political motivations that were the very basis of the mission; obedience to Pope Leo XIII, who had expressly desired such a project, and to the Republic, that had strongly desired to grant to the Benedictines the custody of the Abu Ghosh basilica, origin of the Syrian-Catholic seminary.[100] Soon, however the abbots expressed some reluctance to honour these promises. And if they did supply monks, it was only for a limited period of time. It was a loan but no more, since the Benedictines had to observe their vow of stability, and, further, to support the needs of abbeys much affected in their own recruitment by the anticlerical legislation of 1901. In these circumstances, the superiors did not hesitate to remind Jerusalem and the Abbot General of the obligation to return the monks lent,[101] even when they did not stand in the way of the departure of their religious for the Holy Land, at a time when Dom Gariador was circulating among them to choose his recruits.[102] It happened in the end that some of the religious on loan themselves called for their return to France.[103]

On their side, the Jerusalem Benedictines immersed themselves in their own way of life. According to them, in the name of the Syrian mission and of the 1901 agreement, the abbots of the French Province should respect their undertaking and this led them to regularly renew their reminder in these terms. In this respect, the correspondence between Jerusalem and Rome over the entire period was fundamentally marked by this problem. After the first difficulties, certain measures should have made a settlement possible. These stemmed from World War I and the prospects of revival that emanated from it. Now, in order to 'continue the work of the Syrian seminary, the communities that had combined to

---

[99] Subiaco, file 207 b, Gerusalemme Abou Gosch, Palestine, foundations, 1899-1904, Project for the constitution and governance of the communities of Abu Ghosh and of Jerusalem.

[100] *Ibid.*, memorandum on the Holy Land foundation (for the provincial Chapter, 1901).

[101] *Ibid.*, file 207 a, Gerusalemme Abou Gosch, Correspondence with the Curia Generale, letter from D Joseph Marrot, Abbot of Belloc, to the Abbot General, 21 November 1908.

[102] *Ibid.*, file 207 b, Gerusalemme Abou Gosch, foundations. In this file, a correspondence about the opposition of the Abbot of Besalu, provisional refuge for French Benedictines in Spain.

[103] *Ibid.*, file 207 a, Gerusalemme Abou Gosch, Correspondence Ab. Gen. 1910-1950, letter from Fr. Guénolé to the Fr. Procurator, 2 March 1911.

set it up should contribute towards supplying the necessary staff.'[104] The effective resumption of activity led to the problem being raised again, this time with a possibility of success thanks to the improved situation of the Congregation in France itself. Since it should be possible to return to the Metropolitan territory, could a centre of recruitment not be established there specifically devoted to the Syrian mission?[105] Such a solution would offer a double advantage; it would guarantee the regular arrival of new monks, and they would be fully competent to take up the tasks which awaited them in Palestine.

The requests from the Jerusalem Benedictines did not however succeed, to their great disappointment and likewise that of the Sacred Congregation for Oriental Churches, responsible for them since 1917. By virtue of this authority, and noting the resolute opposition of some Abbots to sending their monks to Jerusalem, the Sacred Congregation for the Orient demanded in 1928 that the French Province should take the opportunity of its Chapter meeting in order to solve the problem once and for all.[106] Furthermore, on the question of recruitment a vicious circle was set up; an inflow of new monks was necessary to secure the flourishing of the work in Palestine and then in the Lebanon. But such an inflow was possible only if it came with enough money for their upkeep. But because of the recurrent lack of funds, the arrival of further Benedictines was only foreseeable if they were ready to take on the cost of their keep.[107]

The financial problem of the institution

This extra difficulty led to another point of difference between the Benedictines in France and those in Jerusalem, about the financing of the Syrian mission; for the dependence on the French Province also raised the question of its financial participation. And just as the correspondence from Jerusalem is full of requests about the sending of new monks, so it is also full of financial preoccupations. This emphasis was not in itself

[104] *Ibid.*, letter from D Gariador to the Abbot General, 25 February 1916.

[105] *Ibid.*, letter from D Chibas-Lassalle to the Abbot General, 3 August 1919.

[106] *Ibid.*, file 207 b, Gerusalemme Abou Gosch, foundations, letter from the SCOC to the Abbot General, 17 January 1928.

[107] *Ibid.*, file 207 a, Gerusalemme Abou Gosch, Correspondence, Jerusalem, 1929-1934, letter from D Chibas-Lassalle to the Abbot General, 21 March 1933.

surprising, since the French establishments in Palestine shared a weak financial situation. It is the more striking because it resulted from a lack of understanding between the source, the French Province, and the Jerusalem establishment.

The need for money was sometimes tied to questions of prestige.[108] But it was evident everywhere in the course of the day-to-day progress of the work. It led the Benedictines to seek funds wherever they might be found.[109] It led them also to demand that their contractual source of finance should comply with the contract terms. Funds certainly came regularly from the French Ministry for Foreign Affairs,[110] from Propaganda (later from the SCOC), even from the pope himself,[111] as also from the *Propagation de la foi*; but it was the monasteries of the French Province which were the problem. Their assistance was especially necessary with the prospect of the official income's running down, with the radicalisation of French anticlerical policy;[112] but more generally it was indispensable. The sparse results of appeals for assistance very soon led to a warning on the part of the Jerusalem religious: since the seminary received nothing, it was essential for the *Propagation de la foi* to grant an annual subsidy, without which the project would cease.[113] The lack of any progress in this direction confirmed this viewpoint. In 1915, on a subvention being obtained on the part of Cardinal Gotti, Prefect of Propaganda, it was used to liquidate the seminary's debt.[114] Should this operation not have been seen as heralding the winding up of the project pure and simple?[115]

---

[108] And so, when funds would allow, some sites to be acquired round Abu Ghosh, in order to counter any rival: 'The Jews began to buy in Abougosch *[sic]* and at this very moment they negotiate the acquisition of several sites. If we do not buy now I believe that we shall regret later not to have done so it since it is highly probable that the Jews won't delay laying their hands on it.' (*ibid*., Correspondence with the Curia Generale, letter from D Gariador to the Abbot General, 1st February 1904.

[109] And so D Gariador toured through Austria-Hungary, even trying to gain the attention of the Emperor Franz-Josef for his project, but in vain (*ibid*., letter from D Gariador to the Abbot General, 21 November 1904).

[110] *Ibid*., letter from D Gariador to the Abbot General, 29 January 1906.

[111] *Ibid*., letter from D Gariador to the Abbot General, 22 August 1905.

[112] *Ibid*., letter from D Gariador to the Abbot General, 22 January 1907 and file 207 b, Gerusalemme Abou Gosch, rescripts of the Holy See, Jerusalem, 1900-1959, letter from D Gariador to the Abbot General, 30 June 1907.

[113] *Ibid*., file 207 a, Gerusalemme Abou Gosch, Correspondence with the Curia Generale, note by D Benoît on the financial situation of his seminary, Rome, 29 June 1909.

[114] *Ibid*., letter from D Gariador to the Abbot General, 26 January 1915.

[115] *Ibid*., letter from D Gariador, then in Vitailles, to the Abbot General, 31 July 1916.

The problematic status of the project

The revival of the seminary after the First World War did not result in the problem's being overcome; it even increased its scope. As already seen, the difference between the Benedictines in France and those in Jerusalem appeared to lie in problems of recruitment and finance. Both difficulties emphasised the further one of the constitution of the Jerusalem foundation. The Syrian-Catholic seminary indeed found its outward recognition in being financially supported first by Propaganda, then by the SCOC, in parallel with the funding supplied by France in the name of its cultural policy. Nevertheless, within the Congregation its status remained unstable.

Two approaches confronted each other. For the Jerusalem Benedictines, that could only create incomprehension. This observation applied to the pre-war period; wasn't their situation a gift for all the Benedictines, since, contrary to what happened in France, the project benefited from the wholehearted support of the Republic? Consequently, should the project not be enlarged to make a still more secure refuge?[116] Their faith in the value of their project was still more evident at the point of time when it was revived. But it was just then confronted by a policy based on the previous obstacles as well as on recent developments.

The latter put in question the very existence of the Syrian mission. As explained by the Jerusalem Benedictines, their foundation constituted a refuge, it was partly an answer to the need to escape the hot winds of the French anticlerical legislation; this was the main explanation for the project's initial success, when the abbey of Belloc had been able to place there some of its expelled monks. At the present time, the fact that the Republic took an attitude of goodwill would lead to the Congregations' being recognised on Metropolitan territory. If that should lead, on the one hand, to the creation of centres of recruitment and training for the Syrian mission, should it not, on the other hand lead also to the final return to France of the French Benedictines? And would this not make the Palestinian foundation redundant?

---

[116] *Ibid.*, file 207 a, Gerusalemme Abou Gosch, Correspondence with the Curia Generale, letter from D Gariador to the Abbot General, 11 January 1909.

This new deal, evidently contested by the Jerusalem Benedictines,[117] strengthened the hesitant abbots in their attitude towards the Syrian mission. After the already mentioned marks of ill will, a first report was drafted in July 1924 by the Abbot Visitor, Dom Maurus Etcheverry:

> 'The future of [the] Jerusalem [foundation] seems to me very obscure and very uncertain. The Province will only support this project as long as it finds some advantage there and even if it does find an advantage, it will only offer meagre support. However people are needed almost immediately. I do not see from where they can be taken.'[118]

This was indeed a real problem, so far as it was not bound only to the circumstances:

> 'It was a mistake to make the Jerusalem foundation a work of the Province. The consequences of this mistake have not been felt too strongly until now because the 1902 expulsion took to Jerusalem a sizeable group of religious from Belloc. I fear that they [the consequences] will make themselves felt more and more henceforth.'

This problem of recruitment was linked to that of finance, which made it more complicated:

> 'If Jerusalem could become self-sufficient financially, this would be so much the better. But will it be enough? The future will tell. But I shall continue to ask: supposing that it won't be enough, who should support Jerusalem?'

---

[117] By a like reasoning it would effectively lead to an unilateral rupture of the agreement concluded with the Republic, whereas the latter promised at the same moment the means of resuscitating the project: 'Everything around us here cries out to us that there is urgency; and the burning emulation of similar projects, to reorganise quickly and to the best of our ability. Also, the great sympathy, encouragement and truly generous help of France in its official and formal capacity. We have offered it our hand and it has given freely against the promise—on our part—of taking up again and developing the project as soon as possible. It is a matter, then, also of keeping one's word.' (Subiaco, file 207 a, Gerusalemme Abou Gosch, Correspondence Ab. Gen. 1910-1950, letter from D Chibas-Lassalle to the Abbot General, 3 August 1919).

[118] *Ibid.*, Correspondence with the Curia Generale, letter from D Maur Etcheverry, then in Buckfast, to the Abbot General, 21 July 1924.

After this warning from within, the crisis broke at the time of the Provincial Chapter of 1925. To the need for the Province to assume its responsibilities was added also the pressing need to settle the constitution of the Palestinian foundation. The state of affairs was critical:

> 'the Monastery of Mount of Olives remains three quarters unbuilt, the annual budget is in deficit, the staffing is insufficient, especially regarding the French components, and there is no regular means of recruitment.'[119]

Furthermore, if this foundation is a work of the Province, it is outside the Congregation's constitution. It was neither affiliated to any abbey nor was it independent since it was not self-sufficient. Consequently,

> 'So far as it will not emerge in one way or another from this state of dependence, it seems that its connections to the Province should be on the pattern, *mutatis mutandis* [...], of a daughter house with the mother house.'

Without taking into account that:

> 'we do not begin to fulfil the condition of the agreement with the French Government that two thirds of the staff should be French; this could lead us into trouble and could end in the cutting off of the subsidy that we now get from the Government.'

Frank reflections provoked by this situation resulted in a radical solution. Since the Abbots refused any further involvement, the Jerusalem mission was declared independent. Faced with this decision, going with an unlikely situation,[120] the Jerusalem Benedictines retained their own

[119] *Ibid.*, file 207 b, Gerusalemme Abou Gosch, foundations, Missio palestinensis, pro-memoria of the Abbot Visitor to the Provincial Chapter, 1925.

[120] In his mémoire (*op. cit.*), the Abbot Visitor had suggested it conditionally, the conditions not being fulfilled 'The solution to all the difficulties would be if the Jerusalem House was rich enough to build the rest of the Monastery,—to have trained in an European House the monks who would be necessary for its recruitment or to fairly compensate the Provincial Houses which would send out trained people to support its Syrian Seminarists: that day, it would then be an independent House like any other House of the Province and it would reintegrate with the common framework.'

approach, refusing that of the Chapter's Abbots; and they knew how to use their submission to the SCOC for their own ends. Writing a letter full of obedience in reaction to the decision, Dom Gariador pointed out that he had informed this dicastery, since the Chapter's decision concerned it in the first place.[121] Asked for its opinion, the SCOC adopted an inflexible position: it neither wanted to nor could it, give the responsibility for the seminary to another Congregation or another Order. Quite logically it:

> '1° Regrets that it cannot approve the decision taken by the Chapter of the French Province to declare the Jerusalem house independent, considering that this house lacks staff as well as means of subsistence;
> 2° Since we have to deal with a situation going back 25 years, originally accepted in view of firm undertakings of which the text is in the possession of this S. Congregation, as well as with present necessities for which it is urgent to provide a solution, [the SCOC] calls upon the good will of the Superiors of the Province and relies on their devotion at the present time.'

With this implication of the SCOC in the internal affairs of the Congregation, divergence between the two Benedictine approaches was unavoidable. If the Chapter agreed that the responsibility for the Palestinian project had been imposed by the French Province,[122] the Jerusalem Benedictines refused to admit this assertion, relying on the records.[123]

Charfet seminary: an opportunity for Jerusalem?

At first, fortune did not seem to spare the seminary, since it was heavily damaged by the earthquake which shook Palestine in July 1927.[124] But Mgr Tappouni's proposal on the subject of responsibility for the Charfet seminary seemed to be a mark of destiny. The trust expressed by the Syrian-Catholic

---

[121] *Ibid.*, file 207 a, Gerusalemme Abou Gosch, Correspondence with the Curia Generale, letter from D Gariador to the 'Révérendissimes Pères capitulaires', 13 October 1925.

[122] *Ibid.*, file 207 b, Gerusalemme Abou Gosch, foundations, letter from D Maur Etcheverry to Mgr Giobbe, 17 October 1925.

[123] *Ibid.*, letter from D Gariador to D Maur Etcheverry, 2 December 1925.

[124] *Ibid.*, file 207 a, Gerusalemme Abou Gosch, Varia, correspondence, Jerusalem 1904-1930, The 'Mission palestinienne' in 1927, and letter from D Chibas-Lassalle to the Abbot General, 15 July 1927.

Patriarch confirmed the situation of the Jerusalem Benedictines henceforth in the religious landscape of the Levant. The prospect of settling in the Lebanon and of creating a Syrian-Benedictine Province seemed manna from heaven for them. Thereby, all the recurrent problems—recruitment, financing, status—would find their solution. In an enthusiastic letter, Dom Chibas-Lassalle summed up the advantages of the proposal:

> 'It would guarantee a providential and unexpected solution to the "Jerusalem question" and would be the happiest outcome for the French Province, which would find itself unburdened from then on, from the moment that indigenous recruitment, thereby made possible and normal, would save it from having to guarantee new monks for our Palestinian houses.'[125]

Quite reasonably, this project was welcomed by the French Province, who gave it a free hand for a trial period of four years. But behind these promises and beyond the real achievements, a success that meant a coming together both of political and religious approaches, the Benedictines had to pay a heavy price for the new undertaking. In fact, they were soon confronted by an exacerbated repetition of the problems met in Jerusalem. Whereas the number of students increased considerably (with the minor seminary in Jerusalem and the major in Charfet), there were still only a few Benedictines continuously available, which increased their workload all the more.[126] Furthermore, the hoped-for indigenous recruitment was nil, which resulted in the ambitious project for a Syrian-Benedictine Province being gradually given up. Besides, very soon warning remarks were made of interference by the Syrian-Catholic clergy in the Benedictine administration;[127] and whereas in 1930 it was believed that the Benedictines had power to control both the problems and also the Oriental hierarchy, it was exactly the opposite that now happened. The Benedictines were placed under the patriarch, in 1935 raised to the

---

[125] *Ibid.*, Correspondence, Jerusalem, 1929-1934, letter from D Chibas-Lassalle, then in Bétharram, to the Abbot General, 11 November 1929.

[126] *Ibid.*, letter from D Chibas-Lassalle to the Abbot General, 8 January 1933.

[127] *Ibid.*, Correspondence Ab. Gen. 1910-1950, letter from D Chibas-Lassalle to the Abbot General, 3 August 1919: 'Our Seminary will always suffer from its unusual situation regarding the Syrian Rite. Otherwise, it is good to maintain a certain distance from the Patriarch, Mgr Rahmani, an intriguing personality, who, as a neighbour, would be a threat. There is only one fear; that our Seminary comes to absorb his own, with which for several years it has been able to maintain excellent relations.'

rank of cardinal, who knew exactly how to make use of the jurisdiction of the French Ministry for Foreign Affairs and also that of the Sacred Congregation for the Oriental Church. In this context, faced always with the lack of financial means, and by some inefficiency at the Quai d'Orsay in paying its grants,[128] the seminary depended more and more on that Congregation, spiritually[129] as well as materially.[130] The latter, quite satisfied with an outcome which allowed for further improvement in a collaboration which favoured this Oriental Church, faithfully transmitted Mgr Tappouni's desires for a greater investment by the Benedictines.[131]

World War II did not allow the situation to improve. As during the first conflict, the Benedictine teaching staff was reduced by mobilisation. Resort was indeed had to a number of Syrians, which made indigenous recruitment seem real. But this solution was provisional; furthermore, despite the interest of the French Authorities, both Vichyists and Gaullists, the official funding did not measure up to the need.[132]

---

[128] Archives of the White Fathers, Rome, fourth period: Birraux 1936-1947, file 255, Sainte Anne, file RP Portier 1936-1939, letter from P. Portier [head of Sainte-Anne] to Mgr Birraux [General of the White Fathers], 17 August 1937: 'The Syrians Seminary, led by the Benedictines, had only a 5.000 francs subvention.'

[129] *Ibid.*, Third period: Voillard 1922-1936, file 142, Sainte Anne, note on Sainte Anne Seminary to the TRP Supérieur Général, 24 May 1926: about the request by the SCOC that the seminary of the Mount of Olives should be the only one for the Syrian Church (and that Sainte-Anne should be the only one for the Melkite Church). Some time later, the Benedictines feared being placed under the orders of the Apostolic delegate in Palestine, the situation of the White Fathers after May 1929 (*ibid.*, file Ste Anne et la Sacrée Congrégation Orientale, handwritten note by P. Portier about the 1929 decree putting Sainte-Anne seminary under the control of the Apostolic delegate in Palestine).

[130] Subiaco, file 207 a, Gerusalemme Abou Gosch, Varia, correspondence, Jerusalem 1904-1930, letters from D Chibas-Lassalle to the Abbot General, 15 July 1927 and 11 June 1930.

[131] *Ibid.*, Correspondence, Jerusalem, 1934-1949, letter from the SCOC to the Abbot General, 21 November 1936, Tisserant.

[132] Therefore, one anonymous Jerusalem Religious was ashamed about the fact that the Abu Ghosh archaeological excavations, led by P. de Vaux from the École Biblique, went on at great expense, whereas the Syrian seminary remained in need: 'Personally I am shocked when I see that 400 pounds were given to Fr Alexandre's excavations [...] whereas the very same Benedictines direct an important seminary that would use this amount for a far superior purpose.' In fact, this 'institution is [...] very necessary for France, since its students, educated according to our culture, must together become the Syrian priests and school heads. [...] An exceptionally important generosity would be both good propaganda and a valuable help in order to enlarge recruitment.' (Archives of the Assumptionist institution Notre-Dame de France, deposited in Saint-Peter in Gallicantu, Jerusalem, 4: relations with the military authorities, inventory of the main communities, with their aims and needs, w.d. (May 1944?), anonymous notes called: Bénédictins de la Pierre qui Vire, Abougoche (sic) and Bénédictins français, Jérusalem).

After the second world war, exacerbation of the problems of the Syrian-Catholic seminary

Whereas the aftermath of World War I had meant the revival of the project, the aftermath of World War II meant the revival of the questions. An early report set out the list:

> 'The situation at Jerusalem is as precarious as it could be. Besides the duties proper to monastic life, there are serious responsibilities, that would call for a numerous staff, well grounded both in religion and academically. In practice, the community has to live by begging, soliciting members from the various monasteries; often these members are obtained only with difficulty and, when they are obtained, they aren't always the best, or to say the least they aren't the most apt for the kind of work in which the Jerusalem community specialises.'[133]

To put it plainly, nothing had changed since the Chapter of 1925: the Syrian seminary remained a problem yet to be solved and which would lie in setting up a proper novitiate, as other foundations had done before achieving independence. Such a step would provide the way out of a burdensome situation, with an illegal house not in accord with the constitutions of the congregation, and which had been 'morally forced on the French Province'.[134] This impossible set-up was due to the peculiar Palestinian situation, to the agreement concluded with France, and to the attitude of the prior, Dom Chibas-Lassalle, who seemed set on this impasse enduring, as shown by his unconcern over the house's autonomy, which was shared by the Abbot Visitors and Generals. All this was exacerbated by the desire of some abbots to get rid of certain monks by sending them to Jerusalem.

The outcome is clear:

> 'Whether the abnormal and paradoxical status of Jerusalem be based on fact or fiction, whether open or secret, it cannot, I feel, be tolerated any longer, both out of regard for our Rules, and out of justice to the other Houses of the Province. It is

[133] Subiaco, file 207 a, Gerusalemme Abou Gosch, Correspondence, Jerusalem, 1934-1949, letter from the Abbot General to D Chibas-Lassalle, 14 October 1945.

[134] *Ibid.*, Pro-memoria on Jerusalem, October 1945, D Marie-Ephrem Bouillet (Abbot Visitor).

> high time to put a stop to a state of affairs which has for so long given rise to dissension and discord ... '

Under such direct attack, Father Chibas-Lassalle falls back on the same arguments as before:

> 'I have the painful feeling that this decision will necessarily deal a mortal blow to the foundation, by destroying its original character as a provincial foundation based on provincial collaboration.'[135]

Furthermore, in his view, this undertaking was quite in accordance with the Constitutions of his religious order and would allow an unprecedented collaboration between the Holy See, the French government and the Syrian-catholic patriarch. And, finally, he called for a canonical visitation to resolve the issue.

This visitation, envisaged by Father Chibas-Lassalle as the chance to save an enterprise closely linked to his name, lent all its weight to a monastic solution of the issue. An on-the-spot review of the situation led the Visitor, Dom Bouillet, to uncompromising conclusions. While he recognised the value of the work, which he described as one of the finest forms of apostolate,[136] he saw little else to praise. In fact, the work itself had had meagre success: after 45 years it had only produced 45 priests in the Syrian-catholic rite.[137] This was even less acceptable given the outstanding efforts by the Province in general and the Jerusalem Benedictines in particular. The latter had an even higher price to pay, since the very work they did led to a neglect of monastic observance which should have been the basis of their apostolate. While the community, whose status remained unresolved, 'could not enjoy that family character, with its common formation and common spirit, that Our Holy Father Benedict intended and provided for, so the monks found it difficult to settle down and find fulfilment.'

---

[135] *Ibid.*, letter from D Chibas-Lassalle, then in Paris, to the Abbot General, 15 October 1946.

[136] *Ibid.*, Correspondence with the Curia Generale, report on the situation of our houses in Palestine and Lebanon, 30 December 1947.

[137] As a comparison, the last available statistics about Sainte-Anne, dated 1931, give the number as 130 students since 1882, of whom 6 became bishops (in *Jubilé cinquantenaire de la fondation du séminaire grec-melkite catholique à Jérusalem—1882-1932—Appel aux anciens et aux amis de Sainte-Anne*, Harissa, w.d. [1931]).

The visitor went on to say that besides being incompatible with monastic life, the organisation of the seminary was flawed:

> 'If I may say so, we have put "the cart before the horse" by opening the institute before training the staff, and before setting up the monastic family that would have charge of it; nor afterwards was there ever serious concern with the structure of this family: hence the lack of suitable personnel.'

Further factors lead to an incontrovertible conclusion:

> 'Half a century's experience has shown our monastery and the duties of our Benedictine life to be incompatible with the demands of the Syrian Seminaries. It is time we recognised quite simply that our fathers were wrong in wanting to shoulder a task, barely reconcilable with our own obligations, and quite beyond our abilities.'

And so the French Benedictines decided to give up Charfet, and consequently Jerusalem—an irrevocable decision, especially since Mgr Tappouni was also considering doubling the size of his seminary by uniting it in Charfet, so as to avoid the complexities of the new Middle-Eastern borders, but also so as to have greater control over the vast enterprise that he wished to make exclusively his own. Such things only further threatened an already unfortunate experience.[138]

---

[138] Subiaco, file 207 a, Gerusalemme Abou Gosh, Correspondence, Jerusalem, 1934-1949, letter from Dom Marie-Ephrem Bouillet to Dom Chibas-Lasssalle, 20 March 1947: ' ... concerning our monasteries, it is clearly God's will that they should be places of prayer and schools of perfection: the main issue is not to have any particular institution, but to guarantee our monks as full a monastic life as possible; charitable activities, however splendid they are, must never occupy the first place, because if observance is regularly sacrificed to the good work, the proper order will be reversed and lead to disorder. Can we not admit among ourselves and without casting blame, that we have such a disorder in Jerusalem, where almost all the observances and customs of our province have been progressively sacrificed to ensure the better running of the Seminary? And what about Charfet where for 16 years our fathers have been living without any monastic observance? [...] I have the greatest esteem, not to say veneration, for H E Cardinal Tappouni, whom I consider a most fetching and attractive personality. But I have to confess that it is rather disturbing to be so dependent on someone, who, not being a monk, does not understand our needs or difficulties. Very soon Provincial Chapter won't be able to elect any other prior than the Cardinal's candidate; so as to please the Cardinal we shall be forced to leave our monks in unacceptable circumstances at Charfé *[sic]*; besides, the Province won't be able to end an agreement that has outlived its natural life, etc., etc ... Where do we go next? [....] Dear Father, you cannot imagine how hateful such interference is from people outside the Order; far from being helpful, they only do harm ... If only the Lord would free us from such things, how we would bless Him! Oh for the freedom to be simply and fully monks!'

Clash between religion and politics

In the hope of transforming the building on the Mount of Olives into a straightforward abbey, the Benedictines presented Mgr Tappouni,[139] at the HOC,[140] and the French Government with their plan to make these purely internal changes.

On the religious side, the Syrian-Catholics and the HOC, such a decision produced some exasperation, but it was on the whole accepted. Besides terminating the Benedictine involvement,[141] an order had to be found who might take on the work. Though such a logical step should have been taken relatively quickly, there arose unexpected delays. For those communities, approached about taking over from the Benedictines, backed off from the undertakings already made by the Benedictines and the ensuing labour.

But it was the clash between the political and the religious positions which proved the greatest problem. In this context it is interesting to note that until this very date, according to the archives, the French diplomats had no idea of the disagreements within the Benedictine province. Even if these debates were purely internal to the Benedictine Order, it is strange that news of them did not spread beyond these confines, given the close relations between the French Foreign Office and the monks of Jerusalem and Lebanon.

For the diplomats the withdrawal of the Benedictines from educating the Syrian-Catholic clergy only gradually sank in. First, they had to recognise the transferral of both major and minor seminaries to the Lebanon following on the sudden deterioration in Palestinian politics, a decision shared by the White Fathers who sent their students to Rayak. But when in 1949, after the first Israeli-Arab war, the French Province resisted the return of the minor seminarians to Jerusalem, the French Consul General there recognised the reality of the situation, namely that keeping the seminary in the Lebanon would mean the end of Benedictine

---

[139] *Ibid.*, Letter from Dom Bouillet to Mgr Tappouni, 4 May 1947.

[140] *Ibid.*, Letter from the Abbot General to the HOC, 15 June 1949.

[141] With some canonical, even if not very grave, snags concerning the ownership of the property on the Mount of Olives, Mgr Tappouni, supported by the HOC, claimed that it had been acquired through Vatican funds and so should revert to the Congregation, and so remain in the hands of the Patriarchate of Antioch. This the Benedictines had to accept, though with promise of compensation (*ibid.,* file 207 b, Gerusalemme Abou Gosh, file, Palestine Mission, suppression, 1950-1953, letter from the Vicar General to the Jerusalem community, 3 February 1951).

presence and activity in the Holy Land. He saw no reason to prevent such a return.[142] Moreover, the argument from lack of staff was not valid:

> 'Moreover, the question of a shortage of French Benedictine vocations [...] does not arise. They have just re-opened St Benoit sur Loire, and all their monasteries, especially La Pierre qui Vire, are flourishing at present.'

Indeed, in the diplomat's eyes, the good faith of the Benedictines was the only issue at stake, since their presence in Jerusalem had been such a success:

> 'I find their decision surprising and upsetting. I believe it was based simply on a monastic desire to follow St Benedict's Rule (It is odd that they have discovered this incompatibility, if indeed there is one, 46 years after founding the seminaries in Jerusalem!) and taking little account either of the role of the French Church in the Middle-East, or even of the Church's role in general.'

In fact, he continued, 'the Benedictine decision took no account of the real situation in the Church,[143] and totally ignored political reality; since this rash decision [...] risks losing for France the privilege of training the Syrian-Catholic clergy in the Middle-East. Our language, our position, our reputation have gained from this more than words can say. It would be ironical to lose all these advantages, simply though the ill-considered decision of the *French* Province of the Benedictines of the Primitive Observance.'

More serious still, this will affect the French position in the present debates over the future of Palestine:

---

[142] 'The monastery of Siloe, apart from a few Israeli shells and a period of occupation by the Arab Legion, lifted several months before, was lucky to have suffered little from the war. It is in the Arab zone where conditions are excellent, and *nothing at present would prevent* the return of the minor seminary, or the major one for that matter, to Jerusalem' (MAE, Paris, Levant, 1944-1960, Palestine, 427, Questions religieuses, mosquée du Rocher, Abou Gosh, 31 August 1944-10 December 1952, letter from the French Consulate Grneral in Jerusalem [578/AL] to the FO, 17 October 1949, Deciry).

[143] 'If I may venture onto purely Church territory, it cannot be denied that the French Benedictines have made a valuable western contribution to the Syrian-Catholic Rite clergy, by providing a religious discipline and a moral strength, of which the Eastern Church, perhaps for climatic reasons or because of local weaknesses, has particular need.'

> 'From the view-point of our present political position—as well as that of the Vatican—concerning the Jerusalem question, the closure of the seminary in Siloe would be just as catastrophic. We can only seriously defend the principle of internationalisation if we can point to our interest in the Holy Places and link them with French religious institutes, with which we are concerned. The closure of the seminary in Siloe would prove to both Jews and Arabs that we set little store by the spiritual importance of the Holy City since we consider that priests of the Syrian-Catholic rite can equally well follow their studies elsewhere ... and under another's direction.'

After outlining the 'threefold structure of priestly education in Jerusalem by French orders' (White Fathers for the Melkite Church, Betharram Fathers for the seminary of the Latin Patriarchate, and Benedictines for the Syrian-Catholic Church), the diplomat finished his analysis with a *cri de coeur*:

> 'To destroy such a harmony would be catastrophic. In the East to give up any post is to lose it for good. At times we may reluctantly give one up from absolute necessity. It does not seem to be so in the present case: the clear joint interests of the Roman Church, the Eastern Church, the French Benedictines and of France itself must permit the Syrian-Catholic seminary to reopen its doors in Jerusalem.'

And so the monks' plan to retain a purely contemplative presence was rejected out of hand by the French, since it would provide no substitute.[144] Completely absorbed in their political world, the officials of

[144] By the end of the 19th century France already experienced problems with the purely contemplative communities which wanted to settle in the Holy Land, such as the Poor Clares or the Sisters of Marie Reparatrice; and these were among the first to see their subsidies reduced by the French Foreign Ministry in the 1920's. The Benedictines were aware from the beginning that the maintenance of such a monastery could not depend on French financial aid, since they no longer fulfilled French political objectives. (Subiaco, Correspondence with the General Curia, brief report on the canonical visit to our houses in Palestine and the Lebanon, 12 December 1947, Dom Bouillet). Likewise, in their search for successors, the French rejected the Sisters of Marie Reparatrice as insufficiently active (MAE Levant 1944-1960, Palestine 472 Questions religieuses, mosquée du Rocher, Abou Gosh, 31 August 1944-10 December 1952, telegram from the MAE [256-57] to the French Consulate General in Jerusalem, [779-80] to the French Embassy in Beirut,[448] to the French Embassy to the Holy See, 2 September 1952).

the Quai d'Orsay were backed by the Jerusalem Benedictines who could not face up to the closure of their mission.[145] Just as in 1925 when he defended his views before the HOC, Dom Chibas-Lassalle, in his address to the French Foreign Ministry, distinguishes between Benedictines in France and Benedictines in the Holy Land; the decision to close the mission was taken in France, divorced from the actual situation, and it depended solely on the Abbot Visitor, Dom Bouillet.[146]There was every hope of his not being re-elected at the 1952 Chapter, which would lead to the reversal of the decision and the continuance of the Syrian Mission. Thus far the French diplomats could only be reassured by the continual postponement of the seminary's closure, caused by the failure to find successors for the Benedictines; and they continued to follow this line towards the monks.[147] Nevertheless the train of events belied the rather naive expectations of the Jerusalem Benedictines, as Dom Bouillet was confirmed in his post. At the Quai d'Orsay they accepted the inevitable:

> 'Since his authority can no longer be challenged, he has put in hand his chosen plan.'[148]

Presented with the resolution of the French Province, the French had no option but to accept the end of the Benedictine settlement in Jerusalem. They also had to find successors to the Benedictines, which proved extremely difficult. For if Paris and its diplomats in Jerusalem were especially attached to keeping the old order going, the Quai d'Orsay had to face facts which bore no resemblance to the end of the 19th century. Aided by the very French Mgr Tisserant, prefect of the HOC, a diplomatic

---

[145] Subiaco, file 207 a, Gerusalemme Abou Gosh, Correspondence, Jerusalem, 1934-1949, letter from Dom Chibas-Lassalle, Beirut to the Abbot General, 15 July 1947.

[146] MAE Levant 1944-1960, Palestine 472 Questions religieuses, mosquée du Rocher, Abou Gosh, 31 August 1944-10 December 1952,telegram from the French Consulate general in Jerusalem (27-29) to the MAE, 25 January 1952, Neuville.

[147] Official France reacted at once to the appointment of a Spanish superior in Jerusalem, in contravention to the convention of 1901, and threatened to withdraw the subsidy (*ibid.*, telegram from the French ambassador to the Holy See [4 bis-5 bis] to the MAE, 16 January 1952, d'Ormesson) The Benedictines backed down and appointed a French monk. (Subiaco, file 207 a, Gerusalemme Abou Gosh 31 August 1934-10 December 1952, telegram from the MAE [256-7] to the French consulate general in Jerusalem. [779-80] to the French embassy in Beirut, [448] to the French embassy to the Holy See, 2 September 1952).

[148] MAE, Levant 1944-1960, Palestine 427, Questions religieuses, mosquée du Rocher, Abou Gosh, 31 August 1944-10 December 1952, letter from the French consulate general in Jerusalem (380/AL) to the MAE, 22 July, Sablière.

offensive was mounted, like that of 1899-1900, between Jerusalem, Paris, Rome and Beirut. Several congregations and orders were sounded out: Dominicans, who had been accustomed to such work in Mosul;[149] Assumptionists, already settled in Jerusalem and whose huge hospice of Notre-Dame de France had just been largely destroyed by the Israeli-Arab conflicts;[150] the White Fathers, responsible over decades for the education of the Melkite clergy.[151] Alarmed by the responsibilities shouldered by the Benedictines, themselves at sea over the new situation in Palestine, suffering the same problems over man power as the Benedictines, or pleading the incompatibility of such an undertaking with their constitutions, these communities declined the official invitation. And after many efforts to find French religious equal to the task, with Mgr Tappouni declaring frequently how much he valued his special relationship with France,[152] Paris had no choice but to accept the Catholic position. Assumptionist Fathers indeed, a congregation of French origin, took over from the Benedictines at Charfet in 1950, but it was the Dutch province of the congregation which took on the work, because of the abundance of vocations in the Netherlands at the time, unlike in France. In Jerusalem after fresh reports of the closure of the minor seminary, the Benedictines effectively abandoned their post without being replaced by any other order.

This drew recriminations from the ultra-Catholic and French consul René Neuville:

> 'I regret that the Department could not persuade the Benedictines of Encalcat to continue the mission they have conducted for 46 years, or, that failing, obtain from Cardinal Tisserant a French order to replace the Benedictines. Cardinal Tappouni wasquite in favour of one or the other solution; it is deplorable that it is the French who could not meet his wishes.'[153]

---

[149] *Ibid.*, letter from the French Embassy to the Holy See (437/AL) to the MAE 27 October 1949, d'Ormesson.

[150] *Ibid.*, telegram from the French Embassy in Beirut (106-108) to the MAE 2 February 1951, du Chayla.

[151] *Ibid.*, telegram from the French Consulate general in Jerusalem (106-107) to the MAE, 7 April 1951, Neuville.

[152] *Ibid.*, letter from the French Embassy in Beirut (381/AL) to the MAE, 25 April 1950, du Chayla.

[153] *Ibid.*, letter from the French consulate general in Jerusalem (38/AL) to the MAE, 17 January 1951, Neuville.

Faced with the inevitable closure of the seminary in Jerusalem, the French redoubled their efforts to provide an effective presence in so prominent a part of the city, and so avoid a vacuum. But the suggested remedies, (a French hospital,[154] the house of a French religious order,[155] or some establishment linked to one,[156] even the site of the French Consulate if their government would buy or rent it),[157] anything that would prevent Mgr Tappouni from selling the building to an international institution, came to nothing.[158] The building remained in the hands of the Syrian-Catholic Church and the Benedictines left the location in 1953.[159] From then on the seminary stayed closed and the French flag no longer floated above this *Mount of Scandal*.[160]

---

[154] *Ibid.*, Letter from the French Embassy to the Holy See (57/AL) to the MAE, 22 January 1952, d'Ormesson.

[155] *Ibid.*, letter from the French consulate general in Jerusalem (247/AL) to the MAE, 9 April 1952, Neuville: the Consul General is thinking of the Sisters of the Rosary, whose intake was Arab: 'So the loss of influence that we have suffered through the closure of the Syrian seminary would be largely offset, and in a similar field.'

[156] *Ibid.*, telegram from the French consulate general in Jerusalem (333-337) to the MAE, 6 August 1952, Sablière: reflection on the settlement of the Lazarists shortly expelled from China.

[157] *Ibid.*, letter from the French consulate general in Jerusalem (506/AL) to the MAE, 11 September 1952, Sablière.

[158] The prelate was then engotiating with the UNRWA (United Nations Relief and Works Agency), interested in the house in order to settle a technical school (*ibid.*, telegram from the French consulate general in Jerusalem (268) to the MAE, 22 June 1952, Neuville).

[159] Subiaco, file 207 b, Gerusalemme Abou Gosh, file, Palestinian Mission, suppression, 1950-1953, authorisation of the Abbot General 10 October 1953. One should note that the possibility of their replacement, in the last resort, by the Benedictines of Chevetogne was rejected both by the French, who did not want the Belgians and were suspicious of their offers to accept French supervision (MAE, Paris, Levant 1944-1960, Palestine 427, Questions religieuses, mosquée du Rocher, Abou Gosh, 31 August 1944-10 December 1952, telegram from the French Consulate General in Jerusalem [249-54] to the MAE, 7 June 1952, Neuville) and by the HOC, who did not want religious to be dependent on the insubstantial assurances of Mgr Tappouni (*ibid.*, letter from the French ambassador at Beirut (864/AL) to the MAE, 14 July 1952, Balay).

[160] Unoccupied thereafter, the building of the Syrian-Catholic seminary was entrusted to the Secours catholique français following on Pope Paul VI's visit to Jerusalemin 1964. At the same time as they closed the mission on the Mount of Olives, the Benedictines left Abou Gosh. Things here were more complicated still because of its status as national property. The number of congregations approached by the French was even greater than before, and the failure to find a buyer for the land acquired by the Benedictines around the church, spurred the French government into taking on the ownership. It was only in 1959 that an agreement was signed between the French State and the Lazarists, who only stayed for a few years. In 1976 the church was entrusted to the care of the Olivetan Benedictines of Le Bec Hellouin, who still remain there. Since 1999 this foundation has become an independent abbey named Sainte-Marie de la Resurrection.

Conclusion

The final chapter of a long drawn-out saga, the Benedictines' announcement that they wished to close the Syrian mission was greeted with dismay by the French diplomats. On the one hand, it meant the breaking off of the 1901 agreement, indeed allowed for in the terms of the accord, but hard to envisage in reality (the general impression being given that the French authorities alone had the right to renounce the entente). On the other hand, along with the worsening of the political situation in Palestine, it was a symbol of the end of the Ottoman era which lingered on throughout the British Mandate, while France could barely bring itself to give up its old prerogatives. Finally, the end of the Benedictine presence was the first rift in the vast French network which had been built up throughout the 19th century, and a sign of the divergence between the component political and religious elements. This was indeed a collision between two viewpoints, the political and the religious, which could continue in tandem as long as they were complementary, and one did not cross the other.

The meeting between the French government and the French Benedictines, leading to the occupancy of the basilica of Abu Ghosh and of the Syrian-Catholic seminary first in Jerusalem and then in Charfet, resulted from the convergence of political and religious interests. For several decades the two concerns had a common objective—politics took on the cloak of eternity while still with an eye to the real world and its demands, while the monks demonstrated a patriotism verging on outright chauvinism, without losing sight of their religious mission.

At the end of the day the alliance between the two interests could not hold. The Jerusalem Benedictines pursued their own end come what may, following their own religious logic, aiming for a Christian hold over what might become a new Latin Kingdom, and resulting in the union of all the Churches. But their compatriots holding to a different religious logic, kept their counsel for the entire period: their long term view being that the Syrian Mission, however useful in the short term, was incompatible with their own *raison d'être*. Faced with this internal contradiction, they paid lip-service to the religious ideal while secretly rejecting it: French officialdom stays within its old modes of thought. The two ideals are opposed to each other: they can co-exist while they share common interests (religious expansion by reviving old Benedictine traditions in the East, working for the benefit of France, the need to find refuge for monks expelled from France). But they come into opposition when the interests diverge: when the Benedictines feel that their vocation as monks is no longer in Palestine, when they decide to give up their position in the name of spiritual values, while the French authorities cannot bear to give up a single French foothold.

THE RELIGIOUS POLITICS OF THE FRANCISCANS IN THE HOLY LAND BETWEEN THE CRIMEAN WAR AND THE FIRST WORLD WAR[1]

Giuseppe Buffon

In the vortex of nationalism

The impact of European nationalism on the Middle East undeniably took place on the occasion of the Napoleonic campaign in Egypt (1798-1799), a campaign understood as a venture of liberation, or rather of civilization,[2] of a region which Europe considered to be the 'mother of ancient civilization'. While France took the side of modernisation, supporting the reforms of Mohamed Ali (1812-1849), Great Britain attempted to increase its own commercial power to keep control of the Persian Gulf coast and the Red Sea. France concentrated on the political scene, whilst England preferred to operate in the economic arena. The competition between these two nations would have a significant influence on the history of Jerusalem, at least in regard to the Arab-Israel conflict.[3]

After Muhamad Ali conquered Palestine (1831-1832), the competing European nations also began to take an interest in 'The Holy Places'. The French, had chosen Egypt as a stronghold from which to expand their influence, and, thanks also to their Algerian campaign,

---

1 Abbreviations and initials: AA.EE.SS. = Vatican Secret Archive, Archives of the Congregation of Extraordinary Ecclesial Affairs, Vatican City; ACPF = Archive of the Congregation for the Evangelization of Peoples, formerly *De Propaganda Fide*, Vatican City; ACTS = Archive of the Holy Land Custody, Jerusalem; ACTSP = Archive of the Commissariat of the Holy Land of Paris, Paris; AGOFM = General Archive of the Order of Friars Minor, Rome; AMAE = Archive of the Minister of Foreign Affairs, Paris; AMAEN = Archive of the Minister of Foreign Affairs, Nantes; AOM = Acta Ordinis Minorum; CCC = Commercial Consular Correspondence; CPC = Political Consular Correspondence; MD = Memories and Documents; ff. = papers.

2 R Owen, 'Egypt and Europe: from French Expedition to British Occupation', in A. Hourani, Ph D S Khoury, M C Wilson, *The Modern Middle East: a Reader*, Berkeley, Los Angeles, 1993, 111-124.

3 R Heacock, 'Jerusalem and the Holy Place in European Diplomacy', in Anthony O'Mahony (ed.), *The Christian Heritage in the Holy Land*, London, 1995, 202-209.

consolidated their position above all within the Arab world.[4] With her growing interest in the Arab question, the issue of the Holy Places also came to assume national, and no longer only religious, importance. The diffusion of a greater tolerance, in virtue of the reforms promised by Muhamad Ali, induced Jerusalem to open the doors to foreign consuls and to new religious communities, especially Protestant ones,[5] and Constantinople to welcome ambassadors and bankers.[6] Consequently, alongside the millenarian Protestant movement, supported above all by Germany, headway was made in the Jewish world, encouraged by Lord Palmerston himself. He invited the Ottoman emperor to welcome the return of the Jews, suggesting that their resources would increase the economic capacity of the Porte, thereby helping to confront the revolutionary movement of Mohamad Ali.[7] Some millenarian groups envisioned a Judeo-Christian kingdom for Jerusalem, others, ultramontanes and legitimists, the establishment of the ancient Latin Kingdom, while the Germans, by contrast, seemed largely inclined to an international regime.

As for religious politics, the French favoured the Greek Catholics, while Russia responded with support for the Orthodox. The recognition of the Greek Catholics in 1831 by the Porte marked a diplomatic success for France. The Ottomans found themselves pressed between the innate tendency to support the Orthodox and the aims advanced by Russia. The pretext, from which the Crimean War originated, matured, in fact, within the Christian confessions, due to the rule of the Orthodox under the aegis of Russia. The Russians had been interested in Palestine since the 18th century, but their attention to the Middle East increased notably during the first part of the 19th century. The Orthodox in Palestine had already overtaken the Latins, from both the numerical perspective and in terms of patrimony. Consideration should also be given to the fact that Russian pilgrims now flocked into Palestine in ever-greater numbers. Subject to pressures from the Russian side, and following the Protestant

---

4 H Laurens, *Le royaume impossible—La France et la genèse du monde arabe*, Paris, 1990, 84-115.

5 T Prein, 'La querelle du Muristan et la fondation de l'église du Rédempteur à Jérusalem', in D Trimbur et R Aaronsohn (eds), *De Bonaparte à Balfour. La France, l'Europe occidentale et la Palestine 1799-1917*, Paris, 2001, 345-360.

6 S Mardin, 'Religion and Secularism in Turkey', in A Hourani, Ph D S Khoury, M C Wilson (eds), *The Modern Middle East*, 348-358.

7 B Tuchman, *Bible and Sword: England and Palestine from the Bronze Age to Balfour*, New York, 1984, 175-223.

example, after 1843 the Orthodox patriarch of Jerusalem was no longer elected at Constantinople, but in Jerusalem. Subsequently, after the conflict between the Porte and Greece on the one side, and Russia on the other, the latter supported the local candidate, an ethnic Arab, with the intention of creating an ally, and with a view to winning the protectorate over the Orthodox. From this moment on a new interest in the Holy Land and Jerusalem arose on the part of the French and the Church of Rome, leading in 1847 to the installation once more of a Latin patriarch. This increased friction between religious groups, brought closer the possibility of the conflict of 1853.[8]

The Crimean War was, essentially, the result of conflict between Russia and France, while the Porte maintained its *status quo*. It followed that only the local community was interested in defining the appurtenance of the Holy Places. France, in fact, acted under the pressure of internal politics and with the objective of provoking division between Austria and Russia, pursuing revenge for what happened at the Congress of Vienna. Russia, for her part, by requesting to protect the Orthodox, tried to strengthen her influence where she was present, supporting the movements of independence. England, instead, while seeking neutrality, also found herself involved in the conflict, if only to protect her access to the commercial routes to India. The Kingdom of Sardinia, needing support for national unification, was likewise obliged to participate in the conflict. The Crimean War does however clearly illustrate the instrumental use of the question of the Holy Places on the part of European nations.

The only result of the conflict was to assure another sixty years of life for the Ottoman empire, thanks to the long period of non-belligerence among the European nations, with the Crimean war, providing the state of equilibrium necessary for European politics in the East for the next sixty years.[9] The instrumentalisation of religion by nationalism for political reasons, already present at the Crimea, became ever clearer in the following decades; only the change in political equilibrium following the First World War could allow the possibility of a different approach.

Between the Congress of Vienna and the First World War, the Crimean War undoubtedly turned out to be the most important event in the context of the relationships between the major powers. It widely tested

---

[8] D Hopwood, *The Russian presence in Syria and Palestine (1843-1914)*, Oxford, 1969, 33-45; 65-72.

[9] A J P Taylor, *Europe: Grandeur and Decline*, London, 1967, 67-77.

their understanding and capacity to manage the international context. It was defined as the *preventative war*, in as much as it sought to block the Russia protectorate over the Orthodox of the Ottoman empire, and what is more, it *anticipated* the wars of succession related to an Ottoman empire already in terminal agony.[10] The two claimants, France and England, would continue to refine their aims over the next half century: France was interested in building an empire in the Mediterranean, the *Mare Internum*; England in defending its route to India, through its protection of Protestants and Jews.

Religion and politics

Le Nouvelliste of 29 January 1892 published an article entitled 'Les Catoliques en Orient et le protectorat de la France' about a conference by Léon Duguit, a Law professor at the University of Bordeaux. The reporter, having just returned from a trip in the East, notes with particular emphasis how, for the Orientals, that is the Turks, only entities of a religious nature exist, be it Greek (Russian), Protestant (English), or Catholic (French), and how, as a consequence, it would also be necessary for France to project her role in the East as religious and Catholic. Professor Duguit expanded on the history of the protectorate, from the beginning to the epoch of the Crusades, until the phenomenon of capitulation from 1535 until 1740. Paraphrasing Paul Bert in his passage 'l'anticléricalisme n'est pas un article d'exportation', he illustrated the means by which French influence in the East was affirmed by the export of her institutions: pilgrimages, hospitals, schools and orphanages. The speaker had words of praise for the Jesuit University of Beirut, the schools of the Christian Brothers in Cairo and the founding of their law faculty, and the cultural initiatives of the Dominicans. He did not forget to cite France's rivals: Germany, England, but above all Russia, 'qui se presente aujourd'hui en Orient comme la plus grande puissance religieuse du monde', as well as Italy's failure in her continual attempts to replace France in its protective role. Lastly, the Franciscan custodians of the Holy Sepulchre are defined

[10] R Heacock, 'La Palestine dan les relations internationales 1798-1914', in D Trimbur and R Aaronsohn, *De Bonapate à Balfour*, 37-39.

[11] A comment by Prof Duguit on the same conference, published in an article in the periodical *La Croix de Bordeaux* (31 May 1892). The author, a certain J Rouvier, engages in polemics about the affirmation of the speaker, regarding the aversion of the Franciscans with regard

as 'les plus grands ennemis de la France'.[11]

Less than a month later, *La Croix*, in a Supplement of 16 February 1892, published the summary of another conference on French politics in the Holy Land, 'La France en Palestine'. This time the speaker was a certain Antoine Sallès, who, the author emphasized, did not have to exert himself to convince his audience that, in the East, politics and religion were inseparable.

The Franciscan Frediano Giannini, then *Custos* of the Holy Land, took part in 1903 in a symposium on Franciscan influence in the Levant, at which he declared his aversion to dealing with politics. His insisted his reasons for this were well motivated, not due to incompetence, or to the fact that politics were not present in the Holy Land. Rather, he insisted, the topic is omnipresent in the Holy Land, 'one no longer speaks [of politics] only in pharmacies but even in nursery schools'; continuing, 'it enters everywhere, even in the way one wears their beard!' The Franciscan, seeming, as it were to want to draw attention to the change in the institution to which he belonged, insisted that he did not want to speak out because, he convincingly declared, 'I also want to have my politics, which consists essentially in keeping myself far from it, *cogitatione, verbo et opera*.'[12]

On the other hand it is understandable that the politics of the Custody could not be the same as that, for example, of France, or of Russia, or of any other national power present in the territory. It is plausible that, in the official sense of the term, the politics of the Custody ceded to the Apostolic See, that is to the Propaganda, or perhaps rather to the Secretary of State. Even though the Custody had its own politics, essentially 'the politics of religion,' that does not mean that the two elements, 'politics' and 'religion' would necessarily be separate. In the Holy Land, in fact, there is no religious event that does not carry political weight and there is no political event which does not have religious significance. The precedence in processions, for example, the omission of some formula during a liturgy, an imprecision regarding the way of blessing, or the use of holy water, that is all those practices called 'liturgical honours,' could give credit to diplomatic

---

to France: 'if it was truly so', he insists, the French Bishops surely would have reacted. The Custody, however, he continues, 'is not composed exclusively of Italians', the vicar is French. The same Custody would not be contrary to the protectorate and the consul, on his part, does not appear discontent with the Franciscans. Besides, some French Franciscans, requested by the Custody would be leaving shortly for the Holy Land.

[12] F Giannini, *La Custodia di Terra Santa*, Livorno, 1903, 10-11.

controversies, and become a matter of international politics. Even the most simple gestures of the religious community assume a political significance: the cleaning of windows, the arrangement of candelabras, crucifixes, the lighting of lamps, not to speak of the building of walls, the maintenance of doors, the preparation of cemeteries, the repair and construction of chapels and other initiatives relating to patrimony.

In other words, what has been said so far demonstrates how the development of the theme of the title does not permit a treatment of anything less than the entire history of the Custody. In fact, the religious politics of the Franciscans in the Holy Land are nothing other than the history *tout court* of their presence in the Middle East. While not eschewing a degree of summarisation, it appears useful to refer to a double *Memorandum* addressed by the Congregation of Propaganda Fide to the French Ambassador to the Holy See.[13] Important principally for its length of more than 50 pages, which makes it one of the richest files—the Spanish case aside[14]—among those recovered from research undertaken in the archive of the Congregation of Extraordinary Ecclesiastic Affairs (the section of the Secretary of State dealing with relations with States) connected to the historical period in question.[15]

Another primary element, in my opinion, is represented by the sources from which the said documentation comes. These consist of a series of letters and reports sent to the Propaganda by a *Custos* of the Holy Land, Fr Giacomo de Castelmadama, who could be defined as the initiator of a movement to awaken the political conscience of the Custody. The same documentary evidence reveals, for example, the attempt made by this religious to appeal to other nations, almost setting a challenge to France, the protecting nation, to give proof of greater effectiveness. The attitude of Castelmadama, who appears to have decided to act in a different manner from that of the Custody in the past, depended also, in part, on the general situation in which the Franciscans found themselves

---

[13] AA.EE.SS., *Francia* 1891-1897, pos. 869-874, fasc. 453, *Terra Santa. Memorandum e Pro-Memoria rimessi al Signor Ambasciatore di Francia, il 18 luglio 1891 e il 18 luglio 1897*, March 1898, ff. 27-57 (1-57).

[14] Regarding this theme see the concluding part of the present study.

[15] With the intention of finding documentation of a political-diplomatic character regarding the Custody of the Holy Land between the War of Crimea and the First World War, we have inspected the most significant sources in this regard, i.e. those relative to France, Spain, Austria, Turkey, Russia and Germany. The outcome of the investigation on Austria, Turkey, Russia and Germany proved irrelevant or almost nil.

in the Holy Land. Since the foundation of the Latin patriarchate (1847), a Franciscan had been named for the first time as prelate for the See of Jerusalem.[16] Further evidence of the importance of this documentation is offered by the French reaction to the *Memorandum*. France found herself, perhaps, for the first time, having to defend herself from an accusation that could give rise to undue discussion on the future of her role as the protector of Catholics.

Shortly after receiving the first *Memorandum* (1891), the Foreign Minister, at the behest of the government, sent a special appointee to the Holy Land, with the duty to discern elements favourable or adverse to maintaining the protectorate.[17] In this initiative, it seems a prelude could be found to what would happen in the imminent First World War.

A last observation, not insignificant for the time frame, could be conjectured from the contents. The document limited itself essentially to the religious politics of France and those of Russia, the two great nations in contention (through the instrumental use of religion) over the political area of the Middle East, from the Crimean War until the First World War. For these and other reasons, which we hope to examine later, we hold that the double *Memorandum* can be consider as a privileged perspective, from which to arrive at a summary of the religious politics of the Custody at the end of the Ottoman empire.

The '*Memorandum—promemoria of the S. C. of the Propaganda to the Lord Ambassador of France (1891-97)*'

1. The text presents at least three thematic sections. The first addresses the arguments for the titles which permitted France to assume the role of protector, resulting from the defence and recovery of the Holy Places—an obligation that they must not disregard, so as not to suffer the extinction of the protectorate and the consequent loss of corresponding political privileges. The second refers to the progress of non-Catholic religious groups, such as Protestants, Jews and Orthodox, considered a threat as much for the mission as for the Holy Places, and the support that they were assured from nations such as Germany, England, America, and above

[16] For more information on this theme see our *Les Franciscains en Terre Sainte (1869-1889) Religion et politique. Une recherche institutionnelle*, Paris, 2005, 201-211.

[17] AMAE, CPC, *Turquie-Jérusalem* 23, Ledoulx, consul of France at Jerusalem, A Spuller, Minister of Foreign Affairs, 14 October 1891, 145-169.

all Russia. The third largely addresses a list of violations to the *status quo* of the Holy Places, beginning with the theft of the star of Bethlehem (1847), held to be the pretext that triggered the Crimean War, and continuing as far as to include contemporary events (1897).

The *Memorandum* starts, however, with the reminder of the merits acquired by France in defence of the 'rights of Catholics' in Palestine. The 'first born daughter of the Church', having established primacy precisely through recovering 'with arms and money the most precious monuments of the Holy Religion', came to be considered the protector of the Holy Places. Maintaining these privileges was subordinate, naturally, to the persistence of the 'religious interest to protect', and above all to the efficacy of the 'guardianship and defence of such interests.' Obviously it concerns, 'Catholic interests', as the author of the *Memorandum* seems anxious to clarify, interests that could not be 'restricted to one or another nation', being pertinent rather to 'all the Catholic nations'. To clarify therefore, letters were sent which made it evident that: 'the work of the Holy Land is an international issue and constitutes a patrimony of all Catholics.'[18] The proof for such an affirmation would have been more than evident: the pilgrims visiting the Holy Places come from every nation; the offerings that are needed for the maintenance of the mission and the care of the shrines arrive there from all parts of the world; and lastly the Franciscan Custody, already composed '*ad antiquo* by religious of various nations', had been later recognized as an international organisation by the Constitutions of Benedict XIV and other pontiffs.

The *Memorandum* represents, therefore, an admonition to France not to cede to the temptation of nationalism, in order not to compromise her position as protector. In other words, a diplomatic action, excessively concentrating on the exclusive defence of national interests could create jealousy on the part of other Catholic powers. The instrumentalisation of the protectorate conceived for the defence of religious interests of an international character would, by undertaking actions of a purely national, political nature, have offered other nations an opportunity to request intervention for the protection of the Holy Places.[19]

---

[18] *Terra Santa. Memorandum e Pro-Memoria rimessi al Signor Ambasciatore di Francia*, 28v.

[19] 'Therefore, wanting to regard the Holy Land as belonging not to the entire Catholic world but to one or more nations in particular, would be the most grave error and could give rise to fatal consequences. From this false concept, that is, that different governments could claim a pretext to assert a right of intervention to protect the Holy Places in reason of the part that the respective nations had in their maintenance.' *Ibid.*

Until that moment, continued the text of the *Memorandum*, France could have maintained the privileges proper to the protectorate by virtue of a tacit approval from the other Catholic powers, thanks to the recognition attributed by the Porte, and by an ancient tradition of the administration of religious affairs regarding the Holy Places. The Congress of Berlin (1878), despite recognizing the privileged situation of France in the Holy Land, had in some ways, limited its rights, granting to other nations also the faculty to 'defend there the persons and the institutions on which its own subjects depend'. With respect to other nations, France still kept the rights relative to the administration of the *status quo* of the Holy Places. From the text of the *Memorandum* seems effectively to emerge the fact that the only advantage over other nations that France could still enjoy was the future Assizes of Berlin, consisting in an assignment of a strictly religious nature, which means to say in the defence of the *status quo* of the Holy Places. In other words, if the government of the Republic wanted to continue to enjoy a special, privileged status in the Middle East, it would have to abandon its nationalistic goals, and interest itself principally in religious questions. 'The glorious duty that France has in practice today, above all, consists in forcefully demanding that no government, including the local government, harms the *status quo*, and upon this base she must found her defence of the Catholic services in the Holy Places.'[20]

If, however, the 'protectorate' had the right of citizenship in Palestine only in order to defend the *status quo*, the violations of the latter would sound like a denunciation in their regard.[21] It seems to be with this intention that the text of the *Memorandum* listed the results obtained by other religious confessions during the last forty years. It then set out a long list of data regarding different nations and religious groups connected to them. The document expressly cites Prussia, present in Jerusalem from 1854, with a consulate, a hospice, a hospital and a school, and which from 1866 gradually developed through personnel, buildings, and territorial property, 'a flowering colony at Caifa, at the foot of Carmel, Jerusalem, Sharon, Nazareth, and Jaffa'; England, in Palestine from 1854, with an

[20] *Terra Santa. Memorandum e Pro-Memoria rimessi al Signor Ambasciatore di Francia*, 29r–29v.

[21] '[...] in this period of time the interests of Catholics in Palestine lost ground rather than gained it. Unkind souls could insinuate the idea that France, to whose powerful support the present situation was due, had, in later times reduced its fervour, and subordinated its duty of Protectress of Catholic interests in those parts in regards to another order'. *Terra Santa. Memorandum e Pro-Memoria rimessi al Signor Ambasciatore di Francia*, 29v.

extended Anglican mission 'at Nazareth, Bethlehem, Naplusa and on the ancient coast of Phoenicia; the American Protestants were active through schools, orphanages, hospitals, and agricultural colonies at Jaffa and Beirut; the Jews with their 'alarming progress' at Jerusalem where 'a magnificent synagogue arose, a Rothschild hospital, a Montefiore hospice, and a number of homes owned by them' on Lake Tiberias.

2. 'But all this is nothing—the text of the *Memorandum* states—compared to the difficult conditions in which the faithful were placed by the powerful influence of Russia, whose progress in Palestine was more like a military invasion than a religious mission.'[22] There are numerous pages from the document dedicated to the history of the presence of Russia in Palestine, beginning with the Crimean War. The report immediately emphasizes the success obtained 'by a special Commission' [the Russian Society in Palestine], with its principal sees at Petersburg and Moscow. It would seem in a large part to be composed of distinguished members of the Russian aristocracy and presided over by no less than two brothers of the Czar, the dukes Sergius and Paul. Its juridical status was not that of a mere private association, but rather 'almost' that of a 'governing association', the beneficiary of incoming revenue, in addition to the collections of 'taxes imposed on possessions and public contracts'. At this point the author seems intent on pointing out the involvement of the initiative of government organs, a sort of 'nationalism at the service of religion', almost an admonition to the 'protector', who instead seems to instrumentalise religion for the goals of national politics.[23] The 'apparent' and 'real' goals of the Committee can be summarized in three points: '1) Orthodox influence (propagation of the schism); 2) scientific exploration (economic, military, etc.); 3) Russian pilgrimages (colonization)'.[24]

A detailed description follows of a long series of various accomplishments: a basilica, a hospital, two hospices built outside of the port of Jaffa; 'another splendid edifice' on the Eastern side of the Mount of Olives; 'a stupendous bell tower, that seems rather an observatory for military observations', erected on the apex of the same Mount; 'towers similar' in construction to St John on the Mount, on the Mountain of

---

[22] *Terra Santa. Memorandum e Pro-Memoria rimessi al Signor Ambasciatore di Francia*, 31r–31v.

[23] 'This Committee obtained a rich booty of collections and taxes imposed on possessions and on public contracts, which reveals strong reliance on the Muscovite government [...]. It is no wonder that extraordinary sums were sent each year in Palestine to effect the occupation plan.' *Terra Santa. Memorandum e Pro-Memoria rimessi al Signor Ambasciatore di Francia*, 31v.

[24] *Terra Santa. Memorandum e Pro-Memoria rimessi al Signor Ambasciatore di Francia*, 31v–32r.

the Visitation, at Hebron and at Jaffa; 'establishments of relief founded at Ramleh, Jericho, Bethany and Nazareth'; 'a university with castle walls' in the construction phase at the Holy Sepulchre; a 'Seminary for Russian Clerics' projected for Nazareth.

On the basis of this document the Russian Orthodox presence in Palestine was three thousand. They managed some flourishing agricultural colonies at St John on the Mount, Jericho and Colonia, as well as thirty schools with about five hundred students. 'It seems, therefore—declared the *Memorandum*—the intention of this Power is to invade the Holy Land gradually and almost secretly. It bears the same, if not greater enthusiasm than there was in opening the way to Central Asia and to the Bosphorus.'[25]

The author of the *Memorandum*, besides thus expressing apprehension for the achievements already undertaken by the Russians, seems to look with still greater concern to what they would be able to obtain in the future. Their influence on the local authority was rather considerable: 'Some time ago a governor of Jerusalem, Revouf Pascià, won over by them, agreed to everything without taking into account the French protection of Catholics.'[26] The population would be easy prey to their proselytism, founded on the strength of money: 'those poor people sell their sympathies, and with the money surrender their faith and reason, intellect and affection'. The Orthodox hierarchy would undergo considerable pressure due to the large debt owed to the Petersburg government: 'it will take just a little to Russianise the Greek Synod, and the rights of the Greeks will pass to the Muscovites.'[27]

3. Before such exuberant Russian initiatives, the *Memorandum* again proposes the appeal to France set forth in the initial part of the text. 'Only France can weigh in the balance and impede what the feared catastrophe would bring about. To be able to succeed, however, it is necessary that the Protectorate, in which the Catholics place their hope, keeps its religious, and therefore universal character, without assuming a character restricted to its own national politics; this would take care, not only of their national interests, but of the whole Catholic world.'[28] France is reminded, yet again, of the duty which derives from her responsibility as the protecting nation,

---

[25] *Terra Santa. Memorandum e Pro-Memoria rimessi al Signor Ambasciatore di Francia*, 32v.

[26] *Terra Santa. Memorandum e Pro-Memoria rimessi al Signor Ambasciatore di Francia*, 33r.

[27] *Terra Santa. Memorandum e Pro-Memoria rimessi al Signor Ambasciatore di Francia*, 33v.

[28] *Ibid.*

that is, to put in second place 'politics and national interests', with a view to giving precedence to the advantage of 'an international and Catholic nature'. Only working in this way, would they have been able to avoid the 'narrow-minded national race, which was evident already, with all the deplorable consequences that could be easily foreseen'. The orientation of the protectorate, however, appears not to conform to that set out in the *Memorandum*. 'Now it is painful to say it—the text continues—but a considerable number of persons believe they can support an entire order of facts to show that lately France leans perhaps too much to limiting herself to safeguard only her national interests, thus almost placing a limit on the universal representation of common interests.'[29]

The organs of the French government, including their delegates in the Holy Land were, however, not the only ones to work in a manner excessively inclined towards nationalism. Public opinion in France, the French institutes, and the pilgrims that went to the Holy Land, would also have fallen short of 'that magnanimous sentiment with which they embraced all the nations', demonstrating hostility 'especially against the Italian Catholic element, mainly against the Franciscan Order'. The document continues with some allusions to the political origins of certain pilgrimages that would have annoyed the sensitivity of 'other nations', of the Muslim population, and of the Turkish government, before returning to the matter of the Custody, attacked, above all in France, in parliament and by the newspapers. 'It is sorrowful to see the interests of the Custody in the Holy Land, or those of the patriarchate, bitterly attacked by public figures. It has been called at Paris, in the public Parliament, an Italian work, and one is led to believe it by French journalism, even the most straightforward. Rather, as already mentioned, by reason of its international nature, the institution and the men who comprise it is absolutely unquestionable.'[30]

The Franciscan Custody, to defend the rights of Catholics in the Holy Places, had no one else to address but France, nor would France permit them to do otherwise. With this intention therefore, 'the affairs of Jerusalem' are cited by which the Custos addressed other nations, to the regret of the French government. From what can be surmised, the manoeuvre of the Custody seems to have encountered no bias on the part of Pontifical authorities, who seem, rather, to give it a silent assent, intending to direct a veiled threat to France; if in the future, the

---

[29] *Terra Santa. Memorandum e Pro-Memoria rimessi al Signor Ambasciatore di Francia*, 34r.

[30] *Terra Santa. Memorandum e Pro-Memoria rimessi al Signor Ambasciatore di Francia*, 34v.

'protector' would not give due attention to Catholic interests, that is to those of the Custody, this would certainly not stop it attempting to seek other political partners.[31]

4. Beginning from this point, the *Memorandum* dedicates many pages to the theme of the *status quo*, or better, to a list of violations of the same. If France was made protector for the defence of the rights of Catholics, rights which, beginning with the Congress of Berlin (1878), were clarified to coincide with the maintenance of the *status quo*, each violation of the latter meant a threat to the legitimacy of her position as protector. The text spends more than a page in explaining how even the minimum violation results in a grave threat to Catholic interests.[32] And this is verified exactly because, in the particular situation of the Holy Land, a territory under the Turkish regime, 'rights are continually offended' for the fact that each mutation of a factual nature determines an alteration in the juridical order. The list of violations seems subdivided into different blocks.

In the first of these, which begins with the removal of the silver star in the Grotto of the Nativity in 1847 and extends to the restoration of the large cupola of the Sepulchre in 1862, seven episodes corresponding to the alterations of the rights of Catholics can be found: in 1853, the Greeks open the wall on the left side of the choir of the Basilica of St Helen at Bethlehem; in 1855, the extension of taxes was repealed for the workers employed in the care of the convents [from Latin conventus, often rendered in English as monastery] and shrines; in 1856, there arose the question of the cistern of David; in 1857, the Greeks brought a large quantity of rocks into the square of the Basilica of Bethlehem; in 1861, the Armenians attempted to impede the Latin procession from the door of Joinville to the Grotto of the Nativity; during the night in 1861 the Greeks, created a door next to the Sepulchre of the Virgin.

---

[31] 'She [the Custody] awaits from France whatever support, whatever defence, and has no one else to ask. Nor in the event that they could ask, would France permit it. It is known how sorry the French government is that in the affair of Gethsemane the Custos of the Holy Land should have threatened to address other consulates at least for the protection of the Religious from different nations'. *Terra Santa. Memorandum e Pro-Memoria rimessi al Signor Ambasciatore di Francia*, 35r.

[32] 'A span of earth that is lost; a restoration that is permitted either to the Porte, or to heterodox sects; a religious ceremony that one of these sects attempts unduly to carry out; a change that takes place in whatever of the shrines, will lead things, little by little, to end by stripping Christians of their ancient rights over the Holy Land'. *Terra Santa. Memorandum e Pro-Memoria rimessi al Signor Ambasciatore di Francia*, 35v.

The gravity of these episodes would not be comparable, according to the author of the *Memorandum*, to details relating to the restoration of the cupola, for which 'Russia unfortunately undertook the expenses', excluding the Holy See and expressly manifesting 'the desire to follow the work alone'. Among the consequences of this event was recognized primarily the successive interference of the Russian clergy in the offices of the Holy Sepulchre, and other 'deplorable facts [which] have continued in the last twenty years, and threaten ever more closely the rights of Catholics in the Holy Land'. The tone of the narration itself from this moment seems rich in drama: 'In fact, in 1861, the property rights of the Cistern of St Helen are lost [...]; in 1863 the extension of the payment of the contributions and taxes, expenses and customs charges are lost [...]; in 1865 the exclusive right of possession of the Grotto of Milk is lost [...]; to this one can add the loss of rights regarding the Silver Star placed over the site of the Nativity (1886) [...]; from 1870-71 there is the deplorable loss of the right of pilgrimage to and the right to officiate at the Church of St James on Mount Sion.'[33]

The facts of 25 April 1873, regarding the Grotto of the Nativity, constitute a second turning point, and a further escalation. 'But wanting to pass over these losses, certainly one cannot omit to make a special mention of the uproars and injuries brought about by the Greeks on 25 April 1873.'[34] It is exactly in regard to this episode that the author of the *Memorandum* makes explicit for the first time, 'a well marked weakness' on the part of the French consulate. 'The religious had recourse to the consulate but obtained nothing'. Successively, that is between 1875 and 1879, during the consulate of Patrimonio, the friction between the Custody and the Consulate returned. 'The facts that concern the last ten years (1880-1890) show how in this time unfortunately the situation has worsened.'[35]

The gravest violations to the *status quo,* however, are recorded as beginning from 1886, corresponding to the increased influence exerted by the Russians in the Holy Land. 'Before the present times the Russians interfered with the Greeks celebrating at the Holy Sepulchre. During the Turkish-Russian war the Muscovites, exiled from Jerusalem, later returned and assisted at the anniversaries of the feasts of the Czar in the offices

---

[33] *Terra Santa. Memorandum e Pro-Memoria rimessi al Signor Ambasciatore di Francia*, 39v-40r. (passim).

[34] *Terra Santa. Memorandum e Pro-Memoria rimessi al Signor Ambasciatore di Francia*, 40v.

[35] *Terra Santa. Memorandum e Pro-Memoria rimessi al Signor Ambasciatore di Francia*, 41v.

celebrated by a Greek bishop. But in 1888 with the Archdukes Sergius and Paul present in Jerusalem, the Russian Archimandrite celebrated in their presence at the Holy Sepulchre, by the will of the said Archdukes.'[36]

On 18 July 1897 the ambassador of France to the Apostolic See was sent another *Promemoria,* in addition to the *Memorandum* of 1891. These two documents form a single item, as the numbering of the pages indicates. The *Promemoria* is intended entirely to treat concerns regarding the Russian presence, while with regards to the *Memorandum* one can note a greater precision. For example, there is no further mention in a generic way of a 'special Committee', but of the 'Russian community present in Palestine'. The connection between Russia and Arab nationalism also appears there with a certain clarity, 'The principal scope of the Russian community, with the construction of numerous large buildings, churches and schools throughout Palestinian territory, is to prepare the terrain to substitute the Greek-Hellenistic schismatic element with the Arab-Fozian, that must, in its turn, prepare the way for the true Russians.'[37]

More detail is also provided regarding the economic situation of the Greek hierarchy, deprived of the revenue of Bessarabia, which had fallen into the hands of the Russians. The way in which the Russians interfered with the administration of the Holy Places, paralyzing the activity of France, is detailed. 'When questions arise—and they often do—between the Greeks and the Latins, Russia is solicited to intervene by means of her consulates and always takes up the defence of the adversaries of the Catholics.'[38] By now the future of the French protectorate would depend almost exclusively on its relationship with Russia. In fact, not by chance, one of the gravest events, among those denounced by the *promemoria* refers to the killing of a Franciscan at the Grotto of the Nativity (1893), which took place directly at the hands of a *cavas* of the Russian Society in Palestine. The assassination would remain unpunished: 'the protector that would let such a grave affair end thus loses not a little of its prestige'.

The absolute novelty of the *promemoria*, compared with the *Memorandum*, seems to be in the fact that it contains, although covertly, allusion to the French-Russian alliance as the latest reason for the flexibility of the French diplomacy. 'One knows, as is already well-known in Jerusalem, of the intervening negotiations regarding the agreements

---

[36] *Terra Santa. Memorandum e Pro-Memoria rimessi al Signor Ambasciatore di Francia*, 43v.

[37] *Terra Santa. Memorandum e Pro-Memoria rimessi al Signor Ambasciatore di Francia*, 47v.

[38] *Terra Santa. Memorandum e Pro-Memoria rimessi al Signor Ambasciatore di Francia*, 48r.

made between the French and Russian representatives. One cannot not recognize the abandonment of the incontestable rights of Catholics on the side of the protecting Power to the advantage of the growing and invasive influence of Russia in the East.'[39]

DENOUNCING NATIONALISM

The criticism of nationalism, as an element harmful to Catholicity, to the mission, and above all to the safeguarding of the Holy Places, clearly constitutes one of the central themes of the *Memorandum* just illustrated. This is one of the themes which also recurs, in an almost obsessive way, in the personal correspondence of Fr James de Castelmadama with his Minister General and with the Congregation of Propaganda. He took the opportunity to write a letter to the Minister General in the spring of 1889 regarding an article published in the periodical *Studi Religiosi* by the Society of Jesus, where the nationalism of the Jesuits was targeted. The latter, 'angry because of the somewhat harsh attitude of the Ottoman empire in their regard, are trying, by means of a flurry of dismal forecasts concerning the future of France in Palestine, to urge the government of the Republic to promote their interests at the Porte, representing them as those who alone can be an effective bulwark of defence against the dark future of the great nation in the East!'[40]

The Custos' accusation seems directed less at the initiative as such, than to the ambiguity of the arguments used by the priests of the Society. It appears that the Jesuits were proposing themselves to France as partners in stopping that which was being referred to as the 'Israelite flooding [of the Holy Land].' It was an absurd proposal, according to the Custos, because it was a matter of an already spreading phenomenon, which the Porte above all 'does not want to repress', being joined in this by other nations, which 'know it and see it [...] and which can do nothing [about it]. What

[39] *Terra Santa. Memorandum e Pro-Memoria rimessi al Signor Ambasciatore di Francia*, 49r. The text of the document proposes the same argument again in the following sections: 'The complex of facts, of different times and places, makes evident that the French government in these last years has shown itself too inclined to favor Russia in the various dissensions that took place between the Catholics and the schismatics in Palestine, with manifest damage to her prestige and of her influence'. *Ibid.*, 50r.

[40] AGOFM, *Terra Santa* 19, 433r: *Giacomo da Castelmadama, custode, a Bernardino da Portogruaro, ministro generale*, 10 April 1889.

could then the Jesuits do?' Their real purpose, according to the Custos, would be to discredit the Custody, which 'they call 'Italian,' I know not whether with greater impudence or greater ignorance'. And while the Consul wanted it French 'and all French', the Custos still continues, 'the Jesuits, in whatever nation they are, make themselves all French if things go well for France, make themselves German if it is useful to be German, Spanish if it is worthwhile for Spain and so forth. They are all less than Catholics. [...] they are like a bat, now a mouse, now a bird, and they get along well and receive the praises of everyone. I do not envy them. We like to be straightforward with everyone, to call white, white, and black, black, to whoever asks our opinion, long live St Francis who formed us to such frankness.'[41]

To the diplomatic skill of the Jesuits, judged as opportunist, the Franciscans seems to oppose a type of anti-nationalism, or better a non-political nature, as the exclusive characteristic of the Custody. He, in contrast to the missionary efficacy and, yes, the politics of the company, seems almost bound to seek a plausible alternative ideology for the Franciscan organisation, an alternative that demonstrates a perception of the concept 'Catholicity'. The Custody was, in fact, composed not only of Italian religious—which qualifies the attribution of 'Italian' by the Jesuits—but also of Spanish and a certain number of German/Austrian and French nationals, as the *Memorandum* itself notes, while the Jesuit presence in the Middle East was exclusively French. However, at this moment its aim was to convince the organs of *Propaganda* that the 'game of nationalism' could be deleterious for Catholicity.

The target of Castelmadama's letter, however, is not simply the Jesuits, who had been presented only as an opposing figure with respect to the Custody. The real focus for his criticism of nationalism was the Brothers of the Christian Schools,[42] at that time experiencing a General Visitation, led by Fr Hugonis. Their strategy was exactly the same as that adopted by the Jesuits, although it did not reach the same level. They also were obliged to a type of ideological dependence on the French government, because they received their economic support from them.

---

41 *Giacomo da Castelmadama, custode, a Bernardino da Portogruaro, ministro generale*, 10 April 1889.433v. The Institute of the Brothers of the Christian Schools, commonly known as the De La Salle Brothers, founded in France by John Baptist de la Salle (1651-1719).

42 *Giacomo da Castelmadama, custode, a Bernardino da Portogruaro, ministro generale*, 10 April 1889, 433v-434r.

'It must be said—the Custos specifies—that they cannot, in fact, trust themselves, because of their craftiness in accomplishing their objectives, which can rightly be called shadowy, that they are so trained to ask help and protection from this France, in whose service they are, to the harm of their institute and of the very morals of Christ which is no longer known today except as a very simple means to be protected by the Church, and nothing more. However with impunity they calumniate, horribly betray, monstrously deceive, shamefully corrupt, they mix the good with the bad indiscriminately, sanctify every means that can bring about their always political and never religious, always national and never Catholic goal.'[43]

At this point it must be said that for French diplomacy the Christian Brothers were considered their privileged agents since through them France could determine a 'plan of nationalization' for the Holy Land, already conceived in the years previous to the defeat of Sedan (1870).[44] The difficult years following the Franco-Prussian conflict (1870-1871) did not permit its fulfilment. In fact it was only in 1876, and by the initiative of the Custody, that the Christian Brothers reached the Holy Land with the objective of joining the Franciscans in administering the schools, where they could stand up to the work of the Protestants that so worried the authorities of Propaganda. The news about the successes obtained by these 'non-Catholic Prussians' diffused in the newspapers beyond the Alps played a primary role. The Catholic and militarist right, who had already seen their national pride humiliated precisely at Sedan, had been not only the moving force in this, but also the probable ambassador to the Roman ecclesiastical authorities.

The Christian Brothers, hardly a year after their arrival in the Holy Land, had already established relationships with the French consulate authorities, gaining, in exchange for a certain economic aid, a discrete autonomy from the Custody. French diplomacy considered this a great success, obtained exactly when it needed to confront the nationalism of the other European powers like Russia, but above all Italy, which bordered what was then the Middle East, and that in the future would be able to find

---

[43] For the events concerning the rapport between the Christian Brothers and the Custody, the summary given here is developed more amply elsewhere (*Les Franciscains en Terre Sainte 1869-1889) Religion et politque. Une recherche institutionnelle*, Paris 2005, 99-118.178-182.208-211.

[44] 'One must absolutely cut away from all that has to do with worldly politics, from which we must show ourselves to be completely estranged, our only politics must be that of Christ'. AGOFM, *Terra Santa* 14, 391r: *Bernardino da Portogruaro, ministro generale, a Camillo da Rutigliano, pro segretario delle Custodia*, 12 April 1876.

allies in the Italian religious of the Custody. In effect, some members of the organisation attempted to join the government in a venture to finance schools in the Jaffa region, but were blocked by the Minister General, who did not want any compromise with politics.[45] In the following years in order to sustain the work of the Christian Brothers, discourses and articles tried to convince the public of the benefits of religious nationalism, especially its French variant. The patriotism taught in the schools of the Christian Brothers constituted the expression of the better Catholicism. Every other nationalism in the Middle East, especially Italian, would have been considered an attack against religion.

It is only since 1879 that the Custody began to react to the spread of French nationalism through the religious congregations.[46] Doubts arose amongst the authorities of the Custody that the Propaganda might have changed its attitude in regards of the Franciscan institution, giving credit to the promises of French nationalism. The change of the Pontificate too would have served to endorse such suppositions. In the years 1884-1885 there is a break in the forward thrust previously characteristic of the expansion of the Christian Brothers' school network. The Custody itself seemed to adopt counter measures, appealing to an alternative strategy. It attempted to obtain from the Apostolic See permission to establish Italian and Franciscan institutes in the Holy Land, with the precise objective of breaking the French monopoly, but the results were not as hoped.

With the passing of 1885-1886, the dispute with the French religious institutes became apparent,[47] becoming an 'open war' in 1888,

---

[45] The Custos, Fr Gaudenzio da Matelica, expressed himself, in regards to this, in the following terms: 'What shall I say? On my part, if I side with the sorrowful enterprise that She has approved, I cannot do otherwise than to side with her resignation. The door is open, Revd Father, France seeks to multiply the French institutes in Palestine; and when will the Patriarch of Jerusalem also be French!!! This is a monopoly, of which I do not now know how to explain the consequences! I am not contrary to France nor to the French, but *uniquique suum*! I would like to see if some other non-French institute would try to come to this country! With what difficulties! Oh! How would our observations be gladly welcomed. But as to this this, enough for today.' AGOFM, *Terra Santa* 16, 38r: *Gaudenzio da Matelica a Bernardino da Portogruaro, ministro generael*, 5 February 1879.

[46] 'The other evening five Sisters of Charity, of course all French, arrived in Jerusalem, to establish themselves there definitively. It is well known that they came, not for a true need, but rather to satisfy the government of the Republic, who were displeased to see the establishment of the Third Order Franciscans (Italian!) in Jerusalem. From here it won't take much for the Lazzarists to follow'. AGOFM, *Terra Santa* 18, 236: *Guido da Cortona, custode, a Bernardino da Portogruaro, ministro generale,* 5 May 1886.

[47] AGOFM *Terra Santa* 19, 410r: *James of Castelmadama, Custos, to Bernardino from Portogruaro, Minister General*, 13 March 1889r.

with the mandate of Fr Castelmadama as governor. The religious expressed himself in these terms: 'The Friars of the Christian Schools try to interfere everywhere to take the schools away from us and the Lord Consuls lack little to recommend them to the Custody [...] I have responded that it is a norm to increase the schools in the Holy Land for the good of the peoples of this mission, but as these are paid for by the Holy Land they want them to be directed by their missionaries. [...] I have written to the respective principals that they do all in their power to keep the schools open and running, which must not be closed even if a thousand Christian Brothers should come, as long as there is one student attending.'[48]

In other letters Castelmadama specifies with greater clarity the reasons for which he held it his duty to reopen the schools of the Custody, particularly where they were closed in order to grant space to those of the Christian Brothers. The principal reason for such an initiative seems to relate essentially to the question of confessionalism, an element deemed of capital importance by the Latin community, which considered it a primary component of their identity. 'I must still grant this request—affirms Castelmadama—because the Pastor saw that some students of the Gallican schools [underlined in the original] know nothing about the catechism, and need to be confirmed! The heads of the families know that the profit is nothing and that corruption is great, however they entrust them to the Holy Land because they want to reopen her schools. Until now I have been quiet and I have not wanted to concern myself, having enough else to do than to concern myself with reopening the schools of Jerusalem: but from here on I will do so if the heads of the families present me with requests, and when I have a good number I will send them to Propaganda and we will see if they are content that the Holy Land reopens the school for Latins.'[49]

---

[48] AGOFM *Holy* Land 19, 410r: *Giacomo da Castelmadama, custode, a Bernardino da Portogruaro, ministro generale*, 22 May 1889; The same Custos, already in an earlier letter, expressed himself towards the Christian Brothers, in rather negative terms: 'Never will the Holy Land call certain people to run their schools. The Holy Land is aware that when it gave over the other schools it had to repent and repent greatly; and it has had to rush to institute other schools to keep them for herself and pay doubly. It had to do this in Alexandria; thus it was bound to do in Jerusalem, because the Latins came to beg me to open our schools; this I must still do in Jaffa [...] we have been obliged to have the Christian Brothers enter, to condescend to the will of our interested protectors'. AGOFM *Terra Santa* 19, 454r: *Giacomo da Castelmadama, custode, a Bernardino da Portogruaro, ministro generale*, 8 May 1889.

[49] G Rigault, *Histoire générale de l'Institut des Christian Brothers des Écoles Chrétiennes VIII. La Fin du XIX siècle: l'Institut en Europe et dans les Pays de Mission*, Paris, 1951, 455.

The claims against the schools of the Christian Brothers, on behalf of the parents belonging to the Catholic community (Latin), mentioned by the Custos in the document cited above, evidently landed in great number on the desks of Propaganda, so much so that in 1890 it decided, to the great surprise of the Christian Brothers, to promulgate a specific rule for the schools in Palestine. Fr Raphaëlis, Assistant General, wrote in these terms: 'Et maintenant, l'on nous présente 'un règlement dont l'adoption aurait pour conséquence immédiate non pas la multiplication des écoles, telle que la souhaite le Souverain Pontife, mais la ruine certaine des établissements déjà en activité.'[50] The norms of the Propaganda foresaw that the Christian Brothers would dedicate themselves to the education of the 'non-Catholics', save with rare exceptions, and only with the consent of the patriarch, to whom responsibility for surveillance, discipline, method and programs was transferred. Furthermore, the teaching was to be imparted in the Arabic language and no longer in the French. The Christian Brothers thought the measure was an initiative brought about by the adversaries of French influence in the Middle East and asked, concernedly: 'Et la France, avec nos écoles amoindries, réduites à rien, que dira-t-elle?... Si je me soumets de coeur et d'âme à tout ce que la Sainte Eglise décidera, je suis mortifié d'être assujetti aux caprices des ennemis de mon pays.'[51]

The mission in the Holy Places and the demands of Catholicity

Another letter of Castelmadama to the Minister General, shortly after the one considered above, again takes up the theme of nationalism, defended and propagated thanks to the religious congregations sent to the Holy Land by the initiative of national governments, in particular the French. The first accusation formulated by the Franciscan is directed to address the 'pontifical court' and in a more explicit way to the Congregation of the Propaganda Fide, in which he reproved the propensity to 'favour political interests and national competition', rather than 'attend as they should to religious interests and to the love of the holy places of redemption.'[52] On

[50] *Ibid.*, 457.

[51] AGOFM, *Terra Santa* 19, 441 rv: *Giacomo da Castelmadama, custode, a Bernardino da Portogruaro, ministro generale*, 24 April 1889.

[52] AGOFM, *Terra Santa* 19, 390: *Bernardine da Portogruaro, ministro generale, a Giacomo da Castelmadama*, 1 March 1889.

the other hand, the same Minister General, Fr Bernardine of Portogruaro, had had a way to personally ascertain what Castelmadama affirmed, just as he sought to reach the Propaganda with another of his protests regarding the French agents. 'It has been decided to send a copy of his letter to His Holiness—he had written some days prior to the Minister General—There was nothing else to do, from the moment that in the Propaganda they always repeated to us: *The Holy Father cannot upset France* [thus emphasized in the original text].'[53]

Therefore, Castelmadama reasoned, granting entrance to such religious institutions into Palestine, showed exactly the lack of careful consideration of the consequences that their 'national character' could have had. Such consequences would have become evident only in a later moment but the Custody had made it known from the beginning. 'Although the Custody had given warning, nonetheless they were not listened to. Although the Propaganda knew it, they did what was necessary not to turn against the Firstborn Daughter'. The Custos observed therefore that institutions born in a national territory with a national character must exercise their work within the nation in which they originated. The Custos, perhaps without seeing it, touched here on one of the central themes of the missionary characteristics of the XIX century, which aimed to transplant the characteristics of the local church into missionary territory. He proposed, however, with the principle of the 'Catholicity of the missions', a sort of de-nationalization of the missionary presence. 'The mission is essentially Catholic, and the institutions threaten its catholicity in this, that they want to subordinate it to the national idea and inclination'.

To this proposal the Custos called into question the Consul, Patrimonio, accusing him of having convinced the French government to make use of religious institutes with the goal of 'making France prevail in the East'. The Franciscan held the diplomat largely responsible for the marriage between religion and politics, a compromise in which religion would be severely penalized. In other words, the raison d'être of these religious institutions in the Holy Land would consist only in a political goal, so much so that politics enjoyed predominance even in their internal life. 'It is for this reason—Castelmadama affirmed—even though the institution is Catholic, that here in Palestine it bears only a French character. Here they cannot survive if they are not French; here they cannot be superior unless

---

[53] AGOFM, *Terra Santa*19, 442r: *Giacomo da Castelmadama, custode, a Bernardino da Portogruaro, ministro generale*, 24 April 1889.

they are French or obtain a title unless they are French and so forth. Are they Augustinians? they must be French; are they Dominicans? they must be French; are they Brothers of Christian Schools? they must be French; are they Sisters of Charity? they must be French; are they Brothers or Sisters of Sion? they must be French; are they Poor Clares? they must be French: all French. Why? They have considered it, has Rome considered it? Has it been considered, whether they consider it or not, it is certain that Rome knows about it. Now knowing it how can they legitimately persuade themselves that these institutions are for the good of the Catholic cause, that must be treated with care in the mission?'[54]

The Catholic character of the mission in Palestine would be required, it seems to the Custos, by reason of the Holy Places. It would be these Places and the demands of their conservation, in the way that they are the destination of pilgrimage for the Catholic world, more so than any missionary character, which required the most absolute opposition to nationalism in Palestine. However, this mark of the Catholic mission would prove difficult to accomplish for the reason that 'the French government, as is well-known, makes every effort for the protection of French institutes and the minimum defence of the rights of the Custody.'[55] This is one of the passages in the letter of the Custos that comes closest to the text of the *Memorandum*.

However, the accusations of the Franciscan are not limited to branding the faults of the national protector, they are also directed anew to the workings of Propaganda, which is inclined to favour the requests of the French institutes to the detriment of the Custody and, in any case, to Catholicity. The tone of the letter at this point is heated: 'If Rome believes that the Franciscan Order is not able to do all that these institutes came to do, it must, in such an ugly hypothesis, think to excise the national character in those institutions that they, in their wisdom deem necessary, in order to do that good which, according to appearance is believed they

[54] 'The Catholic mission is impossible because the national idea is favoured in her activity, so alive in the French, and greatly protected, to the harm of Catholic ideas, by the French government who, as is well known, makes every effort to protect French institutes and hardly any effort for the defence of the sacred rights of the Custody, who must sustain the rights of the Latin Church in the East'. AGOFM, *Terra Santa* 19, 442v: *Giacomo da Castelmadama, custode, a Bernardino da Portogruaro, ministro generale*, 24 April 1889.

[55] AGOFM, *Terra Santa*19, 442v–443r: *Giacomo da Castelmadama, custode, a Bernardino da Portogruaro, ministro generale*, 24 April 1889.

do.'[56] However, it seems the Custos wants to push the Apostolic See to make a clear choice, to select an option, without which, as he himself affirms, there would be a scission in the Holy Land, or better yet a schism, since two churches are concerned. 'Otherwise there will be two missions here, and almost two churches, one represented by the patriarch, the other represented by the Consul: that made up of priests from the Latin patriarchate and from the Custody, and the other from the French institutions. It is certain that when the patriarch goes to celebrate he is only accompanied by a few priests and by us. All those other institutions court the Lord Consul. He is often sick for the celebrations that are held at the Most Holy Sepulchre by the patriarch or by the Custos, but God help us if he is absent from a celebration in some chapel of Sisters or of the Christian Brothers.'[57]

As can be easily seen, this treats of a threat to which the Roman authorities could not remain insensitive. The reasoning of Castelmadama supported by data and arguments, as if he had to supply other elements to demonstrate a theorem, leads him to state that in the Holy Land there was truly a legion of religious congregations whose principal scope coincided with sustaining French national politics. If it was not so, the Custos seems then to ask, 'why so many institutions that have the same scope? If there is one orphanage that is enough, why must there be four or five, from as many different institutes? If six Sisters are enough, or ten, to maintain 60 or 100 orphans, why must there be 20, 30 or 40? They have a hospital where the Sisters of St Joseph serve, why do they want the Sisters of Charity here? And so forth.'[58]

The Custos seems really convinced of the fact that these institutions were none other than agents of French politics. A similar argument had been put forward at least ten years prior by the Minister General, through a response to the Propaganda, which had asked him about the opportuneness of the White Fathers' entrance into the Holy Land. The eloquence of the Minister General, at that time, although clear, had not been as brutal as that of the Custos, who could, however, avail himself of data, of facts and of a ten year experiment and not only suppositions. In

---

[56] AGOFM, *Terra Santa* 19, 443r: *Giacomo da Castelmadama, custode, a Bernardino da Portogruaro, ministro generale*, 24 April 1889.

[57] *Ibid.*

[58] ACPF, *Terra Santa* 25: *Bernardino da Portogruaro, ministro generael, a Franchi, prefetto di Propaganda*, 18 November 1877 (copy in AGOFM, *Terra Santa* 15, 292-298v).

fact, the Minister General had limited himself to putting questions to the Vatican dicastery, about the various goals, such as the pastoral or liturgical aims of the new foundation, while affirming the absence of a real need for that type of activity in the Holy Land. His reasoning regarding the goals mentioned above, rather than dictating definite conclusions, was meant to leave the final verdict to his interlocutor—a verdict that, ten years later, was altogether clear in the Custos' mind: It was all the work of 'nationalism'.[59]

The final part of Castelmadama's letter became almost an address, in which the religious appeared to focus, unknowingly, on one of the most marked defects of the mission of the 1800s, marked by political colonialism. For Castelmadama the Custody naturally constituted the one antidote for the nationalization process, which, with the religious creed, would have been able to twist both the culture of peoples and their future political order. 'The Custody is hated because it is not ready everywhere to Frenchify the East. We do not want to Frenchify anyone, as we do not want to Italianize anyone. We only want to make of these people the Church of Jesus Christ with the nationality that they have by nature and not other than that which is theirs. It is not expedient to us, nor might it be expedient to us to change the nation of the natives. It would be a true betrayal. We do not want to do it because, one day, who knows when, these people have to return to society, they will recognize that they were not betrayed by us, as unfortunately happened with the Americans, who today hate religion because of how its ministers, imposed their foreign nationality even though they did it for necessity. The Catholic idea is what we must show, or show again, to the people; the Catholic idea, pure, genuine, vast, which the Divine Master preached, neither shadowed nor limited by national passions.'[60] The Custos was persuaded that the sincerity of the government could not be believed, that they claimed to support religion in missionary territory while in the country itself they persecuted it. Their religious politics could not be other than ambiguous, their use of religion was merely instrumental. If this was the politics of the government, what could be the outcome of the 'religion' propagated by their religious allies? How then, can one not think that certain passages of

---

[59] AGOFM, *Terra Santa* 19, 444r: *Giacomo da Castelmadama, custode, a Bernardino da Portogruaro, ministro generale*, 24 April 1889.

[60] AGOFM, *Terra Santa* 19, 442v: *Giacomo da Castelmadama, custode, a Bernardino da Portogruaro, ministro generale*, 24 April 1889.

the *Memorandum,* regarding nationalism and catholicity, were not derived from the epistolary text of Castelmadama, a significant representative of the position of the Middle East Franciscan mission?

The nationalization of the collections

Castelmadama's correspondence which we have referred to above, had been, in reality, written in reaction to the proposal set forth by more than one party to divide the collection gathered in favour of the Holy Places, destined until then for the Custody alone, among all the religious congregations in Palestine. His reasoning on the catholicity of the mission in the Holy Land, by virtue of the fact that it was collected principally by the Custody of the Holy Places, aimed to exclude the possibility of using the offerings gathered for other purposes than precisely the care and the upkeep of the shrines of redemption, the patrimony of catholicity. 'It is impossible to keep up the Holy Places if the money shared by so many institutions, and by the many others that long to come, as is too easily permitted, is not enough for the prime intention for which it is sent by the Catholic world. The ugly day will come when the Greeks, the Armenians and the Russians will steal the Holy Places.'[61]

The nationalism demonstrated by the goals of such institutions, the greater part of which were of French origin, was expressed by the Custos with the object of making it understood that to pour the money of catholicity into the pockets of French institutes meant to favour the nationalization of the mission, that is, to collaborate with the political interests of France. 'Now—the Custos urged—if the government called them, let the government maintain them and maintain them *opifare.* Or if there is some institute that came by itself, it has thus declared that they can support themselves. [...] The others are all maintained by the French government and led in their manoeuvres by the French Consulate.'[62]

In regards to this, however, Castelmadama was still more explicit in a letter to the Minister General written on the same day, with the goal of replying to certain questions, put forward by the Propaganda regarding

[61] AGOFM, *Terra Santa* 19, 444v: *Giacomo da Castelmadama, custode, a Bernardino da Portogruaro, ministro generale,* 24 April 1889.

[62] AGOFM, *Terra Santa* 19, 500r: *Giacomo da Castelmadama, custode, a Bernardino da Portogruaro, ministro generale,* 24 April 1889.

the administration of the collection. He, on the particular point of the eventual decision regarding the sharing of the collections, expressed himself thus: 'What will happen by the decision that will be taken according to the norms already adopted? It will happen that the Holy Land must have always a penny in the bank, and when it will have to ransom a shrine, it will not be able to. The Greeks, the Armenians, the schismatic Copts will buy it, the Russians will buy it, and not the Holy Land. It is obliged to maintain the French mission, destined to teach the French language [...] Russia absolutely wants possessions in Palestine: it ardently aspires to conquer the Holy Places; it wants to conquer them. Money is not lacking to her: it is surely lacking to the Custody, which comes from Rome, by Rome herself being obliged to maintain the French institutes, or those of whatever other nation wants to send here, celibates though they be.'[63]

The observations on the collection that Castelmadama had transmitted through his letters to the Minister General were delivered by the same, to Fr Maria da Brest, commisssary of the Holy Land in Paris, who had the task of drawing up a *memoria* to present to the Propaganda, in defence of the Custody's point of view regarding the specific matter of the collections. The same *memoria* therefore had been sent to the French Consulate in Jerusalem and from there to Paris, together with a comment from the Consular authority.[64] The diplomat suggested that France should propose that the Apostolic See should follow the example of some episcopates, such as those in Germany, which had its own organization to collect offerings and that then shared them between the patriarchate, the Franciscans and other religious institutes, such as those of the Sisters of St Joseph. It had in mind, however, a 'nationalized' model, with agencies collecting the offerings as an alternative to the system of the Commissariate administered by the Custody under the control of the Apostolic See, that constituted, instead, a sort of international organisation.

Another observation by the Consul, in response to a certain provocation by Fr da Brest, refers to the friction between nationalism and internationality. In fact, the priest, in retaliation for the division of the collection, had threatened an eventual division of the protectorate itself. In other words, if nationalization of the offerings were adopted,

---

63 AMAE, CPC *Turquie Jérusalem* 20, 70-120r: *Ledoulx, console di Francia a Gerusalemma, a Spuller, ministro degli esteri*, 8 March 1890.

64 AMAE, CPC *Turquie Jérusalem* 20, 72rv: *Ledoulx, console di Francia a Gerusalemma, a Spuller, ministro degli esteri*, 8 March 1890.

they would also have been able to adopt the same resolution for the protectorate, forcing France to share it with the other national powers. The response of the diplomat was rather swift, affirming that the Custody would not have gained any advantage by thinking, as a consequence of the subdivision of the funds, to divide the protectorate among the 23 nations which composed it. Instead, for reasons concerning the financing of the French institutes, the Consul, insisted on the fact that they, in a stay of only thirty years in the Holy Land, had profited civilization in a much greater measure than the Custody had been able to in seven centuries. In conclusion, the Consul wondered just how his fellow-countryman had been able to put forward similar proposals, so dissonant with the patriotic spirit which should distinguish each son of the Republic. Could his long term among the ranks of the Custody, in contact with Italians and Spanish, have produced such a contagion with the 'nonchalance, impéritie et indifférence, de ses con Christian Brothers italiens et espagnols?'. In this regard the diplomat expressed himself thus: 'L'attachement que ce religieux porte à l'ordre de St François lui fait oublier le souci de la dignité et des intérêts de la Nation à laquelle il appartient; nous nous placerons à un point de vue tout différent pour ne point partager sa manière de voir et pour décliner ses propositions.'[65] The agents of French diplomacy, as sustainers of the religious politics of the government, represent however, a type of interface with the Custody, like the background of a picture upon which it is still easy to distinguish the contours and the tones of the image.

From the collections ... to Italianize

The debate around the collections, once it reached the public scene—that is having crossed the threshold of the chambers of parliament and fallen

[65] 'Depuis sa fondation, la Custodie de Terre Sainte est ouverte à tous les Christian Brothers Mineurs, sans distinction de province ou de nationalité [the type is large and bold in the original]; et la sollicitude des Pontifes romains a fait en sorte que, international dans la composition de son personnel, elle revête le même caratère dans son administration. Il convenait qu'il en fut ainsi. Le Christ est à toutes les nations [...] Son internationalité fait la force de la Custodie franciscaine, constitue une de ses plus puissantes raison d'être. Elle n'est ni italienne, ni espagnole, ni française, elle est catholique dans toute la force et tout le sens du mot '*catholique*' comme Eglise elle-même. Catholique c'est-à-dire internationale.' *Les missions Franciscaines Françaises. La Custodie de Terre-Sainte*, Paris, 1922 (ACTSP, Dossier n° 18, 0017).

prey to the press—often assumed a critical tone against the Italianism of the Custody and even of the Apostolic See. These controversies also almost certainly refer to the expressions of the *Memorandum*, regarding the accusations of 'public men' and journalists aimed at the Custody, stigmatized as Italian. Among the envelopes deposited in the archives of the Commissariate of the Holy Land in Paris, there is a classification with the emblematic title of 'gallophobia'; this largely consists of manuscripts of articles published by various journals, with the precise goal of defending the Custody from accusations of connivance with Italian politics. Attached to this documentary material, is also a pamphlet, still in draft form, dated 1922, in which is affirmed, almost in apologetic tones, its international character as the distinctive element and the raison d'être of the Custody.[66]

The public debate on the collections was held, in all probability, as a consequence of a pamphlet published by Fr Charmetant, director of the Institution of the Schools of the East (one of the French organizations for the collection of offerings), under the title *Les Aumônes destinée aux Lieux Saints* (Paris 1890). It seems useful to remember that exactly in this period in France a campaign of parliamentary debates which had seen committed supporters of the financing of rigorously French missionary congregations came to a close. One of the arguments most exploited in the course of the discussions, besides naturally, that of the known nationalism of the French religious, was a type of bill of indictment against the various attempts to substitute France by other nations, such as Austria, but above all Italy.[67]

On 8 January 1891, the *Journal des Débats*, under the title 'Le protectorat catholique de la France et la propagande italienne en Orient', published an article that raised a true polemic. On the 12th of the same month, the same paper, together with the aforementioned article put out a correction on the part of Charmetant, who, in his turn, in order to calm the waters, also published in other organs of the press; on 17 January in the *Estafette*, on the 18th in the *Rebublique Radical*, on the 21st in the *Avenir di Alençon*. On 15 January *l'Univers* published a type of defence of the Custody, reproducing a document/letter of thanksgiving on behalf of the inhabitants of Aleppo for the services rendered by the Franciscans during the cholera

---

[66] For more detail on the event, see *Les Franciscains en Terre Sainte (1869-1889). Religion et politique*, 242-249.

[67] The same letter was published by *Le Monde*, 14 January 1891.

epidemic.[68] Again on March 2nd, the *Univers*, returned to the argument with a reply, signed by the secretary of the Latin patriarchate of Jerusalem. *Le Petit Journal* of 15 March hosted the contribution of a certain Sergy, entitled 'La France d'autr-Mer', reproducing the outline of the argument used by the article mentioned in *Journal des Débats*. On 16 March the *Journal des Débats* re-kindled the polemic with a new article by the anonymous author who had written the piece of January 8th. The Vice Commissary of the Holy Land in Paris, Fr Victor-Bernardine[69] responded to this latest piece on March 22nd, again in the *Univers*. Also on March 22nd, *Le Petit Journal* published a new article by Sergy: 'L'influence française dan les pays d'Orient'. The list, which could be prolonged with other notices, is perhaps already sufficient to indicate the extent of the matter.

The polemic centred, naturally, on the use in the Holy Land of the collections raised in France through organizations such as the Institution of the Schools of the East, directed by Charmetant, and above all The Propagation of the Faith in Lyon. The suitably anonymous correspondent from Syria, author of the January 8 article, held it inconceivable that the directors of the Propagation of the Faith would not directly administer the funds, two thirds of which came from French contributors, rather sending them to the Latin patriarch of Jerusalem, who at that time was Italian, and had spent a large part of the money in accomplishing personal projects, all inspired by the most rigorous Italian style, building churches and convents to the benefit of the Italians. What is worse, according to this author, 'les Pères franciscains de Terre sainte, ennemis acharnes de l'influence française, en reçoivent la plus grande part'. If there were not a sufficient number of Franciscans to hamper the French religious, the prelate would not have hesitated to have recourse to 'laïques, libre—penseurs ou athées, pourvu qu'ils soient Italiens et qu'il soient prêts à faire la guerre, dans leurs écoles, à l'influence de la France'. In brief—the anonymous

[68] The editor of the *Univers* had presented the intervention of the Franciscans in these terms: 'En réponse à de nouvelles accusations portées par le *Journal des Débats*, contre les franciscains de Terre Sainte qui, d'après ce journal, distribueraient de préférence aux missions italiennes les subsides venues en leurs mains de toutes les parties du monde catholique, mais surtout de France, ce journal a reçu la lettre suivante qu'il n'a pas publiée.'

[69] 'Pourquoi ne fait-il pas comme le R. P. Charmetant, qui ayant eu plus d'une fois à constater les dilapidations des évêques italiens et à en souffrir, mais étant obligé par l'autorité de Rome de centraliser les sommes qu'il envoie à ses missionnaires dans les mains de ces mêmes patriarches, a pris cette mesure de simple prudence, de prévenir directement chacun des destinataires intéressés et de forcer la main aux patriarches italiens jusqu'à ce qu'il ait reçu de ces eux-mêmes le récépissés.' *Journal des Débats*, 8 January 1891.

correspondent from Syria accused—French money went to fatten the purses of the enemies of France. To the management of the Propagation of the Faith therefore came the suggestion to follow the example of Fr Charmetant, who in his publication (most probably the above mentioned pamphlet) had criticized the use of money on the part of the Italian bishop.[70] The director of the Institute of the Schools of the East, differing from the policy of the Propaganda, which obliged the Apostolic See to centralize the money in the hands of the Italian bishop, would, rather, have asked that the patriarch of Jerusalem be able to have receipts for the money consigned to the various religious communities, in order to verify the equity of the distribution.

Charmetant, as already stated, was in a hurry to publish the retractions, with which he affirmed that the method of the receipts was not his initiative, but rather a practice already in use for some time by the administration of the Schools of the East. He therefore corrected the false information regarding the distribution of funds handled by the Propagation of the Faith, asserting that the money would not have been transferred to the patriarch of Jerusalem, but directly to the attorneys of the various religious congregations resident in Paris.[71] Charmetant, besides distancing himself, considered it his duty to take up the defense of the patriarch and of the Franciscans: 'il est donc injuste d'accuser les évêques italiens ou les religieux franciscains de détourner à leur profit, ou pour les écoles italiennes, les fonds que la France catholique vers pour le deux tiers dan les caisses de la Propagation de la Foi. C'est M. Crispi lui même, qui se charge de faire concurrence à l'influence française sur le terrain des écoles: son gouvernement, bien que très obérè, consacre chaque année 1,800,000 francs aux établissements italiens du basin oriental de la Méditerranée, tandis que le parlement français, malgré les efforts des nos amis, qui demandaient davantage, n'a voté que 500,000 fr. pour les missions religieuses françaises de l'univers entier.'[72]

[70] On the politics of financing the missions, administered by the three largest associations appointed for that task, the Propagation of the Faith, the Holy Infancy and the Institution of the Schools of the East, see C Prudhomme, *Stratégie missionaire du Saint-Siege sous Léon XIII (1878-1903). Centralisation romaine et défis culturels*, Rome, 1994, 411-439.

[71] *Journal des Débats*, 12 January 1891.

[72] Je remarque d'abord que le correspondent du *Journal des Débats* n'est pas très au courant de l'administration des diocèses d'orient. Il confond les délègués et les patriarches [...] Qu'on ne s'en étonne pas. Correspondent occasionnel n'est autre qu'un commis-voyageur d'une maison de Paris, lequel vient assez souvent en orient.' *Univers*, 2 March 1891.

The other attack against the positions held by the correspondent of the *Journal des Débats,* was directed to the Latin patriarch's secretary, don Legrand, apostrophized by the journalist with the title of 'committed traveler'.[73] He, who was not even French, seems to have revealed himself as completely ignorant of the material in question, confusing, for example, the patriarch with his delegate, or mistaking his place of residence, or even the difference between one and the other. Also the information would seem to be false concerning the money that Propaganda received from the Franciscans, who 'ne reçoivent *absolument rien* (the original is in italics) de se côte.'[74] All the other news regarding the patriarch was false too, and it does not seem appropriate to indulge it on this occasion.

The anonymous correspondent from Syria, not satisfied by the reactions to his article of 8 January, deemed to reply, increasing the level of denunciation. 'Les franciscains italiens sont les ouvrières les plus actifs de la guerre sourde mais acharnée que les patriarches latins et les agents consulaires italiens ont, d'accord entre eux, engagés depuis longtemps contre l'influence française.'[75] He said that he was convinced of the existence of a secret pact between Crispi and Card. Simeoni, Prefect of the Propaganda, an accord designed to favour the interests of Italy abroad. A rumour that began at the Spanish Square the previous summer would confirm it. The double imperative of Propaganda, as reported by none other than the *Journal des Débats*, would turn out to be unequivocal: 1. interdiction of French religious to open schools in places where those of the Custody already existed; 2. prohibition of French school congregations from registering non-Catholic students to their courses. The measures of the Propaganda, according to our author, were aimed at undermining the work of the Christian Brothers and of the Jesuits, who in the East, except in the case of Albania (under the protection of Austria), were all French. Therefore the Propaganda would have been taking the side of the Franciscans, that is, of the Italians, and sharing their aversion to France. The work of confessionalization of the schools in the East seems, on the part of Propaganda, to be interpreted as an astute hit in favour of Italian

---

[73] *Ibid.*

[74] *Journal des Débats*, 16 March 1891.

[75] 'Votre «correspondent occasionnel» de Smyrne, qui déjà le 8 janvier nous avait 'etonné par la gravité de ses communications, nous fait aujourd'hui les révélations les plus stupéfiantes. A l'en croire, l'Eglise, avant d'être catholique est italienne. C'est très sérieux! eyez plutôt.' *Univers* 22 March 1891.

foreign politics. The schools administered by the French institutes in Palestine, and in particular those of the Christian Brothers, were, in fact, largely attended by non-Catholics.

It is with the same sarcastic tone that Fr Victor-Bernardin, the vice commisary of Paris, appears to reply to the journalist of the *Journal des Débats.*[76] Would the Catholic Church, including the pope, who underwrites all that comes forth from the Propaganda, seem therefore to be placed at the service of Italian foreign politics? Would the Franciscans of the Custody seem to be exclusively Italian? It is a pity then that a Pontifical document, fresh off the press, defines the international organisation as composed of religious coming from twenty eight different nations! As for the other excuses, continued the Franciscan, it would be sufficient to consult the articles of Charmetant, and those that appeared in the *Croix*, newspaper of the Assumptionists, also considered victims of the Franciscans.

Perhaps the only subsequent intervention of significance in the polemic was an observation of Sergy, in an article that appeared in the *Petit Journal* of 22 March. He noted that the advancement of Italy was due not to the action of Italian religious, but to the inertia of the consular body—slow, and, in his opinion, interested exclusively in questions of a political order, completely ignoring the commercial component, which was left to be the exclusive domain of the Germans and the English.

The debate took its stand, therefore, poles apart from the position assumed by Castelmadama. If the Custos had sought to convince the Apostolic See not to nationalize the collection for the Holy Land, by availing himself of the concept of catholicity/internationality, French journalism, on the other hand, sought to gain public support for its own country through the concept of anti-Italiansim. However, in both cases the ends at stake were always nationalism and/or internationalism.

An appendix to the polemic of Italiansim

'For many years the Mission of the Holy Land was mistreated by many journals, especially French, in a truly unworth and disgraceful way [...]. Recently a certain Giovanni Bonnefon, welcoming the occasion of the Eucharistic Congress to be held in Jerusalem, has criticized Mons. Piavi,

[76] *I nemici de Terra Santa*, in *Oriente Serafico*, 31 May 1893, 289-290.

and has said many coarse things [...]. The motive of this uproar is neither more nor less the spirit of nationality, put in the middle to alienate from us the generous souls of good French Catholics, beloved as ever of the Missions in the Holy Land.'[77]

This text is taken from an article which appeared in the review *Oriente Serafico*, a periodical published by the Franciscans of Umbria (Italy) from 1890. The review had never made a secret of its patriotism, and sustained the Italianism of the Custody with all its might. 'This mission that was founded by the greatest Italian Saint, that was always composed in large part by Italian religious, and which carries the Italian stamp in order to be more easily universal; this mission, I say, has but to glory and to delight in the benevolence of Italy.'[78] The periodical, due to its own Italianism, was particularly sensitive to the attacks launched by other journals against its fellow-countrymen, especially in connection with Franciscans such as Mgr Piavi. It had decided, therefore, to translate, annotating with its own comments, the article of Bonnefon entitled 'Un ennemi de la France', which appeared in the review *L'Eclaire*, 16 March 1893. In it Piavi was described as the enemy of France, and also branded as a strenuous opponent of the Eucharistic Congress of Jerusalem. His aversion to France, a logical consequence of his Italian identity, was brought to a head even before his nomination as patriarch of Jerusalem when, as Apostolic Vicar of Aleppo, he had a hymn performed in honour of Garibaldi to feast the entrance of the Piedmont troops into Rome, through the breach of Porta Pia. His anti-gallic sentiments would have grown after he was created Apostolic Delegate of Beirut. How his anti-French spirit, that is his Italianism, could then be connected with his aversion to the Eucharistic Congress, the author explains in the following way: 'in these days, the Franciscan is annoyed because the presidency of the Congress has been entrusted to Card. Langènieux, Archbishop of Rheims. Mgr Piavi has manifested his own remonstrance to the pope; he has sold his carriages and his horses and is prepared to leave Jerusalem. But since his manoeuvres have not moved anyone, he has hung on to the only resource that remained, that of relying on the house of Savoy, to this column of the temple broken and thrown upon the atrium. He sought approbation through denying Congress participants the use of his Church, which in the previous year

[77] *Appunti sulla Missione di Terra Santa*, in *Oriente Serafico*, 15 August 1893, 465.
[78] *I nemici de Terra Santa*, in *Oriente Serafico*, 31 May 1893, 294-295.

had been offered to a French pilgrimage; and he was applauded for having closed the doors in the face of Card. Langènieux.'[79]

The articles dedicated by the review to the defence of Piavi were only the first in a long series of contributions, which must in a certain way have accompanied the development of an event considered central to the history of the Franciscans in the Holy Land: the first visit to Palestine on the part of the Minister General.[80] The above mentioned magazine, which circulated more than any other within the Franciscan environment, seems to have followed the event. Witness is given by the number of articles—ten in one year dedicated to the Holy Land, three of which relate the trip of the Minister General—the publication of a booklet on the principal data relating to the activity of the Franciscan Custody *(Relazione sullo stato attuale della S. Custodia di Terra Santa)*,[81] and a diary of the trip in instalments issued by magazine's press, probably the work of the same secretary of the Franciscan Superior,[82] a year after the Minister General's visit,

The visit to the Holy Land of this General, Fr Luigi da Parma, the first such visit since the beginning of the Custody, seems to represent, for the magazine, the best occasion not only to publish the work of the Franciscans in the Middle East, but also to defend it above all from the accusations of Italianism, which is to say of a phobia against the French. For example, on the 15 September 1893, the magazine, with reference to the earlier polemic on Pavia, published an article entitled *I Francescani di Terra Santa sono nemici della Francia*. The author, alluding to the French accusers, affirmed: 'And why take aim especially at the Italians? Because, they say, they are the most relentless enemies of France. But, however, is it really true that the Franciscans in the Holy Land, and especially the Italians are enemies of France? Nothing is more false. The Italians are not

---

[79] Alfonse Padrenostro, *Il primo Ministro generale dei Francescani che va in Terra Santa*, in *Oriente Serafico*, 30 April 1893, 5-8.

[80] Cipriano Verdiani, *Attuale stato della Custodia di Terra Santa*, in *Oriente Serafico*, 31 October 1893, 625-638; 15 November 1893, 660-665; 15 December 1893, 719-723; 31 December 1893, 738-740.

[81] *Il viaggio del Rev.mo P. Luigi da parma Min. Gen. di tutto l'Ordine de' Minori in Oriente nel 1893*, in *Oriente Serafico*, 15 January 1894; the same year the diary of the trip of this Minister General was published in French: *De Rome à Jérusalem. Note de voyage par le RME Père Louis de Parme Ministre Général de tout l'Ordre des Christian Brothers Mineures*, Vanves près Paris 1894. The publication was by the Franciscan Missionaries of Mary, with the goal of diffusing news on the Franciscan mission of the Custody in the Holy Land.

[82] *Oriente Serafico*, 15 September 1893, 529-530.

against the French because they still recognize France as the protector of rights over Catholics. And then since, if the French were to fall out with the Italians, would they not do likewise with the Arabs, the Spanish or the Germans? The aversion to the Custody depends on the fact that France would be able to replace the Franciscans with the sons of St Louis.'[83] The author accused French politics of having constructed an anti-French polemic, even to the creation of the myth of the Italian phobia of France, with the aim of convincing French citizens of the need to substitute the Italian, and anti-French, Franciscans, with religious loyal to the Rebuplic. 'Are the Franciscan in the Holy Land enemies of France?—harangued the author—A thousand times no. They only oppose, as is their duty, those accursed French, who threaten the rights and the propriety of their mission. Lastly those French, and not the Franciscans, are the enemies of France. They are [enemies] of her religion, since they attempt to bring the firstborn Daughter of the Church against the Holy See [...]. They are [enemies] of her politics, since they work to attract the malevolence and the jealousy of the other Powers.[84]

The trip of Fr Luigi da Parma to the Holy Land, however, did not pass unobserved even in Palestine, in fact quite the contrary. The French Consulate, with two reports of 21 April and 4 June 1893, of 6 and 7 pages respectively, described in minute detail to the Minister of Foreign Affairs the preparations made by the Custody in view of this event. The ceremony in the Holy Land was of great importance, being the index of the level of honor that one intends to attribute to a famous person, or better, to his office. What is more, the places assigned in the procession and in the reception also carried a very high value, above all from the political point of view. Hence, the French diplomat must exercise all his wit to be able to make known in time the eventual injuries to the positions assumed, that is to the honor assigned to the protector. He cannot ignore the fact that it involved the first visit of a Minister General; he had noted it to Paris by the level of emphasis expressed by him concerning the enthusiam that such an event raised in the members of the Custody and of the description of the great preparations planned for the occasion. One detail over all attracted his attention, and that of the Minister of Foreign Affairs, he had had the foresight to underline in emphasis: 'Je ne crois pas inutile d'ajouter que ces

[83] *Oriente Serafico*, 15 September 1893, 532.

[84] AMAE, CCC 8, 101rv: *Ledoulx, console di Francia a Gerusalemme al Ministero degli esteri*, 21 April 1893.

dispositions [...] donnent lieu à des commentaires peu favorable à notre cause; on insinue notamment que le déplacement insolite du Ministre général des Franciscains a pour but principalement de combattre, dans l'esprit des communions dissidentes, le prestige que notre Nation doit gagner de l'arrivée prochaine du cardinal Langénieux en qualité de Legat *a latere* de sa Sainteté.'[85] So wrote the Consul in his first report to Paris. The same Consul, drawing up a second report, reached the conclusion, with some slight shadow of doubt that 'il était peut-être également dans les intentions du Conseil supérieur des Franciscains de provoquer en faveur de l'Ordre Séraphique une démonstration destinée à contrebalancer celle qui a signalé [...] l'arrivée du cardinal Langénieux.'[86]

However, if the Eucharistic Congress was celebrated at Jerusalem under the presidency of a French Cardinal and with the open opposition of the Franciscan patriarch, the Custody and the whole Franciscan Order had wished, or perhaps had had to take revenge through the extraordinary event represented by the visit on the part of a Minister General, the first in its history.[87] Did the magazine *Oriente Serafico*, which in the meantime had published a report on the state of the Custody, perhaps believe it was participating in some way in this gesture of compensation, ransoming the Custody from the accusation of a French imprint on their Italianism? If, on the level of research, it is difficult to find an answer to this query, the Consul of Jerusalem would have been able to respond to it without difficulty, if he should have felt that it was the same magazine that had first published the 'Relation sur l'Etat Actuelle de la sacré Custodie Franciscaine [...] qu'il contient [...] à l'égard de la Puissance protectrice des insinuations et des attaques qui me paraissent mériter d'être signalées.'[88] That the attitude of this *Relazione,* together not only with the magazine published by the Franciscans of Umbria, but above all with the trip of the Minister General to Jerusalem, was intended as an emblem of Italian revenge, was obvious from the fact that this *Relazione* was written 'par le T. R. P. Cyprian Verdiani,

---

[85] AMAE, CCC 8, 124v: *Ledoulx, console di Francia a Gerusalemme al Ministero degli esteri,* 21 April 1893.

[86] On the Eucharistic Congress of Jerusalem the volume of C Soetens is fully valid, *Le Congres eucharistique international de Jérusalem 1893 dans le cadre de la politique orientale du pape Léon XIII,* Louvain, 1977.

[87] AMAEN, *Jérusalem Consulat Général* 64, n. 457: *Ledoulx, console di Francia a Gerusalemme al Ministero degli esteri,* 20 September 1893.

[88] Cipriano Verdiani, *Attuale stato della Custodia di Terra Santa,* in *Oriente Serafico,* 30 November 1893, 689.

secrétaire du ministre général des Franciscains dans la visite en Palestine'. This detail had worried above all the Consul of France at Jerusalem: 'Je ferai remarquer en autre que cette publication, certainement connue et tolérée par le ministre général de l'Ordre, emprunte à la personnalité de l'auteur, aux fonctions qu'il remplissait dans la visite du ministre une autorité et une porté particuliéres'. The anti-French polemic nourished by the visit by the Superior of the Franciscans to the Holy Land would, however, have continued to produce its unhappy effects through the publication of the *Relazione* on the state of the Custody, compiled and signed precisely by someone who had accompanied the minister on his pilgrimage to the Holy Places.

The themes of the polemic do not differ from those already mentioned, that is the criticism of the Irenaenism professed in the schools of the French institutes, and that of the inefficacy of the protectorate. Verdiani had particularly insisted on the confessional option of the Custody, in opposition to the relativism of the French school congregations, taking up the same argument that appears in the diary of the visit of the Minister General, published, as one will remember, in the *Oriente Serafico*. 'Some modern persons think that the proximity of Catholics and non-Catholics in the school is a means to gain the non-Catholics to Catholicism, but the holy Custody does not believe so, because from long experience with the Eastern non-Catholics the contrary is taught [...]. It seems that also the parents of the Eastern Catholics are of this mindset, since in general they voluntarily send their children to Franciscan schools, rather than to the others where children of other religions are accepted. It must not be a wonder then if the said schools are very well attended and truly flowering, as appears from the following statistic.'[89]

The other argument which exercised French diplomatic authorities was linked to the question of Gethsemane, something also recalled in the *Memorandum*, and an event in the course of which the Custos had threatened to have recourse to other consuls, indirectly denouncing French diplomats of inefficiency. The despatch of the Consul, having reached the desks of the Foreign Minister, was transmitted to the French ambassador to the Apostolic See, in order to convey a protest to the General

---

[89] AMAEN, *Jérusalem Consulat Général* 64, n. 612: *Ministero degli esteri a Guillois, gerente del consolato di Francia a Gerusalemme*, 17 November 1893 (letter attached—30 October 1893—of the French Ambassador to the Apsotolic See, Lefebre de Béhaine).

Curia of the Franciscans, and perhaps also to the Propaganda.[90] Father Verdiani, under pressure from the Attorney-General of the Franciscan Order, Fr Raphael Delarbre d'Aurillac, a Frenchman, was obliged to give his apologies at the same time as his attestation of ignorance. The ambassador of France had already secured that if it came to press in a new edition, the passages concerning him as suspect of 'Gallophobia' would be suppressed.

Internationality opposed and manipulated

Father Verdiani, in his booklet, *Stato attuale della Custodia di Terra Santa*, written in response to the criticisms directed at Italianism launched by the French press, had brought to light on an official public level, perhaps for the first time, the characteristic of internationality as a distinctive element of the Custody, almost as an antidote against any temptation to nationalism. 'We confess it, our hearts bleed each time that we are obliged to read, either in newspapers or in seriuos periodicals, less than appropriate words regarding the Franciscan Holy Custody [...]. The mark of internationality that really and legitimately belongs to the Holy Custody is the reason for its prosperity and fecundity, let alone a powerful stimulus for its impassioned and life-giving work in the Eastern countries [...] its intrinsic constitution makes it superior to any national competition or party, and renders it suitable to guard and broaden the interests of Catholicism and of true civilization that are the interests of everyone.'[91]

This internationality, which the Custody intended to emphasise as its distinguishing characteristic in order to reject the accusation of 'Italianism'—when and to what extent was it challenged by the '*avances*' of the Italian government, as the French seemed to affirm? In other words, what were the responsibilities of the Italian government regarding the accusation of Italianism addressed to the Custody? Italy set foot for the first time in Palestine in 1869 with the visit of Prince Amodeo, Duke of Savoy, to the Holy Places. French remonstration followed immediately, notwithstanding that in regards to the duke the Custody considered itself to have offered an informal welcome with very little ceremony. The Minister

[90] *Oriente Serafico*, 31 October 1893, 625.

[91] For other details on the Italian presence in Palestine, one can also consult *Les Franciscains en Terre Sainte (1869-1889) Religion et politique*, especially 359-372; 469-472.

General was urgently summoned by the Secretary of State to resolve the accusation of 'aversion to the French'.[92] The Custos, interrogated on the facts, responded, protesting that he felt targetted by the representatives of the European powers who seemed to have taken siege, along with him, the whole Franciscan mission. This refrain is also met with a certain frequency on the mouths of the Custoses in successive years, like a red thread that accompanies the political history of the Custody, at least until the First World War.

On the vigil of the conclusion of the Triple Alliance (1882) Italy made its presence felt in Palestine, almost as if it wanted to take revenge on France for the defeat undergone in the affair of Tunis. The Italian Consul, De Donato, profitting from the funeral of an Italian religious, sought a clash with the authorities of the Custody, with the accusation of not having received an official invitation from them. He knew he could count on retaliation, or on the prospective of the withdrawal of the government pension to Italian religious, and upon the closure of the Commissaries in the Holy Land (understood also to include the novitiate convents), present on the national territory. The authorities of the Order did not cede to the blackmail, protesting their non-political stance and referring the interlocutor to the Secretary of State, the political organ of the ecclesiastical institution.

In 1880 the Italian parliament presented a report on the Italian schools abroad, in which it spoke at length of the Middle East mission and the Custody in particular, citing the writings of Franciscans such as, for example, that of Fr Remigio Buselli, entitled *I luoghi santi e la Palestina* (Rome 1880).[93] Other references were to a letter that Fr Graziano de Carli, attorney of the Franciscans in Hu-pé (China), had sent in 1878 to the King of Italy, request the financing of Franciscan missions in China, as the French government had already done for some time with their compatriots.[94] The suspicion of 'Gallophobia' in regards to the Italians

---

[92] *Relazione al parlamento sulle scuole italiane all'estero*, Rome 1889. Regarding this documentation see M Carmody, 'The Observant Branch of the Order of Friars Minor and Italian Foreign Policy, 1880-1890', in *Archivum Franciscanum Historicum*, 98/1-4 (2005), 769-794.

[93] *Relazione al parlamento sulle scuole italiane all'estero*, 177-182.

[94] In relation to the events regarding Italy in Palestine, in the period following the First World War, see the following: S Minerbi, 'L'Italie contre le protectorat religieux français en Palestina, 1914-1924', in *Asian and African Studies* 4 (1968), 23-56; A Gabellini, *L'Italia e l'assetto dellle Palestina, 1916-1924*, Florence 1997; A Giovannelli, *La Santa Sede e la Palestina. La Custodia di Terra Santa tra la fine dell'impero ottomano e la guerra dei sei giorni*, Rome, 2000 (in particular; 14-20; 24-28; 63-72).

came, however, to maturity in a later period, that is towards the end of the 1880's, coinciding with the mandate of Fr Castelmadama. Such an impression seemed to manifest itself following a series of events that are set out here in schematic form:

—1887, the prince of Naples, Vittorio Emmanuele went to visit the Holy Places raising not a little apprehension in the ranks of French diplomacy, which recorded his every move both within the shrines and elsewhere, together with each of his meetings, in order to compare it with the ceremony reserved for Prince Rudolf of Austria some time before, with the pretext of ascertaining to what extent they dared to push the Custody in this regard;

—1888, the pre-occupation of the Quai d'Orsay focusses on the projects and the initiatives of the Association for the Diffusion of Christianity and of the Italian Society in the East;

—1889, the fears of the French agents increase on the subject of the Italian schools in the Middle East, an element that inflames parliamentary debates; apprehensions already abated at the beginning of the Crispi era increase, absolutely contrary to any collaboration with religious institutes;

—1891, the press campaign against the Italian ecclesiatics begins and, in particular, against the Franciscans, as already amply illustrated above.

Italy also attempted in successive years to interest itself in the Custody, but it did so with greater vigor of all just after the war, intensifying the battle against the French protectorate.[95] Furthermore, the Apostolic See, in the person of Card. Gasparri, Secretary of State, requested the Italian authorities not to let the occasion pass, given the Italianism of the Custody. General d'Agostino, at the time responsible for the Italian troops in the Middle East, in his turn invited the Custody to free itself from the slavery of the nations and, in a specific way, to break with the of protectorship of France. Military interventions were judged inopportune by the same Italian authorities. The Custos, on his part, held them to be the cause of difficulties that the Custody experienced with regard to the British government. The Franciscans on the other hand, were treated with respect during the war years, precisely because of their international institution, and they certainly did not intend to now renounce this, their specific characteristic. The

[95] ACTS, *Segreteria di Stato di S. Santità* I, 1908-1949, 78-79: *Diotallevi, custode, al card. Gasparri, segretario di stato*, 19 February 1920.

attitude of the Apostolic See in their regard appears at least uncertain: in 1917 Cardinal Gasparri had written to the Custos to inform him of the end of the French protectorate and therefore the cessation of liturgical honours; in 1918, the same cardinal, radically changing his approach, had ordered the continuance of the the usual liturgical honours; in 1919, during the visit of Card. Giustini (1919), the same Secretary of State, under the pressure of France and Spain, accused him of nationalism. The response of the Custos at this point could only reiterate the statement based on the experience of so many predecessors: '[...] the powerful of the land seem to have chosen the Custody as their expiatory goat when they do not obtain what they have not always devoutly desired.'[96]

The Italian Consul in Jerusalem, nonetheless, possessed his own precise strategy, which he described in these terms: 'All of our sympathy must go to the Custody [...] because she in the end, notwithstanding the French protection, has remained an Italian institution and with a strong number of convents and schools spread throughout Egypt, Palestine, Syria, and Armenia certainly makes a contribution to the Italian Propaganda in those regions.'[97] The diplomat, who deemed it necessary to take the opportunity of the conclusion of the world war to ask for the cessation of the French protectorate did not, however, judge it advantageous to promote the request for an Italian protectorate. The Custody, in his opinion, had to maintain an international status, as in past centuries. With an international rule, yet allowing each friar the freedom to retain his own nationality, the Custody had in practice shown itself to be an Italian institution, and its convents, schools etc. 'would become effectively Italian in spirit and in intent'. According to the Italian diplomat, the Peace Conference of San Remo (1920) would have guaranteed the Custody its international stautus, thereby excluding the interference of the great Catholic powers. He held that such a proposal would have been pleasing to the Apostolic See, well accepted in London, and that, once accomplished, it would have permitted to Custody to keep its Italian character intact.

In view of the Peace Conference, the Custos was sent a written invitation to preside at the council, with the proposal of the old idea of

---

96 Historic Archive of the Minister of Foreign Affairs, Rome, aff. Pol 1919-1930, Syria, pacco 1564, *Relazione del console d'Italia a Gerusalemme*, 18 August 1919, cited by A Giovannelli, *La Santa Sede e la Palestina*, 69 note 119.

97 AMAE, CPC *Turquie Jérusalem* 23, 97-119v: *Ledoulx, console di Francia a Gerusalemme, a Spuller, ministro degli esteri*, 3 October 1891.

a collective protectorate: a protectorate of honor and not of defence, to be entrusted to different consuls. The Italian government was, however, almost by nature averse to the religious protectorate. At San Remo, Nitti declared himself favourable to the mandate and opposed to France keeping old privileges. Italy, however, had attempted to attract the Custody into its orbit until the last; it would do so also in the following years through the politics of finance, or by trying to press for a numerical increase in Italian personnel. Lastly, Italy, in this predicament, had attempted to manipulate the concept of internationality through its representative in Jerusalem.

The French reaction to the Memorandum

If Italy possessed its own vision of the internationality of the Custody and of the resulting advantages to benefit national interests, France also had her own point of view. Italy and France, after all, could be considered as two sides of the same coin, thesis and antithesis of the same logic: nationalism. Was Italy not perhaps the most strenuous adversary of the protectorate, and the power most feared by French diplomacy? Italian diplomacy could sustain, in its own way, a form of internationality of the Custody since it could count on a high number of compatriot religious; French diplomacy, however, due to the meagre number of French in the Custody, did not succeed in its intent to nationalize Palestine, found itself bound to surrender to England its role as avenger of internationality, and thus to betray the trust of those who had put their last hopes in France. It looked, naturally, to the Apostolic See which, through the *Memorandum* mentioned above, had intervened since 1891 regarding its intentions over internationality. Would it not then come naturally to the French government to consider something which thus far it would not have had to, how to defend its nationalism, at least as regarding the *Memorandum*, showing how it was not prejudicial to the protectorate? This insistence on the Italian case should not be surprising. Consider in this regard, that the ambassador of France to the Apostolic See, in his presentation of the *Memorandum*, warned his colleagues not to interpret the document as the result of pressures exercised by the Triple Alliance, inclined to eliminate the protectorate, nor even more, as a consequence of the influence of religious, especially Italian religious, dominated by nationalism. Such an affirmation by the ambassador, appears to clearly mark the presence of a certain stress on the part of French diplomats, a perspective according to which every attempt to criticize nationalism beyond the Alps risked being interpreted as anti-French Italianism. Each call for a greater respect of the international regime, and therefore of the demands of the protectorate, was considered as French phobia.

The documents that we now intend to analyse as expressions of French reaction to the *Memorandum* are the text of two reports of the French Consul at Jerusalem. The first, drawn up 3 October 1891, relates directly to the *Memorandum*, analysing it point by point.[98] The second, of the 14 October can be considered only as an indirect response to the pontifical document.[99] In fact, it relates to disappointment in respect to a mission ordered by the Minister of Foreign Affairs to verify the conditions suitable for the maintenance of the protectorate.[100] However, the fact that the initiative was decided in the immediate wake of the publication of the *Memorandum*, leads one to think that they are in some way connected.

The consul addressed the theme of accusations of nationalism, i.e. the Custody's attempt at internationality, addressed to him by the *Memorandum*, with the intention of reversing the direction of the question so as to attribute greater responsibility for feeding nationalistic controversies to the Custody. If the *Memorandum* aimed to illustrate the consequences that French politics, irrespective of the internationality of the Custody, had had on the protectorate, as reaffirmed by the treaty of Berlin (1878), the consul insisted on calling attention to the nationalist strategy of the Custody, which had known how to manoeuvre to its advantage the ambiguity contained in the dictates of Berlin. He explained how the sixth paragraph of article 62 of the treaty left space for a degree of uncertainty, especially when compared with the affirmation of the following paragraph. While the intangibility of the right of France relative to the protectorate of the Holy Places was assured, the right to protect their own citizens was also granted to other nations. If the Catholic powers —the diplomat therefore concluded—had hesitated to exploit the ambiguity of Berlin, it was the Custody who 'a été la seul jusqu'a se jour

---

[98] AMAE, CPC *Turquie Jérusalem* 23, 145-169r: *Ledoulx, console di Francia a Gerusalemme, a Spuller, ministro degli esteri*, 14 October 1891.

[99] AMAE, CPC *Turquie Jérusalem* 129: *Rapport du comte de Sercey sur le protectorat et la subvention des éscoles*, February 1892.

[100] AMAE, CPC *Turquie Jérusalem* 23, 106r: *Ledoulx, console di Francia a Gerusalemme, a Spuller, ministro degli esteri*, 3 October 1891.

à la diriger (ambiguïté du Traité) contre nous.'[101] In the Consul's opinion, examples confirming this argument are not lacking, and he cited precisely those in the *Memorandum* relating to Gethsemane. It regarded, as will be remembered, Castelmadama's threats of having recourse to the consulates of other Catholic powers, which were meant to spur the French agent to more effective action.

The consul returned again to the argument of the protectorate and the interference of the other Catholic nations in his dispatch of 14 October. The motive behind his reasoning was still the Treaty of Berlin, but the focal point of the argument was built on a close examination of the historical basis of the protectorate. While France, the Consul observed, could count on the capitulation, and on the mandate conferred to it by the Apostolic See, would the Porte, committed for centuries to France, now have to make itself available and open to other nations? And could the Apostolic See, on its part trust other powers? Would it be able to count on the loyalty of the pontifical authority? How was the news of their nearing the Quirinal [which means to say Italianism] understood? The consul then continued by citing those titles which could be useful to other nations in view of possible revindications of the rights of the protectorate. Austria could bring pressure through the Treaties with the Porte of 1699, 1739 and 1791 and on other concessions snatched from France, including some parishes of Smyrna, in Upper Egypt, and elsewhere. Spain, instead, could advance claims in view of the services rendered to Catholicism in Syria and in Palestine, and of the so-called Royal Dividends of Charles III (1772), to prove its rights of ownership on some convents and shrines. Italy, lastly, could reconstruct its links with the Maritime Republics, Genoa and Venice, or to the Dukes of Naples, or also to the royal title of Jerusalem, attributed to the Sardinian monarchy. The Consul, however, reserved a rather disturbing hypothesis as the conclusion of his reasoning: 'and what would happen if these powers would favour collective action against France, interpreting what was signed at Berlin to their advantage?' The shadow of the Custody, although not explicitly named by the document, seems to inspire the comments of the consul, who, only some days before, had

[101] On this event see: *Les Franciscains en Terre Sainte (1869-1889) Religion et politique*, 192-196; 197-200; H Goren, 'The German Catholic "Holy Sepulchre Society": Activities in Palestine', in Y Ben-Arieh and M Davis (eds), *Jerusalem in the Mind of the Western World. 1800-1948*, London, 1987, 155-172.

accused the Franciscan institute of exploiting the ambiguity of Berlin to organize an alternative to the protectorate, that is to say a type of collective, international protectorate.

Returning to the arguments of the report of 3rd October, we see more clearly that the consul had shifted the accusation of nationalism, that is of the attempt at internationality, to the Propaganda itself. In fact, the diplomat accused the pontifical dicastery of favouritism with regard to Germany, evidencing the lack of clarity with which the events concerning the German colonies of Emmaus were handled,[102] and in particular, the affair of the hospital of St Charles.[103] On both occasions, the Apostolic See had granted an appropriation in the Holy Land to religious that did not intend to refer to the French protectorate, and thus could constitute a serious danger for French interests in Palestine, opening the way for other nations, in this case Germany.

On the other hand, in the consul's opinion, they considered themselves justified in their favouritism of France with regard to French religious institutes—another aspect of nationalism, harmful to the duties of the protectorate—on the basis that such organisations constituted the most active part of the fight against Protestantism. The diplomat warned that the support given to French congregations could not be defined as 'nationalism', but rather the most valid service that it could offer to catholicity in the Holy Land, which means that it was not 'nationalism' but, rather, efficient pastoral care. Pilgrimages were the only political support that France could use to strengthen its position as protector; however, they also refused every accusation of nationalism.

The consul had also defended with all his might the politics of the pilgrimages in his dispatch of 14 October, indicating in addition to the advantages drawn on the internal political field: 'Ces derniers [the pilgrims], à leur retour de France propagent autour d'eux la connaissance qu'ils ont acquis dans la ville sainte de l'importance de nos éstablissements

---

[102] For more details: *Les Franciscains en Terre Sainte (1869-1889) Religion et politique*, 196; H Goren, 'Du «conflit des drapeaux» à la «contestation des hospices»: l'Allemagne et la france catholique en Palestine à la fin du XIXe siécle', in D Trimbur and R Aaronsoh, *De Bonaparte à Balfour*, 325-344.

[103] AMAE, CPC *Turquie Jérusalem* 23, 159v: *Ledoulx, console di Francia a Gerusalemme, a Spuller, ministro degli esteri*, 14 October 1891. On Catholic pilgrimages in the Holy Land at the end of the XIX century it is useful to consult: *Les Franciscains en Terre Sainte (1869-1889) Religion et politique*, 213-230; C Nicault, 'Foi et Politique: Les pèlerinages français en Terre sainte (1850-1914)', in D Trimbur and R Aaronsohn, *De Bonaparte à Balfour*, 295-324.

nationaux, de la loyauté et de la libéralité avec lesquelles nous exerçons notre protectorat.'[104]

However, with respect to the dilemma between the protectorate and religious institutes, between privileges coming from tradition and the advantages of modern nationalism, he expressed himself with cautious circumspection. An excessively sudden abandonment of the protectorate, he suggested, especially without a guarantee of the maintenance of national interests related to it, would appear as a sort of admission of impotence. A voluntary retreat from the duties assumed through the protectorate would affect the rapport with the Apostolic See, thus also incurring a loss of the moral advantages derived from papal support. The Apostolic See, although it complained of France, would have had not a few difficulties in contriving an alternative to the protective power. In conclusion, it seems to the Consul, the end of the Protectorate was signalled, even if the date of its death was still not decided. Therefore an alternative was proposed, which would have consisted in the maintenance of the finances of the national establishment, but giving, at the same time, the impression of caring for the interests of other institutes, that is of the Custody, so that the project for the future would remain secret. The final result of the multiplication of national establishments and their empowerment was to discourage the rival powers from competing for the protectorate. An all-French Palestine would have consented not only to a painless renunciation of the privileges of the protectorate, but would have also ensured the distancing of interference on the part of other nations.

The importance of this document, written in relation to the *Memorandum*, consists, in our judgement, in having admitted in a clear way, that international politics, and, therefore a protectorate, was unsustainable on the part of France. The decision of its end was decided, even if it was decreed only twenty years later. We will limit ourselves in this epilogue to recall, in a schematic way, the principal moments.[105]

—1918: the rapport between France and the Custody still formally correct—the Custos obtains 25,000 franks;

[104] A sufficiently detailed treatment of events is offered by A Giovannelli, *La Santa Sede e la Palestina*, 31-37; on this theme one may note the following studies: S Minerbi, *L'Italie et la Palestine, 1914-1920*, Paris, 1970; D Fabrizio, 'Il protettorato religioso sui Cattolici in oriente: la questione delle relazioni diplomatiche dirette tra Santa Sede e Impero Ottomano, 1901-1918', in *Nuova Rivista Storica* 82 (1998), 583-626; C Nicault, 'La fin du protectorat religieux de la France à Jérusalem (1918-1924)', in *Bulletin du centre de recherche française de Jérusalem* 4 (1999), 7-24.

[105] AMAE, CPC *Turquie Jérusalem* 23, 104r: *Ledoulx, console di Francia a Gerusalemme, a Spuller, ministro degli esteri*, 3 October 1891.

—1919 January: the Custody asks France for war damages;

—1919 February: the Custody addresses the high commissary for Syria and Palestine, judging the protectorate still valid;

—1919 December: visit of Cardinal Dubois (rapport of the Consul with the French institutes and the favouring of a protectorate in Syria including Palestine);

—1920 March: the Secretary of State authorizes the Custody to receive eventual indemnities for war damages;

—1920 August: the British government declares the end of its protectorate to the Apostolic See as established by the accords of San Remo (the French ambassador does not support the interpretation of San Remo and, to the contrary, wants to maintain the liturgical honours);

1920 Christmas: the *status quo* is maintained because of the suspended underwriting of the peace accords and of the lack of approval of the mandate;

—1922 January: incident at Constantinople during the funeral celebrations of Benedict XV (clash between France, Great Britain and Italy about the liturgical honours);

—1922: the Custodial Vicar, at Paris, exposes to the Minister of Foreign Affairs the delicate question of the scanty number of French religious;

—1922-1923: cool climate between the Custody and France following the publication of the diary of Cardinal Dubois;

—1923 July: article in *Le Correspondant* of Paris about the hostility of the patriarchate and the Custody towards France; response of the Custody, reproving France's accord with Russia, the cause of the loss of shrines;

—1923 end: the Custody proposes a compromise: liturgical honours to France only on national feast days;

—1924, 10 April: telegram of Cardinal Gasparri to the Latin patriarch ordering the suspension of liturgical honours;

—1926: agreement signed between France and the Apostolic See.

The Franciscan vindications and the status quo

In the preceding examination of the French reactions to the *Memorandum*, we have considered it necessary to defer reflections on a passage of the consul's report of 3 October, regarding the *status quo*, as being more connected with the part of the pontifical document relating to the vindication of Catholic rights over the Holy Places. It is this we now intend to cover.

The consul, examining the long list of vindications proposed in the *Memorandum*, principally emphasized the difficulty in the administration of the Holy Places arising from the 'manque absolu, pour la plupart, de documents précis, définitifs et exclusive.'[106] In his opinion, it would therefore have been impossible to find adequate documentary support for the claims presented in the pontifical document. The consul, then explained how the parties in question, that is the Catholics and the Orthodox, had each obtained a certain number of their own privileges (*firmans*) from the Porte, demonstrating the favours enjoyed by both parties thanks to their relative influence on the Ottoman government. To support his thesis, he added some examples, such as that of the Star of the Grotto of the Nativity, replaced in 1852, or of the upholstering of the same Grotto, completed in 1873. The star and upholstery were of Latin fabrication because they came from France, but from the moment that the work in hand was followed by the Turkish authorities, in order to avoid conflicts between the parties, the Greeks maintained that the rights of the respective properties belonged to the sultan, and therefore in part also to them, as they were subject to Turkish protection. The difficulties encountered in the negotiations conducted among the members of the Franco-Turkish commission, following the events of 25 April 1873, and recalled also in the *Memorandum*, would, the consul still insisted, suffice to show the difficulty and the danger of such negotiations. In other words, the diplomat attempted to show the impossibility or at least the inadvisability of France to place herself along side the Catholics in supporting the claims put forward in the *Memorandum*. The consul—as he had already tried to do with other accounts sent to the Minister in the preceding years[107]—intended to shift the question of the Holy Places from the defence of the rights of Catholics to the mere safeguarding of the *status quo*, understood as a type of established order. The protective role

[106] AMAE, CPC *Turquie Jérusalem* 18, 41-60v: *Ledoulx, console di Francia a Gerusalemme, a Flourens, ministro degli esteri*, 26 January 1888; AMAE, CPC *Turquie Jérusalem* 17, 1-12r: *Ledoulx, console di Francia a Gerusalemme, a Flourens, ministro degli esteri*, 17 January 1886; still the same theme see: *Les Franciscains en Terre Sainte (1869-1889) Religion et politique*, 450-453.

[107] AMAE, CPC *Turquie Jérusalem* 23, 105v: *Ledoulx, console di Francia a Gerusalemme, a Spuller, ministro degli esteri*, 3 October 1891.

thus came to be transformed into that of a public order agency, a rather modern role, along the lines of the process of secularization taking place in the territorial nations. 'Malgré ce qu'il présente de contraire à la sainte équité, piusqu'il consacre des usurpations antérieures, le principe du *status quo*, a paru, et est en réalité, le seul mode qui présente quelque garantie à la tranquillité entre les communautés en cause.'[108]

To establish the maintenance of the *status quo* as a principle however, the resolution of the question of the Holy Places would not have been sufficient. The claims of the Catholics expressed in the *Memorandum* demanded, in fact, as we will see shortly, the recovering of the rights pertinent to the *status quo* before its signing in 1852. Instead the consul would seem to hold that it would be impossible to establish a date, for the reasons shown above, since sufficiently clear documents did not exist in order to reach an agreement between the parties. To this proposal, the diplomat posed a different question: 'What date could be established as a point of departure acceptable to the parties? what documentation was able to specify the state of things on that date? given the lack of documents, what witnesses could be called for supplementary proof?' The diplomat concluded that the responses to these various interrogatives would have triggered off an endless process of discussions, ending in exasperation for the contracting parties, and with the only result a worsening of an already very precarious rapport.

Naturally the opinion of the Franciscans, the supposed inspirers of the *Memorandum*, was diametrically opposed, taking as it were the line, of 'vindication' with respect to the list of violations of the Holy Places taken from the pontifical document. The thought of the Franciscans appears clear in the memoir, *Les Lieux Saints à la conférence de la Paix* (1919), edited by Fr Diotallevi, then Custos of the Holy Land, for the peace conference held in Versailles, at the end of the First World War.[109] Although not reproducing in detail the contents of the *Memorandum* of 1891-97, the text of Diotallevi, which in its turn contains a list of claims about the Holy Places, does nevertheless reflect its spirit. He opens his report with the question of the Holy Places, proposing it as 'one of the great questions of European public law', over which different Western powers had disputed, including Venice, Genoa, and Naples, then France, Austria,

---

[108] A copy of the memoir is conserved in AA.EE.SS., *Francia* 1919, pos. 1307-1312, fasc. 692, ff. 3-7 (10).

[109] *Les Lieux Saints à la Conférence de la Paix 1919. Mémoire,* 5.

Spain, and England, and even Poland and Holland, all aiming at awarding to themselves the privilege of protecting the shrines of Christianity. The Franciscan seems, therefore, to reconstruct the stages of a type of 'history of claims', from those of the Cenacle and the Sepulchre, to the work of the sovereigns of Naples and Sicily, Roberto d'Angiò and Sancia (1333), to that of the Basilica of the Nativity, of the Grotto of the Nativity, of the Sepulchre of the Virgin, thanks to the intervention of Queen Giovanna of Naples, and of Lorenzo Celsi, Doge of Venice, and of Pedro IV of Aragon. A list follows of commercial treaties and, with articles regarding the Holy Places, of the capitulations, from those stipulated between Venice and the Sultan of Egypt, to those between that authority and Genoa, which already in the first half of the 15th century could have caused problems at Jerusalem for its own Consul in the protection of pilgrims. Nor to be forgotten are those of 1604 to 1740, signed by the King of France, which definitively sanctioned the protection of the Holy Places.

Diotallevi, however, omitted listing numerous *firmans* obtained in favour of the Custody, thanks to the interest of the European powers, in order to concentrate on listing the 'usurpations' perpetrated by the Custody's counterpart, that is to say the Greek Orthodox. The last 'grave usurpation', according to the indications of the Franciscan, had come about in 1757; the loss undergone by Catholics on that occasion still waited to be ransomed. The question of the Holy Places, relative to the problem of the vindications, was confronted several times without a solution in the course of the first part of the 19th century, to be taken up again with greater vigour in 1850, by the work of the French government, the Spanish, Belgians, Sardinians and Austrians, who were allied to vindicate for the Custody those same rights that they enjoyed in the period before 1757. However, to block the progress of their initiative, Russia intervened on the pretext of defending the rights of the Greeks (Orthodox), and dragged Europe into the Crimean War. For reasons of political convenience, the question of the Holy Places was not addressed in the discussions held on the occasion of the Congress of Berlin (1878), which limited itself to hammering out the principle of the *status quo*. 'Cette grande question des Lieux Saints —the Franciscan confirmed—ne fut donc pas résolue; [...] elle fut seulement renvoyée à des temps plus favorables.'[110]

The maintenance of the *status quo,* established in 1852 and confirmed at Berlin, did not at all satisfy the Custody, who considered it,

---

[110] *Ibid.*

on the contrary, 'un état d'indétermination dan lequel a été laissée l'étendue des droits de chaque Communauté chrétienne, qui a fait que les pauvres Franciscains se sont vus, maintes fois et jusqu'au commencement de ce siécle, exposée sans défense possible, aux agressions de leurs rivaux.'[111] The Franciscan invoked for the Holy Places what already, at the middle of the preceding century, the European powers had reclaimed from the Porte (1850), that is the return to the *status quo* at the moment of the usurpation of 1757, practically corresponding to that reached legally in the course of the 14th century, after the end of the Latin reign. 'La custodie de Terre Sainte demande donc qu'on fasse droit aux demandes que le Gen. Aupick, Représentant de La France à Constantinople, par sa note du 28 Mai 1850, presentait tant au nom de son Gouvernement qu'au nom de la Sardaigne, de la Belgique, de l'Espagne et de l'Autriche'[112]. The vindications presented by Diotallevi at the Peace Conference of 1919 were, therefore, the same as those presented to the Porte in 1850, on the vigil of the Crimean War. The religious specified, in fact, that on that occasion it was preferred not to force the hand of the Turkish government, backed by Russia, for fear of adding to a war that was, however, inevitable. He also affirmed that the Custody intended to address anew its requests at the peace table, 'comme elle le fit bien d'autres fois à la veille des grande traités de paix entre Turquie et les Puissances Occidentales.'[113]

It is worth mentioning another appeal that the Custody had addressed in 1856 to the Emperor Napoleon III, perhaps precisely on the occasion of the Peace of Paris, at the conclusion of the Crimean War.[114] The literary genre of this document appears analogous to that of 1919: the same list of titles in favour of Catholics, the same examination of capitulations and firmans, the same list of usurpations, the same reasoning to demonstrate the plausibility of the claims relative to the *status quo* corresponding to the period before 1757. Also, thanks to this last element, we can therefore affirm that the religious politics of the Custody with respect to the question of the Holy Places in the arc of time between the Crimean War and the end of World War I, present united and virtually unvarying characteristics. The positions of the Franciscans regarding the

[111] *Ibid.*, 6.

[112] *Ibid.*, 5.

[113] ACTSP, Dossier 17, 0003: *A Sa Majesté Napoléon III Empereur des Français: Mémoire secret pour sa Majesté*, s.d., ff. 31.

[114] S Roussos, 'The Greek Orthodox Patriarchate and Community of Jerusalem', in A O'Mahony, *The Christian Heritage in the Holy Land*, 211-224.

'politics of vindications' is re-proposed in contradiction to that of French diplomacy, presented instead noteworthy variations even in employing the same language relative to the *status quo*.

Denunciations in regard to the Franco-Russian Alliance

The Russian chapter, from the Crimean War to the First World War, certainly occupied a place of primary importance with regard to Middle Eastern religious politics. This Russian presence in Palestine seemed to mark the same temporal limits. It relates to a presence, worthy of remembrance, very much linked to the birth and the development of Arab nationalism, which, instead, underwent a sudden arrest around 1920, with the arrival of the English, who appeared to greatly prefer the Greeks, yet always favouring Jewish nationalism.[115]

For what information can be drawn from the Franciscans of the Custody, Russian power represented the greatest threat with respect to the Protestants, Germany, England or the United States, and the true threat to the Catholic interests in the Holy Places. For the Franciscans, Russia constituted a danger not only since they supported their Orthodox counterpart, with the menacing intent to one day substitute them, but also for the fact that, being allied to France, it induced them to give ground in defence of the rights of Catholics. The Franciscans had frequently manifested the conviction that it had been exactly this alliance with Russia that brought France to withdraw the protectorate. Fr Diotallevi, then Custos of the Holy Land, had reaffirmed this on the vigil of the cessation of the French protectorate, writing to the Secretary of State in the following terms: 'How can one be brought to lament, therefore, for the deference lacking to the protector, that in the East boasts its rights, fostering discord, making its exclusivity primary, and disgracefully, has never exercised its duties in the guardianship of the shrines, of which many were lost due to the influence of the protector that favoured friendship with those heterodox looking to the Russians against the Latins?'[116]

It is surprising to also find expressions like this in the rough draft of the *Memorandum* of 1891, in a text that was not reproduced in the official

[115] ACTS, *Segretario di Stato* I, 1908–1948, *Diotallevi, custode, a Gasparri, segretario di stato*, 19 February 1920.

[116] AA.EE.SS., *Francia* 1891, pos. 811-812, fasc. 424: *Memoria sopra gli affari di Terra Santa*, 4 April 1891, (ff 28-73r) 15rv.

version of the document. In it we read: '[...] in a not distant future and much more compromising on its part, it is impossible that many do not have the idea that a weak demeanour favours the part of France, and all the more so if one observes that the Sublime Porte, put in the hands of Russia, would seek the mediation of the French to be indulgent with them, without the odiousness and the responsibility that could be met with other powers. The French mission presenting itself as described above, must with every bit of evidence, distance itself from real suspicions, which, were they to attain a valid foundation, would perhaps influence and enjoin in the minds of many the idea that the friend of our frightful adversary cannot be a very effective advocate.'[117] These affirmations concerning the Franco-Russian Alliance, perhaps too strong for the *Memorandum* of 1891, would have found a place, as was noted before, in the *Promemoria* of 1897.

Russia had directed its attention to the Holy Land since the time of Peter the Great, but only with the treaty of Kuchuk Kainarji, in 1774, did it award a type of protectorate to the Orthodox population of the Ottoman empire. The Russian clergy saw the Holy Sepulchre as the Mother Church of the Orthodox, and Palestine as the model of Christianity. The Russian influence in Palestine, in particular in the affairs of the patriarchate of Jerusalem, became effective only in 1843. Under the effect of pressure exerted by Russian diplomacy, in 1845 Cyril, the Archbishop of Lydda, (of local Arab ethnicity) was elected patriarch of Jerusalem, leading to the independence of the See of Jerusalem and separation from the Phanar (the ecclesiastical authority of Constantinople, under the aegis of the Greeks).[118] To Greek eyes, Russia intended to extend in Palestine the politics favouring independence that had already characterized its intervention in the Balkans, that is, to support the Orthodox Christians, through educative politics, in view of a development in their religious nationalism. Not even the Porte cast a kind glance on the presence of Russia in Palestine, so much so as to be ready to sustain the Greek party on the occasion of the deposition of the Arab Patriarch Cyril as a consequence of his refusal to sign the protocol of the Orthodox conference, in which he declared the Bulgarian Church schismatic, favouring national autonomy. Following the deposition of their patriarch, the Arabs claimed a greater presence in the confraternity of the Holy Sepulchre, and even the participation of the laity in the administration of the finances, let alone a greater support for the

[117] D Hopwood, *The Russian Presence in Syria and Palestine 1843-1914*, Oxford, 1969, 181.
[118] S Roussos, *The Greek Orthodox Patriarchate and Community of Jerusalem*, 215-217.

works of education and social activities in favour of the poor population of their own race. The election of Prokopios by the Greeks unleashed the reactions of the Arabs, which met, however, with the favour of the Russian delegate. Russia was in a good position vis-a-vis the patriarch, always in need of financial resources. Soon, in fact, Prokopios was deposed by the interference of Russian diplomacy, responsible for a degree in imposing the candidate Ierotheos.[119]

The Russian Society of Palestine, founded in 1882, which we will refer to later, had a considerable role in the formation of Arab identity. It provided, in fact, a modern education for the Arabs: in 1886, a school was opened to teach women at Bait Jala; and in 1889, a male college, at Nazareth, so that by 1898 one could count 6,500 students.[120] The nationalism of the Arabic Church was notably strengthened. The national vindications of the Arabs increased further in 1908, following a revolt of Turkish youths. The Patriarch Damianos, favourable to the Arabs, risked deposition by the confraternity of the Holy Sepulchre, in which the Porte was also involved (Ali Ekrem Bey, governor of Jerusalem, had given clear signs of aversion to the Russians);[121] only the furious protests of the Arabs were able to block the deposition, and in the February of 1908 Damianos returned to occupy the patriarchal see.

With the beginning of the First World War, while the Arabs lost the support of Russia, the Greeks fruitlessly attempted to have recourse to the government of Athens, already undergoing secularization. The British government, which did not welcome the intrusions of other powers, sought in different ways to demonstrate its favours in regards to the Greeks. During the controversy between Damianos and the most radical wing of the Arabs, for example, London always sided with the patriarch.[122]

Parallel to the work of the Russian diplomacy in the exercise of its influence on institutions already present in the territory, other initiatives by the government of St Petersburg and of Orthodox Russia tried to bring about its own initiatives through construction, education, culture

[119] K Kedourie, *Religion and Politics, in the Chatham House Version and Other Middle Eastern Studies*, London, 1984, 328-330.

[120] D Kushner, 'Ali Ekrem Bey, governor of Jerusalem', in *International Journal of Middle East Studies* 28 (1996), 352-353.

[121] S Roussos, 'The Greek Orthodox Patriarchate and Community of Jerusalem: Church, State and Identity', in A O'Mahony, *The Christian Communities of Jerusalem and Holy Land. Studies in History, Religion and Politics,* Cardiff, 2003, 44-47.

[122] E Astafieva, 'La Russie en Terre Sainte: Le cas de la Société Impériale Orthodoxe de Palestine (1882-1917)', in *Cristianesimo nella Storia* 24 (2003), 42-43.

and religion in the Holy Land. The first Russian foundation in the Holy Land goes back to 1847, with the institution of what is called the 'Ecclesial Mission of Jerusalem' (Russkaja duxovanaja missiaja v Ierusalime), which can be considered as originating in the national politics of Nicholas I.[123] His accomplishment was obtained by judiciously exploiting a situation connected to the interests of public opinion in the Middle East and in particular in Jerusalem, and even to the gradual awakening of missionary fervour typical of the years 1830-1840, let alone the need to render the counterposition of the patriarchate more efficacious in the face of Catholic and Protestant propaganda. The history of this mission had its beginning, however, in 1843-1844, with the sojourn of the Russian churchman Porphirij Ouspenskij at Jerusalem, on pilgrimage to the Holy Places, and entrusted by the Russian Minister of Foreign Affairs to gather information. It was he who suggested a permanent Russian presence, and a mission under the control of a bishop as the Russian ecclesial representative to the Eastern patriarchate. He was also the first official concerned over the care of the Arab element and its protection before the Ottoman authorities, and who favoured the provision of scholastic education and material aid.[124]

A testimony offered by the English Consul at Jerusalem, delineated in detail the campaign of acquisitions already taking place in those years on behalf of the Orthodox, and their attempts to break Ottoman authority through pecuniary measures. It would seem, according to this diplomat, that the Orthodox, and with them the Russians, wanted to become proprietors of a type of ring which, uncoiling itself, would encompass the city of Jerusalem; many were the lands in Orthodox ownership between Jerusalem and Bethlehem.[125]

The second mission, initiated after the Crimean War, would know a moment of greater development under the guidance of Antonin Kasputin, who openly aimed at the acquisition of terrain, the construction of churches, the development of education policies for the Arabs, and the promotion of archaeological digs. In 1858 the Grand Duke Konstantin sent Pavlovich Mansurov to Palestine, to study the possibility of engaging a Russian maritime transport company in the service of pilgrims. Mansurov suggested the foundation of a consulate as an agent of the same company,

---

[123] K Anderson, 'Pilgrims, Property and Politics: The Russian Orthodox Church in Jerusalem', in A O'Mahony, *Eastern Christianity. Studies in Modern History, Religion and Politics*, London, 2004, 390-393.

[124] M Eliav, *Britain and the Holy Land*, Jerusalem, 1997, 154-161.

[125] D Hopwood, *The Russian Presence*, 71-95.

and the construction of hospices and hospitals, to be used for the care of pilgrims. The programme could have been financed through the offerings for Palestine gathered in the Russian churches. The Grand Duke welcomed the suggestions and looked to found a committee for Palestine under the patronage of the czar. In 1859, the same Grand Duke went to Palestine and promoted the campaign of acquisitions and construction projects suggested by Mansurov. In 5 years an enormous complex of edifices, with a church, a house for the Archimandrite, and the Consular See was accomplished. With the investiture of Duke Kostantin as Viceroy of Poland, the *Committee* dissolved.[126]

Since 1886 the 'campaign of acquisitions' of Kasputin was intensified, but the highest level of Russian initiatives in Palestine was reached only later, with the creation of the *Orthodox Imperial Society of Palestine*. The idea of creating a private organisation to guarantee Russian presence in the Holy Places came about in 1839 and was repressed ten years later by the person responsible for ecclesiastical missions. In 1880 it arose again thanks to Vassili Nikolaevitch Khitrovo, a high official of the Minister of Finances, who came to Palestine for the first time in 1871. He immediately thought of organising a Library of Palestine (1876), with the publication of 100 Russian works concerning the Holy Land. The cultural work proposed by Khitrovo was initially rejected by Kasputin, who could not see its importance and considered it useless, later found its first supporter in the titular of the Russian mission. Kasputin, in a letter dated 3 January 1879, expressed the desire to found a Russian Society in Palestine, on the model of the *Das heilige Land* or the *Der Palestina-Verein*. Kithrovo, encouraged by this proposal, sought support among the members of the imperial family, even gaining the support of the Grand Dukes Sergius and Paul.[127] According to Khitrovo, the

[126] For the supporters of the project, he wrote, in October 1879, a type of pamphlet/notice: in the first part the missionary activity of the Catholics and Protestants during the last 25 years was examined; in the second the results that the Russians produced in the same time period was exposed. E Astafieva, *La Russie en Terre Sainte*, 48.

[127] The study appears in the first number of the *Orthodox Miscellanea of Palestine* (Provoslavnij Palestinskij Sbornik), Saint Petersburg 1881. It treats of one of the first historical, sociological analyses of the process of installation of Catholics and Protestants in the Holy Land, during the course of the XIX century: a study that goes beyond the doctrinal and cultural aspect to examine in further depth the aspects relative to the 'way of life' and to institutional functions. It particularly reaffirms the prerogative of tradition, the privileges derived from ancient origins: if Catholics and Protestants reached the Holy Land in a relatively recent epoch, the Orthodox were present in the region *ab immemorabile*. Regarding future perspectives, the necessity for the Orthodox to have an alliance with the Russians is confirmed, thus as it was for the Catholics allied with France, and the Protestants with Germany and England. E Astafieva, *La Russie en Terre Sainte*, 49-50.

Society would have pursued three goals: 1. the diffusion of information on the Holy Land among the Russian population; 2. the improvement of the living conditions of the pilgrims; 3. political, cultural and material support of the Arab Orthodox. This plan was presented through two conferences, held on 23 and 30 March 1880, in the presence of Grand Duke Konstantin, the director of the Department of Foreign Affairs, and various members of the Council of State.

In the meantime, Khitrovo made a second trip to the Holy Land, where he was able to obtain the latest information on the activity of Catholics and Protestants, which he then gathered in a publication, printed in the autumn of 1881, with the title 'The Orthodox in the Holy Land' *(Provoslavie v Svajatoj Zemle)*.[128] This work, together with the trip of Grand Duke Sergius to Palestine, following the assassination of his father, Alexander II, contributed to bringing about the Orthodox Society of Palestine, which sprang up on 21 March 1882, being renamed in 1889 as the Orthodox Imperial Society of Palestine. Beginning on Palm Sunday, 1886, the Russians organized a day to collect offerings in favour of the Holy Land. From 1893, local departments were established in all the dioceses of the Russian Church to function as agents for the collection of funds and for the diffusion of information about the Holy Land.[129] By 1910 a decline in pilgrimages was noted, while the commitment to Russianise the Arab population through schools, seems to experience a lull. The Russian government held it a duty to distance itself from the traditional system, but the renewal of the scholastic programs, proposed by the Minister in 1914, could not be applied due to the outbreak of the war.

The data presented in this brief review concerning Russian initiatives in Palestine, now enables us to turn with greater clarity to the Franciscan influence on the *Memorandum* of 1891-97. The central part of the document, as stated, seems to be reserved to Russia, especially with regard to its influence on France. In this case, it seems useful to linger

---

[128] From 1883 the society was subdivided into three sections, with distinct duties: a) information/propaganda about the Holy Land, b) pilgrimages, c) the defence of the Orthodox in the Holy Places. The diffusion of the information was put into effect through publications at various levels: 1 scientific, through some publications and reviews such as *Miscellanea Orthodox of Palestine* and the *Bulletin of the Orthodox Society of Palestine*; 2 popular/townsmen, that is literate, with readings of a hagiographic style; 3 popular/rural, that is illiterate, with the help of illustrations and visual media of various types (in the country, for those who did not know how to read, 'reading meetings' were organized). E Astafieva, *La Russie en Terre Sainte*, 53-58.

[129] AGOFM, *Terra Santa* 19, 460-467v: *Giacomo da Castelmadama, custode, a Simeoni, prefetto di Propaganda Fide*, 22 May 1889.

on a particular consideration: while the Franciscan inspiration of the *Memorandum* already seems very probable with regard to the other sections of the document, it appears absolutely certain for the part reserved to the treatment of the Russian question. We offer here as only a single example a comparison between an excerpt taken from the *Memorandum* and one taken from a letter of Fr da Castelmadama.[130]

Memorandum

'On the Western side of the Mount of Olives and precisely above Gethsemane rises another splendid edifice, and at the top of the Mount of Olives soars skyward a stupendous bell tower, that seems to be rather an observatory for military operations. Similar towers are built at St John on the Mount, on the Mount of the Visitation, in Hebron and in Jaffa.'[131]

Letter of da Castelmadama

'On the side of the Mount of Olives to the West, and precisely above Gethsemane, rises another edifice, that attracts the sight of all the pilgrims and at the top of the Mount of Olives itself soars skyward a stupendous Bell tower in which there is a large bell and a small bell. That edifice is a temple and last year the ashes of the defunct Empress Alexandrovna, the mother of the current Muscovite Czar were transported there: the bell tower is a square tower with five very high floors over which is a spire. It is a tower upon which an observatory for military operations is located and from which signals are sent to a nearby site: if one goes to Ain Karen (St John on the Mount) one sees a similar tower constructed on the Mount of the Visitation, and equally in Hebron and in Jaffa, it is easy to guess the aim of such edifices.'[132]

---

130 *Terra Santa. Memorandum e Pro-Memoria rimessi al Signor Ambasciatore di Francia*, 32r.

131 AGOFM, *Terra Santa* 19, 461r: *Giacomo da Castelmadama, custode, a Simeoni, prefetto di Propaganda Fide*, 22 May 1889.

132 AGOFM, *Terra Santa* 19, 461r: *Giacomo da Castelmadama, custode, a Simeoni, prefetto di Propaganda Fide*, 22 May 1889.

Repeated alarming news, referred to in the letter of Castelmadama about the 'Russian danger', was put before the officials of the Propaganda by the Minister General of the Order. The Congregation decided on 20 April 1889, however, to ask the Custos directly for elucidation, requesting that 'he give news of the plots of the non-Catholics in general and of the Russians in particular against Catholic interests in Palestine.'[133] Already, on May 20, the long report of the Franciscan was ready to be sent to the Roman Congregation. It examined, in the first part, some details on the history of the Russian Society in Palestine, substantially the same, except for some statistical data, as that found in the *Memorandum*. Among the elements not included in the text of the *Memorandum*, are for example, some figures relating to the Russian Society; the members of rich families would number 779, among whom 79 belonged to noble families; the financial income, promised by the president, Archduke Sergius, would amount to 'millions of roubles', while in the safe there was only six hundred thousand roubles; other foreseen income would include taxation equivalent to '4% for each possession, or public contract'; the income deposited in 1886 for 'contracts only' amounted to 25,038,803 roubles.

The Custos, in proffering such data, intended to make it understood that what was in prospect was not 'whatever society in particular, but a government society' which enjoyed full support from the part of the imperial authorities. This link to government politics would also explain its success. In other words, the Franciscan seems to want to emphasize the state's public commitment in generously favouring the religious initiative. He continued therefore to list all construction of churches, hospices, and hospitals, the initiative in the field of education and students, the founding of agricultural colonies, the success obtained with pilgrimages and so forth, as was already set out in the presentation of the *Memorandum,* as demonstrated in the comparison of texts given above. The Custos seems to acutely realize the economic commitment of Russia to the benefit of the local Arab population. Unlike others, he was convinced that once results were obtained on a material level, they would also reach the threshold with regard to the recovery of morals. 'They are sent to study this people; and rightly they improve the customs, the tendencies, and that which greatly benefits them to win them over. The

[133] AGOFM, *Terra Santa* 19, 463r: *Giacomo da Castelmadama, custode, a Simeoni, prefetto di Propaganda Fide*, 22 May 1889.

spectators have understood that this is a sensual people and that they are not moved if not by material goods; the promises of material advancement moves them more than what Christian morality presents; but they are Turks. [...] According to the human viewpoint therefore the Russians will have also good moral results.'[134]

Therefore the Custos sustained a religious policy for a colonization of Palestine that in the first place would commit states and nations, but that would renounce nationalistic goals. It was, in fact, nationalism, according to the Franciscan, that rendered the activities of the European powers sterile in comparison to Russia. 'Yes, every nation wants to colonize [...] This type of colonization is done by the English, the Germans, the French, only Spain and Italy are missing [...].'[135]

What was the difference between Russia and the other European nations? How did their politics in the East differ and, in particular, their religious politics? The response given by the Franciscan is very clear: 'They have the goal of the propagation of her Orthodoxy, the others their interests and political goals; they, the acquisition of the Holy Places, the others commerce in the East; they work in unison, the others work against one another devoured by national jealousy.'[136]

Having finished at least the first part of his analysis of the situation the Custos therefore moved on to the formulation of some proposals. One in particular, regarding the foundation of a Catholic Society in Palestine, seems to express yet again the peculiarity of the religious policies proposed by the Custody, that is, its ascending internationality. The Society conceived by the Custos anticipated a principal seat in Rome as the coordinating centre of branches situated in other capitals, and with three goals: the first and absolute the boost 'to assist the international work in the Holy Land' for the maintenance and the acquisition of the Holy Places; the second and the third, related to the promotion of 'colonies and international pilgrimages.' The international pilgrimages would have the goal of making clear the devotion of Catholics for the Holy Places, differing from those of a national character, inclined to mix devotion and particular interests, that is to say nationalist. The Custos said that he was preoccupied by the diminution of

[134] *Ibid.*, 463v.

[135] *Ibid.* AGOFM, *Terra Santa* 19, 465r: *Giacomo da Castelmadama, custode, a Simeoni, prefetto di Propaganda Fide*, 22 May 1889.

[136] AGOFM, *Terra Santa* 19, 465r: *Giacomo da Castelmadama, custode, a Simeoni, prefetto di Propaganda Fide*, 22 May 1889.

the number of pilgrimages: the Russian one, which had taken part in the Easter feast, numerically equalled that of the Catholics for the entire year. Also, as regarded the organization of the colonies, Castelmadama foresaw a distribution marked by internationality. The various groups of colonies must be composed that is, from families of different nationalities: Italian, English, and French. To guarantee the success of such a society, however, it was necessary to eliminate the national character from all societies, to wipe the slate clean of nationalist orientations. 'These societies of a national character render the international work in the Holy Land ineffective. If such societies should continue to keep their independence, the Catholic Society of Palestine would fail at once in its aim. It must not be forgotten that such societies restrict the internationality of the Society of the Holy Land, established in Germany under different names, established equally in France, it also has the right to establish itself elsewhere; and the Work of the Holy Land has been called an Italian organization by Paul de Cassagnac in the public parliament of France; and as such it is truly considered by the French government, and is believed to be such by the French. Here is where these societies tend. They are founded to enhance an existing work and they finish by destroying it.'[137]

Here the Custos seems to attack the nationalization of the collections, that would have destroyed the display established by the commissariates of the Holy Land, appointed to gather offerings and to diffuse information relative to the activity of the Custody. He shows admiration for the strategies employed by the Russian Society for the collection of offerings through the diffusion of the 'accounts of the pilgrims'. In regards to that proposal he also describes, with minute detail, the meetings that were organized on the return of the Russian pilgrims from the Holy Land, the commotion brought about by their accounts, the offerings obtained on those occasions and above all the expansion of a desire to conquer and to ransom the Holy Places, which could raise the fear of an imminent invasion.[138] In the opinion of the Franciscan, no Catholic nation would know how to face up to such a possibility, not weak and isolated France, not Austria, 'threatened in her

---

[137] 'Above all they prepare ardent youth who are directed toward Constantinople to then go and ransom the Holy Places. When the imminent movement of the West breaks forth who can foresee what it will produce in Palestine, where Russia is so well implanted? What wound will be made to Catholicism?' AGOFM, *Terra Santa* 19, 465v: *Giacomo da Castelmadama, custode, a Simeoni, prefetto di Propaganda Fide*, 22 May 1889.

[138] AGOFM, *Terra Santa* 19, 466v: *Giacomo da Castelmadama, custode, a Simeoni, prefetto di Propaganda Fide*, 22 May 1889.

own existence', not Italy, from where in Palestine 'the Catholics are obliged to refuse the offerings'. If Russia succeeded in conquering the Holy Places, the Catholics would be treated by them on the same level as the Polish. 'Not a single Catholic nation could oppose the non-Catholic Russian power, which has great means at its disposal, and only one will that commands it, since they do not have such means at their disposal and contradictory wills that command. Russia is an absolute empire and other European powers have constitutions, which means contradiction of wills [...] France could be a rival, as protector of the Catholic missions in the East; and it has a treaty with her. For this reason they are silent against the Latins.'[139]

To stand up to Russia the European powers would have had needed a coalition, a common effort. The Catholic powers would have found themselves, however, confronted by various difficulties in reaching political unity, because they were divided among themselves exactly over the 'Catholic question'; Catholicism, or better, confessionalism, no longer constituted a point of agreement among the European powers, it seemed to have been substituted by another religion, nationalism. It seems one could say, in conclusion, that 'the Catholic politics of Western Europe' were in crisis and that the crisis was irreversible. The hope of the Custos was uselessly founded on the political and diplomatic ability of Leo XIII and on his capacity to organize international strategy. 'A powerful voice such as that of the Roman Pontiff'—the religious declared—'could shake the torpor of France, Italy, Spain, Austria-Hungary; could dissipate the jealousies that wasted them away, return to characterize the policies that they employ [...] In other times a hermit cried that God wants it, and armies of Crusaders marched in their turn to Palestine.'[140]

The Custos seems to believe in the success of politics moved from the centre, a European politics guided by the Holy See. The politics of the Holy Land must, instead, trust the resources obtained only at a local level, not in an imaginary accord among the nations, thanks to the initiation of the 'Roman centre', but rather to a local play of rivalry among

---

[139] AGOFM, *Terra Santa* 19, 467r: *Giacomo da Castelmadama, custode, a Simeoni, prefetto di Propaganda Fide*, 22 May 1889.

[140] AA.EE.SS., *Spagna* 1912-1914, pos. 1062, fasc. 420-426; Ivi, Spagna 1914-1915, pos. 1065, fasc. 428-429. Other material on the events relating to the Spanish Friars of the Custody is kept in the AGOFM; *Terra Santa* 27-34; *Terra Santa* (letter copy) SJ 144-SJ 145; *Terra Santa, questione spagnola* (in this envelope the documentation is divided into 16 bundles: 12 numbered 'envelopes' and 4 files - 1. Minister General, 2. 1865-1913 [defense of the Apostolic Letter '*Cum ad nos*'], 3. 1866-1877 [questione spagnola e Serafino Milani], 4. 1744-1872 [copy of the Dividend Warrant of Charles III and its consequences].

the various nations, who attempted to control the territory. This type of politics could be administered only by a particular agent, which proved to be precisely the Custody, which, however, was almost constitutionally bound to live with a conflicting regime both from within and without. However, the time of the Medieval Papacy, of supra-national accords appeared to have definitely passed; now it was necessary to come to terms with the complexity of internationalism. The Crusader cry of the Custos expressed a nostalgia for a distant past.

An appendix: the Spanish case

The economic administration of the Custody gave rise to disagreements, brought forth, as usual, by the religious of Spanish nationality. Although it was not an argument contemplated in the *Memorandum* of 1891-97, it cannot be passed over in silence in the present treatment of the religious politics of the Franciscans toward the end of the Ottoman empire. In the investigation conducted in the Archives of the Extraordinary Ecclesiastical Affairs where the *Memorandum* of 1891-97 was found, it was verified that in the sector regarding Spain, various documents are stored concerning the controversies about the administration of the 'Holy Land fund'.[141] This largely relates to documentation dated around the years 1912-1914, during which the question took on a high level of importance. It is, however, the case that some documents introduced as historical evidence supporting certain claims of the Custody actually originate only in the second half of the nineteenth century and precisely after the Crimean War. We ask, then, what was the specific characteristic assumed by Spanish events in the period under consideration by our study?

a) Politicization

In this regard some significant elements from a report of 28 June 1855, sent by the Ambassador of France at the Apostolic See to the French Minister of Foreign Affairs can help us.[142] The text was meant to be an

---

[141] AMAE, CP, *Rome* 1004: 80-100r: *Reyneval, ambasciatore di Francia presso la Sede Apostolica, a Walewski, ministro degli esteri*, 28 June 1855.

[142] AMAE, CP, *Rome* 1004: 85v: *Reyneval, ambasciatore di Francia presso la Sede Apostolica, a Walewski, ministro degli esteri*, 28 June 1855.

answer to the Ministry with regard to some information concerning certain initiatives taken by the Spanish and Austrian Consuls in Jerusalem and Beirut. The diplomat, claiming to have gathered more information, through discussions with Cardinal Antonelli, Secretary of State, and with Cardinal Barnabò, Prefect of the Propaganda, declared himself ready to furnish a detailed report on 'l'affaire des Lieux Saints', that he judges 'si complexe et si peu connue', as to require 'comme indispensable de la présenter dans son ensemble'. The ambassador, to make the importance of the questions raised by the Spanish Consul understood, takes as a point of reference a decree, entitled the Royal Dividends, issued by Charles III, in 1772, with the objective, according to him, of soliciting the process of suspension of the Company of Jesus, already being considered by the Holy See. The provision established that the Spanish sovereigns, as successors of the Angevin king, should exclusively exercise the prerogatives of patronage over the Holy Places and over the other churches and hospices in the Holy Land; consequently, then, all the alms and the donations coming from Spain would go directly into the hands of the Spanish Attorney, and be kept in a separate fund from offerings gathered from other nations (at the time it was an extremely meagre sum). The administration of these sums would be subject to the control of the Madrid government, whose right it was also to nominate the Attorney. 'Malgré les constantes protestations du Saint-Siège'—continued the diplomat—'le Gouvernment Espagnol a maintenu son dire, et quoique hors d'étant de rien protéger, il vient de renouveler tout récemment les déclaration de Charles III, et a envoyé pour la première fois à Jérusalem un Consul fortement imbu des prétentions castillanes.'[143] The Ambassador, after illustrating at length, and in some detail, the initiatives of the Spanish Consul, reached a certain point, where he raised a particular question, as if to induce a pause for reflection on the preceding enumeration of facts: 'On se demande souvent pourquoi l'on voit naître aujourd'hui des difficulté de cette nature'. His answer to the question immediately follows: 'Depuis une dizaine d'années, une véritable révolution s'opère à Jérusalem [...].[144] The very recent creation of consulates on the part of European nations, would generate, in his judgement, political incentives for interference, contrary

[143] AMAE, CP, *Rome* 1004: 88r: *Reyneval, ambasciatore di Francia presso la Sede Apostolica, a Walewski, ministro degli esteri*, 28 June 1855.

[144] AMAE, CP, *Rome* 1004: 89v: *Reyneval, ambasciatore di Francia presso la Sede Apostolica, ao Walewski, ministro degli esteri*, 28 June 1855.

to the interests of France, that is, to its protectorate. The agents of such politics, would have been besides those consulates, the Franciscans of the Custody, who 'recherchaient l'appui des consuls, profitant de leurs dispositions jalouses'. The Apostolic See itself would have sought in vain to dissuade the religious from such initiatives. 'Un noyau de dix ou douze Espagnols—the Ambassador specifies—résistent encore très ouvertement et sont en rébellion déclarée contro le Saint-Siège et contre leur Général. Il prétendent ne relever que de l'Espagne [...] Les ordres, les menaces n'y suffisent pas. Comment employer d'autre armes?'[145] The means employed by the religious to attract the interest of the diplomats, the French legate still insists, 'est celui des aumônes qui demande un explication toute particulière'. The diplomat therefore expounds in detail, the particularities regarding the administration of the offerings, which we will return to later, and those relative to the difference between the protectorate—belonging to the French government, that is the political administration of the territory—and the *patronage*, claimed by Spain, which is founded, instead, on merely economic interests.

At this point, however, it is interesting to note, keeping only to the particular characteristic assumed, in the case of Spain, in the period after the Crimean War, or rather to the eminently political aspect the event took on, in virtue of the arrival of a diplomatic representative in the region. The decision to institute a Spanish Consul at Jerusalem seems, in fact, to be the motive for an initiative launched by the Apostolic See regarding the funds of the Holy Land.[146] This refers to the Brief *Romani Pontifices*, with which on 18 August 1846 Pius IX finally, after various failures, decreed the unification of the funds of the Holy Land and, consequently, the return of a common administration of the economy, under the aegis of the Custody. Thus he reconfirmed what had already been established, since 1746 by Benedict XIV with the brief *In Supremo*.

---

[145] D Fabrizio, *Identità nazionali e identità religiose. Diplomazia internazionale, istituzioni ecclesiastiche e comunità cristiane di Terra Santa tra Otto e Novecento*, Rome, 2004, 191.

[146] For further information in this regard: A Arce, *Expediciones de España a Jerusalén, 1673-1842, y la Real Cedula de Carlos III sobre los Santos Lugares en su ambiente internacional*, Madrid 1958; C De Campo Rey, *Historia diplomática de España en los Santos Lugares (1770-1980), Ministerio de Asuntos Exteriores II*, Madrid 1982; P García Barriuso, *España en la historia de Tierra Santa, Ministerio de Asuntos Exteriores II*, Madrid, 1994; F del Bueyy, *Obra de España en Tierra Santa*, in P Pieraccini, *Dos mil años en busca de la Paz. Jerusalén y sus Comunidades*, Madrid, 2003, 563-665; P Pieraccini, *Cattolici di Terra Santa (1333-2000)*, Florence, 2003, 17-36.

We believe it useful, in the interests of greater clarity, to summarize schematically the principal steps of the secular event.[147]

—Philip V of Spain (1700-1746), for military reasons, takes from the Bank of Naples five million ducats, already destined by the Angevin kings for the maintenance of the Friars of the Custody, to transfer them to the Charitable Institution of Madrid;
—The Custos Paul da Laorino attempts to withdraw from the Spanish Attorney the administration of offerings coming from the Charitable Institution (1742);
—Benedict XIV issues the Brief *In supremo militantis Ecclesiae* (1746);
—Charles III of Spain (1759-1788), issues the Royal Dividends (1772), in which he decrees that collections gathered in Spain must be consigned directly to the Attorney;
—Pius VI, with the brief *Inter multiplices* (1787), establishes that the duty of the Custos, Vicar and Attorney be held in turn by Italian, French and Spanish religious;
—Pius VI, due to the French Revolution, decrees with the brief *Exponi nobis* (1794), that the duty of Attorney be held only by Spanish religious;
—The Custos, Bonaventure da Nola sends a protest to Propaganda (1812), denouncing the work of the Attorney and asking that he be helped by an Italian, so as to guarantee a more equal division of funds;
—The French Ambassador to the Apostolic See joins the chorus of protests against the administration of the Spanish Attorney (1823);
—The Propaganda Fide confronts the situation of the power of the Attorney of the Holy Land (1826), revealing 'the insubordination and the despotism' of the Spanish Friars, who refused to submit accounts of the funds of the Holy Land to the Custos;
—Mgr Perpetuo Guasco, Apostolic Vicar of Egypt and ex-Custos, charged with an Apostolic visit, attempts, in vain, to introduce an Italian into the economic administration;
—The Custos, Fr Cherubino da Civezza, addresses himself to the Propaganda, showing the possibility of an intervention (as proposed in the brief *In supremo militantis Ecclesiae*) given the advent of favourable

[147] For further study of the events summarized in this schematic excursus, it is useful to consult the material kept in the AGOFM, *Terra Santa/questione spagnola*, 1744-1872: copy of the Dividends of Charles III and its consequences.

conditions following the diminution of offerings coming from Spain;
—Pius IX confirms the Benedictine Constitution with the Brief *In Supremo* (1846).[148]

In the years following, the newly elected Latin patriarch of Jerusalem, the energetic Mgr Jospeh Valerga, in order to guarantee an economic base for the initiatives of the patriarchate, had asked several times, in virtue of the authority granted to him by Propaganda, that an account of the administration of the Custody should be submitted to him (1851-1854). The Custos continually defended himself, protesting the difficulty he encountered in obtaining the obedience of the Spanish religious, sustained and protected not only by their Consul, but even by their sovereign. In addition, the intervention of the Propaganda was proposed to inform on the complaints from various parties concerning 'the bad administration of alms', with the invitation to transmit to the patriarch 'the state of what the Holy Land possessed, noting exactly all the money deposited in the fund.'[149]

b) In the wake of internationality with Milani

Father Serafino Milani, Custos and Apostolic Visitor by Pontifical nomination, took up a position of clarifying the terms of the situation absolutely in line with the international criteria often adopted by the authorities of the Custody. With a long and meticulous *Memorandum*, he explained the inconsistency of Spanish pretensions to some convents, in which a friar of that nation acted as superior.[150] The Angevin Kings

---

[148] P Pieraccini, *Cattolici di Terra Santa (1333-2000)*, 25-27.

[149] AGOFM, *Terra Santa/questione spagnola*, 1865-1913, defense of the Apostolic letter *Cum ad nos*: *Il custode di Terra santa, p. Serafino Milani risponde al console generale di Spagna a Beirut*, 5 November 1865, ff 25 unnumbered, by Milani himself (copy of the same in AA.EE.SS., *Spagna 1912-1914*, pos. 1062, fasc. 420-26). This letter of Milani is stamped, with other documentation, attached (A) to the pamphlet *Difesa della Lettera apostolica 'Cum ad nos' … pro manuscripto*, 15-45 (*ibid.*). Still on the Spanish question, in reference to Milani, see: AGOFM, *Terra Santa/questione spagnola 7: Milani al console di Spagna a Gerusalemme*, 22 October 1866; *ivi*, 1866-1877, Spanish Question and Serafino Milani: *Milani al ministero generale*, 13 April 1866; *Milani al console di Spagna a Beirut*, 8 April 1866; *Antonio Bernal de Rlly, console di Spagna a Milani*, 2 April 1866; Milani, *Relazione della visita apostolica in Terra Santa*, Jerusalem 1870, *Milani al ministero generale*, 3 August 1866, 11 February 1868, 20 December 1871 (with enclosures), 5 May 1874.

[150] In order to make it easier to find the piece cited above, we refer to the letter of Milani to the Spanish Consul in Beirut, 5 November 1865, from the pamphlet *Difesa della Lettera Apostolics 'Cum ad nos'…*, 35.

and the Marine Republics still sustained the religious, in exchange for their donations they would have never demanded property rights on the convents: their offerings were none other than 'free donations' to the Roman Church. Instead the Spanish government and the friars acted in the opposite way, with their delegate acting, after the issue of the *Dividends* of Charles III, to hide, or rather subtract the alms coming from Spain from the common administration, the so-called 'common fund',

Concerning the Spanish superiors in some convents, according to what had been established by the Benedictine Bull (1746), Fr Serafino precisely defined the distinction between the functions of 'leadership' and 'property': the fact that a convent was directed by a Spanish religious could not be assumed as sufficiently demonstrative proof of its belonging to the nation to which the religious belonged.[151] What is more, the Custos continues, in the Bull cited, a common basis was established for all the convents of the Custody, excluding any distinction of nationality. In the choice of superiors, then, there was no other criteria than their merits and the needs of the place. The nomination of Spanish religious for certain convents clearly must be subordinate to the principal of suitability. The assignment to some convents of distinct superiors from a determined nation could only constitute a sign of recognition towards their respective governments, wanting to share in the care of the Holy Places. The property shared by convents and hospices was then seen as very favourable, especially on the occasion of armed conflicts engaged in with Turkey by one or other of the European powers, since the Ottoman government could avail itself of the citizens and edifices subject to the enemy nation.

Father Serafino proved, in conclusion, the principle according to which all goods administered by the Custody must belong to 'Catholicism in general'. He also affirmed: 'As all the Catholic powers have participated in the founding or in the maintaining or in the ransoming of these Holy Places, and still do so with their alms and gifts, thus all the Catholic powers have equal right, and all must give a friendly hand to protect them and to maintain them as common patrimony of the sons of the true Church [...] the Franciscans must be in the Holy Land not as members of a party, not as masters in the name of this or that Power or Nation, but as foreigners and pilgrims, as men detached from all, as cosmopolitans.'[152]

---

[151] *Difesa della Lettera Apostolica 'Cum ad nos'...*, 44.

[152] AGOFM, *Terra Santa/questione spagnola*, 1866-1877, questione spagnola e Serafino Milani: Milani, *Relazione della visita apostolica in Terra Santa*, Jerusalem, 1870, 5.

The impassioned intervention of Fr Milani was not, however, followed by an effective resolution of the controversies with the Spanish government. In fact, some years later (1870), he again lamented the inaccessibility of the premises of the Spanish Attorney, who kept the *firmans* and various other documents guaranteeing the rights of the Custody over shrines, convents, hospices, homes and land.[153] These arguments continued later, with more or less severity. At the beginning of the 1880s, for example, a disagreement broke out about the ownership of the hospice in Constantinople, involving in the dispute the Propaganda and the Secretary of State, besides the Spanish and French governments.[154] The controversy reached such an acute level as to lead the Franciscan Minister General *pro tempore* to exclaim: 'We call France overbearing, but with Spain also we are not joking.'[155]

c) Anti-nationalism and the intemperance of Carcaterra

The greatest point of conflict was certainly reached in the years 1912-1915, during the Custodial mandate of Fr Onorato Carcaterra.[156] Some introduction to the event may clarify the choice of this energetic Neapolitan, who introduced a little order and discipline into the ranks of the Custody.

On 9 February 1907, the president of the Holy Sepulchre, persuaded to bring about a licit updating of the rubrics, chose a Mass *pro rege Italiae* and not, as usual, *pro rege Sardiniae*. This measure was judged as Italianising, and denounced by a Spanish religious through recourse to the Apostolic See. Some time later, at the end of the mandate of the Attorney, the Minister General's decision to send a Visitor alarmed the Italian government. Considering it an exceptional measure (that is without respect for the usual expiration of the custodial mandate), they feared that, in time, it could result in the withdrawal of the prerogative of the

---

[153] The argument was treated in *Les Franciscains en Terre Sainte (1869-1889) Religion et politique*, 413-420.

[154] ACTS, *Ministro Generale*, C. 15, 172 (Reg. 11, 60-61): *Bernardino da Portogruaro, ministro generale, a Guido da Cortona, custode*, 30 March 1883.

[155] In reference to the 'Carcaterra case', a consultation of the study of Daniela Fabrizio, *Identità nazionali e identità religiose*, 193-264 is worthwhile due to its rich detail.

[156] AGOFM, *Terra Santa*, Spanish question 12: *Esposto del p. Grammiccia, discreto italiano di Terra santa*, May 1909 (typewritten, 7 pages, not numbered).

role of Custos from the Italians. From the result of the visit emerged the presence of a strong nationalistic spirit, particularly involving the Italians and Spanish, who were re-elected Custos and Attorney respectively.There was also discussion over the imprudence of certain acquisitions undertaken in the name of the Charitable Institution and not of the Custody. In this regard, the discreet Italian, Fr Gramiccia, presented a long memo with detailed accusation in regards to the Attorney.[157] Faced with this complex situation, the Minister General nominated a commission, charged with examining the matter further.[158] However, even the circular that the Minister General sent to the Custody, when this commission's work was done, was not enough to cool tempers.[159] The warning of the superior with respect to the norms established by the internal constitution and its directions regarding the duties of the religious charged with the offices of government, still appeared to be an insufficient measure. Given his gifts of resoluteness and determination could the choice of Fr Carcaterra thus be considered a sign of a passage to a new strategy?

As a condition of his nomination—which, because of the war only came about on 1 March 1912—he asked the Apostolic See to issue a *motu proprio*, whereby the new rule was promulgated for the economic administration and 'national possession' of the convents of the Custody under the Spanish government. He insisted on being granted full liberty of action over the establishments and the seals of the Attorney, and also on the nomination of the conventual superior of the religious by the Custody, to whatever nationality they belonged. Father Onorato was also disposed to initiate a process of revision of the statutes sanctioned by the bull of Benedict XIV, while as regarded the rights of Spain, he considered the report of Fr Milani cited above sufficiently clear.[160] By order of Pius X, who held, in contrast that the Benedictine code (1746) was still valid, the Propaganda prepared the motu proprio *Cum ad Nos* (17 November 1912),[161] establishing the following:

---

[157] AGOFM, *Terra Santa* 30, 81r: *Relazione Bendes e Spada*, 25 April 1910.

[158] AGOFM, *Terra Santa* 30, 93-98: *Dionisio Schuler, ministro generale, a Razzoli, custode*, 24 June 1910; *ivi*, 101—106, D Schuler, *Circolare ai religiosi della custodia di Terra santa*, 24 June 1910.

[159] AGOFM, *Terra Santa/questione spagnola*, packet 'ministro generale', *Carcaterra, custode, a Monza, ministro generale*, 8 March 1912, 3ff.

[160] *AOM* 1913, 31 (amendments to the Cum ad nos, proposed by Carcaterra and by the Minister General, in AGOFM, *Terra Santa/questione spagnola* 10: *Remarks and notes regarding Cum ad nos*, 1; *Monza al commissario di Terra Santa*, 4 November 1912).

[161] AA.EE.SS., *Spagna* 1912-1914, pos. 1062, fasc. 421: *Sardi, ambasciatore di Spagna presso la Sede Apostolica, a Merry del Val*, 20 January 1913.

—reunification of the fund, with three keys entrusted distinctly to the Custos, to the Vicar and to the Attorney (art 2);
—full responsibility assigned to the Custos and to the 'discretionary' on the administration of alms (art 3);
—control of the workshops (art 4);
—prohibition of local superiors to use private seals, different from that represented in the insignia of the Holy Land (art 5).

The formulation of article 6, on the Spanish rights of superiorship in some convents (Jaffa, Ramleh, St John on the Mount, Damascus and Nicosia), by leaving space for ambiguity in interpretation, became the principal motive of conflict between the Custos and the Roman authorities, that is to say, the Minister General and the offices of the Propaganda. The Apostolic Letter *Cum ad Nos* immediately met with opposition from the Spanish friars, to the extent that some asked to return to their own provinces, and others to transfer to St John on the Mount. The Secretary of State also received protests on the part of the government of Madrid.[162]

On 16 January 1913, Carcaterra reached Jerusalem, bringing with him the Apostolic Letter.[163] Strengthened by Pontifical prerogatives, he arranged an inspection of the Attorney, substitution of the seals representing the arms of Spain with those inscribed with the emblem of the Holy Land, and the nomination of new superiors. In the application of this last provision, a great fuss arose in the convent of Jaffa, where instead of a Spanish religious, it was an Italian one, who, however, was not permitted even to read the decree of nomination. The rising tone of protest on the part of the Spanish provoked the immediate intervention of their government. The Minister General wrote to the Custos, recommending prudence, as well as correcting him on his interpretation of article 6, which was not to be understood as a deviation of privileges common to Spain.[164] The Secretary of State, Card. Merry del Val intervened on 3rd February ordering the suspension of *Cum*

---

[162] On the work of Carcaterra, Custos of the Holy Land, also bear in mind the *Diario del Governo del Rev.mo p. Onorato Carcaterra OFM custode di Terra Santa e visitatore apostolico. 14 gennaio-14 marzo 1913* (pro manuscript) in AGOFM, *Terra Santa/questione spagnola* 11.

[163] AGOFM, *Terra Santa* (letter-book SJ 145), 55: *Monza, ministro generale, a Carcaterra*, 6 February 1913.

[164] AA.EE.SS., *Spagna* 1912-1914, pos. 1062, fasc. 421: Merry del Val a Carcaterra, 3 February 1913.

ad Nos.[165] A primary factor for the understanding of the event is the fact that the correspondence coming from Rome underwent a considerable lapse of time before reaching the Holy Land. In the meantime, consular agents came on the scene, retracting the passports of the Spanish religious, thus prohibiting them from being transferred to other convents: those in Jaffa, for example, were prevented from reaching their assigned destination (Larnaca) and forced to remain. In Jerusalem, the consular agents even gave them orders on the station platforms in order to block the departure of any friar of Spanish nationality.

Carcaterra sent the correspondence between the Spanish consul in Jerusalem and the ambassador of Constantinople to Rome, to make them aware of the level of interference of the Madrid authorities and the insubordination of the friars.[166] He asked his superiors for a sign of their resolve, even threatening his departure. The religious wrote to the Italian consul, requesting his intervention with the Apostolic See in defence of national interests. On 22 February 1913, Carcaterra, true to his threat, left for Naples. Rome, in reality, did not allow the time necessitated by local circumstances, or by the slowness of communications.[167] Only when Carcaterra reached Naples could he be updated on the letter of the Minister General, and on the prohibition to leave the Holy Land. In the diplomatic diatribe between the Apostolic See and Spain, the Minister General seemed more inclined to sacrifice the individual than to defend not so much the principle of justice, but that of the institutional equilibrium of the Custody, that is, if you will, its equidistance from nationalism, or better yet, its internationality. Therefore he ordered Carcaterra to remain in Naples, precisely to keep him far from Rome. He felt the decision of his superior as a true injustice, effectively denying him the right of personal defence.

On 27 March, Merry del Val wrote to the Minister General and the patriarch of Jerusalem, ordering the restitution of the Spanish superior in Jaffa, previously removed by the Custos, and the restitution of the seals with the Spanish arms.[168] In this way the Apostolic See seemed to want

---

[165] AGOFM, *Terra Santa/questione spagnola* 1: *Carcaterra a Monza*, 16 February 1913.

[166] The correspondence coming from Rome was intercepted and blocked by the Turkish authorities. Telegrams had undergone the same fate, the (official) reason being the failure of the telephone lines. AGOFM, Terra Santa/questione spagnola 1, Carcaterra to Monza, 27 February 1913; Diario del Governo del rev.mo p. Onorato Carcaterra, 28-29.

[167] AGOFM, *Terra Santa/questione spagnola* 2, *Merry del Val, segretario di stato, a Monza,* 27 March 1913; *ibid.* 2, *Merry del Val a Camassei, patrarca latino di gerusalemme*, 27 March 1913.

[168] ACTSP, File 18, 0007: *Notes du service anglais de contre espionnage à Jérusalem. Intelligence Département*, s.d. 5.

to please the new conservative Spanish government, showing obvious appreciation for having abandoned certain positions of ecclesial politics judged as excessively liberal. France also rejoiced in the measures taken. They, in fact, after having broken off diplomatic relations with the Apostolic See, met with not a few difficulties in putting a stop to Italian policies in the Middle East, especially in the organization of the Custody.

Among the documents kept in the packet on 'Gallophobia' in the archive of the commissariate of the Holy Land of Paris, there is one regarding a kind of report by British secret services,[169] in which some serious accusations are levelled at certain attempts of Carcaterra, such as those intended to substitute the French Protectorate with the Italian.[170] Another document appears to be a report on a possible revision of the Benedictine statutes, with observations clearly contrary to the role assumed by the Italians in the government of the Custody and showing instead very favourable evaluations with regards to the Spanish religious.[171] Nationalist counter-positions, resulted, however, in involving and altering the internal rapport between the different organs of the Franciscan institution itself.

Carcaterra had the directives of 27 March communicated to him by the Minister General himself, who, by threatening his deposition, imposed full obedience. Father Onorato, then decided to immediately address his delegate to Jerusalem, Fr Gramiccia, ordering him to employ the objection of conscience, but he received a clear refusal. This religious, though demonstrating his obedience to the Minister General, could not evade a profoundly bitter expression before provisions which would leave the Custody disbanded. 'I say frankly—he wrote to Gramiccia—that it breaks my heart to assist daily in such subtle provocations of some, who,

---

[169] On the collaboration between the French secret services and the English in the years close to the First World War one can consult the study of Yigal Sheffy, 'Une convergence f'inters: la collaboration entre les service secret français et britannique au Levant pendant la Première Guerre mondiale', in D Trimbur et R Aaronsohn, *De Bonaparte à Balfour*, 89-107.

[170] ACTSP, File 18, 0008: *Ladislas Maye, vicario custodiale*, [reserved letter on the updating of the statutes of the Holy Land], 26 Janauary 1912.

[171] AGOFM, *Terra Santa* 31, 479 (479-480r): *Gramiccia, preseidente custodiale, a Monza, ministro generale*, 13 June 1913. The same, 10 April, had affirmed, 'The triumph and systematic victory brought about by some fanatics and rebels to the dispostions contained in the pontifical letter 'Cum ad Nos', has produced in our other Religious such a grave pessimism that one also feels pushed to threaten them to do likewise […]'. AGOFM, *Terra Santa/questione spagnole*, packet 'ministro generale': *Gramiccia a Monza*, 10 April 1913. In the same tone as the latter see also: *ivi, Terra Santa/questione spagnola* 2: *Gramiccia a Monza*, 20 April and 26 April 1913 (both confidential).

even though they should be ashamed to, live with religious, considering the evil that they have done to the Church of God, to the Order and to the Custody. They, instead, are self-assured and arrogant; it seems to them that they have won [...] always sauntering with their meddlesome Consul, they are the reason the other religious groan and suspect still greater evils.'[172] The government of the Custody turns out unsustainable, as long as that state of things endured, that is to say, the indecision of higher authorities.

The decision on 27 March, in an environment external to the Custody, gave rise to different reactions. While, for example, for the Apostolic See it treated of concessions, for the Spanish, it represented only the beginning of the advancement of further demands. The Spanish Attorney, in fact, having just returned, demanded the right of supervising the tailor's workshop, asking for the return of a Spanish brother who had driven away by Carcaterra because of various abuses. Besides, in the convent of Jaffa, for the upcoming festivities for the arrival of the new Consul, the figures of the Custos and patriarch were withdrawn and substituted with Spanish royalty. The morbose line recommended to Gramiccia by the Roman authorities did not pay off: 'The Spanish religious, meanwhile'—declared the friar—'make themselves overbearing, convinced they can rely on His Eminence, the Cardinal Merry del Val and their government [...]. It is already eight months that I tolerate the daily presence of the Spanish Consul in the procurator's office, often accompanied by a lawyer; it is already eight months that I tolerate the continuous pressures of Spanish religious at their Consulate [...].'[173] The situation would continue in the same climate for several months.

The Italian government also intervened with the Apostolic See on the Spanish question, obtaining the promise that the Apostolic Letter *Cum ad Nos* was going to be enforced fully, including the interpretation given by Carcaterra to article 6.[174] The pressures of the Spanish government,

---

[172] ACTS, *Ministro generale* 1913-1921, *Gramiccia a Monza*, 20 September 1913.

[173] P Piaraccini, *Cattolici di Terrasanta*, 34.

[174] AGOFM, *Terra Santa/questione spagnola* 1,3, *Carcaterra a Monza*, 13 July 1913. Further documentation regarding the interpretation by Carcaterra of the Apostolic Letter *Cum ad nos* in AGOFM, *Terra Santa/questione spagnola* 10. Carcaterra had proposed a systematic defense of his work, always based on *Cum ad nos*, on 12 March 1913, with a letter to the Secretary General (AGOFM, *Terra Santa/questione spagnola* 1,2), to which he also attached a series of documents, to testify to the problems which arose following the emanation of the Royal Dividends of Charles III (see this documentation in *Terra Santa/questione spagnola* 7). All of this documentary material is stamped, successively, in the above cited *Difesa della lettera apostolica 'Cum ad Nos'* [...].

however, were such as to induce the Pontifical authorities to change once more, and even to return to the previous position.

Carcaterra, already dismissed because of his reactions to the pontifical provision of 27 March, from his 'exile' in Naples kept the dialogue going with the Minister General, insisting that he was defender and advocate, not of his person, but rather of the institution, namely the Custody. 'Defending Carcaterra from the accusation of having interpreted wrongly art. 6 of the Pontifical Letter, I have taken up the defence of the Custody: in fact, since—violating the text of the article—he got as far as giving him an interpretation different from the true one, which remained as the principal font of disorders in the Custody, the other dispositions of the Pontifical Letter would not have but an ephemeral effect. The most reverend Fr Carcaterra can be accused, calumniated, condemned, deposed, it doesn't matter, because Carcaterra will pass. The Custody, instead, must remain and to remain and live it absolutely, urgently needs to be cared for effectively, radically, courageously, from the evils that threaten its existence.'[175]

The primacy of merit, which means to say of the efficacy of the national privileges, constituted for Carcaterra the key of interpretation of the Pontifical brief. In the opinion of the religious, however, it was necessary to absolutely expel all nationalism from the government of the Custody; it was necessary to commit every effort to expel every nationalist contamination from its organization. However, faced with such convictions and theories on the institution of the Custody, some questions arise: was this plan accomplishable? was it conformed to reality? did it not smack perhaps of excessive innovation? could the Custody carry out its traditional role by completely withdrawing from the games of national rivalry?

In order to accept promotion to the episcopacy, Carcaterra, made it a condition that he should be consecrated in Jerusalem, a celebrative gesture that would have enabled ratification of his work as something welcomed by the Apostolic See. In this way, the religious always argued, the new Custos would have been able to take up his work, beginning from the interpretation that he intended to give it in article 6. The congregation of Propaganda remained unsettled before such resistance. On 1st October 1913, finally, Carcaterra decided to offer his felicitation to the new Custos, Fr Cimino, thereby relieving the diffused state of tension.[176]

---

[175] *Diario del governo del rev.mo p. Onorato Carcaterra*, 25-26.

[176] AA.EE.SS., *Spagna* 1912-1914, pos. 1065, fasc. 428: *Verbale dell'ingresso in procura di p. Cimino, custode in Terra santa*, 13 January 1915.

However it was only in March that Cimino was allowed to leave for the Holy Land, because during that time the relationship between the Apostolic See and Spain remained difficult, wherefore the Pontifical dicastery was not easily able to define the terms of his mandate.

In the meantime, Benedict XV crossed the Pontifical threshold. With Card, Gasparri, the new Secretary of State, called to occupy the place of the Spanish Merry delVal, Spain found herself deprived of a valued ally. On 2 November, the Secretary of State communicated with Cimino to make known the nomination of the 'Discretorium' [the Custos' council], provoking immediate reaction from the Spanish consul. The outgoing attorney, on the other hand, received orders from his national government not to consign to the newly assigned attorney the attorney's office or the objects belonging to the Charitable Institution. On 15 December Spanish seals were placed on the attorney's office, while various Spanish religious abandoned their own places, enclosing themselves in the convent of Jaffa. Promptly informed of the facts by the new Custos, the Apostolic See responded without delay. On he 12 of January, Fr Cimino was telegraphed from Rome with the order to break the seals and to enter the office of the attorney, in the presence of the patriarch, the Italian Consul and the new attorney.[177] A reconciliation with the Spanish government came about only in the spring of 1915. The claims of privileges when put forward in the future, were never again to cause quarrels as bitter as those related above, which were also influenced by the war situation and the closing of many religious houses since March 1915.[178]

The other controversy between the Custody and Spain broke out after this liberation, when religious were permitted to arrogate to themselves immovable property, which first was registered in the name of singular religious, considered as physical persons. What happened was the transferring of ownership of 26 houses in Jaffa, paid for, as a Spanish religious warned, with money administered by the Spanish government.[179] The Franciscans provided the British Mandatory administration with a list of their properties, including 26 houses mentioned above, but the Spanish Consul complained and claimed the ownership of those houses

[177] AGOFM, *Terra Santa* (letter-book SJ 145), 213: *Cimino, ministro generale, a Nicolini, delegato custodiale*, 5 June 1915.

[178] The events in question have been the object of deeper examination on the part of A Giovannellli (*La Santa Sede e la Palestina*, 48-63) and D Fabrizio (*Identità nazionale e identità religiose*, 264-294).

[179] *Ibid.*

for his country. Italy and France were also involved in the controversy. The Custody suggested forwarding a claim to all the Catholic states concerning property belonging to a corporation of international character. In this case, as previously, the Franciscans held themselves victims of the temporising of the Apostolic See, who, aiming to carve out a space in the international scene, had no intention of finding themselves at risk of becoming enemies of Spain, before a certain understanding was re-established with France and Great Britain.

THE EREMITICAL TRADITION IN THE MARONITE CHURCH: A CONTEMPORARY REVIVAL

Guita G Hourani and Antoine B Habchi

It is not easy to write about the life of people who have chosen silence, and to mention them when they do not want to leave their names to posterity, having decided to remain unknown, erased from people's memories. To meet the Maronite hermits requires a long procedure; informing the Secretariat of the Lebanese Maronite Order (OLM), receiving permission from the Superior of the monastery to which the hermitage belongs, and getting the necessary consent of the hermit himself who has chosen silence in order not to disrupt his quest for humility.[1]

In this article we intend to look at the eremitical experience as lived within the Maronite Church. There are four hermits in the contemporary Maronite Church, three monks and one nun. There is a programme to introduce lay people to the eremitical tradition of the Maronite Church through the holding of 'Eremitical Days' organized and led by the Antonine Sisters. Finally, a group of Latin-rite American monks has been attracted to the eremitical spirituality of St Sharbel, who had himself lived this experience in Annaya.[2]

---

1 See our previous statement on the subject: 'The Maronite Eremetical Tradition', *The Heythrop Journal,* Vol. 45, no.4, 2004, 451-465.

2 On the 8th of May 1828 in a village in the mountain of Bekaa' Kafra, Charbel was born in a poor Maronite family. As early as his childhood, his life revealed a call to 'bear fruit like a noble Cedar of Lebanon.' Charbel 'grew and became strong; he was full of wisdom, and God's blessings were upon him'. At the age of 23 he entered the Monastery of Our Lady of Mayfouk (in Northern Byblos), where he became a novice. After two years of novitiate, he was sent in 1853 to the Monastery of St Maron, where he took his monastic vows of poverty, chastity and obedience. Charbel was then transferred to the Monastery of Kfifan, where he studied philosophy and theology. His ordination took place in 1859, after which he was sent again to the Monastery of St Maron. During his 19 years in this monastery, Charbel carried on his sacerdotal ministry and his monastic duties in an edifying manner. He consecrated himself totally to Christ with an entirely devoted heart to live in silence before the Infinite. In 1875, Charbel was authorized to become a hermit at the hermitage of Ss Peter and Paul next to the monastery. His 23 years of

Reflection on eremitical spirituality in the Maronite Church turns out to be a very delicate and difficult issue especially in the absence of written texts and other information which might facilitate the study of this school of spirituality rooted in history and revealed through the actual experience of the Maronite Church.Yet the monastic and eremitical life is at the origins of the Maronite Church in the person of its patron St Maron (Maroun)[3] who was 'an anchorite saint ... living in the 4th and 5th centuries on a mountain situated, in all probability, in the region of Apamea in Syria Seconda.'[4]

---

solitary life were spent in a spirit of total abandonment of the self to God; the Eucharist became then, the center of his life and of his spirituality. Despite the fact that this hermit did not have a place in the world, the people had a big place in his heart. Through payer and penitence, he offered himself as a sacrifice so that the people would open their hearts to God. On the 16th of December in 1898 while he was reciting the liturgical prayer 'Father of Truth', Charbel had a heart attack and passed away on Christmas Eve. Through faith, this hermit received the word of God and through love he continued the mystery of Incarnation. The night of his burial, his Superior wrote: 'Because of what he will do after his death, it is needless to talk about his way of life.' Several months after his death, a strong light was seen surrounding his tomb. The abbots opened the tomb to find his body still intact. Since that day a liquid similar to blood flows from his body. The experts and the doctors were incapable of explaining medically the reasons for the incorruptibility and the flexibility of his body. In the years 1950 and 1952, his tomb was again opened and his body looked as if it were alive. The spirit of Charbel still dwells in the minds of many people. His miracles include numerous healings of the body and the spirit. Thomas Merton, The American hermit, writes in his journal: 'Charbel lived as a hermit in Lebanon. He was a Maronite. He was dead. Everybody forgot him. Fifty years after his death, his body was still intact and in a short period he performed more than 600 miracles. He is my new companion. My life has witnessed a new turning point. It seems to me that I was asleep for 9 years... and before that I was dead.' Upon the closing of the Second Vatican Council on the 5th of December in 1965, Charbel was beatified by Pope Paul VI, who said: 'a Hermit ... from the Lebanese Mountain is declared among the blessed ... a new eminent member of the monastic sanctity enriches, through his example and his intercession the whole Christian people ... May he help us understand, in a world greatly fascinated by wealth and riches, the essential value of poverty, penitence and asceticism in order to free the soul when it is elevated to God ...' On the 9th of October in 1977, during the world Synod for the bishops, Pope Paul VI canonized Blessed Charbel who then became St Charbel. M Hayek, *Father Charbel or the Path of Silence*, Paris, 1956; P Daher, *Charbel: A Man Crazy about God*, 2nd edition, Lebanon, 1993; C Benedict, *Saint Charbel: Mystic of the East*, 3rd edition, USA, 1997; and M C Vincent, *Saint Charbel*, USA, 1992.

3 To have an idea about the history of the Maronite Church, see P Dib, *History of the Maronite Church*, Beirut, 1962. On the life of St Maron, see Theodoret of Cyrrhus, *A History of the Monks of Syria*, translated by R M Price, Kalamazoo, 1985.

4 A Festugière, *Christian and Pagan Antioch, Libanius, Chrysostom and the Monks of Syria*, Library of the French Schools of Athens and Rome, fasc. 194, Paris, 1959, 229.

St Maron led 'a life of penitence and prayer in the open air near a temple for the pagans which he converted to a Church.'[5] This way of life attracted a group of people to become his disciples. Gathered around him, they formed the nucleus that would become the Maronite Church, for their life centred on the monastery dedicated to the memory of their master, namely the Monastery of St Maron situated in the vicinity of Apamea.[6] The fact that it had these origins has 'conditioned and guided the life of the Maronite community. A unique fact in Christian history is that a monastic community has become the principal organizer of a Church, giving birth to a patriarchate which has been granted by tradition the prestigious title of Antioch.'[7] This double historic reality, that of St Maron and that of the monastic grouping of his disciples, determines the eremitical spirituality of the Maronite Church. This spirituality and way of life characterizes the Maronite Church and its believers who appreciate the ascetic life of its founders.

There can be no understanding of the eremitical life in the contemporary Maronite Church without a precise analysis of its origins and of its historical evolution. These reveal a subtle mixture of tradition and adaptation. The eremitical life in the Maronite Church is comparable to a cell in the human body: it constitutes all the essence of its life, of its origins, and it reflects its identity. As identity evolves in history, so the eremitical life nowadays represents not only the contemporary identity of the Maronite Church but also the consequences of the transformations experienced over time: confusion and ambivalence. In other words, the analysis of the evolution of the eremitical life rightly takes into consideration the itinerary of a Church and of a people, the Maronites.

Maronite spirituality

The Maronite Church belongs to the family of Antiochian Syriac Churches and has forged its own spirituality within Syriac spirituality.[8] The spirituality of these Syriac Churches is rooted on the one hand in waiting

---

[5] P Dib, 'Maronite', *Dictionary of Catholic Theology (DTC)*, t. X, 1928, 1.

[6] G Tchalenko, *Ancient Villages of Northern Syria*, Archaeological and Historical Library of the Beirut French Institute of Archaeology, t.1, Paris, 1958, 229.

[7] I Dalmais, 'The Antiochian Hermitage of the Maronite Church', *Melto* 3, 1967, 61.

[8] A Atiya, *A History of Eastern Christianity*, New York, 1980; and D Attwater, *The Christian Churches of the East*, London, 1961.

for the return of Christ, described by Michel Hayek as a 'purgatorial state,'[9] and on the other hand in that meditation on the Scriptures which is the basis for all their liturgical traditions.

This spirituality is based on pneumatic mysticism, which is developed in three stages: corporal, psychological and pneumatic.[10] Maronite spirituality, in spite of being affiliated with, and heir, to Syriac spirituality, has distinguished itself from the latter with certain traits acquired throughout its own history. These specific traits are the memory relative to its Patron and his disciples, its faithfulness to its monastic character, and attachment to the land of the birth of Christianity. Maronite spirituality has an ecumenical character toward other Christians. It also has a spiritual universalism that stemmed from its belonging to the universal Catholic Church and from the spread of its own faithful in the world through emigration. The Maronite Church is also unique among Eastern Christianity in not having an 'Orthodox' branch—all Maronites are in union with Rome. Its universalism has also been manifested through its promotion of conviviality in multi-ethnic and religious communities and its favouring a dialogue with the Muslim world.

The cross is at the center of Maronite spirituality. It 'is fused with the person of Jesus Christ who died and who rose from death. It is just like Him, powerful, victorious, glorious, a source of light, provider of life and source of immortality.'[11] This vision of the crucified Christ comes as a great consolation to Maronites because it allows them to understand and internalize the persecutions which they endured and which they consider as sufferings joined to those of Jesus on the Cross. But this is not everything, since the Maronites, in joining their sufferings to those of Jesus on the Cross, find in this all their hope for victory and glory. It is the Cross itself that allows them to give a meaning to their suffering, transforming their weakness into strength, their persecution into victory and their death into Resurrection.

The attachment of Maronites to Lebanon shows their attachment to the sacred character of the land. Settling in North Lebanon has become a vocation. Making a refuge out of these mountains and settling in the deep

---

[9] M Hayek, 'Maronite (Church)', *A Dictionary of Spirituality*, t.X, 1978, 631-44.

[10] I Dalmais and A Guillaumont, 'Syriac (Spirituality): The early centuries', *A Dictionary of Spirituality (DS)*, XIV, Paris, 1990, 1440.

[11] G Sacre, 'The service of the Feast of the Cross in the Maronite Liturgy', *Parole de l'Orient* 12, 1984/5, 232.

and steep-walled Valley of Qadisha, the Maronites were able to conserve 'what they received and make it productive. Here lies their originality; here could be the testimony which they are to give in the ecumenical chorus.'[12]

Lebanon has the character of a promised land which offers nothing to the Maronites but 'summits, deserts and wild valleys', a country which is 'incessantly contested and periodically abandoned for the sake of a new exodus. Would it be able, as St Maron did when he transformed a pagan temple to a sanctuary in a mountain near Cyr (Cyrrhus), to transform the prominent places in Lebanon of Phoenician mythology into oratories and hermitages?'[13] The close, sacred relationship, formed between the Maronites and the land of Lebanon, transformed the land of refuge into a Patriarchal See of the Catholic Church. From Since then, the patriarch himself has become the symbol of their unity. Michel Hayek noted that 'the Maronite worked, constructed and planted as he celebrated a liturgy: all this economic life had a sacramental taste, a liturgical flavour: the vine and the wheat for the wine and the bread of the Eucharist, the olive tree for refining the holy oils, the mulberry tree for weaving altar cloth and wedding gowns. Everything is a sign of the great beyond.'[14]

The eremitical tradition in the Maronite Church

The Syriac eremitical tradition is the work of individuals who chose to live in solitude and not the result or outcome of cenobitic life. On the contrary, the numerous disciples eager for this life in solitude were the ones who very early on urged their masters to organize a cenobitic structure.[15] The eremitical tradition in the Maronite Church that began with the Syriac Fathers took a particular form with St Maron, who himself decided to live in solitude.[16] This way of life was, however, subject to changes throughout history, particularly with the Muslim conquests, and also as a consequence of monastic reform at the end of the 17th century.

[12] Dalmais, 'The Antiochian Heritage', 65-6.

[13] Hayek, 'Maronite (Church)', 639.

[14] M Hayek, 'L'Eglise Maronite et la Terre', *Deuxième Congrès Maronite Mondial*, New York, October 1980, n p.

[15] Sh Abou Zayd, *Ihidayutha: A Study of the Life of Singleness in the Syrian Orient: From Ignatius of Antioch to Chalcedon 451 A.D.*, Oxford, 1993, 303.

[16] Theodore of Cyrrhus, *A History of the Monks of Syria*, trans. R M Price, Michigan, 1985, 117-9.

Several disciples led the same life as that of St Maron and came to be called 'Beit-Maroun',[17] or the community of Maroun. From the beginning several different terms were used for hermits in the Maronite tradition. First of all, in the times of Aphrahat and St Ephrem, the term 'i h i d o y ô', which means the single ascetic and also the hermit isolated from the people, was employed. Other Syriac terms are used to indicate 'solitaries' such as 'n ϕ k r î t î' or anchorites, 'modebroyé' or hermits, 'b î l Λ' or weepers.[18] There is also 'h b î s Λ', or recluse, from the verb 'h b a s' which means 'to imprison', 'to retreat', or 'to withdraw to a solitary place'. The substantive is 'h î b s ô' and describes the solitary who withdraws to, and imprisons himself in, a hermitage or in an isolated place in the desert for the love of God, ' E s t ϕ n ô y ô' or Stylite, 'ô n w ô y ô' or ascetic.[19] To indicate the solitary or solitaries who lived in the heart of the Maronite Church, the Maronite tradition has kept the term 'h b î s Λ', which corresponds to the term 'hermit'. This term applied to Maronite hermits should not be taken in the strict sense of recluse. By 'h î b s ô', 'we do not mean to say the recluse who avoids people but the hermit who leads a way of life which allows him to carry on a mission.'[20] The choice of this term reflects the socio-political condition of the Maronites: persecuted by their co-religionists and by the new conquerors, they withdrew to Lebanon and especially to the Valley of Qadisha. This feeling of uncertainty, which threatens faith, calls upon the sacrificial martyr to protect the faith of the community. Thus, the hermit offers himself as a sacrifice on the Lord's altar to save the community.

The Church from its beginnings has passed from the stage of 'the red martyr' to the stage of 'the white martyr'; the Maronite hermit retreated to the Valley of Qadisha holding concurrently both attributes. He is the red martyr because of his seclusion imposed by the conqueror. However, defending the faith of all the community leads him equally to be a martyr; the will to become a hermit makes of him in this case a white martyr.

Moreover, the hermit becomes for Maronites the anchoring point for the relationship between God and his people. He helps to maintain

---

[17] B Naaman, *La Maronité Théologie Et Vie : Des Montagnes de Cyr aux Plaines de l'Apamène*, Kaslik, 1971.

[18] B Sfeir, *Les Ermites dans l'Eglise Maronite*, Kaslik, Lebanon, 1986, 112-3.

[19] Sfeir, *Les Ermites*, 114.

[20] Sfeir, *Les Ermites*, 114.

two kinds of relationships in his spiritual life; a vertical relationship, which, makes him, as a white martyr, lead his community to God through his prayer, and a horizontal relationship, because he is sacrificing himself for the sake of his community. In this sense, the Maronite hermit emulates Christ and transforms the Eucharist into daily living: He is sacrificing himself on the Cross to save his community, and to redeem it by taking its sins upon himself. He constitutes himself as a meeting point between God and his people.

What strengthens even more the role of the hermit is his continuous presence throughout Maronite history. Douwaihi points out in his annals the existence of several hermits: Peter the Hermit in 1228,[21] John of Qnat[22] and several others located in the hermitages of the Valley of Qadisha in modern times such as Gabriel of Ehden,[23] Yunan al Matriti, Bishop Youssof of Jaj,[24] Malka al Bukfani,[25] the hermit Barakat,[26] and Bishop Sarkis ar-Rizzi.[27] The presence of these hermits in the Qadisha was not limited to autochthonous hermits. There has been also the almost continuous presence of foreign hermits from Ethiopia, Jerusalem, Egypt and Europe.

There is, too, a link between the hermitage and ecclesiastical authority in the Maronite Church. For centuries monks were in charge. 'The first patriarchs and bishops were chosen from the Monastery of Beth Maroun … The patriarch and his bishops were committed to monastic obligations and without taking monastic vows, they practiced chastity, poverty, obedience and severe asceticism and they cultivated the land.'[28]

Many bishops and patriarchs have indeed led the eremitical life and several of them were called out of their hermitages to serve and guide their people of whom we can name Mikhaël ar-Rizzi (1567-1581), Sarkis ar-Rizzi (1581-1596) and Yussof ar-Rizzi (1596-1608).[29] Furthermore, bishops led the austere life of hermits without dwelling in hermitages. Prior to the synod of Mount-Lebanon in 1736, the patriarch abstained from

---

21 Vat. Syr. 215, fol. 24r.
22 Vat. Syr. 215, fol. 53r.
23 Vat. Syr. 215, fol. 102v.
24 Vat. Syr. 215, fol. 111r.
25 Vat. Syr. 215, fol. 114r.
26 Vat. Syr. 215, fol. 128v.
27 Vat. Syr. 215, fol. 141v.
28 Hayek, 'Maronite (Church)', 639.
29 Mahfouz, 'La vie érémitique dans l'église maronite', *Melto* 2, 1966, 172-3 ; Sfeir, *Les Ermites*, 144-71.

eating meat, wore a monastic habit and led an austere life. This highlights the function of responsibility and leadership fulfilled by the hermits, a fundamental reference point for the community. Even today, the austere way of life, the monastic habit and the cowl remind the Maronite religious authorities, the bishops and patriarchs, of their true identity.

This austere way of life was not the preserve of the ecclesiastical hierarchy only; it was also practiced by the believers, the common Maronite people: 'Until the reorganization of the religious life in 1700, being a monk meant nothing more than a radical commitment to the institution which was the community itself. The people lived according to the liturgical calendar and shared the monastic austerity. They fasted a great deal, abstained from many things and recited daily hymns and prayers even at midnight.'[30] Nor was the eremitical life exclusively reserved for monks and hermits. All Maronite people led a daily eremitical life in work, prayer and obedience to their Church and devotion to their spiritual authorities. This is why the Maronite people were known to be a monastic people.[31] It was around the monasteries that the Maronite community was formed and reformed. Its diffusion followed the path of the monastic foundations; working the land and praying as their main activities like those of the monks.

Everything took place 'as if this community was a vast abbey with affiliates everywhere headed by an abbot, who was the patriarch, surrounded by bishops who were his assistants, while the people formed a kind of third order. All were committed to the same evangelic principles with certain attenuations for the laity and an extreme rigour for the hermits.'[32] This mentality and this popular aspect date back to the early beginnings of monastic tradition, to the 'Banat' and 'Banay Quomo' (Sons and Daughters of the Covenant), who were members of 'a secular ascetic movement within the Syriac Church formed by young men and women who devoted their virginity and their sexual continence to God as an expression of their struggle against sin.'[33]

---

30 Hayek, 'Maronite (Church)', 639.

31 Interview with the former Superior General of the Antonine Order, Sister Clémence Helou, Monastery of Our Lady of Deliverance, 'Ain 'Alaq, 18 August, 2003.

32 Hayek, 'Maronite (Church)', 639.

33 Abou Zayd, Ihidayutha, 101; and J-M, Fiey 'Cénobitisme féminin ancien dans les élises syrienne orientale et occidentale', *L'Orient Syrien* 10, 1965, 281-306.

Maronite hermits in today's Church

A continuous presence of hermits in the Maronite Church maintains this characteristic tradition even now. However, the second half of the twentieth century saw a decline in the numbers of hermits and hence an absence of masters and disciples of the eremitical tradition. This has threatened the eremitical tradition itself. There has nonetheless been a continuation of the eremitical life in the Maronite Church, particularly in Lebanon. Yaakoub Bou Maroun, a monk of the Lebanese Maronite Order, became a hermit in Tamiche on 26 November 1926. Antoun Tarabay, a monk from the Mariamite Order also entered the eremitical life in 1949 in the hermitage of St Elisha in the sacred Qadisha Valley, that is to say before the death of the hermit Bou Maroun on 17 February 1958.[34]

Father Tarabay remained in his hermitage until 1983. Struck with hemiplegia, which prevented him from staying there, he was transferred to Zouk Mosbeh, where he died in 1998.[35] A year before Father Tarabay left his hermitage, Antonios Chayna, a monk of the Lebanese Maronite Order, was authorized to start living in the hermitage of St Boula[36] in the Valley of Qadisha. This period of stagnation was followed by a certain renaissance; there are now four hermits who live in different hermitages in Lebanon, in the Qadisha, in Tamiche and in Ayto. In the Valley of Qadisha there are four large monasteries to which are joined hermitages: the Monastery of Qannoubîn, for a long time a patriarchal residence, the Monastery of St Anthony of Kozhaya, the Monastery of Our Lady of Hawqa and the Monastery of St Elisha.

---

34 L Dagher, *Kashf Al-Khafa'*, 'An Mahabis Lubnan Wa Al-Hubasa' ('Aperçu historique sur la vie des ermites et les ermitages au Liban'), Beyrouth, 1923, deuxième édition, 1988, 144-6.

35 B Sfeir et G Hourani , 'The Maronite Hermits: From the fourth to the twentieth Century', *Journal of Maronite Studies (JMS)*, [http://www.mari.org/JMS/October99/ The_Maronite_Hermits.htm], vol. 3,no. 4 (October 1999). Retrieved July 30 2003.

36 Dagher, *Kashf Al-Khafa'*, 65-69. Amba or St Boula known as the anchorite Paul of Thebes. He was an Egyptian who around 250 AD withdrew to the desert because of the persecution of the Emperor. He led in the desert a life of prayer and asceticism and died in 343 AD. His feast day in the Maronite Church is on the 5th of February. B Dagher, *Al-Sinksbr Al-Mbrûn bi-Hasab Al-Kanisa Al-Intakiyya Al-Mbrûniyya* ('The Synaxarion according to the Rite of the Maronite Antiochian Church'), Lebanon, 1962, 11.

Antonios Chayna

Father Antonios Chayna[37] was born in 1920 in a village called Bqarqacha in Northern Lebanon. On 15 August 1935, he started his monastic life in the Lebanese Maronite Order in Kfifan,[38] at that time the monastery for novices in the Order. He was ordained priest on 16 July 1952 in Strasbourg in France at the age of 32, that is to say, seventeen years after he started his monastic life. Apart from the spiritual path, he undertook a long period of study. He studied philosophy and theology in a Jesuit university. He later pursued his studies in general theology in Strasbourg and in moral theology in the Gregoriana in Rome. He completed his studies and obtained a doctorate in moral theology. He taught moral theology at the Holy Spirit University in Kaslik, Lebanon, from 1957 to the time when he started his hermitage in 1982. He was successful both as an administrator and as a spiritual guide. He was master of novices in his Order from 1958 until 1968, then General Assistant of the Order from 1968 until 1974.

Between 1974 and 1977, he occupied several positions; at the same time he was a professor at the Holy Spirit University in Kaslik, taught courses at the seminary of Karm Saddé and was in charge of the general management of Caritas in Lebanon. Between 1977 and 1982, he was superior of the Monastery of St Anthony Kozhaya, the motherhouse of the Order, a monastery that has always been central to several hermitages in the Sacred Valley of Qadisha. On the feast of Pentecost 1982, Father Chayna decided to give up all responsibilities and become a hermit at St Boula's, a hermitage under the tutelage of the Monastery of St Anthony Kozhaya at an altitude of 1110 meters. The hermitage had been established in 1716 by Father Abdallah Car'ali on the western side of the Monastery of St Anthony Kozhaya to cater for the needs of the monks who sought the life of solitude and silence. Since its establishment hermits have resided there almost continuously.[39]

It should be noted that with the reform of the Lebanese Maronite Order on 10 November 1965, during Father Chayna's time as novice

---

[37] The information about the hermit Chayna was given to us by the superior of the Monastery of St Anthony of Kozhaya, Reverend Father Youssef Tannous.

[38] A village in Northern Lebanon where the Monastery of Ss Justin and Cyprian is located as well as the tomb of St Ni'matallah Kassab al Hardini.

[39] A Mokbel, *Dayr Mar Antûnyûs Kuzihayya* ('The Monastery of Saint Anthony Kozhaya'), 2000, Lebanon, 49-53.

master, monastic life changed from a solitary one to cenobitic, while respecting the spirit of the eremitical tradition.

Sister Mary-Jesus Abboud

Sister Mary-Jesus was born in Tlayl (Akkar) in 1941 and baptized on 11 January 1942 in her village. On 13 April 1968 she entered the Monastery of St Simon The Stylite in Ayto under the guidance of Father Joseph Farah. She took her first vows on 23 July at the same monastery. On 6 October 1974, she took her perpetual vows at the Monastery of St Joseph in Jrabta. She returned to the Monastery of St Simeon The Stylite in Ayto in 1975. From that date, she continuously expressed to her superiors her desire to live as a hermit. On 25 July 1993 she started her eremitic life at the hermitage of her convent.[40]

The Monastery of St Simeon The Stylite is in the district of Zghorta in North Lebanon located at an altitude of 950 meters. According to tradition, the convent was built in the sixth century on the ruins of a Roman temple, during the period of the expansion of Christianity in Lebanon. In the tenth century the convent sheltered Maronite monks who followed the Rule of St Anthony the Great. Between the sixteenth and eighteenth centuries the convent went through a period of decline. At the end of the first half of the nineteenth century it underwent a monastic renewal under the direction of Bishop Paul Moussa, who consecrated it to the nuns. The nuns observed the Rule of the Aleppine Order approved by the Holy See in 1732. From 1863 the convent was put under the direction of the Lebanese Maronite Order (or the Baladite Order), which separated from the Aleppine Order. It is a small hermitage attached to this convent that shelters Sister Mary Jesus Abboud.

On 7 August 1984 the Lebanese Maronite Order of nuns was instituted and took charge of the convent.[41] Both oriental and occidental eremitical currents inspire the spirituality of the nuns. In the cloister, the nuns lead a life of prayer, contemplation and work. They pray four times

---

[40] The information about the hermit Mary-Jesus was given to us by Reverend Father Elie Hanna, Rector of the Holy Spirit University, in Chekka on the 20 September, 2003. He is currently writing the history of the Monastery of St Simeon The Stylites in Ayto.

[41] Interview with Reverend Father Elie Hanna.

a day and attend Mass daily. They recite the offices and rosary and read spiritual books.[42]

The Lebanese Maronite Order decided to change the statutes of the nuns, adding the function of missionaries to their contemplative vocation. They establish retirement homes for old people with no income and no family.

Hermit Yuhanna Khawand

Born on 10 May 1936 in Saydoun, David Khawand was baptized on 7 June the same year. He went to the state primary school of Saydoun, then to the Monastery of Our Lady of Victory in Ghosta. He did his secondary studies at the scholasticate of the Lebanese Maronite Order in Kaslik, after entering the seminary of the Order on 13 October 1947 under the guidance of Father Paul Hatem. On 22 July 1951 he became a novice in the monastery in Ghosta under the direction of Father Simon Awad. He took his first vows on 29 June 1953 and his perpetual vows on 17 January 1958. He was ordained priest in Rome on 4 December 1964. Father Yuhanna Khawand was engaged in university teaching from 1970 until he entered the hermitage of Tamiche. He taught general introduction to the Bible and exegesis of the New Testament as well as Greek, Hebrew and Syriac. He made a major contribution to the process of liturgical reform in the contemporary Maronite Church, and participated in the Arabic translation of the Greek New Testament, edited in 1992 by the Pontifical Faculty of the Holy Spirit University in Kaslik.

Before he entered the hermitage in Tamiche, he several times visited the Monastery of St Anthony Kozhaya, where he observed the rule of solitude, and similarly visited the hermit Father Chayna to benefit from his personal experience. His aspiration to the eremitical life is long-standing; he says that he was present during the funeral of the hermit Yaakoub Bou Maroun in 1958 and held a candle that he blew out and hid in his pocket after the burial. Bou Maroun was the last hermit from the Lebanese Maronite Order before Chayna started life in his hermitage in 1982. The disappearance of hermits within the Lebanese Maronite Order saddened Father Khawand. The candle itself was lost, but when he started

[42] Interview with Reverend Father Elie Hanna.

his hermitical life in 1998 he felt that the candle was lit again. What had long kept him from taking this step towards eremitical life was a keen sense of responsibility, especially towards his Order. Nevertheless, he finally started life in his hermitage in Tamiche on 17 January 1998.[43]

The Monastery of Our Lady of Tamiche is situated in the Metn district. It was built in 1673 by the bishop of Aleppo, Gabriel el Blouzani, to serve as the Episcopal Seat for the diocese of Aleppo. In 1704, Bishop Gabriel was appointed patriarch and his nephew Mikhael el Blouzani was ordained bishop and his successor in Aleppo. Bishop Mikhael el Blouzani stayed in the Monastery of Our Lady of Tamiche until 1724, when he resigned because of old age. He decided to transfer the property of the monastery to the monks of the Lebanese Maronite Order in 1727.[44] In 1841, the Egyptian army burned down the monastery and its two hermitages.[45] In 1926 the abbot of the Monastery of Tamiche, Father Youssef Saadé el Ghostawi, built a new hermitage fifteen minutes away on foot from the monastery in a region called Ain Kattine at an altitude of 350 meters. The first hermit who lived in it was Father Jacques Abi Maroun. Hermit Yuhanna Khawand currently occupies this hermitage.[46]

Dario Escobar Montanya Sanchez

Born on July 7 1934 in La Estrella-Colombia, a village adjoining Medellín, Colombia in South America, the third of the seven sons of Horacio and Lucila Escobar. He entered the novitiate of the Congregation of Jesus and Mary on 8 February1955 in Bogotá, the capital of Colombia. There between 1956 and 1963 he pursued university studies in theology, philosophy and pedagogy. He was ordained priest and in 1974 went to the United States to finish his studies, specializing in psychology. He practiced this profession until 1990. His professional experience was

---

[43] The information about hermit Khawand was given to us by the Pontifical Faculty of the Holy Spirit University in Kaslik, by the secretariat of the Maronite Lebanese Order and by Reverend Father Joseph Azzi, professor at the Pontifical Faculty of Theology of the Holy Spirit University in Kaslik.

[44] L Bleibel, *Tarikh Al-Rahbaniyya Al-Lubnaniyya Al-Maruniyya* ('History of the Maronite Lebanese Order'), t.I, Egypt, 1924, 133–4.

[45] M Karam, *Kisat Al-Mulkiyya fi Al-Rahbaniyya Al-Lubnaniyya Al-Maruniyya*, Beirut, 1972, 221.

[46] Information provided by the Monastery of Tamiche.

centered especially on teaching but also on therapy and spiritual guidance to relationships in crisis. Between 1974 and 1988 he taught theology in different seminaries and in the diocesan scholasticate of the Congregation in Colombia, Venezuela and Spain. He wished to become a hermit in the United States but the bishop of the region did not approve his wish. However, he met Father Boutros Tayyah (later the Maronite Bishop of Mexico). Father Tayyah informed him about the eremitical life in Lebanon and encouraged him to find his vocation there.

In 1990, he moved to Lebanon to become a monk in the Lebanese Maronite Order. However, being a Latin priest, he had to receive a Pontifical authorization to adhere to an Order of an Oriental rite. He stayed at the Monastery of St Anthony Kozhaya from 25 March 1990 until 28 November 1992, waiting for the permission from Rome to enter the novitiate. On 28 November 1992 he went to the Monastery of Ss Justine and Cyprian in Kfifan, where he did his novitiate from 14 December 1992 until 14 December 1993. On 17 January 1997, he took his perpetual vows at the Monastery of Our Lady at Tamiche. On 4 January 1999 he moved to Annaya, staying there until 28 July 1999, and then moving to the Monastery of Jennine, in North Lebanon, where he stayed there for almost a year. On 9 July 2000 he returned to the Monastery of St Anthony Kozhaya waiting for the authorization to begin his life as a hermit. He entered the hermitage of Our Lady of Hawqa,[47] August 15 2000.[48] This hermitage is at an altitude of 1200 m, an hour by foot from the Monastery of St Anthony Kozhaya, to which it belongs. Foreign visitors considered it as 'the pearl of the Valley.'[49]

Our Lady of Hawqa is a grotto where a monastery was built in the seventeenth century. According to Douwayhi, following the Turcoman conquests, the Christians sought refuge in the grottos of the Valley. The cavern of Hawqa, which is adjacent to the monastery, would have remained inaccessible to the Turcomans had they not been assisted by a Maronite traitor from the region. By diverting the flow of the stream of St Simeon, he caused a flood in the grotto, and Maronites hiding there perished. When

---

47 *Hawqa* is a Syriac word which means levels, stairs. Sfeir, The Hermits, 51.

48 The information about hermit Escobar was given to us by the superior of the Monastery of St Anthony Kozhaya, Reverend Father Youssef Tannous.

49 'La'iha bi Al-Istikshafat Wa Al-Iktishafat Allati Kamat Biha Al-Djam'iyya Al-Lubnbniyya L'il Abhath Al-Djawfiyya Fî Mintataqat Wadî Kadîsha' ('List of the sites explored and discovered by the Group of Studies and Subterranean Research of Lebanon in the Valley of Qadisha'), *Subterranean Lebanon*, V, March 1998 , note 12 , 314.

the Turcomans later withdrew, the traitor went to the grotto, spending his life there in severe penitence to save his soul. After his death, the inhabitants cut the rock to form a path to the grotto and called the grotto Our Lady of Hawqa.[50] In 1624, thanks to the protection of Emir Fakhreddine, Patriarch Yuhanna Makhlouf transformed the grotto into a seminary,[51] however the seminary closed in 1633 due to the severity of its location and was reoccupied only with the arrival of Father Dario Escobar.[52]

The lay movement, 'eremitical days' in Qannoubîn

The contemporary Maronite Church has initiated a unique experience. Maronites, lay and religious, are encouraged to experience the eremitical life.[53] The idea came about through the influence St Sharbel has on contemporary spirituality. The Antonine Sisters invited young men and women of twenty years old and above to live an eremitical experience of twenty-four hours in a hermitage within the Valley of Qadisha. Upon arrival at the monastery each participant was informed about the modes of the eremitical life and the history of the valley and about the programme itself. Two or more people more, of the same sex were grouped in each hermitage. The twenty-four hours had to be spent in prayer and solitary contemplation. Participants took with them only the provisions of the hermit as provided by the Sisters, including their lunch of bread and water. They slept on the floor. All participants including the nuns followed the programme. Four times a day—eight in the morning, noon, six in the evening and midnight—were consecrated to prayer, incense offering, intercession and supplication. At the end of these eremitical hours, each participant was invited to share his/her experience with the others, filling in a questionnaire composed of six themes: Whom do you seek during this day in which you are isolated from people and work? How did you spend the hours as a hermit? Have you contemplated the beauty and the

[50] Vat Syr. 215, fol. 66r.

[51] Vat Syr. 215, fol. 66r.

[52] Dib, *History of the Church*, 145. However, Pope Urban VIII granted funds for the construction of the Maronite college in Rome which received the best Maronite students.

[53] His Beatitude Patriarch Mar Nasrallah Sfeir requested that the Antonine Sisters be present in the Monastery of Our Lady of Qannoubîn. This monastery was the patriarchal residence between 1450 and 1823 but it was abandoned after the patriarchal residence was moved to Diman and then to Bkerke. Since then the sisters are present there every year between May and October.

silence of nature? Did this setting help you to pray? After having lived the eremitical experience can you show us the way of salvation? Would you live this experience again? This entire programme took place under the supervision of the Antonine Sisters, who cleaned the hermitages, planned the days and prepared the prayer book *Prayer in the Valley of Qadisha*. Each person had to bring with him/her the Bible, prayer books and a pen and a notebook in case he/she wanted to write about his/her contemplation, as well as a torch and a blanket. Participants were to eat one meal of bread and water but were also allowed to eat wild herbs from the fields surrounding the hermitage in emulation of the hermits before them.

The first programme took place during the week 9 to 16 July 2000. Upon receiving the participants, the sisters accompanied them to the chosen hermitages where they isolated themselves. They only met with the other people in the group when the church bell rang in the Sacred Valley of Qadisha announcing prayer time.

Ninety-two participants who underwent the first experiment of 'Eremitical Days' expressed their positive opinion about the program. Fifty-six were women, of whom thirty-six were single, seventeen were nuns and three were married. These formed 60.8 percent of the whole group. There were thirty-six men, of whom eleven were single, twenty were seminarians, one was a monk and four were married. At the end of the 'Eremitical Days' the Maronite Patriarch Nasrallah Boutros Sfeir celebrated Mass in the presence of the participants, who were able to testify to their experience before the assembly. In the questionnaires, all participants showed their desire to relive the eremitical days and expressed interest in having it extended for more than twenty-four hours.

In 2001, there were no plans to run the programme because of repair work carried out at the Monastery of Our Lady of Qannoubîn. But in 2002, there were sixty-six participants during the two weeks from 19 August until 8 September: fifteen percent had come for the second time. Almost all were enthusiastic about the experience and expressed their wish to repeat it. From 25 July 2003 until 31 August 2003 the programme was planned again, this time for forty-eight hours. There were one hundred and twelve participants.[54]

---

[54] The information about the 'Eremitical Days' is provided by the former Superior General of the Antonine Sisters, Sister Domenique Halabi, at the Monastery of Our Lady of Qannoubîn, on the 4 August 2003. Sister Halabi played a major role in the planning of the program and the initiation into the 'Eremitical Days'. In the year 2000 she was herself the coordinator of this program.

This movement depends on of the Maronite eremitical life within the physical and historical context of the SacredValley of Qadisha. Situated in North Lebanon; the valley stretches for sixteen kilometers from the foot of the Cedar Mountains to the village of Torza. Being narrow, it snakes its way and widens progressively to take the form of a basin, becoming then a fertile matrix. The valley became a land of refuge for the Maronites with its deep and steep dales and slopes, and with their diligence it was transformed into orchards and settlements. Once settled, their monastic grottos became their symbol. In that valley, the Maronites preserved what they were conferred with and they have made it bear fruit. There lies their originality.[55]

Maronite monks in the West

There is increasing interest in Oriental Christian spirituality in the Western Christian tradition. There are hundreds of thousands of Maronites who now live outside Lebanon. As a consequence, a greater knowledge and awareness of the Maronite tradition has rooted itself in the Catholic Church in different parts of the world. This is an important development in the spiritual currents that feed the Catholic tradition. One example of the Maronite monastic and eremitical tradition taking root is the Monastery of the Most Holy Trinity of Petersham, Massachusetts. Fascinated by Maronite spirituality and especially by the life of St Sharbel, a group of Latin-rite monks decided to associate themselves with the Maronite tradition. On 8 September 1978, they established a Catholic Oriental monastic community, that of the Maronite Monks of the Most Holy Trinity Monastery or the Maronite Monks of the Adoration. Their establishment was approved canonically by the Holy See and put under the direction of the Maronite diocese of St Maron in Brooklyn, New York.[56]

Monks of the Maronite Adoration form a contemplative community, which consecrates all its life to prayer and the Adoration of the Eucharist. It is a contemplative, enclosed community which tries to

---

[55] Dalmais, *The Antiochian Heritage*, 65-6.

[56] The Maronite Monks of Most Holy Trinity Monastery of Petersham Massachusetts, official Internet site of the monastery, [http://www.maronitemonks.org/Introduction.htm], Retrieved 29 July 2003.

harmonize and combine the two currents of religious life, coenobitical and eremitical.[57] They try to live their universal apostolate of service and prayer for the glory of God and live the spirituality of Sts Sharbel and Ni'matallah Kassab al Hardini.[58] The order has two monasteries; the mother monastery called the Most Holy Trinity and a second established in 2000 at Nova Scotia in Canada called Our Lady of Grace. Several hermitages have been built in a serene environment next to the monastery for the use of the monks.

The legislation relative to the hermits

Before the monastic reform at the end of the 17th century, there were not any rules for the organization of the hermitical life despite the fact that the term hermit or solitary was mentioned several times in the 'Nomocanon'. In practice, 'anchoritic life is considered as superior to cenobitical life.'[59] During this period the regulations about hermitical life were concerned in the conservation of tradition. This conservation of tradition was provided by empirical teaching or apprenticeship. Each hermit shared hermitical life, in the beginning, with a trained hermit, and learned himself the rules and the practices of hermitry.

This 'ordered disorder' put the rules for the organization of the hermitical movement in the second place and gave the chance for the hermit to be in the first place, while letting him find his way through means, which he deemed appropriate and able to bring him even closer to God. This excluded the existence of a school which unifies hermitical practice but offered on the other hand, a continuous richness and innovation in hermitical life. It is with the monastic reform of 1695 that a new law relative to the organization of the hermitical life is written by the monk 'Abdallah Car'ali. It is composed of 11 articles.[60]

---

[57] The Maronite Monks of Most ... [http://www.maronitemonks.org/Introduction.htm], Retrieved 29 July 2003.

[58] The Maronite Monks of Most ... [http://www.maronitemonks.org/Introduction.htm], Retrieved 29 July 2003.

[59] G Mahfoud, *The monastic organization in the Maronite Church*, Beirut, 1967,126.

[60] Bleibel, *Tārīkh Al-Rahbānīyyā*, t.I, 411-2.

'Article 1. He who wishes to lead solitary life has to be in good health and has to have spent five years in the order after the solemn profession; and his vocation (to become a hermit) has to be steadfast.

'Article 2. He shall remain subjected to the obedience of the Superior of the Monastery to which belongs the hermitage. At the hermitage, there cannot be more than three (hermits) and less than two hermits.

'Article 3. They have to keep the Holy Sacrament in the chapel of the hermitage and they have to visit it very frequently day and night.

'Article 4. They have to be assiduous in manual work in order to avoid idleness as it is the root of all evil. If they do not have any manual work to do, they have to consecrate their time to prayer and meditation.

'Article 5. They shall visit the monastery of their brothers on feast days, that is, on the feast of the Nativity, at Easter, on the feast of St Anthony and if they wish, they can have (on these days) their lunch in the common refectory with the community.

'Article 6. They have to forbid absolutely the entrance of women to the enclosure and they have to avoid seeing the laity frequently.

'Article 7. Everything which is for their use, concerning food, beverages, clothes, bed, etc… has to be imbued with a spirit of absolute poverty. They shall never use a razor to cut their hair, that is, they have to grow their hair and never cut it, such as the Lord did.

'Article 8. They have to fulfil permanently the obligation of fasting until noon; they shall eat lunch which is sent to them from the monastery; they shall never eat meat. However, they can have in the evening, a light dinner, if they want. But during the period in which they fast and abstain from things, they shall fast until sunset, in such a way that they eat only once (a day). They shall totally abstain from eating all kinds of fruits and drinking all sorts of alcoholic beverages.

'Article 9. They shall always remain silent. Should there be any need to talk, their conversation shall be brief and in a low voice.

'Article 10. They shall not sleep more than five hours; they shall spend the rest of the night in prayer and meditation. They shall recite the divine office in the big book of hymns (11).

'Article 11. They shall not leave the hermitage unless authorized by the superior (of the monastery) (12)'

These rules relevant to hermitical life specify the conditions of admission to this life, the program of a hermitical day as well as the practices related to working the place, the number of people that should occupy it, work, the relationship of the hermit with the Order and with the people, the quality of food, clothing, sleep and physical appearance.

It is worth to point out that these rules unite the hermit to the hierarchy on which he depends. Thus, he is no more free to do the activity which he deems suitable, he has to follow from now on the directives of the Superior. Even the choice of becoming a hermit is no more an individual choice, it becomes a community consent since the abbot (especially that of the monastery to which belongs the hermit) have to take the opinion of the monks to grant him the authorization to lead a hermitical life. The interest and the needs of the community come here into play since the authorization granted to a monk to isolate himself in a hermitage, means that the order has to be able to manage without the services done by him until now.

An important change relative to the location and the number of hermits coexisting in the same hermitage, has also taken place. While the hermit lived before in a quasi absolute solitude, Car'Ali requires that for favorable reasons, there should be two to three hermits who live in the same hermitage which belongs to the monastery. Moreover, even if they become hermits, they have to continue obeying the abbot of the monastery. Anyway, their relationship with the community continues by means of obligatory visits which the hermits have to pay to the monastery on certain feast days. However, they have to avoid seeing frequently the laity and renounce seeing women in an absolute and obligatory manner. The Superior of the monastery has to visit continuously the hermit to evaluate his spiritual and physical evolution. As for the food, it has to be eaten in such a way that he stays alive. The habit has to be quite rough. In all this practice, the mortification of the body through asceticism and sleep, which should not be more than five hours a day, plays an important role in paving the way for the soul in quest Christian perfection.

This new law in organizing and institutionalizing hermitical life, holds in itself ambivalence related to identity. Abdallah Car'ali, in conserving the oriental tradition relative to hermitry, was greatly influenced by the Latin tradition. In fact, he was impressed by the book of the practice of Christian Perfection[61] written by St Alphonse Rodrigues.[62] This institutionalization of hermitry which takes a rigid context without changing the identity of the organization limits the spirit of oriental hermitry in uniting it only to the monastic community. Thus, every person is not directly authorized to become a hermit and moreover, the hermit is no more capable of tracing alone his path to God, this path being considered as unique and unified, concise and precise. Also, the idea of absolute solitude originating from the Syriac tradition (Ihidayutha) disappears since it is henceforth forbidden that a hermit lives alone in a hermitage. The rule (of at least two monks and at most three monks living in a hermitage) became then the compromise between absolute solitude and the big community, between the Syriac path and the Basilian path. This reconciliation between contradictions may cause confusion. It is furthermore, a problem which would increase with the centuries until nowadays. It is reflected in a contradiction between the written texts and practice in real life. The constitution of the Order in 1732, which is approved by Rome, adopts these same articles while making some amendments which are not fundamental.[63]

This ambivalence related to identity appears also clearly in the legislations of the Lebanese Synod in 1736. These legislations refer to tradition yet, because of tradition, they are opposed to the rules proposed by the Bishop Abdallah Car'ali. The end of the second chapter of the fourth part states the legislation relative to the hermits. It does not discuss the details relevant to hermitical life but it raises two important issues:

The first issue concerns the lay hermits who have never experienced monastic life. For these hermits, the Synod deems necessary the authorization of the bishop of the region where they attempt to withdraw from public life. This authorization has to take before into consideration the opinion of the neighboring monasteries. If the

---

61 This book was translated into French by Regnier de Marais, Versailles, 1813.

62 St Alphonse Rodriguez was born in Spain in the village of Segovia in 1533. After the premature death of his father, he had the consecrate his time to commerce and got married arround1560. Upon the death of his wife and children, he becomes a brother in the Order of the company of Jesus in 1571. In the same year he was sent to Palma de Mallorca. Until his death, he was the porter of the college of the company. Tried by hard spiritual battles, he received also from God the gift of eminent charisma. He died in Palma in 1617. He was canonized by Leon XIII in 1888. His feast day is in October 31 in the Latin Church. History of the company [http://www.jesuites.com/histoire/saints/alphonserodriguez.htm]. Retrieved 23 September 2003.

63 Mahfoud, *The Maronite organization*, 278-80.

authorization is granted, they can isolate themselves in a place for hermitry but they cannot establish a monastery.[64]

The second issue is that of the monks of the pre-reform of 1695. These monks must spend a small period at the monastery (however, this period is not set to five years as it was provided for in the law of Car'ali).

The monks who followed the old regulations and who lived in big monasteries without being part of any congregation or regular Order needed the authorization of the Superior of the monastery to adopt hermitical life.[65]

The comparison between this Synodal legislation related to hermitry and the reform proposed by Car'ali calls for several remarks. First of all, we notice an ambivalent evolution of the hermitical life. In fact, the reform, which newly governs all the monastic life, which regularizes and even institutionalizes hermitical life is largely imbued with the Latin influence, despite the fact that it continuously refers to the Syro-Maronite Oriental tradition.

This reform which lies, however, within the scope of the continuity of the monastic life within the Maronite Church, creates a certain resistance since this new organization conveys unconsciously a change, which affects the soul and the spirituality of the community. Also, despite the fact that this organizational reform gets the approval of all the authorities of that time, and that it is rationally considered as a positive evolution for the Maronite Church, it remains unacceptable to some people who live according to the old regulations.

While the regular hermitry as it is conceived by Car'ali is henceforth accessible to monks alone, the Synod of Mount-Lebanon continues to make legislations in favour of the lay hermit. Thus, we notice that hermitry in the Maronite Church , before the law of Car'ali, was a hermitry of the people, that is , the spiritual community was put in the forefront, whereas with Car'ali it became a technical and selective hermitry.

The law of Car'ali governing hermitical life and especially the necessity for an authorization granted by the Superior of the monastery to begin hermitage, led to a quantitative development of this kind of

---

64 *Al-Madjma' Al-Lubnānī* 1736 ('The Lebanese Synod' 1736), IV, Chapter II, point 1, 460-1.

65 *Al-Madjma' Al-Lubnānī* 1736, IV, Chapter II, Point 22, 497-9.

life to the detriment of the quality of this vocation, to such a point that people spoke of 'false hermits.'[66] This problem required the intervention of the first assistant ofThe Maronite Lebanese Order, Ignace Bleibel, who reformed hermitical life by writing 13 new articles.

In the rules of Bleibel, we notice the presence of two new principles (the first and third articles). The first article requires that the authorization to adopt hermitical life be granted not only by the Superior of the monastery but also by the Superior General of the Order. This new rule aims essentially at making the access to hermitical life more difficult, while hoping also to give it back its authenticity.

The third article mentions the necessity to give a certain precedence to the eldest monks who wish to become hermits.

Apart from these two articles, Bleibel states again the early notions but stresses on the importance of salvation and the necessity for asceticism. Here also, five articles out of 13 (articles 3,4,5,6 and 7) allude to the necessity of the presence of two or three hermits in the hermitage but in different cells.[67] The legislation governing hermitical life of the Maronites remained the same until the amendments made by the Maronite Lebanese Order in 1974. These rules did not attach a great importance to hermitical life, which is barely mentioned in the third chapter of the first part (article 13); this article points out that solitude at the hermitage is a characteristic specific to the Maronite Lebanese Order.[68]

In the year 2003, within the scope of an overall revision of the rules of the Order, the conditions of the hermitical life were revised and discussed in the first part, in chapter V, from article 104 to article 115.[69]

'Art.104 The life of hermits, the most pure manifestation of asceticism, is the culmination of religious life which consists of treading in the footsteps of Jesus Christ and consecrating oneself totally to Him; hermitical life has witnessed a continuous bloom in Our Maronite Lebanese Order. Being conscious that the vocation for hermitical life is a particular grace from the Holy Spirit to elevate the people of God, our Order gives it a well deserved attention.

---

[66] Mahfoud, *ibid*.

[67] Dagher, *Kashf Al-Khafa'*, 52-5.

[68] *Qawānîn Al-Rahbānîyya Al-Lubnānîyya Al-Mārûnîyya* ('The statutes of the Maronite Lebanese Order'), 1974, 3.

[69] *Qawānîn Al-Rahbānîyya Al-Lubnānîyya Al-Mārûnîyya* ,2003,25-7. Al-Lubnaniyya, 2003, 25-7.

'Art.105 §1. The hermit devotes himself totally to the contemplation of celestial things and separates himself radically from people and the rest of the world.

§2. The hermit remains a member of the community of the monastery to which belongs the hermitage and obeys his Superior within the limits of the constitution of the Order. He only leaves the hermitage upon his Superior's authorization and for a major reason.

'Art. 106 The conditions required for a monk to become a hermit:

1. Having the permission of the Superior General and the consent of the General Council.

2. Having lived at least ten years of perpetual profession.

3. Being at least forty years of age.

4. Having the reputation to observe meticulously the constitution of the Order and of the monastic life,

5. Being endowed with a spiritual and corporal aptitude which allows him to meet the requirements of the hermitical life.

Art.107 The Hermitage chosen by the monk with the consent of the General Council has to be separated from the monastery, appropriate for hermitical life and away from public life. The hermitage can accommodate at most three hermits, each having his own cell. However, they meet together to celebrate Divine Liturgy and recite the divine office.

Art .108 The hermit shall keep the Holy Sacrament permanently in the chapel of the hermitage where he spends most of his time in adoration, contemplation and praying from the heart. He shall recite the seven prayers each in its time.

Art.109 The hermit shall visit the monastery during the feasts of Christmas, Easter, and the Patron Saintt of the Monastery, Saint Anthony the Great, to participate in the religious ceremonies, in the divine office and in the renewal of vows. He shall also visit the monastery during the canonical visit paid by the Superior General or his delegate.

Art.110 Without neglecting his spiritual readings, the hermit shall practice a useful manual and intellectual work. Out of respect for the atmosphere of meditation, silence and contemplation, the laity are not allowed to step into the enclosure, however, they are allowed to visit the chapel.

Art.111 The hermit shall fast and abstain from things known in the Maronite tradition. He shall try hard to mortify himself and dominate his senses, internally as well as externally, while respecting the virtue of prudence, the guide of virtues.

Art. 112 The hermit shall eat once a day. He could eat, if necessary and in case of sickness, a second light meal. He shall not eat meat unless he is sick and unless the Superior gives him the permission to do so. The Superior must appoint a monk or a lay person to provide for the hermit, on a daily basis, all that he needs from the monastery to survive.

Art. 113 The hermit shall sleep only five hours per day. He could sleep for an extra hour if need be.

Art. 114 The Superior shall pay a visit to the hermit at least once a month to check his progression or his regression on the spiritual and corporal level while giving him proper fraternal advice. The Superior shall appoint a confessor who shall help the hermit in his spiritual ascension. The monastic community shall support the hermit through its prayers and shall sympathize with him especially in case of sickness, while showing him charity and fraternal support.

Art. 115 § 1. Should the hermit get sick, his colleague, if there is any, shall console him in saying comforting words useful for the salvation of his soul and for increasing his love to God. If his sickness gets aggravated, the Superior shall take care of him adequately.

§2. The Superior General, with the consent of the General Council may for a just cause, end the hermitical life of the hermit even if this is against the will of the latter.[70]

The amendments do not alter the spirit of the rules but bring only formal modifications. Article 106 requires in the first point that the authorization to begin hermitage be granted by the Superior General and the General Council, whereas the preceding law limited the authorization to the consent of the Superior General. The second point of this same article requires that the monk lives ten years of perpetual profession at the monastery before entering the hermitage, whereas the preceding law required that the monk lives only five years. Article 112 mentions that the hermit shall eat one meal a day. But if need be or in case of sickness, he can have a second meal, whereas the preceding law stated that the hermit shall have only one meal.

---

[70] *Qawānîn Al-Rahbānîyya Al-Lubnānîyya Al-Mārûnîyya.*

Article 113 states that the hermit shall sleep only five hours a day but he can sleep for an extra hour if he wants to, whereas the preceding law stated that the hermit shall sleep only for five hours.

A quick analysis of the evolution of rules allows us to notice a certain leniency in the rules guiding daily life, thus making the living conditions of the hermit quite easier. But in general, the other rules maintain the obligation of remaining silent, of living asceticism and of the coexistence of two or three hermits in the same hermitage.

The female hermitical legislation

Female hermitical legislation is as old as that of the male hermitical life. Theodoret of Cyrrhus, while reporting the life of St Maron, confirms the presence of three women disciples: Domina, Marana and Cyra.[71]

There were certainly in the Church nuns who led the life of a recluse. Etienne-Evode Assemani, in describing in his catalogue the Oriental manuscripts of the Laurentian Library of Florence[72] presents to the reader under number II an old Syriac Bible written by a certain Theodoret before the 9th century...[73] On the same page of this manuscript, Patriarch Jeremiah wrote personally this following obituary: 'The recluse nun, daughter of Dawud (David) has found eternal rest and departed from this world full of evils to the other world full of happiness on Friday 6 November 1199 AD.'[74]

Also, Patriarch Stephen Douwaihi, in his Annals, mentions that a nun called Sarah, who led a solitary life and who endured the strictness of ascetic life, participated also in the costs for enlarging the monastery of St Elisha.[75] Several of these nuns belonged to feudal families and were

---

[71] Theodoret, *A History of the Monks*, 183-9.

[72] E E Assemani, *Bibliothecae Mediceae Laurentianae et Palatinae Codicum Manuscriptorum Orientalium Catalogus*, 1742, 25.

[73] 'This Bible belonged long ago to the archbishop Clement then to his sons Barsawma, Solomon and Philip. These three granted it to the Monastery of Mar Sarkis (St Serge) in Hardin in the diocese of Tripoli. Afterwards, it was offered to the monasteries of Our Lady of Yanuh and Our Lady of Qannubin, which are patriarchal seats. There, it became the private property of Patriarch Irmia (Jeremiah) al-Amiti. This patriarch granted it, in his turn, with the possessions of two of his parents, Yussef (Joseph) and Dawud(David) to the Monastery of Our Lady of Yanuh ...', Sfeir, *The Hermits*, 103-4.

[74] Sfeir, *The Hermits*, 104. Cf. E A W Budge, *The Book of Governors, The Historia Monastica of Thomas Bishop of Marga A.D. 840*, London, 1893.

[75] Vat. Syr. 215, fol.110r.

financially supported by their parents.[76] Until the beginning of the 18th century, there were recluse nuns in cells next to monasteries.[77]Despite the fact that there were nuns who led the life of hermits, we notice that there weren't any specific rules governing female hermitry. The same traditions and later, the same rules were applied to and by the hermits regardless of their sex. In 2003, a law specific to the Maronite Lebanese Order for the nuns is issued and thus constitutes a legislation specific to the hermitical life of the nuns. We notice that the legislation of the female hermitical life is completely new. This new legislation is not even approved by Rome since the revision of the law for the Maronite Lebanese Order for the nuns was made and sent to Rome in 2003 waiting to be approved by the Holy See.

The legislation related to women followed the same procedures as that related to men. The rules that are to govern female Orders were inspired from the rules established in male Orders starting from the 17th century. The legislation related to the hermitage (Chapter IV, Articles 84-92) conforms to that of the monks of the Maronite Lebanese Order except for what is related to the necessary period, after taking the first vows at the monastery and before starting hermitage, which must be fifteen years (Article 86).[78]

The legislation does not state precisely the number of hours that should be consecrated to sleep. However, it is mentioned that sufficient time should be provided for sleep and rest (Article 89).[79]

The Hermitical legislation of the Maronite Monks of Most Holy Trinity in Petersham (USA)

The rules related to the hermitage of the Maronite Monks of Most Holy Trinity in Petersham in the United States, which figure in Title 5—Our Eremitical Orientation and Our Life as Hermits[80]—almost conform with those of the Maronite Lebanese Order except that the Maronite monk

[76] Helyot, *Monastic Order*, 895.

[77] T Spidlik and J Sainsaulieu, 'Hermits', *Dictionary of Ecclesiastical History and Geography (DEHG)*, t.XV, 1963, 769.

[78] Interview with Reverend Father Eli Hanna.

[79] Interview with Reverend Father Eli Hanna.

[80] The Maronite Monks of Most [http://www.maronitemonks.org/Typicon.htm]. Retrieved 29 July 2003.

of that American Order must lead six years of community life at the monastery before he can start his hermitage.[81] It is also worth to point out that in accordance with the rules of this Order, every person who wishes to adhere to the Order can keep his own confession.[82]

The practice of hermitical life in the Church today

In spite of our interviews with the hermits, it was very difficult to be able to specify the organization of their daily life since they refused, because of their humility, to talk about themselves. However, thanks to the testimonies of the Father Superior, of people who see them on a daily basis and of the believers who come for confession and spiritual orientation, it was possible for us to understand how they lived their daily life and their hermitical experience. This experience reflects a spirituality which is clarified at the same time, by the Maronite hermitical tradition and the new rules related to hermitry written in 2003.

The reasons for getting engaged in hermitical life for today's hermits do not seem to be very complex to the hermit Chayna. It is a call from God, an invitation to seek Christian perfection. He thinks that choosing to become a hermit in monastic life is an invitation from God to take a path of a professional specialization just like it would happen in secular life; 'we choose what we love to do.' The hermit Chayna aspires to become closer to God, to live his life close to Him in solitude and in prayer. The choice to become a hermit is neither an escape nor a compensation for a failure. According to what he said, he was a university professor and a renowned judge. In answering the 'why' question which intrigues the young people, he points out that success to him does not lie in worldly and social recognition but in the fact of taking up a much more important challenge, which is that of attracting everybody to his hermitage in order to bring them closer to God. The sense of satisfaction which appears in his words and on his face reflects his state of mind: he was able to achieve, in part, his mission since, isolated in his hermitage, he is henceforth even more recognized and much freer than he was in the world. He is sought

81 The Maronite Monks of Most [http://www.maronitemonks.org/Typicon.htm]. Retrieved 29 July 2003.

82 The Maronite Monks of Most [http://www.maronitemonks.org/Vocations.htm]. Retrieved 29 July 2003.

after by tourists, emigrants and journalists. To him this is satisfactory because he is able to spread even more the word of God.

With the hermit Khawand, the reason for hermitry acquires a historical aspect. It is to him a goal at which he has always aimed to achieve consciously and unconsciously. Since 1958, date of the funeral of the last hermit of the Maronite Lebanese Order, Father Yaacoub Abi Maroun, he lived constantly the temptation to become a hermit. As we mentioned before, the blown out candle hid in his pocket, which he took with him in his luggage during his trips was lost. However, even its loss remains significant since it incited him to light another bright candle, and to transform his life into a hermitical one. Thus, hermitry is the new candle which replaces that which he lost and hence, he is faithful to tradition. But what he has always wished for is becoming a hermit in the sacred valley, a wish which was not granted by the general council of the Order. The hermitage of Tamich is situated in a very noisy context especially with the development of the region of Nahr el Kalb which is a place with great tourist attractions and where there are restaurants hosting singers that sing until dawn worldly music which invades the hermit's privacy. Moreover, Khawand has always wished to be a disciple of the hermit Chayna, to serve him and be initiated to hermitry with him but this latter did not accept, being convinced that tradition requires an absolute solitude. To the hermit Chayna, two or three hermits sharing the same hermitage alter the principal objective of hermitical life.[83]

In fact, how can a hermit like Father Chayna live in absolute solitude while receiving throngs of people every day, from the early morning until early afternoon, to listen to their problems, share their difficulties and guide them spiritually? Furthermore, to the hermit Chayna, the true hermitical life is that which consists of living in absolute solitude since tradition does not allow a coexistence of several hermits in the same hermitage. To him such coexistence shows an ignorance of tradition. An old hermit teaches the disciple the methods of hermitry and this latter applies them afterwards in solitude.

But Khawand, ecstatic about the Bible, takes a path which is characteristic of him, he writes the Bible in poetry (Lebanese dialect). This ecstasy puts him in a transcendental state. He looks at the people with a

[83] Interview with the hermit Chayna at the Monastery of St Anthony Kozhaya, 20 September 2003. The hermit had to leave temporarily his hermitage because he fell down and fractured his hip.

deep smile emanating from a deeply serene face, praising God in his hymns, which could be verbalized or lived mentally. Upon looking at him in this state, we could see the divine peace of mind: divine providence.

This same providence manifested itself in his family life, strengthened his convictions and enlightened him to take his way towards the hermitage. St Charbel has played an important role since he interceded for his brother who was seriously ill and who is healed today. It was to him a sign: the life of Charbel as well as his spirituality has captivated him.

For the hermit Escobar, hermitry is a choice which is well thought-out, premeditated and well sought-after. All his life's pathway in Colombia has led him to the sacred valley. In spite of practicing university teaching and spiritual orientation for married couples, he has always been fascinated by solitary life. He sought this kind of life everywhere and found it only in Lebanon. This is why he came to Lebanon several times before he decided to stay in there for good. Moreover, he constantly did everything to become a hermit. In Lebanon, he started his monastic life from zero since he decided to be a hermit within the Maronite Lebanese Order, where an experienced, Father Antonios Chayna, could enlighten him to take the right path. Accordingly, he had to respect the rules and spend 10 years of cenobitical life before starting his hermitage. However, the Father Superior and the general council have granted him a privilege in authorizing him to start his hermitage after 6 years spent in monastic life only. He was overwhelmed with joy because he had 4 extra years to live his life as a martyr since this is how he understands hermitry. In fact, hermitry to him is a slow martyrdom, a martyrdom which testifies in its daily practice to his faith. As such, the martyrdom which he seeks is not an escape from society but a sacrifice for the society just like the martyrs of the early centuries of Christianity, whose example was one of the primary causes of conversion to Christian faith.

This aspiration to sacrifice oneself, this striving for martyrdom take a new dimension in the sacred Valley and especially in his hermitage in Hawqa. Occupying the hermitage in the center of the valley, at an equal distance from its two ends, he is in 'The heart of the valley' as he likes to say. He holds the entire Valley in his heart and the whole world as well even if it is far away. He holds in his heart his family, his country, the Lebanese community and peace in the world. He praise for the world so that it may come even closer to God. He is a martyr in the hermitage next to the martyrs of Hawqa, 'Our martyrs' as he likes to say, joining thus his life as a hermit with the historical heritage of martyrs. The history of the Maronites and their martyrs are his. Hermitry in this sense become similar to resistance. Resistance to the conqueror is a horizontal dimension of hermitical life. The vertical dimension is then a struggle against evil, wrong and the temptation of the devil. In the cold of the snowy December nights, he listens to the noise of doors opening and closing, of footsteps, and of voices. He resists temptation and he plunges even more in prayer and in martyrdom to lead his soul to salvation.

As for Sister Mary-Jesus, the reason why she chose why to become a hermit are very simple, reflecting the simplicity of her life and away from all theorization. Hermitry for her is a means to consecrate oneself to God and to remember the people in one's prayers. Her aspiration to hermitry corresponds to life in the cloister which all the nuns lead at the convent and which was modified to become as the perfect living example of what Jesus said to Nicodemus on the necessity to be born again.

These characteristics cannot be perceived in Sister Mary-Jesus and this is not because she does not have them but because we are not able to see her face and its expressions. Her head, always inclined while she looks at the floor as if she is reminding herself of her mortal nature, is covered with the veil and her arms are crossed. She keeps herself in the background but she is not forgotten. Anything which is not a hymn of praise to the Lord does not have a place in her life. She inspires humility with her calmness while she is immersed even in corporal silence, expressing her love to God. When she speaks in accordance with the wish of her Mother Superior, she surprises her interlocutor and requires that he gathers all his energy and capacity to find a voice, an echo of what is being said since centuries, which comes from hermitical tradition, is lively, and reflects a vivid example which is far from historical stories.

Their role model is certainly Jesus Christ but each is fascinated by a saint. Mother Mary has a central place in their life; however, other saints form a hermitical example, like St Charbel, for the hermits Chayna and Khawand.

Their hermitage is very ordinary. The hermitage of Boula is made up of a church, the hermit's cell carved, in part, from the rocks. As it is forbidden to us to enter inside, we cannot describe it but perhaps there is nothing in there to describe since it is quite ordinary. After we made our investigation, we knew that the hermit sleeps on the floor and not on a bed.

The hermitage of Hawqa is made up of two cells next to the Church, which is quite separated from the hermitage. The hermit sleeps on the floor and puts his head on a rock instead of a pillow. The hermitage of Tamich is made up of three cells; one of them is for the hermit's use. The three cells are parallel and give access to the hall, which in turn gives access to the Church. We notice immediately the books and the manuscripts piled up everywhere, even on the bed. However, we see also the sweets and the candies which the hermit receives as gifts from his visitors and which he gives to the children and to the poor.

The hermitage of the nun is next to the monastery, a few seconds away on foot. It is made up of a very ordinary cell which is not inhabited by the hermit all year round since the Mother Superior insists that Sister Mary-Jesus sleeps in the monastery during the winter season because of the problem of humidity which is not yet solved and which could be harmful to the health of Sister Mary-Jesus.

Their spiritual readings have undoubtedly the Bible in common but remain very diversified. The hermit Chayna reads a lot about the life of the Maronite hermits and about the tradition of their hermitry. The hermit Khawand is interested in the Church Fathers and in the history of the hermits through which he learns to become a hermit himself. He is interested also in reading the Psalms and the life of the Virgin Mary. The hermit Escobar, who is in love with the Virgin Mary, sends her every day a letter and sometimes he sends her two letters. He reads especially the writings of St Augustine, St Paul, St John of the Cross and St Theresa of Avila.

As for the hermit Sister Mary-Jesus, she is interested in the life of saints, especially those of the Oriental tradition such as Charbel, Rafqa and Hardini. Also, she reads the life of Occidental saints if their biography is in Arabic.

Despite the fact that their spirituality is commonly reflected in the simplicity of daily life and practice, it reveals itself as being divergent in as regards the sources of inspiration and awareness.

The hermit Chayna reflects traditionalism in his hermitical conception. A definite traditionalism since upon listening to his homilies during Mass and to his answers to the questions of the believers, he seems to be very dogmatic. The Virgin Mother occupies a central place in his spirituality. The church of his hermitage is all covered with icons and pictures of saints.

The hermit Khawand[84] prefers a biblical hermitry to a spirituality which is essentially traditional, especially to what is related to the mortification of the body and the excess of asceticism. His spirituality focuses on the Bible, the Old and the New Testament, and is inspired especially from the Psalms. This is well understood especially when we learn that Father Khawand is a poet and a hymn composer. In fact, he writes poems and prays while chanting, using the traditional formula of the sung Lebanese poem (the zaggal).

The hermit Escobar[85] talks about a spirituality which finds its sources in the Latin world. He applies the Carmelite spirituality, especially that of St Theresa of Avila, his prayer is Christocentric and it centres on the Word. The interior of the church of his hermitage is very plain without any pictures or icons, just having the Cross without Jesus Christ on it.

Sister Mary-Jesus[86] does not spend all her days in the hermitage since she is summoned to participate in reciting prayers and offices with her community, after that she withdraws into her cell to pray alone. She constantly invokes God's help for the people in her prayers to such a point that she was named Apostle of the people and missionary like St Theresa of Child Jesus. She devotes herself to the spirituality of the Cross and lives the sufferings of Christ, a blooming joy in her daily life. Besides, the example of the nun who preceded her is significant. This nun is St Rafqa who endured all her sufferings in joining them to those of the Christ.

The day of the hermit is spent in silence, prayer and penitence. All the hermits pray seven times a day as the law requires.

Apart from reciting the offices, they celebrate Mass daily, pray the rosary and praise God. The hermit Khawand is distinguished from the others by his constant use of the word 'mamnoun', a word of thanks said to God. The hermit Escobar practices a lot of contemplation and believes that every work done by the hermit is synonymous with prayer.

Finally, the hermit Chayna spends his time in reciting prayers dedicated to the Virgin Mary. We were not able to know about their acts of penance in details because of their humility, however, we made an investigation and we were able to gather bits of information about the

[84] Interview with the hermit Khawand, Hermitage of St Anthony the Great, Tamich, 12 August 2003.

[85] Interview with the hermit Escobar, Hermitage of Our Lady of Hawqa, Sacred Valley, 4 August 2003.

[86] Interview with the hermit Sister Mary-Jesus, Hermitage of St Simeon, Ayto, 4 August 2003.

issue. The hermit Chayna wears 'goatskin' and sleeps on the floor just like the hermit Escobar who lays his head on a rock instead of a pillow. However, he is not convinced that great penance makes saints. To him saintship is very simply in daily life, in the little things and in every work achieved for the glory of God.

For the hermit Khawand, the idea differs slightly. He believes that penance constitutes a means and not a finality and the biblical concept of the human being is not that of sufferance.

As for Sister Mary-Jesus, her penance is well supervised by her Mother Superior who worries a lot about her health and fragile nature. Her act of penance is especially related to food and sleep. However, she insists eating the leftovers.

The hermit spends part of his day performing manual work. The hermit Chayna cultivates tomatoes and vines. The hermit Escobar cultivates potatoes, courgettes, vines and pumpkins. As for Sister Mary-Jesus, she cultivates roses and various flowers. Her garden is not vast but she has small terraces next to her hermitage. She works also with the other nuns in sewing and in producing the Marsapan (sugar candy).

The hermit Khawand plants citrus trees but the water shortages prevent him from taking care properly of his garden. This is why he asked the father Superior to give him the permission to consecrate himself to intellectual work and abandon manual work. He was granted the authorization and hence he is now able to devote his time to research work and composing liturgical hymns. The hermit Chayna is assisted by novice to help him in the cultivation work, as he is getting old. The hermit Escobar, who cultivates the land in spring and in summer, replaces that manual work by an intellectual work when winter comes since the snow prevents him from working the land.

The visits of the lay believers remain numerous in spite of the instructions dictated in the law. The hermit Chayna constantly receives throngs of people gathering around his hermitage since four o'clock in the morning, especially in summer and during the weekends. He opens his door at ten to seven to invite the people to celebrate Mass and at the end of the celebration, the people leave the Church and wait for their turn in a small corridor to meet the hermit. He first invites the people to confess and once confession is over, he invites them to examine their conscience while reciting the Ten Commandments. Afterwards, he asks the questions related to the purity of their words spoken and to the recitation of the rosary. He receives people until noon and sometimes until one o'clock in the afternoon since he does not send away the people who come to see him from far away.

The hermit Escobar receives the people especially in summer, a period during which the religious tourists are numerous in the Valley of Qadisha. During the winter season he receives nobody because of the snow. Certain villagers or monks come to see him from time to time, to make sure that he is in good health. The hermit Escobar converses easily with the people in several languages and answers their questions concerning all that is religious and spiritual. Having a sharp sense of humour, he jokes using some Lebanese or Arabic terms such as *habibi*, that is, beloved.

The hermit Khawand, although he is much sought after, wishes that the Father Superior would only authorize him to receive a few visitors so that he may consecrate his time to prayer and writing.

Sister Mary-Jesus is very strict about the visits issue, she would rather receive nobody. We were only able to converse with her thanks to her total submission to her vow of obedience. She only gave us five minutes with the possibility of not answering our questions. She receives people only in Church and does not look the visitors in the eye. Her answers are not explicit and they are limited to a word or two.

The visits of the lay believers always break the silence and the solitude of the hermits, a solitude which is very dear to them. Sister Mary-Jesus does not leave the Convent unless her Mother Superior orders her to do so, in order to go and see the doctor. The same goes for the other hermit. The hermit Chayna who fell down and broke his hip, had to stay at the hospital. He later stayed, for a rest cure in the cloister of the monks of the monastery of St Anthony Kozhaya, waiting for his recovery to go back to the hermitage. Apart from the medical visit, the hermits do not leave their hermitage unless the Father Superior tells them. They all praise the benefits of solitude, to Sister Mary-Jesus; solitude allows her to give all her attention to God and to pray. To the hermit Chayna, solitude provides him with a suitable atmosphere for prayer, to give all his attention to God and to contemplate. To the hermit Khawand, solitude allows him to feel the presence of God; it is a dialog with God in silence which allows him to become addicted to the Creator and to his presence.

Conclusion

The Maronite spirituality essentially hermitical and its origins go back to the Syriac traditions. This spirituality has remained faithful to tradition throughout centuries of deep changes and great challenges. All these changes have not altered the original spirit even if the have give this spirituality a form which is more adaptable to challenges. The Maronite hermitical spirituality is characterized since the beginning by the spirituality of the Cross one the one side and hermitry in the open air on the other side.

The spirituality of the Cross since its beginning until nowadays remains the mark of the Maronite spirituality. For the Maronites, contemplating Jesus Christ crucified is at the same time a sign of support from the Son of God for the suffering of His people and a tendency towards glory through Resurrection.This experience was deeply lived in the history of this community through the persistence of this minority having all these characteristics and inserted into a totalitarian world which accepts others only if they are inferior to it otherwise it rejects them.Thus, the Maronite spirituality is born from of the passage from crucifixion to Resurrection. From this angle, the sufferings of Christ are only significant with the Resurrection.The sufferings are present but wait for the Resurrection, which becomes a horizon providing hope.The spirituality of the Cross combines suffering with hope; it is the spirituality of hope par excellence. Crucified on the Cross of a martyred Christian Orient, the Maronite internalizes suffering waiting for the Resurrection. It is the spirituality of the Holy Saturday.[87] It is the spirituality of the passage and passage is always a common identity to all.We convey suffering without being assimilated into the world of darkness but in hoping for glory.This state embodies the human condition on earth waiting for eternal life with Jesus Christ.

As for the specific characteristic of the Maronite hermitical life in the open air, it remains present while being transformed and marked by a certain symbolism. Transformation is the result of the evolution of the historical context which allows this hermitry to be characterized at the same time by a spiritual dimension and a historico-social dimension. Hermitry in the open air and particularly one of its elements, Stylitic hermitry is synonymous with the detachment which symbolizes the shortening of the path towards God.

---

[87] M Hadaya, *The Maronite Office of Holy Saturday,* Lebanon, 1995.

Stylitic hermitry is reminiscent of the spirituality of the Cross since the hermit remains in a suspended position, being above the ground and not having reached the sky yet. It is a situation in which the hermit waits, seeks, is liberated and aspires to God. This Stylitic hermitry which is an emancipation from all imprisoning setting, from all closed space, is transformed with the Muslim conquest to a voluntary prison-hermitage since the hermit chooses himself his own liberating prison. Hermitry in this sense goes from one extreme to the other. In such a case and in such changes, where do we find then faithfulness to tradition? In fact, the geography of the hermitages provides an answer to this sacred question. The hermitages of the sacred valley, especially those occupied at present by the hermits and also the other hermitages of Ayto and Tamich are situated in valleys, neither in the deep side of the valley nor on the highest point of the slopes. They are rather situated on the mountain side, as if suspended from a column in an intermediary position and in a hanging situation. They are hermitages in the open air, detached from earth but not attached to the sky. Thus, it is not preposterous that the Colombian hermit be extremely delighted with the central position occupied by his hermitage, which is situated in the very middle of the two access ways of the valley. It is even a passage way for the believers who cross the valley on foot. The hermit waits for those who travel a long way to share with him the celebration of Mass and the liturgy. As for the historico-social dimension, it appears clearly in the intersection of two vertical and horizontal lines in the sacred valley: The hermitages are on the intersection of these two lines. The hermit carries the anxiety and the suffering of his people but he is well attached to the vertical line to carry his people to God. He is this martyr who, through his sacrifice, constitutes the link between his people and God. The spirituality of the Cross is always present in the Maronite Church with an attenuation of the rules for the ascetic while hermitical life in the open air is replaced by indoor hermitry. It is the change in continuity. Several elements come to highlighted but they mark also the birth of a tension begotten by change and continuity, reform and tradition.

The first element is that of the transformation of the natural hermitry into institutional hermitry. The simple characteristic of natural hermitry as well as its spontaneity and the multiplicity of the practices leading to God are transformed into dictated rules which in advance tell the hermit about the context of his profession. This does not prevent the hermit from being aware of the importance of the rules which come to organize hermitical life and not to abolish it.

Dualism in this context is transmitted through divorce which happens nowadays in certain levels between the hermitical rules and practices. This divorce is manifested particularly in the authorities who make legislations and who promulgate various contradictory rules relative to the organization of hermitical life. There is, first of all, the law which requires that two or three hermits live in the same hermitage but in different cells and which authorizes simultaneously three hermits to live in three different hermitages. Also, rules have developed hermitry, which was based on very harsh condition for corporal asceticism, in transforming it today into a less harsh asceticism. Attenuating the conditions of the material life is not only based on the will for attenuating the suffering of the body but rather on the will of better understanding the sacrament of salvation in the context of the rationalization, which facilitates for the contemporary hermit the action of transcending the body while seeking the perfection of the soul.

However, dualism is present at other levels, since certain hermits such as Chayna and Mary-Jesus remain convinced of the validity of the traditional conception off Maronite hermitry based on real corporal asceticism.

The third element gives concrete expression to the passage form a community hermitry , which implies all the ecclesiastical hierarchy and the Maronite people, to an individual hermitry marginalizing not only the lay people of this world but also the hermits within the ecclesiastical hierarchy. This element gives rise to a dualism between the monastic reform and the hermitical tradition. The monastic reform of 1695 and its amendments grants the privilege of hermitical life only for those who lived a monastic profession, whereas the Maronite hermitical tradition received with open arms the lay people who were trying to form a pact with God just like the case of 'Bnay and Banat Quyomo.' This ambivalence appears today in the new experience of the 'Hermitical Days' which was by the way, well assimilated by the lay people. The best proof for that is the incessantly increasing numbers of participants. The positive reaction of the lay people to the invitation of the Antonine Sisters is a criterion which allows us to notice that tradition continues to be lived, even unconsciously, since it resurfaces in critical moments. At this moment, we notice a faithful attachment of the people to its tradition. The last element concerns the choice of hermitical life. While Maronite hermitry is a voluntary choice, it was transformed throughout history into a reactional choice, faced especially with the accumulating problems and challenges to which the people were subjected in the socio-political context. In the beginning, hermitry in the open air was a decision for abandoning oneself. St Maron was inventive in following himself a new hermitical path. This decision was gradually transformed into a reaction to the Muslim conquest since the hermit, having no choice, looks for a secure hermitage and imprisons himself in a closed space. Nowadays, hermitry reveals itself as a mainstay of a society which must take up new challenges. The number of hermits is incessantly decreasing but we are witnessing a certain renaissance especially after the big crises. This is how the saintship of Charbel and Rafqa who have lived during the second half of the 19th century could be inscribed in the context of the 1860 crisis. The four contemporary hermits of the Maronite community redeem their people after the crisis Lebanon ha experienced at the end of the 20th century.

The dualism in these elements of change hinges on tradition and reform which have to coexist in the contemporary Maronite spirituality. The conscious reform invades tradition. This latter resurfaces unconsciously, surpassing all rules at the critical moment. Hermitical life nowadays moves between two tendencies, that of tradition and that of reform, the first being hermitically centred and the second hierarchically centred. The hermitical spiritual identity remains waiting: suspended between an omnipresent tradition and a non integrated reform. This spirituality is in a state of rediscovery and renaissance.

We have attempted to describe the eremitical life as an expression of Maronite spirituality, which at its core identifies Church and community. The eremitical current has recently been revived within the Maronite heartland of Lebanon—the Sacred Valley of Qadisha. There has also been a developing interest in the eremitical tradition from laity and religious, a continuing sign of a particular spirituality's witness to the identity of this Oriental Catholic Church. There are also signs that the Maronite tradition is taking root in the West, for it has a universal value not only for the Maronite Church but also for Catholicity itself.